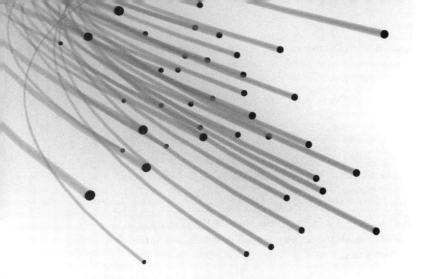

Intelligent Systems

Systems

Principles, Paradigms, and Pragmatics

Robert J. Schalkoff
Clemson University

JONES AND BARTLETT PUBLISHERS
Sudbury, Massachusetts
BOSTON   TORONTO   LONDON   SINGAPORE

World Headquarters

Jones and Bartlett Publishers
40 Tall Pine Drive
Sudbury, MA 01776
978-443-5000
info@jbpub.com
www.jbpub.com

Jones and Bartlett Publishers
Canada
6339 Ormindale Way
Mississauga, Ontario L5V 1J2
Canada

Jones and Bartlett Publishers
International
Barb House, Barb Mews
London W6 7PA
United Kingdom

Jones and Bartlett's books and products are available through most bookstores and online book-sellers. To contact Jones and Bartlett Publishers directly, call 800-832-0034, fax 978-443-8000, or visit our website www.jbpub.com.

Substantial discounts on bulk quantities of Jones and Bartlett's publications are available to cor-porations, professional associations, and other qualified organizations. For details and specific discount information, contact the special sales department at Jones and Bartlett via the above contact information or send an email to specialsales@jbpub.com.

Production Credits:
Publisher: David Pallai
Acquisitions Editor: Timothy Anderson
Editorial Assistant: Melissa Potter
Production Director: Amy Rose
Senior Marketing Manager: Andrea DeFronzo
V.P., Manufacturing and Inventory Control: Therese Connell
Composition: Northeast Compositors, Inc.
Cover and Title Page Design: Kristin E. Parker
Cover and Title Page Image: © Harper/ShutterStock, Inc.
Printing and Binding: Malloy, Inc.
Cover Printing: Malloy, Inc.

Library of Congress Cataloging-in-Publication Data
Schalkoff, Robert J.
  Intelligent systems : principles, paradigms, and pragmatics / Robert J. Schalkoff.
     p. cm.
  Includes index.
  ISBN-13: 978-0-7637-8017-3 (hardcover)
  ISBN-10: 0-7637-8017-0 (ibid.)
 1. Intelligent agents (Computer software) 2. Intelligent control systems. 3. Expert systems (Computer science) 4. Artificial intelligence. I. Title.
  QA76.76.I58S323 2009
  006.3—dc22

                        2009027414

6048
Printed in the United States of America
13 12 11 10 09   10 9 8 7 6 5 4 3 2 1

For all my teachers—
- *My parents*
- *My daughters*
- *The nuns at St. Philomena's*
- *My professors*
- *My colleagues and mentors*
- *My friends*
- My penis

Contents

15 Neural Networks (Part 3): Self-Organizing Systems

Preface

A Long Time Ago, in a Galaxy Far, Far Away...

A field
emerged
called Artificial
Intelligence (AI).
Practitioners were di-
verse and interested in topics ranging from understanding
and quantifying (natural) intelligence
to developing systems that exhibited some
form of "intelligent" behavior and could possibly "learn." Some early practitioners were good
Lisp and Prolog programmers. Applications ranged from
medicine to robotics. Over the years, the field experienced a
roller-coaster ride of popularity. Toy systems were built, programs
beat world masters at chess, and the really hard problems stayed that
way. Along the way, newer and "hotter" technologies came along, such as
fuzzy systems, genetic approaches, and artificial neural networks. In some cases,
the evolution of AI became recast as "Computational Intelligence" or "Evolutionary"
Computing. Over time, the realization grew that many of the goals were the same
and that the two sets of technologies were intertwined. A somewhat different field called
Intelligent Systems began to emerge. This book is a snapshot in the evolution of Intelligent Systems.

Overview

Intelligent Systems: Principles, Paradigms, and Pragmatics explores the theoretical and practical
underpinnings of a field called Intelligent Systems (IS), and provides an introductory-level, hands-on
perspective on IS technology. The objective is to enable a full understanding of IS topics and related
supporting tools and technologies. No previous experience in this area is assumed, although readers
are expected to have minimal familiarity with discrete mathematics and some exposure to modern
programming languages, such as C. Since this is a teaching text dedicated to those new to the field,

efforts have been made to provide the reader a soft start. Clearly, there is more material than can be covered in one semester—the choice of specific topics is left to individual instructors. Many of the exercises in each chapter, combined with the implementation examples in the text, serve as good starting points for projects or extended self- study.

The book presents topics that are generally considered "core" IS concepts (although the "core" is debatable); it cannot be an encyclopedia or bibliographic summary of all IS-related research work ever produced. We take a much more practical approach and consider the development of *systems with intelligence*. Emphasis on the conceptual approach explains the organization of the text. In addition, the book attempts to make the important distinctions between theory and practice that are often a major factor in the choice, implementation, and ultimate success of IS algorithms.

The IS area is becoming more important in both the undergraduate and graduate curricula in Computer Science and Engineering. While the primary objective of the text is to provide a teaching tool, it is possible that practicing engineers and scientists will also find the clear, concept-based treatment useful in updating their backgrounds. Hopefully, this will provide the fundamental conceptual and algorithmic tools necessary to confront the industrial application-driven challenges of this rapidly expanding and emerging field.

Important First Principles

The following is the author's philosophy. Things a reader should consider before entering into a study of IS are:

1. IS embodies a form of computation that appears, at best, to be based upon an inexact and ambiguous model (similar to human reasoning). Some aspects of IS are therefore close to "exploratory programming."

2. IS models are seldom complete.

3. IS is a rapidly maturing discipline with a strong interdisciplinary nature. Algorithms and data structures that were popular yesterday are now considered obsolete. Today's algorithms are under scrutiny, and tomorrow's algorithms are on the horizon.

4. There is more than one way to achieve an IS.

5. There is more than one way to study IS.

Approaches to Developing Intelligent Systems (IS)

At the outset, we make the following claims. The elaboration of the first three is essentially the remainder of the book.

1. **Developing IS Involves Science.**

2. **Developing IS Involves Engineering.**

3. **Developing IS Involves Software**.

4. **Developing IS Requires Credentials**. In almost any endeavor, there are "talkers" and "doers." The IS developer needs to be both, with an emphasis on the latter. Specifically, IS developers:

   - Need to have or have access to application-specific expertise;
   - Need to be cognizant of the myriad of available IS design approaches varying applicability, tradeoffs, and costs;
   - Need to realize there probably exists more than one viable solution approach;
   - Need to realize there probably exists more than one viable implementation;
   - Need to realize that new problems probably have similarities with previously solved problems; and
   - Probably need to use or develop some software.

Audience

It is possible to use this text while deemphasizing implementation aspects. In the author's opinion, however, the "hands on" or practical experience gained by developing and modifying working systems is an invaluable aspect of any IS course. Learning the jargon of IS is one thing; development of an ability to appreciate and experiment with the underlying concepts is a higher goal. Many of the ideas in IS are in fact only fully understood when the complexities and limitations of the problem present themselves to the student through hands-on experience.

The material presented herein is suitable for a first course in IS. This first exposure may occur anywhere from the junior level undergraduate to first year graduate level.

History

In 1988, I wrote my first "AI" book.[1] At that time, AI emphasized a rule-based paradigm, implemented in Lisp or Prolog, with long discussions on uncertainty, learning, and search. Since that time, ontologies, the ubiquitous agents concept, fuzzy, neural, genetic, swarm, and other technologies have come into being. In addition, useful tools like Soar and CLIPS have become available. This book incorporates these concepts, and suggests that a single, simple, simplistic approach to IS is insufficient.

Intelligent systems research and development has fostered many "hidden" applications that often go unnoticed. This includes airline reservation systems, voice recognition, robotic toys for entertainment, and realistic animation. Intelligent, interactive, humanoid robots have yet to appear. In addition, many of the original and underlying problems are still with us. On the bright side, at least we no longer confuse intelligent systems success with chess-playing ability.

It is impossible for a man who takes a survey of what is already known, not to see what an immensity in every branch of science yet remains to be discovered.

Thomas Jefferson, Monticello, June 18, 1799

---

[1] *Artificial Intelligence: An Engineering Approach*, McGraw Hill.

Acknowledgments

I would like to thank Tim Anderson at Jones and Bartlett Publishers for believing in this project. In addition, thanks are due to Amy Rose, Melissa Potter, and the Jones and Bartlett staff for producing a polished, readable text.

The trials of students at Clemson University who used draft versions of the text are appreciated.

Finally, the recognition of those who consider textbook production a bona fide and respectable academic venture is especially appreciated.

## chapter 1

Introduction to Intelligent Systems

1.1 What Is Intelligent Systems (IS)?

Principles: elementary truths, laws, or assumptions

Paradigms: a set of practices, often concerning an intellectual discipline

Pragmatics: practical considerations

Intelligent system: good question

Intelligence through Computation. Early computer pioneers realized almost immediately that the emerging computer had capabilities beyond number crunching [Neu58]. The Intelligent Systems (IS) field seeks to achieve *intelligent behavior through computation*. If useful and generally applicable "intelligent behavior" models and algorithms were available, this book would be much shorter and possibly superfluous. Therefore, this book considers a number of technical approaches aimed at developing autonomous *systems with intelligence*.

What Is Intelligence? *This is a surprisingly difficult question.* In fact, it has recently been cited as one of the five "deep" questions in computing [Win08]. For this reason, we defer to either the reader's own definition or the myriad of definitions provided by dictionaries (see the problems), psychologists, philosophers, or even other IS researchers.

1.1.1 Key Topics or Themes

Any computation requires a representation of some entity (e.g., as a concept or as a numerical quantity) as well as a procedure for manipulation. Representation and manipulation (and learning) are key elements of IS. Obviously, we cannot manipulate something unless it is adequately represented.

Throughout this text, three terms (*representation*, *manipulation*, and *learning*) provide a common denominator for much of the study. The following are the three most relevant questions:

- How is the knowledge (or intelligence) represented?

- How is it manipulated?

- How is it learned (or acquired)?

1.1.2   IS: A Practical Definition?

A somewhat whimsical, yet illustrative, definition of Intelligent Systems (IS) might be:

> *"IS can be defined as the field which attempts to get real machines
> to behave like the ones in the movies."*

IS: An Engineering Viewpoint.   From an engineering viewpoint, we might argue that IS is about generating representations, inference procedures, and learning strategies that automatically (autonomously) solve problems that were heretofore solved by humans. Thus, IS is the engineering counterpart of cognitive science. Cognitive science is a blend of philosophy, linguistics, and psychology.

1.1.3   Some Significant Preliminary Questions

Of the many possible questions related to IS, we introduce a few:

1. Should the (biological) structure of the human brain be the template for an IS implementation?

   Interestingly, aspects of artificial neural network (ANN) IS implementations are motivated by the massive parallel computing capabilities of relatively simple biological cells called neurons. This, of course, assumes we are successful in understanding the human brain at a level that allows implementation of relevant processes.

2. Should the (functional or behavioral) structure of the human brain be the template for an IS implementation?

   This, of course, assumes we are successful in understanding the human brain functionality at a level that allows emulation of the relevant functions.[1]

3. Should the collective behavior of human (or other) populations be a template for IS emulation?

4. Should the evolution of human (or other) populations be a template for learning?

5. Is intelligent behavior necessarily based upon logic or logical reasoning?

6. Is intelligent behavior necessarily based upon formal rules?

7. Is intelligent behavior necessarily based upon the ability to learn?

   As noted in Chapter 16, there is a significant difference between learning and training.

8. What are the right (or "best") questions to ask? Are we asking them?

What Are Some IS Applications?   The short answer to this question is to list reasonably well-agreed-upon application **areas**, such as: robotics (including path planning and vision), engineering design, manufacturing, medical diagnosis, language understanding, security and defense, electronic commerce, (general) expert systems, and learning systems.

A Myriad of Other Definitions and Opinions.   A library of introductory information about a strongly-related topic (artificial intelligence [AI]) is available at http://www.aaai.org/AITopics/aitopics.html

---

[1]Actually, this applies to just about any domain. There is yet to be a "universal language."

Is It an IS or Just Software?   From a historical perspective, IS researchers have been persistent. Funding lulls, disappointing resulting capabilities of systems, realization of the difficulty (and computational complexity) of many problems have not stopped many researchers from continuing efforts in IS. While the machines of the movies do not yet exist (I think), significant IS-derived applications are apparent. This raises an interesting dilemma: Once an IS problem is solved and the application is fielded, does it no longer qualify as IS? In other words, is it now just software?[2]

1.1.4 IS: A Psychology–Based Viewpoint

It would be impossible to attempt to succinctly summarize hundreds of years of accumulated, diverse, and often contradictory research on human psychology. Nonetheless, a few snippets are included to help provide some perspective, and perhaps to motivate or validate certain IS representational strategies.

Early Work.   The study of the mind is probably almost as old as man. Certainly, psychologists have studied human reasoning and behavior since the time of Aristotle. One particularly important psychologist was William James (1890). Many of his basic insights into human behavior have survived the test of time. His two volume set [Jam90] is considered a research milestone and gives some indication of how an engineering approach to developing IS might proceed. Lest we anticipate this work will answer all questions regarding human behavior and, more naively, assume that algorithms will result, we need to note that according to James "...thought works under strange conditions."

James noted that high-level biological reasoning systems, including the human brain, are not designed principally to think abstractly. Rather, they are designed to facilitate the survival of the overall system. Thus, an engineering characterization of human cognitive ability is that of a system that performs reasonably well, according to some performance criteria, with reasonable resources, and in a timely fashion. A corollary to James' philosophy is that the human brain is only as well developed as it needs to be.

Another important result from James' work is that mental concepts need to be studied in the context or environment in which they occur. For example:

◆ Reasoning processes are not developed in a vacuum. (This is a consequence of nature and man, including man's reasoning and survival ability, evolving together.)

◆ Reasoning processes may be adaptations of previous strategies.

◆ Reasoning processes are often application-dependent.

Modern Thinking.   Current thinking is summarized in [Lev02]. Readers interested in a very thorough and readable overview, with a specific application to human interpretation of music, should consult [Lev06].

---

[2]I would suggest avoiding questions such as these, and focus on the objective: **intelligent behavior via computation**.

Modern psychologists have expounded on early work in many divergent (and often conflicting) ways. For example, the early idea of memory as a one-to-one mapping of a visual image into a biological "picture" is now widely questioned, since (1) there does not appear to be an identifiable place in the brain for storing this picture; (2) the picture exists as a thought; and (3) most likely a set of related features and exemplars is stored, not a verbatim "picture."

Other modern concepts include:

1. The notion of *perceptual completion*, (leading to cognitive completion). Human auditory and visual systems are adept at this. Certain (recurrent) ANN structures also capitalize on this behavior.

2. The notion that probability and uncertainty enter the process. For example, some premier perception psychologists (Herman von Helmholtz, Richard Gregory, Irvin Rock, and Roger Shepard) have argued that perception is a process of inference which incorporates probabilistic reasoning. For example, human reasoning is adept at determining the most likely state of the world given incomplete or ambiguous auditory/visual input.

3. The notion that perceptual processes involve feature extraction followed by feature integration.

4. The notion that mental processes are sequential, compositional, and *both* top-down and bottom-up in structure. Apparently top-down and bottom-up processes work together.

The last remark is noteworthy. Using a music perception example, *bottom-up processing* starts from low-level data. Sound features are extracted from raw audio (eardrum) signals, and then pitch, timbre, loudness, etc. are extracted. This low-level building block information is then integrated into a higher-level representation involving form and content, i.e., an impression or mental image of the musical passage.

Conversely, *top-down* processing is guided by expectation. Suppose, in the musical example, you knew you were in an outdoor arena. Based upon experience (both long and short term), you might not expect to hear a classical composition, but rather predict a rock music production. This suggests that a prediction of what could come next could be used to reinforce the hypothesized form and content of the current reasoning scenario.

1.1.5 Two Approaches to IS Development

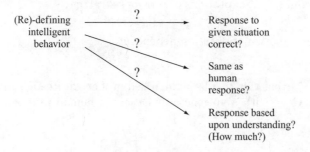

Figure 1.1 Questioning IS Development Approaches

The "Traditional" Way.   This may be thought of as "early AI." Characteristics of this approach include:

- It is based upon attempts to identify and implement a deep "understanding" of the problem. Thus, we often attribute system failure to an "incomplete" model or implementation.

- It uses explicit representation of declarative and procedural knowledge (and is commonly "rule-based").

- The attempt is to develop rich, complex, structured world models.

- Many realizations are brittle.

A More Opportunistic Attitude (the "Modern" Way).   Characteristics of this approach include:

- An attempt to solve the problem using any way that "works."

- The use of parameterized models that can *learn, adapt, or be trained*. Thus, *training* becomes a major component of system design.

- Allowing for uncertainty and allowing modeling uncertainty.

A possible shortcoming is the lack of an **explanation**. Nonetheless, significant efforts in linking neuroscience with computational models are underway [Col05].

An attempt at unifying these approaches is based upon a very macroscopic viewpoint. Specifically, in either approach, much development effort is spent doing two things:

- **quantitatively** determining desired IS behavior or response; and

- developing and modifying models and mechanisms to achieve this desired behavior.

1.2 Key Events and a History of Artificial Intelligence/Intelligent Systems (AI/IS)

1.2.1 A Timetable of Key Events

First, we present an admittedly incomplete and perhaps controversial timetable of some significant and related historical events in the evolution of IS.

1847 George Boole develops a mathematical symbolic logic (later called Boolean algebra) for reasoning about sets of objects.

1937 Alan Turing and Alonzo Church independently postulate a thesis, later called the Church–Turing thesis, that all problems that a human can solve can be reduced to a set of algorithms.

1945–1956 Symbolic artificial intelligence (AI) began to emerge as a recognized scientific endeavor. Norbert Wiener at MIT proposed the field of cybernetics and led to the postulate that intelligence is the process of receiving and processing information to achieve goals.

1949 Hebb suggested a way in which a certain type of artificial neuron might learn.

1950 Turing proposed the Turing test, to test for the realization of machine intelligence.

1956 A two-month summer conference was held at Dartmouth University, organized by John Mc-Carthy (see the following). Although consensus was not achieved on many topics, the participants hypothesized:

> *Every aspect of learning or any other feature of intelligence can in principle be so precisely described that a machine can be made to simulate it.*

1958 John McCarthy developed the Lisp program at MIT for AI work.

1965–1975 Edward Feigenbaum and Robert K. Lindsay at Stanford built DENDRAL, perhaps the first expert system. DENDRAL's use was in mapping the structure of complex organic chemicals from data gathered by mass spectrometers.

1966 ELIZA tricks users into believing the Turing test has been passed.

1969 Minsky and Papert publish "Perceptrons, An Introduction to Computational Geometry," a disparaging treatise on the lack of potential for ANNs.

1970s First practical demonstration of the use of fuzzy logic for process control.

1971–1972 Alain Colmerauer and Phillipe Roussel write the computer language, Prolog (for PROgrammation en LOGique).

1972 Edward Shortliffe and others write MYCIN, an expert system to diagnose infectious blood diseases.

Late 1970s First commercial expert system, XCON, was released. XCON was used to help configure VAX computer systems, and grew to more than 3000 rules.

1980s Fuzzy logic is introduced in a system used to operate subway trains in Japan.

1987 XCON grows to 10,000 rules.

1990s Efforts to use ontology begins.

1997 Deep Blue, an IBM supercomputer, beats Gary Kasparov, world champion of chess.

2002 The Computing Research Association and National Science Foundation initiate a conference series on "Grand Research Challenges in Computer Science and Engineering." Many of the "Grand Research Challenges" involve topics considered fundamental or strongly related to IS. For example, one area involves building cognitive partnerships of human beings with software agents and robots to enhance individual productivity and effectiveness.

Summer Dartmouth Conference, 1956.   As noted previously, this conference may be the clearest indicator of the emergence of modern-day AI thrusts. As quoted from the proposal document:

> *We propose that a 2 month, 10 man study of artificial intelligence be carried out during the summer of 1956 at Dartmouth College in Hanover, New Hampshire. The study is to proceed on the basis of the conjecture that every aspect of learning or any other feature of intelligence can in principle be so precisely described that a machine can be made to simulate it.*

Note the entire document is available online at http://www-formal.stanford.edu/jmc/history/dartmouth/dartmouth.html as well as other sites.

Key areas investigated at the conference are now familiar topics and include:[3]

1. Automatic Computers

2. How Can a Computer be Programmed to Use a Language

3. Neuron Net

4. Theory of the Size of a Calculation

5. Self-improvement

6. Abstractions

7. Randomness and Creativity

1.2.2   Grand Research Challenges in Computer Science and Engineering Related to IS

With the leadership of the Computing Research Association and financial assistance from the National Science Foundation, a conference series on "Grand Research Challenges in Computer Science and Engineering" was initiated. In the Summer of 2002, a group of about 65 researchers from the public and private sectors convened to discuss the specific and urgent research challenges related to building computing systems of the future. The resulting document is available at http://www.cra.org/Activities/grand.challenges/

The Five Overall Areas and Topics Related to IS.   The five areas noted in the Grand Challenges are:

1. **Create a Ubiquitous Safety.Net.** Providing a ubiquitous Safety.Net will save lives and minimize damage from disasters through timely prediction, prevention, mitigation, and response.

2. **Build a Team of Your Own.** Building cognitive partnerships of human beings with software agents and robots will enhance individual productivity and effectiveness.

3. **Provide a Teacher for Every Learner.** Tutoring each individual in a tailored, learner-centered format will enable people to more fully realize their potential.

---

[3]Topical headings are used.

4. Build Systems You Can Count On. Assuring reliable and secure systems from the regional electric grid to an individual's heart monitor will allow us to rely on information technology with confidence.

5. Conquer System Complexity. Building predictable and robust systems (with billions of parts) will enable broader and more powerful applications of information technology.

Many of the conclusions regarding technical objectives and direction in computing are related to computational intelligence. A few are summarized here:

◆ Data fusion and analysis: The ability to fuse related data from multiple sources to derive useful information is critical. Analysis and interpretation of collected data in conjunction with information databases (that could often be out of date and/or have partial or incorrect information) are essential.

◆ Ability to predict, prevent, mitigate, and respond to emergencies, coupled with research in augmented cognition: Augment human cognitive capabilities by developing machines capable of offloading human thought processes, yielding cognitive systems capable of actively supporting individuals in pursuing their goals and solving problems as they arise while planning for the future.

◆ Build a team of your own composed of robots and agents functioning as active partners: These systems enhance individual cognitive abilities by supplementing memory and problem-solving capabilities and by providing direct access to relevant data, expertise, guidance, and instruction. They work toward shared goals while understanding enough about the task, the individual, and each other to assist, mentor, cooperate, and monitor as needed.

◆ Incorporation of cognitive capabilities into both programs and machines, that is, to upgrade them from the status of automation tools to that of cognitive systems. Capabilities include:

  – Understanding tasks and tools as well as the context in which they are embedded

  – Acquiring knowledge by learning from experience and/or instruction

  – Representing their acquired knowledge in visual displays and in appropriate human and formal languages

  – Tracking the evolution of their environment over time and inferring critical consequences of what is known and sensed

  – Acting in a goal-oriented manner, while solving problems as they arise and planning for future contingencies

  – Operating over extended periods of time and across a broad range of domains

◆ Cognitive tutors: It has been demonstrated that it is possible for an automated tutor to improve student performance by roughly one standard deviation from the mean for some high school mathematics students. Significant human effort is required to develop the specialized knowledge; significant progress must be made in crafting knowledge representations that are both interoperable and reusable. The knowledge representations that underlie such tutors should also be designed to incorporate new knowledge about a subject area [Che05].

◆ Build systems with billions of parts: The limiting factor is software, not hardware. Every year, Moore's Law continues to pay its dividend, yielding ever higher raw performance per dollar. Software is still being written at the same manual pace and has progressed only incrementally since the 1950s. Software organization hits a "complexity barrier" somewhere above 10 million lines of code. Without better ways of producing and structuring software, the complexity barrier will constrain our ambitions for system behaviors.

◆ Building self-sustaining software today: Among the research challenges are:

  – Understanding and controlling emergent behavior

  – Learning in multi-agent systems

  – Negotiation and optimization

  – Architectures and networks

  – Programming languages and computational models

1.3 An Elusive Model Yields an Elusive Goal

Some aspects of IS concern **developing and relating mental models to real-world computation**. Surprisingly, we appear to know a great deal more about our physiological functioning (e.g., operation of the heart, immune systems, and nutrition) than the underlying operation of our conscious and subliminal mental processes.

1.3.1 The Mind and (Versus?) the Brain

The brain is a biological computer containing approximately 100 billion neurons (although the argument is often made that not a large percentage are used). In the brain, each neuron is connected to 10^3 to 10^4 other neurons. Note that as the number of neurons increases, the number of possible interconnections grows exponentially.

One IS design strategy could be based upon emulation of the intelligence exhibited by the human "mind." For purposes of argument, suppose we adopt the oft-cited mind–brain relationship: "the mind is what the brain does." In other words, the working brain is the hardware and the mind is the set of processes running on this hardware. Computationally, these processes might be assumed to be due to some large set of "software" running on the brain. In other words, the "mind" is the biological processing itself.

Cognitive neuroscientists attempt to identify and understand the thought processes of the mind. This includes memories, emotions, responses, and experiences, and how they are stored. Furthermore, cognitive neuroscientists attempt to unify this cognitive model with the underlying biological signal processing.

The IS design objective thus becomes describing these mental processes (in effect, reverse-engineering the software) in a manner that permits replication on nonbiological hardware with the same macroscopic behavior. In fact, functional MRIs (fMRIs) have been used for this purpose [Fri05].

The difficulties with this approach are numerous. For one, as noted in Section 1.3, identifying the mental processes corresponding to the higher-level biological computation is somewhere between extremely difficult and impractical. In addition, the analogy itself is probably too simple. The brain and the mind have a somewhat circular coexistence; the mind can influence the brain and vice versa.

Furthermore, the brain (and the mind) are both highly malleable and flexible; computer hardware is (currently) not.

Unexplainable Processes.   Underlying IS efforts is an implicit assumption that human-like reasoning is a form of computation that may be identified and consequently automated. There are numerous examples of consistently successful managers (including presidents and coaches) who consistently make correct decisions based upon unexplainable inner (or "gut") feelings. What is clearly lacking in general are algorithms that describe the reasoning process and thereby facilitate the mechanization of reasoning.

The IS "Singularity."   Since the early 1970s, predictions for the IS field have often been bold (and many are still unrealized). One of the more recent and interesting predictions is related to *the IS "singularity."* This event is predicted to occur shortly after the first IS with superhuman intelligence is realized. Briefly, the prediction is that the autonomous evolution of superintelligent machines (with consciousness) will usher in a new era of productivity and economic growth. A comprehensive summary of the concept and proponents is found in [Zor08].

1.3.2 Puzzle Solving (Riddles) and Intelligence

There is a spectrum of opinion concerning what constitutes (automated) intelligent behavior. We digress briefly to evaluate the utility of approaching IS systems development using problem domains taken from well-known puzzles and games. Examples are the games of tic-tac-toe, chess, the "fox and chickens" puzzle, the Tower of Hanoi puzzle, and a plethora of similar "brain teasers." Many are used in this text.

There is relatively little doubt that explicit formulations and solutions to many of these puzzles are complex. However:

- ◆ The solution to many typical puzzles may be accomplished by an (relatively unsophisticated) exhaustive search procedure, whereas humans often formulate a more elaborate or "clever" solution;

- ◆ The representation of many real-world IS problems is considerably more complex than that of puzzles. For example, in practical problems, many more constraints are applicable, uncertainty is present, and conflicts may arise requiring further definition of the problem. The representation for a puzzle, however, may be as simple as the state of a chessboard.

- ◆ It is not clear that solutions to puzzles extrapolate to solutions to realistic problems.

Nevertheless, the study of IS solutions to puzzle-like problems has some merit. For example, solutions to puzzles illustrate important concepts such as combinatorial explosion of possible states and the use of search. Furthermore, these solutions provide vehicles to explore the representation and programming details of more realistic symbolic manipulation problems. Finally, they may be used to illustrate the utility of solutions guided by heuristics.

1.3.3 Data Versus Knowledge

There is a significant distinction between data and knowledge. Computers manipulate data at almost unimaginable rates; in the domain of intelligent behavior computers are clueless as to the meaning or significance of the data.

The Internet is a seemingly inexhaustible source of (mostly unstructured[4]) data. Autonomously making sense of this data, in tasks such as intelligent search, data mining, or national security is still a very primitive endeavor. Search engines (e.g., Google) match words or phrases. What is needed are intelligent *analysis or understanding* engines. Matching of data is a quantum leap away from semantic analysis of information.

1.3.4 Semantic Computing

The processing of structed data (and design and use of data structures) is not new. The emerging field of Semantic Computing [She07] addresses the processing of, and interaction with, unstructured, semistructured, and structured data using semantics. Key aspects are the identification, extraction, relating, and understanding of syntactic structures.

One could argue that many proposed IS applications fundamentally involve the automated semantic interpretation of sensor data. This data could be audio (speech understanding), visual (computer vision), or other (data mining of web data).

Semantic Computing incorporates elements of software engineering, multimedia data processing, user (language and visual) interface design, Natural Language Processing (NLP), computational linguistics, and AI. An example is using natural language to retreive content from multimedia sources, e.g., "show me all images on my computer containing aircraft." As expected, this is a significantly challenging application. Automated sensor-based security and data mining are also currently popular applications.

1.3.5 IS and Game Theory

What Is Game Theory?   Game theory is a branch of applied mathematics that explores representation and manipulation of games. We define a game as a situation wherein "players" (or agents) choose actions in an attempt to achieve some goal. This goal is often to "win" or to optimize some quantifiable measure.

Most readers are familiar with simple games (e.g., tic-tac-toe, checkers). More advanced game theory applications include the development of military strategy, economic and business modeling,[5] and not surprisingly, intelligent systems. For example, an auction may be considered a multiplayer game.

Components of Game Theory.   A game must have a quantitative representation of the game state, the criteria to be optimized (if any), and the effect of the player's actions on these entities. To this end, many of the representational schemes presented in this book are applicable.

A significant aspect of game theory is that the costs or benefits of a particular action are not fixed, *but they are dependent upon the actions of other players or agents.*

---

[4]Although XML is making inroads.

[5]Mathematician John Nash won a Nobel Prize in this area and inspired the book and movie *A Beautiful Mind.*

Other attributes of games are noteworthy:

1. In a *zero sum* game, the sum of some measure of benefit to the players remains constant. Card games involving betting, such as poker, typify this attribute.

2. A game may be *simultaneous* or sequential. In simultaneous games, the players choose actions simultaneously; there is not an "order" in which the game is played. In sequential games, there is an ordering of the allowed player's actions (and usually previous actions are known to the players).

3. A game may or may not have a finite number of possible states and/or action-choice sequences.

1.4   Distinguishing Characteristics of IS Problems

Consider the following problems:

1. Finding the maximum of a set of numbers

2. Computing A^{-1}, given matrix A

3. The Traveling Salesman problem (TSP)

4. Map coloring using a fixed number of colors (e.g., 3)

In the first problem, we know a solution (or solutions) exist. Ignoring efficiency, the problem is solvable. In the second problem, a solution may or may not exist. For example, if A is not square, our definition of inverse may need to be generalized. Even in the case where A is square, invertability is not guaranteed. *However, tests (computations) exist that allow us to check this prior to attempting to compute the inverse* (i.e., determining the rank of A). If the matrix is invertible, many computational techniques are available. Problems 3 and 4 are members of a class of problems more appropriate for IS. In these problems, one of two things may occur:

1. There are (e.g., brute force) solution approaches, but:

   (a) It may not be possible to determine if a solution exists without attempting to find one.
   (b) Even if a (conventional) solution exists, the computational complexity required in the solution is such that constraints on processing time may not be met. In this case, the conventional solution may be useless.

For example, suppose we could overcome the computational cost of the TSP by employing a recurrent neural network. The network may converge to a solution 75% of the time in a few iterations. Thus, the computational cost is low, but the quality of the solution must be evaluated.

The trade-off is between:

◆ Exact (conventional) solutions to problems whose solutions may not exist; and

◆ Nontraditional solutions to problems that sometimes work or provide suboptimal, but perhaps useful, solutions.

Thus, many times IS approaches may be a "last resort." This example also suggests the "knowledge-intensive vs. computer-intensive" spectrum of approaches and thus raises the (old) questions of search and computational complexity.

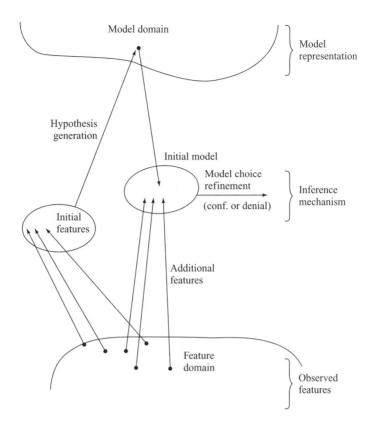

Figure 1.2 Another IS Theme—Model Unification

Model Unification.   Another underlying theme commonly encountered in IS applications is the unification of observations with a predetermined model. This is shown in Figure 1.2.

Search.   Problems associated with computational complexity and search are (typically) inherent in the implementation of IS. Many IS applications, when approached "traditionally," are NP complete,[6] and therefore exhibit characteristics of exponential growth and combinatorial explosion. This is especially apparent in empirical solution approaches employing trial-and-error (e.g., generate-and-test), or random selection.

To avoid this pitfall, the formulation of solution strategies to search-based problems using an intelligent component is desirable. This may be viewed as trading brute-force computation for "insight" or "cleverness" in the solution procedure. Thus, **knowledge facilitates (efficient) search**.

---

[6]NP stands for Nondeterministic Polynomial time. This is explored in Chapter 3.

1.5 The Turing Test

A reasonable question is: "How would you know if an IS is intelligent?" British mathematician Alan Turing addressed the potential for a computer to serve as a "mechanical brain" [Tur50]. Turing provided a test intended to both answer and circumvent this question. We paraphrase Turing's test (or game) as follows:

> Consider two rooms, one containing a (wired) computer terminal, used by a human. Call this Human A. The wire extends into the other room. Human A cannot tell what is in the other room, i.e., what Human A's computer terminal is connected to. Two possibilities exist:
>
> 1. The wire is connected to another terminal, at which Human B resides and communicates with Human A via the terminal.
> 2. The wire is connected to a computer running an "intelligent" program; no human is involved in the second room.
>
> Basically, Turing said that if Human A, after extensive conversation via the terminal, cannot tell whether the other room contains Human B or a computer program, *and if the other room in fact contains a computer*, the computer (program) passes the Turing test.

In any practical case, the domain of discourse is limited. For example, Human A cannot ask "Are you a computer?"

Remarks.   It is arguable whether the goal of an IS is to pass the Turing test. In addition, some claim the Turing test is too weak; others claim it is chauvinistic. A more comprehensive analysis of the Turing test is available at http://plato.stanford.edu/entries/turing-test/

1.6 Where Is the Field of IS Going?

Predicting trends in IS technology is very tricky. However, a few observations are probably useful:

1. As much of the reading in this chapter suggests, and as exemplified by the remainder of the text, the field of IS is not homogeneous. *Many* technologies now contribute to the field, including mathematical logic, production systems, evolutionary computing, and neural networks.

2. A corollary to the previous remark is that no single IS architecture or technology has yet proven to be the all-encompassing solution. Instead, it is now recognized that the opportunistic *fusion* of many representation, manipulation, and learning approaches provides a more versatile solution avenue.

3. Much effort is being put into the development of large knowledge bases, in a structured (and manipulable) form. Part of the motivation is to develop systems that embody "common sense" and/or are not "brittle." This effort also allows the reuse of information, and avoids the "reinvention of the wheel" for each new IS system. Chapter 8 discusses knowledge ontologies and related tools.

4. The distinction between games and real IS problems is now understood and accepted.

5. Computational architectures (both hardware and software tools) for IS development continue to evolve and standardize. Thus, Lisp programming ability is no longer a prerequisite for IS development.

6. Many issues remain open. This includes cognitive modeling and the development of mathematical foundations and characterizations for IS technologies.

1.7 Quantitative Tools for IS Development

Some Available Tools.   There is an adage that says "If the only tool you have is a hammer, then every problem looks like a nail." This adage is applicable, by analogy, to IS development. While we no longer equate AI/IS with programming in a "historically AI/IS-oriented" language (e.g., Lisp, Prolog) or environment (e.g., Soar, CLIPS, OPS5), it is still true these tools have a significant utility in some IS problem domains. Moreover, there has probably never been a time in history when so many well-developed and mature tools are available to the IS practitioner, including:

- Updated and standardized versions of Prolog and (Common) Lisp

- C and C++ libraries for IS use

- Shells for production system development, including CLIPS and Soar

- Neural network simulators

- Genetic algorithm simulators

- Tools to build quantitative, manipulable ontologies (e.g., see the Protege Ontology Editor in Chapter 2)

- Standardized representations of ontologies and "common sense"

- Parallel architectures to combat computational complexity

Some of these tools are good, some are difficult to learn, and some are vehicles to allow nonprogrammers to develop IS programs. A complete listing of available tools for all languages is impractical. We highlight a few tools and related approaches in this book. We also strongly assert: *The notion that IS should be taught or implemented using a single tool, development environment, or language is nonsense.* Actually, this assertion applies to just about any problem domain, since there is yet to be a "universal language."

Programming Paradigms.   Although one could argue that any programming paradigm and/or language is suitable for IS development purposes, experience has shown that some are more favorable. A wide variety of programming paradigms exist [Sch07]. Relevant examples include:

1. Procedural (probably the best-known; found in languages such as C and Java)

2. Functional (e.g., Lisp)

3. Declarative (e.g., Prolog)

4. Object-oriented (which allows complex systems to be modeled as modular components that can be easily reused to model other systems or to create new components)

5. Rule-based (which allows knowledge to be represented as rules that specify a set of preconditions that must hold and, if so, a set of actions to be performed)

6. Parallel programming (e.g., MPI, CUDA)

As noted, the set of candidate languages and development systems for IS development includes scripting (PERL, Tcl/Tk/), C/C++, Prolog, Lisp/ML, OPS5, CLIPS, Soar, and MATLAB. It is noteworthy that IS development seems to favor the rule-based paradigm (CLIPS, Soar), with some attention given to the declarative approach (Prolog). These are shown in subsequent chapters.

1.8 Organization of the Text

In this text, we visit a number of often interrelated IS topics. It is not necessary to explore the chapters in numerical order; however some are prerequisites for others. In addition, the Appendices summarize important background material, some or all of which may be familiar to the reader.

- Chapter 2 provides a look at a number of underlying IS themes, including knowledge representation and manipulation, ontologies, and expert query.

- Chapter 3 explores the abstract notion of an IS state space, IS computational complexity, and the role of search in IS applications.

- Often, the perception of intelligent behavior is based upon the simultaneous satisfaction of a large number of constraints. This is typical of problems in scheduling, temporal reasoning, and games. Chapter 4 considers (nonstructure-based) constraint satisfaction problems (CSP) in IS.

- Chapter 5 explores structure-based CSP problems, including natural language (NL) understanding.

- Chapter 6 introduces the mathematical underpinning of rule-based inference as a representation and manipulation tool. The notion of a production system is introduced.

- Chapter 7 introduces the CLIPS production system architecture and software, and Chapter 8 fuses the CLIPS paradigm with more advanced production system topics such as hierarchical and modular representations and the Rete algorithm. The fuzzy capabilities of CLIPS are introduced.

- Chapter 8 extends the production system notion to include integration with ontologies and modular representations, system consistency, and other forms of reasoning. In addition, this chapter introduces the concepts of agents and distributed IS paradigms.

- Chapter 9 introduces the Soar architecture, including philosophy and pragmatics. Soar is more complex, powerful, and flexible than CLIPS.

- Chapters 10 and 11 consider the representation and manipulation of IS knowledge representations containing uncertainty.

- Chapter 12 covers planning in IS.

◆ Chapters 13, 14, and 15 address the biologically inspired IS approach of ANNs. Biological inspiration is also considered in Chapter 17, in the forms of genetic and swarm algorithms.

◆ Chapter 16 addresses learning in IS.

1.9 Practice or Introductory Exercises

1. To gain some insight into the quantitative challenges in IS, develop (or research) definitions for each of the following:

    1. cognition
    2. knowledge
    3. understanding
    4. learning
    5. intelligence
    6. intellect
    7. rational
    8a. reason (verb)
    8b. reason (noun)
    9. think
    10. perception
    11a. memory
    11b. remember
    12. consciousness

2. Section 1.1.3 indicated a number of IS *application areas*. Using the Web, find a specific application example for each of these areas:

    ◆ robotics
    ◆ engineering design
    ◆ manufacturing
    ◆ medical diagnosis
    ◆ language understanding
    ◆ security and defense
    ◆ electronic commerce
    ◆ expert systems
    ◆ learning systems

3. Apply the three questions from Section 1.1.1 to each of your sample applications in the previous exercise.

4. One exciting and popular application area for IS is the production of realistic video games [BB08]. These games involve complex, autonomous opponents and may incorporate machine learning. Using the Web, research this area and find several current applications.

## chapter 2

First Steps in IS: Representation, Ontologies, and Obtaining Expertise

2.1 Representation in IS

2.1.1 Knowledge Representation and Related Definitions

A (knowledge) *representation* is a scheme or approach used to capture the essential elements of a problem domain. A *manipulable representation* is one that facilitates computation, and, for our purposes, is the only one worthy of further consideration. In manipulable representations, the information is accessible to other entities (e.g., inference engines), which use the representation as part of the overall computation.

Development of the representation may involve the process of *knowledge engineering*. This may include expert query. The issues involved in the development of a detailed knowledge representation are complex, interrelated, and problem and goal-dependent.

2.1.2 Human Reasoning: Classes, Categories, Concepts, and Chunking

In Chapter 1, Section 1.1.4, the role of psychology and cognitive science in IS was summarized. Modern psychology includes the study of the notions of categories (classes) and concepts. Categorization (or classification) is a basic capability of high-level biological systems [Ros99]. Whereas every object is unique, different objects may be conceptualized and/or treated similarly as members of a class or category. Aristotle argued that humans define categories by a set of characteristic features, in a formal, rigid definition of the category. Modern philosophy[1] (and pattern recognition) seems to refute this notion of category membership in two ways:

- Category (class) membership is not all-or-nothing (crisp), but rather fuzzy; and

- Category membership is determined by resemblance to one or more exemplars for the category. In other words, there is no single, all-encompassing set of features that define a category. Instead, a (possibly dynamic) set of category exemplars provide a reference point for membership in the category.

---

[1]Professor Eleanor Rosch has written extensively on the subject.

Chunking. Chunking is related to the study of memory theory, i.e., paradigms for how categories are defined, formed, and learned (or stored) in the human brain. For example, creating related "chunks" of information from experience is fundamental to human learning. New situations may be approached by recalling similar stored "chunks" identified in previous situations [GLC+01]. This aspect of cognitive science is not lost on IS development; the Soar system (Chapter 9) implements a form of this type of learning.

2.1.3   Declarative Versus Procedural Representations

Knowledge representation approaches may be subdivided into declarative (i.e., the representation of facts and assertions) and procedural (i.e., the storing of actions or consequences) representations. An alternative characterization of this representational dichotomy is knowing "what" (declarative) vs. knowing "how" (procedural).

The specifics of an application may dictate a preferred approach. A reasonable postulate is that versatile, intelligent systems may need to use both.

Declarative schemes include logic-based and relational approaches. Relational models may lead to representations in the form of trees, graphs, or semantic networks. Logical representation schemes include the use of propositional logic and, more importantly, predicate logic.

Procedural representational schemes store knowledge in how to do things. They may be characterized by formal grammars and usually implemented via procedural or rule-based (production) systems.

Declarative Versus Procedural Knowledge: Examples. The difference between declarative and procedural schemes may be illustrated by a simple example. A table of logarithms is an **explicit enumeration** of this (numerical) domain knowledge and would be considered a declarative representation. On the other hand, a stored sequence of actions indicating **how to compute** the logarithm of a number would be considered a procedural representation. This example illustrates tradeoffs in using declarative vs. procedural knowledge representations. Declarative representations are usually more expansive (and expensive), in the sense that enumeration may be redundant and inefficient. However, modification of declarative representations is usually quite easy; one merely adds or deletes the knowledge. Procedural representations, on the other hand, may be more compact, at the expense of flexibility.

2.2   Tools for Representation
2.2.1   Discrete Mathematics: Using Relations and Properties

Binary Relations. If A and B are sets, a binary relation from A to B is a subset of $A \times B$, where $A \times B$ denotes the Cartesian product of the sets A and B. This definition is mathematically precise; it is referred to as a binary relation since it only involves two sets.

Relation Properties. A relation from set A to set B may be represented by a set of ordered pairs, $\{(a_i, b_i)\}$, where $a_i \in A$ and $b_i \in B$. There are three properties of prime importance for a relation R:

1. reflexive: R is reflexive if $\forall a \in A, \quad (a, a) \in R$

2. symmetric: R is symmetric if $\forall (a, b) \in R,\quad (b, a) \in R$

3. transitive: R is transitive if $\forall (a, b) \in R$ and $(b, c) \in R,\quad (a, c) \in R$

Using Relations in IS Representations. Suppose our knowledge representation involves a relation between two entities, x and y. x and y may be symbols, numbers, actions, or concepts. Consider, for example,

"attribute R of object x has value y"

For representation purposes, one view might be that x and R are arguments to a function, denoted f, which returns y, i.e., $y = f(x, R)$. This relation may also be viewed as the ordered triple (R, x, y), which is in the (attribute, value) form or (A, O, V) format. This is read as "the A of O is V." An alternative is to view this mapping as a relation, denoted R, (in the strict mathematical sense), i.e.,

x is related to y by relation R

or $R = \{(x, y)\}$ or graphically $x \xrightarrow{R} y$.

2.2.2 Digraphs to Semantic Nets

The use of graphical constructs (directed graphs or digraphs) to enumerate both numerical and symbolic relations among sets of entities is common.[2] A semantic network, or simply semantic net, is a labeled digraph used to describe relations (including properties) of objects, concepts, situations, or actions. Semantic nets are ideal visualization tools that are widely used in IS to facilitate knowledge representation. Knowledge in a semantic net may be naturally organized to reflect hierarchies and thus enable inheritance.

Unfortunately, for most reasonable representations of our knowledge about even a very restricted domain, the overall semantic net is usually a large and highly interconnected entity.

2.2.3 Semantic Net Examples

A semantic net represents objects as nodes (shown as circles) and relations as labeled arcs (or edges). For "real-world" entities, they are usually quite complicated. A relatively simple semantic net for a "blocks world" situation is shown in Figure 2.1. Figure 2.2 shows a portion of a semantic net for a typical vehicle description.

Observe from these figures that:

1. The semantic net consists of many different edge labels or relations, such as "is-a," "has-attribute," "used-for," "adjacent-to," etc.

2. The semantic network may contain redundant or "derivable" information. For example, the "left_of" and "right_of" arcs between two nodes shown in Figure 2.1, while correct, are unnecessary, since given one, the other may be deduced. In addition, the enumeration of other

---

[2]In fact, as we show later, ontology editors may produce these graphical constructs, or even allow the development of ontologies graphically.

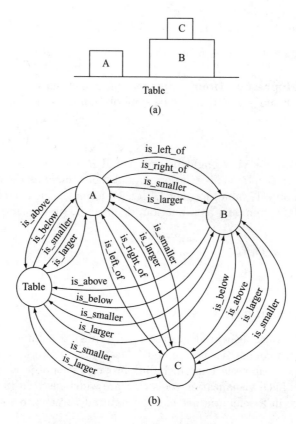

Figure 2.1 Semantic Net for "Blocks World"

information, such as the transitivity of a relation (e.g., on_top_of) allows the deduction of additional arcs. This approach often allows development of a desired representation in the form of a "skeletal" semantic net and a set of underlying explicit rules.

2.3 The Semantic Web: Concepts and Relationships, Not Just Data or Words

Throughout history, the *circulation of knowledge* has been fundamental for technical advancement of society. Printed academic journals and books, as well as (relatively recent) online publications made knowledge available to an audience capable of using it and, in turn, advancing it. However, printed media, while useful to humans, is not as useful for IS applications, since it is not a directly manipulable form of knowledge. To foster IS objectives, we might say we desire the *circulation of manipulable knowledge*.

The World Wide Web Consortium (W3C) is an international and vendor-neutral consortium that works to develop web standards, protocols, and guidelines that facilitate long-term growth for the

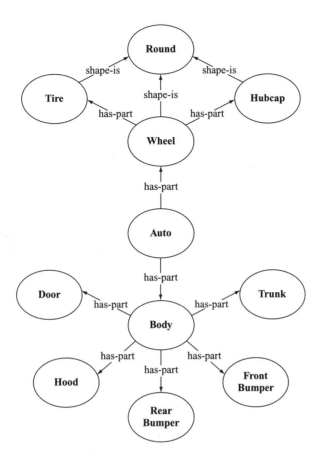

Figure 2.2 Portion of a Semantic Net for "Automobile"

Web. One significant enhancement of interest is the representation of *metadata*, that is, information about information.

The Semantic Web is a collaborative effort led by W3C with participation from a large number of researchers and industrial partners. The goal of the Semantic Web is to provide a common framework that allows data to be shared and reused across application, enterprise, and community boundaries. This, of course, includes knowledge representations in structured format. The Semantic Web is based on the Resource Description Framework (RDF, described below), which integrates a variety of applications using XML for syntax and Uniform Resource Identifiers (URIs) for naming. The URL is http://www.w3.org/2001/sw/

2.4 Structuring the Representation: Frames and Object-Oriented Representations

In both human and IS reasoning domains, structured representations are commonly used. One way to enforce structure is by using frames. In general, a frame is a general data structure implemented as collections of slots. Slots are frame components used to store variables that characterize the frame. Slots allow the embedding of interframe relations in the frame representation and thus provide "hooks" to link frames.

2.4.1 Frame Slots, "is–a," and Inheritance

Slot names in frames often (but are not required to) correspond to relation names. The all-important "is-a" frame link or slot is probably the most used slot. *"is-a" facilitates hierarchical representations and the inheritance of information.* This can lead to an object-oriented representation.

Hierarchical representations are efficient in the sense that redundancy of information is minimized and inheritance is facilitated. In addition, they allow the modeling and visualization of the structure and complex relations between entities.

A common approach to hierarchical frame representation is to create "generic" or type frames to represent abstractions of specific entities, and then create instance frames to represent specific instances of these generic types. The instance frames are linked to the type frames via the instance relation. This approach allows slots and their default values to be inherited by the instance frame from the type frame.

Inheritance with Exceptions.   The "is-a" relation is quite useful for hierarchical representations. Unfortunately, its generality often precludes its practical use. In order to correctly represent the situation where "almost all a's are b's," the concept of inheritance with exceptions or qualified "is-a" statements is relevant.

2.4.2 Object–Oriented Approaches

In a structured, hierarchical representation, many of the general attributes of an entity may be attributable to classes to which the entity belongs. Thus, we tend to take an object-oriented approach to representation development where:

1. Objects belong to classes. Each object is an instance of a class and all objects in a class share attributes (with generally different values for those attributes).

2. Classes can be subclasses of other classes. The subclass relationship is usually one of specialization.

A Simple Hierarchically Structured Representation.   Consider a representation for Jesse, a type of dog known as a Golden Retriever, who is 3.5 years old, etc. In exhaustive query of Jesse's owner, we ascertain the hierarchical, "is-a," based representation shown in Figure 2.3. In this figure, properties of superclasses, such as golden retriever, dog, mammal, etc., which may be inherited, are shown.

Inheritance is used in a class-based hierarchy to allow objects to acquire information from other objects in the representation.

For example, in the representation of Figure 2.3, Jesse inherits properties such as having four legs, from the fact that Jesse "is-a" dog. Similarly, the entity Jesse inherits the property of being warm-blooded, due to the fact that a dog "is-a" mammal. The "is-a" relation shown in this hierarchy to implement

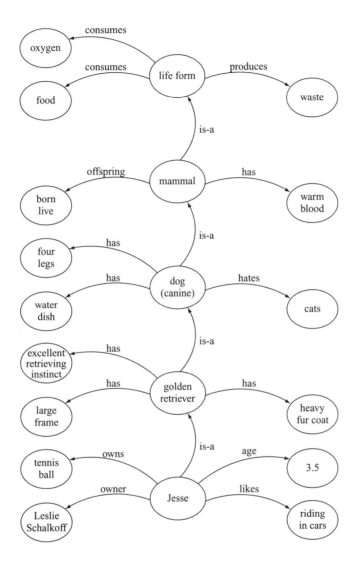

Figure 2.3 Hierarchical Representation of Jesse

inheritance has the transitive property. Using inheritance, a particular object (or instance of a class) inherits attributes from the superclasses to which the object belongs. Therefore, an "is-a" based representational structure allows the quantification of Jesse's characteristics using:

1. A property list (or equivalent structure) that stores properties or property values unique to Jesse

2. A record of Jesse's membership in other classes (via "is-a")

3. The transitive property of "is-a"

2.5 Ontologies: Concept and Tools
2.5.1 Background and Motivation

The task of determining the structure of a domain's knowledge and representing this knowledge in manipulable form is daunting. Novice developers might choose to start the process with an open text editor, a blank screen, and lots of randomly generated and loosely coupled ideas. This approach, aside from being somewhere between inefficient and impractical, is unlikely to yield any real success.

A historically interesting Lisp-based tool for knowledge base development is the CLASSIC knowledge representation system. Many of the underlying considerations, such as choice of concepts, implementing hierarchical class relations, etc. are still relevant. A tutorial and related Lisp implementation is available at the URL http://www.bell-labs.com/project/classic/papers/ClassTut/ClassTut.txt.

Another issue is the potential reuse and sharing of collectively-developed knowledge bases. The inefficiencies of building reasonably well-known knowledge bases from "scratch" have led to efforts to develop large, reusable ontologies. One active area is the representation of nonspecialized, i.e., "everyday" knowledge or "common sense."

2.5.2 What Is an Ontology and Why Do I Care?

There are many definitions of "ontology." Often, the abstract definition of "a specification of a conceptualization" is used. Historically, ontology is the theory of objects and their relationships. However, to facilitate IS discussion, we claim:

> An ontology is a formal characterization of concepts in a domain of discourse.

For our purposes, it is probably reasonable to extend the ontology definition to a "**(machine) manipulable** formal characterization." Ontologies exist for many domains, including medicine, engineering, and business.

Reasons for developing an ontology include:

◆ To capture domain knowledge

◆ To explore any underlying structure of the available domain knowledge

◆ To be able to visualize, manipulate, reuse, and update or extend the representation

◆ To be able to share representation information. In a world of large, decentralized knowledge, this may lead to an alternative, practical, and functional definition for an ontology: *a way for a community to agree on common terms and structure for representing knowledge in a domain.*

Developing an Ontology: Steps and Questions

It is important to note that there is often no optimal way to define an ontology. Alternatives, with different structures resulting from different concept choices, may exist. The process of ontology development, like many IS endeavors, is iterative. Perhaps the first step in developing any ontology is a search to determine if the ontology, or a similar, perhaps reusable one, already exists.

An ontology typically is based upon **concepts** (usually implemented as **classes**). Classes often spawn **subclasses**, and hierarchical parts of an ontology may result from super- and subclass relationships. Properties of classes are represented in **slots**. Inheritance is commonly used. Therefore, the practical elements of ontology development "from scratch" include [NM]:

♦ Defining concepts (classes). It is advisable to choose concepts or classes to be related to those encountered in the actual application.

♦ Defining the relationships among these classes (including hierarchies)

♦ Defining slots and value restrictions (if any) and ranges

♦ Determining default values

Developing an Ontology: Scope and Competency

A series of questions [NM] fundamental to the development of a specific ontology are:

1. What is the domain of the ontology? What knowledge domain is it intended to cover?

2. What is the purpose (use) of the ontology?

3. Who is the intended user of the ontology, and what information will they be using/seeking?

The answers to these questions should have a dominant role in the guidance of the ontology design process. The last question introduces the notion of a set of *competency questions*. The knowledge base built upon the ontology should be able to answer the competency questions. Another viewpoint is that these questions test the scope of the resulting ontology.

2.5.3   Ontologies and Knowledge Bases

Since an ontology may be viewed as a hierarchically structured set of entities for describing a domain, it may be used as a skeletal foundation for a *knowledge base* [BR97]. More importantly: *Adding instances of classes to an ontology yields a knowledge base.*

2.5.4   Standardization of Ontology Formats

The development of standardized representations for ontologies is proving quite useful, especially when integrated with web applications. Ontological information may be shared and modified (extended) without starting from scratch. Thus, many (not all) of the standardized representations are designed for web integration and based upon markup languages. Using a standardized representation format, IS applications can have a common understanding of the underlying knowledge, and semantic or knowledge-based interoperability is enhanced.

Some Popular Standardized Formats

Open Knowledge Base Connectivity.   Open Knowledge Base Connectivity (OKBC) is an API (application programming interface) for accessing knowledge bases stored in knowledge representation systems (KRSs). OKBC was developed under the sponsorship of DARPA's High Performance Knowledge Base program (HPKB). OKBC is the successor to the Generic Frame Protocol representation. For more information, the home page is http://reliant.teknowledge.com/HPKB/.

Resource Description Framework.   The Resource Description Framework (RDF) is a framework (and a language) for web-based information representation. The RDF syntax is based upon XML syntax.

The structure of any expression in RDF is a collection of triples. Each RDF triple consists of a subject, a predicate, and an object, and are conventionally written in that order. The predicate is also called the *property* of the triple.

In an RDF triple:

♦ The subject is an RDF URI reference[3] or a blank node

♦ The predicate is an RDF URI reference

♦ The object is an RDF URI reference, a literal, or a blank node

Since each triple may be represented by a digraph, the similarity of the RDF representation with the information contained in a semantic net is obvious. The set of all RDF triples in the representation is called an RDF graph.

Section 2.5.4 shows an example of RDF. An excellent resource for RDF syntax, semantics, and extensions is http://www.w3.org/TR/2004/REC-rdf-concepts-20040210/.

OWL.   The Ontology Web Language (OWL) describes a language for web-representable ontologies. The semantics of the OWL language allow inferences about elements contained in ontologies. An OWL ontology may include descriptions of classes, properties, and their instances. OWL is another component of the Semantic Web activity; Section 2.5.4 shows an example of an OWL representation. Further details are available at http://www.w3.org/TR/owl-guide/.

An Example: Comparing Underlying Representation Formats

Consider the elementary and minimal semantic knowledge representation shown in Figure 2.4.

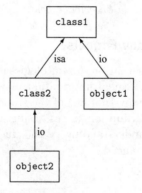

Figure 2.4 Simple (Generic) Knowledge Representation Used to Show Standardized Representation Formats

---

[3]A constrained UNICODE string.

```
(defclass class1                    ([object1] of  class1
(is-a %3ASYSTEM-CLASS)              )
(role concrete)
(single-slot %3ANAME                ([object2] of  class2
(type STRING)                       )
;+ (cardinality 0 1)
(create-accessor read-write)))

(defclass class2
(is-a class1)
(role concrete)
(single-slot %3ANAME
(type STRING)
;+ (cardinality 0 1)
(create-accessor read-write)))
```

Figure 2.5 Snippets of Protege `pins/pont` File Representations Corresponding to the Semantic Net of Figure 2.4. Note class structure information is held in the `pont` file (left) and instance information is stored in the `pins` file (right). This format is compatible with CLIPS COOL (Chapter 8).

`*.pins/*.pont` **Format.** First, we show snippets of the Protege `pins/pont` representation for the simple network in Figure 2.4 and Figure 2.5. Two files are required; one for the class structure (`pont`) and the other for instances (`pins`).

Figure 2.6 shows snippets of the OWL representation corresponding to Figure 2.4. Similarly, Figure 2.7 shows snippets of the corresponding two part RDF representation.

```
<?xml version="1.0"?>
<rdf:RDF
    xmlns:rdf="http://www.w3.org/1999/02/22-rdf-syntax-ns#"
    xmlns:xsd="http://www.w3.org/2001/XMLSchema#"
    xmlns:rdfs="http://www.w3.org/2000/01/rdf-schema#"
    xmlns:owl="http://www.w3.org/2002/07/owl#"
    xmlns="http://www.owl-ontologies.com/unnamed.owl#"
  xml:base="http://www.owl-ontologies.com/unnamed.owl">
  <owl:Ontology rdf:about=""/>
  <owl:Class rdf:ID="class2">
    <rdfs:subClassOf>
      <owl:Class rdf:ID="class1"/>
    </rdfs:subClassOf>
  </owl:Class>
  <owl:ObjectProperty rdf:ID="to-class2"/>
  <class1 rdf:ID="object1"/>
  <class2 rdf:ID="object2"/>
</rdf:RDF>
```

Figure 2.6 Standardized OWL Representation for the Network of Figure 2.4

```
<?xml version='1.0' encoding='UTF-8'?>
<!DOCTYPE rdf:RDF [
 <!ENTITY rdf 'http://www.w3.org/1999/02/22-rdf-syntax-ns#'>
 <!ENTITY a 'http://protege.stanford.edu/system#'>
 <!ENTITY rdf_ 'http://protege.stanford.edu/rdf'>
 <!ENTITY rdfs 'http://www.w3.org/2000/01/rdf-schema#'>
]>
<rdf:RDF xmlns:rdf="&rdf;"
 xmlns:rdf_="&rdf_;"
 xmlns:a="&a;"
 xmlns:rdfs="&rdfs;">
<rdfs:Class rdf:about="&rdf_;class1"
 rdfs:label="class1">
<rdfs:subClassOf rdf:resource="&a;_system_class"/>
</rdfs:Class>
<rdfs:Class rdf:about="&rdf_;class2"
 rdfs:label="class2">
<rdfs:subClassOf rdf:resource="&rdf_;class1"/>
</rdfs:Class>
<rdf:Property rdf:about="&rdf_;to-class2"
 rdfs:label="to-class2">
<rdfs:range rdf:resource="&rdfs;Class"/>
</rdf:Property>
<rdf:Property rdf:about="&a;_name"
 rdfs:label=":NAME">
<rdfs:domain rdf:resource="&rdf_;class1"/>
<rdfs:domain rdf:resource="&rdf_;class2"/>
</rdf:Property>
</rdf:RDF>
```

```
<?xml version='1.0' encoding='UTF-8'?>
<!DOCTYPE rdf:RDF [
 <!ENTITY rdf 'http://www.w3.org/1999/02/22-rdf-syntax-ns#'>
 <!ENTITY rdf_ 'http://protege.stanford.edu/rdf'>
 <!ENTITY rdfs 'http://www.w3.org/2000/01/rdf-schema#'>
]>
<rdf:RDF xmlns:rdf="&rdf;"
 xmlns:rdf_="&rdf_;"
 xmlns:rdfs="&rdfs;">
<rdf_:class1 rdf:about="&rdf_;object1"
 rdfs:label="object1"/>
<rdf_:class2 rdf:about="&rdf_;object2"
 rdfs:label="object2"/>
</rdf:RDF>
```

Figure 2.7 Standardized RDL Class (left) and RDF Instance (right) Representations for the Network of Figure 2.4

The Availability of Ontology Editors

Coupled with the notion of standardized ontology representations is the concept of an ontology editor. Without careful engineering, ontologies may be poorly constructed and difficult to maintain. Using an ontology editor frees the knowledge engineer (at least initially) from the details of IS implementation and opens the world of ontology development to a wider group (including nontechnical experts themselves).

There are at least 30 well-known ontology editors, many of which are open source. A table may be found at http://www.xml.com/pub/a/2004/07/14/onto.html. In Section 2.6, as well as Chapter 8, we explore the popular Protege ontology editor.

2.6 The Protege Ontology Editor

Protege is a free, open-source, extensible, platform-independent environment for creating and editing large ontologies and knowledge bases in various representation formats. Protege also facilitates the visualization of ontologies using a number of plugins. It is a java application with MS Windows, linux, and Mac OS X ports. The Protege home page is http://protege.stanford.edu.

Protege supports the development of ontologies that are frame-based (object-oriented) using the OKBC. In the frame-based representation, an ontology consists of:

1. A set of classes organized in a subsumption hierarchy;

2. A set of slots associated with each class; and

3. A set of instances of the classes.

Protege also supports development using the OWL. The OWL language incorporates formal semantics that allow the derivation of logical consequences, i.e., new facts not explicitly present in the ontology. Defining a class with attributes using OWL is not as direct as the frame-based approach. The OWL and frame-based distinctions are addressed in the problems. Note that a "full" installation of Protege (3.4 or later) supports both formats.

We introduce simple Protege examples and some underlying implementation issues in this Chapter. Many other features and examples of Protege use are included in Chapter 8.

2.6.1 Protege Examples

Card Games

Figure 2.8 shows the use of Protege in defining an ontology for a set of card games. A graphical representation of the resulting class hierarchies is shown in Figure 2.9. One of the attractive features of Protege is the ability (using so-called plugins) to graphically display and input elements of an ontology.

A More Complex Protege Ontology Example

Consider the ontology view shown in Figure 2.10. This ontology was inspired by the hierarchical representation of Figure 2.3. We reuse this ontology in Chapter 8 to show integration with CLIPS COOL. A graphical representation of the ontology, including instances, is shown in Figure 2.11.

Figure 2.8 An (Incomplete) Ontology for Card Games Produced Using the Protege Ontology Editor

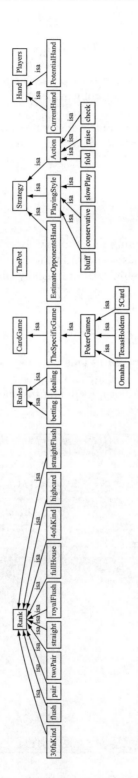

Figure 2.9 Graphical Representation for the Card Games Ontology (Produced Using Protege)

2.6.2 Alternate Representation Formats Using Protege

Our primary interest is in using the Protege `pins` and `pont` representational formats (incorporated in files ending with these extensions). This allows direct importation of the Protege-based knowledge representation into CLIPS. One of the more noteworthy aspects of Protege is the ability to import and export a number of standardized ontology representations, including CLIPS, OWL, RDF, XMK, and HTML. For example, the HTML representation (shown displayed on a browser) for the Protege-based ontology shown of Figures 2.10 and 2.11 is shown in Figures 2.12 and 2.13.

2.7 Ontological Reasoning and "Common Sense" Implementations
2.7.1 CYC (OpenCYC)

The objectives of CYC Corporation's CYC effort is "Formalized Common Knowledge." OpenCyc is the open source version of what is claimed to be the world's largest and most complete general knowledge base and commonsense reasoning engine. It may be used as the basis of a wide variety of IS applications. Versions for both Linux and Windows XP operating systems are available.

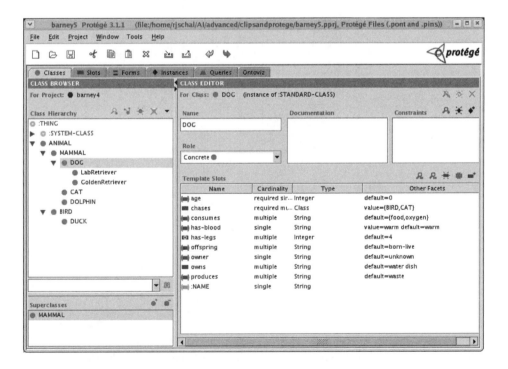

Figure 2.10 Protege Structured Representation (Class View Shown) Example

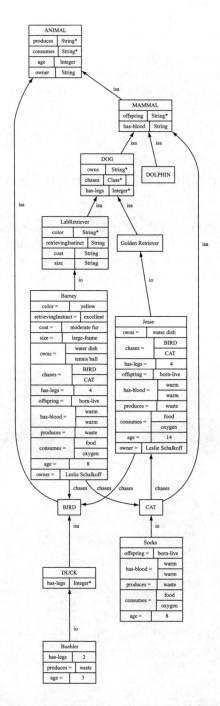

Figure 2.11 One Graphical View of the Ontology of Figure 2.10 Produced Using the Protege OntoViz Plugin

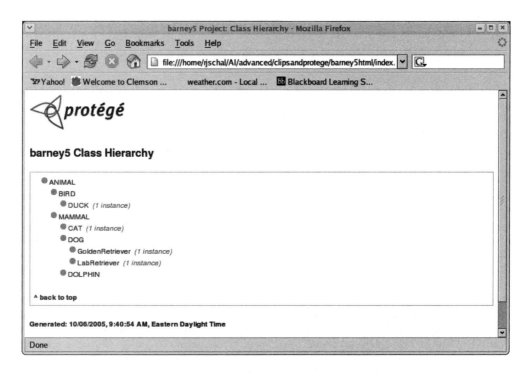

Figure 2.12 HTML Representation for the Ontology (Main Window)

Sample Database.   For illustration, the first few entries in the CYC open database (file `omcsraw.txt`) are shown in Figure 2.14. The (open) CYC home page is http://www.opencyc.org/ and the Sourceforge project page is http://sourceforge.net/projects/opencyc/.

2.7.2 Common Sense (MIT)

The Open Mind common sense database, a product of the MIT Media Lab, is comprised of approximately 600,000 statements, such as:

> People do not walk on their heads.

For more information, see http://commonsense.media.mit.edu/.

2.8 Expert Systems
2.8.1 What Is an Expert System?

The term expert system is used to indicate a subset of IS that is restricted to specific task domains.

> Expert systems (ES) are programs that attempt to emulate the behavior of human experts, usually confined to a specific field.

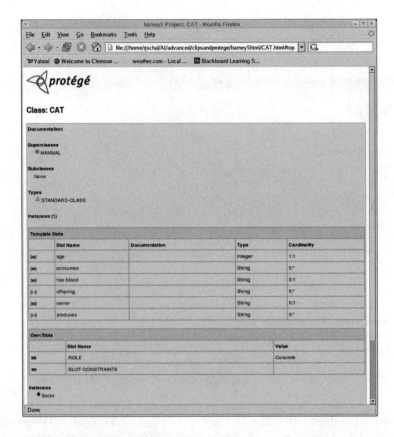

Figure 2.13 HTML Representation for the Ontology (After Clicking on "cat")

Expert system shells and knowledge acquisition systems have been developed using disparate approaches to knowledge representation and manipulation as well as user interfacing. A sample ES structure is shown in Figure 2.15.

The following are typical attributes of an ES:

1. Knowledge is usually represented in declarative form to enable easy reading and modification. Most ESs use IF-THEN structures for representation, thus, rule-based ES predominate.

2. There is usually a clear structure to the knowledge representation (this excludes neural expert systems).

3. There is a clear distinction between the knowledge representation and the control or manipulation mechanism.

4. A significant user I/O interface, to allow query, advice, explanation, and interaction with the ES is provided.

5. A user knowledge acquisition or knowledge modification module is often provided for extension of the ES.

```
dogs are mammals

dogs are small

dogs cannot fly

dogs live in dog houses

A box can hold things

A flag is for displaying in public the political group of the owner of the flag

A goldfish is a type of carp that makes a nice pet

A lawn is a place outside where grass grows

A nightgown is a long, loose garment worn to bed

A roach is an insect

A unicycle is a vehicle with one wheel that is moved by pedals

A wheel is a circular object that rotates around its center

Ants are social insects

At night the sun is not visible

Coral reefs are warm, clear, shallow ocean habitats that are rich in life

George washington was the first president of the united states
```

Figure 2.14 Sample CYC Database Entries

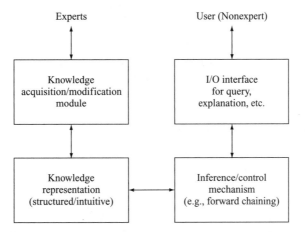

Figure 2.15 Overall Expert System Structure Indicating Both Development Phase (Knowledge Engineering) as Well as System Interface to Nonexpert

2.8.2   Rule-Based Implementations

Many expert systems are implemented using the rule-based paradigm, where knowledge is encoded in IF-THEN form. Rule-based expert systems are typically:

1. Based upon IF-THEN (implication) based representations of knowledge obtained from expert query

2. Applied in narrowly defined problem domains

An example of a rule from the DENDRAL [LBFL80] expert system follows. DENDRAL is one of the oldest ES, having been developed in 1964 (in Lisp). A typical production in DENDRAL [HK85] is:

```
IF
the molecule spectrum has two peaks at masses x1 and x2
such that

x1 + x2 = M + 28            AND

x1 - 28 is a 'high' peak    AND

x2 - 28 is a 'high' peak    AND

at least one of the x1 or x2 is high

THEN

The molecule contains a ketone group.
```

Another sample rule, taken from an online technical support example, is

```
if 'symptom' = 'Label Designer hangs on converting databases dialog'
            and ('BackTrack Version'  <=  '4.10')

            and 'second edition' = 'yes'
            and (operating_system = 'Windows 98 Second Edition'
            or operating_system = 'Windows 98')
        then problem = 'Win 98se.'
```

2.8.3   How Long Does It Take to Become an Expert?

The (human) acquisition of expertise is, by some references, quite slow. For example, in the United States a so-called high school education is obtained at approximately 18 years of age. This raises serious concerns in the development of an IS with similar capability. How long would/should it take?

From psychological studies of expertise acquisition [ES91] [Eri05], the emerging opinion is that approximately 10,000 hours of practice is required to achieve the level of "expert" or master *in any discipline*. Note that this represents a level of effort of approximately 20 hours per week for 10 years. While many of the studies relate to athletic and musical expertise, it is nonetheless worrisome that the "10K hours argument in psychology" could translate into "?K hours argument in IS."

2.8.4 The Appeal of Expert Systems

The development of ES is motivated by a number of factors, including:

1. Expert-level knowledge is a scarce and expensive resource.

2. ES make expert behavior available to a large audience. This is especially true of those implemented using the Internet.

3. The integration of the expertise of several experts may lead to ES that outperform any single expert.

4. ES are not motivated to call in sick, leave a company for better working conditions, or demand huge salaries (although their development and maintenance costs are often substantial).

The potential for expert systems is enormous. Declining development costs have led to numerous efforts in developing both small, easily modified ES, as well as large systems.

However, the quantification coding of human insight, compassion, motivation, guessing ability, and learning capabilities is still an elusive goal. Often the ES design process requires a minimum of new technology and a large amount of engineering judgment.

2.8.5 The Expert System Knowledge Engineering Process

The first questions an expert system developer must ask are the following:

1. Are bona fide experts available whose performance is significantly better than that of amateurs?

2. Can their expertise be automated?

3. Does it make practical and economic sense to develop an ES?

It does little good to determine a representation before meeting with the expert(s). The development of expert systems proceeds with the consulting of an expert (or group of experts) with the aim of developing a manipulable knowledge base. This is often referred to as Knowledge Engineering (KE). The first phase of the process consists of the formation of a database of domain-specific knowledge. In the expert interrogation process, the formulation of "good" questions is paramount. Fortunately, experts often articulate problem-solving methodologies in terms of IF-THEN structures. Moreover, an expert may volunteer rationalizations of the resulting rules, i.e., "I conclude this because...." This type of explanatory production is also desirable.

Knowledge Engineering

The development of an expert system is almost always an iterative task, involving the cycle of expert query, the database formation development of the inference strategy, verification of system performance, etc. The gap between the concept of an ES and a finished, delivered product may be enormous. The necessary application-specific selection of a reasoning structure, interviewing of experts, development of a prototype, refinement, user training, and documentation may take several years.

One of the most important aspects of ES development is verification of system operation. A set of test cases is developed and used by both the ES and the human experts. When responses differ, modifications to the system and perhaps additional expert consultation are required.

The ability of an ES to provide the user with an explanation is also important. An expert system response such as

"patient has disease x"

is probably insufficient, even if it is correct, since no explanation of the inference process is provided. An explanation may be as simple as indicating the sequence of rules used, or may be as complicated as indicating all possible inference paths considered and the logic that leads to the most appropriate response or conclusion.

The Role of the "Knowledge Engineer"

The knowledge engineer is responsible for knowledge acquisition. As noted, sources of knowledge are varied and include the expert, or more typically, expert(s), as well as the end-user. Another often overlooked source is the literature.

The Knowledge Elicitation Cycle

The phase of knowledge acquisition specific to expert(s) is referred to as knowledge elicitation. This phase may involve long and tedious sessions between knowledge engineers and experts. The overall objective is to identify the expert's relevant knowledge/problem-solving skills and convert this into a "manipulable" form. This phase is arguably one of the most complex and arduous tasks in building the ES. Recall the various types of knowledge (e.g., procedural, declarative, or heuristic) that might be encountered at this point.

Format of the Query.   There are several possible formats for the knowledge elicitation effort, including:

1. An interactive exchange of ideas. This is the **Interview** method.

2. Observation of the expert(s) solution to a problem. This is the **Case Study** method.

The expert query effort is almost always exploratory in nature and an iterative process. Following this stage, the knowledge engineer is responsible for analysis and codifying of the elucidated knowledge.

Parts of the Knowledge Elicitation Cycle.   Knowledge elicitation may be viewed as a four-part cycle, with the following (sample) distributions of effort:

1. **Collection**: From basic to specific knowledge; 5–10% of effort.

2. **Interpretation**: Review and identify key elements of the acquired knowledge; 20% of the effort.

3. **Analysis**: Determine relevant/key concept relationships, structures, and how the knowledge may be applied to the problem; 70% of the effort.

4. **ES design**. 20% of the effort.

Notice there is no clear endpoint to this process.

Difficulties in Knowledge Acquisition.   There are many potential pitfalls in this process, including:

1. Expert(s) are unaware of the underlying knowledge

2. Expert(s) are unable to articulate knowledge

3. Expert(s) provides knowledge that is:

    ◆ irrelevant

    ◆ incomplete

    ◆ incorrect

    ◆ inconsistent (especially with multiple experts)

4. Social problems, e.g., fear of replacement, fear of change, skepticism of technology exist.

Knowledge Acquisition/Engineering Procedures

The Expert Interview.   Once an interview is scheduled with the expert(s), it should be structured. Guidelines are listed here:

1. Have an agenda.

2. Work from generalities to specifics.

3. Employ good question design and varying question types:

    ◆ direct questions ("Is xxx true?")

    ◆ indirect questions ("What parameters do you consider?")

    ◆ probes ("Can you explain...")

    ◆ prompts ("Can we return to...")

4. Employ active listening.

5. Bring or acquire previous case studies.

6. Bring an audio/video recorder.

7. Generate a transcript from the interview.

8. Allow the expert(s) to review the transcript.

After the Interview.   Following the interview(s), the process consists of:

1. Analysis of the transcript(s).

2. Determination of the structure and representations for the knowledge (the model).

3. Follow-up with the experts for verification of the model.

2.8.6 Production Systems for Expert System Implementation

The rule-based and production system concepts are commonly used to implement expert systems. When rules are extended to become more general productions (see Chapter 6), a production system results. Production systems may be developed with a minimum of specialized programming using "canned" shells. Examples of such production system shells are CLIPS (Chapter 7) and Soar (Chapter 9).

2.9 Exercises

1. There are many classifications of knowledge. Define and give an example of each of the following:

    (a) Intensional knowledge
    (b) Extensional knowledge
    (c) Metaknowledge

2. In developing an IS, an oft-asked question is: *What type of knowledge is "Common Sense" and how do I represent it?* Research this topic and provide an answer.

3. Consider the "is_a" and "can-be" relations.

    (a) What properties does each relation have?
    (b) Derive a relationship between statements using "is_a" and statements using "can-be."

4. Composers and musicians use sheet music to archive musical works. Is sheet music a declarative or a procedural representation?

5. Develop a hierarchical frame representation for the entity "house." Include entities such as door, window, street address, driveway, etc. Consider value inheritance and default values in your representation.

6. Distinguish between **value inheritance** and **default inheritance** in frame representations.

7. As shown in the text, a prototypical "automobile" frame could contain, among other information, the fact that an automobile has four wheels. However, there may be exceptions where we have reason to believe otherwise, and therefore wish to override this inherited information. Discuss and compare several alternatives for implementing exceptions, including

    (a) via additional frame slots
    (b) via multiple defaults

8. Consider the use of a frame-structured representation with slots labeled "more-general" and "more-specific." Discuss how this structure could:

    (a) Lead to a hierarchical representation structure; and
    (b) Facilitate the focusing of diagnostic inference.

9. Consider an alternative structured representation based upon the *typical* attributes of an entity. For example, instead of representing "all elephants are gray" or equivalently

$$(\forall X) \text{ elephant } (X) \rightarrow \text{ gray } (X)$$

we choose to represent

    "*typical* elephants are gray."

Can this approach be quantified and extended? How are exceptions handled?

10. Using Protege (and good judgment), develop an ontology for the concept: *Computer Engineering and Science (undergraduate college-level) Course.* Based upon this, extend your ontology with instances to realize a knowledge base. Show (using the graphical features and associated plugins in Protege) graphical depictions of the relations between elements of your ontology.

Be sure to develop answers to the basic questions posed in Section 2.5.2, and develop competency questions.

11. Would you consider an ontology produced by Protege to be the basis for a declarative or a procedural knowledge representation? Explain.

12. Using Protege, develop an ontology for a world consisting of two blocks, Block1 and Block2, as shown in Chapter 9, Figure 9.22. Both blocks are situated on an $n \times n$ checkerboard at initially different locations. Each block may sense its location as well as the location of the other block. In addition, each block may move into an empty adjacent cell. The objective (motivation) of Block2 is to move toward and overtake Block1 (get to the same location). Block1 has a very different objective (motivation)—that is, to not be overtaken or caught.

13. Using Protege, develop an ontology for the domain of programming languages. Keep in mind that they may differ in terms of paradigm, language constructs, intended application, ease of use/learning, etc.

14. Section 2.1.3 considered declarative vs. procedural representations. In this context, is a Makefile (used in conjunction with the make utility) a declarative or a procedural representation?

15. Must a semantic net based solely upon an "is-a" link or relation yield an acyclic, hierarchical graph?

16. The fact that all dogs are mammals may be represented in logic by the statement

$$(\forall X) \quad \text{dog}(X) \rightarrow \text{mammal}(X)$$

How would you represent this in Prolog?

17. More general logical representations, which relate class values, are possible. For example, *if the class of entity X is t1, then the value of property p1 (of X) is v1* may be written:

$$(\forall X) \quad \text{class}(X, t1) \rightarrow p1(X, v1)$$

Convert this to a Prolog representation.

18. Suppose you are developing an ontology in Protege. How would you determine whether the OWL or the frames-based representation is most appropriate for your ontology?

19. We have noted that realistic ontologies tend to be very large (for example, in terms of number of frames and instances). As a practical matter, is there a limit to the size of an ontology developed in Protege?

20. Develop a Protege ontology to be used for temporal reasoning. Elements should include concepts such as time, measures of time (years, months, days, etc.), and instances such as January, Tuesday, etc.

21. Using Protege, develop an ontological representation of the semantic net shown in Figure 2.2.

22. Is there a difference between a knowledge representation and a knowledge base?

23. One definition sometimes proposed for an ontology (Section 2.5.2) is *"a taxonomy with multiple link types, each with precise meaning."* Is this definition accurate?

## chapter 3

Search and Computational Complexity in IS

3.1 Why Do We Care about IS Problem Computational Complexity?

The concepts of computational complexity and search have a strong link to the practical aspects of IS development. An algorithm used to solve an IS problem is of little use if it cannot provide a solution, for a reasonable problem size, in reasonable time, and using reasonable computing resources. The term "reasonable" is used here to denote practical or problem-dependent limits. For example, in processing television images, it is necessary (in the United States) to complete processing of a frame of data in $\frac{1}{30}$ sec., regardless of the image resolution. Moreover, if the problem scale changes (e.g., the resolution of a digital image doubles), it is important to be able to predict the required increase in the computational time required for processing (or the additional computational resources necessary to achieve the processing result in the same time).

We often focus on the complexity of an algorithm in terms of required computations as a function of the problem size. However, computational resources (as a function of problem size) such as the *space bounds* of the computation also warrant consideration. For example, space bounds could include the amount of available memory required (without swapping). Before exploring the concepts of computational complexity and search, we digress to introduce the notion of an IS *state space*.

3.2 The Concept of a System State Space

Readers familiar with linear algebra may have been introduced to the concept of a vector space. A similar concept that is extremely important in IS is the notion of a system *state space*.

3.2.1 System State Representation

The system state, or state description, contains the set of all information, in the context of the chosen representation, which describes the current status of the system. The system state is a somewhat abstract concept until we consider specific examples of state representations. States S_i and S_g denote the initial and goal states, respectively, of a system.

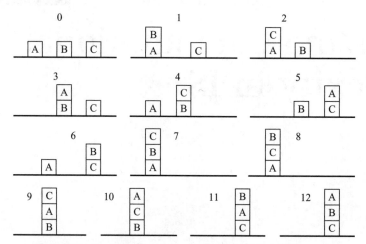

Figure 3.1 System States in the "Blocks World" Scenario

3.2.2 The System State Space

The system state space or problem space is the domain of all possible system states. Consider the graphical depiction of the "blocks world" situation in Figure 3.1. Each of the 12 (numbered) possible system states corresponds to a unique configuration of the three blocks on the table. As we show in Figure 3.2, operators such as "put Block A on Block B" are used to change the system state.

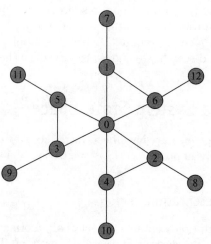

Figure 3.2 State Space and State Relationships for the "Blocks World" Scenario of Figure 3.1

3.2.3 Satisfying Goals via State Manipulation with Operators

Mechanisms for state modification or transformation are denoted operators, productions, or actions and are used to link the initial and goal states. Operators (or productions or actions) are a means to control or change the system state. Operator application is constrained by appropriate system states, and operator application generally changes the system state. A typical example of operators are rules and productions. This yields the very important observation:

> **Operators, agents, actions, etc.,** *change the system state.* **Many IS problems may be characterized as the search for a sequence of suitable operators to link (or satisfy) specified initial and desired problem subspaces.**

Operator and State Manipulation Example.   Consider a set of operators such as "put Block A on Block B," or "remove Block A from Block C" in the "blocks world" example. Use of any of these operators (where applicable), maps the present state into another state. This is shown in Figure 3.2.

Since the number of possible operator sequences to be explored in the development of a solution is usually large, solution methods that do not require enumeration of all possible sequences are desirable. This again suggests a problem in searching for a sequence of solution steps. If we begin at S_i and proceed (hopefully) toward S_g, data-driven or forward search is employed. Conversely, working from S_g to S_i ("backward") exemplifies goal-directed search. Hybrid strategies are also possible. Search problems are closely related to those of optimization.

3.2.4 Nondeterminism: Unreachable States

The previous sections may have left the impression that IS analysis simply involves enumeration of the problem state space and, given operators, subsequent path-finding computations. Unfortunately, as illustrated in Section 1.4, the problem is more complex. Figure 3.3 illustrates the situation wherein it is obvious to the human observer (the reader should ask "how?") that a solution does not exist. Automation of this capability is elusive and tricky.

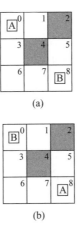

(a)

(b)

Figure 3.3 Subspaces of a Problem State Space That May Not Be Linked by the Operators of Section 3.3.2

3.3 Computational Complexity
3.3.1 Complexity Functions

In order to study the efficiency and behavior of algorithms and corresponding implementations, two entities are required:

1. A model of the computation; and

2. A complexity measure.

A hierarchy of complexity functions exists. Following the approach of [Tar83], we denote an efficient algorithm as one whose worst-case running time is bounded by a polynomial function of the problem size. Tractable problems have efficient algorithms; intractable problems do not. We note that even tractable problems become gradually unusable. This is shown in Figure 3.4.

In computing program execution time estimates on the basis of operations/sec and total required operations, it is useful to note that 10^8 seconds $= 3$ years. From Figure 3.5, observe how the complexity of seemingly innocuous problems, when scaled to larger n, often results in unacceptable computing times.

We define an algorithm as polynomial time (P) if its complexity function is polynomial. A nonpolynomial time algorithm has a complexity function that dominates every polynomial function.

Referring to Figure 3.5, for example, we note that the exponential function dominates any polynomial, and is thus nonpolynomial. A useful consequence of this categorization is that nonpolynomial

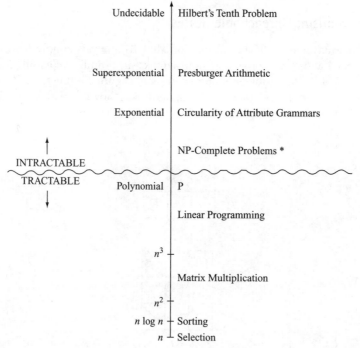

Figure 3.4 The Spectrum of Computational Complexity

Growth	1	20	50	100	1000	10,000	100,000	1,000,000
				n(Size)				
n	1×10^{-6} sec	20×10^{-6} sec	50×10^{-6} sec	1×10^{-4} sec	1×10^{-3} sec	1×10^{-2} sec	0.1 sec	1 sec
n^2	1×10^{-6} sec	4×10^{-4} sec	2.5×10^{-2} sec	1×10^{-2} sec	1.0 sec	1.67 min	2.78 hours	11.6 days
n^3	1×10^{-6} sec	8×10^{-3} sec	2.5×10^{-3} sec	1.25×10^{-1} sec	16.8 min	11.6 days	3.17×10^5 CENT	—
2^n	2×10^{-6} sec	1.05 sec	35.7 years	4.02×10^{14} CENT	—	—	—	—
exp (n)	2.7×10^{-6} sec	8.10 min	1.65×10^6 CENT	—	—	—	—	—

Figure 3.5 Sample Growth of Problem Complexity (one step $= 10^{-6}$ sec.)

time algorithms, as n increases, get large (unmanageable) at an alarming rate. A large class of problems are nonpolynomial. Using the best methods known, the complexity of nonpolynomial problems grows exponentially. An example is the so-called "Traveling Salesman" problem. From Figure 3.4, it is clear that the modification of algorithms (with reasonable heuristics, for example) to avoid nonpolynomial (or worse) complexities is desirable. This may lead to algorithms that do not guarantee a solution, but may execute with P complexity.[1]

3.3.2   An Example of the State Space and IS Problem Complexity

Refer to an $n \times n$ "checkerboard," as in Figure 3.6 (here $n = 3$). The state space for this problem is depicted, with the pictorial representation of states labeled S_i. Each state may also be designated by the location of Blocks A and B, (i.e., the initial state is (A4, B8)) and knowledge of the (assumed persistent) extent of the checkerboard and the blocked locations. Operators such as move up, move left, etc., are used to modify the state of the system. Often the state space is infinite or practically infinite.

In each state, there are p "blocked" locations, with q blocks ($q \leq n^2 - p$), and no unreachable states. Therefore, the number of possible states in the system state space is:

$$|S| = \prod_{j=0}^{q-1}(k - j) \tag{3.1}$$

where $k = n^2 - p$.

Analysis.   The simple 12-state example of Figure 3.6 does little to illustrate potential state growth and consequent search problem complexity as a function of n, p, and q. Whereas the number of distinct states for this problem (denoted as the cardinality of the state space or $|S|$) grows as indicated by

---

[1] A very interesting trade-off!

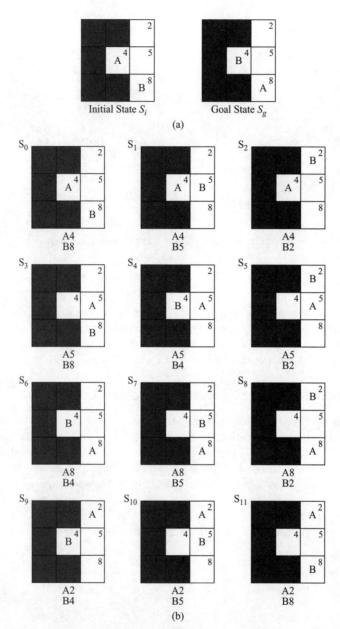

Figure 3.6 The (Simplistic) "Checkerboard" Problem. (a) Sample Initial and Goal States. (b) Graphical Depiction of the States.

Equation 3.1, a few computations illustrate the significant practical limitations to brute-force based solutions due to this complexity. For example, when $n = 3$, $p = 0$, and $q = 4$, $|S|$ jumps to 3024. More significantly, for the seemingly innocuous problem where $n = 10$, $p = 0$, and $q = 10$, $|S|$ is

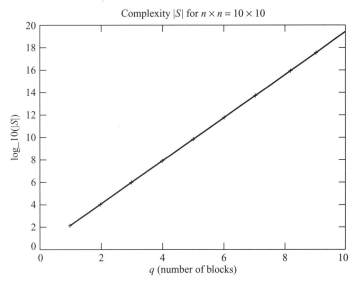

Figure 3.7 Growth of the "Checkerboard" Problem State Space

an astonishing 62,815,650,955,529,469,952. The plot of Figure 3.7 further illustrates the situation. Additional ramifications are addressed in the exercises.

3.4 Search

Intuitively, to search means to look for something. We refine this notion in the following sections. Search is a fundamental element of many computer solutions [Knu73]. In IS problems, many search strategies may be employed. The choice of a particular approach (explicitly or implicitly) may determine whether we achieve a practical, working solution or a computation-bound, impractical one.

3.4.1 To Search or Not to Search

The concepts of search and IS have historically had a tenuous relationship. While some view search as fundamental to IS, others view IS as a means to eradicate search from certain problems. No look at IS would be complete without an examination of the fundamental component that underlies most IS algorithms—namely the process of search. Inefficient ("uninformed") algorithms often amount to brute-force search and are easily defeated by combinatorial explosion.

3.4.2 Problem Representation

The first entity necessary to consider the search process is a problem representation. There are several scenarios that allow study of search, as a function of the chosen representation. For example, we may choose to show the problem space, given a state space representation in terms of a graph representation. If we showed the evolution of the system using either (perhaps conditional) rule firings or operator applications, the state of a system in the graph (problem state) representation could be a position (node) in the graph. Here we have assumed specification of initial and goal states. As we shall see, many search algorithms are based upon a performance measure (estimator of distance between initial and goal states).

3.4.3   Definition of a Search Problem (P)

A search problem, P, is characterized by a 4-tuple:

$$P = \{D, S_i, T, G\}$$

where

D is a set of system states that represent the problem state-space;

$S_i \in D$ is a starting state;

$T = \{t_1, t_2 \cdots\}$ is a set of transformations (e.g., operators, rules);

     and

$G \subset D$ is a set of goal states.

A solution to D, denoted T_s, is a sequence of $t_i = t_1, t_2, \cdots t_p$ with the property that

$$t_n(t_2(t_1(S_i))) \in G$$

Note that D and T may be finite or countably infinite. We may partition D into two mutually exclusive subsets:

1. Those $D_r \subset D$ where $\exists$ a T_s such that

$$t_n \cdots (t_2(t_1(S_i)) \in D_r$$

     These are so-called *reachable states*.

2. Those $D_{ur} \subset D$ for which no T_s exists such that

$$t_n \cdots (t_2(t_1(S_i)) \in D_{ur}$$

     These are *unreachable states*.

If

$$G \cap D_r \neq \emptyset$$

then P is solvable. Unfortunately, it is difficult, at best, to ascertain that P is solvable before attempting a solution.

3.4.4   State–Space Graphs

A state-space graph (SSG) is a digraph that enumerates D and T. Specifically, nodes of the SSG represent elements of D, and directed arcs represent elements of T, i.e., each t_i. T generates an arc in the SSG between nodes d_i and $d_j \in D$ to indicate $d_j = t_i(di)$.

3.4.5 Search Costs and Heuristics

Using the SSG, a search cost function, C, is a mapping of all arcs onto the set of non-negative real numbers. More intuitively, C is a mechanism to associate a cost measure with a path through the SSG. Typically, C is used along with a search heuristic/algorithm to identify paths with low cost.

3.4.6 Graphical Representations for Search

We take a more detailed look at the graphical representations that may be employed in IS problems. Note that the principal utility of this abstraction is in conveying the complexity of the solution process, and in comparing alternative solution approaches. Once a problem representation has been chosen, the problem space, within which the search process occurs, may be explored. In order to develop a unified approach that is applicable to a number of IS problems, often graphical abstractions are chosen. Particular states of the system are represented by nodes in a digraph, and the edges in the graph, that link nodes (or states) represent the application of a state modification entity (i.e., a rule or operator). Note that this graphical representation does not assume certain system properties, such as decomposability or commutativity. If these properties exist, however, modifications, partitioning, or simplifications of the graph are possible. Thus, in large-scale problems, this graph is both large and complex.

Nodes are interpreted as states. A state might be the current contents of a system database. Actions (rule firings or planning operator applications) on all possible states, describe a graphical construct showing a linked sequence of system states. In most problems, one such state, denoted S_i, represents the system initial state, and one (or more) denote the goal state, S_g.

3.4.7 Example: A Graphical Representation of State Propagation

Consider the following simplistic rule-based system:

Initial (database) facts: $a\ b\ g = S_i$.

System operators (rules) are shown as follows:[2]

Rule 1	IF	a	b	THEN	c
2	'	b	g	'	d
3	'	a	c	'	e
4	'	e	d	'	f
5	'	d	g	'	f

Suppose the objective is to produce a state that contains fact **f**. Figure 3.8 (a) shows a combined inference net for the system. More importantly, Part (b) shows the search space and possible paths that lead from S_i to (one) S_g. Note the nine possible paths (rule-firing sequences) are shown in Table 3.1.

---

[2]Note "THEN" means "Add the fact."

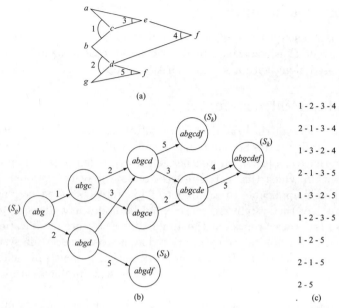

1 - 2 - 3 - 4

2 - 1 - 3 - 4

1 - 3 - 2 - 4

2 - 1 - 3 - 5

1 - 3 - 2 - 5

1 - 2 - 3 - 5

1 - 2 - 5

2 - 1 - 5

2 - 5

(c)

Figure 3.8 Problem Search Space. (a) Inference Net for Rules. (b) Search Paths Through State Space Using Forward Chaining. (c) Possible Rule-Firing Sequences.

1 - 2 - 3 - 4

2 - 1 - 3 - 4

1 - 3 - 2 - 4

2 - 1 - 3 - 5

1 - 3 - 2 - 5

1 - 2 - 3 - 5

1 - 2 - 5

2 - 1 - 5

2 - 5

Table 3.1 Possible Rule-Firing Sequences Leading to Goal States.

3.4.8 From Graph to Tree Representations

Since two states may often be "linked" by more than one state modifier (or agent or action or operator), the nodes in the problem state graph may have several arcs linking them. This is shown in Figure 3.9.

This makes analysis difficult, therefore the graph is often converted into a tree. The price of this modification is "expansion" of the graph into a structure where tree nodes are not unique (since graph nodes are replicated). One node must be specified as the root (this is usually either the initial or goal state), and the remaining nodes or states appear at some level in the tree. In this expansion, however, the multiplicity of sequences leading from the root state to any other specified state may easily be seen.

3.4.9 Example: Another Graphical Representation of Search

We use the Prolog unification mechanism to illustrate the search path in a Prolog database. The example is taken from Appendix B.[3] A CLIPS version appears in Chapter 7. The sample database is shown in Figure 3.10. The relationship of the database clauses is shown in Figure 3.11.

The order in which the database is searched is shown in Figure 3.12.

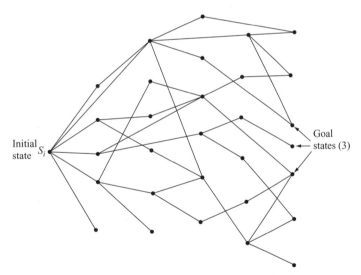

Figure 3.9 Problem State Space as a Graph

---

[3]The reader should review the discussion of the Prolog unification mechanism contained in this Appendix.

```
/* tenure-search.pro */

gets_tenure(Faculty) :- publishes(Faculty),
                            gets_research(Faculty),
                                teaches_well(Faculty).

publishes(Professor) :- does_research(Professor),
                            documents_research(Professor).

gets_research(Researcher) :- writes_proposals(Researcher),
                                gets_funded(Researcher).

teaches_well(Educator) :- prepares_lectures(Educator),
                             lectures_well(Educator),
                                gets_good_evaluations(Educator).

/* simplistic database to illustrate search */

does_research(rjs).
documents_research(rjs).
writes_proposals(rjs).
gets_funded(rjs).
prepares_lectures(rjs).
lectures_well(rjs).
gets_good_evaluations(rjs).
```

Figure 3.10 Prolog Database for Search Example

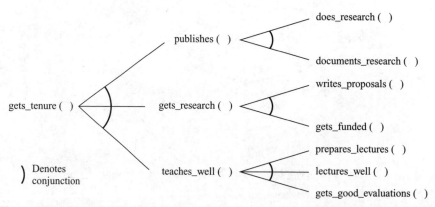

Figure 3.11 Graphical Representation of Clause Dependencies in a Prolog Database

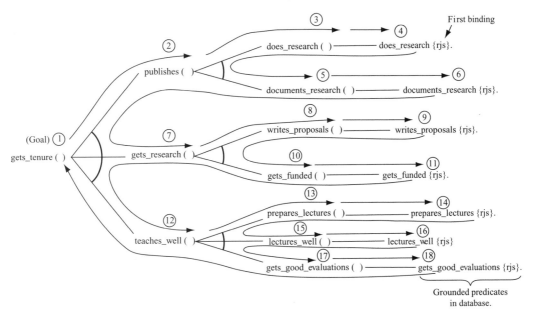

Figure 3.12 Search Order for the Database shown in Figure 3.10

3.5 Searching the Problem State Space

The primary difficulty in search is that of combinatorial explosion. Since several choices are available at each problem step, a technique to prune the possible paths to be explored is necessary. Notice also that this pruning algorithm may "prune out" the (or an) optimal solution if it is not chosen carefully. Thus, we are faced with an optimality vs. practicality situation.

3.5.1 Example of Search and State-Space Paths

Using the checkerboard problem of Figure 3.6, Figure 3.13 illustrates the process of finding a path from S_i to S_g. Here "C" denotes a cycle, and the state is shown as a node indicating the position of Blocks A and B.

3.5.2 The Explosion of Operator Choices

The example of Section 3.5.1 suggests that many search problems could be solved simply by problem state enumeration followed by application of a graph path-finding algorithm. Unfortunately, this is impractical (or impossible, in problems whose state space has infinite cardinality).

Figure 3.14 illustrates the situation for the games chess and Go. The game of Go is considerably more complex in both state space cardinality and operator choices per state (turn). Notice the state space for the Go game [Hsu07] is comprised of 10^{170} states. Furthermore, after only three moves in Go, an exhaustive consideration of all possible moves involves eight million possibilities. This spawns a need for search techniques and heuristics to make the problem manageable. Commonly, branch-and-bound search techniques are employed.

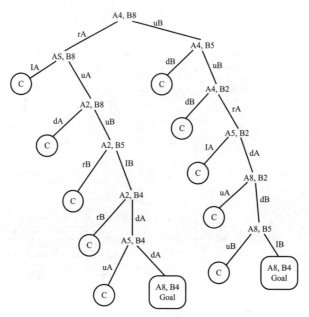

Figure 3.13 Search Paths Example

Chess Versus Go

Grid Size	
8 × 8	19 × 19

Average Number of Move Choices Per Turn	
35	200–300

Length of Typical Game	
60 moves	200 moves

Number of Possible Game Positions	
10^{120}	10^{170}

Explosion of Choices
(starting from average game position)

35	Move 1	200
1225	Move 2	40,000
42,875	Move 3	8,000,000
1,500,625	Move 4	1,600,000,000

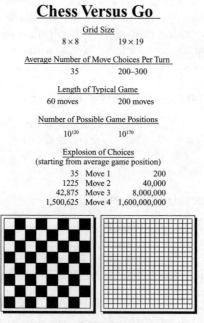

Figure 3.14 The Complexity of Chess and Go Games. From [Hsu07].

3.6 Heuristics

3.6.1 What Is a Heuristic?

The word heuristic comes from the Greek root which yields the word "eureka." Although heuristics are an old concept, the mathematician George Polya popularized the use of heuristics in his book *How to Solve It* [Pol73]. Another classical reference is [Pea84].

A heuristic is a technique that:

♦ Is designed to solve a problem that ignores whether the solution exists or can be proven to be correct

♦ Usually produces a good or "acceptable" solution

♦ Solves a simpler problem that contains the solution of the more complex problem

Search problems, like many other aspects of IS, are often not easily able to be described in a form that leads to immediate mathematical derivations of optimal solutions. Typically, heuristics are employed.

3.6.2 Definitions

A heuristic is a strategy (that often defies detailed analysis of its properties, such as proof of applicability in all situations) or algorithm used to aid in the efficient solution of a problem. Often heuristics are developed by trial and error, in conjunction with a number of reasonable approximations, simplifications, or reasonable guesses. The lack of an ability to prove the worthiness of a heuristic (in all applications) does not preclude its use. Moreover, many IS problems could not be solved without the development of heuristics. The development of heuristics is more art than science. (This is not necessarily bad, since, as was indicated earlier, logic is not the only basis for the development of intelligent systems.)

A second definition is:

"Involving or serving as an aid to learning, discovery, or problem solving by experimental and esp. trial-and-error methods" (Webster's 9th Collegiate Dictionary)

Another definition is [Len82]:

"Compiled hindsight...used to guide future behavior."

A practical definition is [Bid03]:

" 'Rules of thumb' intended, but not guaranteed, to aid in the solution of a problem."

3.6.3 Applications

When we use a graphical problem space description, we note that heuristics are used to prune (i.e., limit the branches explored in the search tree). We note also that heuristics are often "tuned" for a particular application; success in one IS implementation using this heuristic does not necessarily translate into success in even closely related implementations.

Heuristics are often crucial to practical[4] solutions to problems. They are often intended to do many things:

♦ Provide *computational savings* or *conceptual simplicity*. This is almost always at the expense of accuracy or precision. A good example is the use of a model that is known to be inexact or inaccurate. In this case, the model is a heuristic that is intended to foster understanding of the true model.

♦ Direct the attention of the problem-solving mechanism in a beneficial direction

The field of Heuretics is the study of informal, judgmental "rules of thumb." This includes the study of heuristics.

3.6.4 Sample IS Heuristics

Here are a few:

1. Use the first applicable rule/production found.

2. Use the most specific (general) rule/production found.

3. Use the least (most) recently used rule/production.

4. Choose the action that changes the state the most.

5. Pick an action randomly.

More commonly, a combination of heuristics is employed.

3.6.5 Why Use Heuristics?

Heuristic search techniques attempt, via a heuristic, to guide and limit the search process. The heuristic often employs some measure of search cost. Often, the success of the heuristic approach is predicated upon formulation of a good cost measure. One example is an estimate of the disparity, or distance, between the current state (S_c) and the goal state (S_g), i.e., a state difference function, denoted $D(S_c, S_g)$.

Why Not Just Choose a Performance Measure and Employ Optimization?   The astute reader may question the amount of attention devoted to the concept of search and search algorithms. Instead, suppose we approach the problem as follows:

♦ Formulate a measure indicating the difference or closeness of a state, S_c to the goal state, S_g. Denote this measure $D(S_c, S_g)$. Assume $D(S_c, S_g)$ is minimum when $S_c \subset S_g$.

♦ Treat D as an objective function and use any well-known minimization technique to find the succession of states leading to S_g. In other words, the search algorithm is guided by choosing operators that map S_c into S_{c+1} and minimize $D(S_{c+1}, S_g)$. Intuition suggests that we would move monotonically toward the goal.

---

[4]Non-brute force search.

There are several problems with the attempted strategy:

1. This approach does not guarantee a good path toward the goal state. This is due to the locality of the decision process.

2. In all but trivial applications, $D(S_{c+1}, S_g)$ does not exist in any useful form. Moreover:

   ◆ Even if an approximation to $D(S_{c+1}, S_g)$ were available, it would probably contain numerous local minima and lack differentiability.

   ◆ Even if $D(S_{c+1}, S_g)$ were available, minimization would, at best, be guided by direct search[5] (or "derivative free") methods.

3.6.6 The Power, Application, and Properties of Heuristics

Despite the remarks of the previous section, heuristics and cost measures are commonly used. For one, heuristics may mean the difference between a practical IS and one whose practicality is limited by computational cost and lack of scalability. Heuristics may serve to suggest plausible actions/operators or to eliminate implausible actions/operators.

Properties of heuristics [Len82] (or what might be called "heuristics about heuristics") include:

1. The generalization/specialization hierarchy of concepts induces a similar structure on heuristics.

2. If heuristic H is relevant to concept C, then H is also relevant to specializations of C.

3. Appropriateness and 0th order theory:

   (a) If H is useful in situation S, heuristics similar to H would be useful in S.

   (b) If H is useful in situation S, H would be useful in situations similar to S.

   (c) Thus, the "appropriateness" function $appropriate(H, S)$ is continuous in both arguments and slowly varying so

   $$appropriate(H, S) \approx appropriate(H', S')$$

   where H' is similar to H and S' is similar to S.

3.6.7 Machine Learning of Heuristics

While heuristics are often employed by the IS designer, there is considerable interest in machine learning of heuristics. [Pri93] summarizes many of the relevant concerns.

---

[5]R. Hooke and T.A. Jeeves. Direct search solution of numerical and statistical problems. *Journal of the Association of Computing Machinery, 8*, 212–269, 1961.

3.7 Informed Versus Uninformed ("Blind") Search

Systematic (e.g., depth-first or breadth-first) or random search strategies are "blind" in the sense that selection of the next state is not guided by any attributes of the current state or the goal state (unless the current state is the goal state) or any of the past states explored. Thus, they are referred to as uninformed search procedures. As might be expected, it is not unusual for uninformed strategies to spend significant computational resources searching through irrelevant subspaces.

If some guidance could be imparted to the search, perhaps using heuristics, the process would be termed *informed search.* This guidance could be in the form of entities such as state evaluation functions, path pruning algorithms, operator confidence measures, or heuristics. Informed search is used in all but trivial IS applications.

3.8 The Computational Cost of Search

We begin by illustrating an important and often non-obvious computational ramification of search in IS systems. When we begin to explicitly employ search strategies for the optimization of IS algorithms, we must consider the computational cost of the search strategy in view of the efficiency gains in the overall algorithm. For example, a search strategy that led to significantly shorter or more direct paths in backward chaining is of questionable utility if the total (i.e., to completion) computation time consumed by the search algorithm far exceeds the time saved in the inference process. In other words, a second-order consideration is the efficiency of the search algorithm and its effect on the overall IS system computation.

Figure 3.15 illustrates this relationship. As an example, suppose that a backward-chaining rule-based system employed a search mechanism to identify the next rule that was closest to "optimal"

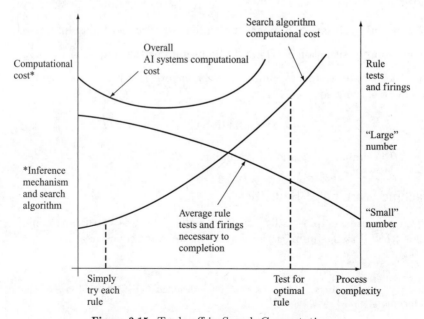

Figure 3.15 Trade-off in Search Computation

in that it could be successfully fired. If the algorithm exhaustively examines the rules, refers to the past history of rule-firing success, etc., a great deal of computation may be expended in determining whether to actually check the rule antecedents for possible firing. At some point it may be computationally more efficient to simply check the rules directly. Thus, there exists a point of diminishing returns wherein the search algorithm actually becomes counterproductive from the point of overall IS performance.

Thus, the IS engineer must consider the economies of search algorithms in the process of system design. This is why heuristics are so important—their effect may be almost as beneficial as a far more complex search algorithm.

3.8.1 The Computational Complexity of Forward Propagation of States

We present another very simple example of the combinatorial explosion that may occur in the process of generating a search tree in an IS implementation. First, we consider the forward propagation of states, i.e., starting at state S_i, we generate all possible successors to this state, by considering all applicable state modification operators. In this example, assume we are considering a rule-based production system. Suppose at state S_i, representing stage i in the problem space generation process, we have n_i total system facts, and m_i applicable rules. We will assume that m_i is constant with respect to i. In addition, assume the firing of each of the m_i applicable rules generates $(m_i/k_i)n_i$ new facts. Again, assume k_i is independent of i, i.e., $k_i = k \forall i$. Thus, at stage $i + 1$ we have:

$$n_{i+1} = n_i(1 + m_i/k)$$

total system facts. Note that it is reasonable to expect that

$$(1 + m_i/k) > 1$$

therefore the number of system facts is monotonically increasing with i. Given n_0 facts at stage n, the number of facts propagates to stage p $(p > 0)$ as

$$n_p = n_0(1 + m_i/k)^p$$

For example, if $n_0 = 100$, and we assume $m_i/k = 1.3$, at stage $p = 10$ we have

$$n_{10} = 100(2.3)^{10} = 414,265$$

total facts. The preceding quantity, $(1 + m_i/k)$, is referred to as the branching factor, denoted b, and is explored in the problems. The distance p is referred to as the solution depth. Referring to Figure 3.16, we observe this effect graphically, in that the tree grows rapidly for succeeding stages.

3.8.2 Backward State Propagation

Figure 3.17 indicates the use of backward state propagation. Suppose we are implementing a backward-chaining algorithm, are at state S_g, and therefore must identify possible precursors to state S_g. In other words, by considering the effect of state-modification operators, we determine a set of system states $\{S_{g-1}\}$, which might exist and lead directly to S_g. We repeat this process for $\{S_{g-2}\}$, etc., until one of the states in the back-propagated set is S_i.

We note that the combinatorial explosion that potentially occurs in the previous two examples was derived in the basis of expansion of the problem space one stage (i.e., level of the tree) at a time.

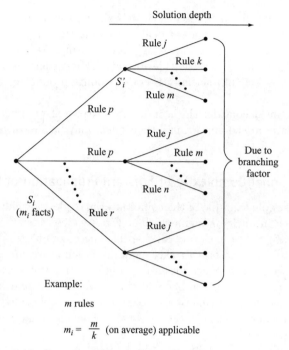

Example:

    m rules

$$m_i = \frac{m}{k} \quad \text{(on average) applicable}$$

Figure 3.16 Growth of Search Space (forward state propagation)

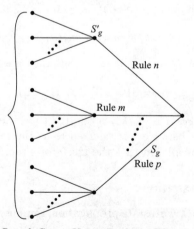

Figure 3.17 Search Space Using Backward State Propagation

3.9 Common Search Algorithms

3.9.1 Brute Force ("Uninformed") Algorithms

So called brute force approaches do not require any particular problem-solving skill or heuristics. All that is required is S_i, S_g, a problem representation, and the set of rules or operators. Several of the systems we develop in this text employ these approaches.

Trial and Error Approaches

This method is the most obvious and probably the least efficient and least informed search strategy. We randomly select state modification operators and, following application, check to see if the goal state has been reached. In this manner, we might "stumble" onto a solution, if one exists, and we are both persistent and lucky. For simple problems (i.e., those with a very small problem space), this may be sufficient. Note, however, that the IS never concentrates attention on a strategy or solution path to pursue. The selection of the next operator is (almost) independent of previous choices.[6] The use of generate-and-test in solving Constraint Satisfaction Problems (CSPs) in Chapter 4 is an example of this strategy.

3.9.2 Systematic Search Strategies

Systematic approaches usually involve a deterministic order in which nodes of the problem space search tree are explored. Several are illustrated in Figure 3.18. Depth-first and breadth-first are two extremes in this space of possible search algorithms.

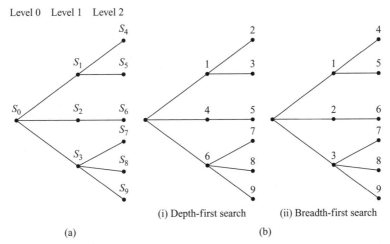

Figure 3.18 (a) Problem Search Space. (b) Search Space Path or Order Using Depth. (i) Depth-first search (ii) Breadth-first search.

---

[6]Except for the effect of new facts produced by its successor.

Breadth–First ("Vertical") Search

A simple problem search space is shown in Figure 3.18(a) The breadth-first search path through this space is illustrated in Figure 3.18(b)(ii). Note that breadth-first search generates all nodes in the problem space tree at level i prior to exploration of the nodes at level $i + 1$. The computational complexity of any search algorithm is a function of the number of nodes investigated. The complexity of breadth-first search up to level q, therefore, is

$$C_{breadth-first} = 1 + b + ... + b^q$$

where b is the branching factor. The complexity of this approach is exponential, since $e^x = 1 + x + \frac{x^2}{2} + \frac{x^3}{3!} + \cdots$.

Notice that since breadth-first search examines all nodes in the problem space tree at level i prior to investigating level $i + 1$, the path of shortest length is found. If path length is the metric used to measure (or compare) search algorithm performance, then breadth-first search is optimal. However, if all the goal states are a large distance from the start node and the number of alternative paths to store is large, breadth-first search may be impractical due to both time and memory requirements.

The general rule is that if the search has b branches at each node and goes to depth d, then there are approximately b^d nodes to explore. In these path/state problems, the branching factor b corresponds to the number of states adjacent to a given state, and the depth d corresponds to the path length, which is bounded by the number of legal states if the search is restricted to simple paths. For example, there are 2^{58} nodes in a balanced binary tree of depth $d = 58$.

Depth–First ("Horizontal") Search

Depth-first search explores all paths in a branch before considering alternative branches. It may be shown that the depth-first approach to level d generates the same number of nodes as in the breadth-first search (in a different order, however), and therefore has the same complexity. One interesting characteristic, however, is that it only requires storage of the current path, which is a function of the depth, d. For this reason, depth-first search is often preferred to breadth-first search. Figure 3.18(b)(i) illustrates the path or sequence and compares it with the breadth-first search.

Forward–Backward or Bidirectional Search

This strategy involves starting both at S_i and S_g and working forward from S_i and backward from S_g, until a common state, S_c or states that "link" S_i and S_g is found. Thus, two breadth-first searches are required, although it is hoped that the combinatorial explosion in each remains limited before S_c is found. This is illustrated by merging Figures 3.16 and 3.17.

3.10 Other Search Approaches (Informed Search)

Many reasonable combinations and modifications of the preceding algorithm are possible. For example, depth-first search could be combined with breadth-first search in a number of ways. One example of this is depth-first with iterative deepening. An alternative is the incorporation of one or more heuristics.

The Means–End Approach

Means-end is a valuable heuristic that may be employed in a variety of ways. The basic approach is to select operators that seem to provide a means to some end, most often the goal. For example, an often problem-specific and heuristic measure $D(S_c, S_g)$ is used, at each step, to choose an operator that makes the decrease in $D(S_c, S_g)$ largest.

Best–First

Best-first search considers all the nodes that have been examined up to the current time, and proceeds by expanding the one that, *according to a heuristic*, is closest to the goal. In this sense, the best-first approach does not explicitly consider the cost of getting to node n, but rather only the estimated remaining cost. Intuitively, the search proceeds by "following the best guess." Thus, best-first search may proceed in depth-first fashion. Again, a function or heuristic to compare two transformations (or their resulting states) is necessary.

The Branch–and–Bound Search Approach

Practical solutions to many problems may be obtained by using a breadth-first (or best-first) search with some form of heuristically-guided pruning. A search technique known as branch-and-bound (B&B) is often applied to discrete and combinatorial optimization problems and games. The solution is found by elaborating on the best set of paths found so far. Clearly, B&B requires a measure of goodness, so that "best" may be quantified. Unfortunately, general goodness measures are often difficult to find.

B&B starts in a feasible region of the state space, called the root problem, and systematically enumerates a subset of the problem state space by considering succeeding states. Each solution in the feasible region is attributed with a measure of goodness. Assume it is desired to minimize this measure (e.g., often path length is used for illustration). The feasible region is subdivided into some number of subregions. The B&B search algorithm is applied recursively to these subregions. If a solution is found in a subregion, it is a feasible (but not necessarily optimal) solution to the full problem. The goodness measure attached to this feasible solution is then used to prune the remainder of the search tree by examining the costs associated with unexpanded nodes in the feasible region. If the lower bound for a node exceeds the best known feasible solution goodness measure, the node and any subsequent subtrees can be removed from consideration. The B&B search proceeds until all nodes have been explored or pruned.

The A* Algorithm

The A* algorithm is a combination of the best-first and B&B procedures. It is based upon formulating a figure of merit (again often heuristic) for node n by tallying the actual (minimal or optimal) cost of the path from the initial state to node n (denoted $g(n)$) and the *inferred or estimated* (minimal) cost from node n to the goal, denoted $h(n)$. If there is no path from node n to the goal, $h(n)$ is infinite. Similarly, if no path between the initial state and node n exists, then $g(n)$ is infinite. Therefore, the overall cost metric at node n is:

$$f(n) = g(n) + h(n)$$

which represents the cost of the optimal path that includes node n. In terms of traditional optimization problems, $g(n)$ is the "cost to date" and $h(n)$ is the "cost to go." The objective is to find the optimum path, i.e., one that yields a minimum f and links S_i and S_g. One difficulty, and thus limitation of this approach, is the determination of a good estimator for the quantity $h(n)$.

3.11 Exercises

1. Referring to the "checkerboard" problem representation of Section 3.3.2, consider the four operators whose effect upon the system state space is somewhat obvious:

   (a) $move - up - x$,

   (b) $move - down - x$,

   (c) $move - left - x$, and

   (d) $move - right - x$

   where x is the name of a block, i.e. $x \in \{A, B\}$ in Figure 3.6. Characterize each operator as a relation on the system state, both as a set and graphically.

2. Develop a three-dimensional plot of the number of distinct states for the "checkerboard" problem of Section 3.3.2 as a function of n and q for the case $p = 0$. Hint: use a logarithmic scale for $|S|$.

3. The game of Go is played on a rectangular board of any size, but a board with 19 lines by 19 lines is commonly used. Surprisingly, Go is an old game; it originated in China over 3000 years ago. Worldwide, Go is and has been one of the most played games.

   In game theory terminology, Go is a zero-sum, deterministic strategy board game, thus putting it in the same class as chess and checkers. Although the rules of Go are simple, the skill required to become a good Go player (or to develop good Go-playing software strategies) is significant. Whereas current computer programs are capable of defeating skilled human chess players, a mediocre Go player may easily defeat the current crop of Go-playing programs.

   (a) Look up and become familiar with the rules for playing Go.

   (b) Determine (look up) the computational complexity of Go. How does it compare to chess?

   (c) Explore (human) strategies for playing Go.

   (d) Consider the implementation of a Go-playing program using some form of state prediction and search.

   (e) At http://www.gnu.org/software/gnugo/ you will find GNU Go, a freely distributed program that plays the game of Go. Download, build, and experiment with the program. What is the playing strategy implemented in GNU Go?

4. Estimate the computational complexity of the following problems, applications, or algorithms (and cite any assumptions used):

   (a) The board game of checkers

   (b) Processing an $n \times n$ image on a pixel-by-pixel basis

   (c) Implementation of a multilayer, feedforward ANN (see Chapter 13)

(d) Unsigned analog-to-digital conversion with an n-bit result

(e) Inversion of an (assumed invertable) $n \times n$ matrix

(f) Factoring an integer

(g) Labeling an image

(h) Sorting a list of n real numbers

5. Label and show a direction for each of the arcs in Figure 3.2 corresponding to the operator(s) used.

6. As noted, Prolog implements depth-first search. How does the use of the cut (!) operator affect Prolog's search strategy?

7. In CLIPS (Chapter 7), a variety of conflict resolution strategies are available. How does each strategy affect CLIPS search for a goal state? Would you say CLIPS implements informed search?

8. In Soar (Chapter 9), preference-based operator selection is a complex process used to determine the next Soar state. If Soar is not able to select a unique operator, an impasse occurs and a substate is generated (subgoaling). How would you characterize the search strategy in Soar? Would you say Soar implements informed search?

## chapter 4

Constraint Satisfaction Problems, Part 1

In this chapter we explore a number of Constraint Satisfaction Problems (CSPs) and related solution approaches and implementations. Often, the perception of intelligent behavior is based upon the simultaneous satisfaction of a large number of constraints. In fact, one role of a CSP solution may be thought of as providing *coherence* to an observed situation. Coherence may mean making sense of text, images, or events, or, more generally, constructing an interpretation that "fits." It is a concept studied by philosophers and psychologists.

In the simplest form, a CSP involves assigning values to variables so some constraint (or set of constraints) is satisfied. A more formal definition is provided in Section 4.1.3.

This chapter focuses on nonstructural constraints, which are common in many, but not all, CSP problems. This includes applications in diverse areas such as machine vision, belief maintenance, temporal reasoning, labeling, map coloring, planning and scheduling [Fox90], [KL90], diagnosis, power system protection, and game playing.

In other chapters, a number of alternative solution strategies for this class of problems is considered. This includes Genetic algorithms, Swarm approaches, (Recurrent) Neural networks,[1] and Production systems.

In Chapter 5 we consider grammar-based CSPs, including natural language understanding. Finally, the parallel solution of CSPs is an important, open problem [Sar93].

4.1 Nonstructural Constraint Satisfaction Problems (CSPs)

4.1.1 A Simple Introductory Example: Map Coloring

Many CSPs are simple to articulate. For example: "Given a map with regions delineated (examples are shown in Figures 4.8 and 4.26) and a set of possible colors, assign colors to the regions such that no two regions that share a boundary have the same color." This is the famous map coloring problem, and is treated in detail in Section 4.7.

---

[1]See Section 14.8.7 of Chapter 14.

4.1.2   Another CSP Example: Numerical Constraint Satisfaction

This is another familiar and easy-to-visualize example. Consider the solution of a set of linear equalities of the form:

$$x + y = 6 \tag{4.1}$$
$$3x - y = 2 \tag{4.2}$$

Each of these equations constrains the numerical solution of assignment of values to variables x and y. Furthermore, each equation alone is insufficient constraint information for a unique solution. More precisely, each equation constrains the n-dimensional numerical solution space to an $n - 1$ dimensional subspace. In this example, with $n = 2$ variables, each equation therefore constrains the solution to a line. The satisfaction of the conjunction (AND-ing) of these constraints (in this example, the intersection of the constraint lines), yields the global solution space. In this example, if the constraint equations are linearly independent, these constraint lines are forced to be noncollinear, thus a unique solution is obtained at their intersection. This is shown in Figure 4.1.

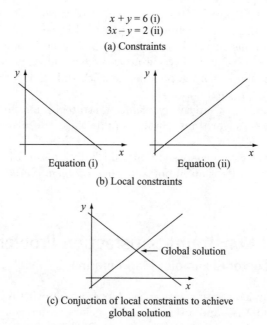

$x + y = 6$ (i)
$3x - y = 2$ (ii)

(a) Constraints

Equation (i)   Equation (ii)

(b) Local constraints

Global solution

(c) Conjuction of local constraints to achieve
global solution

Figure 4.1   Example of a Numerical CSP

4.1.3 Formal Definition

A Constraint Satisfaction Problem (CSP) is defined [XL00], [Mac92] as a tuple (U, D, C) where

- A finite set $U = \{u_1, \ldots, u_n\}$ of variables;

- A domain, D_i with d_i elements or values for each variable u_i (note a variable can only be assigned a value from its domain and that different variables may have different domains); and

- A set, C, of constraints among variables. Often a constraint takes the form of a k-ary relation. For $2 \leq k \leq n$ a constraint $C_{i1,i2,\ldots,ik}$ consists of a subset $\{u_{i1}, u_{i2}, \ldots, u_{ik}\}$ of U and a corresponding relation $R_{i1,i2,\ldots,ik} \subseteq D_{i1} \times \ldots \times D_{ik}$ where $i1, i2, \ldots, ik$ are distinct. $C_{i1,i2,\ldots,ik}$ is a k-ary constraint and k-ary relation $R_{i1,i2,\ldots,ik}$ specifies all the allowed tuples of values for variables $u_{i1}, \ldots, u_{ik}$, which are compatible. We show several examples of $k = 2$ (binary relations) in the following section.

Constraint $C_{i1,i2,\ldots,ik}$ is satisfied if the tuple of values assigned to variables $u_{i1}, \ldots, u_{ik}$ is an element of the relation $R_{i1,i2,\ldots,ik}$. A *solution* to a CSP is an assignment of a value to each variable (from its domain) such that all constraints are satisfied. In other words, a solution is a problem-consistent assignment of variables to values. A specific CSP can have zero solutions, a unique solution (one), or many solutions. A CSP that has a solution is called *satisfiable*; otherwise it is *unsatisfiable*.

As noted, many important applications, such as planning, resource scheduling, parsing, and engineering design can be cast within the framework of CSPs. There is much research into the computational cost and properties of CSPs. In general, CSPs are computationally intractable, specifically they are NP-complete [Dec98].

4.2 CSPs as Propositional Satisfiability (SAT) Problems

In a broad sense, propositional satisfiability (SAT) is the problem of determining an assignment for the variables in a proposition-based formula such that the formula is true (or satisfied). A CSP may be formulated as a SAT problem.

Introductory Example. Consider the following situation, derived from [Hay79]:

> *You are chief of protocol for the embassy ball. The crown prince instructs you either to invite Peru or to exclude Qatar. The queen asks you to invite either Qatar or Romania or both. The king, in a spiteful mood, wants to snub either Romania or Peru or both.*
>
> *Can you formulate a guest list that will satisfy the prince, the king, and the queen?*

This is an easy-to-visualize example of a propositional satisfiability (SAT) problem. Let P, Q, and R be Boolean variables that are true if and only if we invite Peru, Qatar, and Romania, respectively. Note this means the search space requires evaluation of 2^3 *possible* guest lists. Satisfaction of the prince requires that $P \cup \neg Q$ be true. Satisfaction of the queen requires $Q \cup R$ be true. Satisfaction of the king requires $\neg R \cup \neg P$ be true. Thus, the overall problem is to find assignments to the binary variables P, Q, and R such that G is true, where

$$G = (P \cup \neg Q) \cap (Q \cup R) \cap (\neg R \cup \neg P) \tag{4.3}$$

This example is continued in the Exercises.

4.3 SAT: Definition, Properties, and Solutions

A SAT instance (or problem) [SS00], denoted C, is a formula in propositional logic. For standardization, conjunctive normal form is used, i.e., C is a set ("bag") of m clauses connected by conjunction (AND).

In C, a clause is a disjunction of literals. Each literal is a Boolean variable or its negation. The total set of variables used in C comprise a set of n symbols, V. This form was shown in Equation 4.3.

An *assignment* is a mapping from V to either true or false. If an assignment may be found that makes C true, this assignment is a solution to the SAT. A SAT for which a solution exists is said to be *satisfiable*.

The SAT decision question or decision problem is that of determining whether a solution exists. (Note that this may be different from actually determining a solution, although finding a solution certainly answers the decision question.)

4.3.1 k-SAT

The k-SAT problem is the SAT problem restricted to clauses containing k literals. It is of significant concern that the k-SAT problem for $k \geq 3$ is NP-hard.

4.3.2 SAT Solutions

The dominant solution approach to SAT is some form of search, usually with heuristics. Many times the search has a random component, such as randomly generating possible assignments and testing to see if they are solutions. Another technique is (perhaps randomly) modifying portions of the assignment and subsequent testing. This is a form of local search.

The WSAT algorithm [SC94] is one popular local search-based strategy. Pseudocode for WSAT is shown in Figure 4.2. Many others (Davis-Putnam, GSAT, TSAT, WalkSAT, and hybrid approaches) have been proposed.

4.3.3 SAT Properties

The relationship between SAT solution computational (search) cost and the structure of some SAT problems has been investigated for some time. Often, assignments are randomly generated and evaluated for specific values of k. It has been noted [SS00] that certain distributions of SAT instances (C) may be parametrized by a "control" parameter. As this parameter is changed, a sharp threshold or "phase transition" in the probability of there being a solution occurs. Problem instances generated with this parameter less than the critical value (the so-called underconstrained region) have a high probability of the existence of a solution. Conversely, instances generated with this parameter greater

```
WSat(C, Max-tries, Max-flips, p)
  for i = 1 to Max-tries
    T := a random assignment
    for j = 1 to Max-flips
      clause := an unsatisfied clause of C, selected at random
      v := Select-variable-from-clause(clause, C, p)
      T := T with v's value 'flipped'
      if T is satisfying
        return T
      end if
    end for
  end for
  return 'no satisfying assignment found'
```

Figure 4.2 The WSAT Local Search Algorithm (Pseudocode)

than the critical value (the so-called overconstrained region) have a low probability of the existence of a solution. It has also been observed that control parameter critical value(s) are often associated with a peak in the computational cost of search.

For example, using the SAT terminology of Section 4.3, the control parameter m/n (clauses/variables) has been investigated. As this ratio increases, at a certain value the probability of satisfiability (for randomly generated SAT problems) exhibits a sharp transition.

4.4 A (Somewhat) Obvious Solution to CSPs: Generate-and-Test (GAT)

One possible approach to solving problems of this type is to simply generate (perhaps randomly) possible assignments and then to evaluate the constraint(s) to determine if they are satisfied. This is an example of generate-and-test (GAT). GAT is a search strategy based upon exploring points in the problem state space and evaluating the suitability of these points. As noted in Section 4.9, GAT may be inefficient or even impractical in many cases.

4.5 Constraint Programming and a Role for Prolog in CSPs

Mapping a CSP directly to a suitable programming language introduces the broader topic of *constraint programming* [Apt03, Ros06]. Constraint programming uses constraints as the basis of a programming language designed to solve CSPs.

The semantics of Prolog, especially Prolog's unification mechanism (see Appendix B), suggest a useful role in the implementation of CSP solutions. Since Prolog is an implementation of logic programming, and logic allows the formulation of constraints (as shown by the SAT problem), it is not surprising that CSPs and SAT problems are solvable using Prolog [Rob92]. Note that computational efficiency must also be considered.

From the Prolog viewpoint, many CSPs or SAT problems may be implemented using a set of variables, and a set of predicates, the conjunction of which the instantiated variables must satisfy.

The reader may wish to review Appendix B before continuing.

4.6   The Labeling (Assignment) Problem

Labeling problems are a commonly encountered form of a CSP. In this section, we explore and extend an image-based example.

4.6.1   Labeling Complexity

Given n objects to be labeled and the set of m possible labels on each, note that, without further constraints, m^n *possible and valid* labeling solutions exist.

4.6.2   Image Labeling Example

This problem is also solved using CLIPS; see Chapter 7. We assume the input is a segmented image of the form shown in Figure 4.3. As Figure 4.3 indicates, we consider the labeling of six regions, denoted as R1, R2,...,R6. There are five possible labels for each of these regions, i.e., members of the set:

$$\{car, road, trees, grass, sky\}$$

Note that an exhaustive enumeration of the unconstrained labeling of these regions thus yields $5^6 = 15,625$ possibilities.

Definition: Adjacency.   For simplicity, first consider a single binary constraint, namely that of region adjacency. Two regions that share a boundary are said to be adjacent. This is an easily extracted relation involving the image regions of Figure 4.3. Adjacency is a symmetric relation that is easily depicted graphically via an adjacency graph. The observed region adjacency graph (in terms of unlabeled regions R_i) for the sample segmented image of Figure 4.3 is shown.

Constraints Regarding Adjacency.   The next step is developing a set of constraints on allowable labels pairwise as a function of whether the regions are adjacent or not. For example, it makes sense to allow two adjacent regions to have the labels "car" and "road," i.e., it does not violate human intuition when viewing an image wherein a car is adjacent to a road. On the other hand, if a labeling indicated a car were adjacent to grass (the driver is driving off the road) in the image, we would not allow this labeling.

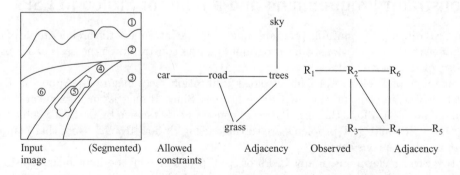

Figure 4.3 Sample Image and Labeling Constraints

```
label 'car' is allowed on an adjacent region with label 'road'
label 'road' is allowed on an adjacent region with label 'grass'
label 'grass' is allowed on an adjacent region with label 'trees'
label 'road' is allowed on an adjacent region with label 'trees'
label 'sky' is allowed on an adjacent region with label 'trees'
```

Figure 4.4 Allowable Labels on Adjacent Regions (symmetry of relation is not enumerated)

Allowable Labels. We therefore generate the set of compatible labels shown in Figure 4.4 and graphically in Figure 4.3. Note adjacency is a symmetric relation; we only show half of the allowed label pairs.

4.6.3 CSP Solutions in Prolog

Database for Labeling Problem

The essential database (using **only** the `adjacent-to` constraint) is shown in Figure 4.5. The reader should verify that there are 42 solutions to this problem, without any other constraints or measures to be optimized. Although we have considerably reduced the solution space, we have not reached our goal of a consistent labeling that would be produced by a human observer. To do this, additional constraints are employed to further constrain the solution space.

```
/* label.pro */
/* basic image labeling solution in Prolog */
/* database of allowed adjacency constraints */

adj-to(car,road).
adj-to(road,grass).
adj-to(road,trees).
adj-to(sky,trees).
adj-to(grass,trees).

adjacent-to(X,Y) :- adj-to(X,Y).
adjacent-to(X,Y) :- adj-to(Y,X).

/* observations of adjacency  */

goal([R1,R2,R3,R4,R5,R6]):-
adjacent-to(R1,R2),
adjacent-to(R2,R6),
adjacent-to(R2,R3),
adjacent-to(R3,R4),
adjacent-to(R2,R4),
adjacent-to(R4,R6),
adjacent-to(R4,R5).
```

Figure 4.5 Skeletal Prolog Image Labeling Solution

4.6.4 Adding Unary Constraints

We consider first the incorporation of the unary constraint that the region labeled "sky" must be the uppermost region in the segmented image. We add this observation, or assumed extracted information, to the goal statement (assuming that image processing techniques may be used to extract this information) and to the database as a fact, indicating a second relation (or in this case a property) "highest." In addition, we add a second unary constraint. Assume several time observations or samples of the image were available. Using this data, it is possible to determine if a region exhibited motion, i.e., it was moving. (As an aside, this is nontrivial with "real" images.) This motion is an attribute only possible on a region labeled "car." This modification and the result are shown in Figures 4.6 and 4.7.

```
/* label2.pro */
/* addition of write and fail to print all solutions */

highest(sky).
moving(car).
adj-to(car,road).
adj-to(road,grass).
adj-to(road,trees).
adj-to(sky,trees).
adj-to(grass,trees).

adjacent-to(R1,R2) :- adj-to(R1,R2).
adjacent-to(R1,R2) :- adj-to(R2,R1).


goal :- highest(R1),
        moving(R5),
        adjacent-to(R1,R2),
        adjacent-to(R2,R6),
        adjacent-to(R2,R3),
        adjacent-to(R3,R4),
        adjacent-to(R2,R4),
        adjacent-to(R4,R6),
        adjacent-to(R4,R5),
        write('Solution is'),nl,nl,
        write('region 1 is bound to  '),write(R1),nl,
        write('region 2 is bound to  '),write(R2),nl,
        write('region 3 is bound to  '),write(R3),nl,
        write('region 4 is bound to  '),write(R4),nl,
        write('region 5 is bound to  '),write(R5),nl,
        write('region 6 is bound to  '),write(R6),nl,nl,
        fail.
```

Figure 4.6 Prolog Image Labeling Solution Incorporating Two Unary Constraints (Unique Solution)

```
?- ['label2.pro'].
% label2.pro compiled 0.01 sec, 2,976 bytes

Yes
?- goal.
Solution is

region 1 is bound to  sky
region 2 is bound to  trees
region 3 is bound to  grass
region 4 is bound to  road
region 5 is bound to  car
region 6 is bound to  grass


No
?-
```

Figure 4.7 Result of Prolog-Based Image Labeling with Binary and Unary Constraints

4.6.5 Adding Global Constraints

In this section, we extend the labeling problem by incorporating selected global constraints. These include:

1. At most one region is labeled with label L;

2. At least one region is labeled with label L; and

3. Only one region is labeled with label L.

As shown in the Prolog solution, the formulations of these constraints in Prolog are interrelated.

Prolog Formulation

The Prolog database shown as follows is used to solve this problem. Output (solutions) are shown in the following section.

```
/* CONTENT: label-global.pro      */
/* CONTENT: labeling problem with global constraints */
/* CONTENT:     - at most one region is labeled with label L.  */
/* CONTENT:     - at least one region is labeled with label L. */
/* CONTENT:     - only one region is labeled with label L.     */
/* note: does not include "highest" or "moving"     */

/* database */

adj-to(car,road).
adj-to(road,grass).
adj-to(road,trees).
adj-to(sky,trees).
adj-to(grass,trees).
```

```
        adjacent-to(R1,R2) :- adj-to(R1,R2).
        adjacent-to(R1,R2) :- adj-to(R2,R1).


        at_most_one(L,[R1,R2,R3,R4,R5,R6]):-
                not(repeated_in(L,[R1,R2,R3,R4,R5,R6])).

        at_least_one(L,[R1,R2,R3,R4,R5,R6]):-
                    member(L,[R1,R2,R3,R4,R5,R6]),!.

/* note: cut in above predicate eliminates */
/* redundandant solutions */

        exactly_one(L,[R1,R2,R3,R4,R5,R6]):-
                    at_least_one(L,[R1,R2,R3,R4,R5,R6]),
                    at_most_one(L,[R1,R2,R3,R4,R5,R6]).



/* part (i): at most one 'trees' in goal1 */

        goal1 :-
                adjacent-to(R1,R2),    /* the observations */
                adjacent-to(R2,R6),
                adjacent-to(R2,R3),
                adjacent-to(R3,R4),
                adjacent-to(R2,R4),
                adjacent-to(R4,R6),
                adjacent-to(R4,R5),
                at_most_one(trees,[R1,R2,R3,R4,R5,R6]),
                write_soln([R1,R2,R3,R4,R5,R6]),
                fail.

/* part (ii): exactly one 'car' in goal2  */

        goal2 :-
                adjacent-to(R1,R2),
                adjacent-to(R2,R6),
                adjacent-to(R2,R3),
                adjacent-to(R3,R4),
                adjacent-to(R2,R4),
                adjacent-to(R4,R6),
                adjacent-to(R4,R5),
                exactly_one(car,[R1,R2,R3,R4,R5,R6]),
                write_soln([R1,R2,R3,R4,R5,R6]),
                fail.



/* part (iii): at least one trees in goal3 */

        goal3 :-
                adjacent-to(R1,R2),
                adjacent-to(R2,R6),
                adjacent-to(R2,R3),
                adjacent-to(R3,R4),
```

```
                adjacent-to(R2,R4),
                adjacent-to(R4,R6),
                adjacent-to(R4,R5),
                at_least_one(trees,[R1,R2,R3,R4,R5,R6]),
                write_soln([R1,R2,R3,R4,R5,R6]),
                fail.


/* all of the above constraints together */

        goal4 :-
                adjacent-to(R1,R2),
                adjacent-to(R2,R6),
                adjacent-to(R2,R3),
                adjacent-to(R3,R4),
                adjacent-to(R2,R4),
                adjacent-to(R4,R6),
                adjacent-to(R4,R5),
                exactly_one(car,[R1,R2,R3,R4,R5,R6]),
                at_most_one(trees,[R1,R2,R3,R4,R5,R6]),
                at_least_one(trees,[R1,R2,R3,R4,R5,R6]),
                write_soln([R1,R2,R3,R4,R5,R6]),
                fail.



/* auxiliary (new) predicates */

/** this yields more compact solution display */

write_soln([R1,R2,R3,R4,R5,R6]):-
                write('R1='),write(R1),write(' '),
                write('R2='),write(R2),write(' '),
                write('R3='),write(R3),write(' '),
                write('R4='),write(R4),write(' '),
                write('R5='),write(R5),write(' '),
                write('R6='),write(R6),nl.

/* repeated_in.predicate description */
/* predicate to tell if a list */
/* contains a specific repeated item */

repeated_in(X,[X|R]):-member(X,R).
repeated_in(X,[_|R]):-repeated_in(X,R).
```

Prolog Results

```
?- goal1.                                          R1=road R2=trees R3=grass R4=road R5=grass R6=grass
R1=car R2=road R3=grass R4=trees R5=road R6=grass   R1=road R2=trees R3=grass R4=road R5=car R6=grass
R1=car R2=road R3=grass R4=trees R5=sky R6=grass    R1=sky R2=trees R3=road R4=grass R5=road R6=road
R1=car R2=road R3=grass R4=trees R5=grass R6=grass  R1=sky R2=trees R3=grass R4=road R5=grass R6=grass
R1=road R2=grass R3=road R4=trees R5=road R6=road   R1=sky R2=trees R3=grass R4=road R5=car R6=grass
R1=road R2=grass R3=road R4=trees R5=sky R6=road    R1=grass R2=trees R3=road R4=grass R5=road R6=road
R1=road R2=grass R3=road R4=trees R5=grass R6=road  R1=grass R2=trees R3=grass R4=road R5=grass R6=grass
R1=road R2=trees R3=road R4=grass R5=road R6=road   R1=grass R2=trees R3=grass R4=road R5=car R6=grass
```

```
R1=grass R2=road R3=grass R4=trees R5=road R6=grass   R1=sky R2=trees R3=grass R4=road R5=grass R6=grass
R1=grass R2=road R3=grass R4=trees R5=sky R6=grass     R1=sky R2=trees R3=grass R4=road R5=trees R6=grass
R1=grass R2=road R3=grass R4=trees R5=grass R6=grass   R1=sky R2=trees R3=grass R4=road R5=car R6=grass
                                                       R1=grass R2=trees R3=road R4=grass R5=trees R6=road
No                                                     R1=grass R2=trees R3=road R4=grass R5=road R6=road
?- goal2.                                              R1=grass R2=trees R3=grass R4=road R5=grass R6=grass
R1=car R2=road R3=grass R4=trees R5=road R6=grass      R1=grass R2=trees R3=grass R4=road R5=trees R6=grass
R1=car R2=road R3=grass R4=trees R5=sky R6=grass       R1=grass R2=trees R3=grass R4=road R5=car R6=grass
R1=car R2=road R3=grass R4=trees R5=grass R6=grass     R1=grass R2=road R3=grass R4=trees R5=road R6=grass
R1=car R2=road R3=trees R4=grass R5=trees R6=trees     R1=grass R2=road R3=grass R4=trees R5=sky R6=grass
R1=car R2=road R3=trees R4=grass R5=road R6=trees      R1=grass R2=road R3=grass R4=trees R5=grass R6=grass
R1=road R2=grass R3=trees R4=road R5=car R6=trees      R1=grass R2=road R3=trees R4=grass R5=trees R6=trees
R1=road R2=trees R3=grass R4=road R5=car R6=grass      R1=grass R2=road R3=trees R4=grass R5=road R6=trees
R1=sky R2=trees R3=grass R4=road R5=car R6=grass       R1=trees R2=road R3=grass R4=trees R5=road R6=grass
R1=grass R2=trees R3=grass R4=road R5=car R6=grass     R1=trees R2=road R3=grass R4=trees R5=sky R6=grass
R1=trees R2=grass R3=trees R4=road R5=car R6=trees     R1=trees R2=road R3=grass R4=trees R5=grass R6=grass
                                                       R1=trees R2=road R3=trees R4=grass R5=trees R6=trees
No                                                     R1=trees R2=road R3=trees R4=grass R5=road R6=trees
?- goal3.                                              R1=trees R2=grass R3=trees R4=road R5=grass R6=trees
R1=car R2=road R3=grass R4=trees R5=road R6=grass      R1=trees R2=grass R3=trees R4=road R5=trees R6=trees
R1=car R2=road R3=grass R4=trees R5=sky R6=grass       R1=trees R2=grass R3=trees R4=road R5=car R6=trees
R1=car R2=road R3=grass R4=trees R5=grass R6=grass     R1=trees R2=grass R3=road R4=trees R5=road R6=road
R1=car R2=road R3=trees R4=grass R5=trees R6=trees     R1=trees R2=grass R3=road R4=trees R5=sky R6=road
R1=car R2=road R3=trees R4=grass R5=road R6=trees      R1=trees R2=grass R3=road R4=trees R5=grass R6=road
R1=road R2=grass R3=trees R4=road R5=grass R6=trees
R1=road R2=grass R3=trees R4=road R5=trees R6=trees    No
R1=road R2=grass R3=trees R4=road R5=car R6=trees      ?- goal4.
R1=road R2=grass R3=road R4=trees R5=road R6=road      R1=car R2=road R3=grass R4=trees R5=road R6=grass
R1=road R2=grass R3=road R4=trees R5=sky R6=road       R1=car R2=road R3=grass R4=trees R5=sky R6=grass
R1=road R2=grass R3=road R4=trees R5=grass R6=road     R1=car R2=road R3=grass R4=trees R5=grass R6=grass
R1=road R2=trees R3=road R4=grass R5=trees R6=road     R1=road R2=trees R3=grass R4=road R5=car R6=grass
R1=road R2=trees R3=road R4=grass R5=road R6=road      R1=sky R2=trees R3=grass R4=road R5=car R6=grass
R1=road R2=trees R3=grass R4=road R5=grass R6=grass    R1=grass R2=trees R3=grass R4=road R5=car R6=grass
R1=road R2=trees R3=grass R4=road R5=trees R6=grass
R1=road R2=trees R3=grass R4=road R5=car R6=grass      No
R1=sky R2=trees R3=road R4=grass R5=trees R6=road      ?-
R1=sky R2=trees R3=road R4=grass R5=road R6=road
```

4.6.6   Adding Optimization to the Formulation

This is an introduction to constrained optimization. The now-familiar image labeling problem (using **only** the adjacent-to constraint) is used. There are 42 solutions to this problem, without any other constraints or measures to be optimized. Consider additional problem specifications (both individually and together) of the form:

1. Maximize the number of regions labeled "car"

2. Maximize the number of regions labeled "trees"

This problem is not simple, but it is solvable. The basic difficulty in this problem is the generation of solutions and development of a "how-many-in-soln" predicate.

Prolog Formulation

```
/* file: label-optim.pro */
/* modified CSP (labeling) problem */
/* some of these preds may be built-in in some Prologs */


/* database of constraints, as before*/

adj-to(car,road).
adj-to(road,grass).
adj-to(road,trees).
adj-to(sky,trees).
adj-to(grass,trees).

adjacent-to(X,Y) :- adj-to(X,Y).
adjacent-to(X,Y) :- adj-to(Y,X).

/* a predicate  to calculate the occurences of an element in a list */
/* form:  how-many(Element,List,Occurences) */

/* if List is empty;  Occurences is 0 */

how-many(A,[],0).

/* if element is same as head of the list, increase number by 1 */

how-many(A,[A|B],K1) :- how-many(A,B,J1),!,K1 is J1+1.

/* use recursion if doesn't match with the head of the list */

how-many(A,[_|B],K2) :- how-many(A,B,K2).

/* predicate to find the largest of two numbers */
/* form: largest(A,B,C) */
/* Compares A and B, and gives C as the largest number */
/* SWI Prolog claims to have a "max/2" predicate    */

largest(J,A,K) :- J>A,K is J.
largest(J,A,K) :- A>=J,K is A.

/* predicate to find the largest element (number) in a list */
/* assumes nonnegative entries    */

largest-elem([],0). /* by definition  */
largest-elem([A|B],K):-largest-elem(B,J),largest(J,A,K).

/* predicate to find number of occurences (K) of A in each solution */

how-many-in-soln(A,K):-goal([R1,R2,R3,R4,R5,R6]),how-many(A,[R1,R2,R3,R4,R5,R6],K).

/* produce all solutions, and then select K number of occurences of A */

soln(A,K):-goal([R1,R2,R3,R4,R5,R6]),
        how-many(A,[R1,R2,R3,R4,R5,R6],J),
        K=:=J, /* succeeds when K evaluates to a number equal to J  */
        write_soln([R1,R2,R3,R4,R5,R6]).
```

```
/* find all solutions and store the number of occurences in each solution in L */
/* find the largest number in L (call this number G) */
/* then check the results with that number of elements */
/* (G number of A) */

/* use built-in predicate: findall(+Var, +Goal, -Bag)
   Creates  a  list  of  the  instantiations  Var gets  successively  on
   backtracking  over Goal and unifies the  result with Bag        */

optmzed_soln(A):-findall(X,how-many-in-soln(A,X),L),largest-elem(L,G),soln(A,G).

/* observations */

goal([R1,R2,R3,R4,R5,R6]):-
adjacent-to(R1,R2),
adjacent-to(R2,R6),
adjacent-to(R2,R3),
adjacent-to(R3,R4),
adjacent-to(R2,R4),
adjacent-to(R4,R6),
adjacent-to(R4,R5).

/* goals */
/* goal1:       maximize the number of regions labeled car */
/* goal2: maximize the number of regions labeled trees */
/* goal3: both objectives   */

goal1:-optmzed_soln(car),fail.

goal2:-optmzed_soln(trees),fail.

/* this is somewhat inefficient; computes the solutions 2x   */
/* determines for intersection of goals 1 and 2 in soln. space   */

goal3:- findall(X1,how-many-in-soln(car,X1),L1),largest-elem(L1,G1),
        findall(X2,how-many-in-soln(trees,X2),L2),largest-elem(L2,G2),
        goal([R1,R2,R3,R4,R5,R6]),
        how-many(car,[R1,R2,R3,R4,R5,R6],K1),K1=:=G1,
        how-many(trees,[R1,R2,R3,R4,R5,R6],K2),K2=:=G2,
        write_soln([R1,R2,R3,R4,R5,R6]).


/* printing utility */

write_soln([R1,R2,R3,R4,R5,R6]):-
                write('R1='),write(R1),write(' '),
                write('R2='),write(R2),write(' '),
                write('R3='),write(R3),write(' '),
                write('R4='),write(R4),write(' '),
                write('R5='),write(R5),write(' '),
                write('R6='),write(R6),nl.
```

Prolog Results

```
?- goal1.
R1=car R2=road R3=grass R4=trees R5=road R6=grass
R1=car R2=road R3=grass R4=trees R5=sky R6=grass
R1=car R2=road R3=grass R4=trees R5=grass R6=grass
R1=car R2=road R3=trees R4=grass R5=trees R6=trees
R1=car R2=road R3=trees R4=grass R5=road R6=trees
R1=road R2=grass R3=trees R4=road R5=car R6=trees
R1=road R2=trees R3=grass R4=road R5=car R6=grass
R1=sky R2=trees R3=grass R4=road R5=car R6=grass
R1=grass R2=trees R3=grass R4=road R5=car R6=grass
R1=trees R2=grass R3=trees R4=road R5=car R6=trees

No
?- goal2.
R1=trees R2=road R3=trees R4=grass R5=trees R6=trees
R1=trees R2=grass R3=trees R4=road R5=trees R6=trees

No
?- goal3.

No
?-
```

4.7 The Map Coloring Problem

4.7.1 Background and History

The map coloring problem is another popular CSP example. It is very similar to labeling. The objective is to color the regions in a given map using a predefined number of colors such that adjacent regions (i.e., sharing a border) have different colors. This problem has a rich history and raises numerous theoretical issues.

The problem may be approached via graph theory. In this interpretation, the graph vertex coloring problem is a CSP with the objective to color the vertices of a graph using a predefined number of colors so that the vertices that are connected by an edge have different colors.

The map or graph coloring problem belongs to a class of problems that are called NP-hard problems, for which no efficient solution method is known. The TSP is another example.

In the mid-1800s this problem was popular within a group of mathematicians since it was a challenging and unsolved problem. It was common knowledge among practicing mapmakers, even at that time, that four colors were sufficient to color a map. This wasn't actually proved, however, until 1976.

Furthermore, as we explore later, even though four colors are enough to color any map, some maps can be colored with fewer than four colors. In this problem we consider the use of three colors as well as four, and then extending the formulation to minimize the actual number of colors used. Note that a method to determine exactly how many colors are needed for a given map is itself a challenging problem.

The so-called four-color theorem states that any map in a plane can be colored using four colors in such a way that regions sharing a common boundary (other than a single point) do not have the same color. F. Guthrie first conjectured the theorem in 1853 and communicated it to the famous deMorgan.

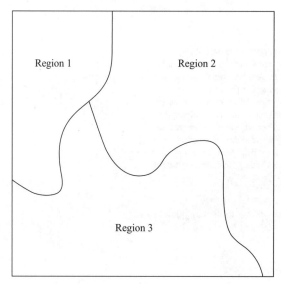

Figure 4.8   Map to be Colored

In 1878, Cayley wrote the first paper on this conjecture. A series of fallacious proofs followed. The conjecture that four colors were sufficient was finally proved by Appel and Haken in 1977 [AH77] in a computer-assisted proof.

4.7.2   Prolog-Based Solution Approaches

Refer to the map to be colored in Figure 4.8. We will use this simple map to develop Prolog-based map coloring CSP results.

Prolog Formulation.   A Prolog formulation for the map of Figure 4.8, using three colors (abbreviated as "r," "g," and "b") is shown as follows:

```
/* mapcolor1.pro */
/* first map case (3 regions) */
/* 3 colors; r,g,b */
/* write and fail used to print all solutions */

adj-to(r,g).
adj-to(r,b).
adj-to(b,g).

/* symmetry of adjacency relation */

adjacent-to(R1,R2) :- adj-to(R1,R2).
adjacent-to(R1,R2) :- adj-to(R2,R1).

goal :- adjacent-to(R1,R2),
        adjacent-to(R2,R3),
        adjacent-to(R1,R3),
```

```
        write('Solution is'),nl,nl,
        write('region 1 is colored:  '),write(R1),nl,
        write('region 2 is colored:  '),write(R2),nl,
        write('region 3 is colored:  '),write(R3),nl,
        fail.
```

Results using this formulation are shown here.

```
?- ['mapcolor1.pro'].
['mapcolor1.pro'].
% mapcolor1.pro compiled 0.00 sec, 1,888 bytes

Yes
?- goal.
Solution is

region 1 is colored:  r
region 2 is colored:  g
region 3 is colored:  b
Solution is

region 1 is colored:  r
region 2 is colored:  b
region 3 is colored:  g
Solution is

region 1 is colored:  b
region 2 is colored:  g
region 3 is colored:  r
Solution is

region 1 is colored:  g
region 2 is colored:  r
region 3 is colored:  b
Solution is

region 1 is colored:  b
region 2 is colored:  r
region 3 is colored:  g
Solution is

region 1 is colored:  g
region 2 is colored:  b
region 3 is colored:  r

No
?-
```

This effort is continued in the exercises, using different region data and a varying number of colors.

4.8 Another Framework for CSP Assignment Problems and Alternative Solution Approaches

4.8.1 A General Representational Framework

Using the notation of Section 4.1.3, the labeling problem consists of

1. A finite set $U = \{u_1, u_2, \ldots, u_n\}$ of n objects (variables) to be labeled together with a domain, D_i, of labels (or values) for each object;[2]

2. A finite set $\Gamma = \{\lambda_1, \lambda_2, \ldots, \lambda_m\}$ of m possible labels; and

3. A constraint (formulated below), here based upon a $k = 2$-ary adjacency relation.

Each $D_i \subseteq \Gamma$ is denoted Γ_i. As noted, restrictions on D_i may be used to implement unary constraints. Note the set of unconstrained labelings or assignment values consists of all elements of

$$\underbrace{\Gamma \times \Gamma \times \Gamma \times \Gamma \cdots \times \Gamma}_{n \text{ times}}$$

Constraining the overall labeling by considering objects pairwise yields a $k = 2$-ary CSP, based upon a relation R_{sol}:

$$R_{sol} \subseteq (U \times \Gamma) \times (U \times \Gamma) \tag{4.4}$$

Sets, Vectors, and Matrices for Problem Representation. One of the motivations in this section is to develop data structures that facilitate the solution of CSPs by an iterative computation. It is convenient to represent set membership using binary vectors. Each element of the binary vector corresponds to an element of the set. With this convention, the Cartesian product of two sets (or a set with itself) may be computed as the outer product of two binary vectors. This operation yields a binary matrix. Referring to set Γ, to facilitate computation we define a corresponding binary vector

$$\underline{\Omega}_i = [l_1 \; l_2 \cdots l_m]^T \tag{4.5}$$

where

$$l_k = \begin{cases} 1 & \text{if } \lambda_k \text{ compatible with } u_i \\ 0 & \text{otherwise} \end{cases} \tag{4.6}$$

$\underline{\Omega}_i$ may be used to enforce any unary constraints. Furthermore, as we show in Section 4.8.3, $\underline{\Omega}_i$ may be iteratively propagated to determine a limit set for the solution.

---

[2]Recall an object can only be assigned a value from its domain and different objects may have different domains. This provides a mechanism for the enforcement of unary constraints, as shown in the Prolog formulations.

Denoting Γ_i as the set of λs corresponding to elements in $\underline{\Omega}_i$ that are 1, the set of values for a unary-only constrained labeling assignment would be a subset of $\Gamma_1 \times \Gamma_2 \times \cdots \times \Gamma_n$. Taken pairwise, assignment values in this case would be elements of set $\Gamma_{ij}^{\text{unary}}$, where

$$\Gamma_{ij}^{\text{unary}} \subseteq \Gamma_i \times \Gamma_j$$

To represent this, *permissible* pairwise labelings (based upon unary constraints only, i.e., without any consideration of k-ary relational constraints) would correspond to elements in P_{ij} that are 1, where

$$P_{ij} = \underline{\Omega}_i \cdot \underline{\Omega}_j^T \tag{4.7}$$

4.8.2 Enforcing *k* = 2 Object Label Compatibility

The Constraint. It is useful to restate the $k = 2$-ary constraint. To achieve a labeling (assignment of labels to objects):

- ◆ Unary constraints may be defined for all objects. Nonadjacent objects are only subject to the unary constraints.

- ◆ For every pair of objects, *if the objects are adjacent*, the corresponding labels must satisfy a relational or compatibility constraint.

- ◆ The overall solution requires an assignment such that all relational (pairwise) and unary constraints are satisfied.

A corollary to this is that if two objects do not satisfy the adjacency relation (i.e., are not observed to be adjacent), then, for these two objects, only the unary constraints are of concern.

Define label compatibility c_{kl} as follows:

$$c_{kl} = \begin{cases} 1 & \text{if } \lambda_k \text{ is compatible with } \lambda_l \\ 0 & otherwise \end{cases} \tag{4.8}$$

Therefore, label pairs for which $c_{kl} = 1$ are a subset of $\Gamma_i \times \Gamma_j$. From this we derive a $m \times m$ binary matrix, C, where

$$C = [c_{kl}]$$

A sample C matrix for the label compatibility constraints given in Section 4.6.2 is shown in Figure 4.9. Note that C is a symmetric matrix with a zero diagonal.

Furthermore, referring to Equation 4.7, to get the overall constraint matrix for any two distinct objects, u_i and u_j, we define binary matrix Ω_{ij} as follows:

$$\Omega_{ij} = P_{ij} \otimes [\neg rel(i,j)E \oplus C] \tag{4.9}$$

$$C = \begin{array}{c} \\ \lambda_1 \\ \lambda_2 \\ \lambda_3 \\ \lambda_4 \\ \lambda_5 \end{array} \begin{array}{ccccc} \lambda_1 = \text{car} & \lambda_2 = \text{grass} & \lambda_3 = \text{road} & \lambda_4 = \text{trees} & \lambda_5 = \text{sky} \\ \left[\begin{array}{ccccc} 0 & 0 & 1 & 0 & 0 \\ 0 & 0 & 1 & 1 & 0 \\ 1 & 1 & 0 & 1 & 0 \\ 0 & 1 & 1 & 0 & 1 \\ 0 & 0 & 0 & 1 & 0 \end{array} \right] \end{array}$$

Figure 4.9 C Matrix for Problem of Section 4.6.2. Derived from Label Compatibility Graph of Figure 4.3.

where $rel(i,j)$ is used to represent a general binary relation (here $rel(i,j) = Adj(i,j)$) and

$\otimes$ denotes element-by-element (Kronecker product) matrix multiplication;[3]

$\oplus$ denotes element-by-element logical OR;

E is an $m \times M$ matrix of all 1s; and

$\neg$ denotes the logical NOT operator.

$Adj(i,j)$ is a binary function[4] used to enforce the observed adjacency relation. $Adj(i,j) = 1$ if objects u_i and u_j are adjacent, otherwise $Adj(i,j) = 0$. Note a Ω_{ij} matrix exists for every pair of objects where $i \neq j$.

4.8.3 Iterative CSP Solutions via Constraint Propagation: Introducing Discrete Relaxation

The formulation of Section 4.8.1 is used as a foundation to show two iterative approaches to achieve a CSP solution. Rules for the so-called Label Discarding and Label Retention Approaches are introduced. These approaches are related to the Arc Consistency Algorithm #3 (AC-3 for short) proposed by Mackworth [Mac92]. In addition, extension of this framework leads to continuous, probabilistic formulations.

The basis for these strategies is an iterative form of search, wherein the problem state space is successively and systematically refined (ideally narrowed) to yield a solution space. Both cases may be formulated within a graph-based format.

A Graphical Representation of the Solution Process

We begin with a digraph, G, whose arcs represent the relation-based constraint. Here adjacency is used. Note that the symmetry of the relation we are considering, i.e., adjacency, allows us to ignore the arc direction; this is not true in general. The observed relational constraint between nodes is indicated as arcs in G.

---

[3]In this case equivalent to an element-by-element AND operation.

[4]Alternately, it may be viewed as an $n \times n$ upper-triangular matrix with row and column indices corresponding to regions $R1$ through $R6$.

Furthermore, (using the notation of Section 4.8.1) each node has an associated set of labels, denoted Γ_i. Members in Γ_i are denoted by λ. We obtain Γ_i for all i by considering the elements of $\underline{\Omega}_i$, which are nonzero. In the special case where

$$\underline{\Omega}_i = [1\ 1\ 1 \ldots 1]^T \ \forall \ i$$

(i.e., any label is possible on any object u_i), $\Gamma_i = \Gamma$ and Γ_i has m members.

In this formulation, we are seeking labelings constrained by the binary relation (i.e., observed adjacent objects). This corresponds to node pairs in G connected by an arc. Notice an arc exists for every pair of objects u_i and u_j for which $Adj(i, j) = 1$. Interobject label compatibility constraint is represented by denoting Γ_{ij} as the set of all label pairs (λ, λ') that satisfy

$$\Gamma_{ij} = \{(\lambda, \lambda') |\ \Omega_{ij} = 1\} \tag{4.10}$$

where Ω_{ij} is given by Equation 4.9.

With the mathematical framework established, we now state two versions or interpretations of the iterative CSP algorithm. Note that the iteration is over nodes in G, with possible modification of Γ_i at each node. Define the neighbors of node i to be all the other nodes directly connected to node i via an arc in G.

The Label Retention Rule (LRR)

Retain label $\lambda \in \Gamma_i$ at node i if $\exists$ a label λ' such that $(\lambda, \lambda') \in \Gamma_{ij}\ \forall$ neighbors of i.

The Label Discarding Rule (LDR)

Discard label $\lambda \in \Gamma_i$ at node i if $\exists$ a neighbor j (of i) such that **every label** $\lambda' \in \Gamma_j$ is incompatible with λ, i.e., $(\lambda, \lambda') \notin \Gamma_{ij}\ \forall\ \lambda' \in \Gamma_j$.

The Limit Set and Remarks

The rules in Section 4.8.3 should be studied closely. One (retention) looks for support *at all neighbors*; the other (discarding) looks for lack of support *at some neighbor*.

Given that we iteratively apply one of these approaches over the nodes of G, the question of algorithm termination is important. For one, if any Γ_i becomes empty, the algorithm could (or should) stop and report that no solution is possible. However, consider the case where the algorithm, when applied over nodes $i = 1, 2, \ldots, n$ produces *no further change* in the Γ_i. This yields the limit set, i.e., the set consisting of

$$\{\Gamma_1^c, \Gamma_2^c, \ldots, \Gamma_n^c\}$$

where Γ_i^c is the set of remaining labels on object u_i upon algorithm termination.

An important observation is that even when every Γ_i is nonempty, the limit set does not, by itself, necessarily indicate possible solutions. In the case where each Γ_i consists of a single element, the unique solution is found by assigning each object u_i the single label found in Γ_i. Where the cardinality of one or more Γ_i is greater than 1, additional search is necessary to enumerate the solutions. This procedure is, nonetheless, a powerful tool for elimination of extraneous search.

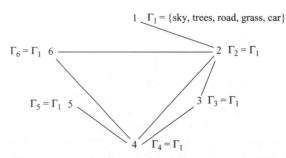

Figure 4.10   Starting Point for Iterative Labeling (no unary constraints applied)

Handworked Examples of LRR/LDR

We apply the LDR to the image labeling problem of Section 4.6.2. Note that even this simple example requires several iterative steps; only illustrative glimpses of the solution are shown.

Unary Constraints: $R1$ Must be Sky and $R5$ Must Be Car.   Figure 4.10 shows a possible starting point. *Unary constraints have not yet been applied.*

After application of both unary constraints ($R1$ must be sky and $R5$ must be car) and several iterations, Figure 4.11 results. Finally, the limit set corresponding to a unique solution is shown in Figure 4.12.

Limit Set Obtained from Unary Constraint: $R1$ Must Be Sky.   This result is shown in Figure 4.13. The use of this limit set is considered in Section 4.8.3.

The reader is encouraged to compare the limit sets from the two previous examples (Figures 4.12 and 4.13) with those obtained from the MATLAB/Octave implementation described in Section 4.8.3.

Example: Use of the Limit Set

This example should help explain the role (and limitations of) the limit set in a CSP. Consider the image labeling problem of Section 4.6.2, with the adjacency constraint shown in Figure 4.3. We

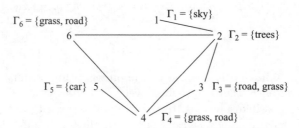

Figure 4.11   Intermediate Point in Solution. Unary Constraints Applied ($R1$ must be sky and $R5$ must be car)

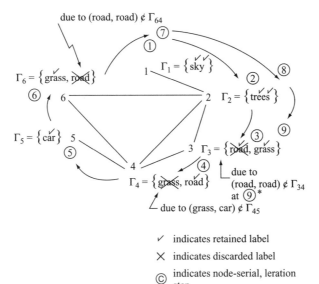

Figure 4.12 Final Iterations to Limit Set (two unary constraints—unique solution)

also use the single unary constraint "highest." Recall that using Prolog, we find that there are five solutions to the CSP in this case. First, we solve for the limit set using the LRR. Here $\Gamma_1 = \{sky\}$ and $\Gamma_j = \Gamma \; j \neq 1$. The limit set is shown in Figure 4.14.

Incorporating the Limit Set in Prolog.   Here we use the limit set to develop a more efficient Prolog solution and show the result. This is shown on the right side of Figure 4.15. In addition, both Prolog CSP formulations in Figure 4.15 have been modified to obtain runtime statistics, using SWI-Prolog's `statistics` predicate. This predicate has the prototype `statistics(inferences, -Value)`, and returns the total number of passes via the call and redo ports since Prolog was started as the value of variable `Value`.

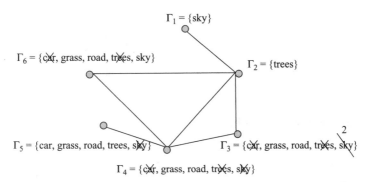

Figure 4.13 Limit Set Obtained with Single Unary Constraint $R1$ Must be Sky (non-unique solution)

$$\Gamma_1 = \{sky\}$$

$$\Gamma_2 = \{trees\}$$

$$\Gamma_3 = \{road, grass\}$$

$$\Gamma_4 = \{road, grass\}$$

$$\Gamma_5 = \{trees, road, car, grass\}$$

$$\Gamma_6 = \{road, grass\}$$

Figure 4.14 Limit Set Using Constraint $\Gamma_1 = \{sky\}$ and $\Gamma_j = \Gamma\ j \neq 1$

Results. Notice from the performance results in Figure 4.16 that the unmodified Prolog solution required 219,842 subgoal call and redo invocations. The limit set-based version, however, required 7694 subgoal call and redo invocations. In other words, the limit set-based solution required only 7694/219,842 or 3.5% of the search required by the unmodified solution. Thus, the example provides a clear sign that restricting the possible label sets by preprocessing had a positive influence on the run-time behavior and efficiency of the solution.

In addition, notice the preceding limit set (the single unary constraint) produces 32 6-tuples. These would need to be verified to identify possible solutions in the limit set-modified Prolog implementation. By comparison, the single unary constraint requires the highest region to be labeled "sky"; thus there are $5^5 = 3125$ possible tuples to be explored in the unmodified Prolog approach. This produces a ratio of search-related computation of $\frac{32}{3125} = 0.01$, i.e., the limit set-based solution should require only 1% of the brute-force search solution.

Propagating $\underline{\Omega}_i$

While the handworked solutions using LRR/LDR are useful for illustration of the iterative solution process, a more automated procedure is desired. While developing the notation for the overall problem in Section 4.8.1, it was noted that vector $\underline{\Omega}_i$ (corresponding to current label set Γ_i on u_i) may be iteratively propagated. Once unary constraints are incorporated into the label sets through $\underline{\Omega}_i^1$, $\underline{\Omega}_i^k$ may be propagated as follows:

$$\underline{\Omega}_i^{k+1} = \otimes|_{i\neq j}(\Omega_{ij}\underline{\Omega}_j^k)\ \forall i = 1, 2, \ldots, n \tag{4.11}$$

where Ω_{kj} was defined in Equation 4.9 and the operator $\otimes|$ denotes element-by-element AND-ing of the resulting $n-1$ $\Omega_{ij}\underline{\Omega}_j^k$ vectors.[5] Note Ω_{ij} is constant and may be precomputed. Equation 4.11 basically implements the LDR iteratively. When $\underline{\Omega}_j^{k+1} = \underline{\Omega}_j^k\ \forall j$, the limit set is obtained.

The iterative formulation of Equation 4.11 is also very significant in that it suggests a nonbinary extension incorporating the notion of *label support*. This is treated in Section 4.10.

Relaxation Implementation Using MATLAB/Octave

The formulation of Equations 4.9 and 4.11 in MATLAB/Octave is straightforward and facilitated by the availability of multidimensional arrays.

---

[5]Here we adopt the MATLAB/Octave interpretation of a binary element having value 0 or some nonzero value.

```
/* label2b-time.pro */
/* just one of two unary constraints (highest) */
/* addition of write and fail to print all solutions */
/* timing version   */

highest(sky).
adj-to(car,road).
adj-to(road,grass).
adj-to(road,trees).
adj-to(sky,trees).
adj-to(grass,trees).

adjacent-to(R1,R2) :- adj-to(R1,R2).
adjacent-to(R1,R2) :- adj-to(R2,R1).


goal :- highest(R1),
        adjacent-to(R1,R2),
        adjacent-to(R2,R6),
        adjacent-to(R2,R3),
        adjacent-to(R3,R4),
        adjacent-to(R2,R4),
        adjacent-to(R4,R6),
        adjacent-to(R4,R5),
        write('Solution is'),nl,nl,
        write('region 1 is bound to  '),write(R1),nl,
        write('region 2 is bound to  '),write(R2),nl,
        write('region 3 is bound to  '),write(R3),nl,
        write('region 4 is bound to  '),write(R4),nl,
        write('region 5 is bound to  '),write(R5),nl,
        write('region 6 is bound to  '),write(R6),nl,nl,
        statistics(inferences,Number),write(Number),nl,
        fail.
```

Version without limit set

```
/* label-limit-set-time.pro */
/* uses limit set to prefilter solutions and
   reduce thrashing      */
/* Gamma_i determined from Gamma_1={sky} (highest) */
/* addition of write and fail to print all solutions */
/* timing version   */

adj-to(car,road).
adj-to(road,grass).
adj-to(road,trees).
adj-to(sky,trees).
adj-to(grass,trees).

adjacent-to(R1,R2) :- adj-to(R1,R2).
adjacent-to(R1,R2) :- adj-to(R2,R1).


goal :- gamma1(Gamma1), member(R1,Gamma1),
        gamma2(Gamma2), member(R2,Gamma2),
        gamma3(Gamma3), member(R3,Gamma3),
        gamma4(Gamma4), member(R4,Gamma4),
        gamma5(Gamma5), member(R5,Gamma5),
        gamma6(Gamma6), member(R6,Gamma6),
        adjacent-to(R1,R2),
        adjacent-to(R2,R6),
        adjacent-to(R2,R3),
        adjacent-to(R3,R4),
        adjacent-to(R2,R4),
        adjacent-to(R4,R6),
        adjacent-to(R4,R5),
        write('Solution is'),nl,nl,
        write('region 1 is bound to  '),write(R1),nl,
        write('region 2 is bound to  '),write(R2),nl,
        write('region 3 is bound to  '),write(R3),nl,
        write('region 4 is bound to  '),write(R4),nl,
        write('region 5 is bound to  '),write(R5),nl,
        write('region 6 is bound to  '),write(R6),nl,nl,
        statistics(inferences,Number),write(Number),nl,
        fail.


/* the (previously determined) limit set */

gamma1([sky]).
gamma2([trees]).
gamma3([road,grass]).
gamma4([road,grass]).
gamma5([trees,road,car,grass]).
gamma6([road,grass]).
```

Version incorporating limit set

Figure 4.15 Original and Limit-Set-Modified Prolog Solution Formulations with Run-Time Statistic Monitoring

```
?- ['label2b-time.pro'].                          ?- ['label-limit-set-time.pro'].
% label2b-time.pro compiled 0.00 sec, 2,788 bytes % label-limit-set-time.pro compiled 0.00 sec, 4,316 bytes

Yes                                               Yes
?- goal.                                          ?- goal.
Solution is                                       Solution is

region 1 is bound to  sky                         region 1 is bound to  sky
region 2 is bound to  trees                       region 2 is bound to  trees
region 3 is bound to  road                        region 3 is bound to  road
region 4 is bound to  grass                       region 4 is bound to  grass
region 5 is bound to  trees                       region 5 is bound to  trees
region 6 is bound to  road                        region 6 is bound to  road

219642                                            7261
Solution is                                       Solution is

region 1 is bound to  sky                         region 1 is bound to  sky
region 2 is bound to  trees                       region 2 is bound to  trees
region 3 is bound to  road                        region 3 is bound to  road
region 4 is bound to  grass                       region 4 is bound to  grass
region 5 is bound to  road                        region 5 is bound to  road
region 6 is bound to  road                        region 6 is bound to  road

219668                                            7331
Solution is                                       Solution is

region 1 is bound to  sky                         region 1 is bound to  sky
region 2 is bound to  trees                       region 2 is bound to  trees
region 3 is bound to  grass                       region 3 is bound to  grass
region 4 is bound to  road                        region 4 is bound to  road
region 5 is bound to  grass                       region 5 is bound to  trees
region 6 is bound to  grass                       region 6 is bound to  grass

219791                                            7512
Solution is                                       Solution is

region 1 is bound to  sky                         region 1 is bound to  sky
region 2 is bound to  trees                       region 2 is bound to  trees
region 3 is bound to  grass                       region 3 is bound to  grass
region 4 is bound to  road                        region 4 is bound to  road
region 5 is bound to  trees                       region 5 is bound to  car
region 6 is bound to  grass                       region 6 is bound to  grass

219816                                            7626
Solution is                                       Solution is

region 1 is bound to  sky                         region 1 is bound to  sky
region 2 is bound to  trees                       region 2 is bound to  trees
region 3 is bound to  grass                       region 3 is bound to  grass
region 4 is bound to  road                        region 4 is bound to  road
region 5 is bound to  car                         region 5 is bound to  grass
region 6 is bound to  grass                       region 6 is bound to  grass

219842                                            7694

No                                                No
?-                                                ?-
```

Figure 4.16 Run-Time Statistics for Original and Limit-Set-Modified Prolog Solutions

Octave Code and Results.   A straightforward implementation of the iterative solution approach is shown in Figure 4.17. Sample results for two different initial unary constraint cases are shown in Figure 4.18. Case 1 only incorporates a unary constraint on $u1$ (sky), and indicates multiple solutions. Case 2 incorporates both unary constraints on $u1$ and $u4$ (sky and road, respectively), and leads to a unique labeling.

Observe, as the MATLAB/Octave source indicates, that the label order in the omega vectors is "car," "grass," "road," "trees," "sky." This facilitates comparison with the handworked solutions.

```
%% label.m; iterative labelling formulation
%%  image example

%% label order in omega vectors:
%%       car grass road trees sky

%% initial label sets (D_i) and unary constraints
%% enforce (only) unary 'sky' label on u1
%% requires
omega(:,1)=[0 0 0 0 1]';

%% u2-u6 can have any label

omega(:,2)=[1 1 1 1 1]';
omega(:,3)=[1 1 1 1 1]';
omega(:,4)=[1 1 1 1 1]';
omega(:,5)=[1 1 1 1 1]';
omega(:,6)=[1 1 1 1 1]';

%% display omega with unary constraints only
printf("\nInitial omega (before iteration) is: \n");
omega

%% form Pij

for i=1:6
  for j=1:6
   if(i!=j)
    P(:,:,i,j)=omega(:,i)*omega(:,j)';
   endif
  endfor
endfor

E=ones(5);

%% use A to represent adjacency constraint
%% rows/cols of A indexed from R1 (u1) to R6 (u6)

A=[0 1 0 0 0 0;1 0 1 1 0 1
 0 1 0 1 0 0; 0 1 1 0 1 1;
 0 0 0 1 0 0;0 1 0 1 0 0]

% C from allowed pairwise labelling (if adjacent) graph
%% label order in omega vectors:
%%       car grass road trees sky

C=[0 0 1 0 0;
 0 0 1 1 0;
 1 1 0 1 0;
 0 1 1 0 1;
```

```
 0 0 0 1 0]

%% form omegaij

for i=1:6
  for j=1:6
   if(i!=j)
    omegaij(:,:,i,j)=P(:,:,i,j) & ((!A(i,j)*E)|C);
   endif
  endfor
endfor

%% iteratively update ui using omegaij and ui

count=0;

while(1)
count=count+1;
%% store old omega
omega_old=omega;

%% get updated omega ui from uj; j!=i
%% this updates uses the newest ui for each update,
%% i.e., asynchronously

tmp=ones(5,1);

for i=1:6
  for j=1:6
    if(i!=j)
      tmp = (omegaij(:,:,i,j)*omega(:,j)) & tmp;
    endif
  endfor
  omega(:,i) = tmp;
  tmp=ones(5,1);
endfor

%% check for convergence

if(omega==omega_old)
printf("\nfinal omega is: \n");
omega
break
endif

%% display new omega at iteration count
printf("\nomega at iteration %d is: \n",count);
omega

endwhile
```

Figure 4.17 Iterative Image Labeling Formulation Using MATLAB/Octave

Case 1: unary constraint on $u1$ (sky)

```
octave:7> label.m

Initial omega (before iteration) is:
omega =

   0   1   1   1   1   1
   0   1   1   1   1   1
   0   1   1   1   1   1
   0   1   1   1   1   1
   1   1   1   1   1   1

A =

   0   1   0   0   0   0
   1   0   1   1   0   1
   0   1   0   1   0   0
   0   1   1   0   1   1
   0   0   0   1   0   0
   0   1   0   1   0   0

C =

   0   0   1   0   0
   0   0   1   1   0
   1   1   0   1   0
   0   1   1   0   1
   0   0   0   1   0

omega at iteration 1 is:
omega =

   0   0   0   0   1   0
   0   0   1   1   1   1
   0   0   1   1   1   1
   0   1   0   0   1   0
   1   0   1   0   0   0

omega at iteration 2 is:
omega =

   0   0   0   0   1   0
   0   0   1   1   1   1
   0   0   1   1   1   1
   0   1   0   0   1   0
   1   0   0   0   0   0

final omega is:
omega =

   0   0   0   0   1   0
   0   0   1   1   1   1
   0   0   1   1   1   1
   0   1   0   0   1   0
   1   0   0   0   0   0
```

Case 2: unary constraints on $u1$ and $u4$ (sky and road)

```
octave:7> label_case2.m

Initial omega (before iteration) is:
omega =

   0   1   1   1   1   1
   0   1   1   1   0   1
   0   1   1   1   0   1
   0   1   1   1   0   1
   1   1   1   1   0   1

A =

   0   1   0   0   0   0
   1   0   1   1   0   1
   0   1   0   1   0   0
   0   1   1   0   1   1
   0   0   0   1   0   0
   0   1   0   1   0   0

C =

   0   0   1   0   0
   0   0   1   1   0
   1   1   0   1   0
   0   1   1   0   1
   0   0   0   1   0

omega at iteration 1 is:
omega =

   0   0   0   0   1   0
   0   0   1   0   0   1
   0   0   1   1   0   0
   0   1   0   0   0   0
   1   0   1   0   0   0

omega at iteration 2 is:
omega =

   0   0   0   0   1   0
   0   0   1   0   0   1
   0   0   0   1   0   0
   0   1   0   0   0   0
   1   0   0   0   0   0

final omega is:
omega =

   0   0   0   0   1   0
   0   0   1   0   0   1
   0   0   0   1   0   0
   0   1   0   0   0   0
   1   0   0   0   0   0
```

Figure 4.18 Results Using MATLAB/Octave

4.9 Investigating Solution Efficiencies
4.9.1 Considering Search

It is evident that numerous alternate procedures are available for the solution of CSPs, in particular SAT and labeling formulations of the problem. Each solution may be characterized in terms of an underlying search strategy. Therefore, the computational complexity, and thus efficiency, of the solution depends upon the computational complexity of the underlying search algorithm.

4.9.2 GAT

As described in Section 4.4, GAT is a strategy wherein the problem state space is investigated by enumeration and testing. To fully enumerate the entire space (this assumes the problem has a state space with finite cardinality) is often impractical. In addition, while exhaustive enumeration may not be necessary to generate a solution (we might get "lucky" early in the process), to conclude there is no solution yields the worst-case computational cost, i.e., a complete search.

For example, recall that the specific image labeling problem of Section 4.6.2 has a state space of $5^6 = 15,625$ possible labelings. In addition, Section 4.6.3 indicates that using **only** the `adjacent-to` constraint yields 42 solutions to this CSP. Assume a specific, possible assignment is only generated and tested once. The probability of randomly generating (essentially guessing) a solution at the outset of the procedure is $\frac{42}{15,625}$ or about 0.26%.[6]

4.9.3 GAT with Heuristic Guidance

This is exemplified by the WSAT approach, wherein local solution subspaces are explored by random toggling of values in a specific clause. Heuristics, as noted in Chapter 3, are intended to aid in the efficient solution of a problem. The lack of an ability to prove the worthiness of a heuristic does not preclude its use.

4.9.4 Backtracking

Backtracking essentially performs a depth-first search of the problem state space. This was exemplified by the Prolog solutions previously developed. Although backtracking is preferable to GAT, it still suffers from exponential complexity. Since it is based upon depth-first search, one of the major shortcomings of using backtracking in CSPs is that the *depth-first search, as the problem state space is explored, may keep failing for the same underlying reason.* This is easy to see using the Prolog labeling solution. Consider the goal:

```
goal :- adjacent-to(R1,R2),
        adjacent-to(R2,R6),
        adjacent-to(R2,R3),
        adjacent-to(R3,R4),
        adjacent-to(R2,R4),
        adjacent-to(R4,R6),
        adjacent-to(R4,R5).
```

Recall Prolog attempts unification of the subgoal clauses in the order in which they appear in the tail of this clause. This yields backtracking. Suppose a label or value, e.g., `car` is assigned to region or variable R2 at the outset (i.e., when unifying `adjacent-to(R1,R2)` with the database) of the unification process. Referring to the database in Figure 4.5, observe numerous backtracking points are generated. If, in fact, `car` assigned to region or variable R2 is not a valid variable assignment in

---

[6]Note that this probability will increase, albeit slowly, as possible solutions are generated, tested, and discarded.

the ultimate solution space due to subsequent incompatibilities, Prolog will nonetheless spend lots of computational effort in investigation of the alternatives in the subsequent search. In a sense, we would like to "fail early" in the process, so that search effort is not wasted on (ultimately) unproductive areas of the problem space.

4.9.5 Constraint Propagation

Iterative constraint propagation approaches attempt to overcome the shortcoming of backtracking, as described in Section 4.9.4. It is a powerful tool for elimination of extraneous search. Further computation is necessary to determine actual solutions. It is noteworthy that even when every Γ_i is nonempty, no solution may exist.

4.10 Extension to Continuous/Probabilistic Formulations
4.10.1 "Relaxing" and Extending Several Aspects of Discrete Relaxation

In the discrete relaxation approach illustrated in Section 4.8.1, pairs of labels on objects are either: (i) compatible; or (ii) incompatible; i.e., only one of two cases is possible. Membership of a label pair in Γ_{ij} is a binary valued function, i.e., a label pair is either a member of the set of compatible label pairs, or not. For computational purposes, this information is encoded in Ω_{ij}.

Revisiting and Reinterpreting Ω_{ij}. The matrix Ω_{ij} in Equation 4.9 contains only values of 0 or 1. For a specific pair of objects (i, j), a value of 1 in position (k, l) of matrix Ω_{ij} indicates that the label corresponding to position l in vector $\underline{\Omega}_j$ is compatible with the label corresponding to position k in $\underline{\Omega}_i$. Similarly, a value of 0 in position (k, l) of matrix Ω_{ij} indicates that the label corresponding to position l in vector $\underline{\Omega}_j$ is not compatible with the label corresponding to position k in $\underline{\Omega}_i$. This was the basis of the label set updating strategy implemented by Equation 4.11, namely, element k in $\underline{\Omega}_i$ is 1 only if the projection of row k of Ω_{ij} is nonzero for every neighbor of u_i.

"All Compatible Label Pairs Are Not Equal"

Recall from the constraints in our previous labeling example that labels "road" and "grass" on adjacent objects (regions) are as allowable as the labels "road" and "trees" or "road" and "car." All three pairs were allowed by the constraints (an arc existed for each allowable pair in Figure 4.3; none was preferred or "better" in any sense).

An extension (which yields so-called continuous relaxation) is to allow compatibilities to be represented by nonbinary values that indicate relative preferences (or perhaps reflect known joint probabilities). For example, in the preceding case, suppose it was known that the label "road" on a region, while allowing "trees," "grass," or "car," strongly suggested or supported "car" over both "grass" and "trees." The continuous relaxation formulation allows the representation of this preference. Conversely, label pairs that are not allowed (an arc does not exist in Figure 4.3) are equally "unallowed."

An Alternate View of the Label Compatibility Graph. This reasoning leads to a viewpoint where the arcs in Figure 4.3 are extended to include all possible label pairs, but are weighted. For example, positive weights might correspond to allowable or preferred label pairs; negative weights correspond to unallowed or nonpreferred pairs.

The continuous formulation allows a more general and extended encoding of relational information, and may lead to more efficient solutions (i.e., quicker algorithm convergence). Due to extension of set membership from the binary case, continuous relaxation is conceptually related to fuzzy set theory (Chapter 11).

Quantifying Label Support

In the extended (continuous) formulation, label pairs are no longer thought of as simply being compatible or incompatible, but rather label combinations on adjacent objects are viewed as positively or negatively (or neutrally) supporting compatibility.

Merging the two "support"-based strategies leads to another approach for quantification of the constraints on pairwise labels on objects u_i and u_j. For example, consider the previous label constraints and observed adjacent regions u_i and u_j. Label "sky" on u_i may be positively supported if there is a label "trees" on u_j, but negatively supported by the label "car" on u_j. This is akin to a compatibility "reward or punishment" measure, in contrast to the previous "allowable" strategy.

Label Support Function.   Since the extended constraint satisfaction process is based upon propagation of local support for labels, we postulate a *support function*, $s_{ij}(\lambda)$, for objects u_i and u_j with respective labels λ and λ'. An example might be:

$$s_{ij}(\lambda, \lambda') = \begin{cases} 1 & if (\lambda, \lambda') \in \Gamma_{ij} \ AND \ Adj(i,j) = 1 \\ -1 & if (\lambda, \lambda') \notin \Gamma_{ij} \ AND \ Adj(i,j) = 1 \\ 0 & if \, Adj(i,j) = 0 \end{cases} \qquad (4.12)$$

Notice the last case represents support neutrality.

A Continuous Formulation.   It is not necessary that the support for all compatible label pairs be the same positive value nor is it necessary that the support for all incompatible label pairs be the same negative value. Consider some cases:

1. Suppose label "sky" very strongly suggests or supports label "trees."

2. Suppose labels "road" and "car" support each other more than the pair "road" and "grass."

3. Suppose labels "car" and "sky" have stronger, or more negative support than "car" and "trees."

Thus, a more general formulation is to allow

$$a \leq s_{ij}(\lambda, \lambda') \leq b \qquad (4.13)$$

The Limit Set, Support, and Probability

A label suitability or confidence measure for label λ on object u_i, denoted $P_i(\lambda)$, is defined as

$$P_i(\lambda) = \begin{cases} 1 & \text{if } \lambda \in \Gamma_i \text{ in the limit set} \\ 0 & \text{if } \lambda \notin \Gamma_i \text{ in the limit set} \end{cases} \tag{4.14}$$

Furthermore, the strength of a constraint will be denoted using $s_{ij}(\lambda, \lambda')$, from Equation 4.12 or Equation 4.13.

Allowing the confidence measure in Equation 4.14 to take on values over a continuous range spawns a continuous (as opposed to discrete) constraint satisfaction problem. $P_i(\lambda)$ denotes confidence in the assignment of label λ to object u_i. Normalizing $P_i(\lambda)$ such that

$$0 \leq P_i(\lambda) \leq 1 \ \forall \ i, \lambda \tag{4.15}$$

and

$$\sum_{\tau} P_i(\tau) = 1 \ \forall \ i = 1, 2, \ldots, n \tag{4.16}$$

allows $P_i(\lambda)$ to be interpreted as a probability.

Cumulative Support

In terms of the preceding measures, the cumulative support for label λ on object u_i denoted $S_i(\lambda)$, is given by:

$$S_i(\lambda) = \sum_{j \neq i} \sum_{\lambda'} s_{ij}(\lambda, \lambda') P_j(\lambda') \tag{4.17}$$

As noted, it is often necessary to normalize $S_i(\lambda)$, e.g.,

$$S_i(\lambda) = \frac{1}{n} \sum_{j \neq i} \sum_{\lambda'} s_{ij}(\lambda, \lambda') P_j(\lambda') \tag{4.18}$$

In the limit set, a label, λ, which has positive support from many neighbors, will thus have a large value of $S_i(\lambda)$.

4.10.2 An Algorithm for Propagating $P_i(\lambda)$

The only remaining step is to form an iterative procedure that allows modification (propagation) of the $P_i(\lambda)$ values $\forall \ i, \lambda$ using $s_{ij}(\lambda, \lambda')$. An iterative solution procedure modified from [HZ83] is:

Iterative Stochastic Labeling Algorithm.

1. Initialize $P_i^{(k)}(\lambda)$ for $k = 0$.

2. Form $S_i^{(k)}(\lambda)$ using $P_i^{(k)}(\lambda)$.

3. Normalize or modify $S_i^{(k)}(\lambda)$ so that the quantity $(1 + S_i^{(k)}(\lambda))$ is nonnegative.

4. Form

$$P_i^{(k+1)}(\lambda) = \frac{P_i^{(k)}(\lambda)[1 + S_i^{(k)}(\lambda)]}{D^{(k)}}$$

where

$$D^{(k)} = \sum_\lambda P_i^{(k)}(\lambda)[1 + S_i^{(k)}(\lambda)]$$

5. Stop when (if) values of $P_i^{(k)}(\lambda)$ converge. Generally this implies

$$P_i^{(k+1)}(\lambda) \approx P_i^{(k)}(\lambda) \ \forall \ i, \lambda$$

Of course, other formulations are possible.

4.10.3 Examples and Extensions

We now consider an example of the previous approach to image region labeling. First, we must determine $s_{ij}(\lambda, \lambda')$. Observe that i, j, λ, and λ' take on discrete values. Thus, for implementation purposes, we will develop a matrix of values for $s_{ij}(\lambda, \lambda')$.

Note that the choices of label compatibility coefficients are neither unique nor optimal. Many choices and alternatives are possible; we show some simple choices for comparison with previous results.

Consider three cases:

Case 1: Regions i and j are adjacent $(Adj(i, j) = 1)$. In this case selection of $s_{ij}(\lambda, \lambda')$ could be *based upon* the previously developed label compatibility matrix for adjacent objects, i.e., C shown in Figure 4.9.

Cases 2: Regions i and j are not adjacent. A simplistic interpretation for this case is that no positive or negative supporting (conflicting) information is possible, therefore one might conclude that the zero matrix is appropriate.

Case 3: $i = j$. Here, assigning any nonzero weight makes little sense, since the only effect of a nonzero (positive or negative) weight would be a reinforcement of our choice of a label. Thus we set all matrices in this case equal to the zero matrix.

On this basis, an obvious choice for one $s_{ij}(\lambda, \lambda')$ is just an elaboration of Ω_{ij} from Equation 4.9 for all i, j, λ, and λ'.

Adding a Heuristic to $s_{ij}(\lambda, \lambda')$

Since there exists considerable freedom in choosing $s_{ij}(\lambda, \lambda')$, other a priori information may be incorporated. For example, consider the cases where $s_{ij}(\lambda, \lambda')$ reflects the number of neighbors of a particular region or u_i. For example, if:

1. $Adj(i,j) = 1$ AND

2. Labels λ and λ' are compatible under adjacency AND

3. The **number of regions** that region i is observed to be adjacent to is $>$ the **number of labels** that label λ is allowed to be adjacent to.

Note constraint #3 is a heuristic. This is shown in Figure 4.19 and used in the examples that follow.

		1	2	3	4	5	6
		→ i					
		0 0 0 0 0	0 0 1 0 0	0 0 0 0 0	0 0 0 0 0	0 0 0 0 0	0 0 0 0 0
		0 0 0 0 0	0 0 0 0 0	0 0 0 0 0	0 0 0 0 0	0 0 0 0 0	0 0 0 0 0
1	j	0 0 0 0 0	0 0 0 0 0	0 0 0 0 0	0 0 0 0 0	0 0 0 0 0	0 0 0 0 0
		0 0 0 0 0	0 0 0 0 0	0 0 0 0 0	0 0 0 0 0	0 0 0 0 0	0 0 0 0 0
		0 0 0 0 0	0 0 0 1 0	0 0 0 0 0	0 0 0 0 0	0 0 0 0 0	0 0 0 0 0
		0 0 1 0 0	0 0 0 0 0	0 0 1 0 0	0 0 1 0 0	0 0 0 0 0	0 0 1 0 0
		0 0 1 1 0	0 0 0 0 0	0 0 1 1 0	0 0 1 1 0	0 0 0 0 0	0 0 1 1 0
2		1 1 0 1 0	0 0 0 0 0	1 1 0 1 0	1 1 0 1 0	0 0 0 0 0	1 1 0 1 0
		0 1 1 0 1	0 0 0 0 0	0 1 1 0 1	0 1 1 0 1	0 0 0 0 0	0 1 1 0 1
		0 0 0 1 0	0 0 0 0 0	0 0 0 1 0	0 0 0 1 0	0 0 0 0 0	0 0 0 1 0
		0 0 0 0 0	0 0 1 0 0	0 0 0 0 0	0 0 1 0 0	0 0 0 0 0	0 0 0 0 0
		0 0 0 0 0	0 0 1 1 0	0 0 0 0 0	0 0 1 1 0	0 0 0 0 0	0 0 0 0 0
3		0 0 0 0 0	0 0 0 0 0	0 0 0 0 0	0 0 0 0 0	0 0 0 0 0	0 0 0 0 0
		0 0 0 0 0	0 0 0 0 0	0 0 0 0 0	0 0 0 0 0	0 0 0 0 0	0 0 0 0 0
		0 0 0 0 0	0 0 0 1 0	0 0 0 0 0	0 0 0 1 0	0 0 0 0 0	0 0 0 0 0
		0 0 0 0 0	0 0 1 0 0	0 0 1 0 0	0 0 0 0 0	0 0 1 0 0	0 0 1 0 0
		0 0 0 0 0	0 0 1 1 0	0 0 1 1 0	0 0 0 0 0	0 0 1 1 0	0 0 1 1 0
4		0 0 0 0 0	1 1 0 1 0	1 1 0 1 0	0 0 0 0 0	1 1 0 1 0	1 1 0 1 0
		0 0 0 0 0	0 1 1 0 1	0 1 1 0 1	0 0 0 0 0	0 1 1 0 1	0 1 1 0 1
		0 0 0 0 0	0 0 0 1 0	0 0 0 1 0	0 0 0 0 0	0 0 0 1 0	0 0 0 1 0
		0 0 0 0 0	0 0 0 0 0	0 0 0 0 0	0 0 1 0 0	0 0 0 0 0	0 0 0 0 0
		0 0 0 0 0	0 0 0 0 0	0 0 0 0 0	0 0 0 0 0	0 0 0 0 0	0 0 0 0 0
5		0 0 0 0 0	0 0 0 0 0	0 0 0 0 0	0 0 0 0 0	0 0 0 0 0	0 0 0 0 0
		0 0 0 0 0	0 0 0 0 0	0 0 0 0 0	0 0 0 0 0	0 0 0 0 0	0 0 0 0 0
		0 0 0 0 0	0 0 0 0 0	0 0 0 0 0	0 0 0 1 0	0 0 0 0 0	0 0 0 0 0
		0 0 0 0 0	0 0 1 0 0	0 0 0 0 0	0 0 1 0 0	0 0 0 0 0	0 0 0 0 0
		0 0 0 0 0	0 0 1 1 0	0 0 0 0 0	0 0 1 1 0	0 0 0 0 0	0 0 0 0 0
6		0 0 0 0 0	0 0 0 0 0	0 0 0 0 0	0 0 0 0 0	0 0 0 0 0	0 0 0 0 0
		0 0 0 0 0	0 0 0 0 0	0 0 0 0 0	0 0 0 0 0	0 0 0 0 0	0 0 0 0 0
		0 0 0 0 0	0 0 0 1 0	0 0 0 0 0	0 0 0 1 0	0 0 0 0 0	0 0 0 0 0

Figure 4.19 $s_{ij}(\lambda, \lambda')$ Values Used (see text)

Example #1: Equal $P_i^{(0)}(\lambda)$

Initial label probabilities $P_i^{(k)}(\lambda)$ for $k = 0$ are shown in the following table to be equal.

Initial Probabilities (Case 1).

	car	grass	road	trees	sky
region1	0.2000	0.2000	0.2000	0.2000	0.2000
region2	0.2000	0.2000	0.2000	0.2000	0.2000
region3	0.2000	0.2000	0.2000	0.2000	0.2000
region4	0.2000	0.2000	0.2000	0.2000	0.2000
region5	0.2000	0.2000	0.2000	0.2000	0.2000
region6	0.2000	0.2000	0.2000	0.2000	0.2000

Sample results using these values and $s_{ij}(\lambda, \lambda')$ cited here are shown in Figure 4.20. Note the converged solution is ambiguous.

Example #2: Deriving $P_i^{(0)}(\lambda)$ from Unary Constraints

In this case we modify $P_i^{(k)}(\lambda)$ for $k = 0$ so the initial condition on **region1** indicates certainty of the correct label being "sky" and the initial condition on **region5** indicates certainty of the correct label being "car."[7] Thus the initial assignments are:

Initial Probabilities (Case2)

	car	grass	road	trees	sky
region1	0.0000	0.0000	0.0000	0.0000	1.0000
region2	0.2000	0.2000	0.2000	0.2000	0.2000
region3	0.2000	0.2000	0.2000	0.2000	0.2000
region4	0.2000	0.2000	0.2000	0.2000	0.2000
region5	1.0000	0.0000	0.0000	0.0000	0.0000
region6	0.2000	0.2000	0.2000	0.2000	0.2000

Figure 4.21 shows the labeling results, which are observed to correspond with our previous solutions.

---

[7]Compare this with the use of the unary "highest" and "moving" constraints in the discrete relaxation and Prolog formulations.

The probabilities at iteration   3:

	car	grass	road	trees	sky
region1	0.2860	0.1427	0.1427	0.1427	0.2860
region2	0.0486	0.1412	0.3808	0.3808	0.0486
region3	0.2010	0.4837	0.0572	0.0572	0.2010
region4	0.0486	0.1412	0.3808	0.3808	0.0486
region5	0.2860	0.1427	0.1427	0.1427	0.2860
region6	0.2010	0.4837	0.0572	0.0572	0.2010

The probabilities at iteration   6:

	car	grass	road	trees	sky
region1	0.3966	0.0690	0.0690	0.0690	0.3966
region2	0.0049	0.0374	0.4764	0.4764	0.0049
region3	0.1050	0.7805	0.0048	0.0048	0.1050
region4	0.0049	0.0374	0.4764	0.4764	0.0049
region5	0.3966	0.0690	0.0690	0.0690	0.3966
region6	0.1050	0.7805	0.0048	0.0048	0.1050

The probabilities at iteration   9:

	car	grass	road	trees	sky
region1	0.4632	0.0246	0.0246	0.0246	0.4632
region2	0.0003	0.0061	0.4966	0.4966	0.0003
region3	0.0374	0.9248	0.0002	0.0002	0.0374
region4	0.0003	0.0061	0.4966	0.4966	0.0003
region5	0.4632	0.0246	0.0246	0.0246	0.4632
region6	0.0374	0.9248	0.0002	0.0002	0.0374

The probabilities at iteration   12:

	car	grass	road	trees	sky
region1	0.4884	0.0077	0.0007	0.0077	0.4884
region2	0.0000	0.0008	0.4996	0.4996	0.0000
region3	0.0117	0.9765	0.0000	0.0000	0.0117
region4	0.0000	0.0008	0.4996	0.4996	0.0000
region5	0.4884	0.0077	0.0077	0.0077	0.4884
region6	0.0117	0.9765	0.0000	0.0000	0.0117

The probabilities at iteration   15:

	car	grass	road	trees	sky
region1	0.4965	0.0023	0.0023	0.0023	0.4965
region2	0.0000	0.0001	0.4999	0.4999	0.0000
region3	0.0035	0.9929	0.0000	0.0000	0.0035
region4	0.0000	0.0001	0.4999	0.4999	0.0000
region5	0.4965	0.0023	0.0023	0.0023	0.4965
region6	0.0035	0.9929	0.0000	0.0000	0.0035

The probabilities at iteration   18:

	car	grass	road	trees	sky
region1	0.4990	0.0007	0.0007	0.0007	0.4990
region2	0.0000	0.0000	0.5000	0.5000	0.0000
region3	0.0011	0.9979	0.0000	0.0000	0.0011
region4	0.0000	0.0000	0.5000	0.5000	0.0000
region5	0.4990	0.0007	0.0007	0.0007	0.4990
region6	0.0011	0.9979	0.0000	0.0000	0.0011

The number of iterations = 19

The converged probabilities:

	car	grass	road	trees	sky
region1	0.4993	0.0005	0.0005	0.0005	0.4993
region2	0.0000	0.0000	0.5000	0.5000	0.0000
region3	0.0007	0.9986	0.0000	0.0000	0.0007
region4	0.0000	0.0000	0.5000	0.5000	0.0000
region5	0.4993	0.0005	0.0005	0.0005	0.4993
region6	0.0007	0.9986	0.0000	0.0000	0.0007

Figure 4.20 Case1 (equal a priori probabilities) Results—Ambiguous Solution

The probabilities at iteration   3:

	car	grass	road	trees	sky
region1	0.0000	0.0000	0.0000	0.0000	1.0000
region2	0.0427	0.0990	0.2234	0.5996	0.0353
region3	0.2000	0.4916	0.0542	0.0542	0.2000
region4	0.0353	0.0990	0.5996	0.2234	0.0427
region5	1.0000	0.0000	0.0000	0.0000	0.0000
region6	0.2000	0.4916	0.0542	0.0542	0.2000

The probabilities at iteration   6:

	car	grass	road	trees	sky
region1	0.0000	0.0000	0.0000	0.0000	1.0000
region2	0.0041	0.0141	0.0911	0.8895	0.0012
region3	0.1008	0.7904	0.0040	0.0040	0.1008
region4	0.0012	0.0141	0.8895	0.0911	0.0041
region5	1.0000	0.0000	0.0000	0.0000	0.0000
region6	0.1008	0.7904	0.0040	0.0040	0.1008

The probabilities at iteration   9:

	car	grass	road	trees	sky
region1	0.0000	0.0000	0.0000	0.0000	1.0000
region2	0.0003	0.0011	0.0227	0.9759	0.0000
region3	0.0353	0.9291	0.0002	0.0002	0.0353
region4	0.0000	0.0011	0.9759	0.0227	0.0003
region5	1.0000	0.0000	0.0000	0.0000	0.0000
region6	0.0353	0.9291	0.0002	0.0002	0.0353

The probabilities at iteration 12:

	car	grass	road	trees	sky
region1	0.0000	0.0000	0.0000	0.0000	1.0000
region2	0.0000	0.0001	0.0050	0.9949	0.0000
region3	0.0110	0.9780	0.0000	0.0000	0.0110
region4	0.0000	0.0001	0.9949	0.0050	0.0000
region5	1.0000	0.0000	0.0000	0.0000	0.0000
region6	0.0110	0.9780	0.0000	0.0000	0.0110

The probabilities at iteration 15:

	car	grass	road	trees	sky
region1	0.0000	0.0000	0.0000	0.0000	1.0000
region2	0.0000	0.0000	0.0011	0.9989	0.0000
region3	0.0033	0.9934	0.0000	0.0000	0.0035
region4	0.0000	0.0000	0.9989	0.0011	0.0000
region5	1.0000	0.0000	0.0000	0.0000	0.0000
region6	0.0033	0.9934	0.0000	0.0000	0.0033

The probabilities at iteration 18:

	car	grass	road	trees	sky
region1	0.0000	0.0000	0.0000	0.0000	1.0000
region2	0.0000	0.0000	0.0002	0.9998	0.0000
region3	0.0010	0.9980	0.0000	0.0000	0.0010
region4	0.0000	0.0000	0.9998	0.0002	0.0000
region5	1.0000	0.0000	0.0000	0.0000	0.0000
region6	0.0010	0.9980	0.0000	0.0000	0.0010

The number of iterations = 18

The converged probabilities:

	car	grass	road	trees	sky
region1	0.0000	0.0000	0.0000	0.0000	1.0000
region2	0.0000	0.0000	0.0002	0.9998	0.0000
region3	0.0010	0.9980	0.0000	0.0000	0.0010
region4	0.0000	0.0000	0.9998	0.0002	0.0000
region5	1.0000	0.0000	0.0000	0.0000	0.0000
region6	0.0010	0.9980	0.0000	0.0000	0.0010

Figure 4.21 Case2 (unequal a priori probabilities) Results—Note a Unique Labeling Is Obtained

4.11 Summary

The symbolic and numerical manipulation methods presented all share a common characteristic in that they involve search for a consistent global problem solution. This suggests the utility of developing additional constraints (or heuristics) that may be employed to limit the search. The evaluation of relaxation labeling convergence is shown in [FER81].

4.12 A More Comprehensive CSP: Electric Power System Protection Analysis

This section provides another example of an IS development effort that may be cast as a CSP. It provides a useful exercise in the formulation of a CSP and the corresponding Prolog implementation.

4.12.1 Background and Motivation

The operation of our massive, highly interconnected, and surprisingly reliable electric power system is complex, and requires the attention of many skilled engineers. However, electromechanical devices such as relays and breakers can and do fail to operate correctly, therefore redundancy or "backup" is designed into the protection scheme. In particular, when elements of the protection system operate, (specifically relays and their corresponding line circuit breakers) it is necessary for a power system protection engineer to determine the location of the fault in order to correct the situation and restore service to customers. Given a properly designed system, possible fault locations (i.e., lines in our example) must satisfy a number of constraints. The engineer must examine and interpret the overall operation or state of the protection system with knowledge of these constraints. It is also possible that some protection elements failed to operate and thus required backup from other elements. In a complex system with hundreds of lines and when many possible interpretations exist, this is a nontrivial problem.

4.12.2 Objectives

The application concerns the development of a reasoning system for power system protection. Protection of an electric power system involves developing a strategy to operate ("open") appropriate circuit breakers in the event a fault occurs. For simplicity, a fault may be considered a shorting of a circuit to ground, usually resulting in abnormally high currents through various power system circuit elements. These currents can cause significant mechanical and thermal damage to elements of the system. A simplistic model of a circuit breaker is that of a robust switch, which is used to isolate the faulted section of the system (one or more lines) by removing one or more sources of current.

Using the constraints imposed by:

- The topology of a specific power system, and

- A properly designed power system protection scheme,

an explanation or interpretation of the state of the system as a CSP is formulated. The corresponding implementation of this CSP is then developed in Prolog.

4.12.3 Simple Power Protection Background

The basic arrangement of a simple electric power generation and distribution network is shown in Figure 4.22. This graphical representation is denoted by a one-line diagram. The system has sources of power (generators) and lines that interconnect generators and loads. Loads, for example, may be large industrial plants, or residential customers. Each line is protected by a circuit breaker at each end. It is important to note that each breaker only "sees" in one direction, as shown in Figure 4.23. It is also important to note that this "sight" (or domain of protection) may extend, directionally, beyond the corresponding breaker and thus enable some overlapping of protection to other lines. This is referred to as backup.

4.12.4 Problem Formulation

Our goal is the development of an IS system to observe and "reason" about these aspects of power system protection, specifically:

1. To identify, given: i) the power system network topology; ii) the locations of generators, and iii) the breaker status information (i.e., either in service (s) or operated (o)), all possible fault scenarios. This includes fault locations (lines) and cases of circuit breaker primary operation or backup.

2. To identify correct vs. incorrect operation. Correct operation means that the appropriate breaker(s) has operated; incorrect means either the incorrect breakers have operated or (logical OR) the correct breakers have not operated. We henceforth assume that incorrect breaker function is a failure to operate. It is highly unlikely that breakers that are not supposed to operate incorrectly do so (i.e., rarely do breakers simply decide to open for no reason and electrically isolate a section

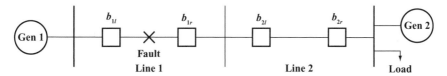

Figure 4.22 Simple Case of Power Protection System

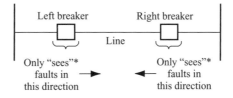

Figure 4.23 Simplified Directional Characteristics

of a line). In essence, we want to take the same information available to a power system protection engineer and automatically generate the same conclusions. As we will see, the unification mechanism in Prolog allows us to examine this situation from several viewpoints.

3. To identify the elements that are in error, i.e., faulty.

We begin, as in most IS problems, by considering a subcase of the problem and then attempting decomposition of the larger problem into one that is solvable via the subcase. We begin our description of the protection problem in Prolog with the following knowledge.

4.12.5 Prolog Description of System Topology

First, consider the case of a single (transmission) line. A line is protected by two circuit breakers; one at each end. In the normal state, there is no reason (except for scheduled maintenance, which we ignore) for either breaker to be in a state we refer to as "operated" or, electrically speaking, open. We refer to this case as a line in service, or in the normal state and denoted by a capital "S" on the one-line diagram. When a fault occurs on the line, if the line is connected to a source of generation at either end (a source of generation includes connection to another line that is in service connected to a generation source, etc.) the breaker at that end is designed to operate. This status is denoted by "O" on the one-line diagram. Note this takes into account the directionality of the protection scheme. Thus, at this point we could summarize the state of **Line_x** with the following sample Prolog description that relates lines and breaker labels (names or numbers), corresponding operational states (O, S), and the existence of a fault. These are meant to be simple examples that are refined in the succeeding sections. This is done by the incorporation of the facts in the Prolog database:

```
protected_by(Line_x, Breaker_l, Breaker_r).
generation(Breaker_l).
generation(Breaker_r).
```

By way of example, a sample interpretation rule for the left-line breaker might be:

```
correct_oper_left(Line_x, Breaker_l, Breaker_r) :-
    protected_by(Line_x, Breaker_l, Breaker_r),
    fault(Line_x),
    generation(Breaker_l),
    operated(Line, Breaker_l).
```

Since each line has two circuit breakers, we consider the rightmost one similarly via:

```
correct_oper_right(Line_x, Breaker_l, Breaker_r) :-
    protected_by(Line_x, Breaker_l, Breaker_r),
    fault(Line_x),
    generation(Breaker_r),
    operated(Line, Breaker_r).
```

4.12.6 Breaker Backup

To fully appreciate the complexity of the situation, we now add the additional facts:

1. Breakers are designed to provide backup for other breakers that may fail to operate. Recall the assumption that the only type of operational failure of a breaker is failure to operate when required. Backup for this type of operational failure is accomplished by modifying the time-current characteristics of the protection system; it is not imperative that this be understood in the context of the current example. Referring to Figure 4.22, we merely note that if a fault exists on Line 2 and breaker b_{2l} fails to operate (we denote this by "m" for malfunction) then breaker b_{1l} operates, providing backup for b_{2l}. A similar remark may be made for b_{2r} and b_{1r}; the directionality of the protection must still be observed.

2. The breakers will only operate if sufficient current causes an alarm. This requires that the line containing the breaker be supplied with a source of current or "generation," which may occur in either of two ways:

   (a) The line is directly connected to a generator; or

   (b) The line is connected to an adjacent line that supplies current (i.e., the adjacent line has generation). This in turn requires the adjacent line to be either connected to a generator or itself connected to a line supplying current. (The reader may notice the beginning of a transitive relation.)

   Thus, to develop a Prolog representation for the system, we need the following:

1. The network topology, i.e., the line interconnection. This representation, due to the directionality of the protection scheme, needs to account for the left-right relationship of lines.

2. An indication of the location of generators.

3. An indication of the status of all breakers in the system.

Temporarily, we assume that only a single fault is under consideration.

4.12.7 Detailed Prolog Description Derivation

In this section we revise and extend our approach from that shown in the preceding section, and develop a more general framework in Prolog for fault location, and protection system operation interpretation. To take the development further, assume the two-line system shown in Figure 4.24 is used.

The important assumptions used in the description development are:

1. Only one breaker malfunction is possible;

2. The malfunctioned breaker has backup breaker(s);

3. Only a single line fault is possible; and

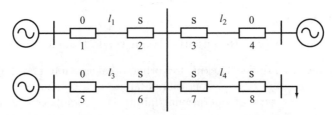

Figure 4.24 Sample Power System Used for Examples

4. The relays (breakers) have the aforementioned directional protection characteristics.

Thus, in the Prolog formulation we seek to represent:

1. The topology of the network;

2. The current breaker status; and

3. Rules regarding correct (primary and backup) breaker operation.

Note we also embed a goal ("run") in the Prolog database, to avoid entering large amounts of data at the Prolog interpreter prompt.

General Network Topology Description

First, we develop a general topology description based upon a somewhat self-explanatory clause of the form:

```
protected_by(Line,Breaker1,Breaker2)
```

The system shown in Figure 4.24 therefore yields the following facts:

```
protected_by(line1,1,2).
protected_by(line2,3,4).
protected_by(line3,5,6).
protected_by(line4,7,8).
```

Furthermore, a clause of the form:

```
connect(Breaker1_name,Breaker2_name)
```

means that `Breaker1` is connected to `Breaker2` through a bus. (In our simplistic formulation, we assume that it is not possible for a bus to become electrically isolated from lines, i.e., it is assumed that it is "hardwired" into the system. In real systems, the bus itself has another special type of differential protection. This extension is addressed in the problems.) From the sample network of Figure 4.24, the Prolog database contains:

Description of Line Connections for Figure 4.24

```
connect(2,3).
connect(2,6).
connect(2,7).
connect(3,6).
connect(3,7).
connect(6,7).
```

Similarly, the fact

```
generation(Breaker_name)
```

means that there is a source of generation directly connected to the breaker. Note that this is only a part of the representation, since we later show how generation propagates via line interconnections and breaker status. In our example, the facts regarding generator locations are:

Description of (Direct) Sources of Generation (Generators)

```
generation(1).
generation(4).
generation(5).
```

Breaker Status Description

The predicate

```
operate(Breaker_name)
```

is used to represent the situation that the given breaker has operated. In our system, we choose the following scenario for illustration:

```
operate(1).
operate(4).
operate(5).
```

This formulation implies breakers that are not specified as "operated" are assumed in service. The reader is encouraged, using the previous description of breaker operation and fault locations, to manually determine all possible fault locations and corresponding protection system interpretations before proceeding. We now turn our attention to the development of Prolog database rules.

Connectivity Rules

The rule "connection" is used to represent the symmetric property of connectedness, i.e., the relation "Breaker1 connected to Breaker2" implies that the relation "Breaker2 connected to Breaker1" also exists. Note, connection is a symmetric relation that must be encoded carefully.

```
connection(B1,B2) :- connect(B1,B2).
connection(B1,B2) :- connect(B2,B1).
```

Locating Corresponding Breakers Via Rules

It is useful to be able to locate, given the topology of the network and the names of a specific line and one of the line's breakers, the name of the other breaker. Rule

```
other_breaker(known_breaker_name,unknown_breaker_name)
```

gives the unknown breaker's name, using the following approach:

```
other_breaker(B1,B2) :- protected_by(_,B1,B2).
other_breaker(B1,B2) :- protected_by(_,B2,B1).
```

Two rules are included so that we are not forced to consider which end of the line the known breaker is on.

Generation Constraints and Corresponding Prolog Rules

One of the most important rules, i.e., rule

```
has_gen(B)
```

is used to indicate that Breaker B has a (direct or indirect) source of generation. Therefore, B may need to operate under certain fault conditions. A "generation-less" breaker does not need to consider operation; there is no current to interrupt. The first rule deals with the case in which Breaker B is connected directly to a source of generation. The second rule deals with the case of generation transitivity in which Breaker B is connected to Breaker B1 of Line L, Line L is protected by Breakers B1 and B2, and Breaker B2 has generation. This is stated as the two-rule set:

```
has_gen(B) :- generation(B), !.

has_gen(B) :- connection(B,B1),
              other_breaker(B1,B2),
              has_gen(B2), !.
```

We employ the cut "!" operator to achieve an efficient solution. A breaker may have generation from many sources; we only care about the first time we establish (through unification) that a breaker has generation.

"has_gen" Example for System of Figure 4.25(a).

```
?- consult(gen).
yes
?- has_gen(1).
Breaker 1 is connected to a generation directly.

yes
?- has_gen(2).
Breaker 2 is not connected to a generation directly,
  but it is connected to breaker 3
  and breaker 3 protects a line  with breaker 4.
Breaker 4 is not connected to a generation directly,
  but it is connected to breaker 5
  and breaker 5 protects a line  with breaker 6.
Breaker 6 is connected to a generation directly.

yes
```

"has_gen" Example for System of Figure 4.25(b).

```
?- consult(gen2).
yes
?- has_gen(2).
Breaker 2 is not connected to a generation directly,
  but it is connected to breaker 3
  and breaker 3 protects a line  with breaker 4.
Breaker 4 is connected to a generation directly.

yes
```

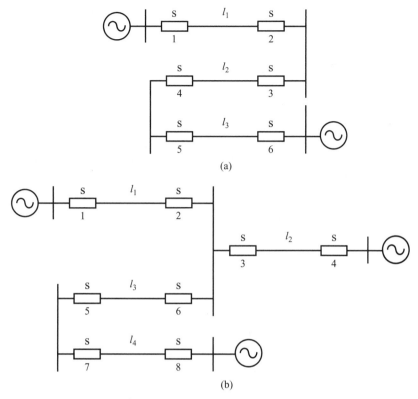

Figure 4.25 Power System Topology Used for "`generation`" Examples

Backup Breaker Operation Constraints and Prolog Description

The role of a backup breaker is described in the Prolog database. For example, predicate

```
back_up(B1,B2)
```

is used to represent the fact that Breaker B2 is one of B1's backup breakers. Note that B1 may have any number of backup breakers, which are a function of the power network topology. Backup operation is specified via the constraint:

```
back_up(B1,B2) :- not(generation(B1)), /* no backup for generators */
            connection(B1,B3),
            other_breaker(B3,B2),
            has_gen(B2).
```

In assessing protection system operation, the rule `backup_did_not_work(B1,B2)` signifies that back-up breaker, B2, of Breaker B1 did not operate as a back-up breaker. This constraint, formulated as a Prolog rule, is:

```
backup_did_not_work(B1,B2) :- back_up(B1,B2),
                              not(operate(B2)).
```

Determination of Fault Locations Through Electrical Isolation

In order to determine a possible fault location, we assume that electrically isolated lines (i.e., those with generation cutoff) are candidates for fault locations. This is done via rule `no_source_coming(B1)` that is true when the generation source is cut off from the side of the line containing Breaker B1. This constraint leads to the three Prolog-rule set:

```
no_source_coming(B1) :- not(has_gen(B1)).
no_source_coming(B1) :- has_gen(B1),
                        operate(B1).
no_source_coming(B1) :- back_up(B1,_),
                        not(backup_did_not_work(B1,_)).
```

which is used for this specification.

The heart of the matter, in this CSP, is that *electrically isolated lines are candidate fault locations.* Prolog predicate `elect_isolated` is used to represent this constraint and thus determine possible fault locations and corresponding interpretations. The Prolog rule constraining a line containing a fault location to have no generation is:

```
elect_isolated(L,B1,B2) :-
              no_source_coming(B1),
              no_source_coming(B2), !.
```

Rules for Interpretation and Display

Rule `printout` gives the interpretation of correct and incorrect (primary) breaker operation:

```
printout(B) :- has_gen(B),
               operate(B),
               write('Breaker '),
               write(B),
               write(' operated correctly.'),nl, !.

printout(B) :- has_gen(B),
               not(operate(B)),
               write('Breaker '),
               write(B),
               write(' malfunctioned.'),nl,
               not(printbackup(B)), !.
```

For output, the rule "`printbackup(B)`" prints all correct operations corresponding to backup breakers. Note it always evaluates to FALSE due to the final fail predicate in the body. This is a way to force the Prolog unification mechanism to exhaustively find, and enumerate, all possible successful unifications. The rule is:

```
printbackup(B) :-
                back_up(B,B1),
                operate(B1),
                write('Breaker '),
                write(B1),
                write(' operated correctly as a back-up
                breaker.'),
                nl,fail.
```

Finally, we incorporate our overall goal in the database:

```
run  :-  protected_by(L,B1,B2),
         elect_isolated(L,B1,B2),
         write('Possible Fault Location is on line '),
         write(L),nl,
         printout(B1),
         printout(B2),
         nl,nl,
         fail.
```

Notice again the use of fail, which, together with the predicate `protected_by`, as well as the topological description, forces an assessment of the status of each line.

4.12.8 Listing of Overall Prolog Program

Note this listing contains the topology corresponding to Figure 4.24.

```
/* file: power1.pro

This program finds the fault locations in a power system
network and gives the interpretation of the breaker operation.


Key assumptions are:
  1) only one possible breaker malfunction,
  2) the malfunctioned breaker has to have backup breakers.
  3) only line fault is possible,
  4) the relay has direction characteristic.


The database consists of:
  1) topology of the network,
  2) the current breaker status,
  3) rules,
  4) goal. */
```

```
/* 1) topology data for system*/


protected_by(line1,1,2).
protected_by(line2,3,4).
protected_by(line3,5,6).
protected_by(line4,7,8).

connect(2,3).
connect(2,6).
connect(2,7).
connect(3,6).
connect(3,7).
connect(6,7).


generation(1).
generation(4).
generation(5).



/* 2) breaker status */

operate(1).
operate(4).
operate(5).

/* 3) rules for breaker operation and interpretation */


connection(B1,B2) :- connect(B1,B2).
connection(B1,B2) :- connect(B2,B1).


other_breaker(B1,B2) :- protected_by(_,B1,B2).
other_breaker(B1,B2) :- protected_by(_,B2,B1).

has_gen(B) :- generation(B), !.
has_gen(B) :- connection(B,B1),
              other_breaker(B1,B2),
              has_gen(B2), !.


back_up(B1,B2) :- not(generation(B1)), /* no backup for generators */
                  connection(B1,B3),
```

```
                    other_breaker(B3,B2),
                    has_gen(B2).


back_up_not_work(B1,B2) :- back_up(B1,B2),
                           not(operate(B2)).


no_source_coming(B1) :- not(has_gen(B1)).
no_source_coming(B1) :- has_gen(B1),
                        operate(B1).
no_source_coming(B1) :- back_up(B1,_),
                        not(back_up_not_work(B1,_)).


elect_isolated(B1,B2) :- no_source_coming(B1),
                         no_source_coming(B2), !.


/* printbackup(B)-prints all correctly operating backup breakers and
   fails */


printbackup(B) :- back_up(B,B1),

                  operate(B1),

                  write('Breaker '),

                  write(B1),

                  write(' operated correctly as a back-up breaker.'),

                  nl,fail.


/* printout gives the interpretation of breaker operation */


printout(B) :- has_gen(B),
               operate(B),
               write('Breaker '),
               write(B),
               write(' operated correctly.'),nl, !.


printout(B) :- has_gen(B),
```

```
                       not(operate(B)),
                       write('Breaker '),
                       write(B),
                       write(' malfunctioned.'),nl,
                       not(printbackup(B)), !.


/* 4) goal */


run  :-  protected_by(L,B1,B2),
         elect_isolated(B1,B2),
         write('Possible Fault Location is on '),
         write(L),nl,
         printout(B1),
         printout(B2),
         nl,nl,
         fail.
```

4.12.9 Sample Results

Using the sample system of Figure 4.24, with the breaker status as shown, the Prolog formulation generates the dialog shown here.

```
?- ['power1.pro'].
% power1.pro compiled 0.00 sec, 5272 bytes


Yes
?- run.
Possible Fault Location is on line1
Breaker 1 operated correctly.
Breaker 2 malfunctioned.
Breaker 4 operated correctly as a back-up breaker.
Breaker 5 operated correctly as a back-up breaker.


Possible Fault Location is on line2
Breaker 3 malfunctioned.
Breaker 5 operated correctly as a back-up breaker.
Breaker 1 operated correctly as a back-up breaker.
Breaker 4 operated correctly.


Possible Fault Location is on line3
Breaker 5 operated correctly.
Breaker 6 malfunctioned.
Breaker 1 operated correctly as a back-up breaker.
Breaker 4 operated correctly as a back-up breaker.
```

```
Possible Fault Location is on line4
Breaker 7 malfunctioned.
Breaker 1 operated correctly as a back-up breaker.
Breaker 4 operated correctly as a back-up breaker.
Breaker 5 operated correctly as a back-up breaker.

No
?-
```

4.12.10 Summary: Expert System for Electric Power System Protection Interpretation

This section showed how the "expert" interpretation of an electric power system protection scheme could be cast as a CSP. The corresponding Prolog description and implementation of the expert system is straightforward and based upon problem decomposition and incremental development and refinement. The solution presented is not unique—the reader is encouraged to develop alternative (and perhaps more efficient) solutions. The exercises provide other cases for Prolog development and testing.

4.13 Extensions

Chapter 5 continues our look at CSPs, focusing on problems constrained by structure. This leads to expert systems for Natural Language (NL) understanding and related topics. The implementation of constraint satisfaction solutions using the neural network computational paradigm is shown in Chapter 14.

4.14 Exercises

1. Referring to the "guest invitation" CSP problem in Section 4.2:

(a) Determine all possible (unconstrained) guest lists.

(b) By enumerating and evaluating each possible guest list, find all solutions to this problem. How many solutions exist?

(c) Use Prolog to formulate and solve this problem. Show all solutions.

(d) Suppose the constraints are augmented to add that the minimum number of invited dinner guests is two. Revise your Prolog solution to the previous part to accommodate this revision. Show the revised set of solutions.

(e) Suppose the crown prince is disowned by the royal family and therefore his constraint is no longer valid. How does the solution space change?

2. SAT Properties were considered in Section 4.3.3. In particular, the control parameter m/n (clauses/variables) was shown to be an important parameter. As this ratio increases, at a certain value the probability of satisfiability (for randomly generated SAT problems) exhibits a sharp transition. Consider a constant numbr of problem variables. As the ratio of clauses to variables increases, it is postulated that many randomly-generated SAT problems sharply transition from a high probability of a solution existing to a much lower value. Intuitively, does this makes sense? Can you think of a sample problem where this occurs?

3. Using the notation of Section 4.1.3, formulate the labeling problem as a CSP.

4. Repeat the labeling problem solution (in Prolog) using just the adjacency constraint together with the unary constraint:

   the largest region must be labeled "grass"

   Here assume $R3$ is observed to be the largest region.

5. Consider an alternative formulation of the previous labeling or SAT/optimization problem in Prolog using the Prolog `bagof` and/or `findall` predicates.

6. Revise the Prolog solution to the labeling problem in Section 4.6.4 to allow:

   (a) The constraint relation to be reflexive, i.e., a pair of adjacent regions could be labeled (*car, car*).

   (b) A negative formulation, i.e., formulation of constraints such as `cant-be-adj-to(sky,road)`. Assume the goal still uses positive observations of adjacent regions, i.e.,

   ```
   goal :- highest(R1),
           moving(R5),
           adjacent-to(R1,R2),
           adjacent-to(R2,R6), ...
   ```

7. As noted in Section 4.6.1, there are $5^6 = 15,625$ possible solutions to the unconstrained image labeling problem.

   (a) Formulate the unconstrained problem in Prolog and determine the number of solutions found. (Hint: first draw a graph showing allowed labels on adjacent regions. This graph should indicate a symmetric and reflexive relation.)

   (b) A somewhat obvious, but uninformed solution is to use the goal predicate as specified in Figure 4.5 together with the fact:

   ```
   /* anything allowed adjacent-to anything */
   adjacent-to(_,_).
   ```

   Does this approach work? Explain your answer.

8. Repeat the labeling example of Section 4.8.3, but do not employ unary constraints. Show the limit set, and indicate how the 42 possible solutions could be obtained from this set.

9. Compare and contrast the iterative label discarding and label retention (LRR/LDR) strategies. Are they really two distinct strategies, or are they related?

10. Compare the iterative LRR/LDR strategies with the Prolog solution. Is the Prolog formulation similar to either strategy?

11. Determine the limit set for the image labeling problem using the relational (adjacency) constraint and the single unary constraint $R1 = sky$. (You may do this by hand or by modification of Prolog. Note this limit set is also shown in the MATLAB/Octave solution.) There are five solutions. Using this limit set, determine $\Gamma_1 \times \Gamma_2 \times \cdots \times \Gamma_n$. What is the relationship of the five solutions to this set?

12. In the limit set-based solution of Figure 4.15 (right side), the filtering provided by the limit set was implemented by first restricting labels on regions (variables) before the adjacency constraint was tested. This was done via a revision of the goal as follows:

```
goal :- gamma1(Gamma1), member(R1,Gamma1),
        gamma2(Gamma2), member(R2,Gamma2),
        gamma3(Gamma3), member(R3,Gamma3),
        gamma4(Gamma4), member(R4,Gamma4),
        gamma5(Gamma5), member(R5,Gamma5),
        gamma6(Gamma6), member(R6,Gamma6),
        adjacent-to(R1,R2),
        adjacent-to(R2,R6),
        adjacent-to(R2,R3),
        adjacent-to(R3,R4),
        adjacent-to(R2,R4),
        adjacent-to(R4,R6),
        adjacent-to(R4,R5), .....
```

This resulted in a savings of almost 97% of the search computation. Could you suggest an even better placement of the **gamma** predicates to further reduce the computational cost of search?

13. Repeat the previous problem using the label retention rule and using only the adjacency constraint together with the unary constraint:

    the largest region must be labeled "grass"

Here assume $R3$ is observed to be the largest region.

14. Refer to Figure 4.26. This, along with Figure 4.8, will be used to test your extended map coloring CSP results.

    Part 1: The objective of this part is to use Figure 4.26 with three colors (RGB) and develop a logic-based (Prolog) implementation of the coloring solution. Specifically do all of the following:

    (a) Using three colors, how many solutions are there?
    (b) State the coloring problem constraints in Prolog.
    (c) State the observed data in Prolog.
    (d) Implement the solution.
    (e) Assess the Prolog result.

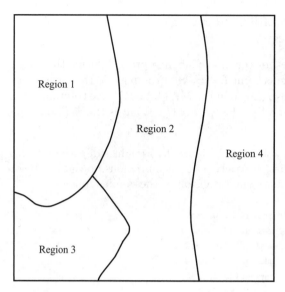

Figure 4.26 Second Map for Verification

Part 2: Repeat the effort of Part 1 (see Figure 4.26), but using four colors (RGBW).

Part 3: Repeat the effort of Part 2 (four colors), but use Figure 4.8.

Part 4: This effort repeats the efforts of Parts 2 and 3, but using *up to four colors*. In other words, *minimize the total number of colors used*. This must be done by the addition of another Prolog constraint to implement this measure of optimization.

15. Using the segmented image regions shown in the labeling problem of Figure 4.3, develop a map coloring solution following the structure of the previous exercise.

16. Apply the LDR/LRR approach to the map coloring problems given in the chapter.

17. Repeat the previous map coloring CSP problem, but add the unary constraint:

    The largest region must be labeled "blue"

18. Discuss the similarity of the map coloring and image labeling CSPs.

19. If the three-color map coloring problem of Section 4.7 is solved using the LDR/LRR with $\Gamma_i = \Gamma = \{red, green, blue\} \forall i$, what is the limit set?

20. In the image labeling problem, constraints on allowed pairwise labels were shown using an undirected graph. This was shown in Figure 4.3. Similarly, in the map coloring problem the allowed pairwise color constraints on adjacent map regions may also be shown using an undirected graph.

    (a) Draw this graph for the cases of $n = 3, 4, 5$ colors.

    (b) Determine the number of arcs as a function of n.

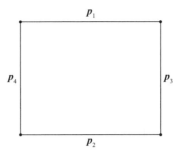

Figure 4.27 Geometric Figure Labeling CSP

21. Must Ω_{ij} in Equation 4.9 be symmetric?

22. Consider the application of constraint-based labeling to geometric figures in the plane. An example is shown in Figure 4.27. The set of objects to be labelled is U, where

$$U = p_1, p_2, p_3, p_4$$

and the set of possible labels is

$$\Gamma = \{t, b, ls, rs\}$$

corresponding to "top," "bottom," "left side," and "right side," respectively.

(a) Using the binary constraint "connected to" (or, equivalently, "intersects"):

    i. Attempt labeling of this figure. Show the observed "connected to" relational graph. How many solutions exist?

    ii. Repeat the previous problem but incorporate the unary constraint "topmost" on p_1.

(b) Develop Prolog and MATLAB/Octave representations for the previous cases and show the results.

23. Another famous CSP is the eight-Queens puzzle. There are many online references and resources available for this problem (e.g., http://en.wikipedia.org/wiki/Eight_queens_puzzle). Look up this problem and:

(a) Develop a quantitative formulation of the constraints.

(b) Show a Prolog solution.

24. Notice in Equation 4.11, i.e., $\underline{\Omega}_i^{k+1} = \otimes|_{i \neq j}(\Omega_{ij}\underline{\Omega}_j^k)$ that updated values of Ω_i are available and used (in the MATLAB/Octave solution) immediately. This was referred to as an asynchronous update. An alternative is to "freeze" $\underline{\Omega}_i^k$ and use these values in Equation 4.11 until all $\underline{\Omega}_i^{k+1}$ have been computed. This is termed a synchronous update. Comment on the advisability and consequences of using one approach over the other. Show examples to justify your solution.

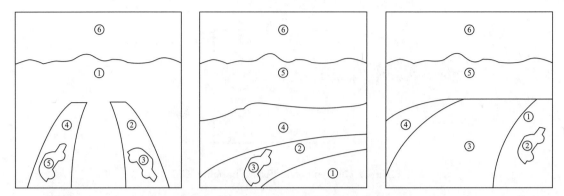

Figure 4.28   Additional Images for Labeling CSP

25. Label the images of Figure 4.28, using

   (a) Prolog

   (b) Iterative Relaxation (LRR/LDR)

In each case show all solutions.

26. Using the LRR/LDR on the *rightmost* image in Figure 4.28, with $\Gamma_i = \Gamma = \{car, road, grass, trees, sky\}$ 4 and $\Gamma_4 = \{trees\}$, what is the limit set?

27. For the power system shown in Figure 4.29, modify the Prolog topological description and obtain fault location(s) and interpretation(s) for the following cases (recall "O" denotes open or operated; "S" indicates closed or in service):

Breaker	Case 1	Case 2	Case 3	Case 4
1	O	O	O	S
2	S	O	S	S
3	S	S	S	O
4	O	S	S	S
5	S	S	O	S
6	S	S	S	O
7	S	S	S	S
8	S	S	S	S

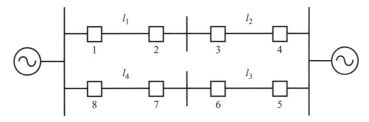

Figure 4.29 Modified System Topology for Power System Protection Interpretation CSP

28. Repeat Problem 27 for each of the topologies in Figure 4.30(a) with the following cases of breaker status:

Breaker	Case 1	Case 2	Case 3
1	S	S	O
2	S	S	S
3	S	O	O
4	S	S	S
5	O	S	S
6	O	O	S

29. Repeat Problem 27 for each of the topologies in Figure 4.30(b) with the following cases of breaker status:

Breaker	Case 1	Case 2	Case 3
1	O	O	S
2	S	S	S
3	S	S	S
4	O	S	S
5	S	S	O
6	S	S	S
7	S	S	S
8	S	O	O

30. In the power protection CSP of Section 4.12, a somewhat "negative" formulation of several constraints (especially concerning backup operation) was shown. Examples are:

```
backup_did_not_work(B1,B2) :- back_up(B1,B2),
                              not(operate(B2)).
```

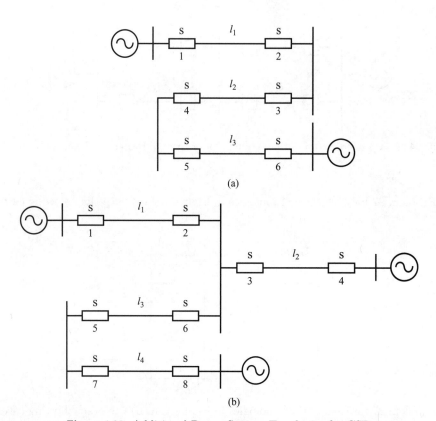

Figure 4.30 Additional Power System Topologies for CSP

and

```
no_source_coming(B1) :- back_up(B1,_),
                        not(backup_did_not_work(B1,_)).
```

Investigate the possibility and consequences of converting this representation to a more positive formulation, i.e., one without the use of the **not** predicate.

31. Discuss the feasibility of implementing CSP solutions in parallel. (This is a very open-ended problem.)

CSPs, Part 2: Structural Approaches Leading to Natural Language Understanding and Related Topics

5.1 Introduction

In Chapter 4, we explored an important class of constraint satisfaction problems common to many IS applications. In this chapter we extend our look at constraint satisfaction-based IS formulations and consider CSPs that involve structural, or *structure-based* constraints. This includes natural language (NL) understanding, an important IS application area.

5.2 What Types of Problems Have Structural Constraints?

Our examination of modeling in Chapter 1 indicated that many IS applications exhibit a strong dependence on a clearly defined structural model. Most noteworthy, and emphasized in this chapter, is natural language. However, many other problem domains have structural concerns. As we show, some of the language structure-based modeling and solution approaches (e.g., grammars) are also applicable in these domains. Examples include:

1. Music, as shown in the following paragraph;

2. Line drawings, as shown in Figure 5.1;

3. Signals, such as the cardiac EKG signal shown in Figure 5.2; and

4. Mechanical assemblies, typically shown in "exploded views" or drawings.

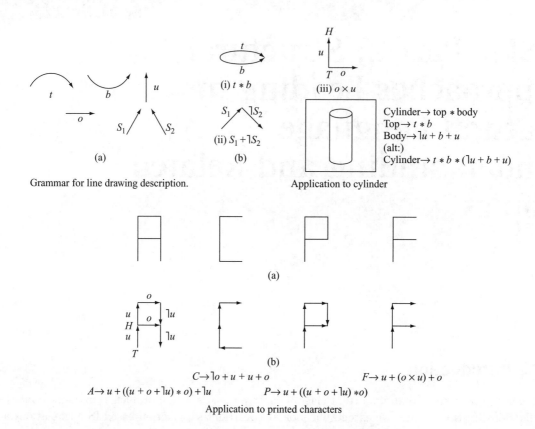

Figure 5.1 Structural Interpretation of Line Drawings

Structure, Computer Music, and CSPs.   Open Music [Ope] is a visual programming and development environment for computer-aided music composition. As shown in the example of Figure 5.3, Open Music facilitates constraint programming and allows music composition to be treated as a CSP. Constraint satisfaction formulations can be defined and integrated into Open Music using a graphical interface. They may be solved using a number of different constraint solvers, including the Oz[1] constraint language [HLZ96]. Oz provides a programming interface that allows the interactive exploration of search trees and implementation of parallel search.

---

[1]http://www.mozart-oz.org/

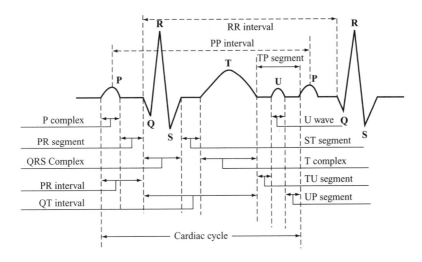

Figure 5.2 Structure of Cardiac EKG Waveform (from [TS90]). Courtesy of P. Trahanias and E. Skordalakis. Syntactic pattern recognition of the ecg. IEEE Transactions on Pattern Analysis and Machine Intelligence, 12(7):648–657, 1990.

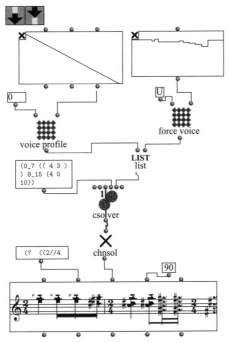

Figure 5.3 (Graphical) Formulation of Music Composition as a CSP Using the Open Music System ([Ope]; from the web page)

5.3 Natural Language and Structure

Determination of structure often leads to the recognition, or more importantly, the determination of the meaning of an entity. For example, on one level, an English sentence is merely a string of words. (These can and have been randomly generated by computer, leading to "nonsense" prose.) On a higher level (one that implies "intelligence") once the structure of the sentence (i.e., the noun and verb phrases) have been identified, it is possible to ascertain "who did what to whom." Thus, in the interpretation of the sentence, we identify lay entities (i.e., the subject), relationships, or action (e.g., the verb) and interpret the sentence in the context of other a priori information about these entities.

Natural language understanding is a dynamic field of study. Important early references include [Bob67], [Cho56], [Win83], [Win72], [HS84], [BG84], and [All95]. More recent and general references include [JM00], [Pin94], and [CP92]. Covington [Cov94] shows a Prolog-based approach.

We develop a general and formal mathematical description of languages. It is worth noting that the descriptor's "language" and "sentence" connote a far broader meaning than "spoken words," for example we might apply the same approach to computer languages as well as languages used to describe music and the structure of visible objects.

Achieving natural interactions between human and machine requires a machine to understand and generate language. Likewise, understanding human communication requires the understanding of how language is interpreted by humans. The nature of human language raises many challenging issues for language processing systems: natural language is often incomplete and imprecise, leaving much unstated and assumed, and its meaning is context-dependent. "Jack took a drink" could imply he was thirsty or he is a thief. It is therefore natural to investigate algorithms for syntactic parsing, and to determine both the grammatical structure and perhaps deeper structure of text.

In this chapter we will emphasize NL applications and string grammars. Formal grammars may be viewed as procedural representations. Several Prolog-based tools, including language generators and parsers, are used or developed. The syntactic description and analysis approach, however, is easily extended to more complex knowledge representations, including relational approaches.

5.4 Early NL Understanding Efforts

Two significant events mark the early history of this field:

1. McCarthy's research proposal (see Section 5.4.1); and

2. ELIZA.

5.4.1 McCarthy's Proposal

As mentioned in Chapter 1, J. McCarthy, then with Dartmouth College, proposed a summer research project on artificial intelligence (AI) in August, 1955. In the document, McCarthy noted:

> *I propose to study the relation of language to intelligence.*

Moreover, one of the significant thrust areas was outlined as follows:

2. How Can a Computer be Programmed to Use a Language

It may be speculated that a large part of human thought consists of manipulating words according to rules of reasoning and rules of conjecture. From this point of view, forming a generalization consists of admitting a new word and some rules whereby sentences containing it imply and are implied by others. This idea has never been very precisely formulated nor have examples been worked out.

5.4.2 ELIZA

A Sample Conversation with ELIZA

One of the most famous (or should we say notorious?) examples of simplistic NL analysis is Weizenbaum's ELIZA program [Wei65], which emulates (some might claim "imitates" or even "ridicules" is a better descriptor) conversation with a Rogerian psychologist. An example of a conversation with ELIZA follows:

```
lisp> (load "eliza.lsp")
;; Loading file eliza.lsp ...
;; Loading of file eliza.lsp is finished.
t
lisp> (top-level)

    Welcome to the ELIZA program. The following
    guidelines should help your conversation along:

        1: Punctuation should not be used. Periods, commas, apostrophes, and
           question marks only confuse ELIZA now.

        2: ELIZA understands simple declarative sentences and questions best.

        3: When you are done, simply type 'goodbye' at the 'input>' prompt
           and ELIZA will know you want to stop.
input>my AI class is not going very well

YOUR AI CLASS IS NOT GOING VERY WELL

input>right

DOES THAT HAVE ANYTHING TO DO WITH THE FACT THAT YOUR AI CLASS IS NOT GOING VERY WELL

input>sure does

I AM NOT SURE I UNDERSTAND YOU FULLY

input>the class is very slow to comprehend even the simplest concepts

PLEASE GO ON

input>they do not want to do homework

WHAT DOES THAT SUGGEST TO YOU
```

```
input>they have other interests besides AI

DO YOU FEEL STRONGLY ABOUT DISCUSSING SUCH THINGS

input>no

ARE YOU SAYING NO JUST TO BE NEGATIVE

input>yes

YOU SEEM QUITE POSITIVE

input>no

YOU ARE BEING A BIT NEGATIVE

input>yes

YOU ARE SURE

input>yes

I SEE

input>How should I fix the class?

WHY DO YOU ASK

input>because I would like everybody to be successful

DO YOU REALLY MEAN EVERYONE

input>yes

I UNDERSTAND
```

The Significant Limitations of ELIZA

Unfortunately, ELIZA's responses are not determined through understanding of user input, but rather a simple pattern-matching approach is used to determine system response. The program recognizes particular patterns in the user input and then selects and modifies one of a stored set of replies for response. This behavior is evident in the "shallow" conversation in Figure 5.4, where ELIZA clearly rephrases many of the patient's statements as questions and then poses them to the patient.

ELIZA References and Availability of Source Code

The original ELIZA paper is available electronically via several sites, including the ACM Digital Library. An HTML version of the original paper is online at http://i5.nyu.edu/~mm64/x52.9265/january1966.html. Numerous ELIZA implementations and variations are available in many languages. This includes:

1. The CMU Artificial Intelligence Repository at ftp://ftp.cs.cmu.edu/user/ai/0.html

2. A JavaScript applet at http://www.manifestation.com/neurotoys/eliza.php3

Emacs ELIZA

A version of ELIZA, called "Doctor" is included with the Emacs editor. Snippets of the Lisp source code are shown in Figure 5.4. Sample use of Emacs ELIZA is shown in Figure 5.5.

```
(doctor-type '(i am the psychotherapist \.
 ($ please) ($ describe) your ($ problems) \.
 each time you are finished talking, type \R\E\T twice \.))
  (insert "\n"))


.
.
.

(make-local-variable 'continue)
  (setq continue '((continue)
  (proceed)
  (go on)
  (keep going) ))
  (make-local-variable 'relation)
  (setq relation '((your relationship with)
  (something you remember about)
  (your feelings toward)
  (some experiences you have had with)
  (how you feel about)))
  (make-local-variable 'fears)
  (setq fears '( (($ whysay) you are ($ afraidof) (// feared) \?)
(you seem terrified by (// feared) \.)
(when did you first feel ($ afraidof) (// feared) \?) ))
  (make-local-variable 'sure)
  (setq sure '((sure)(positive)(certain)(absolutely sure)))
  (make-local-variable 'afraidof)
  (setq afraidof '( (afraid of) (frightened by) (scared of) ))
  (make-local-variable 'areyou)
  (setq areyou '( (are you)(have you been)(have you been) ))
  (make-local-variable 'isrelated)
  (setq isrelated '( (has something to do with)(is related to)
    (could be the reason for) (is caused by)(is because of)))
  (make-local-variable 'arerelated)
  (setq arerelated '((have something to do with)(are related to)
    (could have caused)(could be the reason for) (are caused by)
    (are because of)))


.
.
.

(make-local-variable 'shortlst)
  (setq shortlst '((can you elaborate on that \?)
(($ please) continue \.)
(go on\, don\'t be afraid \.)
(i need a little more detail please \.)
(you\'re being a bit brief\, ($ please) go into detail \.)
(can you be more explicit \?)
(and \?)
```

```
(($ please) go into more detail \?)
(you aren\'t being very talkative today\!)
(is that all there is to it \?)
(why must you respond so briefly \?)))


.
.
.

(make-local-variable 'replist)
  (setq replist '((i . (you))
(my . (your))
(me . (you))
(you . (me))
(your . (my))
(mine . (yours))
(yours . (mine))
(our . (your))
(ours . (yours))
(we . (you))
(dunno . (do not know))
;;  (yes . ())
(no\, . ())
(yes\, . ())
(ya . (i))
(aint . (am not))
(wanna . (want to))
(gimme . (give me))
(gotta . (have to))
(gonna . (going to))
(never . (not ever))
(doesn\'t . (does not))
(don\'t . (do not))
(aren\'t . (are not))
(isn\'t . (is not))
(won\'t . (will not))
(can\'t . (cannot))
(haven\'t . (have not))
(i\'m . (you are))
(ourselves . (yourselves))
(myself . (yourself))
(yourself . (myself))
(you\'re . (i am))
(you\'ve . (i have))
(i\'ve . (you have))
(i\'ll . (you will))
(you\'ll . (i shall))
(i\'d . (you would))
```

Figure 5.4 Snippets of Emacs ELIZA Source (note the responses to various input phrases)

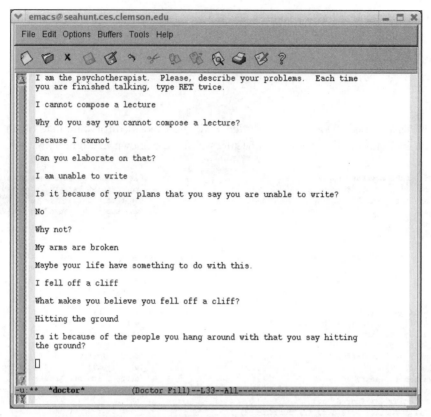

Figure 5.5 Example of Emacs Lisp-Based "Doctor" (ELIZA)

5.5 Natural Language Understanding: Grammars

We begin a study of grammars and parsing approaches with a simple example.

5.5.1 Example: Sentence Formation As Productions (Rewrite Rules)

Consider the following sentence:

```
The program crashes the computer.
```

Temporarily ignore the significance of the capital letter at the beginning and the period at the end and concentrate on the formation and structure of this sentence. The sentence was produced according to the following rewrite or production rules:

```
1. <sentence>
2. <noun phrase> <verb phrase>
3. <adjective> <noun> <verb phrase>
4. the <noun> <verb phrase>
```

```
 5. the program <verb phrase>
 6. the program <verb> <noun phrase>
 7. the program crashes <noun phrase>
 8. the program crashes <adjective> <noun>
 9. the program crashes the <noun>
10. the program crashes the computer
```

More specifically, the sentence was formed using a sequence of rewrite or production rules. Note also the gradual elimination of intermediate entities such as "noun" and "adjective." This sequence could be determined by cataloging each of the preceding rewrites or substitutions. We now seek a formal definition of this process.

Language utility involves both generation and recognition. In the case of a spoken language, consider a speaker and a listener. One generates sentences in the language; the other recognizes them (otherwise the conversation is, at best, one-sided). Although one might question their utility, we will consider language generators as well as recognizers.

5.5.2 The Phase Structure (String) Grammar

A phase structure grammar (PSG) consists of the following four entities:

1. A set of terminal or primitive symbols (primitives), denoted V_T (or, alternately, Σ). In many nonlinguistic applications, the choice of this set is one of the most significant challenges.

2. A set of nonterminal symbols, or variables, which are used as intermediate quantities in the generation of an outcome consisting solely of terminal symbols. Often this set is denoted as V_N (or, alternately, N). In the previous example, nonterminals were shown enclosed in < >, e.g., <noun>. Sets V_T and V_N are disjoint.

3. A set of productions, production rules, or rewriting rules, denoted P, which allow substitutions. It is this set of productions, coupled with the terminal symbols, which principally gives the grammar its "structure."

   The application we investigate in Section 5.6.3 employs string grammars, where P is used to generate sentences consisting of linear or one-dimensional strings of terminals. Note that this does not restrict the representation to one-dimensional. The production or rewrite rules in G for a string grammar are of the general form:

$$S1 \rightarrow S2$$

   which means String $S1$ "is replaced by" String $S2$. A phase structure grammar [AMK88] requires $S1$ to be in the positive closure set of $(V_T \cup V_N)$ *and contain at least one nonterminal* [Sch07]. $S2$ is an element of the closure set of $(V_T \cup V_N)$.

4. A starting (or root) symbol, denoted S, where $S \in V_N$. In the previous example, S = <sentence>.

   Thus, using the preceding definitions, we formally denote a phase structure grammar, G, as:

$$G = (V_T, V_N, P, S)$$

5.5.3 $L(G)$

The language generated by G, denoted $L(G)$, is the set of all strings where:

1. Each string consists solely of terminal symbols; and

2. Each string was produced from S using P.

5.5.4 Grammar Modes

A grammar may be used in one of two modes:

1. Generative: The grammar is used to create a string of terminal symbols using P; a sentence in the language of the grammar is thus generated.

2. Recognition (analytic): Given G, one seeks to determine:

    i. If the sentence was in fact generated by this grammar; and, if so,

    ii. The structure (usually characterized as the sequence of productions used) of the sentence.

5.5.5 Grammar Types and Productions

Type 0 (Free).   This grammar has no restrictions on the rewrite rules, and is of little practical significance.

Type 1 (Context-Sensitive).   This grammar typically exhibits productions of the form:

$$A \ S1 \ B \rightarrow A \ S2 \ B$$

meaning String S2 replaces String S1 in the context of Strings A and B. Spoken languages are considered context-sensitive, in the sense that subjects and verbs and verbs and objects must exist for strings in the language to be grammatically correct and have sensible semantics.

Type 2 (Context Free).   This grammar restricts productions to have a single nonterminal on the left-hand side. Thus, context-sensitive replacements as shown above are not possible. As we show, this is a serious limitation when it is desirable to achieve sensible or meaningful semantics.

    Grammar types other than string grammars exist and are characterized by their terminals and nonterminals (as opposed to constraints on P). These are useful in two-dimensional higher applications, in that the structure of the terminals and nonterminals is higher than one dimension. Thus, productions in these grammars are more complex, since rewriting rules embody operations more complex than simple one-dimensional string modifications. For example, in two-dimensional cases standard "attachment points" are defined. Two of the more popular are tree grammars and web grammars [Fu82].

5.5.6 Syntax, Semantics, and Context

In our initial work, we consider *context-free string grammars*. This allows the use of the productions in P independent of the context, or meaning, or relationships among the nonterminal symbols. In contrast, a higher-level grammar imposes constraints on the meaning of strings produced, i.e., it enforces semantics. This is a more complex concept, some ramifications of which are considered later and in the problems.

5.5.7 Graphical Aids

The use of graphical constructs for a grammar in either the generative or analytic mode is common. In the generative mode we show a derivation tree, whereas in the analytic mode we use a parse tree. Given a sentence, for practical purposes (and as long as the sentence is in the language of the grammar), these entities are the same. It is merely a question of whether we start from the root node or the leaves in the tree. This is shown in Figure 5.6.

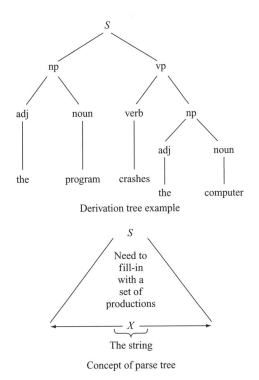

Derivation tree example

Concept of parse tree

Figure 5.6 Derivation and Parse Trees

5.6 Sentence Generation and Recognition Using Prolog

To construct a generator or a parser for any language, it is first necessary to quantify the language to be parsed, in terms of primitives and allowable productions.

5.6.1 The Initial Grammar Model

Initially, we consider the so-called "verb model" of the basic sentence. In this model, there is a relationship[2] between the subject and object in a sentence. Specifically, the subject acts upon the object.

Assume words are the basic building blocks and are used to represent concepts. The next-larger syntactic unit is the phrase, and we show two types. A sentence is built (and recognized) using phrases.

We consider the specification of a grammar and the use of Prolog to generate and recognize the language of the grammar.

5.6.2 Grammar G1

Consider the following grammar $G1 = (V_T, V_N, P, S)$
  where

$$V_T = \{the, program, crashes, computer\}$$
$$V_N = \{sentence, adj, np, vp, noun, verb\}$$

and P consists of the following six productions:

$$(i) \quad sentence \rightarrow np \quad vp$$
$$(ii) \quad np \rightarrow adj \quad noun$$
$$(iii) \quad vp \rightarrow verb \quad np$$
$$(iv) \quad noun \rightarrow computer|program$$
$$(v) \quad verb \rightarrow crashes$$
$$(vi) \quad adj \rightarrow the$$

with starting nonterminal $S = sentence$. The symbol | has the meaning "or," from the Backus-Naur Form (BNF) syntax.

Given the preceding productions and symbols (terminal and nonterminal), it is relatively simple to develop a Prolog language generator and parser. Note that we are generating or parsing sentences entered, for simplicity, in list form. Each word (terminal) in the generated sentence is an atomic element of a list. The reader may wish to review Prolog and the Logic Grammar Notation (LGN; Appendix B) before considering the following section.

---

[2]In the problems, we force this to be a sensible, or semantically meaningful, relationship.

5.6.3 Sample Results for a Simple Grammar

Prolog LGN Formulation

```
/* prolog LGN formulation of sentence gen/parser */
/*  for first example */
/* file: gener-lgn.pro  */

sentence --> np, vp.
np --> adj, noun.
vp --> verb, np.
adj -->[the].
noun --> [program].
verb --> [crashes].
noun --> [computer].
```

Sample Results (as a Language Generator)

```
?- ['gener-lgn.pro'].

Yes
?- sentence(What,[]).

What = [the, program, crashes, the, program] ;

What = [the, program, crashes, the, computer] ;

What = [the, computer, crashes, the, program] ;

What = [the, computer, crashes, the, computer] ;

No
?-
```

Sample Results (as a Parser)

```
?- ['gener-lgn.pro'].

Yes
?- sentence([the, program, crashes, the, computer],[]).

Yes
?- sentence([the, dog, crashes, the, computer],[]).

No
?- sentence([the, program, crashes],[]).

No
?- sentence([the, computer, crashes, the, program],[]).

Yes
?-
```

5.6.4   Showing Structure and Extending the Language

Suppose grammar $G = (V_T, V_N, P, S)$ where

$$V_T = \{the, a, system, program, computer, crashes, runs\}$$
$$V_N = \{sentence, adj, np, vp, noun, verb\}$$

and P consists of the following productions:

$$sentence \rightarrow np \ vp$$
$$sentence \rightarrow np \ verb$$
$$np \rightarrow adj \ noun$$
$$vp \rightarrow verb \ np$$
$$noun \rightarrow system | computer | program$$
$$verb \rightarrow crashes | runs$$
$$adj \rightarrow the | a$$

with starting nonterminal $S = sentence$.

A modified LGN-based generator/parser for this grammar follows, where the numbered changes have been incorporated:

1. The noun phrase following a verb is optional;

2. The sentence structure is indicated using an additional list; and

3. A slightly larger dictionary is used.

To show sentence structure, the LGN formulation incorporates an additional variable, thus yielding an additional argument (a specially structured list) for the relevant predicates. For example, the structure of the sentence:[3]

```
[the, program, crashes, the, computer]
```

is determined to be the two-element structured list:

```
[[[the], [program]], [[crashes], [[the], [computer]]]]
```

where each of the top-level elements indicates a parse for **np** and **vp**, respectively. In addition, each of these elements is itself a structured list indicating the substructure of the top-level elements. Such a list could be used to "diagram" the sentence structure, as is commonly done in elementary school grammar classes. Readers may wish to consult Section B.6.2 of Appendix B for more details.

```
/* revised and extended prolog formulation of sentence gen/parser */
/* shows structure of generated/parsed senetence */
/* file: generate-lgn2.pro */
```

---

[3]Which is represented as a five-element list with all elements at the top level.

```
sentence([Np,Vp]) --> np(Np), vp(Vp).

/* second allowable sentence structure (optional verb phrase) */

sentence([Np, Verb]) --> np(Np), verb(Verb).

np([Adj,Noun]) --> adj(Adj), noun(Noun).
vp([Verb,Np]) --> verb(Verb), np(Np).

/* a slightly larger 'dictionary' of terminals */

adj([a]) -->[a].
adj([the]) -->[the].

noun([program]) --> [program].
noun([system]) --> [system].
noun([computer]) --> [computer].

verb([crashes]) --> [crashes].
verb([runs]) --> [runs].
```

Result as a Language Generator and Parser

Sample use of this grammar in the generative and analytic modes is shown as follows. Note that a very small change in the language sentence structure and dictionary yielded a substantial increase in the cardinality of $L(G)$. The exercises further explore this topic.

```
?- ['generate-lgn2.pro'].
% generate-lgn2.pro compiled 0.00 sec, 2648 bytes

<Use as a parser>

Yes
?- sentence(Structure, [the, program, crashes, the, computer],[]).

Structure = [[[the], [program]], [[crashes], [[the], [computer]]]]

Yes
?- sentence(Structure, [the, program, crashes],[]).

Structure = [[[the], [program]], [crashes]]

Yes
?- sentence(Structure, [the, crashes, program],[]).

No

<Use as a generator>

?- sentence(Structure, Generate, []).

Structure = [[[a], [program]], [[crashes], [[a], [program]]]]
Generate = [a, program, crashes, a, program] ;
```

```
Structure = [[[a], [program]], [[crashes], [[a], [system]]]]
Generate = [a, program, crashes, a, system] ;

Structure = [[[a], [program]], [[crashes], [[a], [computer]]]]
Generate = [a, program, crashes, a, computer] ;

Structure = [[[a], [program]], [[crashes], [[the], [program]]]]
Generate = [a, program, crashes, the, program] ;

Structure = [[[a], [program]], [[crashes], [[the], [system]]]]
Generate = [a, program, crashes, the, system] ;

<and lots of others; this is left to the exercises>
```

5.6.5   Enforcing Meaningful Semantics

Why Is This an Issue?

This section is very significant and may be approached on a number of levels. Our objective is to design and implement a context-sensitive language generator and parser for a modified $G1$ grammar.

Observe that the parser/generator of Section 5.6.3 generates and parses sentences that are grammatically correct. However, some of these sentences have questionable meaning or semantics. This is because the grammar productions do not require or allow replacement of sentence elements that are forced to agree in some meaningful sense.

For example, in a modified Prolog implementation of the $G1$ generator/parser, using a slightly reduced "dictionary" of terminals:

```
adj -->[the].

noun(program) --> [program].
noun(computer) --> [computer].

verb(crashes) --> [crashes].
verb(runs) --> [runs].
```

leads to production of $L(G)$:

```
?- sentence(Structure,What,[]).

Structure = [program, crashes, program]
What = [the, program, crashes, the, program] ;

Structure = [program, crashes, computer]
What = [the, program, crashes, the, computer] ;

Structure = [program, runs, program]
What = [the, program, runs, the, program] ;

Structure = [program, runs, computer]
What = [the, program, runs, the, computer] ;

Structure = [computer, crashes, program]
What = [the, computer, crashes, the, program] ;
```

```
Structure = [computer, crashes, computer]
What = [the, computer, crashes, the, computer] ;

Structure = [computer, runs, program]
What = [the, computer, runs, the, program] ;

Structure = [computer, runs, computer]
What = [the, computer, runs, the, computer] ;

No
```

Notice some of these sentences, while grammatically correct, have questionable meaning or semantics.

Adding Constraints on Replacements Via Relations between Subject, Verb, and Object

Consider the forcing of meaningful semantics by constraints on sentence subject, verb, and object agreement. A more meaningful result might be:

```
?- sentence(Structure,What,[]).

Structure = [program, crashes, computer]
What = [the, program, crashes, the, computer] ;

Structure = [program, runs, computer]
What = [the, program, runs, the, computer] ;

Structure = [computer, runs, program]
What = [the, computer, runs, the, program] ;

No
```

Furthermore, consider the following formulation of [Noun,Verb,Object] constraints to define the semantics of sentences with this structure:

program is an entity capable of running or crashing something (as the subject) and being run, (as the object) but a program may not run or crash itself.

computer is an entity capable only of running something (as the subject) and being run or crashed (as the object), but a computer may not run itself.

plant is something only capable of being run (only exists as an object) i.e., it cannot itself run or crash anything.

Furthermore, consider a very restricted dictionary consisting of:

```
adj -->[the].

noun(program) --> [program].
noun(computer) --> [computer].
noun(plant) --> [plant].

verb(crashes) --> [crashes].
verb(runs) --> [runs].
```

The reader should easily be able to show all sentences generated with semantically unconstrained productions.

Prolog Generator/Parser Modifications

Implementing the prescribed constraints leads to the concept of an *attribute grammar*, where nonterminals have attributes that may be checked. For example, the Prolog source code that follows uses braces ({}) to "protect" Prolog clauses from the LGN. The Prolog inside the braces is not translated, but instead it is appended to a resulting translated clause. The objective is to generate and recognize strings with equal numbers of a's, b's, and c's. Note that this is impossible using only a context-free grammar (CFG).

```
/* file: attrib.pro */
/* example of attributes for context sensitivity */
/* this will generate or recognize strings with
   an equal number of a's, b's, and c's.  */

string --> numAs(M1), numBs(M2), numCs(M3),
{ M1=:=M2, M2=:=M3 }. %% require equal numbers

numAs(M) --> [a], numAs(N), { M is N+1 }.
numAs(0) --> [ ].

numBs(M) --> [b], numBs(N), { M is N+1 }.
numBs(0) --> [ ].

numCs(M) --> [c], numCs(N), { M is N+1 }.
numCs(0) --> [ ].
```

Application of this concept to the NL problem yields the following code.

```
/* revised and extended prolog formulation of sentence gen/parser */
/* subject, verb, object agreement in simple sentences */
/* file: generate-lgn2-agree2.pro  */

/* [Noun,Verb,Object] constraints the semantics for this structure */
/*****************************************************************
 constraints:
            program is an entity capable of running
            or crashing something (as the subject)
            and being run, (as the object) but
            a program may not run or crash itself

            computer is an entity capable only of
            running something (as the subject)
            and being run or crashed (as the object), but
            a computer may not run itself

            a plant is something only capable of being run
            (only exists as an object)
            i.e., it cannot itself run or crash anything
*****************************************************************/
```

```
/* here's a sentence without semantic constraints --
sentence([Noun,Verb,Object]) --> np(Noun), vp([Verb,Object]).
*/

/* use the above semantic constraints */

sentence([Subject,Verb,Object]) --> np(Subject), vp([Verb,Object]),
                                    {agree(Subject,Verb,Object)}.

/* more than just simple enumeration
   but short of a structured representation */

agree(Something,Action,What) :- Something \= What, % no reflexive
                                Something=program,
                                (Action=runs;Action=crashes),
                                checkObject(Action,What).

agree(Something,Action,What) :- Something \= What,
                                Something=computer,
                                Action=runs,
                                checkObject(Action,What).

checkObject(Action,What) :- (Action=runs;Action=crashes),
                            What=computer.

checkObject(Action,What) :- Action=runs,
                            (What=program;What=plant).


/* rest is unaffected except no longer lists */

np(Noun) --> adj, noun(Noun).
vp([Verb,Object]) --> verb(Verb), np(Object).

/* slightly reduced 'dictionary' of terminals */

adj -->[the].

noun(program) --> [program].
noun(computer) --> [computer].
noun(plant) --> [plant].

verb(crashes) --> [crashes].
verb(runs) --> [runs].
```

If the preceding constraints are implemented, using the Prolog parser/generator as shown, the resulting language is:

```
?- ['generate-lgn2-agree2.pro'].
% generate-lgn2-agree2.pro compiled 0.00 sec, 128 bytes

Yes
?- sentence(Structure,What,[]).
```

```
Structure = [program, crashes, computer]
What = [the, program, crashes, the, computer] ;

Structure = [program, runs, computer]
What = [the, program, runs, the, computer] ;

Structure = [program, runs, plant]
What = [the, program, runs, the, plant] ;

Structure = [computer, runs, program]
What = [the, computer, runs, the, program] ;

Structure = [computer, runs, plant]
What = [the, computer, runs, the, plant] ;

No
```

5.7   From a Simple Parse to Structure to Meaning

Once the sentence has been successfully parsed (and the higher-level structure is evident from the parse), the deeper meaning of the sentence may be determined. This is shown in Figure 5.7.

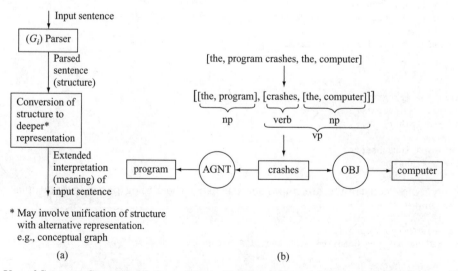

Figure 5.7 Use of Sentence Structural Information in Understanding. (a) Steps (b) Hypothetical Conversion from Parser-Provided Structure to Representation of Meaning

5.8 Feature Structure–Based Representation and Manipulation

This chapter (as well as Chapter 4) emphasize IS situations wherein we seek solutions where "things fit." In more quantitative terms, a CSP is satisfied. Specific examples included CSP (labeling) problems as well as problems with structural constraints imposed via phase structure grammars.

5.8.1 Motivations

In this section, we consider the generalizations and extensions of previous strategies for structural CSPs. This leads to strategies based upon feature structures (FS).

The Limitations of Context–Free Grammars and Term Unification

CFGs are not quite powerful enough for use with natural languages. We are, however, interested in retaining some notion of unification as a general processing strategy. To do this, we seek to define and implement a more general type of representation and unification. One strategy is to look at *Unification Grammars* and *Feature Structures*. This yields a framework for computational semantics that is suitable for parsing and generation.

The Limitations of Prolog and First–Order Logic

The built-in unification mechanism in Prolog is quite useful. Recall, however: *Prolog implements first-order logic.* As simplistic as this statement may appear, it alludes to our interest in higher-order logics and alternative representations. The principal constraint on a first-order logic is that *variables may not be used as placeholders for predicate names.* This is more than an issue of representational convenience; the concept of unification when the predicate names are not constant raises a number of important theoretical issues. As shown in Section 5.8.2, there are potential "workarounds" to allow this type of Prolog representation, however the basic issue of how unification should proceed in this case is complex.

An Extension: The Head–Driven Phrase Structure Grammar

The Head-Driven Phrase Structure Grammar (HPSG) is an approach to grammatical theory that seeks to model human languages more generally as systems of constraints [CFPS06, LM]. Typed FS (defined in the following section) have a central role in this grammatical model. HPSG research is conducted by a consortium of research institutions. Good starting points are http://hpsg.stanford.edu/ and http://www.ling.ohio-state.edu/research/hpsg. An example of the representation of the verb "put" in the HPSG is shown in Figure 5.8.

5.8.2 Feature Structures (FS) and Basic Properties

Unification Grammars and Feature Structures

Unification grammars encode knowledge as a declarative specification of constraints. Within the unification-based grammar framework, a complex data structure referred to as a feature structure

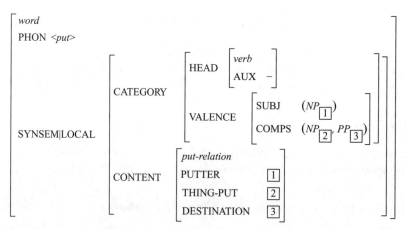

Figure 5.8 HPSG Representation of the Verb "put" (adapted from [ref], tutorial available at http://purl.org/dm/papers/all2-hpsg.pdf)

$$
\begin{bmatrix}
Feature_1 & Value_1 \\
Feature_2 & Value_2 \\
... & \\
Feature_n & Value_n
\end{bmatrix}
$$

Figure 5.9 Very Simple ("Hello World") FS to Illustrate FS Concept

[Kni89, Shi86], or functional description [Kay85], encodes information from various sources as feature/value pairs. Perhaps the simplest FS is shown in Figure 5.9. By noting that values may themselves be FS, more complex (and useful) FS are possible.

FS: Formal Definition. A feature structure may be viewed as a partial function from features to their values [Shi86]. For instance, a function mapping the feature object onto the value *house* and mapping viewpoint onto *top* would be represented in a feature structure notation as shown in Figure 5.10. More complex feature structures contain partial functions from features to values that are themselves feature structures, as shown in Figure 5.11.

FS: Related Definitions and Properties. Feature structures are related to frames (Chapter 8) and are similar in appearance to "record"-like structures in some programming languages. They are useful as a data structure in certain CSPs, especially when operations such as generalization, specialization, and unification are desirable. FS may quantify concepts, as well as instances of these concepts. FS are also potentially useful in information fusion.

Relationship to First-Order Logic

Feature structures resemble first-order logic terms but have several important distinctions [Kni89]. The first difference is that feature substructures are labeled symbolically. First-order terms require strict ordering of information; feature structures lift this restriction by labeling the information and,

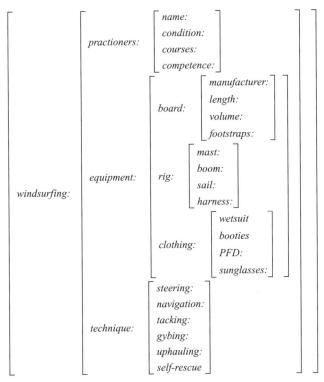

Figure 5.10 Example of Feature Structure (concept: windsurfing)

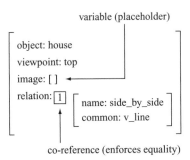

Figure 5.11 Second Feature Structure Example Including Variables and Co-Reference

therefore, the information in the FSs must be considered in an order-independent fashion. The second distinction is that fixed arity is not required. Feature structures may represent partial information. Feature structures containing partial information may be combined into larger structures, assuming no conflict of information occurs. Furthermore, the distinction between function and argument is removed. This aspect of FSs is termed the *demoted functor*. In first-order terms, the functor (function symbol that begins the term) has a special significance. In feature structures, all information has equal status. The last distinction is that variables and co-references are treated separately (see

Figure 5.11). Variables in first-order terms serve two purposes: placeholders for future instantiations and enforcement of equality constraints among different parts of the term. In FSs, these two purposes are served by different means. Co-reference, or marking attributes with the same value label, forces the attributes to share the same value. The FS variable [ ] does not enforce equality constraints, but simply serves as a placeholder that may unify with any other feature structure.

Prolog Implementations

Implementation of FSs may be accomplished in a variety of ways and in a variety of languages, including Prolog, Lisp, and C. The use of some form of "modified" list representation is somewhat obvious. In addition, the demoted functor (see Section 5.8.2) causes a problem with direct implementation in Prolog, since the tendency would be to allow predicate names to also be variables. However, Prolog does supply the "universal term" construct, as shown in Figure 5.12.

```
1 ?- help('=..').
?Term =..  ?List
     List is a list which head is the functor of Term and
     the remaining arguments are the arguments of the term.
     Each of the arguments may be a variable, but not both.
     This predicate is called 'Univ'.  Examples:

         ?- foo(hello, X) =.. List.

         List = [foo, hello, X]

         ?- Term =.. [baz, foo(1)]

         Term = baz(foo(1))


Yes
2 ?- predname(arg1,arg2,arg3)=..Converted_List.

Converted_List = [predname,arg1,arg2,arg3]


Yes
3 ?- predname(arg1,arg2,arg3)=..Converted_List,Get_it_back =.. Converted_List.

Get_it_back = predname(arg1, arg2, arg3)
Converted_List = [predname,arg1,arg2,arg3]


Yes
4 ?-
```

Figure 5.12 Using the Prolog =.. Construct

5.8.3 Feature Structure-Based Manipulation

In this section, we illustrate the power and application of FSs to a recognition problem in computer vision. The process of model-based recognition consists of matching features, which include geometrical, syntactical, and relational information, extracted from a given input image with those of the models. Unification, a common matching method in model-based computer vision [Sch89], is the single operation used to manipulate feature structure-based representations [Shi86].

Posets, Lattices, and Feature Structures

The feature structure-based representation technique relies heavily on the use of lattices for visualization and manipulation. The lattice concept is fundamantal to order theory, where one considers arbitrary partially ordered sets.

A relation R on the set L is a *partial order* if R is reflexive, antisymmetric,[4] and transitive [Lau84]. The symbol $\leq$, rather than R, is often used to denote a partial order. Note that while this symbol looks like the "less than or equal to" symbol, it merely symbolizes whatever relation we are using.

The relation we will use is *subsumption* (defined shortly). Thus, in terms of a (binary) relation, "a subsumes b," $a \rightarrow b$, and $a \leq b$ all mean the same thing.

A *lattice* is a *partially ordered set*, or *poset*, $(L, \leq)$ in which every subset $\{a, b\}$ consisting of two elements has a *least upper bound* (LUB) and a *greatest lower bound* (GLB). The LUB of two elements a and b is called the *join* of a and b, denoted by $\text{JOIN}(\{a, b\})$. Likewise, the GLB of two elements a and b is called the *meet* of a and b, denoted by $\text{MEET}(\{a, b\})$. A nonempty subset S of a lattice L is called a *sublattice* of L if both the $\text{JOIN}(\{a, b\})$ and $\text{MEET}(\{a, b\})$ are contained within the sublattice S whenever a and b are elements of S. A lattice is a special type of lattice, denoted a bounded lattice, if it has a greatest element I and a least element O.

The partial ordering relation used in this work is *subsumption*. As we show, the process of FS *unification* consists of finding a LUB (join) of two structures. Similarly, the process of *generalization* consists of finding a GLB (meet) of two feature structures.

Simple Lattice Example. Figure 5.13 shows a graphical depiction of a simple lattice consisting of elements a through h. The relation is indicated by an (undirected) arc; by convention the direction of the relation is indicated by vertical height. In other words, all edges point upward.[5]

Relevant Definitions [KB84]. Consider three elements, a, b, and c. In what follows, these elements will be FS. The following are important points:

1. a is a *lower bound* for b and c with order relation "$\leq$" iff $a \leq b$ and $a \leq c$.

2. a is a *greatest lower bound* (GLB) for b and c if a is a lower bound for b and c AND if d is any lower bound of b and c AND $d \leq a$.

3. a is an *upper bound* for b and c with order relation "$\leq$" iff $b \leq a$ and $c \leq a$.

---

[4] Antisymmetric: $\forall (x, y) \in R$ *with* $x \neq y$, $(y, x) \notin R$.
[5] This yields a Hasse diagram and helps conceptualization of the "upper" and "lower" bounds concepts.

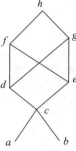

Figure 5.13 Graphical Depiction of a Simple Lattice (Hasse Diagram). Arrows are Implied at *Top* of Arcs.

4. a is a *least upper bound* (LUB) for b and c if a is an upper bound for b and c AND if d is any upper bound of b and c AND $a \leq d$.

In what follows, the ordering relation "$\leq$" is *subsumption*. $a \leq b$ means "a subsumes b." In other words, FS a's information is a subset of that in FS b. If $b \leq a$ and $c \leq a$, then a is an upper bound of b and c. The LUB is, in terms of subsumption, the most general. Compare this with the formal definition of the unification of FS b and c as follows.

GLB/LUB Examples.   Suppose in Figure 5.13 $A = \{a, b, c, d, e, f, g, h\}$ and $B = \{a, b\}$. Upper bounds (UBs) of B in the lattice are c, d, e, f, g, h; the LUB of B is c. Furthermore, if $B_2 = \{d, e\}$, the GLB of B_2 is c.

Unification Using Feature Structures

Unification has been studied in a number of computer-related fields such as natural language processing, logic programming, theorem proving, computational complexity, and computability theory [Kni89]. Abstractly stated, the unification problem is the following: Given two descriptions x and y, can we find an object z that fits both descriptions?

Unification is the basis of information-combining in FSs ([LS92], [Kni89], [Shi86], [Kay85]). Unification of FSs results in a new structure that contains all of the information from the two structures to be unified, assuming no attribute/value pairs contain conflicting information. Figures 5.14, 5.15, and 5.16 illustrate sample FS unification cases. Unification of FSs can be defined with the introduction of the partial ordering relation *subsumption*.

Subsumption.   Recall the ordering relation "$\leq$" used is *subsumption*. $D' \leq D$ means "D' subsumes D." Intuitively, feature structure D *subsumes* feature structure D' (denoted $D \leq D'$) if D contains a subset of the information in D'. More precisely:

A complex FS D subsumes a complex FS D' if and only if $D(l) \leq D'(l)$ for all l contained in the $dom(D)$ and $D'(p) = D'(q)$ for all paths p and q such that $D(p) = D(q)$ [Shi86].

$$
\begin{bmatrix} \text{object: house} \\ \text{viewpoint: front} \end{bmatrix} \sqcup \begin{bmatrix} \text{box: [ ]} \\ \text{triangle: [ ]} \\ \text{relation:} \begin{bmatrix} \text{name: on\_top\_of} \\ \text{top\_component: triangle} \\ \text{bottom\_component: box} \end{bmatrix} \end{bmatrix}
$$

$$
= \begin{bmatrix} \text{object: house} \\ \text{viewpoint: front} \\ \text{box: [ ]} \\ \text{triangle: [ ]} \\ \text{relation:} \begin{bmatrix} \text{name: on\_top\_of} \\ \text{top\_component: triangle} \\ \text{bottom\_component: box} \end{bmatrix} \end{bmatrix}
$$

Figure 5.14 Sample Unification of Feature Structures (houses)

$$
\begin{bmatrix} \text{rig:} \begin{bmatrix} \text{mast: carbon} \\ \text{boom: bic} \\ \text{sail: neil pryde} \\ \text{harness: none} \end{bmatrix} \end{bmatrix} \sqcup \begin{bmatrix} \text{board:} \begin{bmatrix} \text{manufacturer: mistral} \\ \text{length: 355cm} \\ \text{volume: 200L} \\ \text{footstraps: none} \end{bmatrix} \end{bmatrix}
$$

$$
= \begin{bmatrix} \text{rig:} \begin{bmatrix} \text{mast: carbon} \\ \text{boom: bic} \\ \text{sail: neil pryde} \\ \text{harness: none} \end{bmatrix} \\ \text{board:} \begin{bmatrix} \text{manufacturer: mistral} \\ \text{length: 355cm} \\ \text{volume: 200L} \\ \text{footstraps: none} \end{bmatrix} \end{bmatrix}
$$

Figure 5.15 Another Example of FS Unification (windsurfing example)

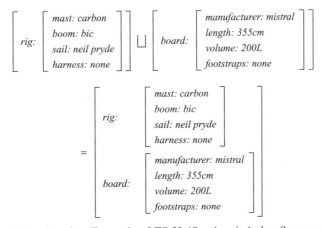

Figure 5.16 Third Example of FS Unification (involves co-reference). Top: Unification defined by Subsumption. Bottom: Graph Unification (adapted from [MCC00]).

The notation $D(l)$ denotes the value associated with the feature l in the FS D and the domain of an FS D, $dom(D)$, consists of the features in the FS D. For example, in Figure 5.11:

D(object) = house

and

Dom(D) = object, viewpoint, image, relation

A feature structure with an empty domain is called an empty feature structure or a variable. A path in an FS is a sequence of features that can be used to pick out a particular subpart of an FS by repeated application and is denoted $D(p)$. In Figure 5.11, an example path (sequence of features) is $D(< relation, common >) = v\_line$. In addition, an atomic feature structure neither subsumes nor is subsumed by a different atomic feature structure. Variables subsume all other feature structures, atomic or complex, because, as the trivial case, they contain no information at all. As a partial ordering relation, subsumption is reflexive, antisymmetric, and transitive.

Recall "a subsumes b," $a \rightarrow b$, and $a \leq b$ all refer to the relation involving FS a and b. Also note that a general FS subsumes more specific ones.

Formal Definition of FS Unification

Unification of FSs D' and D'' is the most general feature structure D, such that D' subsumes D and D'' subsumes D [Shi86]. The partial ordering imposed by subsumption provides a framework or lattice for characterizing unification [Kni89]. Figure 5.17 shows a portion of a lattice containing simple feature structures augmented with two special terms called top ($\top$) and bottom ($\perp$); making the lattice a bounded lattice.

Unification in Lattices.   Unification corresponds to finding the least upper bound (LUB; join) of two feature structures in the lattice.[6] The "join" is a good mnemonic, because that is what we do with the (required consistent) information in the FS. Recall join is viewed as a form of union. If $D' \leq D$ and $D'' \leq D$, then D is an upper bound of D' and D''. The LUB is, in terms of subsumption, the most general FS.

Figure 5.17 shows the unification of FSs within a partial lattice of FSs (arrows point to the unifying FS of two FSs). The top of the lattice ($\top$) is also called the *universal variable* because it is the trivial case of containing no information and subsumes all other FSs in the lattice. The bottom of the lattice ($\perp$), to which all pairs of terms can unify, represents inconsistency. If the greatest lower bound of two terms is $\perp$, then they are not unifiable.

Generalization.   The process of *generalization* consists of finding a GLB (meet) of two FSs. Recall meet is akin to intersection. As shown in Figure 5.17, unification and generalization correspond to traversals in opposite directions in the lattice.

---

[6]In other works involving subsumption and lattices of FS ([Kni89]), the subsumption relation used is the inverse of this, resulting in a lattice that indicates the dual poset $(L, \geq)$. Upper bounds in $(L, \leq)$ correspond to lower bounds in $(L, \geq)$ and vice versa.

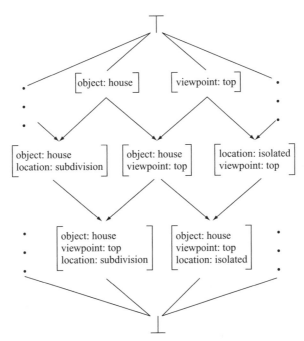

Figure 5.17 Lattice Consisting of Unified Feature Structures. (*Note direction of subsumption relation.*) Unification Corresponds to Moving Down the Lattice; Generalization Corresponds to Moving Up.

Computational Cost of FS Unification

The computational cost and efficiency of systems based on the use of the FS representation has long been of concern to the computational linguistics community [Tro93]. Unification of two FSs has been defined in terms of subsumption ordering. One major obstacle to processing "large" grammars using FS-based frameworks, such as the HPSG, is the time and space cost of the subsumption ordering-based unification process itself. Computationally, it is advantageous to consider *graph unification*, as illustrated in Figure 5.16. Unification of two FSs, represented as directd acyclic graphs (DAGs), is much more computationally efficient using a variation of the Union-Find algorithm [MCC00]. Whereas early algorithms ran in exponential time [Kni89], ones employing graph representations are almost able to achieve linear time [Kog93].

5.8.4 Feature Structure Representation Enhancements

Disjunctive Features

Disjunctive features are characterized by a feature that may be specified by a set of values, at least one of which must be its true value. Disjunctive features are often seen as a logical construct that is useful in describing feature generalizations within the FS representation. There are many useful classes of feature structures that cannot be modeled by using only a single partial FS [Kas93]. Disjunctive features are a way to model these classes of FSs and still maintain the simplicity of the representation.

A sample of a computer vision-based disjunctive feature is shown in Figure 5.18. The curly brackets ({ }) indicate disjunction. The disjunctive feature's value may be any one of the structures inside the brackets. All feature value possibilities are maintained when performing unification.

Range-Valued and Multivalued Features

Another extension to the basic FS is the use of range-valued and multivalued features. The features defined in terms of range-valued and multivalued may take on more than one value. An example of a range-valued feature is also shown in Figure 5.18. To distinguish range-valued from multivalued, the range-valued feature is defined by a range of values, usually numerical in nature. A multivalued feature may be defined by any set of values, not necessarily related as in range-valued features.

5.8.5   Rules as Feature Structures

Rules in a unification grammar define how FSs can be manipulated to build new FSs. A key aspect of unification grammars is that a rule can be represented as an FS [LS92]. Application of a rule proceeds by attempting to unify the FS representation of the rule with the current feature structure representation of system information. Rule application is permitted if the current FS does not violate any constraints represented as feature/value pairs of the rule. The unification process simultaneously enforces the constraints of the rule and builds the new FS that is specified by the rule. Figure 5.19 illustrates the concept.

5.8.6   Lattices of Feature Structures

The lattice of partially ordered feature structures is a very important structuring element and visualization tool. Conceptually, there are three lattices of concern addressed here: the infinite lattice, the enumerated lattice, and the search lattice.

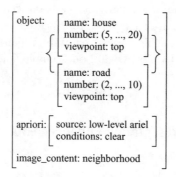

Figure 5.18 Use of Disjunctive and Range-Valued Features to Represent Image Information

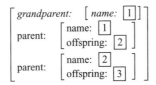

Figure 5.19 "Grandparent" Rule as FS

The Infinite Lattice, L_I

The *infinite lattice*, denoted L_I, is the representation that would exist if all possible models and elements that could be modeled within a physical world were modeled. However, there will always exist more elements than can be physically represented within a computer vision system (a model is always incomplete) and, therefore, this lattice is impossible to realize. The infinite lattice is the conceptual whole from which the subset of elements to be modeled in a computer vision system will be taken.

The Enumerated Lattice, L_E

The *enumerated lattice*, denoted L_E, is the lattice that, in theory, could be produced given the entire set of FS object models, FS rules, and FS inputs modeled. This lattice consists of all FS unification paths that are possible, given the set of objects and object components modeled as FS and the set of rules expressed as FSs. Within sections of the enumerated lattice, locality of information is readily apparent. As shown in Figure 5.20, portions of the enumerated lattice can be identified as containing information about things such as houses, cars, or character information. These areas may overlap where there are areas of common features, such as boxes or circles or the common structure of line information. This locality of information within the enumerated lattice is beneficial in partitioning the rules expressed as FSs into sets for the purposes of unification and search.

The Search Lattice, L_S

The *search lattice*, denoted L_S, is the lattice that is actually produced in the search through the enumerated lattice during the determination of image content. This lattice contains only the FSs and FS unification paths that are produced in the current search through the enumerated lattice to reach a goal. The search lattice is the subset of the enumerated lattice explored during the search to the goal state.

5.8.7 Lattice Processing Directions

One of the most significant and open problems in using FSs is choice of what rules to use and what FSs to unify. This is our old friend conflict resolution, and FSs, in themselves, do little to facilitate this.

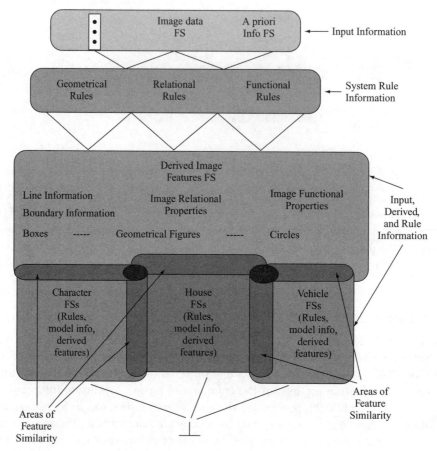

Figure 5.20 Example of Possible Arrangement of Features within a Lattice (image processing/computer vision application)

The Search Problem Within the Lattice of Feature Structures

Search is one of the central issues in problem-solving systems [TB92]. It occurs whenever the system is faced with a choice from a number of alternatives, where each choice leads to the need to make further choices, and so on until the problem is solved.

A general search problem is characterized by the following [Par91, Sch90]: a set of system states that represent the problem state space, a set of initial system states contained in the set of system states, a set of transformations (operators, rules) that can transform one state into another, and a set of goal states contained in the set of system states. Thus, problem solving is represented as finding and applying a sequence of operators that will transform an initial system state, through a sequence of intermediate states, into a system goal state.

Any problem represented by the lattice of FSs still embodies a general search problem. The set of system states that represent the problem state space are contained in L_E. The initial system state is the input data and a priori information input into the system as a feature structure. The set of transformations (operators, rules) that can transform one state into another are the rules expressed as FSs within the enumerated lattice. Finally, the set of goal states contained in the set of system states could be the world models of the objects or scenes possibly contained in the input image. The search problem consists of finding and applying a sequence of FS rules that will transform initial data and a priori information (initial system state) into a system goal state containing the explanation of the input data as an expanded FS.

A possible solution path through the lattice, if it exists, may be visualized for small problems; however, with even modest problems, there are many possible search lattices. The decision of which FSs to unify in the production of a search lattice must be chosen from many possible applicable feature structures in the system. The critical problem-solving step is to determine which grammar rules expressed as FSs are appropriate at the given time and then decide which FSs may be unified with the chosen grammar rule.

FS-Based Generalization

The option of generalization is also available in the search through the lattice. Generalization is often referred to as the dual of unification [Kni89]. Within the lattice framework, unification corresponds to finding the GLB of two FSs contained in the lattice. Alternately, generalization corresponds to finding the LUB of two FSs contained in the lattice. The top of the lattice (T), to which all pairs of terms can generalize, is also called the *universal term* or *universal variable*. Every feature structure contained in the lattice is an instance of this term [Kni89].

Generalization is used to point to common aspects within data and also point to other promising solution paths to explore. Sample generalization operators are shown in Chapter 16, Section 16.3.11. They include the dropping condition operator and the constants to variables operator. The dropping condition operator relaxes conditions required by a grammar rule FS. The constants to variables operator relaxes required values contained in the FS models to variables. In this method, general aspects of a world model or FS grammar rule are retained, but some specifics of the model or rule may be relaxed to allow the unification search path through the lattice to proceed in other directions so that a viable solution may be determined.

5.9 Exercises

1. The list-based output from the Prolog sentence generator and parser is acceptable, but perhaps a more familiar output could be generated. Consider a Prolog predicate to print the resulting sentence (still without capitalization and a period). Suppose we have:

```
alist([my,dog,has,fleas]).
goal :- alist(X), printAlist(X).
```

The desired behavior is as follows:

```
?- goal.
my dog has fleas

Yes
```

2. Modify the Prolog-based language generator and parser for the ($G1$) grammar such that questions are generated and parsed. First, develop the revised grammar, then the Prolog implementation. An example use is shown below:

```
?- question([can, the, program, crash, a, computer],[]).

Yes
```

3. Modify the grammar of Section 5.6.4 to enable formation and recognition of compound sentences using the connectives "and," "or," and "but." For example, the following should be generated and parsed:

```
[a, program, crashes, a, program, and, a, program, crashes, a, program]
[a, program, crashes, a, program, and, a, program, crashes, a, system]
[a, program, crashes, a, program, and, a, program, crashes, a, computer]
 .
 .
 .
[a, computer, runs, the, program, and, a, program, crashes, a, system]
[a, computer, runs, the, program, and, a, program, crashes, a, computer]
[a, computer, runs, the, program, and, a, program, crashes, the, program]
 .
 .
 .
[the, program, runs, a, computer, but, the, program, runs, the, system]
[the, program, runs, a, computer, but, the, program, runs, the, computer]
[the, program, runs, a, computer, but, the, system, crashes, a, program]
```

4. In the preceding problem, can you design a grammar and a corresponding Prolog implementation such that longer (multiple connectives are used) compound sentences are generated?

5. Modify the $G1$ generator/parser so paragraphs are generated and recognized. Recall a paragraph should be longer than one sentence.

6. A student attempted to solve the $G1$ meaningful semantics (context) problem with the following solution:

```
sentence([Subject,Verb,Object]) --> np(Subject), vp([Verb,Object]),
                              {agree(Subject,Verb,Object)}.

agree(program,runs,What) :- What \= program.
agree(program,crashes,What) :- What \= program.

agree(Something, run, program) :- Something \= program.
```

```
agree(computer,runs,Something) :- Something \= computer.
agree(Something, runs, computer) :- Something \= computer.

agree(Something, crashes, computer).

agree(_,runs,plant).
```

Does this accomplish the objective?

7. Modify the $G1$ sentence generator and corresponding parser such that sentences are generated (and parsed) with an optional adverb, and an optional noun phrase as part of the verb phrase. For example, the following are examples of the type of sentences produced:

   'the quarterback accurately throws the ball' 'the quarterback throws accurately.

   Begin your solution by showing the revised productions.

8. Predict $|L(G1)|$ as a function of the number of nouns, verbs, and modifiers.

9. This makes an excellent project. Note that our Prolog parsers and generators require input sentences in (Prolog) list form. After studying Prolog's reading and writing predicates, revise the parser/generator so that sentences to be parsed are input as strings. This requires subsequent conversion into a Prolog list.

   Repeat the effort for generated sentences.

10. Using SWI Prolog, a number of graphical tools are available to help you see the sequence of Prolog goals spawned in the generation or parse of a sentence. Consider the following modification to the previous goal used in Section 5.6.3:

```
/* tracing and goal */

goal :- spy(sentence), spy(np), spy(vp), spy(adj),
        spy(noun), spy(verb), guitracer,
        sentence([the,program,crashes,the,computer],[]).
```

11. In the example of Section 5.6.4, is it possible for a syntactically correct sentence to satisfy both sentence predicates in the Prolog database? Show an example.

12. In Section 5.6.4 it was asserted (but not shown) that a very small change in the language sentence structure and dictionary size yielded a substantial increase in the cardinality of $L(G)$. Determine the cardinality of $L(G)$ in this case.

13. In Section 5.5.2 it was stated that Sets V_T and V_N are required to be disjoint. Discuss the consequences if this constraint does not hold.

14. Show the result of unifying each of the following feature structures:

   (a) $\begin{bmatrix} \text{Feature1} & \text{Value1} \end{bmatrix} \sqcup \begin{bmatrix} \text{Feature2} & \text{Value2} \end{bmatrix}$

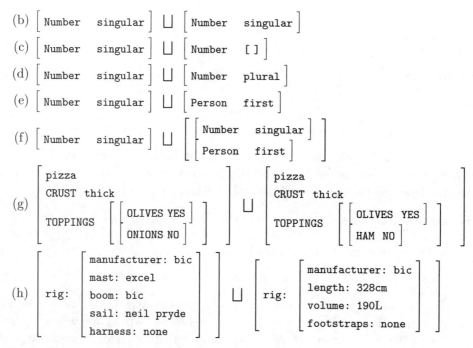

15. Verify the FS unification shown in Figure 5.14 using:

    (a) The definition of subsumption; and

    (b) The concept of a LUB.

16. The purpose of this problem is to compare and contrast the feature structure paradigm with two other IS technologies, namely:

    (a) Ontologies (Chapter 2); and

    (b) Frames (Chapter 8).

Specifically, we are interested in the similarities and differences among the three representational schemes (and their corresponding manipulation strategies, where applicable). Develop a table for comparison. What can you do with one that cannot be done with others? For example,[7] you might address the following issues:

    (a) Consider the concept of *inheritance* as it might apply to each.

    (b) How is each manipulated?

    (c) Can each of these representational schemes be easily modified or updated?

17. Suppose FS a and FS b are unifiable and their unification yields FS c. Must c be unique? (Hint: This may be recast as a question regarding the uniqueness of the LUB.)

---

[7] This is not all-inclusive.

18. This chapter considered the pairwise attempted unification of FS. A reasonable question is whether this is necessary, i.e., can we consider the unification of more than two FS? Specifically, suppose we are interested in determining $a \sqcup b \sqcup c$. Consider several viewpoints:

(a) Successive pairwise unification (e.g., $a \sqcup b$ and $b \sqcup c$, followed by unification of the results).

(b) Observation that a LUB is defined for a set of elements with cardinality greater than 2.

(c) Use of the subsumption definition.

19. Each FS below is "indexed" by a bold numeric label above the FS. This has nothing to do with co-reference, but just makes referring to the FS easier. *Use this label in place of rewriting each FS in this problem.* Using the relation "subsumes," arrange the following FS in a lattice.

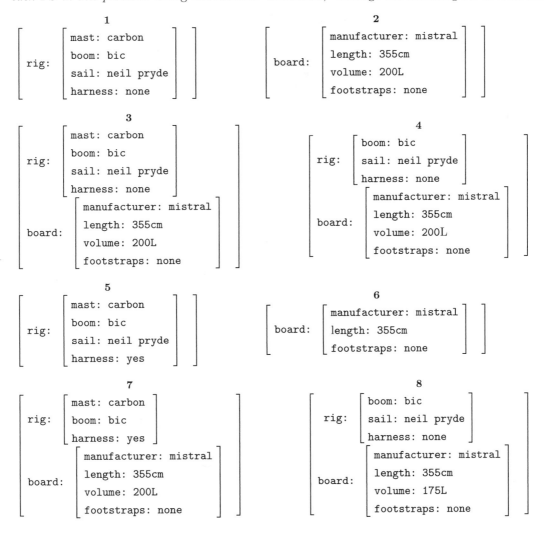

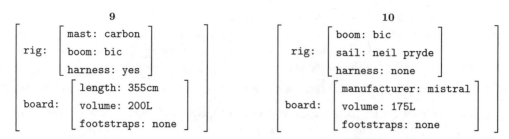

20. Refer to Figure 5.17, which shows the portion of a "house" lattice. Consider now the FS shown in Figure 5.21. As the notes indicate, curly brackets ({ }) indicate disjunction. The disjunctive feature's value may be any one of the structures inside the brackets.

$$\begin{bmatrix} \text{object: house} \\ \text{viewpoint: top} \\ \text{location: } \{ \text{ subdivision, isolated } \} \end{bmatrix}$$

Figure 5.21 House Feature Structure Using Disjunction

Show, clearly and unambiguously, where the FS of Figure 5.21 would be inserted into the lattice of Figure 5.17.

## chapter 6

From Logic-Based Chaining to Production Systems

6.1 Conceptual Background and Motivation

This chapter introduces IS representation and manipulation strategies based upon the rule-based inference paradigm. We approach this topic from both the mathematical (logic) and implementation (software) viewpoints. The rule-based paradigm is powerful, popular, and leads to the notion of a production system. Examples of production systems and implementations are treated in depth in Chapters 7, 8, and 9. In addition, many agents (Chapter 8, Section 8.9) are rule-based [GLC+95], [Kat02].

6.2 The Role of Logic in IS Representation and Manipulation

The discipline of mathematical logic is a subset of discrete mathematics. A systematic study of symbolic logic dates back to Aristotle (384–322 B.C.), however the results that have been of practical importance are credited to George Boole (1815–1864 A.D.), thus the label "Boolean" algebra.

Logic serves both representation and manipulation roles in IS. Logic-based approaches are introduced first for several reasons:

- Logic is familiar to most engineers and computer scientists;

- Logic-based representations are manipulated in a mathematically sound manner;

- Logic embodies the implication connective, which leads directly to the notion of an IF-THEN based rule structure; and

- Logic includes the predicate calculus, wherein we allow variables in the representation. This leads to the important concept of *unification*.

- Logic suggests a number of manipulation strategies for logic-based representations, most notably Modus Ponens (MP). This leads directly to the concept of chaining.

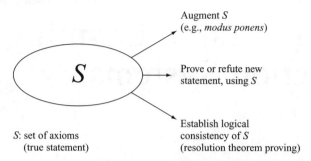

Figure 6.1 Using Logic in IS

Logic Utility.   In logic-based IS representations, facts are stored as axioms. An axiom is a statement that is always TRUE. Typically, in a logic-based approach, the truth value of a statement is to be proved (or refuted). If a logical representation is complete, all the logical consequences that follow from the axioms are derivable (as theorems). This is shown in Figure 6.1.

Limitations of Logic.   Logic can be used to rigorously prove (or disprove) the truth value of statements. At first glance, it appears that if the concepts of reasoning and intelligent behavior could be completely formalized using mathematical logic, IS implementation would be straightforward. Unfortunately, this is not the case for several reasons:

- Humans displaying intelligent behavior do not always reason by making (observable) logical inferences; and

- Logic is too rigorous and inflexible to be of use in all IS problem domains.

- Logic may not capture the "deeper" meaning of statements (see Section 6.3.9).

6.2.1   Inference and the Vocabulary of Logic

The vocabulary of logic includes a plethora of terms such as "statement," "clause," "expression," "proposition," "sentence," etc. Figure 6.2 summarizes the vocabulary of logic, and provides a road map for our initial study.

Statement.   Logic uses mathematical symbols to represent statements. A statement (or a proposition or an assertion) is a declarative sentence that is either TRUE or FALSE.

Inference.   Inference is the process of deducing (new) facts from (other) existing facts.

Deduction.   Deduction is a logically sound and systematic inference procedure.

Induction.   Induction is reasoning from a part to the whole, which, in the context of learning, may involve agglomeration or classification of new information into larger entities.

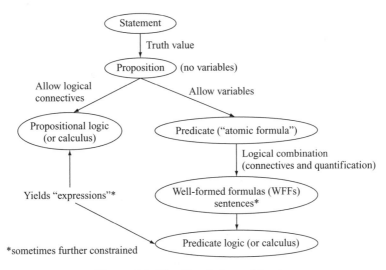

Figure 6.2 The Vocabulary of Logic

6.2.2 Other Logic Families

This chapter concerns classical, binary-valued, first-order logic. Other useful logics exist and are addressed in other chapters. They include multivalued logic, nonmonotonic logic, modal logic, temporal logic, and fuzzy logic.

6.3 Logic–Based Underpinnings of Rule–Based Chaining Systems
6.3.1 The Implication Connective

The reader may wish to review the mathematical basis of implication [KB84] [Joh86]. *Implication is a logical connective.* A basic statement using implication is of the form "IF p THEN q," or "p implies q." Most often, this is written

$$p \rightarrow q \tag{6.1}$$

Implication uses the truth values of statements p and q to form a compound statement in logic. This compound statement has a truth value that is a function of the truth values of p and q. p does not cause q, in fact the underlying *meanings* of statements p and q may be unrelated. The truth table for implication is shown in Table 6.1. Note the equivalence:

$$(p \rightarrow q) \equiv (\neg p \cup q)$$

p	q	$p \rightarrow q$	$\neg p \cup q$
T	T	T	T
T	F	F	F
F	T	T	T
F	F	T	T

Table 6.1 Truth Table for Implication and Equivalence

6.3.2 An Implication-Based IS Rule Example

Consider a simplistic rule of the (abstract) form:

$$\text{IF } p \text{ THEN } q$$

for example: "IF The weather is clear, THEN I can go fishing." Here, p is denoted the rule antecedent ("The weather is clear") and q is denoted the consequent ("I can go fishing"). The rule is of the form $p \rightarrow q$. Moreover, p and q may themselves be compound statements. For example: "IF The weather is clear AND I have my fishing pole AND I do not have to work, THEN I can go fishing AND enjoy myself."

6.3.3 Rule-Based Representation Examples

Rule-based systems are a natural means to express observed knowledge. Thus, a rule-based paradigm is a natural choice for expert system implementation. Rule-based (expert) systems are typically:

1. Based upon IF-THEN-(implication) based representations of knowledge obtained from expert query; and

2. Applied in narrowly defined problem domains.

An example of a rule from the DENDRAL [LBFL80] expert system is shown as follows. DENDRAL is one of the oldest expert systems (ES), having been developed in 1964 (in Lisp). A typical DENDRAL rule might be [HK85]:

```
IF
the molecule spectrum has two peaks at masses x1 and x2
such that

x1 + x2 = M + 28          AND

x1 - 28 is a "high" peak    AND

x2 - 28 is a "high" peak    AND

at least one of the x1 or x2 is high

THEN

The molecule contains a ketone group.
```

Another sample rule, taken from an online technical support example, is

```
if 'symptom' = 'Label Designer hangs on converting databases dialog'
            and ('BackTrack Version'  <=  '4.10')

            and 'second edition' = 'yes'
            and (operating_system = 'Windows 98 Second Edition'
            or operating_system = 'Windows 98')
        then problem = 'Win 98se.'
```

6.3.4 Business Rules and Engines

An emerging application for rule-based representations is in business rules. Almost any business follows rules or constraints that govern the operations of the business. While these rules may be informal, there is a growing trend to formalize, quantify, document, and share these rules with other businesses, customers, and regulatory agencies.

Rules may apply to many facets of the business operation. They may constrain the behavior of the business and its employees, indicate company sales (and refund) practices, define legal behavior, or facilitate the automation of company operations.

For IS purposes, we are interested in rules and rule engines that follow the rule-based chaining paradigm. As a quick web search will show, there are many vendors of business rules software and engines. Some examples follow.

The Rule Markup Initiative.   The objective of this effort is the design of a shared Rule Markup Language (RuleML), permitting both forward (bottom-up) and backward (top-down) rules in XML for deduction, rewriting, and further inferential-transformational tasks. More information may be found at www.ruleml.org/

Drools.   Drools is an open source rules engine, written in Java. Drools uses the Rete algorithm. Rules are expressible in an XML-based syntax. Drools was rebranded as JBoss Rules, and acquired by Red Hat. More on Drools is available at www.ibm.com/developerworks/java/library/j-drools/

IBM CommonRules.   The IBM literature indicates: *CommonRules is a rule-based framework for developing rule-based applications with emphasis on maximum separation of business logic and data, conflict handling, and interoperability of rules.* Information on the current version of CommonRules can be found at http://alphaworks.ibm.com/tech/commonrules

Microsoft Business Rules.   Microsoft BizTalk is a suite of business process management software. Within this software, the business rule engine serves a number of functions, including implementation of forward chaining with an agenda and conflict resolution. For more information, see www.microsoft.com/biztalk.

6.3.5 Implication and Inference: Simple Modus Ponens (MP)

Modus Ponens (MP) is one basis for logical manipulation. MP leads to the concept of chaining, and is based upon the axiom:

$$\{(p \cap (p \rightarrow q)) \rightarrow q\} = T \tag{6.2}$$

Thus, given a rule (which itself is assumed to be TRUE) of the form $p \rightarrow q$, to prove $q \ (= T)$, we must verify $p \ (= T)$ in the database. Typically, Equation 6.2 is shown with the notation

$$
\begin{array}{c}
p \\
p \rightarrow q \\
\hline
q
\end{array}
\tag{6.3}
$$

Proof that Equation 6.2 is a tautology is left to the exercises.

6.3.6 Modus Ponens with Variables

Rules typically involve variables in order to enable a more general representation. For example, a rule indicating "X is the grandparent of Z" in the form of Equation 6.1 might look as follows:

$$[(\text{parent } X \ Y) \cap (\text{parent } Y \ Z)] \rightarrow (\text{grandparent } X \ Z) \tag{6.4}$$

Shared Variables.   In the example of Equation 6.4, notice the use of variables that appear multiple times (i.e., are shared) in the antecedent (i.e., variable Y) and those that are shared across the antecedent and consequent (i.e., variables X and Z). Shared variables are common in representations.

Binding.   Assignment of a value to a variable is called binding. Given a database of clauses of the form **(parent tom sally)**, etc., it is necessary to find a consistent set of bindings for variables X, Y, and Z in order to use the rule in Equation 6.4. Such a set of bindings is called a *unifying substitution*. Determination of unifying substitutions is treated in Section 6.3.7.

Revised MP Formulation for Variables in Rules.   To accommodate rules with variables, MP is revised as follows:

$$
\begin{array}{cl}
p^1 & \text{(statement(s) without variables)} \\
p \rightarrow q & \text{(rule with variables)} \\
(\exists \theta)(p^1 = p\theta) & \text{(unifying substitution)} \\
\hline
q^1 = q\theta &
\end{array}
\tag{6.5}
$$

6.3.7 The Concept and Process of Unification

To be useful, a rule-based IS must allow variables in the representation. Therefore, inference requires finding unifying substitutions (see Equation 6.5). This is the job of a unification algorithm.

Unification.   Unification is a systematic procedure that attempts to make two expressions identical ("unify them") by finding appropriate substitutions or bindings of variables (where necessary) in the expressions. *The basis of unification is* **consistent** *substitution*. This is defined next.

Substitution.   A substitution is a set of assignments of terms to variables, with no variable being assigned more than one term.

A set of expressions is unifiable if and only if there exists one or more (unifying) substitutions that make the expressions identical. Interestingly, substitution does not imply that all variables are assigned constants as their values (to produce grounded predicates), but rather allows the assignment of (other) variables to a variable.

Unification Approaches

The IS "unifier" consists of the implementation of one or more unification algorithms. In unification, two major classes of possible substitutions may occur. They are:

1. A variable may be replaced by a constant; and

2. A variable may be replaced by a variable.

For illustration, we consider the expressions to be unified represented in list form. Of course, other representations are possible. Given two statements to unify, the unification algorithm returns one of two things:

1. A list of the unifying substitutions (that may be empty if there are no substitutions required) and a report of success; or

2. A report of failure (FAIL) if unification is not possible.

Notation.   A single substitution of the term *substitution* for the term *substituted_for* is represented using the syntax (*substitution/substituted_for*). For example, we denote a substitution of the variable R with the constant value t, using the notation (t/R). This indicates that the value of R is bound to value t. An easy way to remember the notation t/R is that it corresponds to the assignment $R = t$ in many imperative languages.

Similarly, substitution of the variable $V1$ for variable $G1$ is denoted $(V1/G1)$. This indicates that the value of variable $G1$ is determined by variable $V1$. Note $V1$ may or may not have a value, or $V1$ may itself be bound to other variables.

Binding Environment.   A list of all current variable substitutions, or bindings, is called the substitution or *binding environment*. Recall when using MP with variables that the goal of unification is to determine a unifying substitution, if possible.

One difficult aspect of unification is achieving a set of consistent substitutions, in the sense that if we come to a unification step where a constant $c1$ has replaced a variable $V1$, i.e., $(c1/V1)$ is on the list of substitutions, then we cannot substitute any other value for $V1$. We could use $V1$ in other substitutions, i.e., $(V1/V2)$ might make sense if $V2$ is currently unbound.[1]

To accomplish unification on lists of elements, rather than single terms, we first determine how to accomplish unification on a single term. Then we employ recursion in the process, as shown in Section 6.3.7.

A Preliminary "Handworked" Unification Example

We use list-based notation for the example. Characters beginning with an uppercase letter are considered variables.

Finding a Unifying Substitution, Θ.   Suppose we are asked to unify statements:

$$p^1 = (left\_of\ block_1\ block_2)$$

and

$$p = (left\_of\ A\ B)$$

A unifying substitution is

$$\Theta = \{(block_1/A), (block_2/B)$$

for which $p\Theta = p^1$.

Using Θ.   Suppose a simple rule is of the $p \rightarrow q$ form:

$$(left\_of\ A\ B) \rightarrow (right\_of\ B\ A)$$

and our database contains

$$p^1 = (left\_of\ block_1\ block_2)$$

To employ forward chaining, we determine Θ, as shown, and given

$$q = (right\_of\ B\ A)$$

we use forward chaining and MP with variables to infer:

$$q^1 = q\Theta = (right\_of\ block_2\ block_1)$$

q^1 may then be added to the database of facts.

---

[1]In this specific case, it might be more efficient, if $V1$ is already bound to $c1$, to also bind (or substitute) $c1$ to (for) $V2$.

A More Complex Example

Consider the slightly more complex (list-based) representation:

$$(parent\ X\ Y) \cap (parent\ Y\ Z)] \rightarrow (grandparent\ X\ Z)$$

$$(parent\ tom\ bob)$$

$$(parent\ bob\ sam)$$

$$(parent\ sam\ mary)$$

consisting of one rule and three facts. **Notice that shared variables in the conjunction of the clauses forming the rule antecedent are involved**. One unifying substitution is:

$$\Theta = \{(tom/X), (bob/Y), (sam/Z)\}$$

which yields

$$q^1 = q\Theta$$

or

$$(grandparent\ X\ Z)\Theta = (grandparent\ tom\ sam)$$

The determination of other possible unifying substitutions is left to the reader.

A General Unifier: Algorithm

We briefly show the skeleton of a general unifier. Computational efficiency is not considered at this point. The more elegant, computationally efficient and almost-universal Rete approach is treated in depth in Chapter 7, Section 7.5. The approach shown here is highly recursive. The desired result is a yes/no answer concerning unification and, if unification succeeds, the resulting binding list (if nonempty). We assume the following data structures:

x,y: Input lists to be unified.

bindings: List of variable bindings so far.

Starting with an initial binding list, attempt to unify the first two corresponding elements of the two lists. If unsuccessful, fail. If successful, record the bindings generated, if any, and pass the (possibly modified binding list result) to the unifier for the remainder of the lists. Repeat until the ends of both lists are reached simultaneously, i.e., the algorithm is applied to a pair of empty lists.

6.3.8   Resolution (Proof by Refutation): An Alternative to MP

Overview

MP is only one possible basis for an inference technique. Here we present another approach based upon *resolution*. This approach also produces new clauses from an initial set, and it may be shown that all logically consistent clauses may be obtained using resolution. Thus, resolution is *logically complete*.

Application

Resolution is used to show that a set of clauses is logically inconsistent, in the sense that the resolution process produces a logical contradiction in the database. *A clause may be proven to be TRUE, in the context of a set of clauses known to be TRUE, by appending the logical NOT of this clause to the set and subsequently finding a contradiction.* Thus, resolution is a means of verifying the validity (i.e., truth value) of new statements by refutation, or contradiction. By arranging the original database in clause form (i.e., we do not allow implication but rather use the truth table equivalent) and adding the negated fact (actually a hypothesis), we are able to verify the truth of the hypothesis if a contradiction is generated.

Strategy

After augmenting the database with the negation of the desired hypothesis, clauses are resolved pairwise[2] in the augmented database until a contradiction is found (or, if none is generated, we conclude that the situation is consistent, and therefore the hypothesis is, in fact, FALSE).

The Basis for Resolution.

$$a \cup b \quad (T)$$

$$\neg a \cup c \quad (T)$$

$$b \cup c \quad (T)$$

which is equivalent to showing

$$[(a \cup b) \cap (\neg a \cup c)] \rightarrow (b \cup c)$$

is a tautology.

A Resolution Application

Consider the following example of resolution-based inference.

---

[2]Notice this does not indicate *which* clauses, i.e., some choice or decisions (search) are still necessary.

Initial Database (D1).   Note all statements are assumed TRUE and the database is (initially) assumed consistent.

$$p1 \quad (c1)$$

$$p1 \rightarrow q1 \quad (c2)$$

$$q1 \rightarrow q2 \quad (c3)$$

The goal is to prove, using D1, that $q2$ is TRUE. Therefore, $\neg q2$ is added to D1, clauses are converted to the form that facilitates resolution, and pairwise resolution proceeds. This yields the revised database D2:

$$p1 \quad (c1)$$

$$\neg p1 \cup q1 \quad (c2)$$

$$\neg q1 \cup q2 \quad (c3)$$

$$\neg q2 \quad (c4)$$

Resolution of clause $(c2)$ with clause $(c3)$ yields $\neg p1 \cup q2$, so the subsequent database D3 becomes

$$p1 \quad (c1)$$

$$\neg p1 \cup q1 \quad (c2)$$

$$\neg q1 \cup q2 \quad (c3)$$

$$\neg q2 \quad (c4)$$

$$\neg p1 \cup q2 \quad (c5)$$

Resolution of $(c4)$ with $(c5)$ yields $\neg p1$, so database D4 is:

$$p1 \quad (c1)$$

$$\neg p1 \cup q1 \quad (c2)$$

$$\neg q1 \cup q2 \quad (c3)$$

$$\neg q2 \quad (c4)$$

$$\neg p1 \cup q2 \quad (c5)$$

$$\neg p1 \quad (c6)$$

Clauses $(c1)$ and $(c6)$ produce a contradiction in the database, specifically $\neg p1 \cap p1$. Therefore, $\neg q2$ is inconsistent with D1, hence $q2$ is TRUE. Alternate sequences of clause resolution are possible and left as an exercise.

6.3.9 Mechanical Implementations of Logic Can Lead to Illogical Results

Logic, while useful as a computational tool in IS, has several limitations:

♦ Logic is "brittle" (this is the subject of another chapter) in the sense that a statement must be either TRUE or FALSE.

♦ The precise and complete underlying meaning of statements must be carefully represented in logic.

A Counterexample.   To show a potential representational flaw in a logic-based representation and manipulation, consider the following:

```
inexpensive textbooks are rare
rare things are expensive
-----------------------------
inexpensive textbooks are expensive
```

Common sense[3] indicates the logically-inferred conclusion in this case is incorrect.

6.4 Chaining, Inference Directions, and Potential Complexities in Chaining

Chaining is a very important component in the implementation of a rule-based inference system. It is typical that the consequents of some rules are the antecedents to others (using unifying substitutions, where necessary). These links form potential "chains," which are logical links or paths through the system rulebase.

♦ A forward-chaining (or antecedent-driven) system attempts to form chains from the initial fact base to a database containing the goal.

♦ A backward or consequent-driven paradigm attempts to (conditionally) form chains backward from a goal database to the initial facts database.

♦ Hybrid strategies involve both forward and backward chaining.

Whether a rule-based system is implemented through forward-, backward-, or a hybrid-chaining paradigm, the inference engine (IE) searches for one or more paths through the problem state space and may therefore explore a large number of redundant or unsuccessful paths in the process. A good IE design uses all available a priori information (such as properties of commutativity and decomposability, if applicable), to avoid needless or unproductive searching.

Referring to Equation 6.2, rule-based inference becomes quite complicated in a number of realistic situations. These include:

---

[3]Note we have not defined "common sense."

1. There exist many rules to choose from, i.e., the database contains multiple rules of the form:

$$p_1 \rightarrow q \quad (= T)$$
$$p_2 \rightarrow q \quad (= T)$$
$$\vdots$$
$$p_n \rightarrow q \quad (= T) \tag{6.6}$$

Thus, we have the initial problem of choosing a rule.

2. The antecedent p in a rule is not a simple statement of the form:

$$p \rightarrow q \tag{6.7}$$

but rather a compound expression involving propositions, e.g.,

$$p = p_1 \cap p_2 \cap p_3 \ldots \cap p_n \tag{6.8}$$

Thus it is necessary for the IE to verify $p_1 \cap p_2 \cap p_3 \ldots \cap p_n$.

3. The antecedent, p, in a rule is not a simple proposition, but rather a *predicate* that involves one or more variables. There may be no bindings or perhaps multiple bindings that would satisfy any this one antecedent. In this case:

$$p = p(X_1, X_2, \ldots, X_m)$$

Now it is necessary to find bindings on $X_1, X_2, \ldots, X_m$ so that $p(X_1, X_2, \ldots, X_m)$ is T.

4. The antecedent p in a rule is of the form of Equation 6.8, but each p_i is a predicate, i.e., contains variables.

$$p_1(X_{11}, X_{12}, \ldots, X_{1j}) \tag{6.9}$$
$$\cap$$
$$p_2(X_{21}, X_{22}, \ldots, X_{2k})$$
$$\cap$$
$$p_3(X_{31}, X_{32}, \ldots, X_{2l}) \ldots$$
$$\cap$$
$$p_n(X_{n1}, X_{n2}, \ldots, X_{nm})$$
$$\rightarrow q$$

This is the previous problem, only compounded by the increased number of predicates and variables, **and the fact that variables may be shared**.

Assuming (shared) variables are involved, there may be no consistent set of bindings on these variables or perhaps many possible bindings that would satisfy all antecedents.

5. There are multiple rules with an antecedent of the form of Equation 6.8, e.g.,

$$p_1 \cap p_2 \cap p_3 \ldots \cap p_n \rightarrow q$$
$$p_1' \cap p_2' \cap p_3' \ldots \cap p_m' \rightarrow q$$
$$\vdots$$
$$p_1'' \cap p_2'' \cap p_3'' \ldots \cap p_q'' \rightarrow q \qquad (6.10)$$

Again, we have the problem of choosing a rule.

All of these circumstances may occur in realistic problems.

6.5 Implementing Rule–Based Chaining

Recall that chaining based upon MP with variables requires finding a unifying substitution, Θ. The process of unification is fundamentally based upon a carefully designed matching algorithm. Thus, matching, or unification, is fundamental in the implementation of a rule-based inference system.

Once rule and fact data structures have been chosen, and the corresponding functions necessary to extract components from these structures (e.g., the antecedent portion of a rule) have been developed, we are ready to implement unification and ultimately rule-based inference systems. The following chapters explore the detailed design and use of more sophisticated systems for this purpose.

6.5.1 The Role and Design of the System Inference Engine

The heart of a rule-based system is a database (consisting of facts and rules) and the corresponding inference mechanism or inference "engine" (IE) that manipulates this database. The IE is responsible for:

1. The selection of relevant rules (or sets of rules, which may pertain to a specific reasoning scenario that the control mechanism determines should be focused upon).

2. Determining the applicability of a given rule, using the criteria of Section 6.4, given the current database. This includes unification of one or more possibly compound statements containing predicates.

3. Execution or firing of the rule(s), and subsequent modification of the database.

4. Determination if the overall system goal has been satisfied.

In practice, the control strategies used to implement conflict resolution (rule selection) are quite diverse. They may range from tests as simple as "fire the first rule that is found to be applicable" to "fire the rule that (according to some heuristic) gets the system closest to the desired goal state."

It is entirely possible for the IE itself to be formed from a rule-based system where metarules (rules about rules) are used to guide the selection of (user) rules.

6.5.2 Computational Elements of Rule-Based Chaining and Examples

Major Computations

Regardless of the chosen implementation language, the following are common elements in the implementation of a rule-based chaining paradigm:

- Designing (or using existing) data structures for rules;
- Designing (or using existing) data structures for facts;
- Checking antecedents and consequents (and possibly a goal) against the facts base;
- Updating or maintaining the facts base;
- Choosing rules that could be used with MP;
- Choosing the chaining direction;
- Implementing conflict resolution strategies (described later); and
- Determining when to stop the IE.

6.6 Extensions to the Simple Chaining Paradigm: Rule Selection, Conflict Resolution Measures, and the Conflict Set

The chaining approach of the previous sections, while a useful first look at the "anatomy" of an IE, is of somewhat limited versatility, since:

1. The matching process cannot invoke other actions, such as checking the value of a variable quantity, determining the meaning of a statement and using that for a match, or invoking a function and causing an additional action. One desirable action might be the loading of an additional (assumed relevant) database.

2. The choice and firing of rules occurs without considering which rules might be "preferable" or "best" (in some sense). Note that alternate inference nets, i.e., paths from the initial to final fact bases, may exist. It is the identification and efficient traversal of these paths that distinguishes practical systems from those that simply employ exhaustive or brute-force search procedures (Chapter 3). For these reasons, the previous simplistic approach is extended to incorporate *conflict resolution*.

6.6.1 The Conflict Set

Consider the following alternative and perhaps more mature strategy for forward-chaining inference:

1. Find all applicable[4] rules.

---

[4]Meaning antecedents are satisfied by unification with the current database.

2. On the basis of some measure and/or computation, determine "good" rules (or perhaps the "best" rule) to fire. Sample definitions of "good" are subsequently presented.

3. Fire this rule or subset of rules and go to Step 1.

This strategy alludes to the process of *conflict resolution,* in the sense that a choice must be made in selecting rules. This selection process determines the path from initial to final databases, and the solution efficiency.

Conflict Set.   The (current) set of applicable rules constitutes the IE conflict set. This set of rules (or productions) is also referred to as the IE "agenda." Forming the conflict set, especially in large systems, is often a computationally intensive process. The conflict set and a conflict resolution strategy are used by the IE with the objective of reaching the goal state as efficiently and as quickly as possible.

Conflict Resolution.   Conflict resolution is the process of choosing "good" rules from the conflict set. This process requires one or more conflict resolution strategies. Many strategies exist, and these strategies are often based upon multiple heuristics.

6.6.2 Possible Conflict Resolution Strategies

Several approaches to conflict resolution exist. Examples are:

1. In choosing rule "a" versus rule "b," examine the antecedents of both rules. If the antecedents of rule "a" are a superset of those of rule "b," then rule "a" is more specialized than rule "b." (Alternately, this means that more constraints must hold for rule "a" to be applicable). Consider, for example, the following two rules:

```
(rule 'specific' (IF   (a b c d))
                 (THEN (j k l)))

(rule 'general'  (IF   (b d))
                 (THEN (p q l)))
```

One strategy is to choose the rule with the stricter precondition (rule "specific" in this case). We choose this rule on the grounds that it is more specialized to the current situation. This is known as specificity-ordered conflict resolution.

2. Examine the conflict set, and choose a rule whose firing moves the facts base (the system state) closer to the goal than any other rule. Of course, this implies we have a specific goal and some metric to measure current-state to goal-state disparity. This is the basis of search algorithm application and associated heuristics to conflict resolution.

3. Choose the rule that has the largest number of consequents, with the assumption that "more is better," i.e., the more additional information that is produced, the closer the system is to the goal.

4. Rank rules according to some measure of "firing desirability" a priori.

5. If rules contain variables (the case considered below), it is possible for a rule to be used repeatedly. In this case, several additional conflict resolution strategies are possible:

    5a. Use the most recently used rule.

    5b. Use the least recently used rule.

    5c. Use the rule with the least (most) number of variables.

The preceding examples are merely suggestions for conflict resolution strategies. Other algorithms and heuristics, perhaps developed from more structured rule and fact bases, are also applicable to a given situation. For example, confidence measures might be used as another guide to conflict resolution. In addition, combinations of the previous example strategies may be used.

6.6.3 Conflict Resolution Examples

We investigate the resulting sequences of rule firings in a forward-chaining system with different conflict resolution strategies. All three cases apply to the following initial database *facts* and rule database *rules*. Lisp notation is used.

```
-> *facts*
(f b g e)

-> *rules*
((rule 1 (IF f b) (THEN s i))
 (rule 2 (IF f b s) (THEN e))
 (rule 3 (IF s j q) (THEN d))
 (rule 4 (IF s e) (THEN a i))
 (rule 5 (IF g f b) (THEN j))
 (rule 6 (IF s a) (THEN p q))
 (rule 7 (IF s e g i) (THEN j k))
 (rule 8 (IF a s j q) (THEN d p)))
```

For each case explored, we assume the goal is to fire rules until no more applicable rules are found. Specifically, for each conflict resolution strategy, we are interested in exploring:

1. The final database, i.e., the contents of *facts* when no more rules are applicable; and

2. The database before and after each rule firing.

The conflict resolution strategies used are arranged into three cases:

Case 1: The first applicable rule is fired and the process of finding an applicable rule restarts on the modified database.

Case 2: The entire conflict set is formed and then all rules in the conflict set are fired. Following this, a new conflict set is formed using the updated database, all rules in the conflict set are fired and the process repeats.

Case 3: Specificity ordered conflict resolution is used. The conflict set is formed, as in Case 2, but only the most specific rule is fired. Then the new database is used to find the new conflict set and, again, the most specific rule is fired. We consider Rule a to be more specific than Rule b if Rule b's antecedent list is contained in the antecedent list of Rule a.

The results are shown in Figures 6.3, 6.4, and 6.5.

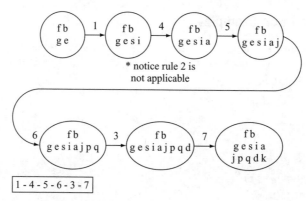

Figure 6.3 Succession of States and Final Database: "Fire the First Applicable Rule"

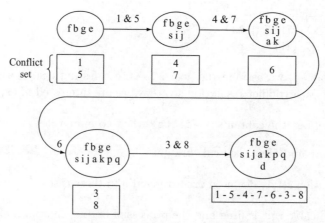

Figure 6.4 Succession of States and Final Database: Form Conflict Set and Fire All Rules

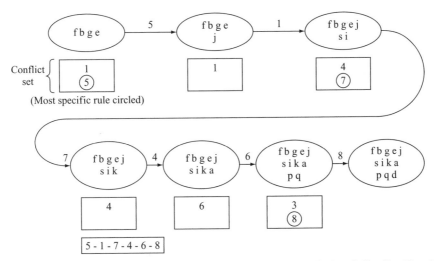

Figure 6.5 Succession of States and Final Database: Specificity-Ordered Conflict Resolution

6.6.4 Conflict Resolution Computational Aspects and Tradeoffs

Forming the conflict set and performing the rule ranking (conflict resolution) requires computational resources. The attempted unification of the conjunction of the antecedents for *each* rule[5] is required. On this basis, the "fire the first rule" is probably computationally justified. However, note that a "good" conflict resolution scheme that involves considerable computation might use fewer overall rule firings (i.e., "good" rules to fire are identified) and therefore may be justified.

6.7 The Production System Paradigm
6.7.1 Programming Paradigms and Production Systems

As noted in Chapter 2, a wide variety of programming paradigms exist. The rule- or production-based paradigm allows knowledge to be represented as rules that specify a set of preconditions that must hold and, if so, a set of actions to be taken. This paradigm, and its application to IS, is the focus of the remainder of this chapter.

6.7.2 A More General Viewpoint: *Rules Trigger Actions*

The use of logic and MP in the previous sections formed the basis of a computational framework for inference and led to the important concept of chaining. A more general, and IS-friendly computational structure, namely the production system (PS) paradigm, might be suggested by an extension of this logic-based chaining framework.

---

[5]This is based upon our view of the inference process, so far. The Rete algorithm, described later, reduces this computational burden.

Example: From a Rule to a Production.   Recall a sample logic-based rule from Section 6.6.3:

`(rule 3 (IF s j q) (THEN d))`

An alternative view of this rule is:

> *IF conditions* s, j, *and* q *are satisfied,*
> *THEN add* d *to the database*

With this viewpoint, rules now have a set of conditions (formerly antecedents) and a set of corresponding actions (formerly consequents).

Strictly speaking, a PS paradigm leaves logic and MP behind and instead provides a CONDITION-ACTION-based computational framework for IS development. "Off the shelf" PS development frameworks, including CLIPS and SOAR are available. CLIPS is treated in Chapter 7; SOAR is the subject of Chapter 9.

6.7.3   Production Systems Architecture

Figure 6.6 shows a somewhat simplistic and generic rule-based production system triad consisting of three entities:

1. A database of information or knowledge (e.g., facts or more complex structures);

2. A set of productions (e.g., rules) that may modify the existing database (and have other effects) and whose applicability is conditioned upon the current database; and

3. A control mechanism (e.g., a production or rule interpreter) that determines the applicability of the productions in the context of the current database, and selects the most appropriate production(s) through a process known as conflict resolution.

Productions Versus Rules and the Computational Structure.   Productions in PSs are specified by a set of CONDITION-ACTION pairs. Specification of conditions in the form of IF statements and actions via THEN yields an extension of the familiar rule-based system representation. Production systems may also be thought of as a subset of pattern-directed systems, which are systems whose

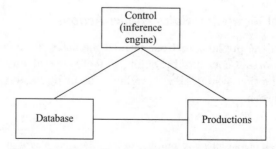

Figure 6.6 Basic Production System Architecture

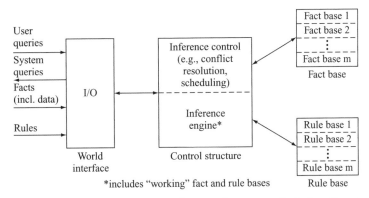

Figure 6.7 More Complex Rule-Based Production System Structure. Includes Structured Rule and Facts Databases and User Interface

production applications are driven by input (or initial) data patterns. Production system operation is based upon a "production cycle" of searching for applicable productions, selecting a particular production, using (firing) the production, and repeating the cycle. Firing of a production usually results in some modification (e.g., addition and/or deletion of facts) of the current database.

Figure 6.7 shows a more realistic rule-based system architecture, which takes into account practical concerns such as user interfacing and structuring and partitioning of the fact and rule databases.

6.7.4 Features of Rule–Based Production Systems

Positive Features. Characteristic of systems employing productions in rule form are the following generally positive features:

1. Expressibility (rules allow the expression of knowledge in a form understood by human experts and at the same time are sufficiently quantitative for symbolic manipulation by machine).

2. Ease of modification of the database (facts and or rules may be added or removed). In addition, the development and implementation of systems that are highly modular is both desirable and straightforward.

3. Ease of exploring the current knowledge base contained in the system (i.e., the encoding of information is in a readable form).

4. Flexibility of processing (the inference mechanism(s) may be chosen to suit the problem).

5. Ease in following the inference mechanism. (The order in which rules were employed may be recorded and traced for an "explanation" of the system's conclusions.)

6. Standardization in terms of a knowledge representation and inference approach.

7. Availability of off-the-shelf software for implementation.

Disadvantages.   Disadvantages include:

1. Inability to predict system behavior for a given problem. (This characterizes many IS computations.) In other words, there may be many solutions, no solution, or a unique solution, and the only way to establish this is via IE search.

2. Inability to force a specific production sequence,[6] as compared to imperative programming.

3. Lack of suitability for all applications.

4. Lack of ability to directly implement "deep reasoning" and "common sense." Note this is a general representational issue, not an inherent shortcoming of the rule-based PS paradigm.

6.7.5 Production System Properties

The general concept of a production system is theoretically and practically important enough to warrant detailed definition and examination of several properties. Given a specific database and a set of productions, production system properties, to some extent, guide the type of inference mechanisms we might employ. In addition, several PS properties enable computational efficiencies, as well as the parallel decomposition of the problem.

Commutative Versus Noncommutative Production Systems

A significant question is the following:

> "Does the order in which the (applicable) productions are applied to the fact database(s) matter?"

When the answer to the question is "no," several useful properties that lead to paradigms for production selection and application result.

One type of specialized PS is the commutative system. We first define a production as applicable in the context of a database, denoted D, if the conjunction of the preconditions or antecedents ("IF parts") for that production are satisfied by D, i.e., the production is eligible for firing. A commutative PS satisfies the following:

1. Any production applicable to D is also applicable to any database derived from D by successive applications of applicable productions. Note that this only applies to productions that are initially applicable to D. Recall, the state of the database will change over time (i.e., as productions occur and D is modified), thus possibly yielding other productions that are applicable in databases derived from D.

2. If a goal is satisfied by D, then it is also satisfied by any database produced by applying any applicable productions to D.

---

[6]Note some expert system shells allow manipulation of IE parameters to accomplish this.

3. The database generated by firing of a sequence of productions applicable to D is invariant to permutations in the sequence. This property should not be construed to mean that if we find a sequence of productions leading from the initial system state to the goal state through a succession of system states that we may arbitrarily reorder this entire production sequence and find that the reordered sequence will also achieve the goal.

The significance of having a PS with the commutative property is twofold:

1. The IE does not need to consider the application of all permutations of production order, i.e., it is possible to avoid many of the solution paths that differ only in the order in which initially applicable productions are applied. For large production bases, this may be a significant number.

2. The commutative property allows use of an IE employing an irrevocable control strategy.

Relation to Planning Systems

A good example of a noncommutative PS is one with the capacity for fact and/or rule removal (retraction) (e.g., use of the Prolog "retract" predicate). Our best example of a noncommutative PS, however, is a planning system (Chapter 12). In planning systems, the order in which productions are invoked is usually critical to the outcome of the system. In other words, achievement of a plan that meets the prescribed goal is highly dependent upon the chosen sequence of operations comprising the plan.

6.7.6 Decomposable Production Systems

Whereas the commutative property of a production system facilitates a limited degree of flexibility in the sequence in which applicable rules are fired, another related property, namely that of decomposability, leads to computationally efficient IE designs. We note that decomposition of IS problems in general is an important and desirable property, since we may then apply a "divide and conquer" approach that involves solution of a set of (hopefully) simpler or smaller problems. *A database, D, is decomposable if it can be decomposed or partitioned into disjoint sets that can be processed independently (perhaps in parallel).* Furthermore, a decomposable PS is one for which both the database and the goal are decomposable. Decomposability is an important production system property for two major reasons:

1. The decomposition allows inferences to proceed in parallel (up to the inputs of the goal decomposition).

2. Decomposition eliminates many of the redundant solution paths and related searches that otherwise might be explored, since the entire fact and rule databases are not involved.

Given an arbitrary production system, identification of the decomposability property (as well as achievement of a suitable decomposition) is often challenging. One algorithm for this is given in [Nil80].

6.8 Production Systems: The Next Step

This chapter introduced the notion of a production system, and illustrated the overall structure and relevant properties. Chapters 7 and 9 explore the "inner workings" of a production system and provide practical examples.

6.9 Exercises

1. Notice the use of MP only employs the first row of the truth table defined in Equation 6.2. Can you think of any other inference strategies (or logic-based constraints) that result from Equation 6.2?

2. Prove Equation 6.2 is a tautology.

3. The basis for inference using resolution is shown in Section 6.3.8. Prove that this is a tautology.

4. (a) An aging IS designer, in a series of flashbacks, envisions two potential new logic-based inference strategies. The first of these is termed "Modus Woodstock" (MW) and is:

$$[(p \to q) \cap (q \to w)] \to (p \to w) \tag{6.11}$$

   Is MW, as defined by Equation 6.11, a tautology? If so, how could it be used for inference?

   (b) The same engineer, in a second flashback, envisions strategy "Modus Woodstock 2" (MW2), as follows:

$$[(p \to q) \cap (q \to w)] = (p \to w) \tag{6.12}$$

   Note here = is a logical connective. Is Modus Woodstock 2 (MW2), as defined by Equation 6.12, a tautology? If so, how could it be used for inference?

5. The following sample database was obtained from thinning a search of the Open CYC database using the term "grandparent." Using this information as a starting point, develop a representation in logic for this concept.

```
the parent of a parent is a grandparent
Some grandparents are mentally ill
parents are the children of grandparents
a grandparent can give presents
Your parents' parents are your grandparents
sometimes grandparents live in a nursing home
grandparents like to have pictures of their grandchildren
grandparents are parents of parents
A grandparent has children
grandparents can ship gifts to grandchildren
```

grandparents are always older than their grandchildren
grandparents are your parents parents
A grandparent is the parent of the parent of a child
A male grandparent is a grandfather
A female grandparent is a grandmother
A person has four grandparents
A grandfather and a grandmother are grandparents
Everyone has grandparents, althought they may no longer be alive

6. (a) What is the fundamental flaw in the example in Section 6.3.9? Is it the fault of the formulation of the statements or is it due to MP?

   (b) How would you resolve it?

   (c) Develop a representation of the silly example of Section 6.3.9 in Prolog. Does Prolog deduce the same result?

7. Section 6.3.8 suggested that alternate sequences of clause resolution are possible. Show an alternate sequence.

8. The intent of this problem is to discover if there is any relationship between resolution-based inference and chaining. Consider the sequence of clause resolutions in Section 6.3.8. Recall that resolution of $\neg p1 \cup q1$ and $\neg q1 \cup q2$ yielded $\neg p1 \cup q2$. However, also recall that

$$\neg p1 \cup q1 \equiv p1 \rightarrow q1$$

and

$$\neg q1 \cup q2 \equiv q1 \rightarrow q2$$

and resolution of these clauses yielded

$$\neg p1 \cup q2 \equiv p1 \rightarrow q2$$

From this, do you see a way to relate the two concepts? Explain in detail.

9. How would you extend resolution-based (proof-by-refutation) inference to allow variables?

10. Section 6.3.6 indicated the logical basis for MP with variables in rules. Can variables be allowed in facts? If so, how would MP be modified for this case? Show an example.

   Hint: consider the fact (equal X X).

11. Using the notation of Section 6.3.7, what is the unification of:

   (a) $(A \ A \ B)$ and $(a \ B \ b)$

   (b) $(A \ A \ B)$ and $(b \ B \ b)$

   (c) $(A \ c \ B)$ and $(a \ A \ b)$

12. Consider the unification of two lists containing shared variables:

$$(A\ A\ B)$$

and

$$(a\ B\ a)$$

Find a unifying substitution.

13. For the example shown in Section 6.3.7, what other unifying substitutions exist for this problem?

14. Develop the general unifier in C. Initially, ignore efficiency. Choose appropriate data structures for the clauses to be unified (including variables). Show the algorithm in pseudocode, then the C implementation with examples.

15. A commutative production system was defined in Section 6.7.5. Using this definition, develop an example of a system that is noncommutative because it allows:

(a) rule removal, e.g., using the notation of Section 6.6.3

```
(rule 1 (IF f b) (THEN (remove rule 2)))
```

(b) fact removal, e.g.,

```
(rule 3 (IF s j q) (THEN (remove d)))
```

16. Many systems, such as CLIPS, are designed principally for forward chaining (antecedent-driven inference). Assume you are given a forward-chaining system implementation (we continue this problem in Chapter 7). The purpose of this problem is to consider using a forward-chaining IE for backward chaining.

(a) Given a prespecified goal, how would you implement backward chaining with this system? (Note: modification of the source code for the forward-chaining IE is not an option.)

Hint: As suggested by [BFKM86], one strategy requires two sets of rules:

　i. control rules that implement backward chaining. These are goal-splitting and goal-fusing rules; and

　ii. rules for handling immediately soluble goals.

The basis of the strategy is to split goals that are not immediately soluble into subgoals and make each of these subgoals the precondition (antecedents) to a rule. Once the conjunction of the subgoals is satisfied, "fusing" productions return to the parent goal.

(b) Show this strategy on the following database:

```
initial dB facts: {a  b  g}

rules:    IF   a  b   THEN   c          (1)

               b  g          d          (2)

               a  c          e          (3)

               e  d          f          (4)
```

17. Suppose your company produces an elegant rule-based software product wherein rules are required to be of the form:

$$(p_1 \cap p_2 \cap ... \cap p_n) \rightarrow q$$

where the p_1 and q are simple statements. The system uses forward chaining.

You discover an exciting and lucrative application, but rules in this application are not in the preceding form. Specifically, two new forms for (assumed true) rules are proposed. In both forms, a, b, c, and d are simple statements.

Case 1:

$$(a \cup b) \rightarrow (c \cup d)$$

Case 2:

$$(a \cup b) \rightarrow (c \cap d)$$

Determine, using logic, if the rule forms in Cases 1 or 2 may be converted into a form for which you can use your product.

18. Benchmarking of rule-based systems, especially when large rule and fact bases are involved, periodically receives attention. Two well-known, and perhaps well-worn, benchmarks are "Miss Manners" and the "Waltz" benchmark. The former yields a CSP (Chapter 4) wherein Miss Manners has invited 16, 32, 64, or 128 guests with various hobbies to a dinner party. She wants to arrange the guest seating so that genders alternate and each guest will have someone on the left or right with a common hobby. The Waltz benchmark involves labeling the lines in a two-dimensional drawing with the constraint that these lines are the projection of edges from a three-dimensional object.

Using the Web as a resource, find and explore implementations of each of these benchmarks.

The C Language Integrated Production System (CLIPS)

7.1 CLIPS: Conceptual Background and Motivation

The C Language Integrated Production System (CLIPS) is a computational structure and language for implementing production systems. CLIPS may be viewed as a descendant of OPS5, an early Lisp-based production system. CLIPS is written in C for portability, interoperability, and speed. It is widely available and has been ported to many different operating systems.

CLIPS is well documented; this chapter merely highlights useful introductory concepts. The reader should become familiar with the documents cited in Section 7.1.5. Acquiring the CLIPS software is addressed in Section 7.8.

7.1.1 CLIPS History

The origin of CLIPS dates back to 1984 at NASA's Johnson Space Center, where the intent was to provide a framework for the development of expert systems. OPS5 was deemed too difficult for widespread adoption, primarily due to the underlying Lisp implementation. After initial development, CLIPS was released outside of NASA in 1986. CLIPS is now maintained independently from NASA as public domain software.

7.1.2 CLIPS Structure

The CLIPS structure is a somewhat expanded version of the generic PS "triad" structure shown in Chapter 6, Figure 6.6. Figure 7.1 shows this expanded structure. Note that if the "agenda," "user interface," and "inference engine" were combined, the triad structure reappears.

Programming Paradigms Supported by CLIPS. CLIPS itself supports three programming paradigms:

1. Forward chaining, rule-based;

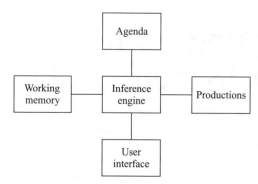

Figure 7.1 CLIPS Structure

2. Object-oriented (via COOL); and

3. Procedural.

Our emphasis is on the first paradigm, although we consider aspects of COOL; especially the integration of Protégé-developed ontologies in Chapter 8.

7.1.3 CLIPS Nomenclature

CLIPS uses some nomenclature that differs from other production system descriptors. The conflict set is referred to as the `agenda`. Note that CLIPS *is based on productions*, although the CLIPS documentation refers to productions as "rules." In addition, CLIPS "facts" are stored in `wm` and may be more elaborate structures than simple facts.

7.1.4 Simplified CLIPS Execution Cycle

The basic execution cycle of the CLIPS IE shown in Figure 7.1 proceeds as follows[1]:

1. If the rule-firing limit has been reached, execution is halted.

2. If the rule-firing limit has not been reached, the top rule on the `agenda` (conflict set) is selected for execution. If there are no rules on the agenda, execution is halted. Otherwise, the right-hand side (RHS) actions of the selected rule are executed. The number of rules fired is incremented.

3. As a result of Step 2, rules may now be activated or deactivated. A new `agenda` is recomputed and the CLIPS IE returns to Step 1.

7.1.5 CLIPS Documentation

The accompanying CLIPS documentation consists of a number of pdf files, as shown in Table 7.1. Of these, the Basic Programming Guide should be considered mandatory reading. In addition, expert systems programming is covered in [KL96] and the use of CLIPS is shown in [GR98].

---

[1]Here we temporarily ignore the concept of focus. The `agenda` is CLIPS nomenclature for the ranked conflict set. The process of determining the `agenda` (conflict resolution) is accomplished with the Rete algorithm and discussed in Section 7.5.

usrguide.pdf	User Guide
bpg.pdf	Basic Programming Guide (Vol. I)
apg.pdf	Advanced Programming Guide (Vol. II)

Table 7.1 CLIPS Documentation

7.1.6 Introductory CLIPS Examples

A Simple CLIPS "Hello World"-type Example

Suppose the objective was to use CLIPS to implement the database:

$$a \cap r \cap s$$

$$a \cap r \rightarrow b$$

We show two possible strategies. The first is based upon the use of ordered facts; the second uses unordered facts. The CLIPS command-line interface is used in both cases.

Implementation Using Ordered Facts. This implementation is perhaps the most straightforward, and therefore shown first and with a minimum of discussion. The CLIPS database is shown in Figure 7.2. Sample use is shown in Figure 7.3.

Implementation Using Unordered Facts. Figure 7.4 illustrates a CLIPS database using the unordered facts representation. A sample operation using the CLIPS database of Figure 7.4 is shown in Figure 7.5.

The examples presented were based upon loading the CLIPS databases from files. The entire CLIPS database may be entered using the command-line interface, as shown in Figure 7.6.

```
;; clips implementation of a sample database
;; file: ars-ordered.clips

;; a rule
(defrule rule1 "simple rule"
  (a)
  (r)
=>
  (assert (b)))

;; initial facts
(deffacts startup
  (a) (r) (s))
```

Figure 7.2 CLIPS Example Database Using Ordered Facts

```
CLIPS> (load "ars-ordered.clips")
Defining defrule: rule1 +j+j
Defining deffacts: startup
TRUE
CLIPS> (reset)
CLIPS> (facts)
f-0     (initial-fact)
f-1     (a)
f-2     (r)
f-3     (s)
For a total of 4 facts.
CLIPS> (run)
CLIPS> (facts)
f-0     (initial-fact)
f-1     (a)
f-2     (r)
f-3     (s)
f-4     (b)
For a total of 5 facts.
CLIPS>
```

Figure 7.3   CLIPS Dialog for the CLIPS Database of Figure 7.2

```
;; clips implementation of a sample database
;; file: ars-clips.clips

;; template for memory
(deftemplate primitive
(slot name))

;; a rule
(defrule rule1
  (primitive (name a))
  (primitive (name r))
=>
  (assert (primitive (name b))))

;; initial facts
(deffacts startup
  (primitive (name a))
  (primitive (name r))
  (primitive (name s)))
```

Figure 7.4   CLIPS Example Database Using Unordered Facts

```
CLIPS> (load "ars-clips.clips")  ;; load the file
Defining deftemplate: primitive
Defining defrule: rule1 +j+j
Defining deffacts: startup
TRUE
CLIPS> (facts)                   ;; see facts- there are none
CLIPS> (reset)                   ;; reset loads facts
CLIPS> (facts)
f-0     (initial-fact)
f-1     (primitive (name a))     ;; note the fact indices f-0, etc.
f-2     (primitive (name r))
f-3     (primitive (name s))
For a total of 4 facts.
CLIPS> (agenda)                  ;; look at the current cs (agenda)
0       rule1: f-1,f-2
For a total of 1 activation.
CLIPS> (run)                     ;; run clips
CLIPS> (facts)                   ;; now look at facts (wm)
f-0     (initial-fact)
f-1     (primitive (name a))
f-2     (primitive (name r))
f-3     (primitive (name s))
f-4     (primitive (name b))
For a total of 5 facts.
CLIPS> (agenda)                  ;; cs (agenda) empty
CLIPS> (exit)                    ;; end of clips use
```

Figure 7.5 Annotated CLIPS Dialog for the CLIPS Database of Figure 7.4

```
CLIPS> (deftemplate primitive
(slot name))
CLIPS> (deffacts startup
  (primitive (name a))
  (primitive (name r))
  (primitive (name s)))
CLIPS> (defrule rule1
  (primitive (name a))
  (primitive (name r))
=>
  (assert (primitive (name b))))
CLIPS> (reset)
CLIPS> (agenda)
0       rule1: f-1,f-2
For a total of 1 activation.
CLIPS> (run)
CLIPS> (facts)
f-0     (initial-fact)
f-1     (primitive (name a))
f-2     (primitive (name r))
f-3     (primitive (name s))
f-4     (primitive (name b))
For a total of 5 facts.
CLIPS> (agenda)
```

Figure 7.6 CLIPS Command-Line Entry and Dialog for the CLIPS Example of Figure 7.4

A Second CLIPS Example: A Constraint Satisfaction Problem

This example introduces the image labeling problem of Chapter 4, Section 4.6.2. This is an example of a Constraint Satisfaction Problem (CSP) formulated in CLIPS. Three **wm** element classes are used, as well as variables in the productions. A version incorporating the "highest" and "adjacency" constraints is shown here. This formulation uses productions **rule1** and **rule2** to implement the symmetry of the "adjacent-to" relational constraint.

The CLIPS source is shown in Figure 7.7. A transcript of the resulting CLIPS session using this formulation is shown in Figure 7.8.

```
;; file: label1r.clips
;; clips version of labeling CSP
;; this version incorporates 'highest' constraint

(deftemplate highest
  (slot reg))

(deftemplate adj-to
  (slot reg1)
  (slot reg2))

(deftemplate labeling
  (slot lab1) (slot lab2) (slot lab3) (slot lab4) (slot lab5) (slot lab6))

;; to elaborate the symmetry of the adj-to constraint

(defrule rulesym
  (adj-to (reg1 ?Y) (reg2 ?X))
  =>
  (assert (adj-to (reg1 ?X) (reg2 ?Y))))

;; the actual labeling rule

(defrule ruleg
  (highest (reg ?R1))
  (adj-to (reg1 ?R1) (reg2 ?R2))
  (adj-to (reg1 ?R2) (reg2 ?R6))
  (adj-to (reg1 ?R2) (reg2 ?R3))
  (adj-to (reg1 ?R3) (reg2 ?R4))
  (adj-to (reg1 ?R2) (reg2 ?R4))
  (adj-to (reg1 ?R4) (reg2 ?R6))
  (adj-to (reg1 ?R4) (reg2 ?R5))
  =>
  (assert (labeling (lab1 ?R1) (lab2 ?R2) (lab3 ?R3)
                    (lab4 ?R4) (lab5 ?R5) (lab6 ?R6))))

(deffacts startup
(highest (reg sky))
(adj-to (reg1 car) (reg2 road))
(adj-to (reg1 road) (reg2 grass))
(adj-to (reg1 road) (reg2 trees))
(adj-to (reg1 sky) (reg2 trees))
(adj-to (reg1 grass) (reg2 trees)))
```

Figure 7.7 Example of CLIPS Use for a Constraint Satisfaction Problem (image labeling)

```
CLIPS> (load "label1r.clips")
Defining deftemplate: highest
Defining deftemplate: adj-to
Defining deftemplate: labeling
Defining defrule: rulesym +j
Defining defrule: ruleg +j+j+j+j+j+j+j
Defining deffacts: startup
TRUE
CLIPS> (reset)
CLIPS> (run)
CLIPS> (facts)
f-0     (initial-fact)
f-1     (highest (reg sky))
f-2     (adj-to (reg1 car) (reg2 road))
f-3     (adj-to (reg1 road) (reg2 grass))
f-4     (adj-to (reg1 road) (reg2 trees))
f-5     (adj-to (reg1 sky) (reg2 trees))
f-6     (adj-to (reg1 grass) (reg2 trees))
f-7     (adj-to (reg1 trees) (reg2 grass))
f-8     (adj-to (reg1 trees) (reg2 sky))
f-9     (adj-to (reg1 trees) (reg2 road))
f-10    (adj-to (reg1 grass) (reg2 road))
f-11    (labeling (lab1 sky) (lab2 trees) (lab3 grass) (lab4 road) (lab5 trees) (lab6 grass))
f-12    (labeling (lab1 sky) (lab2 trees) (lab3 grass) (lab4 road) (lab5 grass) (lab6 grass))
f-13    (labeling (lab1 sky) (lab2 trees) (lab3 road) (lab4 grass) (lab5 road) (lab6 road))
f-14    (labeling (lab1 sky) (lab2 trees) (lab3 road) (lab4 grass) (lab5 trees) (lab6 road))
f-15    (adj-to (reg1 road) (reg2 car))
f-16    (labeling (lab1 sky) (lab2 trees) (lab3 grass) (lab4 road) (lab5 car) (lab6 grass))
For a total of 17 facts.
```

Figure 7.8 CLIPS Results for the Image Labeling CSP Formulation of Figure 7.7

CLIPS Examples Included with Distributions

Most CLIPS distributions are accompanied by a number of examples. Three are especially recommended for the reader to study:

`rpc.clp`: The rock-paper-scissors game;

`animal.clp`: An animal identification system; and

`mab.clp`: The monkey and bananas problem.

We show the monkey and bananas CLIPS source and the corresponding `xclips` execution in Section 7.4.5.

7.1.7 Logging a CLIPS Session

The functions `dribble-on` and `dribble-off` control session logging. The syntax is:

```
(dribble-on <file-name>)
```
and
```
(dribble-off)
```

7.1.8 CLIPS Help

Assuming the file `clips.hlp` is in the CLIPS path, the command (`help [<path>]`) provides help on topics. An example follows. Versions of CLIPS built with a GUI facilitate help via a menu entry.

```
CLIPS> (help function_summary)


FUNCTION_SUMMARY

This section gives a general overview of the available CLIPS functions.

Subtopics:
PREDICATE_FUNCTIONS          DEFRULE_FUNCTIONS
MULTIFIELD_FUNCTIONS         AGENDA_FUNCTIONS
STRING_FUNCTIONS             DEFGLOBAL_FUNCTIONS
IO_FUNCTIONS                 DEFFUNCTION_FUNCTIONS
MATH_FUNCTIONS               GENERIC_FUNCTION_FUNCTIONS
PROCEDURAL_FUNCTIONS         COOL_FUNCTIONS
MISCELLANEOUS_FUNCTIONS      DEFMODULE_FUNCTIONS
DEFTEMPLATE_FUNCTIONS        SEQUENCE_EXPANSION_FUNCTIONS
FACT_FUNCTIONS

FUNCTION_SUMMARY Topic? fact_functions
```

7.2 Selected Syntax, Constructs, and Examples

Extended BNF is used to show the syntax[2] of CLIPS. Note that CLIPS is case-sensitive. This is shown in the example in Section 7.4.4. Furthermore, a string is a sequence of characters that begins and ends with a double quotation mark.

7.2.1 Predominant CLIPS Constructs

The three predominant CLIPS constructs are:

`deftemplate` for defining **wm** structures or templates;

`defrule` for defining productions; and

`deffacts` for defining facts, i.e., creating instances of **wm** templates.

Template Definition Syntax

Non-ordered (or `deftemplate`) facts assign names to each field or slot defined within the fact. The `deftemplate` construct is used to create a template that can then be used to access fields of the non-ordered fact by name.

---

[2]The syntax examples shown here are skeletal and therefore incomplete. They are used to show typical constructs. The CLIPS manual should be consulted for the complete, precise syntax.

The detailed syntax of the `deftemplate` construct is:

```
(deftemplate <deftemplate-name> [<comment>]
   <slot-definition>*)
```

where

```
<slot-definition>          ::= <single-slot-definition> |
                               <multislot-definition>

<single-slot-definition>   ::= (slot <slot-name>
                                     <template-attribute>*)

<multislot-definition>     ::= (multislot <slot-name>
                                          <template-attribute>*)

<template-attribute>       ::= <default-attribute> |
                               <constraint-attribute>
```

Slot default attributes are possible, and are inserted by the CLIPS system when (`reset`) occurs if no explicit values are defined.

`deftemplate` **Examples.**   The CLIPS code fragment:

```
(deftemplate primitive
     (slot element-name1)
     (slot element-name2))
```

declares a `wm` template named "primitive" with a pair of single-slot definitions for slots "`element-name1`" and "`element-name2`."

Some of the more elaborate parts of the `deftemplate` syntax are shown in the following example. This example is continued in Section 7.4.4.

```
(deftemplate faculty
            (slot name)
            (slot teaching_evals
               (default unknown)
               (allowed-symbols excellent good fair poor miserable unknown))
            (slot lecture_quality
               (default unknown)
               (allowed-symbols fantastic excellent good fair
                            poor miserable unknown))
            (slot lecture_prep
               (default yes)
               (allowed-symbols yes no))
            (slot proposal_writing
               (allowed-symbols extensive regular occasional never))
            (slot proposal_funding
               (type INTEGER))
            (slot research_accomp
               (allowed-symbols extraordinary excellent
                            substantial good fair poor))
```

```
        (slot research_publ
           (type INTEGER))
        (slot tenure_status(default UNKNOWN)
           (allowed-symbols tenured untenured fired UNKNOWN))
)
```

Representing Facts

In CLIPS, almost anything may be added to the facts list in **wm** using the **assert** command. Facts may be ordered (the simplest case) or non-ordered (i.e., structured). The vast majority of CLIPS applications appear to use a non-ordered fact representation.

Fact Identifiers.   Time tags are used in the display of working memory, specifically as indices to **wm** elements. This was pointed out in the simple example of Figure 7.5.

deffacts Syntax.   The **deffacts** construct facilitates definition of a list of facts that are asserted whenever the **reset** command is invoked. Facts asserted through **deffacts** may be retracted or pattern-matched like any other fact.

The syntax of the **deffacts** construct is:

```
(deffacts <deffacts-name> [<comment>]
   <RHS-pattern>*)
```

where fact specification for non-ordered facts is constrained by

```
<RHS-pattern> ::= <template-RHS-pattern>

<template-RHS-pattern> ::= (<deftemplate-name> <RHS-slot>*)

<RHS-slot> ::= <single-field-RHS-slot> | <multifield-RHS-slot>

<single-field-RHS-slot> ::= (<slot-name> <RHS-field>)

<multifield-RHS-slot> ::= (<slot-name> <RHS-field>*)

<RHS-field> ::= <variable> | <constant> | <function-call>
```

Syntax for Rules (Abbreviated)

CLIPS rule structure is straightforward. The heart of the rule (production) is a set of condition elements, followed by a set of corresponding actions that *could* be taken if the condition elements are satisfied and the rule is chosen during conflict resolution. Note:

1. The arrow (=>) separates the LHS (condition elements) from the RHS (actions).

2. RHS actions are executed *sequentially*.

Formally, the CLIPS rule or production syntax is:

```
(defrule <rule-name> [<comment>]
    [<declaration>]
    <conditional-element>*
    =>
    <action>*)
```

A rich syntax for condition elements exists, including:

```
<conditional-element>   ::= <pattern-CE> | <assigned-pattern-CE> |
                            <not-CE> | <and-CE> | <or-CE> |
                            <logical-CE> | <test-CE> |
                            <exists-CE> | <forall-CE>
```

and

```
<test-CE>               ::= (test <function-call>)
<not-CE>                ::= (not <conditional-element>)
<and-CE>                ::= (and <conditional-element>+)
<or-CE>                 ::= (or <conditional-element>+)
<exists-CE>             ::= (exists <conditional-element>+)
<forall-CE>            ::= (forall <conditional-element>
                                  <conditional-element>+)
<logical-CE>            ::= (logical <conditional-element>+)
```

Note that a comment is allowed in the rule header (just as in **deftemplate**), beginning and ending with double quotes. The CLIPS Basic Programming Manual provides a more complete reference to the rich vocabulary for articulating productions.

Matching in Single and Multifield Slots

The following are examples of condition elements in a rule, including the use of the CE **test** form.

```
(defrule tenure_decision2
   ?Who <- (faculty (name ?W) (tenure_status untenured|UNKNOWN))
   (or (teaching_performance (name ?W) (rating embarrassment|poor))
       (research_performance (name ?W) (rating poor))
       (publ_performance (name ?W) (rating poor)))
=>
   (printout t tab "faculty member" tab ?W tab "will be fired" crlf)
   (modify ?Who (tenure_status fired)))
(defrule assess_publ_perf1
   (faculty (name ?W) (research_accomp substantial))
   (faculty (name ?W) (research_publ ?how_many))
   (test (> ?how_many 50))
=>
   (assert (publ_performance (name ?W) (rating good))))
```

Use of the **test** form of the CE must be preceded by a **(reset)** command.

Wildcard Matches.   The single field wildcard[3] is "?". A multifield wildcard is denoted by "$?"; it matches zero or more fields.

---

[3]Commonly this is denoted by using "*" in many other languages.

&	and
|	or
~	not

Table 7.2 Connectives in Field Value Constraints

Connectives in Field Value Constraints.   These are summarized in Table 7.2.

Variables in Rules

As shown in previous examples, variables are denoted using a string beginning with the "?". In CLIPS, *variables can have one of two uses.* The first, and most common use is for representational generality, i.e., as a placeholder. Another is binding to a condition element in CLIPS syntax for subsequent modification of wm in a RHS action. This is shown via the following excerpt from the "monkey and bananas" implementation:

```
(defrule unlock-chest-with-key ""
  ?goal <- (goal-is-to (action unlock) (arguments ?name))
  ?chest <- (chest (name ?name) (contents ?contents) (unlocked-by ?key))
  (thing (name ?name) (location ?place) (on-top-of ?on))
  (monkey (location ?place) (on-top-of ?on) (holding ?key))
  =>
  (printout t "Monkey opens the " ?name " with the " ?key
            " revealing the " ?contents "." crlf)
  (modify ?chest (contents nothing))
  (assert (thing (name ?contents) (location ?place) (on-top-of ?name)))
  (retract ?goal))
```

In this example, if production `unlock-chest-with-key` is used, the matched wm element for

```
(chest (name ?name) (contents ?contents) (unlocked-by ?key))
```

is modified to

```
(chest (name ?name) (contents nothing) (unlocked-by ?key))
```

and the matched wm element for

```
(goal-is-to (action unlock) (arguments ?name))
```

is retracted, i.e., removed from the facts list. Another example of this use of a variable is shown in the example in Section 7.4.

Another CLIPS Example: Sorting

This example shows the combined use of several of the aforementioned constructs.

CLIPS Database Formulation for Sorting.

```
;; clipsSort.clips: A Sorting Program for clips

(deftemplate num
    (slot val)
    (slot processed))

(defrule sort
   ?Anum <- (num (val ?V) (processed nil))
   (not (and
              (num (val ?X) (processed nil))
              (test (< ?X ?V))))
=>
   (printout t "the next number is: " ?V crlf)
   (modify ?Anum (processed t))
 )

(deffacts database
  (num (val 170))
  (num (val 77))
  (num (val 127))
  (num (val 16))
  (num (val 119))
  (num (val 103))
  (num (val 101))
  (num (val 18))
)
```

Skeletal Execution.

```
CLIPS> (load "clipsSort.clips")
Defining deftemplate: num
Defining defrule: sort +j+j+j
Defining deffacts: database
TRUE
CLIPS> (reset)
CLIPS> (run)
the next number is: 16
the next number is: 18
the next number is: 77
the next number is: 101
the next number is: 103
the next number is: 119
the next number is: 127
the next number is: 170
CLIPS>
```

The reader is encouraged to repeat this example and set watch levels as well as open browser windows, single step the CLIPS execution, etc., for a more complete appreciation of the solution and the operation of CLIPS.

Functions, Actions, and Commands

There are many available actions and functions that may be used on the LHS and RHS of rules as well as at the CLIPS top-level command prompt. Appendix 1 of the CLIPS Basic Programming Guide lists all the available (built-in) CLIPS functions.

Nomenclature.   The term "function" is used to refer to a function that returns a value. The term "action" refers to a function having no return value but that performs some basic operation as a side effect. The term "command" refers to functions typically used at the top-level command prompt.
   Commonly used actions include:

assert: Adds a fact to the fact-list. Multiple facts may be asserted with each call. The syntax is:

```
(assert <RHS-pattern>+)
```

retract: Removes facts from the fact-list. As expected, retraction of a fact removes all rules from the conflict set that required the deleted fact for activation. The syntax is:

```
(retract <retract-specifier>+ | *)
<retract-specifier> ::= <fact-specifier> | <integer-expression>
```

modify: Modifies template facts on the fact-list. Modification of a fact is equivalent to retracting the present fact and asserting the modified fact. The syntax is:

```
(modify <fact-specifier> <RHS-slot>*)
```

bind: Create new variables or modify the value of previously bound variables on the RHS of a rule. The syntax is:

```
(bind <variable> <expression>*)
```

RHS Actions.   The RHS contains a list of actions to be performed when the LHS of the rule is satisfied. The syntax is:

```
<action> ::= <expression>
<expression> ::= <constant> | <variable> | <function-call>
<function-call> ::= (<function-name> <expression>*)
```

where <function-name> is any symbol that corresponds to a system or user-defined function.

Combining Actions for Realistic Rules: an Example.   The following function, taken from a CLIPS-based blocks world planner, shows the use of unordered facts, variables, and multiple actions in a CLIPS production.

```
(defrule move-block-A-left
?Initial <- (cell (name ?Current-A) (contents A))
  (neighbors (name ?Current-A) (left ?Status))
?Fill <- (cell (name ?Status) (contents empty))
```

```
 (cell (name ?Bloc) (contents B))
 (not (priorState (whereA ?Status) (whereB ?Bloc)))
=>
(printout t crlf "moving block A to " ?Status crlf)
(modify ?Initial (contents empty))
(modify ?Fill (contents A))
(assert (priorState (whereA ?Status) (whereB ?Bloc)))
)
```

CLIPS I/O and Related Functions

(read). The read function may be used to read from a file or stdin, as follows. read stops reading when it encounters any delimiter; readline stops reading when it encounters a CR, semicolon, or EOF character.

```
CLIPS> (read stdin)
hello  ;; this was typed
hello
CLIPS> (readline stdin)
this is a whole line ;; this was typed followed by a CR
"this is a whole line"
```

(printout). (printout) is used for printing. More specifically, printout directs output to a device attached to a "logical name." The symbol t is used to designate stdout, as shown in the following example:

```
CLIPS> (printout t "something to print" crlf)
something to print
CLIPS>
```

Other Actions

(reset): Resets the CLIPS system. This has the following effects[4]:

1. All rules are removed from the conflict set (agenda);

2. All facts are removed from the fact-list; and

3. All facts listed in all deffacts statements are asserted onto the fact-list.

(system): This function allows calls to the host operating system. The syntax is:

```
Syntax
(system <lexeme-expression>*)
```

Moreover,

(clear): clears the CLIPS system by removing all constructs and all associated data structures (such as facts and instances) from the CLIPS environment. Note that clear does not change the current conflict resolution strategy.

---

[4]There are other effects.

(load) and (save): loads and saves CLIPS source files, respectively.

(exit): exits CLIPS.

7.2.2   A Third Example—Prelude to an Expert System

Card games on television apparently attract lots of viewers. Suppose we were charged with developing an expert system to play Texas Holdem Poker. Here we assume two players ("heads up"), i.e., a CLIPS expert system vs. a human player. It is first necessary to generate the two hands; this is shown in Figures 7.9 and 7.10. These examples also illustrate a number of commonly used CLIPS constructs and strategies, including:

1. Control of salience (note the production for checking for duplicates has higher salience than the production used for dealing more cards);

2. Multislot matching ((deck (cards $?D)));

3. The nth$ function ((nth$?X $?D);

4. A "return value constraint" ((dealt (when = (- ?N 1))); and

5. A negated attribute test ((dealt (card-value ?X) (when ~last)))

This example is continued in Chapter 11.

7.3   CLIPS Conflict Resolution and the agenda

7.3.1   Controlling Production System Computation

Recall from Chapter 6 that the rule-based (RB) programming paradigm implemented by a production system differs significantly from (conventional) imperative programming. In the RB paradigm, a sequence of commands is not executed. Instead, a sequence of production firings takes the system from an initial state to a final state. The order of the productions used is (usually) not explicitly specified a priori, since it is necessary that the antecedents or condition elements of the production be satisfied before firing can be considered.

However, *aspects of the production system computation are controllable*. In CLIPS, the production system designer influences the sequence of productions used in several ways:

1. Through control of production salience, i.e., the ability to articulate the relative importance of a production;

2. Through the design of the productions themselves; and

3. Through the choice of conflict resolution strategies used.

```
;; file: cards0f.clips

;;    generate * 2 hands * with 5 community cards
;;    via rule-based programming paradigm
;;    -- using productions (instead of function(s))
;;    might be simpler with a function and list data structure

;; 52 card deck template via multifield slot
;; access with nth$, use 1-52

(deftemplate deck (multislot cards))

;; template for 'used' or previously dealt cards
;; used cards instances in wm initally empty

(deftemplate dealt (slot card-value) (slot when))

;; keep track of how many cards
(deftemplate deal (slot cardNum))

;; templates for 7 card hands

(deftemplate hand1
  (slot holecard1)
  (slot holecard2)
  (slot community1)
  (slot community2)
  (slot community3)
  (slot community4)
  (slot community5)
)

(deftemplate hand2
  (slot holecard1)
  (slot holecard2)
  (slot community1)
  (slot community2)
  (slot community3)
  (slot community4)
  (slot community5)
)

;; reseed the random number generator
;; so each run uses a newly 'reshuffled' deck
;; must do first -- control salience

(defrule reseed
  (declare (salience 1000))
  (initial-fact)
  =>
  (seed (* 10000 (time)))
)

;; deal and record first card (must be unique)

(defrule generate-first-card
  (deck (cards $?D))
  ?Which <-(deal (cardNum 0))
  =>
  (bind ?X (random 1 52))
  (printout t "X= " ?X " or " (nth$ ?X $?D) crlf)
  (assert (dealt (card-value ?X) (when last)))
  (modify ?Which (cardNum 1))
  )

;; remainder of deal

(defrule generate-rem-cards
  (deck (cards $?D))
```

```
  ?Which <-(deal (cardNum ?N))
  (test (< ?N 9)) ;; only 9 (unique) cards needed
  ?Last <- (dealt (when last))
  =>
  (modify ?Last (when ?N)) ;; do this first
  (bind ?Y (random 1 52))
  (printout t "Y= " ?Y " or " (nth$ ?Y $?D) crlf)
  (assert (dealt (card-value ?Y) (when last))) ;; may not be unique
  (modify ?Which (cardNum (+ 1 ?N)))
)
;; check for duplicates -- see if any card matches the most recently dealt (last)
;; if so, remove last card dealt and try again

(defrule filter-duplicates
  (declare (salience 500))
  ?Which <- (deal (cardNum ?N))
  ?PrevLast <- (dealt (when = (- ?N 1))) ;; return value constraint
                                         ;; finds next to last
  ?Last <- (dealt (card-value ?X) (when last)) ;; latest
  ?Dealt <- (dealt (card-value ?X) (when ~last)) ;; not latest
  =>
  (printout t "duplicate detected -- removing" crlf)
  (retract ?Last)
  (modify ?PrevLast (when last))
  (modify ?Which (cardNum (- ?N 1))) ;; try again
)


;; form the hand (lots of variations on this)

(defrule formHand
  (deal (cardNum 9)) ;; done generating cards
  (dealt (card-value ?C1) (when 1))
  (dealt (card-value ?C2) (when 2))
  (dealt (card-value ?C3) (when 3))
  (dealt (card-value ?C4) (when 4))
  (dealt (card-value ?C5) (when 5))
  (dealt (card-value ?C6) (when 6))
  (dealt (card-value ?C7) (when 7))
  (dealt (card-value ?C8) (when 8))
  (dealt (card-value ?C9) (when last))
  =>
  ( printout t "forming the hands" crlf)
  (assert (hand1 (holecard1 ?C1)
                 (holecard2 ?C2)
                 (community1 ?C5)
                 (community2 ?C6)
                 (community3 ?C7)
                 (community4 ?C8)
                 (community5 ?C9)))
  (assert (hand1 (holecard1 ?C3)
                 (holecard2 ?C4)
                 (community1 ?C5)
                 (community2 ?C6)
                 (community3 ?C7)
                 (community4 ?C8)
                 (community5 ?C9)))
)


;; non-ordered fact represents the deck

  (deffacts deckfact "the deck data structure"
  (deck (cards
  '2S' '3S' '4S' '5S' '6S' '7S' '8S' '9S' '10S' 'JS' 'QS' 'KS' 'AS'
  '2C' '3C' '4C' '5C' '6C' '7C' '8C' '9C' '10C' 'JC' 'QC' 'KC' 'AC'
  '2D' '3D' '4D' '5D' '6D' '7D' '8D' '9D' '10D' 'JD' 'QD' 'KD' 'AD'
  '2H' '3H' '4H' '5H' '6H' '7H' '8H' '9H' '10H' 'JH' 'QH' 'KH' 'AH')))

(deffacts noDealYet (deal (cardNum 0))) ;; no cards dealt
```

Figure 7.9 Clips Example of Dealing Two Card Hands for Texas Holdem Card Game—Prelude to Expert System Development

```
CLIPS>(load "cardsOf.clips")
Defining deftemplate: deck
Defining deftemplate: dealt
Defining deftemplate: deal
Defining deftemplate: hand1
Defining deftemplate: hand2
Defining defrule: reseed +j
Defining defrule: generate-first-card +j+j
Defining defrule: generate-rem-cards =j+j+j
Defining defrule: filter-duplicates +j+j+j+j
Defining defrule: formHand +j+j+j+j+j+j+j+j+j
Defining deffacts: deckfact
Defining deffacts: noDealYet
TRUE
CLIPS> (reset)
CLIPS> f-0     (initial-fact) %% wordwrapped for illustration
f-1     (deck (cards '2S' '3S' '4S' '5S' '6S' '7S' '8S' '9S' '10S' 'JS' 'QS' 'KS' 'AS' '2C'
 '3C' '4C' '5C' '6C' '7C' '8C' '9C' '10C' 'JC' 'QC' 'KC' 'AC' '2D' '3D' '4D' '5D' '6D' '7D'
 '8D' '9D' '10D' 'JD' 'QD' 'KD' 'AD' '2H' '3H' '4H' '5H' '6H' '7H' '8H' '9H' '10H' 'JH' 'QH'
 'KH' 'AH'))
f-2     (deal (cardNum 0))
For a total of 3 facts.
CLIPS> X= 28 or '3D'
Y= 17 or '5C'
Y= 8 or '9S'
Y= 7 or '8S'
Y= 13 or 'AS'
Y= 11 or 'QS'
Y= 1 or '2S'
Y= 34 or '9D'
Y= 10 or 'JS'
forming the hands
CLIPS> f-0     (initial-fact)
f-1     (deck (cards '2S' '3S' '4S' '5S' '6S' '7S' '8S' '9S' '10S' 'JS' 'QS' 'KS' 'AS' '2C'
 '3C' '4C' '5C' '6C' '7C' '8C' '9C' '10C' 'JC' 'QC' 'KC' 'AC' '2D' '3D' '4D' '5D' '6D' '7D'
 '8D' '9D' '10D' 'JD' 'QD' 'KD' 'AD' '2H' '3H' '4H' '5H' '6H' '7H' '8H' '9H' '10H' 'JH' 'QH'
 'KH' 'AH'))
f-5     (dealt (card-value 28) (when 1))
f-8     (dealt (card-value 17) (when 2))
f-11    (dealt (card-value 8) (when 3))
f-14    (dealt (card-value 7) (when 4))
f-17    (dealt (card-value 13) (when 5))
f-20    (dealt (card-value 11) (when 6))
f-23    (dealt (card-value 1) (when 7))
f-26    (dealt (card-value 34) (when 8))
f-27    (dealt (card-value 10) (when last))
f-28    (deal (cardNum 9))
f-29    (hand1 (holecard1 28) (holecard2 17) (community1 13) (community2 11) (community3 1) (community4 34) (community5 10))
f-30    (hand1 (holecard1 8) (holecard2 7) (community1 13) (community2 11) (community3 1) (community4 34) (community5 10))
For a total of 14 facts.
CLIPS>
```

Figure 7.10 Log of CLIPS Session Corresponding to Figure 7.9

7.3.2 The agenda

CLIPS refers to the conflict set (cs) as the agenda. The agenda is a list of rules ranked in descending order of firing preference. In other words, the agenda is the list of all rules that have their LHS conditions satisfied (and have not yet been executed). In CLIPS, these rules are said to be *activated*.

When changes to working memory cause a rule to no longer be in the conflict set, it is said to be *deactivated.* One feature of CLIPS that makes a discussion of conflict resolution more complicated is the (optional) incorporation of adjustable rule *salience*, as shown in Section 7.3.3. The CLIPS user may view the status of rules using the function `matches` with syntax `matches <name-of-rule>`.

7.3.3 User-Defined Rule Salience

Placement of rules on the agenda is determined by *salience* or *saliency.* A noteworthy feature of CLIPS is that the user may define the saliency, or priority, of individual rules. This feature allows user specification of the relative importance of rules independent of any conflict resolution scheme. Salience may be dynamically controlled.

The rule with the highest salience (priority) will fire first. The declared salience value should be an expression that evaluates to an integer in the range −10,000 to +10,000. The default salience value for a rule is zero. Also, by default, salience values are only evaluated when a rule is defined.

Salience Example.   The CLIPS source is shown in the following example with three rules listed in order of increasing saliency. As the execution shows, saliency is used to prioritize the rule firings.

```
;; clips sample database for salience
;; template for memory

(deftemplate primitive
(slot name))

;; rules

(defrule rule1
  (declare (salience -1000))   ;; not very important
  (primitive (name a))
  (primitive (name r))
=>
  (assert (primitive (name b))))

(defrule rule2
  (declare (salience 1000))   ;; important
  (primitive (name a))
  (primitive (name r))
=>
  (assert (primitive (name d))))

(defrule rule3
  (declare (salience 9999))   ;; very important
  (primitive (name a))
  (primitive (name r))
=>
  (assert (primitive (name e))))

;; initial facts

(deffacts startup
```

```
       (primitive (name a))
       (primitive (name r)))

CLIPS> (load "ars-clips-sal.clips")
Defining deftemplate: primitive
Defining defrule: rule1 +j+j
Defining defrule: rule2 =j+j
Defining defrule: rule3 =j+j
Defining deffacts: startup
TRUE
CLIPS> (matches rule1)
Matches for Pattern 1
 None
Matches for Pattern 2
 None
Partial matches for CEs 1 - 2
 None
Activations
 None
CLIPS> (reset)
CLIPS> (matches rule1)
Matches for Pattern 1
f-1
Matches for Pattern 2
f-2
Partial matches for CEs 1 - 2
f-1,f-2
Activations
f-1,f-2
CLIPS> (matches rule2)
Matches for Pattern 1
f-1
Matches for Pattern 2
f-2
Partial matches for CEs 1 - 2
f-1,f-2
Activations
f-1,f-2
CLIPS> (matches rule3)
Matches for Pattern 1
f-1
Matches for Pattern 2
f-2
Partial matches for CEs 1 - 2
f-1,f-2
Activations
f-1,f-2
CLIPS> (agenda)
9999   rule3: f-1,f-2
1000   rule2: f-1,f-2
-1000   rule1: f-1,f-2
For a total of 3 activations.
CLIPS> (run)
CLIPS> (facts)
```

```
f-0      (initial-fact)
f-1      (primitive (name a))
f-2      (primitive (name r))
f-3      (primitive (name e))
f-4      (primitive (name d))
f-5      (primitive (name b))
For a total of 6 facts.
CLIPS> (agenda)
CLIPS>
```

7.3.4 Forming the Conflict Set (agenda)

A rule is said to be *activated* if the current state of wm satisfies all the CEs to the rule. In normal operation of the CLIPS execution cycle described in Section 7.1.4, rules may become (or remain) activated or become (or stay) deactivated. A newly activated rule is one that has just transitioned from a deactivated to an activated state. Most often, this is due to the addition (i.e., assertion) of one or more wm elements.

When a rule is newly activated, its placement on the agenda is based (in order) on the following factors:

1. Newly activated rules are placed above all rules of lower salience and below all rules of higher salience.

2. Among rules of equal salience, the current conflict resolution strategy is used to determine the placement among the other rules of equal salience.

3. If a rule is activated (along with several other rules) by the same assertion or retraction of a fact, and the preceding two tests are unable to specify an ordering, then the rule is arbitrarily (not randomly) ordered in relation to the other rules with which it was activated.

The default depth conflict resolution strategy implements a depth-first search by placing newly activated rule instantiations at the top of the agenda. Note that if a new fact in wm activates more than one instantiation of a rule at a time, the order of those instantiations (at the top of the agenda) is arbitrary.

7.3.5 Available CLIPS Conflict Resolution Strategies

CLIPS provides seven user-selectable conflict resolution strategies: depth, breadth, simplicity, complexity, lex, mea, and random. **The default conflict resolution strategy is depth**. A strategy is selected using the set-strategy command, with syntax:

(set-strategy <strategy>)

where <strategy> ∈ {*depth, breadth, simplicity, complexity, lex, mea, random*}. Examples are shown as follows. When the conflict resolution strategy is changed, the agenda is reordered. (get-strategy) returns the conflict resolution strategy currently in use. The descriptions of each apply to *productions of equal salience*. Refer to the CLIPS manual (bpg.pdf) for more detail.

A brief description of each follows:

depth: The depth strategy ranks productions based upon the recency of rule activation. Recency of activation is determined by the highest-valued time tag of the activated production. The most recently activated productions are ranked above all others. If a tie occurs, the agenda ordering of the most recently activated rules is arbitrary. As noted, this is the default strategy in CLIPS.

breadth: The breadth strategy is implemented by placing the newest activations of rules on the bottom of the agenda. Thus, the least recently activated productions are ranked above all others. As in depth, the order of any "ties" is arbitrary.

simplicity/complexity: This agenda ranking is based upon specificity or generality of a production. Specificity is measured in terms of LHS comparisons. For simplicity, the more comparisons, the lower the rule is on the agenda. The complexity ranking is the reverse, i.e., the more specific productions are placed on the agenda above those of lower specificity.

lex: This conflict resolution strategy emphasizes *recency*, but employs a more sophisticated strategy than depth. The lex strategy orders productions based upon sorting the recency of CE instantiation time tags. If necessary, a secondary test is to compare the number of CE tests (a crude measure of specificity).

mea: The basis of this strategy is forming the agenda by sorting (in decreasing order) activated productions using the time tag of their *first* CE.

random: Each activated production is assigned a random number to determine the placement of this production on the agenda.

7.3.6 Conflict Resolution Examples

We use two simple CLIPS databases to show the effect of varying CLIPS conflict resolution strategies. Figure 7.11 illustrates the simpler CLIPS conflict resolution strategies. The CLIPS source file is shown on the left. The resulting agendas, each formed by a different conflict resolution strategy, are shown on the right. Each reordered agenda is shown after revision of the conflict resolution strategy using set-strategy.

The reader should verify the reasonableness of these results, given the conflict resolution strategy descriptions. Figure 7.12 compares the depth, lex, and mea strategies.

7.4 Another Expert System Application Example: "Tenure"

7.4.1 An Application Domain

Consider the development of an "expert" system in CLIPS to automate the role of a college dean. The dean, among other things, is charged with determining which faculty members in his/her college receive tenure, or lifetime employment.

```
;; clips database for simple
;; conflict resolution examples
;; file: "ars-clips-cr.clips"


;; template for memory

(deftemplate primitive
(slot name))

;; rules

(defrule rule1
  (primitive (name a))
  (primitive (name r))
  (primitive (name s))
=>
  (assert (primitive (name b))))

(defrule rule2
  (primitive (name a))
  (primitive (name r))
=>
  (assert (primitive (name d))))

(defrule rule3
  (primitive (name r))
  (primitive (name s))
=>
  (assert (primitive (name e))))

(defrule rule4
  (primitive (name r))
  (primitive (name s))
  (test (< 1 2))
  (test (< 2 3))
=>
  (assert (primitive (name f))))

;; initial facts

(deffacts startup
  (primitive (name a))
  (primitive (name r))
  (primitive (name s)))
```

```
CLIPS> (clear)
CLIPS> (load "ars-clips-cr.clips")
Defining deftemplate: primitive
Defining defrule: rule1 +j+j+j
Defining defrule: rule2 =j=j
Defining defrule: rule3 +j+j
Defining defrule: rule4 =j+j
Defining deffacts: startup
TRUE
CLIPS> (agenda)          ;; empty (no facts)
CLIPS> (get-strategy)
depth                    ;; the default
CLIPS> (reset)           ;; enable facts
CLIPS> (agenda)
0      rule1: f-1,f-2,f-3
0      rule3: f-2,f-3
0      rule4: f-2,f-3
0      rule2: f-1,f-2
For a total of 4 activations.
CLIPS> (set-strategy breadth)
depth  ;; note: returns previous strategy
CLIPS> (agenda)
0      rule2: f-1,f-2
0      rule4: f-2,f-3
0      rule3: f-2,f-3
0      rule1: f-1,f-2,f-3
For a total of 4 activations.
CLIPS> (set-strategy simplicity)
breadth
CLIPS> (agenda)
0      rule2: f-1,f-2
0      rule3: f-2,f-3
0      rule4: f-2,f-3
0      rule1: f-1,f-2,f-3
For a total of 4 activations.
CLIPS> (set-strategy complexity)
simplicity
CLIPS> (agenda)
0      rule4: f-2,f-3  ;; more CE tests
0      rule1: f-1,f-2,f-3
0      rule2: f-1,f-2
0      rule3: f-2,f-3
For a total of 4 activations.
CLIPS> (set-strategy random)
complexity
CLIPS> (agenda)
0      rule1: f-1,f-2,f-3
0      rule4: f-2,f-3
0      rule2: f-1,f-2
0      rule3: f-2,f-3
For a total of 4 activations.
CLIPS>
```

Figure 7.11 CLIPS Database (left) to Illustrate Simple Conflict Resolution Strategies (depth, breadth, complexity, simplicity, and random). Right: Resulting Agenda Positions of Rules Using These Strategies.

```
;; clips database to illustrate
;; strategies depth, lex and mea.
;; file "ars-clips-cr2a.clips"

;; template for memory

(deftemplate primitive
(slot name))

;; rules

(defrule rule1
  (primitive (name f1))
  (primitive (name f4))
  (primitive (name f5))
=>
  (assert (primitive (name f6))))

(defrule rule2
  (primitive (name f2))
  (primitive (name f4))
  (primitive (name f5))
=>
  (assert (primitive (name f7))))


(defrule rule3
  (primitive (name f1))
  (primitive (name f4))
=>
  (assert (primitive (name f8))))

;; initial facts

(deffacts startup
  (primitive (name f1))
  (primitive (name f2))
  (primitive (name f3))
  (primitive (name f4))
  (primitive (name f5)))
```

```
CLIPS> (get-strategy)
depth
CLIPS> (watch activations)
CLIPS> (load "ars-clips-cr2a.clips")
Defining deftemplate: primitive
Defining defrule: rule1 +j+j+j
Defining defrule: rule2 +j+j+j
Defining defrule: rule3 =j=j
Defining deffacts: startup
TRUE
CLIPS> (reset)
==> Activation 0      rule3: f-1,f-4
==> Activation 0      rule2: f-2,f-4,f-5
==> Activation 0      rule1: f-1,f-4,f-5
CLIPS> (facts)
f-0     (initial-fact)
f-1     (primitive (name f1))
f-2     (primitive (name f2))
f-3     (primitive (name f3))
f-4     (primitive (name f4))
f-5     (primitive (name f5))
For a total of 6 facts.
CLIPS> (agenda)
0       rule1: f-1,f-4,f-5
0       rule2: f-2,f-4,f-5
0       rule3: f-1,f-4
For a total of 3 activations.
CLIPS> (set-strategy lex)
depth
CLIPS> (agenda)
0       rule2: f-2,f-4,f-5
0       rule1: f-1,f-4,f-5
0       rule3: f-1,f-4
For a total of 3 activations.
CLIPS> (set-strategy mea)
lex
CLIPS> (agenda)
0       rule2: f-2,f-4,f-5
0       rule1: f-1,f-4,f-5
0       rule3: f-1,f-4
For a total of 3 activations.
```

Figure 7.12 Second CLIPS Conflict Resolution Examples. Here CLIPS conflict resolution strategies depth, lex, and mea are compared.

7.4.2 The Development Process

We begin the development of a CLIPS representation for this decision capability with the following dialog between a typical dean (DEAN) and the CLIPS software developer (CSD).

CSD: Dean, tell me how you decide who gets tenure.
DEAN: That's easy. I award tenure to my faculty who publish,
get research, and teach well.
CSD: Am I correct in my understanding that they must do
all three of these?
DEAN: That's right.
CSD: How does a faculty member "publish?"
DEAN: The faculty member conducts research and documents
the research.
CSD: How does the faculty member get research?
DEAN: The faculty member writes research proposals that
subsequently become funded.
CSD: What does it mean for a faculty member to teach well?
DEAN: That's easy. A good teacher prepares lectures,
delivers the lecture well, and gets good evaluations from the students.
CSD: Is that all there is to it?
DEAN: That's right.
CSD: Thanks for your time and expertise, Dean.

7.4.3 Initial CLIPS Expert System Development Example

Based upon the conversation in Section 7.4.2, the following CLIPS representation was developed.

```
;; first 'tenure' example in clips
;; spartan version (no ranges, defaults, printouts,..

;; TEMPLATES

(deftemplate faculty
        (slot name)
        (slot teaching_evals)
        (slot lecture_quality)
        (slot lecture_prep)
        (slot proposal_writing)
        (slot proposal_funding)
        (slot research_accomp)
        (slot research_publ)
        (slot tenure_status))

(deftemplate teaching_performance
        (slot name)
        (slot rating))
```

```
(deftemplate research_performance
          (slot name)
          (slot rating))

(deftemplate publ_performance
          (slot name)
          (slot rating))


;; RULES

(defrule assess_teach_perf
   (faculty (name ?W) (lecture_prep yes))
   (faculty (name ?W) (lecture_quality good))
   (faculty (name ?W) (teaching_evals good))
=>
   (assert (teaching_performance (name ?W) (rating acceptable))))

(defrule assess_research_perf
   (faculty (name ?W) (proposal_writing extensive))
   (faculty (name ?W) (proposal_funding good))
=>
   (assert (research_performance (name ?W) (rating good))))

(defrule assess_publ_perf
   (faculty (name ?W) (research_accomp substantial))
   (faculty (name ?W) (research_publ adequate))
=>
   (assert (publ_performance (name ?W) (rating good))))

(defrule tenure-decision
   ?Who <- (faculty (name ?W) (tenure_status UNKNOWN))
   (teaching_performance (name ?W) (rating acceptable))
   (research_performance (name ?W) (rating good))
   (publ_performance (name ?W) (rating good))
=>
   (modify ?Who (tenure_status tenured)))

;; FACTS

(deffacts database
(faculty (name pwd)
        (teaching_evals good)
        (lecture_quality good)
        (lecture_prep yes)
        (proposal_writing extensive)
        (proposal_funding good)
        (research_accomp substantial)
        (research_publ adequate)
        (tenure_status UNKNOWN))
(faculty (name dir)
        (teaching_evals good)
        (lecture_quality fantastic)
        (lecture_prep yes)
```

```
          (proposal_writing extensive)
          (proposal_funding good)
          (research_accomp substantial)
          (research_publ adequate)
          (tenure_status UNKNOWN))
(faculty (name lls)
          (teaching_evals good)
          (lecture_quality good)
          (lecture_prep never)
          (proposal_writing extensive)
          (proposal_funding good)
          (research_accomp substantial)
          (research_publ adequate)
          (tenure_status UNKNOWN))
(faculty (name cwd)
          (teaching_evals fair)
          (lecture_quality good)
          (lecture_prep yes)
          (proposal_writing extensive)
          (proposal_funding good)
          (research_accomp extraordinary)
          (research_publ adequate)
          (tenure_status UNKNOWN))
(faculty (name lpr)
          (teaching_evals good)
          (lecture_quality good)
          (lecture_prep yes)
          (proposal_writing extensive)
          (proposal_funding good)
          (research_accomp substantial)
          (research_publ adequate)
          (tenure_status UNKNOWN))     )
```

Sample use with CLIPS is shown in Figure 7.13.

7.4.4 Enhanced CLIPS Development of the Previous Example

Suppose the CLIPS software developer (CSD) from Section 7.4.2 later meets the Dean at the campus pub. The Dean, sitting in front of a table full of empty bottles, calls the CSD over and wishes to expand upon, and clarify, some of his earlier points. On this basis, the following, more comprehensive, database is developed. This expanded example illustrates the use of a number of more sophisticated CLIPS elements, including:

1. Non-ordered fact default values;

2. Restrictions on slot values;

3. (printout);

4. Field value constraint connectives (mostly |);

5. OR-ed condition elements;

```
CLIPS> (load "tenure.clips")
Defining deftemplate: faculty
Defining deftemplate: teaching_performance
Defining deftemplate: research_performance
Defining deftemplate: publ_performance
Defining defrule: assess_teach_perf +j+j+j
Defining defrule: assess_research_perf +j+j
Defining defrule: assess_publ_perf +j+j
Defining defrule: tenure-decision +j+j+j+j
Defining deffacts: database
TRUE
CLIPS> (reset)
CLIPS> (facts)
f-0     (initial-fact)
f-1     (faculty (name pwd) (teaching_evals good) (lecture_quality good) (lecture_prep yes)
        (proposal_writing extensive) (proposal_funding good) (research_accomp substantial)
        (research_publ adequate) (tenure_status UNKNOWN))
f-2     (faculty (name dir) (teaching_evals good) (lecture_quality fantastic) (lecture_prep yes)
        (proposal_writing extensive) (proposal_funding good) (research_accomp substantial)
        (research_publ adequate) (tenure_status UNKNOWN))
f-3     (faculty (name lls) (teaching_evals good) (lecture_quality good) (lecture_prep never)
        (proposal_writing extensive) (proposal_funding good) (research_accomp substantial)
        (research_publ adequate) (tenure_status UNKNOWN))
f-4     (faculty (name cwd) (teaching_evals fair) (lecture_quality good) (lecture_prep yes)
        (proposal_writing extensive) (proposal_funding good) (research_accomp extraordinary)
        (research_publ adequate) (tenure_status UNKNOWN))
f-5     (faculty (name lpr) (teaching_evals good) (lecture_quality good) (lecture_prep yes)
        (proposal_writing extensive) (proposal_funding good) (research_accomp substantial)
        (research_publ adequate) (tenure_status UNKNOWN))
For a total of 6 facts.
CLIPS> (run)
CLIPS> (facts)
f-0     (initial-fact)
f-2     (faculty (name dir) (teaching_evals good) (lecture_quality fantastic) (lecture_prep yes)
        (proposal_writing extensive) (proposal_funding good) (research_accomp substantial)
        (research_publ adequate) (tenure_status UNKNOWN))
f-3     (faculty (name lls) (teaching_evals good) (lecture_quality good) (lecture_prep never)
        (proposal_writing extensive) (proposal_funding good) (research_accomp substantial)
        (research_publ adequate) (tenure_status UNKNOWN))
f-4     (faculty (name cwd) (teaching_evals fair) (lecture_quality good) (lecture_prep yes)
        (proposal_writing extensive) (proposal_funding good) (research_accomp extraordinary)
        (research_publ adequate) (tenure_status UNKNOWN))
f-6     (teaching_performance (name lpr) (rating acceptable))
f-7     (research_performance (name lpr) (rating good))
f-8     (publ_performance (name lpr) (rating good))
f-9     (faculty (name lpr) (teaching_evals good) (lecture_quality good) (lecture_prep yes)
        (proposal_writing extensive) (proposal_funding good) (research_accomp substantial)
        (research_publ adequate) (tenure_status tenured))
f-10    (research_performance (name cwd) (rating good))
f-11    (research_performance (name lls) (rating good))
f-12    (publ_performance (name lls) (rating good))
f-13    (research_performance (name dir) (rating good))
f-14    (publ_performance (name dir) (rating good))
f-15    (teaching_performance (name pwd) (rating acceptable))
f-16    (research_performance (name pwd) (rating good))
f-17    (publ_performance (name pwd) (rating good))
f-18    (faculty (name pwd) (teaching_evals good) (lecture_quality good) (lecture_prep yes)
        (proposal_writing extensive) (proposal_funding good) (research_accomp substantial)
        (research_publ adequate) (tenure_status tenured))
For a total of 17 facts.
CLIPS>
```

Figure 7.13 Sample Use with CLIPS

6. The use of `modify`;

7. `test` and numerical field value constraints; and

8. Case sensitivity (e.g., unknown and UNKNOWN).

```
;; enhanced clips 'tenure' example
;; file: tenure2.clips


;; TEMPLATES

(deftemplate faculty
          (slot name)
          (slot teaching_evals
             (default unknown)
             (allowed-symbols excellent good fair poor miserable unknown))
          (slot lecture_quality
             (default unknown)
             (allowed-symbols fantastic excellent good fair
                           poor miserable unknown))
          (slot lecture_prep
             (default yes)
             (allowed-symbols yes no))
          (slot proposal_writing
             (allowed-symbols extensive regular occasional never))
          (slot proposal_funding
             (type INTEGER))
          (slot research_accomp
             (allowed-symbols extraordinary excellent
                           substantial good fair poor))
          (slot research_publ
             (type INTEGER))
          (slot tenure_status(default UNKNOWN)
             (allowed-symbols tenured untenured fired UNKNOWN))
)

(deftemplate teaching_performance
          (slot name)
          (slot rating
             (allowed-symbols superlative acceptable let_slide poor embarrassment))
)

(deftemplate research_performance
          (slot name)
          (slot rating))

(deftemplate publ_performance
          (slot name)
          (slot rating))


;; RULES
```

```
(defrule assess_teach_perf1
   (faculty (name ?W) (lecture_prep yes))
   (faculty (name ?W) (lecture_quality ~miserable))
   (faculty (name ?W) (teaching_evals ~miserable|~poor))
=>
   (assert (teaching_performance (name ?W) (rating let_slide))))

(defrule assess_teach_perf2
   (faculty (name ?W) (lecture_prep yes))
   (faculty (name ?W) (lecture_quality excellent|good))
   (faculty (name ?W) (teaching_evals excellent|good))
=>
   (assert (teaching_performance (name ?W) (rating superlative))))

(defrule assess_teach_perf3
   (faculty (name ?W) (lecture_prep yes))
   (faculty (name ?W) (lecture_quality miserable|poor))
   (faculty (name ?W) (teaching_evals poor))
=>
   (assert (teaching_performance (name ?W) (rating poor))))

(defrule assess_research_perf1
   (faculty (name ?W) (proposal_writing extensive|regular))
   (faculty (name ?W) (proposal_funding ?dollars))
   (test (>= ?dollars 100000))
=>
   (assert (research_performance (name ?W) (rating excellent))))

(defrule assess_research_perf2
   (faculty (name ?W) (proposal_writing occasional|never))
   (faculty (name ?W) (proposal_funding ?dollars))
   (test (< ?dollars 100000))
=>
   (assert (research_performance (name ?W) (rating poor))))

(defrule assess_publ_perf1
   (faculty (name ?W) (research_accomp substantial))
   (faculty (name ?W) (research_publ ?how_many))
   (test (> ?how_many 50))
=>
   (assert (publ_performance (name ?W) (rating good))))

(defrule assess_publ_perf2
   (faculty (name ?W) (research_accomp fair|poor))
   (faculty (name ?W) (research_publ ?how_many))
   (test (<= ?how_many 25))
=>
   (assert (publ_performance (name ?W) (rating poor))))

(defrule tenure_decision1
   ?Who <- (faculty (name ?W) (tenure_status untenured|UNKNOWN))
   (teaching_performance (name ?W) (rating ~embarrassment|~poor))
   (research_performance (name ?W) (rating excellent))
   (publ_performance (name ?W) (rating good))
```

```
=>
   (printout t tab "faculy member" tab ?W  tab "will be tenured" crlf)
   (modify ?Who (tenure_status tenured)))

(defrule tenure_decision2
   ?Who <- (faculty (name ?W) (tenure_status untenured|UNKNOWN))
   (or (teaching_performance (name ?W) (rating embarrassment|poor))
       (research_performance (name ?W) (rating poor))
       (publ_performance (name ?W) (rating poor)))
=>
   (printout t tab "faculty member" tab ?W tab "will be fired" crlf)
   (modify ?Who (tenure_status fired)))


;; FACTS

(deffacts database
(faculty (name pwd)
         (teaching_evals good)(lecture_quality good)
         (lecture_prep yes)(proposal_writing extensive)
         (proposal_funding 100000)(research_accomp substantial)
         (research_publ 25)(tenure_status UNKNOWN))
(faculty (name dir)
         (teaching_evals good)(lecture_quality fantastic)
         (lecture_prep yes)(proposal_writing extensive)
         (proposal_funding 50000)(research_accomp substantial)
         (research_publ 50)(tenure_status UNKNOWN))
(faculty (name lls)
         (teaching_evals good)(lecture_quality good)
         (lecture_prep no)(proposal_writing extensive)
         (proposal_funding 25000)(research_accomp substantial)
         (research_publ 3)(tenure_status UNKNOWN))
(faculty (name cwd)
         (teaching_evals fair)(lecture_quality poor)
         (lecture_prep yes)(proposal_writing occasional)
         (proposal_funding 5000)(research_accomp fair)
         (research_publ 20)(tenure_status UNKNOWN))
(faculty (name lpr)
         (teaching_evals good)(lecture_quality good)
         (lecture_prep yes)(proposal_writing extensive)
         (proposal_funding 1000000)(research_accomp substantial)
         (research_publ 100)(tenure_status UNKNOWN))
)
```

Using this CLIPS database, the reader should be able to determine who, if anyone, gets tenure and who, if anyone, gets fired.

7.4.5 A CLIPS Planning Example: The Monkey and Bananas (MAB) Problem

The monkey and bananas problem is an excellent toy problem used to illustrate planning and goal-directed chaining. The monkey and bananas CLIPS source is freely available from the CLIPS website. The reader is encouraged to obtain and study this formulation. The corresponding xclips execution of the planner is shown in Figure 7.14.

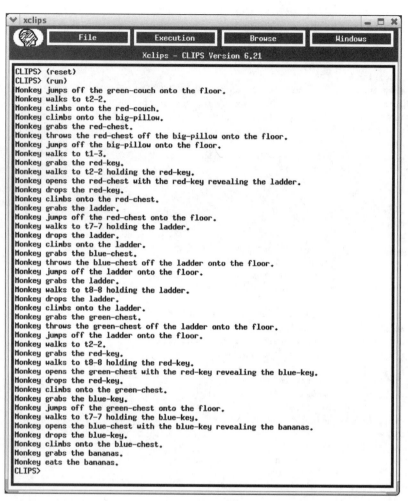

Figure 7.14 Execution of the Monkey and Bananas Problem Using `xclips`

7.5   CLIPS Efficiency and the Rete Algorithm

7.5.1   Motivation

Two empirical observations fuel our desire for an efficient implementation of a production system:

1. In most production systems, *most of the processing time is spent determining which productions are eligible to fire or be used.* Thus, the significant computational cost in a CLIPS system is repeated execution of `recognizeact` cycles to form the next agenda (conflict set).

   In the "recognize" phase of the cycle, production CEs in the system are matched against working memory. In the "act" phase, one or more of the matched productions are fired, possibly changing the working memory, and causing the system to execute the next `recognizeact` cycle (unless a termination condition has been encountered).

2. Much of the production system knowledge base is fixed from cycle to cycle. This suggests that much of the rechecking of CEs at the next cycle is superfluous.

Production System Scalability

A serious criticism of production system implementations is the inability to handle large data sets [Ish91]. This is a serious flaw, since it appears that IS and expert systems benefit from larger and larger knowledge bases. It appears the primary cause of the poor scalability is the combinatorial explosion in the number of possible matches that arise from the need to match conjunctive conditions where each CE can potentially match all of wm.

7.5.2 Computational Complexity

An alternative viewpoint is to consider the computational complexity of the conflict set-forming process. Here we simplify the computational cost estimate by using the average number of CEs per production. Note that the actual computation will be greatly affected by the number of slots (patterns) to be checked in each CE, as well as the effect of (shared) variables. More formally, consider a PS with r productions, each having an average of $\bar{c}$ CE tests and a database of f wm elements. Assume a straightforward, "brute-force" matching strategy is used. The computational complexity in conflict set formation, denoted cc_{cs}, is given by Equation 7.1:

$$cc_{cs} = \mathcal{O}(rf^{\bar{c}}) \tag{7.1}$$

Notice cc_{cs}, is scaled by r, but the significant complexity arises from the $f^{\bar{c}}$ part. Figure 7.15 shows this complexity measure normalized to $r = 1$ and using a semilog scale. The motivation for efficient matching is apparent. We revisit the measure of Equation 7.1 in Section 7.5.9.

Production System Time Response

As noted, a key performance bottleneck in the production system computation is in the production match cycle. This computation is NP-hard, and has proven to be a problem in different areas of production system application. In real-time systems based on productions systems, combinatorial match hinders the achievement of guaranteed response times. Furthermore, in systems that learn new productions, combinatorial match can lead to an actual slowdown with learning [TNR90]. Combinatorial production match also has unfavorable implications for parallelizing production systems [ATG92].

7.5.3 The Computational Model

The computational model for a production system is one of a data-dependent control flow. We next explore whether the computation may be viewed as either "wm-driven" or "pm-driven."

7.5.4 The "Traditional" Viewpoint of Production System Operation

The conceptual framework and the match-act cycle for a production system is shown in Figure 7.16.

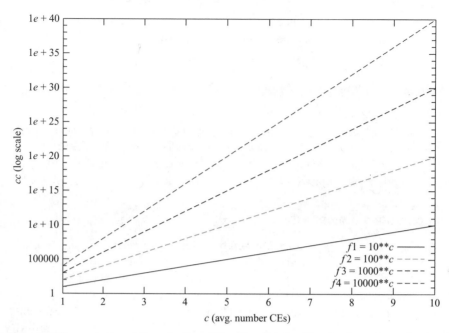

Figure 7.15 Potential Computational Complexity of Forming the Conflict Set from Equation 7.1. Normalized to $r = 1$. (note semilog scale)

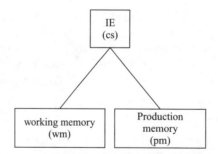

Figure 7.16 A Conceptual Structure of CLIPS Computation

An inefficient and somewhat unintelligent *computational* approach to rule-based inference would be for the pattern matcher, the heart of the IE, to:

1. Start over at each cycle and match all production CEs against `wm`. This is referred to as *iterating over* `wm`;

2. Form conflict set and perform conflict resolution; and

3. Fire a production and go to Step 1.

The inefficiency of this process is apparent when one considers that, in a "typical" production system, less than 1% of `wm` *changes at each cycle.* This property is called *temporal redundancy.* Therefore, the majority of the tests performed by the pattern matcher are superfluous (vis-a-vis the previous match cycle). In other words, wm is assumed **persistent**. The "recheck all antecedents at each cycle" strategy, while straightforward, yields many redundant CE tests at each cycle.

7.5.5   Rete (I) Background

Rete is latin for "net." The Rete algorithm was developed by Dr. Charles L. Forgy at Carnegie-Mellon University. The Rete algorithm is widely used and forms the computational basis for OPS5, CLIPS, JESS, Soar, and numerous commercial rule-based tools. Rete efficiency is asymptotically independent of the number of rules. Rete is several or many times faster than any known, alternative algorithm.

In the principal reference for the algorithm is [For82]. Unfortunately, this paper is more of a comprehensive reference to a specific implementation of the algorithm rather than the approach itself.

In the following section, to illustrate the basic operation of Rete, we assume wm does not contain variables. This restriction is later removed.

7.5.6   Productions and wm Data: Who's In Charge?

One viewpoint of production system operation is shown in Figure 7.17. Notice from Figure 7.17 that each condition element (CE_j) is explicitly checked against wm. In this case, the presumption is that productions are "in charge." This strategy is notoriously inefficient if there are very small changes to the contents of wm at each cycle. In this case, the production system matcher is basically repeating most of the same work at each cycle.

The Rete Viewpoint

The Rete viewpoint differs considerably from Section 7.5.6 and Figure 7.17. One way to visualize the Rete-based computational approach is the following: instead of the production "examining the data in working memory," the data in working memory "notifies the production of changes." Using Rete, the computational cycle is based upon the propagation of *differential* changes to working memory.

Using Rete, changes to wm are communicated to pm through the Rete network. This is shown in Figure 7.18. This approach can be very efficient when wm is persistent. Notice from Figure 7.18 that wm "notifies" each condition element, $CE_j \ldots CE_x$ about their respective status in the conflict set formation. There are two main optimizations possible with Rete: capitalizing on the persistence of wm

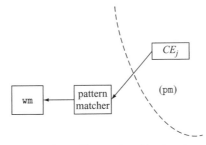

Figure 7.17 One Matching Viewpoint: Productions (re)-Check wm

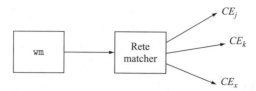

Figure 7.18 Rete Matching Viewpoint: Changes to **wm** are Conveyed to the Production Condition Elements. (This includes the initial formation of **wm**.)

(often called "state saving") and sharing of CE tests. Sharing CE tests employs *structural similarity*. The persistence-based optimization is, by far, the most important.

What Are the Tests in a CE?

Consider a typical (but not very general) production of the form:

```
(defrule rule2
(primitive (element-name1 c) (element-name2 a2))
(primitive (element-name1 ?A2) (element-name2 c))
(primitive (element-name1 c) (element-name2 ?A2))
(primitive (element-name1 b))
(not (primitive (element-name2 b)))
=>
(assert (primitive (element-name1 a2))))
```

Figure 7.19 Sample CLIPS Code for Rete Network

Notice the CE tests (the conjunction of which is implied) either involve matching of **wm** instances with constants or unification with variables.

Possible Efficiencies

In addition to the assumption of temporal persistence of **wm**, other noteworthy sources of potential efficiency in the matching process are based upon observations that

1. Parts of CE tests may be shared with other CEs in the same production; and

2. Parts of CE tests may be shared with other CEs in other productions.

These observations form the framework of the Rete matching algorithm. Rete gains its efficiency by exploiting the fact that only a small fraction of working memory changes each cycle and that common CE tests exist in productions. This reduces the overall number of matching tests performed at each cycle.

The sharing of common parts of CEs in a single production or across different productions reduces the number of tests required to complete the match [Ish88], [ML91]. In practice, however, the computational savings of sharing have turned out to be quite meager relative to the savings due to exploiting **wm** persistence.

7.5.7   How Is Rete Implemented?

Our previous reasoning and the concepts of Section 7.5.6 and Figure 7.18, suggest that an efficient interface between wm and pm that facilitates matching is necessary. Since wm (and possibly pm) will likely change over time (or recognizeact cycles), the nature of the linking mechanism must facilitate this.

The reader should consider the implementor's dilemma in this problem. wm and pm may change, but we desire a means of implementing a unidirectional link for communication between the current incarnations of the two. It is not hard to see that static data structures linking wm and pm would be problematic. Instead, a data-flow network is used. The basic building blocks for the data-flow graph are one- and two-input nodes, as described next.

Data–Flow Graphs

Rete uses a data-flow network derived from decomposing and precompiling the CEs on the LHS of all productions. Many production system interfaces (e.g., CLIPS, Soar) actually provide rudimentary information on the formation of the network. CLIPS, for example, uses +j and =j notation, as shown in Section 7.5.8 to indicate the addition of a new join node or re-use of an existing join node, respectively.

The overall Rete network is generated before the production system is actually run. The entities used to encapsulate and communicate wm changes and that "flow" through the Rete network are *tokens*. A token consists of a tag, a list of WME timetags, and a list of variable bindings. A token tag is either a+ or a− type, indicating the addition or deletion of a wm element. The list of WME timetags identifies the data elements matching a subsequence of CEs in the production. The list of variable bindings associated with a token corresponds to the bindings created for variables in those CEs that unify with wm elements.

Types of Nodes in the Rete Network (Data–Flow Graph) and Token Propagation

Tokens in the Rete network data-flow graph are generally used to communicate changes in wm. There are a number of types of nodes in the Rete network, varying in both structure and function:

1. A root node, which accepts a token and *distributes it to its successors*, are the input nodes at the "top" of the network. Many times this node is not shown, but simply assumed, in the Rete network. This node simply broadcasts the tokens and is of no particular significance.

2. One-input nodes, which are called *alpha* nodes that implement simple tests on the class of the working memory element and specific fields (e.g., slot values). The "top" of the Rete net is composed of alpha nodes. This part of the Rete network possesses no memory. Tokens are passed to succeeding nodes in the network only if the tests at the current node succeed.

3. Two-input (*join*) or *beta* nodes, test for joint satisfaction of CE tests. To accomplish this, two-input nodes compare tokens from different paths and join them into bigger tokens if they satisfy inter-element constraints. These two-input beta nodes implement so-called beta or AND tests and are also responsible for unifying variable values between two condition elements. Beta nodes save wm state.

Each beta node has both two inputs and two memories (left and right; one associated with each input direction). As a token arrives at a beta node, it is stored in the left or right memory. This is how the Rete network maintains state (wm) information. The token is then tested against the opposite memory to see if one or more consistent variable bindings can be achieved. If so, a new token is constructed from the incoming token and the stored token. This new token is then propagated through this beta node to successor nodes. Therefore, the left and right memories associated with the beta nodes store partial matches, making it unnecessary to repeat the entire computationally expensive unification process after each change to wm.

In the case of a negated token (that is, a token resulting from a remove or modify command), the AND node functions in the same way except that the token is removed from the memory node and, if the token satisfies the tests, a new negated token is passed to succeeding nodes so that partial matches will be deleted from memory nodes lower down in the network. If the succeeding node is a production node, then the negated token indicates this production (with a particular instantiation) should be removed from the conflict set.

4. A NOT node is used to implement negated clauses in a production LHS. NOT nodes are structurally similar to AND nodes, but the processing is different. A NOT node must ensure that for a given negated clause, there is no working memory element that matches that clause in such a way that there are consistent variable bindings with the working memory elements matching the preceding LHS clauses. Like the AND node, the NOT node has two memories. One memory is devoted to working memory elements that potentially match the negated clause. The other memory contains a list of tokens corresponding to the nonnegated condition elements of the LHS and, associated with each token, a count of the number of matches that occur in the opposite memory.

A negated token should not be confused with a negated condition element. *A negated token is simply a token indicating* wm *element removal while a negated condition element specifies a* wm *instance that cannot exist if the production is to be included in the conflict set.*

5. Production nodes are at the bottom of the Rete net. If a token arrives at one of these nodes, the production corresponding to the node is placed in the conflict set and instantiated with variable bindings from the incoming token. A production node has no memory, thus only one production firing ever results from a given combination of working memory elements. This implements refraction and inhibits a production sec:exploring-rete-with-clips-jess from repeatedly firing and yielding the exact same actions.

Example Rete Network

Consider the CLIPS code as follows:

```
;; reteEx1r.clips

(deftemplate class1
        (slot attr1)
```

```
            (slot attr2))
(deftemplate class2
            (slot attr1)
            (slot attr2))
(deftemplate class3
            (slot attr1)
            (slot attr2))
(deftemplate class4
            (slot attr1)
            (slot attr2))

(defrule prod1
    (class1 (attr1 ?X) (attr2 12))
    (class2 (attr1 15) (attr2 ?X))
    (class3 (attr1 ?X))
    =>
    (assert (class4 (attr2 1)))
    )

(defrule prod2
    (class2 (attr1 15) (attr2 ?Y))
    (class4 (attr1 ?Y))
    =>
    (assert (class3 (attr1 2)))
    )
```

A Rete network for production "prod1" is shown in Figure 7.20.

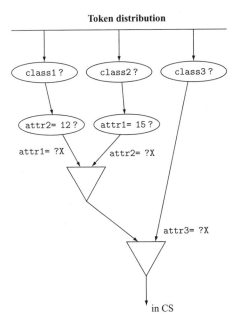

Figure 7.20 Rete Network for Sample Production "prod1"

The exercises consider the Rete network for `prod2` and the combined Rete network.

7.5.8 Exploring the Rete Algorithm with CLIPS

Here we show several simple examples of the operation of CLIPS (and JESS) using the Rete algorithm. In addition, relevant CLIPS source files are cited.

CLIPS Source for the Rete Implementation

Although a detailed exploration of the CLIPS C source code is beyond our scope, we show a few examples of CLIPS implementation of Rete. For illustration, the first CLIPS source file the reader may explore is `rulebld.c`. This file indicates the key to watching Rete algorithm production compilation as a CLIPS file is loaded.

If compilations are being watched (via (`watch compilations`)), a `+j` is printed for each new join used to map the rule CEs to a Rete network. Printing of a `+j` indicates that this CE pattern of the rule could not be shared with another rule.

If the next CE part to be compiled into the Rete network results in a join that can be shared, `=j` is printed. Finally, a carriage return is printed after all of the `=j`'s and `+j`'s necessary to encode each CE have been determined. This explains the role of the mysterious symbols printed during CLIPS file loading.

Case #1: No CE Reduction Possible in Rete Network

The following examples all use ordered facts for simplicity. Consider the very simple CLIPS (or JESS) source file containing a pair of rules as follows:

```
;; file: rete-ex0.clips

(defrule rule0
(a) (b)
=>
(assert (r)))

(defrule rule0.5
(c) (d)
=>
(assert (x)))
```

Notice no redundant `wm` element tests are involved. The CLIPS compilation of this source is shown as follows:

```
CLIPS> (clear)
CLIPS> (load "rete-ex0.clips")
Defining defrule: rule0 +j+j
Defining defrule: rule0.5 +j+j
TRUE
```

Notice no `=t` compilation results are reported.

Case #2: CE Reduction Possible in Rete Network

The next example contains a pair of rules as follows:

```
;; file: rete-ex0.5.clips

(defrule rule0
(a) (b)
=>
(assert (r)))

(defrule rule0.5
(a) (d)
=>
(assert (x)))
```

Here redundant **wm** element tests are involved, in the sense that `rule0` and `rule0.5` share a CE (i.e., (a)). The CLIPS compilation of this source is shown as follows:

```
CLIPS> (clear)
CLIPS> (load "rete-ex0.5.clips")
Defining defrule: rule0 +j+j
Defining defrule: rule0.5 =j+j
TRUE
```

Notice a =t compilation result is reported.

Case #3: Significant CE Reduction Possible in Rete Network

Next consider:

```
;; file: rete-ex0.75.clips

(defrule rule0
(a) (b)
=>
(assert (r)))

(defrule rule0.5
(a) (d)
=>
(assert (x)))

(defrule rule0.75
(a) (d) (e)
=>
(assert (y)))
```

Observe redundancy between `rule0` and `rule0.5` and the significant redundancy between `rule0.5` and `rule0.75` (i.e., two identical CEs). Compilation results reflect this, as shown:

```
CLIPS> (load "rete-ex0.75.clips")
Defining defrule: rule0 +j+j
Defining defrule: rule0.5 =j+j
Defining defrule: rule0.75 =j=j+j
TRUE
```

Case #4: Very Significant CE Reduction Possible in Rete Network

Case #4 is somewhat extreme, but illustrative. Consider the source:

```
;; file: rete-ex1.clips

(defrule rule1
(a) (b) (c)
=>
(assert (r)))

(defrule rule2
(a) (b) (c)
=>
(assert (s)))

(defrule rule3
(a) (b) (c)
=>
(assert (t)))

(defrule rule4
(a) (b)
=>
(assert (u)))
```

Observe the significant redundancy among all rule CEs. Compilation results reflect the ability of the Rete algorithm to encode this set of productions with maximal sharing of tests, as follows:

```
CLIPS>(clear)
CLIPS> (load "rete-ex1.clips")
Defining defrule: rule1 +j+j+j
Defining defrule: rule2 =j=j+j
Defining defrule: rule3 =j=j+j
Defining defrule: rule4 =j=j
TRUE
```

7.5.9 Writing Efficient CLIPS Programs

Concerns Related to Rete and an Example

The Rete algorithm significantly reduces the computational complexity from that of a brute-force matching process (see Section 7.5.2) in conflict set formation. However, careful coding of the productions in an unmodified Rete-based PS implementation (including CLIPS) is still necessary. There are several concerns, including:

1. The computational cost of token propagation, especially at beta nodes; and

2. Memory requirements for the Rete network, especially beta nodes.

To this end, consider the following two-rule CLIPS database.

```
;; to show clips matching efficiency/Rete
;; efficiency-ex1.clips
;; uses ordered facts for simplicity

;; rules

(defrule rule1
(find ?x ?y ?z ?w)
(item ?x)
(item ?y)
(item ?z)
(item ?w)
=>
(printout t tab "rule 1 found" tab "x= " ?x "   y= " ?y "   z= " ?z "   w= " ?w crlf)
)

(defrule rule2
(item ?x)
(item ?y)
(item ?z)
(item ?w)
(find ?x ?y ?z ?w)
=>
(printout t tab "rule 2 found" tab "x= " ?x "   y= " ?y "   z= " ?z "   w= " ?w crlf)
)

;; initial facts

(deffacts startup
(find a c e g)
(item a)
(item b)
(item c)
(item d)
(item e)
(item f)
(item g)
)
```

The individual Rete networks for the productions (without sharing CEs) rule1 and rule2 consist of the same number of alpha and beta nodes. A significant distinction, however, is the location in the corresponding network of the test for CE (find ?x ?y ?z ?w). In rule1, there is an alpha node at the top of the network, whereas in rule2 this CE is tested using a beta node at the bottom of the network. In addition, this beta node for rule2 must consider a number of variable pairings whereas the corresponding test in rule1 only requires an alpha node and results in a single set of variable bindings. Clearly, the formulation of rule1 is preferable. This example is continued in the problems.

Possible Efficiencies

Guidelines for coding productions efficiently include [BFKM86]:

1. Avoid CEs that match many wm elements. To achieve this, add additional attribute (slot) tests, or subdivide the production by adding more wm element classes.

2. Avoid large cross-product comparisons due to shared variables (the example in Section 7.5.9 shows this).

3. Put the most restrictive attribute tests first.

7.5.10 Beyond Rete

Recall that the efficiency of Rete is largely due to an assumption that **wm** changes are small or incremental from cycle to cycle. Rete II was created in the 1980s. The Rete II algorithm is claimed to be as good as the original Rete at handling large numbers of rules, but it is faster than the original algorithm when dealing with large amounts of data or rapidly changing data. In tests, a Rete II-based system (CLIPS/R2) ran a few times faster than a system based on standard Rete (CLIPS 6.04) on moderately complex problems. On complex problems, the Rete II system was over 100 times faster.

Another extension of Rete is TREAT [ML91]. [NGR88] compares TREAT and Rete using several sample problems and using the Soar production system.

Research related to the scalability, computational efficiency, and especially the parallelization of production systems continues to be an active area of research [KC04], [LC02], [LSK98].

7.6 Embedded CLIPS

7.6.1 Embedding a Production System

A realistic production system may need to interface with other applications. As shown in the Advanced Programming Guide, CLIPS supports integration in two ways:

1. CLIPS may be embedded in user code for another application; and

2. CLIPS may call external (user-written) applications.

We only consider the former here.

7.6.2 Sample CLIPS Embedding (Using C)

For simplicity, we only consider embedding CLIPS in a user's C program. We show the creation of a running CLIPS engine, loading a database (the example of Section 7.4 is used), displaying the initial facts, running the CLIPS engine until the agenda is empty, and displaying the final facts.

Source Code with Embedded CLIPS

```
/* embedExample.c

   example of embedding clips in c program

   compilation w/ linking to (assumed static library) libclips:
   gcc embedExample.c -L./ -lclips -lm -o embedExample
*/
```

```
#include <stdio.h>
#include "clips.h"

/* added per Advanced Prog. Guide, Section 4  */
void UserFunctions(void);
void EnvUserFunctions(void *);

int main(
  int argc,
  char *argv[])
  {
   char *filename = "ars-clips.clips";
   InitializeEnvironment();

   printf("\n***** embedded clips example *********\n\n");

   printf("\nLoaded file: %s and reset clips to yield the\n",filename);
   printf("initial facts list:\n\n");

   Load(filename);
   Reset();
   Facts("wdisplay",NULL,-1,-1, -1);

/* run until the agenda is empty */
   Run(-1);

   printf("\nRunning clips until the agenda is empty yielded\n");
   printf("the final facts list:\n\n");

   Facts("wdisplay",NULL,-1,-1, -1);

   return(1);
  }
```

Compilation

A simplistic approach might be to simply replace (or modify) the CLIPS source distribution file `main.c` and rebuild the executable. This is, at best, inefficient and does not fully convey the embedding potential.

A more mature approach consists of creating a static library (`libclips`) for CLIPS using the available makefile:

```
make -f makefile.lib
```

and linking this library with the user application after compilation:

```
gcc embedExample.c -L./ -lclips -lm -o embedExample
```

Results

The following shows the execution of the C program with CLIPS embedded.

```
$ ./embedExample

***** embedded clips example *********


Loaded file: ars-clips.clips and reset clips to yield the
initial facts list:

f-0     (initial-fact)
f-1     (primitive (name a))
f-2     (primitive (name r))
f-3     (primitive (name s))
For a total of 4 facts.

Running clips until the agenda is empty yielded
the final facts list:

f-0     (initial-fact)
f-1     (primitive (name a))
f-2     (primitive (name r))
f-3     (primitive (name s))
f-4     (primitive (name b))
For a total of 5 facts.
```

The reader should compare this facts list with that obtained in Section 7.4.

7.7   Descendants of CLIPS

7.7.1   JESS

JESS is a rule engine and scripting environment written in the java language at Sandia National Laboratories. JESS was originally inspired by the CLIPS expert system shell. The core JESS language is compatible with CLIPS, and many JESS databases are valid CLIPS databases and vice versa. Like CLIPS, the Rete algorithm is used to implement conflict resolution efficiently. JESS adds several features to CLIPS, most notably the implementation of backward chaining. The following simple session uses the CLIPS database:

```
;; template for memory

(deftemplate primitive
(slot name))

;; rules

(defrule rule1
  (primitive (name a))
  (primitive (name r))
=>
  (assert (primitive (name b))))

(defrule rule2
```

```
  (primitive (name r))
  (primitive (name s))
=>
  (assert (primitive (name d))))

;; initial facts

(deffacts startup
  (primitive (name a))
  (primitive (name r))
  (primitive (name s)))
```

and shows that JESS uses:

```
$ java -classpath jess.jar jess.Main

Jess, the Java Expert System Shell
Copyright (C) 2001 E.J. Friedman Hill and the Sandia Corporation
Jess Version 6.1p7 5/7/2004


Jess> (batch "./ars-clips2.clips")
TRUE
Jess> (reset)
TRUE
Jess> (facts)
f-0    (MAIN::initial-fact)
f-1    (MAIN::primitive (name a))
f-2    (MAIN::primitive (name r))
f-3    (MAIN::primitive (name s))
For a total of 4 facts.
Jess> (agenda)
[Activation: MAIN::rule2  f-2, f-3 ; time=4 ; salience=0]
[Activation: MAIN::rule1  f-1, f-2 ; time=3 ; salience=0]
For a total of 2 activations.
Jess> (run)
2
Jess> (facts)
f-0    (MAIN::initial-fact)
f-1    (MAIN::primitive (name a))
f-2    (MAIN::primitive (name r))
f-3    (MAIN::primitive (name s))
f-4    (MAIN::primitive (name d))
f-5    (MAIN::primitive (name b))
For a total of 6 facts.
```

Unfortunately, the distribution of JESS (as of 10/1/2006) is tightly controlled. JESS is not licensed under the GPL, the LPGL, the BSD license, or any other free software or open source license. A nontransferable commercial license is necessary to use JESS software to create derivative works by embedding JESS source code. Readers interested in pursuing JESS should consult the web page.

7.7.2 CLIPS in Java

Java programmers may embed the CLIPS engine in java applications using the CLIPS java native interface (CLIPSJNI). This is addressed in Chapter 10 of the Advanced Programming Manual.

7.7.3 Soar

In Chapter 9, we consider an (arguably) much more complex and powerful production system implementation, namely Soar.

7.8 CLIPS Web Resources and Downloads

There are numerous ways to acquire a recent version of CLIPS. The development website is at http://clipsrules.sourceforge.net/ or http://sourceforge.net/projects/clipsrules/. Moreover, many linux package managers (e.g., the Synaptic Package Manager for Ubuntu) provide an easily installable package.[5] For the Debian/GNU linux version, packages are at http://packages.debian.org/search?keywords=clip

7.9 Exercises

1. The following are salient elements of the CLIPS syntax and semantics. After studying the CLIPS Basic Programming Guide, provide a brief description of the syntax and use of each.

   (a) Ordered vs. non-ordered facts

   (b) `deftemplate`

   (c) `deffacts`

   (d) `defrule`

   (e) The `agenda` (conflict set)

   (f) Pattern matching and condition elements (CEs) in a production

   (g) Wildcard matches

   (h) Variables and their use

   (i) `assert`, `retract`, and `modify`

   (j) `bind`

   (k) `run`, `halt`, and `clear`

   (l) `printout`

   (m) Typed and default slot values

2. Develop a CLIPS representation for the tenure example of Section 7.4.3 using ordered facts. Compare this with the non-ordered facts-based version.

---

[5]The author, however, recommends obtaining and building CLIPS from source. In this manner, customization is possible and embedded versions (See Section 7.6) may be developed.

3. Compare CLIPS representations using ordered vs. non-ordered facts. Discuss:

    (a) Suitability

    (b) Efficiency

    (c) Trade-offs

4. The following information was obtained from thinning a search of the Open CYC database using the term "grandparent." Using this information as a starting point, develop a representation in CLIPS for this concept.

```
the parent of a parent is a grandparent
Some grandparents are mentally ill
parents are the children of grandparents
a grandparent can give presents
Your parents' parents are your grandparents
sometimes grandparents live in a nursing home
grandparents like to have pictures of their grandchildren
grandparents are parents of parents
A grandparent has children
grandparents can ship gifts to grandchildren
grandparents are always older than their grandchildren
grandparents are your parents' parents
A grandparent is the parent of the parent of a child
A male grandparent is a grandfather
A female grandparent is a grandmother
A person has four grandparents
A grandfather and a grandmother are grandparents
Everyone has grandparents, although they may no longer be alive
```

5. In Section 7.3, conflict resolution and saliency of rules were considered. Given the CLIPS database that follows, determine the agenda for each of the available conflict resolution strategies.

```
;; clips sample database for conflict resolution

;; template for memory

(deftemplate primitive
(slot name))

;; rules

(defrule rule1
  (primitive (name a))
  (primitive (name r))
  (primitive (name s))
=>
  (assert (primitive (name b))))

(defrule rule2
  (declare (salience 100))
```

```
   (primitive (name a))
   (primitive (name r))
=>
   (assert (primitive (name d))))

(defrule rule3
   (primitive (name r))
   (primitive (name s))
=>
   (assert (primitive (name e))))

(defrule rule4
   (declare (salience 100))
   (primitive (name r))
   (primitive (name s))
   (test (< 1 2))
   (test (< 2 3))
=>
   (assert (primitive (name f))))

;; initial facts

(deffacts startup
   (primitive (name a))
   (primitive (name r))
   (primitive (name s)))
```

6. In Section 7.5.7, it was claimed that static data structures linking **wm** and **pm** could be problematic. Show the shortcomings of a statically-defined matrix indicating **wm** element to CE connectivity.

7. Use the following CLIPS database to test the **random** conflict resolution strategy.

```
;; clips sample (random) conflict resolution

;; template for memory

(deftemplate primitive
(slot name))

;; rules

(defrule rule1
   (primitive (name a))
=>
   (assert (primitive (name z))))

(defrule rule2
   (primitive (name b))
=>
   (assert (primitive (name z))))

(defrule rule3
   (primitive (name c))
```

```
=>
  (assert (primitive (name z))))

(defrule rule4
  (primitive (name d))
=>
  (assert (primitive (name z))))

(defrule rule5
  (primitive (name e))
=>
  (assert (primitive (name z))))

;; initial facts

(deffacts startup
  (primitive (name a))
  (primitive (name b))
  (primitive (name c))
  (primitive (name d))
  (primitive (name e))
)
```

8. Here we consider a simple example of using CLIPS to convert an "expert" diagnosis paradigm into production system formulation. The diagnostic scenario concerns diagnosing problems when turning on a room light[6] and is summarized as follows:

```
If you turn the switch "on" and the light does not go "on" and other lights
in the house are on, then check the lightbulb.
If you want to check the lightbulb and the lamp fixture contains a standard (any
wattage) lightbulb, then remove the lightbulb and check it.
If you check the bulb and it is OK, then check to see if the lamp is plugged
in.
If you check the bulb and it is bad, then replace the bulb.
```

Implement this paradigm in CLIPS and show sample results.

9. Can you convert the pair of single slot definitions in the simple example of Section 7.2.1 into a multislot definition?

10. State, quantitatively, the difference between the `lex` and `depth` conflict resolution strategies in CLIPS.

11. This problem is based upon the CLIPS example in Section 7.5.9.

    (a) Using the default CLIPS conflict resolution strategy, which production will be fired first?

---

[6]We are being somewhat imprecise (bulb wattage, etc.), but this example is more for the CLIPS introduction than a final expert system design.

(b) Since CEs are AND-ed, does this example and the rules of Section 7.5.9 suggest a reordering strategy for production CEs to optimize the resulting Rete network?

12. An IS engineer was beginning the development of an expert system for a card game. Consider the *syntactically correct* CLIPS implementation shown here.

```
;; file: cardsquiz.clips
;; clips version -1 of expert system for card game

;; 52 card deck template via multifield slot

(deftemplate deck (multislot cards))

(deftemplate printed (slot player))

;; the template for a 7 card hand

(deftemplate hand
  (slot player)
  (slot holecard1)
  (slot holecard2)
  (slot community1)
  (slot community2)
  (slot community3)
  (slot community4)
  (slot community5)
)

;; productions

(defrule do-something
(hand (player ?Who)
      (holecard1 ?X)
      (holecard2 ?Y)
      (community1 ?Z)
      (community2 ?A)
      (community3 ?B)
      (community4 ?C)
      (community5 ?D))
  =>
  (printout t "the hand is" crlf)
  (printout t ?X " " ?Y " " ?Z " " ?A " " ?B " " ?C " " ?D  crlf)
  (assert (printed (player ?Who)))
)

(defrule do-something-else
(printed (player ?Who))
?W <- (hand
      (player ?Who)
      (holecard1 ?X)
      (holecard2 ?Y)
      (community1 ?Z)
      (community2 ?A)
      (community3 ?B)
```

```
        (community4 ?C)
        (community5 ?D))
 =>
(printout t "player " ?Who " folds; deleting the hand" crlf)
(retract ?W)
)


;; non-ordered fact represents the deck

(deffacts deckfact "the deck data structure"
(deck (cards
'2S' '3S' '4S' '5S' '6S' '7S' '8S' '9S' '10S' 'JS' 'QS' 'KS' 'AS'
'2C' '3C' '4C' '5C' '6C' '7C' '8C' '9C' '10C' 'JC' 'QC' 'KC' 'AC'
'2D' '3D' '4D' '5D' '6D' '7D' '8D' '9D' '10D' 'JD' 'QD' 'KD' 'AD'
'2H' '3H' '4H' '5H' '6H' '7H' '8H' '9H' '10H' 'JH' 'QH' 'KH' 'AH')))


;; some hands

(deffacts hand1 "player 1's hand"
(hand (player 1)
      (holecard1 'AH')
      (holecard2 'KH')
      (community1 'QH')
      (community2 '10H')
      (community3 '5C')
      (community4 '6S')
      (community5 'JH')))

(deffacts hand2 "player 2's hand"
(hand (player 2)
      (holecard1 '5S')
      (holecard2 '5D')
      (community1 'QH')
      (community2 '10H')
      (community3 '5C')
      (community4 '6S')
      (community5 'JH')))
```

This file is loaded into CLIPS, as shown in the following example. *Fill in the blanks for answers 1–5.*

```
CLIPS> (clear)
CLIPS> (facts)

<answer #1 here>

CLIPS> (load "cardsquiz.clips")
Defining deftemplate: deck
Defining deftemplate: printed
Defining deftemplate: hand
Defining defrule: do-something +j
Defining defrule: do-something-else +j+j
Defining deffacts: deckfact
Defining deffacts: hand1
```

```
Defining deffacts: hand2
TRUE
CLIPS> (facts)

<answer #2 here>

CLIPS> (reset)
CLIPS> (facts)

<answer #3 here>

CLIPS> (run)

<answer #4 here>

CLIPS> (facts)

<answer #5 here>
```

13. A problem in Chapter 6 considered using a forward-chaining inference engine for backward chaining. Show an implementation of this in CLIPS, given the following database:

```
initial dB facts: {a  b  g}

rules:    IF    a  b   THEN   c          (1)

                b  g          d          (2)

                a  c          e          (3)

                e  d          f          (4)
```

14. This problem considers the sample CLIPS database of Section 7.5.7.

    (a) Draw the Rete network for production "**prod2**".

    (b) Merge the preceding results with the network of Section 7.5.7 into the single Rete network.

15. This exercise will appeal to C developers. Using the CLIPS source (Version 6.24), recompile the code (**setup.h**) with the **DEVELOPER** directive set to 1. This produces a CLIPS version with two new functions. These functions are **show-joins** and **rule-complexity**. The former facilitates visualization of the CLIPS implementation of the Rete network, as shown in the following.

```
CLIPS>  (load "reteEx1.clips")
Defining deftemplate: class1
Defining deftemplate: class2
Defining deftemplate: class3
Defining deftemplate: class4
Defining defrule: prod1 +j+j+j
Defining defrule: prod2 +j+j
TRUE
```

```
CLIPS> (show-joins prod1)
 1 :
 2 : (fact-jn-cmp-vars1 p 1 1 0)
 3 : (fact-jn-cmp-vars1 p 0 2 1)
CLIPS> (show-joins prod2)
 1 :
 2 : (fact-jn-cmp-vars1 p 0 1 1)
CLIPS> (rule-complexity prod1)
7
CLIPS> (rule-complexity prod2)
4
```

16. This problem provides a look at CLIPS conflict resolution strategies and the corresponding search ramifications. Chapter 3, Section 3.4.7 considered the following simplistic rule-based system:

Initial (database) facts: $a\ b\ g = S_i$.

System operators are shown below[7]:

```
rule 1    IF  a   b    THEN  c

     2    IF  b   g    THEN  d

     3    IF  a   c    THEN  e

     4    IF  e   d    THEN  f

     5    IF  d   g    THEN  f
```

Suppose the goal is to produce a state that contains fact **f**. Chapter 3, Figure 3.8(b) showed the search space and possible paths that lead from S_i to (one) S_g. The nine possible paths (rule-firing sequences) are repeated here.

```
1 - 2 - 3 - 4

2 - 1 - 3 - 4

1 - 3 - 2 - 4

2 - 1 - 3 - 5

1 - 3 - 2 - 5

1 - 2 - 3 - 5

1 - 2 - 5

2 - 1 - 5

2 - 5
```

Possible Rule-Firing Sequences Leading to Goal States

---

[7]Note "THEN" means "Add the fact."

(a) Implement this as a CLIPS production system, with the productions named after the corresponding rule (e.g., `rule1`, `rule2`, etc.). Include one or more productions to check if `wm` contains the chosen CLIPS representation of `f`.

(b) For each of the following conflict resolution strategies:

    i. `depth`

    ii. `breadth`

    iii. `random`

show the sequence of rules used and discuss the corresponding search strategy.

17. This problem tests your understanding of simple CLIPS syntax. A student was attempting to implement a language generator in CLIPS. The productions are:

$$S \rightarrow AB$$

$$S \rightarrow C$$

$$A \rightarrow C$$

$$A \rightarrow a$$

$$B \rightarrow b$$

$$B \rightarrow c$$

$$C \rightarrow d$$

where S is the starting symbol and $\rightarrow$ means "may be replaced by." The student figured that ordered facts would lead to the simplest implementation and designed the following CLIPS database:

```
;; clips implementation of a simple grammar
;; uses ordered facts and
;; fact that clips is case sensitive
;; chains to find L(G)
;; file: sab.clips

;; productions in G

(defrule rule1
   (S)
=>
   (assert (AB)))

(defrule rule2
   (S)
=>
   (assert (C)))
```

```
(defrule rule3
  (A)
=>
  (assert (C)))


(defrule rule4
  (A)
=>
  (assert (a)))

(defrule rule5
  (B)
=>
  (assert (b)))

(defrule rule6
  (B)
=>
  (assert (c)))

(defrule rule7
  (C)
=>
  (assert (d)))

;; initial facts
(deffacts startup (S))
```

Show the CLIPS operation with this design. Is $L(G)$ generated? If not, how would you suggest changing the CLIPS implementation to achieve this goal?

18. The implementation of CLIPS is quite involved. However, given the CLIPS source, it is possible to profile the running code. For example, using **gprof**, a version of clips may be compiled to generate profiling information at runtime. Using the CLIPS example in 7.1.6, which implements the image labeling problem of Chapter 4, a snippet of the **gprof** output is shown as follows. This snippet shows the function call structure.

```
index % time   self  children    called    name
               0.00    0.00       1/33          CommandLoop [5]
               0.00    0.00       1/33          EnvClear [15]
               0.00    0.00       2/33          PerformMessage <cycle 1> [19]
               0.00    0.00       6/33          ExecuteIfCommandComplete [6]
               0.00    0.00       8/33          LoadConstructsFromLogicalName [12]
               0.00    0.00      15/33          EnvRun <cycle 1> [9]
[1]    100.0   0.00    0.01      33         PeriodicCleanup [1]
               0.00    0.01       8/8           RemoveEphemeralAtoms [3]
               0.00    0.00       8/8           FlushMultifields [301]
               0.00    0.00       8/8           RemoveGarbageFacts [307]
               0.00    0.00       8/9           CleanupInstances [285]
-----------------------------------------------
```

```
              0.01    0.00    32/32        RemoveEphemeralAtoms [3]
[2]    100.0  0.01    0.00    32           RemoveEphemeralHashNodes [2]
              0.00    0.00    32/32        RemoveHashNode [126]
--------------------------------------------------

              0.00    0.01    8/8          PeriodicCleanup [1]
[3]    100.0  0.00    0.01    8            RemoveEphemeralAtoms [3]
              0.01    0.00    32/32        RemoveEphemeralHashNodes [2]
```

Revise your CLIPS executable to enable profiling and test the results on some of the simple examples in this chapter. Most importantly, *where does a running CLIPS system spend most of its time?*

19. The CLIPS labeling example of Section 7.1.6 uses production `rulesym` to implement the symmetry of the "adjacent-to" relational constraint. However, Figure 7.8 shows that four of the five possible labelings are found before the (car, road) and (road, car) labeling constraints are put into `wm`.

   (a) Why does this occur (provide a detailed answer)?

   (b) Modify the CLIPS source in order to achieve complete "elaboration"[8] of the "adj-to" relational constraint in `wm` *prior to* use of production `ruleg`. Show your results.

   (c) Why does infinite recursion not occur when using production `rulesym`?

20. CLIPS provides the actions `undeffacts` and `undefrule`. Study their syntax and semantics, and suggest a practical use for each.

21. JESS is also based upon the Rete algorithm, and provides a similar visual indication when building the Rete network. However, both one- and two-input nodes compilations are indicated. Repeat the CLIPS examples in Section 7.5.8 using JESS.

---

[8] As is done in the Soar elaboration cycle (Chapter 9).

Extended Production System Representation and Manipulation Approaches, Including Agents

Chapter 2 introduced the IS representation challenge. In this chapter, we revisit and extend a number of concepts related to developing and using IS knowledge representations, including:

- Practical use of subsets of the available data;

- Collaborative IS reasoning (Blackboards);

- Representation integrity;

- Fusion of the structured representation with the manipulation process (e.g., developing overall IS implementations solutions by using Protégé and CLIPS together);

- The notion of distributed and autonomous IS "Agents;" and

- Incorporating temporal reasoning in an IS.

8.1 Modular Production System Development Approaches

Another central issue in the design of an efficient inference system is how to effectively concentrate the attention of the system on a salient and manageable amount of knowledge (i.e., rules and facts). This is referred to as opportunistic problem solving and involves automation of a "use what is most appropriate and ignore the rest" problem-solving methodology. This type of approach leads to computationally efficient inference. One risk, however, is that the potential use of incomplete information (due to the exclusion by default of other facts and rules) may lead to logically unsound conclusions. This is the subject of nonmagnetic reasoning (see Section 8.6).

Inference often requires a significant amount of computational effort for unification or matching of symbolic structures. If we simply represent "everything we know" in terms of massive rule and fact bases (so-called "monolithic structures"), a great deal of IE computational effort may be involved in searching through (and perhaps applying) rules that, although strictly applicable, do little to advance the system state toward a goal. A better strategy is to focus using an "information lens." Subdividing a representation into manageable "packets," frames, or modules facilitates this objective.

8.2 Implementing Modular Representations in CLIPS

8.2.1 Introduction

As noted, database structuring enables the focusing of the inference process and facilitates efficiency. CLIPS support for the modular development is via the **defmodule** construct. **defmodule** may be used to restrict access to **deftemplate** and **defclass** constructs. Modular structuring of the CLIPS database restricts only certain facts (and instances) and rules to be used. Thus, CLIPS inference is correspondingly restricted, or focused. Via modules, CLIPS could implement the blackboard paradigm. By default, all CLIPS constructs are contained in the module **MAIN**.

8.2.2 Module Definition Syntax

The syntax of the **defmodule** construct is:

```
(defmodule <module-name> [<comment>]
     <port-spec>*)
<port-specification> ::= (export <port-item>) |
                         (import <module-name> <port-item>)

<port-item>              ::= ?ALL |
                             ?NONE |
                              <port-construct> ?ALL |
                              <port-construct> ?NONE |
                               <port-construct> <construct-name>+

<port-construct>         ::= deftemplate | defclass |
                             defglobal | deffunction |
                             defgeneric
```

Note the syntax allows for modules to export and import elements of other modules. This is analogous to the abstract data type (ADT) concept.

8.2.3 Specifying the Module for a Construct

CLIPS constructs are tagged to a module when the construct is defined. This includes the **deffacts**, **deftemplate**, **defrule**, **deffunction**, **defclass**, and **definstances** constructs. The specific module corresponding to the construct is specified by including it in the construct name, as shown in the following section. The module must be declared via a **defmodule** before loading any module-specific constructs.

8.2.4 Examples of Module Specifications: Different Knowledge Domains

For illustration, consider the module-based versions of two simple examples used previously. The first is a CLIPS sorting implementation and the second is the "hello world" or "ars" database. Two modules, named **SORT** and **ARS**, respectively, are used.

The SORT Module.

```
;; clipsSort-dm.clips
;; modular version of sorting implementation

(deftemplate SORT::num
    (slot val)
    (slot processed))

(defrule SORT::sort
  ?Anum <- (num (val ?V) (processed nil))
  (not (and
              (num (val ?X) (processed nil))
              (test (< ?X ?V))))
=>
    (printout t "the next number is: " ?V crlf)
    (modify ?Anum (processed t))
 )

(deffacts SORT::database
 (num (val 170))
 (num (val 77))
 (num (val 127))
 (num (val 16))
 (num (val 119))
 (num (val 103))
 (num (val 101))
 (num (val 18))
)
```

The ARS Module.

```
;; clips ars module-based implementation
;; file: ars-clips-dm.clips

;; template for memory
(deftemplate ARS::primitive
(slot name))

;; a rule
(defrule ARS::rule1
  (primitive (name a))
  (primitive (name r))
=>
  (assert (primitive (name b))))

;; initial facts
(deffacts ARS::startup
  (primitive (name a))
  (primitive (name r))
  (primitive (name s)))
```

8.2.5 Module Visibility

The constructs of one module may not be used by another module unless the constructs are specifically exported and imported. When started, CLIPS defaults to the MAIN module. The focus command may be used to change the module focus, as shown in the following example.

A particular construct is said to be visible (or within scope of a module) if that construct can be used by the module. The following example shows the error produced when attempting to load module-specific constructs for an undefined module.

```
CLIPS> (load "ars-clips-dm.clips")
[PRNTUTIL1] Unable to find defmodule ARS.

ERROR:
(deftemplate ARS::primitive
[PRNTUTIL1] Unable to find defmodule ARS.

ERROR:
(defrule ARS::rule1
[PRNTUTIL1] Unable to find defmodule ARS.

ERROR:
(deffacts ARS::startup
FALSE
CLIPS
```

This error is easily corrected by defining the module ARS. As the following example shows, there is potential confusion when using reset to initialize the facts database, since the reset and clear commands make the MAIN module the current focus. Also note that module-specific facts may be viewed by the extended facts command.

```
CLIPS> (defmodule ARS)
CLIPS> (load "ars-clips-dm.clips")
Defining deftemplate: primitive
Defining defrule: rule1 +j+j
Defining deffacts: startup
TRUE
CLIPS> (facts)        ;; none for module MAIN
CLIPS> (facts ARS)  ;; none for module ARS (yet)
CLIPS> (reset)        ;; module focus is MAIN
CLIPS> (facts ARS)
f-1      (primitive (name a))
f-2      (primitive (name r))
f-3      (primitive (name s))
For a total of 3 facts.
CLIPS> (run)
CLIPS> (facts ARS)  ;; nothing happened- empty agenda for MAIN
f-1      (primitive (name a))
f-2      (primitive (name r))
f-3      (primitive (name s))
For a total of 3 facts.
CLIPS> (focus ARS)  ;; make ARS the focus
TRUE
```

```
CLIPS> (run)
CLIPS> (facts)      ;; as expected
f-1      (primitive (name a))
f-2      (primitive (name r))
f-3      (primitive (name s))
f-4      (primitive (name b))
For a total of 4 facts.
CLIPS>
```

Each module has its own Rete network for its rules and its own agenda. When **run** is invoked, the agenda of the module that is the current focus is used. This was shown in the previous example.

8.2.6 Example: Changing Focus

The following example show a production that changes the module focus.

```
;; focus-mgr.clips

(defmodule ARS)
(defmodule SORT)

(defrule      MAIN::focus-manager
   =>
   (load "ars-clips-dm.clips")
   (load "clipsSort-dm.clips")
   (reset)
   (printout t "changing focus to module ARS" crlf)
   (focus ARS)
   (printout t "facts in module ARS are:" crlf)
   (facts)
   (printout t "changing focus to module SORT" crlf)
   (focus SORT)
   (printout t "facts in module SORT are:" crlf)
   (facts)
   (halt)
)
```

Operation is as follows:

```
CLIPS> (clear)
CLIPS> (load "focus-mgr.clips")
Defining defmodule: ARS
Defining defmodule: SORT
Defining defrule: focus-manager +j
TRUE
CLIPS> (reset)
CLIPS> (run)
Defining deftemplate: primitive
Defining defrule: rule1 +j+j
Defining deffacts: startup
Defining deftemplate: num
Defining defrule: sort +j+j+j
Defining deffacts: database
```

```
changing focus to module ARS
facts in module ARS are:
f-1      (primitive (name a))
f-2      (primitive (name r))
f-3      (primitive (name s))
For a total of 3 facts.
changing focus to module SORT
facts in module SORT are:
f-4      (num (val 170) (processed nil))
f-5      (num (val 77) (processed nil))
f-6      (num (val 127) (processed nil))
f-7      (num (val 16) (processed nil))
f-8      (num (val 119) (processed nil))
f-9      (num (val 103) (processed nil))
f-10     (num (val 101) (processed nil))
f-11     (num (val 18) (processed nil))
For a total of 8 facts.
CLIPS>
```

8.3 Object–Oriented (OO) Representation, Production Systems, and CLIPS COOL

Object-oriented (OO) representations and production systems are two different things. However, they may be combined, as we show here. Elements of the CLIPS Object-Oriented Language (COOL) are used for illustration.

The reader is encouraged to review the relevant CLIPS Basic Programming Guide sections for an introduction to COOL. A number of new functions and concepts are introduced in the examples that follow. We then show the combined use of CLIPS and Protégé.

8.3.1 COOL Class Syntax

The syntax of the COOL `defclass` construct is:

```
(defclass <name> [<comment>]
  (is-a <superclass-name>+)
  [<role>]
  [<pattern-match-role>]
  <slot>*
  <handler-documentation>*)
```

8.3.2 Sample Class Hierarchy in COOL

We begin by defining a hierarchy of classes to reflect and build upon the structure of Figure 2.3. A CLI version of CLIPS is used for illustration.

```
CLIPS> (defclass LIFE-FORM (is-a USER)
(slot consumes (default food))
(slot produces (default waste)))
CLIPS> (defclass MAMMAL (is-a LIFE-FORM)
```

```
(slot offspring (default born-live)))
CLIPS> (defclass DOG (is-a MAMMAL)
(slot has (default four-legs)))
```

8.3.3 Examining the COOL Classes

```
CLIPS> (describe-class MAMMAL)
=================================================================================
*********************************************************************************
Concrete: direct instances of this class can be created.
Reactive: direct instances of this class can match defrule patterns.

Direct Superclasses: LIFE-FORM
Inheritance Precedence: MAMMAL LIFE-FORM USER OBJECT
Direct Subclasses: DOG
---------------------------------------------------------------------------------

SLOTS     : FLD DEF PRP ACC STO MCH SRC VIS CRT OVRD-MSG    SOURCE(S)
consumes  : SGL STC INH RW  LCL RCT EXC PRV RW  put-consumes LIFE-FORM
produces  : SGL STC INH RW  LCL RCT EXC PRV RW  put-produces LIFE-FORM
offspring : SGL STC INH RW  LCL RCT EXC PRV RW  put-offsprin MAMMAL

Constraint information for slots:

SLOTS     : SYM STR INN INA EXA FTA INT FLT
consumes  :  +   +   +   +   +   +   +   +  RNG:[-oo..+oo]
produces  :  +   +   +   +   +   +   +   +  RNG:[-oo..+oo]
offspring :  +   +   +   +   +   +   +   +  RNG:[-oo..+oo]
---------------------------------------------------------------------------------
Recognized message-handlers:
init primary in class USER
delete primary in class USER
create primary in class USER
print primary in class USER
direct-modify primary in class USER
message-modify primary in class USER
direct-duplicate primary in class USER
message-duplicate primary in class USER
get-consumes primary in class LIFE-FORM
put-consumes primary in class LIFE-FORM
get-produces primary in class LIFE-FORM
put-produces primary in class LIFE-FORM
get-offspring primary in class MAMMAL
put-offspring primary in class MAMMAL
*********************************************************************************
=================================================================================
CLIPS> (describe-class DOG)
=================================================================================
*********************************************************************************
Concrete: direct instances of this class can be created.
Reactive: direct instances of this class can match defrule patterns.

Direct Superclasses: MAMMAL
Inheritance Precedence: DOG MAMMAL LIFE-FORM USER OBJECT
```

Direct Subclasses:

```
--------------------------------------------------------------------------------
SLOTS      : FLD DEF PRP ACC STO MCH SRC VIS CRT OVRD-MSG      SOURCE(S)
consumes   : SGL STC INH RW  LCL RCT EXC PRV RW  put-consumes LIFE-FORM
produces   : SGL STC INH RW  LCL RCT EXC PRV RW  put-produces LIFE-FORM
offspring  : SGL STC INH RW  LCL RCT EXC PRV RW  put-offsprin MAMMAL
has        : SGL STC INH RW  LCL RCT EXC PRV RW  put-has      DOG
```

Constraint information for slots:

```
SLOTS      : SYM STR INN INA EXA FTA INT FLT
consumes   :  +   +   +   +   +   +   +   +  RNG:[-oo..+oo]
produces   :  +   +   +   +   +   +   +   +  RNG:[-oo..+oo]
offspring  :  +   +   +   +   +   +   +   +  RNG:[-oo..+oo]
has        :  +   +   +   +   +   +   +   +  RNG:[-oo..+oo]
--------------------------------------------------------------------------------
```

Recognized message-handlers:
init primary in class USER
delete primary in class USER
create primary in class USER
print primary in class USER
direct-modify primary in class USER
message-modify primary in class USER
direct-duplicate primary in class USER
message-duplicate primary in class USER
get-consumes primary in class LIFE-FORM
put-consumes primary in class LIFE-FORM
get-produces primary in class LIFE-FORM
put-produces primary in class LIFE-FORM
get-offspring primary in class MAMMAL
put-offspring primary in class MAMMAL
get-has primary in class DOG
put-has primary in class DOG
```
********************************************************************************
================================================================================
```

In addition, we can see the pretty-printed class definition of DOG via:

```
CLIPS> (ppdefclass DOG)
(defclass MAIN::DOG
   (is-a MAMMAL)
   (slot has
     (default four-legs)))
```

Other classes may be examined in a similar fashion:

```
CLIPS> (describe-class LIFE-FORM)
================================================================================
********************************************************************************
Concrete: direct instances of this class can be created.
Reactive: direct instances of this class can match defrule patterns.

Direct Superclasses: USER
Inheritance Precedence: LIFE-FORM USER OBJECT
Direct Subclasses: MAMMAL
```

```
--------------------------------------------------------------------------------
SLOTS     : FLD DEF PRP ACC STO MCH SRC VIS CRT OVRD-MSG      SOURCE(S)
consumes : SGL STC INH RW  LCL RCT EXC PRV RW  put-consumes LIFE-FORM
produces : SGL STC INH RW  LCL RCT EXC PRV RW  put-produces LIFE-FORM


Constraint information for slots:

SLOTS     : SYM STR INN INA EXA FTA INT FLT
consumes : +   +   +   +   +   +   +   +  RNG:[-oo..+oo]
produces : +   +   +   +   +   +   +   +  RNG:[-oo..+oo]
--------------------------------------------------------------------------------
Recognized message-handlers:
init primary in class USER
delete primary in class USER
create primary in class USER
print primary in class USER
direct-modify primary in class USER
message-modify primary in class USER
direct-duplicate primary in class USER
message-duplicate primary in class USER
get-consumes primary in class LIFE-FORM
put-consumes primary in class LIFE-FORM
get-produces primary in class LIFE-FORM
put-produces primary in class LIFE-FORM
********************************************************************************
================================================================================
```

Furthermore, we can get the big OO-picture via two CLIPS functions:

```
CLIPS> (get-defclass-list)
(FLOAT INTEGER SYMBOL STRING MULTIFIELD EXTERNAL-ADDRESS FACT-ADDRESS
INSTANCE-ADDRESS INSTANCE-NAME OBJECT PRIMITIVE NUMBER LEXEME ADDRESS
INSTANCE USER INITIAL-OBJECT LIFE-FORM MAMMAL DOG)
```

and

```
CLIPS> (browse-classes)
OBJECT
  PRIMITIVE
    NUMBER
      INTEGER
      FLOAT
    LEXEME
      SYMBOL
      STRING
    MULTIFIELD
    ADDRESS
      EXTERNAL-ADDRESS
      FACT-ADDRESS
      INSTANCE-ADDRESS *
    INSTANCE
      INSTANCE-ADDRESS *
      INSTANCE-NAME
```

```
USER
  INITIAL-OBJECT
  LIFE-FORM
    MAMMAL
      DOG
```

8.3.4 Creating Instances

At this point, we have no instances of any class. To remedy this we do the following:

```
CLIPS> (make-instance [jesse] of DOG)
[jesse]
```

We can check our representation in numerous ways using COOL functions. For example:

```
CLIPS> (class [jesse])
DOG
```

Although we do not emphasize the message-passing structure that is available, we show a more elaborate creation of another instance:

```
CLIPS> (watch messages)
CLIPS> (make-instance barney of DOG)
MSG >> create ED:1 (<Instance-barney>)
MSG << create ED:1 (<Instance-barney>)
MSG >> init ED:1 (<Instance-barney>)
MSG << init ED:1 (<Instance-barney>)
[barney]
```

8.3.5 Integrating Classes, Instances, and Productions in COOL

Productions and Instances

The basic COOL syntactic constructs used to fuse OO representations and productions are summarized as follows[1]:

```
<pattern-CE>            ::= <ordered-pattern-CE> |
                           <template-pattern-CE> |
                           <object-pattern-CE>

<object-pattern-CE>    ::= (object <attribute-constraint>*)

<attribute-constraint> ::= (is-a <constraint>) |
                           (name <constraint>) |
                           (<slot-name> <constraint>*)
```

As noted, the central issue is relating the features of a production system with a class-oriented knowledge representation. CLIPS (COOL) facilitates this in a straightforward manner, as shown in the following examples.

---

[1]Note that the *setting or changing* of object slot values in a purely OO paradigm requires sending the object messages with predefined accessor methods. We do not cover these concepts here, but refer the reader to the Basic Programming Guide.

Object Slot Values: With and Without Inheritance

The first example is quite simple and does not involve inheritance. Consider the two instances created in Section 8.3.4.

```
CLIPS> (defrule find-dog
?dog <- (object (is-a DOG) (has $?find))
=>
(printout t 'the dog ' (instance-name ?dog) ' has ' ?find crlf))
CLIPS> (run)
the dog [barney] has four-legs
the dog [jesse] has four-legs
```

To show the use of inheritance in the OO-representation, consider:

```
CLIPS> (defrule dog-consumes
?dog <- (object (is-a DOG) (consumes $?what))
=>
(printout t 'the dog ' (instance-name ?dog) ' consumes ' ?what crlf))
CLIPS> (run)
the dog [barney] consumes food
the dog [jesse] consumes food
```

To show inheritance from several super-classes, we use:

```
CLIPS> (defrule dog-several-slots
?dog <- (object (is-a DOG) (has $?find)
                          (consumes $?what)
                          (offspring $?how))

=>
(printout t 'the dog ' (instance-name ?dog)
            ' has ' ?find ' and, through inheritance: ' crlf
            ' offspring are: ' ?how
            ' consumes: ' ?what crlf))
CLIPS> (run)
the dog [barney] has four-legs and, through inheritance:
 offspring are: born-live consumes: food
the dog [jesse] has four-legs and, through inheritance:
 offspring are: born-live consumes: food
```

An alternative to using CLIPS productions for database queries is the COOL instance-set query mechanism described in Section 8.4.7.

Reading and Modifying Object Slot Values

Notice in the two previous COOL production examples, production CEs were able to read instance slot values. More generally, in OO computing, instances of classes (objects) are modified using messages sent to the object invoking slot-specific methods, as shown in Figures 8.1 and 8.2.

In CLIPS COOL, direct modification of instances is both possible and often practical. The `modify-instance` function is used with syntax:

```
(modify-instance <instance> <slot-override>*)
```

```
 (defclass LIFE-FORM (is-a USER)
(slot age (default UNKNOWN)))

(defclass MAMMAL (is-a LIFE-FORM)
(slot offspring (default born-live)))

(defclass DOG (is-a MAMMAL)
        (slot has (default four-legs)))
```

Figure 8.1 Simple Class Definitions to Illustrate Instance Modification

```
 CLIPS> (load "barney-classes2.cool")
Defining defclass: LIFE-FORM
Defining defclass: MAMMAL
Defining defclass: DOG
TRUE
CLIPS> (make-instance [Barney] of DOG)
[Barney]
CLIPS> (send [Barney] get-age)
UNKNOWN
CLIPS> (send [Barney] get-has)
four-legs
CLIPS> (send [Barney] put-age 8)
8
CLIPS> (send [Barney] get-age)
8
```

Figure 8.2 Instance Modification Using Messages and the Class Definitions from Figure 8.1

It is noteworthy that this function still uses a `direct-modify` message to change the values of the instance. A continuation of the example, using the classes defined in Figure 8.1 and the instance defined in Figure 8.2, is shown in Figure 8.3.

Multiple Inheritance in COOL

COOL supports multiple inheritance, using a set of rules defined in the Basic Programming Guide. The example in Figures 8.4 and 8.5 show this feature. Notice that instances [c1] and [c2] inherit a different value from slot "theslot," depending upon the order of superclass specification. Notice

```
 CLIPS> (instances)
[Barney] of DOG
For a total of 1 instance.
CLIPS> (send [Barney] get-age)
8
CLIPS> (modify-instance [Barney] (age dead))
TRUE
CLIPS> (send [Barney] get-age)
dead
```

Figure 8.3 Direct Instance Modification in CLIPS COOL Using `modify-instance`

```
;; sample-defclass2.clips
;; will use instance set query to get
;; inherited slot values of c1 and c2

(defclass A (is-a USER)
(slot slotA (default 1))
(slot theslot (default valA)))

(defclass B (is-a USER)
(slot slotB (default 2))
(slot theslot (default valB)))

(defclass C1 (is-a A B))
(defclass C2 (is-a B A))

;; sample use of definstances
;; notice no slot values overridden

(definstances THE-OBJS
   (c1 of C1)
   (c2 of C2))
```

Figure 8.4 Sample Class Definitions with Multiple Inheritance

```
$ clips
        CLIPS (V6.24 06/15/06)
CLIPS> (load "sample-defclass2.clips")
Defining defclass: A
Defining defclass: B
Defining defclass: C1
Defining defclass: C2
Defining definstances: THE-OBJS
TRUE
CLIPS> (watch instances)
CLIPS> (instances) ;; no instances until (reset)
CLIPS> (reset)
==> instance [initial-object] of INITIAL-OBJECT
==> instance [c1] of C1
==> instance [c2] of C2
CLIPS> (do-for-all-instances
((?anybody C1 C2)) ;; define instance-set template
TRUE ;; test condition
(printout t ?anybody ' has ' slot values as follows:' crlf
 ' slotA:    ' ?anybody:slotA crlf
 ' slotB:    ' ?anybody:slotB crlf
 ' theslot: ' ?anybody:theslot crlf))
[c1]'has'slotvaluesasfollows:'
'slotA:'1
```

Figure 8.5 Annotated Example of Values Inherited with Multiple Inheritance Using the COOL Formulation of Figure 8.4

```
$ clips
'slotB:'2
'theslot:'valA ;; notice multiply-inherited value
[c2]'has'slotvaluesasfollows:'
'slotA:'1
'slotB:'2
'theslot:'valB ;; notice multiply-inherited value
```

Figure 8.5 Annotated Example of Values Inherited with Multiple Inheritance Using the COOL Formulation of Figure 8.4 (continued)

we also use the instance-set query mechanism (described in Section 8.4.7) and the `definstances` construct in this example.

8.4 Protégé, OO–Based Ontologies, CLIPS, and COOL

8.4.1 Protégé Representation Files

A very synergistic relationship exists between Protégé and CLIPS COOL. This is because one file format for Protégé class (`*.pont`) and instance (`*.pins`) representations uses the CLIPS COOL syntax. Perhaps the easiest way for the reader to see this is to start Protégé with an existing ontology in the pins/pont format. Then, use Protégé's "`Export to Format`" command (available under the <u>File</u> menu) to export the ontology in CLIPS format. Following this, compare the original and exported files. Because of this, (with the caveats described in the following sections), it is straightforward to use ontologies developed in Protégé in CLIPS. For a complete description of the CLIPS-Protégé interface, see http://protege.stanford.edu/doc/design/clips.html.

8.4.2 Graphical Representation of the Sample Ontology

To facilitate subsequent examples without listing long files, Figure 8.6 graphically depicts the Protégé ontology (a knowledge base) used. This ontology is used to show both integration with Protégé and instance-set queries.

8.4.3 Importing *.pont Files into CLIPS

Consider the snippet, or portion, of the class hierarchy shown in Figure 8.7. The COOL syntax is evident. As shown in Figure 8.9, the CLIPS `load` command is used with this file.

8.4.4 Importing *.pins Files into CLIPS

Similarly, consider the `*.pins` (Protégé instance representation) for this example. This is shown in Figure 8.8. Importing `*.pins` representations into CLIPS is facilitated by the CLIPS COOL function `load-instances` with syntax:

```
(load-instances <filename>)
```

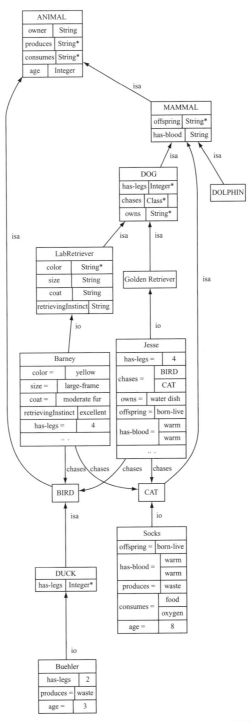

Figure 8.6 Graphical Depiction of the Ontology Used with CLIPS COOL

```
(defclass ANIMAL "Multicellular organisms that ingest food.
They also have their own means of locomotion in at least one phase of their life cycles."
(is-a USER)
(role concrete)
(single-slot %3ANAME
(type STRING)
;+ (cardinality 0 1)
(create-accessor read-write))
(single-slot age
(type INTEGER)
(default 0)
;+ (cardinality 1 1)
(create-accessor read-write))
(single-slot owner
(type STRING)
(default "unknown")
;+ (cardinality 0 1)
(create-accessor read-write))
(multislot consumes
(type STRING)
(default "food" "oxygen")
(create-accessor read-write))
(multislot produces
(type STRING)
(default "waste")
(create-accessor read-write)))

(defclass MAMMAL "Class of warm blooded (usually hairy) animals, that feed their young with milk from the mammary
glands of females. Mammalia include monotremes, marsupials, primates, cats, dogs, bears, hoofed animals, rodents,
bats, seals, dolphins, and whales."
(is-a ANIMAL)
(role concrete)
(multislot offspring
(type STRING)
(default "born-live")
(create-accessor read-write))
(single-slot has-blood
(type STRING)
(default "warm")
;+ (value "warm")
;+ (cardinality 0 1)
(create-accessor read-write)))

(defclass DOG
(is-a MAMMAL)
(role concrete)
(multislot owns
(type STRING)
(default "water dish")
(create-accessor read-write))
(multislot has-legs
(type INTEGER)
(default 4)
(create-accessor read-write))
(multislot chases
(type SYMBOL)
;+ (allowed-parents)
;+ (value BIRD CAT)
(cardinality 1 ?VARIABLE)
(create-accessor read-write)))
```

Figure 8.7 Snippet of COOL Hierarchical Class Representation (Protégé **pont** file format) Corresponding to Figures 2.10 and 2.11. The complete ontology is depicted graphically in Figure 8.6. This file may be loaded directly into CLIPS.

```
; Thu Oct 06 09:28:35 EDT 2005
;
;+ (version "3.1.1")
;+ (build "Build 216")

([Barney] of  LabRetriever

(age 8)
(coat "moderate fur")
(color "yellow")
(consumes
"food"
"oxygen")
(has-blood "warm")
(has-legs 4)
(offspring "born-live")
(owner "Leslie Schalkoff")
(owns
"water dish"
"tennis ball")
(produces "waste")
(retrievingInstnct "excellent")
(size "large-frame"))

([Buehler] of  DUCK

(age 3)
(has-legs 2)
(produces "waste"))

([Jesse] of  GoldenRetriever

(age 14)
(consumes
"food"
"oxygen")
(has-blood "warm")
(has-legs 4)
(offspring "born-live")
(owner "Leslie Schalkoff")
(owns "water dish")
(produces "waste"))

([Socks] of  CAT

(age 8)
(consumes
"food"
"oxygen")
(has-blood "warm")
(offspring "born-live")
(produces "waste"))
```

Figure 8.8 COOL Instance Representation Produced by Protégé Corresponding to Figures 2.10 and 2.11

```
$ clips
        CLIPS (V6.24 06/15/06)
CLIPS> (load "barney5.pont")
Defining defclass: %3ACLIPS_TOP_LEVEL_SLOT_CLASS
Defining defclass: ANIMAL
Defining defclass: MAMMAL
Defining defclass: DOG
Defining defclass: LabRetriever
Defining defclass: GoldenRetriever
Defining defclass: CAT
Defining defclass: DOLPHIN
Defining defclass: BIRD
Defining defclass: DUCK
TRUE
CLIPS> (watch instances)
CLIPS> (load-instances "barney5.pins")
==> instance [Barney] of LabRetriever
==> instance [Buehler] of DUCK
==> instance [Jesse] of GoldenRetriever
==> instance [Socks] of CAT
4
CLIPS> (instance-existp [Barney])
TRUE
CLIPS> (instances)
[Barney] of LabRetriever
[Buehler] of DUCK
[Jesse] of GoldenRetriever
[Socks] of CAT
For a total of 4 instances.
```

Figure 8.9 CLIPS Dribble of Loading "Barney" Class Definitions and Instances

8.4.5 Loading the Protégé Ontology into CLIPS

This is shown in Figure 8.9. Note that the `load-instances` function returns the number of instances loaded.

8.4.6 Combining CLIPS Productions with the Protégé Sample Ontology

As noted and shown previously, productions may use instances as part of condition element tests. Consider the sample production shown in Figure 8.10. CLIPS usage is shown in Figure 8.11.

```
(defrule dog-chases
?dog <- (object (chases $?)) ;; instances of the chaser
?who <- (object (is-a CAT | BIRD)) ;; instances of the chasee
=>
(printout t "the dog " (instance-name ?dog)
          " will chase " (instance-name ?who) crlf))
```

Figure 8.10 Sample Production Using Instances from Ontology

```
CLIPS> (run)
the dog [Barney] will chase [Socks]
the dog [Jesse] will chase [Socks]
the dog [Jesse] will chase [Buehler]
the dog [Barney] will chase [Buehler]
```

Figure 8.11 Using CLIPS with the Production of Figure 8.10 and Instances from the Protégé Knowledge Base

8.4.7 Instance-Set Queries in COOL

In CLIPS COOL, an instance-set is a collection of instances from sets defined by the user. CLIPS provides a query mechanism for use with instance-sets. Six functions are provided. The utility of this mechanism is shown in Figure 8.12. This example is based upon the imported Protégé ontology from Section 8.4. The COOL function `do-for-all-instances` is used to define instance-sets for the DOG and DUCK class, respectively, and then determine DOG instances capable of chasing DUCK instances. The reader should compare this text result with the graphical depiction of the underlying KB in Figure 8.6.

```
$ clips
         CLIPS (V6.24 06/15/06)
CLIPS> (load "barney5.pont")
Defining defclass: %3ACLIPS_TOP_LEVEL_SLOT_CLASS
Defining defclass: ANIMAL
Defining defclass: MAMMAL
Defining defclass: DOG
Defining defclass: LabRetriever
Defining defclass: GoldenRetriever
Defining defclass: CAT
Defining defclass: DOLPHIN
Defining defclass: BIRD
Defining defclass: DUCK
TRUE
CLIPS> (load-instances "barney5.pins")
4
CLIPS> (do-for-all-instances
((?dog DOG) (?duck DUCK))        ;; define instance-sets (template)
(and ?dog:chases ?duck)          ;; instance-set query (predicate)
(printout t ?dog ' chases ' ?duck crlf)) ;; resulting action
;; clips response follows ---
[Barney][Buehler]
[Jesse][Buehler]
CLIPS>
```

Figure 8.12 Annotated Example of Using CLIPS COOL Instance-Set Queries with the Imported Protégé Knowledge Base

8.4.8 Protégé, fuzzyCLIPS, and COOL

The ability to create classes, subclasses, and instances in Protégé and then directly import this representation into CLIPS is quite valuable. This ability provides a structured methodology for the representation development and modification. As is noted in Section 11.6.1, instances of classes used with fuzzyCLIPS, which are defined in Protégé, must be explicitly declared "reactive," i.e., able to be matched against object patterns in the CE to a rule.

8.5 IS Representation/Knowledge Base Consistency

The knowledge base for an expert system is derived from consultation with perhaps a number of different domain experts. One might suspect that this process could lead to the embedding of disparate information in the database, thus not all the expert information is guaranteed to be consistent. Furthermore, under some circumstances it is possible to produce conflicting information. The verification of the knowledge base consistency is a major problem in practical IS development.

For illustration, we concentrate our attention on rule-based systems, and explore techniques for testing the consistency and completeness of a rule set.

8.5.1 Redundancy

In this case, two rules are equivalent in the sense that they satisfy the same preconditions and produce the same conclusion. For example, the rules

$$p(X) \cap q(X) \rightarrow r(X)$$

and

$$p(Y) \cap q(Y) \rightarrow r(Y)$$

are redundant. Redundancy is seldom as easy to spot, due to the use of alternative, but logically equivalent, statements.

8.5.2 Conflicts

In this case, the system contains two or more rules that are applicable, but produce conflicting conclusions. For example,

$$p(X) \rightarrow r(X)$$

and

$$p(Y) \rightarrow \neg r(Y)$$

8.5.3 Subsumed or Subordinate Rules

In this case, two or more rules produce the same consequents, but one has additional preconditions (antecedents). For example, in a system containing

$$p(X) \cap q(X) \rightarrow r(X) \quad (i)$$

and
$$q(Y) \rightarrow r(Y) \quad (ii)$$
it is only necessary to have Rule (ii). Note, Rule (i) is more specific.

8.5.4 Unnecessary Conditions

Consider the following two rules:
$$p(X) \cap q(Y) \rightarrow r(Z)$$
and
$$p(X) \cap \neg q(Y) \rightarrow r(Z)$$

Application of resolution to this pair yields:
$$p(X) \rightarrow r(Z)$$

This situation implies that rules exist in the rule base which, in light of the facts, can never be fired. Clearly, for a rule to be fired, its antecedents must be satisfied. The unreachable condition dilemma occurs in two ways:

1. No subset of the facts in the database will allow firing of the rule; and

2. There is no combination of rule consequents that is able to produce the preconditions necessary to fire the rule.

8.5.5 Circular Rules

This is perhaps one of the most common problems encountered. The careless representation of transitive or symmetric relations in Prolog is a good source of this type of problem. In a more general sense, the problem occurs when the inference net forms a cycle. The following set of rules exemplify this problem:
$$p(X) \rightarrow q(X)$$
$$q(Y) \rightarrow r(Y)$$
$$r(Z) \rightarrow p(Z)$$

8.6 Nonmonotonic Logic

8.6.1 Definition

In many situations, inference must be conducted in light of information that is either of questionable validity or unavailable. In addition, inferences may be based upon assumptions or default values. Assumptions upon which inferences are made may change over time or are found to be incorrect.

In this section we consider nonmonotonic reasoning or nonmonotonic logic [MD80], which are concepts intended to facilitate reasoning with incomplete information, and which may necessitate revision of previous reasoning scenarios when updated or when more complete information becomes available. *A mode of reasoning is* **monotonic** *if it reaches conclusions that are never retracted on the basis of new information.* Nonmonotonic reasoning (logics) do not have this characteristic.

8.6.2   Examples of Situations Involving Nonmonotonic Reasoning

There are many examples of reasoning with incomplete data. For example, suppose in an implementation of frame-based inference, a number of slots contained default values that were used in the inference process, and a number of hypotheses were verified. At some later time it is determined (on the basis of new or updated information) that the actual values of entities used in the inference process differed significantly from those assumed previously. Clearly, the results of the reasoning process using the default values are questionable. In fact, since they are conclusions drawn from incomplete or erroneous data, they are logically unsound. This is an example of a system employing assumptions as to the typical behavior of a number of variables; humans employing common sense seem to know (how) to check the reasonableness of these assumptions and adjust the inference process accordingly.

8.6.3   Soar and Nonmonotonic Reasoning

The Soar production system facilitates nonmonotonic reasoning via **wm** truth maintenance implemented based upon I-instantiation of facts. This is considered in depth in Chapter 9.

8.6.4   Nonmonotonic Reasoning Formalisms

Modifications to classical first-order logic that enable proofs in the face of incomplete or default information are, in general, quite complicated and the subject of continued research. We show this using two simple examples.

A Monotonic Representation and Modus Ponens.

```
IF a, b, c

THEN d
```

A More Advanced ("Common Sense") Representation.

```
IF a, b, c

ASSUMING e, f, g

THEN d

UNLESS h, i, j
```

The difficulty arises when attempting to develop a logic and corresponding sound inference strategy based upon the second "common sense" representation. Thus, nonmonotonic reasoning with some form of possible backtracking may be necessary as part of a realistic knowledge representation [Doy79], [Fil88].

8.7 Reasoning with Time (Temporal Logics and Operators)

Up to this point, our examination of knowledge representation and manipulation has neglected the concept of time, e.g., we ignored the ramifications of tense in statements (or simply considered all statements atemporal). A number of realistic IS problems exist wherein reasoning with time (RWT) is necessary. For example:

1. Statements that were true yesterday may still be true today, but perhaps not tomorrow. Thus, temporal reasoning is a dynamic process.

2. Things we do (and don't do) today cause other things to be in some state at a later time.

3. Humans reason and plan in a world with history, calendars, wristwatches, deadlines, predictions, and other temporal constraints.

A number of fundamental topics are related to RWT, such as temporal logics, interval-based temporal representations, causality, and modal logic.

8.7.1 Characteristics of Temporal Reasoning

Time is a parameter in the reasoning process that must be carefully interpreted and that constrains most practical reasoning. However, the concept of time, as applied to reasoning, is much deeper for several reasons:

1. There exist situations (or reasoning scenarios) other than the "current" one. The situation existing at the present time may influence future states, and itself may be influenced by events occurring in the past.

2. Humans (and some algorithms) have a limited memory capacity in the sense that, over time they forget, i.e., information is removed from the database.

3. The process of planning is intimately related to the concept of time since a plan is comprised of a sequence of actions with a temporal ordering.

4. Causal reasoning does not allow reasoning in the present to require facts in the future. Humans and IS implementations must employ causal reasoning.

8.7.2 Subdivisions of Time

Reasoning with time (RWT) may be point or interval-based. This dichotomy is easily explained by recalling that (fortunately) time is a one-dimensional concept with an ordering that is universally accepted. The three major subdivisions of time, relative to a chosen point (which itself is not stationary) are:

1. The present or "current time," is denoted by t_c. The present may be affected by the past.

2. The past is defined by all values of $t < t_c$, and possibly available to us in the form of "history." The past cannot be changed; there is one past.

3. The future is defined by all values of $t > t_c$, and may be affected by events occurring in the past or present.

8.7.3 Time Intervals and Points

A (time) interval is defined as a set of points and therefore may or may not contain a specified point. Intervals may overlap, i.e., share common points, or may be disjoint (e.g., the past and future intervals are always disjoint). Temporal relations involving intervals may be developed by considering interval-based relations involving "overlapping," "coincident," etc. For example, given intervals I1 and I2, the following predicates are TRUE under the stated conditions:

during (I1, I2): Interval I1 is (completely) contained within interval I2.

before (I1, I2): I1 exists before I2 and there is no overlap.

overlap (I1, I2): I1 begins before I2, and I1 and I2 overlap.

equal (I1, I2): I1 = I2.

meets (I1, I2): before (I1, I2) = T and I2 starts where I1 ends (i.e., no interval between I1 and I2).

These are shown in Figure 8.13.

8.7.4 Possible Implementations of RWT

There exists a multitude of conceptually obvious (and simplistic) implementations of RWT. The fundamental property of temporal logic, in contrast to the classical logic is that in temporal logic, the same statement may have different truth values at different times, i.e., in different worlds, situations, intervals, or "time frames."

Representing the Truth Value of Statements over Time: Temporal Operators (F, P, G, and H)

Our attention is restricted to four possible time-specific aspects of the truth value of a statement, A, which are conveyed by four temporal operators, denoted F, P, G, and H. The truth value of A at time t is denoted A(t). An example situation is shown in Figure 8.14.

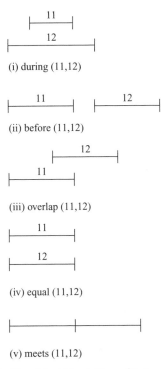

(i) during (I1,I2)

(ii) before (I1,I2)

(iii) overlap (I1,I2)

(iv) equal (I1,I2)

(v) meets (I1,I2)

Figure 8.13 Graphical Depiction of Interval Relations

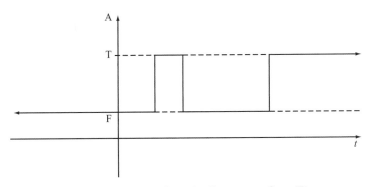

Figure 8.14 Truth Value of a Statement Over Time

Denoting the current time as t_c, the four operators are:

1. F(A): A is TRUE at some future time, i.e., $\exists$ a nonempty set of values $\{t_f\}$ where $t_f > t_c$ and $A(t_f)$ is TRUE for each value.

2. P(A): A was TRUE at some time in the past, i.e., $\exists$ a nonempty set of values $\{t_p\}$ where $t_p < t_c$ and $A(t_p)$ was TRUE for each value.

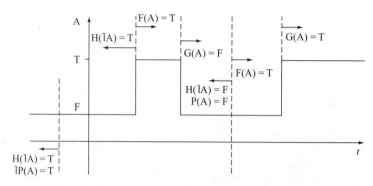

Figure 8.15　Temporal Operators Applied to the Statement Shown in Figure 8.14

3. G(A): A is TRUE at all future times, i.e., $\forall t > t_c$ A(t) is TRUE.

4. H(A): A was TRUE for all past time, i.e., $\forall t < t_c$ A(t) is TRUE.

Figure 8.15 illustrates the use of these operators with the time-varying truth value of statement A, shown in Figure 8.14.

Note the relationships between the F and G and the P and H operators, respectively. G and H are used to form stronger (in the sense of constraints) statements, and therefore F and P are always applicable in situations where G and H, respectively, are.

Example: Representational Utility of Temporal Operators.　Consider the following statements, A and B:

```
A: person X will die (i.e., is alive)
B: person X is alive
```

Given B is TRUE at t_c, we may correctly assert F(A) is TRUE. Furthermore, given B is TRUE at t_c, we may also correctly assert P(B) is TRUE, but not H(B).

Manipulation of Compound Statements Using G, F, A, and P

Manipulation of compound statements involving the G, F, A, and P operators is both possible and desirable. The reader should verify the following tautologies:

$$G(A \cup B) \neq G(A) \cup G(B)$$

$$G(A) \cup G(B) \to G(A \cup B)$$

$$G(A) \cap G(B) = G(A \cap B)$$

Other valid statements (tautologies) are shown in Table 8.1.

The F, P, G, and H operators, combined with the tautologies of Table 8.1 and a notion of temporal relations, form the basis for a manipulable and quantifiable RWT strategy.

1.	$G(A \rightarrow B) \rightarrow (G(A) \rightarrow G(B))$
2.	$H(A \rightarrow B) \rightarrow (H(A) \rightarrow H(B))$
3.	$A \rightarrow H(F(A))$
4.	$A \rightarrow G(P(A))$
5.	$G(A) \rightarrow F(A)$
6.	$H(A) \rightarrow P(A)$
7.	$G(A) = \neg F(\neg A)$

Table 8.1 Valid Statements in Temporal Logic

8.8 IS Collaboration: Blackboards

A formalized mechanism for structuring, or specifically partitioning representations to facilitate distributed IS computation is the blackboard model [Ni89]. This mechanism is so-named as a result of observing how experts, confined to a room and given a problem and a blackboard, might interact and share applicable knowledge in the solution process. In the case of humans, this knowledge might be enumeration of solution approaches, assumptions, constraints, figures, references, etc. Material may be added to or removed from the blackboard by one or more of the experts.

The blackboard model is one vehicle to implement opportunistic problem solving. Figure 8.16 shows the overall concept, which we now explore in more detail.

The collaboration inherent in the blackboard model leads to the notion of distributed agents in Section 8.10.8.

The "blackboard" itself is a type of globally accessible database that serves as a repository of information. In a blackboard system, domain-specific knowledge (often procedural) is partitioned into

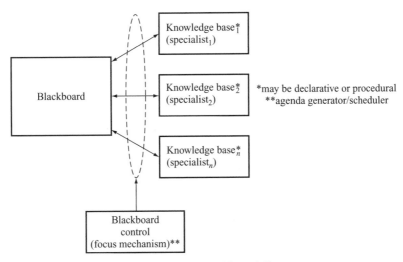

Figure 8.16 The Blackboard Concept

specialists, which are allowed to communicate through the blackboard. These specialists are usually separate and independent. Thus, the blackboard provides a vehicle to agglomerate problem-specific information from a number of databases, without necessitating the use of all of each database. Only information specific to the particular state of a specific problem is extracted and communicated via the blackboard. This may include relevant data or intermediate conclusions. Note that the flow of data between the specialists and the blackboard is bidirectional—specialists may contribute knowledge to the blackboard as well as extract information from it. This allows some computationally advantageous form of local reasoning in the specialists. In addition, the blackboard itself is a dynamic data structure, with information being added or removed over time.

Applications that are candidates for a blackboard solution approach share a number of characteristics, including:

1. A need for an opportunistic problem solving methodology including fusion of expertise;

2. A need for extensive communication between heterogeneous representations and solution approaches;

3. A need to generate and explore multiple hypotheses in parallel;

4. A need to reason on multiple levels of abstraction; and

5. A need to consider external information that arrives sporadically.

8.8.1   Blackboard Control

In the blackboard structure, it is necessary to control the distributed opportunistic reasoning that occurs. Using the human analogy, a "moderator" is required. This mechanism determines, among other things,

◆ Who is "at the blackboard" (i.e., which knowledge source is activated) over time

◆ How long a specialist may control the inference process

◆ Relative weights or significance to attach to statements produced by each specialist

This "moderator" or focusing mechanism is usually implemented in the blackboard control, as shown in Figure 8.16. For example, this control may be implemented by incorporation of a set of preconditions in each specialist, indicating the conditions that must exist for activation of that expert. The specialists may be given relative weights (just as one might choose the opinion of a more qualified person over another less qualified), which govern their activation potential. This provides, to some extent, a means to implement some form of "common sense," by using a high-priority specialist (often referred to as a "demon").

8.8.2   Typical Sequence of Blackboard Operations

A typical sequence of blackboard-based operations are as follows:

1. A specialist changes the blackboard.

2. All specialists then indicate to the control mechanism (the "moderator") their potential contribution to the problem, based upon the revised problem state.

3. The control mechanism then determines the next specialist that is given access to the blackboard. If two or more are applicable, the control mechanism determines a schedule, or agenda, for their participation.

4. This specialist (and perhaps others on the agenda) is allowed to revise the blackboard.

5. The control mechanism determines if the problem has been solved (or perhaps if it is insolvable). If it has, a new problem is sought, otherwise operation resumes at Step 2.

The preceding scenario indicates that the operation of the blackboard system is consistent with our concept of a general production system. The solution approach is clearly data-driven and nondeterministic. We note that the control of assertion and removal of blackboard information suggests that a tentative control strategy (i.e., keeping a copy of previous blackboard states) may be desirable. Furthermore, conflict resolution is involved. We note that the blackboard concept is easy to describe while giving rise to a number of difficult questions in the implementation stage.

8.9 From Production Systems to Distributed, Autonomous Agents

8.9.1 What Is an Agent?

The notion of agents brings together a number of different technologies and research areas, including IS, software engineering, robotics, and distributed computing. Agents are a powerful, natural metaphor for conceptualizing, designing, and implementing many complex, distributed applications.

8.9.2 Definitions

A single, informative, and precise definition of an agent is elusive. In addition, there is significant variation in any attempted taxonomy of agents. There is a great deal of ongoing debate about exactly what constitutes an agent. Vague and useless definitions abound, such as:

"An Agent is something that acts in the world."

Historically, agents emerged as "situated robots." In fact, what we normally perceive as "robots"[2] are easily categorized as agents. From this viewpoint, an agent is something that can perceive its environment through sensors and act upon that environment via effectors. Another somewhat more quantitative definition [WJ95] is:

An agent is an encapsulated computer system that is situated in some environment, and that is capable of flexible, autonomous action on behalf of its user (or owner) in that environment in order to meet prespecified design objectives.

---

[2]assuming we have a "normal" or "typical" idea of what constitutes a robot.

The MIT Media Lab offers the following remarks related to software agents:

> Software agents differ from conventional software in that they are long-lived, semi-autonomous, proactive, and adaptive. Our primary focus is to create software that acts as an assistant to the user rather than a tool, learning from interaction and proactively anticipating the user's needs.

> Trivial software agents include Unix daemons. In contrast, an intelligent agent is capable of flexible autonomous action in an environment.

8.9.3 An Agent Example: NL Understanding

Figure 8.17 shows a simple, reactive agent used to facilitate NL conversation. Reactive (or reflex) agents, as the name implies, sense the environment and, on the basis of internally generated or stored goals, respond accordingly. Commonly, productions may be used to implement this behavior. Conditions correspond to environmental states; actions correspond to the agent response.

8.9.4 An Agent Example: Network Monitoring

ExperNet [Vla02] is a multiagent system for monitoring computer networks, detecting problems, and diagnosing the source of problems. Each agent in the system is responsible for managing a portion of the network, e.g., a single agent manages each subnet. Using multiple agents has many advantages, including fault tolerance and a reduction in the amount of monitoring information transmitted over the network.

Each agent has a modular structure. The "Device" knowledge-base system comprises the expert system shell in which rules are implemented. Device is implemented on top of CS-Prolog II. CS-Prolog II uses an extension of HNMS network management software, called HNMS+, to acquire information about the network. The system also uses a computer monitoring program called BigBrother to gather information about the computer the agent is attached to. This information is used to infer information

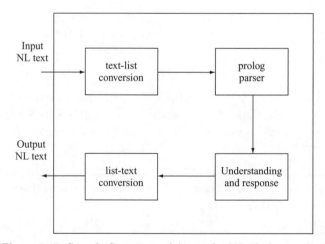

Figure 8.17 Sample Structure of Agent for NL Understanding

about the network's performance. Device provides many interesting features, such as support for multiple rule types (deductive, production, and event-driven rules) and object orientation.

8.9.5 Agent Characteristics

Characteristics of an agent include:

1. An agent has well-defined problem boundaries and interfaces.

2. An agent is embedded in a particular environment.

3. An agent is designed to achieve specific objectives.

4. An agent is autonomous.

5. An agent is flexible and displays (context-dependent) problem-solving behavior. In other words, the agent is reactive.

8.10 Basic Agent Structures and Types of Agents

8.10.1 Generic Structure

The basic agent structure is shown in Figure 8.18.

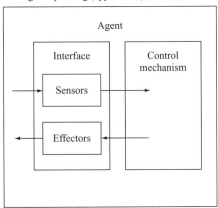

Figure 8.18 Basic Agent Structure

8.10.2 Agent Types

There are many different agent architectures, including:

1. Simple reactive agents (see Figure 8.17)

2. Reactive planning agents

3. Software agents serving as personal assistants

4. Collaborative agents

5. Information-gathering agents

6. Robotic agents

7. Learning agents

8. Mobile agents

9. Belief-desires-intentions (BDI) agents (see Section 8.10.3)

8.10.3 BDI Agents

Belief-desires-intentions (BDI) agents have the structure shown in Figure 8.19 and are characterized by:

1. A database of beliefs consisting of world facts as well as data relevant to the agent's internal state;

2. A set of the agent's goals or objectives (desires);

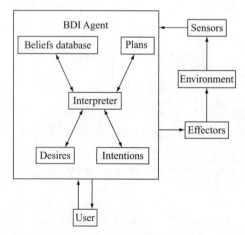

Figure 8.19 Belief-Desires-Intentions (BDI) Agent Structure

3. A set of plans necessary to achieve these goals; and

4. An ordered set of these plans (intentions).

8.10.4 Theoretical Components of an Agent

[TE05] indicates the following components of an agent:

1. A state space, X, together with a set of state variables, x. Specific values of x denote the state of the agent. Elements of x might be entities such as location and speed.

2. A set of *perceived environment variables*, z, indicating the perceived state of the environment. The environment state space is denoted Z. This includes the observable characterisitcs of other agents.

3. A set, A, of allowable actions for each agent. A could include move-left or stop.

4. A set of individual agent-based strategies, S. Each element of S is a function:

$$s : (Z \times X) \to A$$

These strategies form the basis for the agent behavior.

5. A set of utility variables, U for the specific problem. Variables include time and various costs.

6. An objective function, $F : U \to R^m$. Each agent attempts to optimize this function. Notice that F may contain problem constraints, e.g., game rules.

These components serve as a framework for theoretical analysis of agent-based systems and behavior.

8.10.5 Agents and Rule-Based Systems

One connection between agents and expert and rule-based systems is straightforward—expert or intelligent agents may be implemented using a rule-based paradigm. Sample applications are shown in [GLC+95], [Kat02].

8.10.6 Living Organisms As Agents

We are surrounded by a plethora of living entities, most of which satisfy the definition of an agent. Specifically, as shown in Figure 8.20, the definition for an agent includes the human as an agent. This inclusion is important, since it allows the agent-oriented model to facilitate the understanding, simulation, and control of collections of living "agents."

8.10.7 Potential Applications for Agents

While robotics is often mentioned as the typical agent application, [Jen05] indicates applicability in a number of areas, including some that are non-obvious. This includes transportation [BHM97] and scientific data interpretation [GJL+99]. The use of multiple agents to model the spread of disease is shown in [EGK+04]. The Internet seems to offer equal potential for the paradigm, as discussed next.

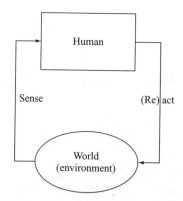

Figure 8.20 The Human "Agent"

Intelligent Agents and the Internet. The Internet is arguably one of the most complex, changing, and unpredictable environments that software designers must deal with. At the same time, Internet applications are arguably one of the most important areas from both technical and economic viewpoints. The Internet may offer one of the best opportunities for the agent paradigm. Numerous purchase tracking and "recommender" systems are currently implemented using agents.

8.10.8 Multiple, Mobile Agents and Distributed Computing

Beyond a Single Agent. Whereas a single agent is capable of independent action, a current trend is the use of multiple agents. A multiagent system is one that consists of a number of agents, which interact with each other (as well as the environment). This is an outgrowth or perhaps natural evolution of the area of distributed artificial intelligence (DAI). The history of DAI dates back to 1980.

A multiagent system consists of a number of agents that interact with each other. The "real world" is a multiagent environment. Usually, in this framework, agents communicate, cooperate, and coordinate with one another.

Mobile Agents. An extension to the distributed agent concept is that of mobile agents. Mobile agents are autonomous, intelligent programs that can move through a network, searching for and interacting with services on the user's behalf. In this sense, security is important, since viruses are included in this definition. Since mobile agents may need to execute on every machine in the network, the agent code needs to be mobile as well. Thus, mobile code systems like Java are popular in this case.

Agents in the Cinema. One of the most interesting and nonobvious applications for agent technology is in motion picture production. Especially significant is the arena of computer-generated (CG) movie scenes. Incorporation of agents as "software actors" has led to more realistic and cost-effective rendering of scenes. For example, "crowd" scenes in *King Kong* (2005) and *The Fast and the Furious: Tokyo Drift* (2005) were generated using Massive software's autonomous agent-based three-dimensional animation software.[3] With this software, the film animator creates agent-based autonomous characters capable of generating reactions to what is going on around them. The Massive software is a framework for designing and running such agents. Agent libraries are available.

8.10.9   Software Agents As a Design Paradigm

Agent-oriented software (AOS) design is considered a supplement for existing (e.g., UML, OO, agile) software design methodologies [ZJOW00]. For example, a software agent could be as simple as a program function. Agent-based computing is emerging as a means for the development of complex software systems in terms of autonomous software agents that exhibit proactive and intelligent behavior, and that interact with one another in terms of high-level protocols and languages. This paradigm is also referred to as agent-oriented software engineering.

AOS as a design paradigm requires:

1. Definition of suitable IS architectures for agents

2. Definition of suitable software architectures for agents

3. Definition of agent communication protocols and languages

4. Coordination models for agent behavior

5. Models for the specification and verification of multiagent systems

6. Methodologies to support developers in an engineering approach to the analysis, design, and verification of single and multiagent systems.

8.10.10   Agent Software Standards

The Foundation for Intelligent Physical Agents (FIPA) is an IEEE Computer Society standards organization. FIPA promotes agent-based technology and, more importantly, the interoperability of agents (through its standards) with other technologies. This includes, for example, interfaces to the Web. Standards and other information may be obtained from http://www.fipa.org/. Of particular significance to developers are the FIPA-2000 agent management and message transport standards.

8.10.11   Tools for Agent-Based Development

Numerous agent development frameworks are available. Some are commercial products; some are free; some are available online. Links to others are given in Section 8.11. For example, [PZG05] provides a survey of Java-based agent development frameworks.

Soar (considered in detail in Chapter 9) is fundamentally an agent-based, problem-solving computational infrastructure. In Chapter 9 the notion of independent, but interacting, agents in a Soar kernel is developed and implemented in C++. Relevant sections of interest for the agent-specific aspects of Soar are Sections 9.11.2 and 9.11.4.

---

[3]http:massivesoftware.com

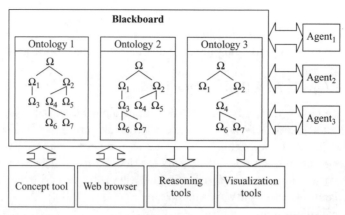

Figure 8.21 Merging Multiple Agents with the Blackboard Concept. From [CVS04]. Courtesy of Wamberto W. Vasconcelos.

8.10.12 Merging Multiple Agents and Blackboards

The common knowledge necessary for multiple agents is often stored in a common location. The blackboard architecture may facilitate this. An application of ontology management using agents and the blackboard together is shown in [CVS04]. Figure 8.21 indicates the structure.

8.11 References

General agent references include [Jen05], [WJ95], [ZJOW00], and [GJL$^+$99]. References for software agents and programming include [Sho93], [Nwa96], [BHM97], [OZ99], [PA98], [BDJT95], and [FFMM94]. Internet resources for agent research and applications abound. The following are good starting points:

> http://www-2.cs.cmu.edu/ softagents/
> http://agents.umbc.edu/
> http://www.fipa.org.

Other sources of information and downloadable agent development software resources may be found at:

> http://www.agentlink.org
> http://www.agentlink.org/resources/agent-software.php

8.12 Exercises

1. Using CLIPS and COOL, develop a hierarchical frame representation for the entity "house." Include entities such as door, window, street address, representation.

2. Can a frame representation (perhaps together with an inference procedure) facilitate object recognition? For example, suppose entities (or features) corresponding to "door," "window," etc., have

been extracted from the raw input data. How would a frame representation for house be used to facilitate either:

(a) Further feature extraction; or

(b) Recognition.

3. One knowledge base inconsistency, indicated in the text, concerns the subsuming of rules. An example is the two-rule pair:

$$p \cap q \to r \tag{8.1}$$
$$q-> r \tag{8.2}$$

(a) Does $\neg p \to r$ logically follow?

(b) What constraints do these Equations place upon p?

4. Show, *using resolution*, that the following database contains an inconsistency:

$$a \tag{8.3}$$
$$a \to b \tag{8.4}$$
$$c \tag{8.5}$$
$$c \to \neg b \tag{8.6}$$

5. Distinguish a logic that is nonmonotonic from one that is inconsistent.

6. The following list contains more advanced elements of the CLIPS syntax and semantics. After studying the CLIPS Basic Programming Guide, provide a brief description of the syntax and use of each. Advanced CLIPS concepts and constructs include:

(a) `set-strategy`

(b) `defmodules`

(c) `deffunction`

(d) `defclass`

(e) `definstances, make-instance`

(f) `browse-classes`

7. In Section 8.5, the issue of developing and maintaining a consistent production system was addressed. Research the topics of metarules and demons and indicate how these concepts could be applied to this task.

8. The importation of Protégé-derived knowledge representations into CLIPS raises the important and larger issue of knowledge representation and production system interoperability. Note that Protégé was not necessary to develop the CLIPS representation. This raises the interesting question:

Is it possible to export COOL class and instance specifications into Protégé?

9. Often, inheritance is overly general, and leads to the concept of inheritance with exceptions. Consider the following (inconsistent) class representation:

   ◆ A civilian **is not** a soldier.

   ◆ A (U.S.) president is a commander-in-chief.

   ◆ A commander-in-chief is a soldier.

   ◆ A (U.S.) president is a civilian.

   Implement this in COOL.

10. Five statements involving the F, P, G, and H operators for RWT and statements A and B follow. Determine whether each is TRUE or FALSE.

$$G(\neg A) = \neg G(A)$$

$$F(A) \to G(A)$$

$$G(A) \to P(A)$$

$$H(A) = \neg P(\neg A)$$

$$[G(A \cup B)] \to [G(A) \cup G(B)]$$

11. Consider the development of a rule-based logic that employs a WHEN construct, as compared with an IF-based antecedent designator. In our previous reasoning we formulated rules or productions with the form:

$$\text{IF statement(s) ... THEN consequent(s)} \tag{8.7}$$

   versus the form:

$$\text{WHEN statement(s) ... THEN consequent(s)} \tag{8.8}$$

   Representation (8.8) is obviously quite useful in a number of representations. The connotation in Statement (8.8) is different from Statement (8.7) in the sense that Statement (8.8) implies that eventually the antecedent is TRUE. How would you integrate this representational tool with a production system? Address related issues such as conflict resolution.

12. How would you revise the production structure to include temporal linguistic descriptors such as:

```
henceforth (subsequently)
until
never
eventually
previously
before, after, and during
```

13. List and explain three attributes of an agent.

14. This problem makes an excellent long-term project. To gain some "hands-on" experience with the agent computational framework (as an alternative to using Soar) explore one of the many downloadable development environments. Many are listed at http://www.agentlink.org/resources/agent-software.php. For example, Agent Factory (http://www.agentfactory.com/) is a framework that supports the development and deployment of agent-oriented applications using Java. Agent Factory is compliant with the FIPA-2000 agent management and message transport standards.

15. This problem makes another excellent long-term project. Consider the development of a multi-agent/blackboard computational framework in Prolog. An agent might be implemented using the predicate `agent`. In addition, each agent may have several possible actions, implemented using the predicate `action`. Actions include reading and writing on the blackboard. The blackboard is implemented as a list of terms.

16. *Mobile* agents are programs that can migrate, via a network, from computational platform (host) to computational platform. As such, they are quite useful for providing uninterruptable computing by reducing the need for a single, reliable platform. As attractive as it seems, however, this capability spawns a number of serious concerns. Perhaps the most significant concern is that of security. For example, a computer virus could be crafted as a mobile agent. Research this topic and provide a synopsis of the security aspects of mobile agents.

17. Compare and contrast the object-oriented programming paradigm (OOP) with that of the agent-oriented paradigm (AOP). Specific features to be considered include architecture, communication capabilities, encapsulation, and reuse.

## chapter 9

Soar

Soar is a computational and philosophical architecture for knowledge representation and manipulation. The objective of this chapter is to develop a working understanding of Soar fundamentals. In addition, we compare and contrast Soar with less sophisticated IS architectures such as CLIPS. Finally, for the more ambitious and computer literate, we look at the internals of Soar interfacing and use of the Soar kernel.

It is of historical note that the name SOAR was originally an acronym for **S**tate **O**perator **A**nd **R**esult. After finishing this chapter, readers should understand the significance and interaction of these three Soar components.

The Soar approach has been applied to different problem domains, including computer manufacturing, solving puzzles, war-game simulations (TankSoar), and natural language processing (NL-Soar). More sophisticated Soar-based blocks-world planning examples are included in Chapter 12.

9.1 Soar Background

Soar may be approached from a number of viewpoints:

- The maintainers of Soar postulate that Soar is a general cognitive architecture for developing systems that exhibit intelligent behavior.

- Soar is a computational environment designed to accommodate an agent-based framework for IS.

- Pragmatically, Soar is based upon the notion of a production system.

9.1.1 Soar History

Soar is not new. Soar was created by John Laird, Allen Newell, and Paul Rosenbloom at Carnegie Mellon University, beginning in 1983. Early efforts leading up to Soar are described in [LNR87], [New90], [New92a], [New92b], and [RLN92]. A major goal of the Soar project is for Soar to be able to implement the full range of capabilities of an intelligent agent. The Soar project is a long-term, multidisciplinary, multi-investigator effort.

Similar Approaches. Soar is not alone. Other cognitive architectures such as ACT-R exist. ACT-R is Lisp-based. ACT-R is described in detail in [TLA06]. For more details, see http://act-r.psy.cmu.edu/.

9.1.2 IS Design and Implementation Using Soar

A common trade-off is writing software from scratch vs. learning the concepts, syntax, and semantics of software written by others. In this respect, the Soar software platform is no different. The good news is that Soar facilitates the representation, manipulation, and learning capabilities required by many IS applications. The bad news is the significant learning curve associated with designing an IS in Soar.

Soar is complicated enough that we investigate it in two passes—the first pass using old, familiar examples from simple production systems and the second pass incorporating more advanced Soar concepts. In both operation and architecture, Soar is considerably more complex than the CLIPS production system considered in Chapter 7. Many of the features of the CLIPS production system could be considered a subset of Soar features.

Soar: Extending the Notion of a State

In Soar, the notion of a state is expanded to distinguish between *internal and external aspects* of the state. This is the basis for the (additional) *state elaboration* cycle in Soar, detailed in the following subsection. Internal changes to the state ("elaborations") may correspond to conscious or unconscious "mental" changes in state due to changes in the external world, such as the acquisition of input. These may be thought of as changes in perception, as opposed to changes in the state corresponding to the actions of operators (yielding external changes in the state).

Soar: Extending the Notion of Productions and Operators

In Soar, productions (rules) are different from operators. In fact, operators are more powerful and more general than productions. Operators are, in essence, based upon productions.

Soar is based upon the concept of applying operators to a state. Specifically, if the current situation is representable as a (Soar) state, goals may be pursued by attempts at transforming this state into a goal state. Productions have a broader role in Soar, i.e., a production may:

1. **elaborate** on the state;

2. **suggest** an operator for use;

3. **compare** two operators for potential use; and

4. **apply** an operator.

In addition, there is a distinction regarding the persistence of the effect of an operator in Soar.

Soar: Expanding the Notion of Conflict Resolution

Conflict resolution is fundamental to production system operation. In Soar, as in CLIPS, only a single operator can be selected for a state at a given time (cycle). A single operator may provide multiple actions. The process of conflict resolution in Soar is far more complex that that of CLIPS, and allows for the creation of an *impasse* when a unique operator cannot be chosen. In addition, an impasse creates one or more new states (substates of the current state) for subsequent resolution of the impasse. This process leads to learning new impasse-resolution behavior or rules in Soar in a process called *chunking*.

Soar: Directly Incorporating Learning

Chunking is one of three learning mechanisms provided by Soar (and the most developed at this time). In addition, reinforcement learning and episodic memory-based learning schemes are under development.

Soar: Implementing Agents Via Kernels

Soar is based upon the notion of an agent (Chapter 8, Section 8.9). Each agent may be implemented using a Soar kernel. Agents may communicate; SML is the current standard for interagent communication. Each agent exists in its own Soar "world"; I/O is used to allow the agent to interact with the "outside" world. This interaction could involve controlling robots or interaction with other agents.

9.1.3 Significant Elements of Soar Philosophy and Pragmatics

The following are some distinguishing elements of the philosophy and pragmatics of Soar.

Philosophy.

1. Soar is explicitly designed to be a *problem-solving system* (as opposed to a general purpose chainer). The Soar architecture has psychological plausibility (one of the original goals was to enable cognitive modeling[1]).

2. Soar emphasizes the concept of a system state. All wm structures are linked to some state and therefore all the current problem short-term knowledge (in wm) is considered an elaboration of this state.

3. Soar distinguishes between an operator and a production. Productions (rules) are used to nominate operators and implement the actions of a chosen operator. In fact, Soar uses productions for a number of different tasks, including state elaboration, operator proposal, impasse resolution (described later), and checking for goal satisfaction.

4. Soar employs *state elaboration*, wherein the problem knowledge is expanded (by other productions) prior to the selection of the next operator.

---

[1] For a discussion of Soar as a candidate Unified Theory of Cognition (UTC), see Allen Newell's *Unified Theories of Cognition* (1990).

5. Soar allows an interface to the "outside" world through an IO state link so that **wm** may also be modified on the basis of interaction with this world (in addition to the use of productions).

6. Elements in **wm** may or may not be **persistent**—those created by operators are persistent whereas those created in state elaboration are not. Soar distinguishes between **wm** persistence or support for a WME produced by a production (I-support) and that produced by operator application (O-support).

7. Soar incorporates *preference-based reasoning*, since operators are *proposed* and evaluated prior to selection. To facilitate this, Soar adds a third memory, namely a "preferences" memory to the architecture.

8. Soar incorporates learning (directly) in both impasse resolution and chunking.

Pragmatics.

1. Soar development is ongoing.

2. Soar (Versions 8.6.1–8.6.4) is integrated with Java for ease of debugging. A visual development environment is provided. This provides easy access to many of the Soar commands and allows examination of many Soar components at runtime.

3. Soar is based upon a freestanding core kernel, written in C++. This kernel may be integrated into other applications. Typically, these applications may be Java, C++, or Tk/Tcl-based. Several instances of the kernel may be running simultaneously and independently and perhaps on different machines.

4. Several independent agents may be implemented (and examined, using separate debuggers) within a single kernel.

9.2 Soar Syntax, Computational Architecture, and Examples

In what follows, we intermingle the discussion of Soar language syntax and semantics and show major features and concepts by example. Many examples employ subtle variations on previous ones (e.g., I vs. O support for the initial state, inhibiting operator proposal, etc.).

The initial "hello world" Soar examples are similar to the simple rule-based examples shown in Chapters 6 and 7. This Section is designed to accompany, not replace, the Soar documentation and resources cited in Section 9.12.

9.2.1 Soar Memory Architecture

Soar incorporates three memories:

1. A working memory;

2. A production memory; and

3. A preference memory.

We summarize the first two in the next section, and elaborate on the third later in the chapter.

9.2.2 States and Working Memory (wm) in Soar

In Soar, a state is a representation of the current or past situation. The running Soar system progresses through a number of states, possibly including substates for impasse resolution and learning. *States are kept in working memory*, which may be thought of as Soar's short-term memory.

Working memory is comprised of working memory elements (WMEs). A basic WME element consists of three entities:

◆ An identifier, which is a unique symbol created by Soar at runtime when a new object is added to wm;

◆ A set of attributes; and

◆ A set of values for the attributes, which may be other objects.

Soar's wm is built upon these triples (although representational flexibility in Soar often obscures this).

Unlike CLIPS, Soar does not require any predeclaration of wm structure. In fact, this structure may change at runtime, as new structures are added and others deleted.

WME structure is governed by syntax of the form:

```
(identifier [^attribute value]*)
```

For example,

```
(state <s> ^thing a ^thing b ^thing d)
```

Notice the preceding example illustrates a multivalued or multiattribute, namely, ^thing. ^thing a, ^thing b, and ^thing d may be thought of as an elaboration of state <s>. Another, less readable way to represent this is:

```
(state <s> ^thing a)
   (state <s> ^thing b)
   (state <s> ^thing d)
```

The latter is the way it would be listed (with time tags and identifiers in alphabetical order) using the Soar wmes command.

9.2.3 Variables in Soar

Variables in Soar follow the OPS5 syntax, i.e., variable names are enclosed in angular brackets. Recall that CLIPS uses a question mark to notate a variable, whereas variables in Prolog syntax begin with an uppercase letter.

9.2.4 Comments and Constants

◆ Soar is case sensitive.

◆ Comments begin with (#) and end with the end of line, e.g.,

```
# this is a comment
```

◆ Constants are enclosed in (|), i.e., |the comment example is here|. This is often useful in text output, as shown by the numerous examples in the chapter.

9.2.5 Hierarchical Representations and Objects

A wm element (WME) object may have a set of attributes. The attribute values may themselves be other objects. Thus wm objects may be linked. The collection of WMEs that share the same first identifier are called an *object* in wm. All wm elements must be linked to a state[2] (either directly or indirectly, i.e., through other objects). Since the state is the root of the wm structure, all objects linked to this state may be considered augmentations of the state.

The use of a hierarchical representation is apparent with wm declarations such as this one, taken from the blocks-world demo:

```
(<s> ^ontop <ontop1> <ontop2> <ontop3>
     ^object <blockA> <blockB> <blockC> <table>
     ^desired <ds>)
  (<ontop1> ^top-block <blockA>
            ^bottom-block <blockB>)
  (<ontop2> ^top-block <blockB>
            ^bottom-block <table>)
  (<ontop3> ^top-block <blockC>
            ^bottom-block <table>)
  (<blockA> ^name A ^type block)
  (<blockB> ^name B ^type block)
  (<blockC> ^name C ^type block)
  (<table> ^name table ^type table)
```

In Soar, when a wm element is created, an integer representing the element time tag is assigned. These may be viewed via the Soar wmes command.

9.2.6 Production Memory (pm) and Production Syntax

Production Components

User-defined and "learned" (from chunking) productions are contained in production memory (pm). A production consists of three required and two optional parts:

1. A name (required). It is conventional to use long, descriptive names for operators to facilitate human interpretation of the Soar program. The Soar reference manual suggests a production

---

[2]wm objects not linked to a state are automatically removed by the Soar architecture.

naming convention. To enhance readability of Soar code, a production name should contain the following elements:

(a) A task name (e.g., move);

(b) A string indicating function (e.g., propose);

(c) The name of the related operator, if applicable; and

(d) Any other relevant information.

2. A set of conditions, denoted the left-hand side or LHS (required).

3. A set of actions, denoted the right-hand side or RHS (required).

4. A documentation string (optional).

5. A type (optional).

Soar production syntax may be summarized as:

```
sp {production-name
    "documentation string"
    CONDITIONS
    -->
    ACTIONS
    }
```

Example. For example, the three required elements are shown in the following:

```
sp {rule2
    (state <s> ^thing e ^thing d)
-->
(<s> ^thing h)
(write (crlf) |h in wm|)}
```

The order of conditions in a production is irrelevant, *except that the first condition must directly test the state.*

LHS Attribute Tests

As the Soar reference manual indicates, there are numerous tests available for attributes and attribute values. This includes **not**, indicated by –, disjunction, indicated by << >>, and conjunction, indicated by { }.

9.2.7 Getting Started with a (Very) Simple Example

Before exploring the more advanced features of Soar, we show a simple use via a simple (and possibly familiar) example.

Soar Source for Example #1

Figure 9.1 shows a simple database of rules and facts comprising Soar Example #1. A log of the resulting Soar behavior is discussed in the next paragraph. The reader is encouraged to run Soar and verify the behavior of this example.

Log of Soar Execution for Example #1

A log of the Soar execution of the source in Figure 9.1 is shown in Figure 9.2. The reader should carefully examine and study each step in the Soar cycle.

```
sp {initial-state
    (state <s> ^superstate nil)
-->
(<s> ^thing a)
(write (crlf) |a in wm|)
(<s> ^thing b)
(write (crlf) |b in wm|)
(<s> ^thing g)
(write (crlf) |g in wm|)}

sp {rule1
    (state <s> ^thing a ^thing b ^thing d)
-->
(<s> ^thing c)
(write (crlf) |c in wm|)}

sp {rule2
    (state <s> ^thing e ^thing d)
-->
(<s> ^thing h)
(write (crlf) |h in wm|)}

sp {rule3
    (state <s> ^thing b ^thing g)
-->
(<s> ^thing d)
(write (crlf) |d in wm|)}

sp {rule4
    (state <s> ^thing a ^thing c)
-->
(<s> ^thing e)
(write (crlf) |e in wm|)}

sp {rule5
    (state <s> ^thing d ^thing j)
-->
(<s> ^thing f)
(write (crlf) |f in wm|)}
```

Figure 9.1 Simple Soar Source for Example #1

```
**** log opened ****

=>WM: (2: S1 ^superstate nil)
=>WM: (1: S1 ^type state)

      0: ==>S: S1
--- Input Phase ---
=>WM: (5: I1 ^output-link I3)
=>WM: (4: I1 ^input-link I2)
=>WM: (3: S1 ^io I1)

--- Proposal Phase ---
--- Firing Productions (IE) ---
Firing initial-state
 -->

a in wm
b in wm
g in wm (S1 ^thing g +)
 (S1 ^thing b +)
 (S1 ^thing a +)
--- Change Working Memory (IE) ---
=>WM: (8: S1 ^thing a)
=>WM: (7: S1 ^thing b)
=>WM: (6: S1 ^thing g)

--- Proposal Phase ---
--- Firing Productions (IE) ---
Firing rule3
 -->

d in wm (S1 ^thing d +)
--- Change Working Memory (IE) ---
=>WM: (9: S1 ^thing d)

--- Proposal Phase ---
--- Firing Productions (IE) ---
Firing rule1
 -->

c in wm (S1 ^thing c +)
--- Change Working Memory (IE) ---
=>WM: (10: S1 ^thing c)

--- Proposal Phase ---
--- Firing Productions (IE) ---
Firing rule4
 -->

e in wm (S1 ^thing e +)
--- Change Working Memory (IE) ---
=>WM: (11: S1 ^thing e)
```

```
--- Proposal Phase ---
--- Firing Productions (IE) ---
Firing rule2
 -->

h in wm (S1 ^thing h +)
--- Change Working Memory (IE) ---
=>WM: (12: S1 ^thing h)

--- Proposal Phase ---

--- Decision Phase ---
=>WM: (18: S2 ^quiescence t)
=>WM: (17: S2 ^choices none)
=>WM: (16: S2 ^impasse no-change)
=>WM: (15: S2 ^attribute state)
=>WM: (14: S2 ^superstate S1)
=>WM: (13: S2 ^type state)

      1:    ==>S: S2 (state no-change)
--- Application Phase ---

--- Output Phase ---
(2: S1 ^superstate nil)
(1: S1 ^type state)
(3: S1 ^io I1)
(8: S1 ^thing a)
(7: S1 ^thing b)
(6: S1 ^thing g)
(9: S1 ^thing d)
(10: S1 ^thing c)
(11: S1 ^thing e)
(12: S1 ^thing h)
(2: S1 ^superstate nil)
(1: S1 ^type state)
(3: S1 ^io I1)
(8: S1 ^thing a)
(7: S1 ^thing b)
(6: S1 ^thing g)
(9: S1 ^thing d)
(10: S1 ^thing c)
(11: S1 ^thing e)
(12: S1 ^thing h)
(5: I1 ^output-link I3)
(4: I1 ^input-link I2)
Current learn settings:
    -on
    -all-levels

**** log closed ****
```

Figure 9.2 Soar Execution for Source of Figure 9.1

An Illustration of the Links Between wm, Production Conditions, and Soar Elaboration

This is shown in Figure 9.3 using the Soar matches command.

```
-- abbreviated log file --                Firing initial-state
soar1> source "/AI/soar-chapter/abg.soar"
******                                    a in wm
Source finished.                          b in wm
soar1> matches rule1                      g in wm=>WM: (8: S1 ^thing a)
>>>> (state <s> ^thing d)                 =>WM: (7: S1 ^thing b)
     (<s> ^thing b)                       =>WM: (6: S1 ^thing g)
     (<s> ^thing a)                       Firing rule3

0 complete matches.                       d in wm=>WM: (9: S1 ^thing d)
                                          Firing rule1
## **** note rule1 cannot be fired ****
                                          c in wm=>WM: (10: S1 ^thing c)
soar1> matches initial-state              Firing rule4
   1 (state <s> ^superstate nil)
                                          e in wm=>WM: (11: S1 ^thing e)
1 complete matches.                       Firing rule2
   1 (state <s> ^superstate nil)
                                          h in wm=>WM: (12: S1 ^thing h)
1 complete matches.
                                          --- END Proposal Phase ---
soar1> run 1 --phase
                                          soar1> matches rule1
--- Input Phase ---                          1 (state <s> ^thing d)
                                             1 (<s> ^thing b)
--- END Input Phase ---                      1 (<s> ^thing a)

soar1> run 1 --phase                      1 complete matches.

--- Proposal Phase ---                    ## **** note rule1 can now be fired ****
```

Figure 9.3 Viewing Production Matches in Soar

"Not" Condition Example

A negated condition element is indicated with a (-) preceding the CE test. A negated condition match will succeed only if there *does not exist* a WME consistent with the indicated test. In other words, it must be absent. For example, to require (in a production LHS) that a state must **not** contain an attribute previous with value thingB, we could write:

```
.
.
   (<s> -^previous thingB)
-->
.
.
```

WME Removal and Examples

Conversely, to remove a WME matching (<s> ^previous thingB), we could write:

```
   .
   .
   .
-->
   (<s> ^previous thingB -)
   .
   .
```

Notice that this action should only be used with WMEs with O-support. If the WME has I-support, the next elaboration will remove it.

It is very important to distinguish between LHS condition syntax and RHS action syntax. This is especially important when symbols are common to both, but have vastly different semantics. For example, the LHS CE (or attribute) test involving not (-) should not be confused with RHS actions involving the same symbol. In the latter case (-) may represent specification of a reject preference, in which case the action is the removal of WME(s) from **wm**.

Limitations of the Simple Example

The source in Figure 9.1 provides a useful introduction to elementary Soar syntax and pragmatics. This simple example, however, does not fully exemplify realistic Soar behavior in that:

♦ No operators are implemented, proposed, or used;

♦ The only augmentations to **wm** are via *state elaboration*; and

♦ No goal or stopping condition is used.

As such, it excludes many available Soar features and the real power of Soar, and does little to convey the full-blown Soar decision cycle.

9.2.8 Arithmetic in Soar

Arithmetic in Soar uses prefix notation, as shown in the fragment of a production RHS in Figure 9.4.

9.3 Digging Deeper into Soar

9.3.1 Long-Term Knowledge in Soar

There are six possible types of long-term knowledge that may be embedded in a Soar program:

1. Knowledge that an operator is appropriate for the current state (Operator proposal);

2. Knowledge that allows operator comparison (Operator comparison);

3. Knowledge to select a single (best) operator; given the knowledge of two (Operator selection);

4. Knowledge about how to apply the operator, i.e., the specific state modifications caused by the operator application (Operator application);

5. Knowledge about elaborations of the state knowledge, without operators, but using productions (State elaboration); and

.
.
.

```
## compute distance
    (<y> ^xloc <xy> ^yloc <yy>)
    (<d> ^bindings <ba>)
    (<ba> ^cell <which> ^contents.name | blockA|)
    (<which> ^xloc <xw> ^yloc <yw>)
-->
    (<s> ^operator <o> +)
    (<o> ^name move-blockA ^b1 <b1> ^t1 <t1>   # save the
                           ^x <x> ^y <y>        # matching
                           ^b2 <b2> ^t2 <t2>)
## remember arithmetic is prefix notation
    (<o> ^sqdist (*
                (- <xy> <xw>)
                (- <xy> <xw>)
                (- <yy> <yw>)
                (- <yy> <yw>)))
## following is for illustration and debugging
    (write (crlf) |*** for operator move-block-A --->|)
    (write (crlf) |for proposed next cell | <y>)
    (write (crlf) |located at | <xy> | | <yy>)
    (write (crlf) |with goal to be at | <xw> | | <yw>)
    (write (crlf) |distance squared is |
                (+ (*
                (- <xy> <xw>)
                (- <xy> <xw>))
                (*
                (- <yy> <yw>)
                (- <yy> <yw>))))
    (write (crlf))
```

.
.
.

Figure 9.4 Soar Arithmetic Example

6. Knowledge about when the goal has been achieved or at least when to stop Soar (Stopping).

Notice the first four types concern operator selection and application, the fifth concerns state elaboration, and the sixth concerns stopping by goal identification.

9.3.2 Simplified Soar Execution Cycle

The Soar computation is based upon a "decision" or "execution" cycle with the following skeletal structure:

1. Apply a selected operator;

2. State elaboration;

3. Propose applicable new operators; and

4. Select a new operator.

Additional steps may involve acquiring external input to `wm` and the creation of substates and resolution of an impasse. These are treated later. Note that the cycle continues until the Soar `halt` action is issued (or the user interrupts the Soar program).

9.3.3 Preference Memory

Unlike its predecessors, Soar has an additional memory used to facilitate conflict resolution. This memory is `preference memory`.

All WMEs have preferences. By default, if the preference for a WME is not specified at the time it is added to `wm`, it is given the acceptable (+) preference. All WMEs with + preference are also available in `wm`. Removal of a `wm` element is achieved by specifying a reject preference or -.

9.3.4 Operator Preference

Control of operator preference is an important part of Soar. In Soar, only a single operator may be selected at each cycle. Approaches such as CLIPS use static conflict resolution schemes to determine subsequent actions when a nonempty conflict set exists.

The procedure used in Soar is more complex, flexible, and dynamic. A preference for an operator is created by a production firing. An operator preference is an absolute or relative measure of the operator's value in the current state. Soar allows the expression of eleven different preference levels. Since operators are linked to states, operator augmentation of states to show preferences allows multiple preferences for the same state. Thus, preference memory, unlike working memory, is not a set and may contain duplicates.

Preferences are described by identifier-attribute-value constructs, for example:

```
(<s1> ^operator rule2 +)
```

indicates operator `rule2` is an acceptable operator in state `<s1>`.

9.3.5 SOAR Operator Preference Syntax and Semantics

Operators may be proposed with the following preference values:

Acceptable: +

Reject (Unacceptable): -

Better, Best: >

Indifference: =

Require: !

as indicated by the Soar BNF syntax:

```
<preference-specifier> ::= <unary-preference> [","]
                         | <unary-or-binary-preference> [","]
                         | <unary-or-binary-preference> <rhs_value> [","]
<unary-pref>           ::= "+" | "-" | "!" | "~" | "@"
<unary-or-binary-pref> ::= ">" | "=" | "<" | "&"
```

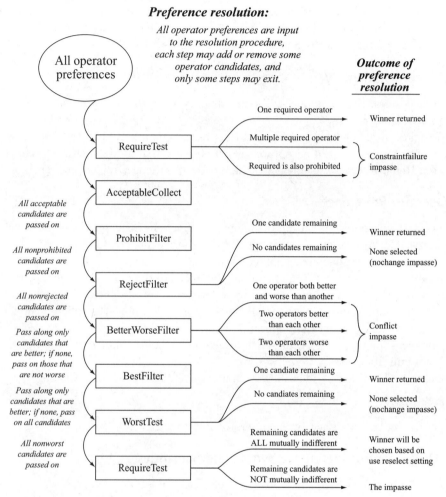

Figure 9.5 Flowchart of Eight-Step Sequential Process Used in Soar Preference-Based Operator Selection (from Appendix D of Soar Manual). Courtesy of John Laird.

More importantly, these preferences are used to rank proposed operators, as shown in Figure 9.5.

For example, the following code shows augmentation of state `<s>` with an operator `<o>` with unacceptable (reject) preference:

```
-->
   (<s> ^operator <o> -)
```

9.3.6 Steps in Soar Operator Preference Resolution

Based on specified operator preferences, Soar employs an eight-step, sequential process to choose among proposed operators and determine the single operator to be applied. This strategy is based upon ranking of proposed operator preferences. Figure 9.5 (from the Soar reference manual, Appendix D) shows this eight-step process used to determine the outcome of the operator selection phase. Note that of the 12 possible outcomes of the process, only four result in automatic selection of an operator. The remaining eight cases generate impasses.

9.3.7 States and State Elaboration

Soar makes significant use of the concept of a *state*. As noted in Section 9.2.2, states are kept in working memory and are subject to elaboration. In Soar, a state is distinguished from the simple notion "the contents of working memory" in the following ways:

1. Only one operator may be applied in a given state;

2. A state may contain many proposed operators;

3. Before selection of an operator, a so-called state elaboration cycle occurs; and

4. Once the elaboration phase is completed, operator selection based upon *preference* occurs.

The State Elaboration Phase.   In this phase, exemplified by the example of Figure 9.1 in Section 9.2.7, the working memory is checked against the productions conditions. Productions whose conditions are satisfied have the wm changes suggested by their actions put in preference memory. The wm contents of productions that matched in a previous cycle but now no longer match are retracted from working memory. Preference memory is checked for inconsistencies and the consistent data is added to working memory. This is the elaboration phase; once wm is unchanging, the Soar interpreter reaches *quiescence*. State elaboration is the significant prerequisite to operator selection.

9.3.8 General Operator Definition

For every operator, at least two productions (rules) must be defined:

1. A rule to propose the operator; and

2. A rule to apply the operator.

9.3.9 I–Support Versus O–Support

The notion of I- and O-support in Soar is an important and fundamental concept. It is important to distinguish between these different types of support.

Once an operator is proposed (by one or more productions, on the basis of wm), its preference persists until wm no longer supports the operator preference. Thus, the preference is said to have instantiation or I-support. Similarly, *WMEs created by state elaboration have I-support*. Operator actions (productions) also change wm, but these actions are persistent over subsequent wm changes. *These changes due to operator actions are said to have operator or O-support.*

9.3.10 Example #2: Operator-Based State Initialization

Figures 9.6 and 9.7 show the modified ontology Soar source from the previous example for *proposal of an operator* to initialize the system state.

The difference between the Soar state initialization examples shown in Sections 9.2.7 and 9.3.10 is very significant with respect to the **wm** support for the WMEs produced:

♦ In the formulation of Section 9.2.7, the initial state was augmented via productions that did not involve operators, i.e., state elaboration. Thus, all WMEs created by this approach have I-support, and therefore will automatically be retracted by Soar when all the conditions necessary to fire the elaboration production no longer hold (the terminology is that the production is no longer "supported").

♦ In the case of the operator-based formulation of Section 9.3.10, *WMEs produced by the operator have O-support* and will thus remain in **wm** until explicitly retracted by an operator. Furthermore, if we were to use a production to retract these WMEs with O-support, state elaboration would put them back in the next cycle.

9.3.11 Soar Operator Life Cycle

The operator "life-cycle" in Soar is comprised of five entities:

1. Proposal: An operator is proposed when the conditions for proposal of the operator hold.

2. Comparison and Selection: When more than one operator is proposed, comparison rules allow operator conflict resolution and subsequent selection of the "best" or preferred operator.

```
# abgr1.soar: agb.soar revised to show operator
# proposal and application
# (and comment syntax)

sp {propose*initialize-state
    (state <s> ^superstate nil)
-->
   (<s> ^operator <o> +)
   (<o> ^name initialize)}

sp {apply*initialize-state
    (state <s> ^operator <o>)
    (<o> ^name initialize)
-->
   (<s> ^thing a)
   (<s> ^thing b)
   (<s> ^thing g)
   (write (crlf) |** state initialized **| (crlf))}
```

Figure 9.6 Soar Source Revised for Operator Proposal and Application

```
**=>WM: (2: S1 ^superstate nil)        (S1 ^thing g +   :O )
=>WM: (1: S1 ^type state)              (S1 ^thing b +   :O )
                                       (S1 ^thing a +   :O )
      0: ==>S: S1                      --- Change Working Memory (PE) ---
--- Input Phase ---                    =>WM: (11: S1 ^thing a)
=>WM: (5: I1 ^output-link I3)          =>WM: (10: S1 ^thing b)
=>WM: (4: I1 ^input-link I2)           =>WM: (9: S1 ^thing g)
=>WM: (3: S1 ^io I1)

                                       --- Application Phase ---
--- Proposal Phase ---
--- Firing Productions (IE) ---        --- Output Phase ---
Firing propose*initialize-state        Current learn settings:
 -->                                       -on
 (O1 ^name initialize +)                   -all-levels
 (S1 ^operator O1 +)
--- Change Working Memory (IE) ---     --- Input Phase ---
=>WM: (7: S1 ^operator O1 +)
=>WM: (6: O1 ^name initialize)         --- Proposal Phase ---


--- Proposal Phase ---                 --- Decision Phase ---
                                       =>WM: (17: S2 ^quiescence t)
--- Decision Phase ---                 =>WM: (16: S2 ^choices none)
=>WM: (8: S1 ^operator O1)             =>WM: (15: S2 ^impasse no-change)
                                       =>WM: (14: S2 ^attribute operator)
      1:    0: O1 (initialize)         =>WM: (13: S2 ^superstate S1)
--- Application Phase ---              =>WM: (12: S2 ^type state)
--- Firing Productions (PE) ---
Firing apply*initialize-state              :    ==>S: S2 (operator no-change)
 -->                                   --- Application Phase ---

** state initialized **                --- Output Phase ---
```

Figure 9.7 Log of Soar Execution of the Source in Figure 9.6

3. Application: The actions of the preferred operator are applied to the state.

4. Termination: When the operator actions are finished, Soar is then ready to repeat the cycle.

As noted, Soar has an additional memory called Preference Memory wherein suggested changes to working memory are stored. In the Soar example of Figure 9.9, this memory is shown on successive cycles.

9.3.12 Example #3: Operator Preference Use

The semantics of operator preference specification were shown in Section 9.3.4. A simple example comparing the (!) and (+) preference is shown in Figures 9.8 and 9.9.

9.3.13 Example #4: Goal State Checking

In Figure 9.10, we add another production to the Soar source of Figure 9.8 employing a right-hand side function interrupt. This production checks to see if the goal state has been reached. A log of the Soar session is shown in Figure 9.11.

```
# abgr2rev.soar
# operator preference example

sp {initialize-state
    (state <s> ^superstate nil)
-->
    (<s> ^thing a)
    (<s> ^thing b)
    (<s> ^thing g)
    (write (crlf) |** state initialized **| (crlf))}

sp {propose*operator1
    (state <s> ^thing a ^thing b)
-->
    (<s> ^operator <o> +)
    (<o> ^name operator1)}

sp {propose*operator2
    (state <s> ^thing a ^thing b)
  -(state <s> ^thing h)  ## no longer proposed afer use
-->
# operator2 is required
    (<s> ^operator <o> !)
    (<o> ^name operator2)}

sp {apply*operator1
    (state <s> ^operator <o>)
    (<o> ^name operator1)
-->
(<s> ^thing c)
(write (crlf) |c in wm|)}

sp {apply*operator2
    (state <s> ^operator <o>)
    (<o> ^name operator2)
-->
    (<s> ^thing h)
    (write (crlf) |h in wm|)}
```

Figure 9.8 Soar Source Revised for Operator Preference

```
watch 5
source "abgr2rev.soar"
*****
Total: 5 productions sourced.
Source finished.

## look at initial state

print <s>
(S1 ^io I1 ^superstate nil ^type state)
step
--- input phase ---
--- propose phase ---
Firing initialize-state
-->
** state initialized **
(S1 ^thing g +)
(S1 ^thing b +)
(S1 ^thing a +)
=>WM: (8: S1 ^thing a)
=>WM: (7: S1 ^thing b)
=>WM: (6: S1 ^thing g)
Firing propose*operator1
-->
(O1 ^name operator1 +)
(S1 ^operator O1 +)
Firing propose*operator2
-->
(O2 ^name operator2 +)
(S1 ^operator O2 !)
=>WM: (12: S1 ^operator O1 +)
=>WM: (11: S1 ^operator O2 +)
=>WM: (10: O2 ^name operator2)
=>WM: (9: O1 ^name operator1)
--- decision phase ---
=>WM: (13: S1 ^operator O2)
      1: O: O2 (operator2)

## show preferences for illustration

preferences S1 operator --names

Preferences for S1 ^operator:

acceptables:
   O1 (operator1) + :I
     From propose*operator1


requires:
   O2 (operator2) ! :I
     From propose*operator2

## next step

step
--- apply phase ---
--- Firing Productions (PE) ---
Firing apply*operator2
-->
h in wm
(S1 ^thing h + :O)
--- Change Working Memory (PE) ---
=>WM: (14: S1 ^thing h)
--- Firing Productions (IE) ---
Retracting propose*operator2
-->
(O2 ^name operator2 +)
```

```
(S1 ^operator O2 !)
--- Change Working Memory (IE) ---
<=WM: (11: S1 ^operator O2 +)
<=WM: (13: S1 ^operator O2)
<=WM: (10: O2 ^name operator2)
--- Firing Productions (IE) ---
--- Change Working Memory (IE) ---
--- output phase ---
--- input phase ---
--- propose phase ---
--- decision phase ---
=>WM: (15: S1 ^operator O1)
      2: O: O1 (operator1)

## look at current state

print <s>
(S1 ^io I1 ^operator O1 ^operator O1 + ^superstate nil ^thing h ^thing a
    ^thing b ^thing g ^type state)

## show preferences

preferences S1 operator --names

Preferences for S1 ^operator:

acceptables:
   O1 (operator1) + :I
     From propose*operator1

## next step

step
--- apply phase ---
--- Firing Productions (PE) ---
Firing apply*operator1
-->
c in wm
(S1 ^thing c + :O)
--- Change Working Memory (PE) ---
=>WM: (16: S1 ^thing c)
--- output phase ---
--- input phase ---
--- propose phase ---
--- decision phase ---
=>WM: (22: S2 ^quiescence t)
=>WM: (21: S2 ^choices none)
=>WM: (20: S2 ^impasse no-change)
=>WM: (19: S2 ^attribute operator)
=>WM: (18: S2 ^superstate S1)
=>WM: (17: S2 ^type state)
      3: ==>S: S2 (operator no-change)

## check preferences -- note same operator proposed
preferences S1 operator --names

Preferences for S1 ^operator:

acceptables:
   O1 (operator1) + :I
     From propose*operator1

## look at newly-created substate and notice impasse

print <s>
(S2 ^attribute operator ^choices none ^impasse no-change ^quiescence t
    ^superstate S1 ^type state)
```

Figure 9.9 Log of Soar Execution of the Source in Figure 9.8. Comments have been added and operator preferences are displayed. Note both **h** and **c** are eventually added to **wm** and a "**no-operator-change**" impasse results.

```
# abgr3rev.soar: to show stopping
# of Soar cycle -- goal is a state containing h
# L.A.E.: compare interrupt with halt

sp {initialize-state
    (state <s> ^superstate nil)
-->
   (<s> ^thing a)
   (<s> ^thing b)
   (<s> ^thing g)}

sp {propose*operator1
   (state <s> ^thing a ^thing b)
-->
   (<s> ^operator <o> +)
   (<o> ^name operator1)}

sp {propose*operator2
   (state <s> ^thing a ^thing b)
-->
# operator2 is required
   (<s> ^operator <o> !)
   (<o> ^name operator2)}

sp {apply*operator1
   (state <s> ^operator <o>)
   (<o> ^name operator1)
-->
(<s> ^thing c)}

sp {apply*operator2
   (state <s> ^operator <o>)
   (<o> ^name operator2)
-->
(<s> ^thing h)}

sp {check*if*done
   (state <s> ^thing h)
-->
(write (crlf) |That's All Folks!| (crlf))
(interrupt)}
```

Figure 9.10 Soar Source Revised for Checking Goal State

```
watch 5
source "abgr3rev.soar"
******
Total: 6 productions sourced.
Source finished.
step
--- input phase ---
--- propose phase ---
Firing initialize-state
-->
(S1 ^thing g +)
(S1 ^thing b +)
(S1 ^thing a +)
=>WM: (8: S1 ^thing a)
=>WM: (7: S1 ^thing b)
=>WM: (6: S1 ^thing g)
Firing propose*operator1
-->
(O1 ^name operator1 +)
(S1 ^operator O1 +)
Firing propose*operator2
-->
(O2 ^name operator2 +)
(S1 ^operator O2 !)
```

```
=>WM: (12: S1 ^operator O1 +)
=>WM: (11: S1 ^operator O2 +)
=>WM: (10: O2 ^name operator2)
=>WM: (9: O1 ^name operator1)
--- decision phase ---
=>WM: (13: S1 ^operator O2)
       1: O: O2 (operator2)
step
--- apply phase ---
--- Firing Productions (PE) ---
Firing apply*operator2
-->
(S1 ^thing h + :O)
--- Change Working Memory (PE) ---
=>WM: (14: S1 ^thing h)
--- Firing Productions (IE) ---
Firing check*if*done
-->
That's All Folks!
--- Change Working Memory (IE) ---
Interrupt received.

Run stopped (interrupted).
```

Figure 9.11 Log of Soar Execution of the Source in Figure 9.10. Note the watch Settings Used.

9.4 Expanded View of the Soar Execution Cycle

The phases of a Soar cycle are **input**, **elaboration (proposal)**, **decision**, **application**, and **output**. Each is summarized here:

input: In this phase, input from the external environment may be obtained and wm (working memory) elements are modified to reflect this information. This may be viewed as changes in "perception."

elaboration: In this phase, wm contents are matched against the condition elements of the productions. All productions that match fire (in parallel) and this process continues until no more rules may fire, a condition called *quiescence*. Note that changes to wm during this phase are just elaborations to the state with I-support. It is during this phase that operators are suggested or proposed. The Rete algorithm figures prominently during this phase.

decision: Quiescence in the elaboration phase marks the start of the decision phase. This is the point wherein proposed operator preferences are evaluated. Recall that Soar allows preferences to be articulated using a rich vocabulary. If possible, the "best" (single) operator is selected at this point. Otherwise, an *impasse* occurs and a substate is generated. Impasse resolution is treated in Section 9.8.

application: In this phase the chosen operator is applied to the system state.

output: Here actions may be conveyed to the external environment.

```
Soar
  while (HALT not true) Cycle;

Cycle
  InputPhase;
  ProposalPhase (also called the Elaboration phase);
  DecisionPhase;
  ApplicationPhase;
  OutputPhase;

ProposalPhase
  while (some I-supported productions are waiting to fire or retract)
    FireNewlyMatchedProductions;
    RetractNewlyUnmatchedProductions;

DecisionPhase
  for (each state in the stack,
       starting with the top-level state)
  until (a new decision is reached)
    EvaluateOperatorPreferences; /* for the state being considered */
    if (one operator preferred after preference evaluation)
      SelectNewOperator;
    else /* could be no operator proposed or */
      CreateNewSubstate; /* impasse */

ApplicationPhase
  while (some operator application productions
         are waiting to fire or retract)
    FireNewlyMatchedProductions;
    RetractNewlyUnmatchedProductions;
```

Figure 9.12 Expanded View of the Soar Cycle

This cycle is shown in Figure 9.12. Note that these stages are viewable when running Soar using the visual debugger.

9.5 Another Soar Example: Revisiting the Image Labeling Problem

Here we revisit the image labeling CSP from Chapter 4. This example is continued in the exercises.

The Soar-based labeling shown produces labelings with O-support, i.e., via operators (not simply state elaboration). We use the adjacency and "highest" constraints; recall from Chapter 4 that there are five solutions to this formulation. The Soar source is shown in Figure 9.13 and the results follow; note the five labelings produced.

```
## file: label1b-oper-rev.soar
## soar version of labeling CSP
## this version incorporates the 'highest' constraint
## operator-based solution(s) augmented to state
## this formulation could be improved (see the problems)

sp {initialize-state
    (state <s> ^superstate nil)
-->
# here are the allowed pairwise labelings
(<s> ^allowed <u> <b1> <b2> <b3> <b4> <b5>)
(<u> ^highest sky)
(<b1> ^reg1 car ^reg2 road)
(<b2> ^reg1 road ^reg2 grass)
(<b3> ^reg1 road ^reg2 trees)
(<b4> ^reg1 sky ^reg2 trees)
(<b5> ^reg1 grass ^reg2 trees)}

## symmetry of adjacency relation
## for compatability w/ prev. solutions
## here implemented by enumeration

sp {rule1
(state <s> ^allowed <b>)
(<b> ^reg1 <X> ^reg2 <Y>)
-->
(<s> ^adjacent <a>)
(<a> ^reg1 <X> ^reg2 <Y>)}

sp {rule2
(state <s> ^allowed <b>)
(<b> ^reg1 <Y> ^reg2 <X>)
-->
(<s> ^adjacent <a>)
(<a> ^reg1 <X> ^reg2 <Y>)}

## the observations

sp {propose*ruleg
(state <s> ^allowed <u>
          ^adjacent <a1> <a2> <a3> <a4> <a5> <a6> <a7>)
(<u> ^highest <R1>)
(<a1> ^reg1 <R1> ^reg2 <R2>)
(<a2> ^reg1 <R2> ^reg2 <R6>)
(<a3> ^reg1 <R2> ^reg2 <R3>)
(<a4> ^reg1 <R3> ^reg2 <R4>)
(<a5> ^reg1 <R2> ^reg2 <R4>)
(<a6> ^reg1 <R4> ^reg2 <R6>)
(<a7> ^reg1 <R4> ^reg2 <R5>)
-->
(<s> ^operator <o> +)
(<o> ^name implement*ruleg)
(<o> ^result <l>)
(<l> ^lab1 <R1> ^lab2 <R2> ^lab3 <R3>
^lab4 <R4> ^lab5 <R5> ^lab6 <R6>)}

sp {implement*ruleg
(state <s> ^operator <o>)
(<o> ^name implement*ruleg)
(<o> ^result <l>)
-->
(<s> ^labeling <l>)}
```

Figure 9.13 Soar Implementation of the Image Labeling Problem (Operator-Based Version)

Operator-Based Labeling Results.   Notice the five solutions are shown in WM elements 54–92 as follows:

```
source "label1b-oper-rev.soar"
*****
Total: 5 productions sourced.
Source finished.
step
--- input phase ---
--- propose phase ---
Firing initialize-state
-->
(B5 ^reg2 trees +)
(B5 ^reg1 grass +)
(B4 ^reg2 trees +)
(B4 ^reg1 sky +)
(B3 ^reg2 trees +)
(B2 ^reg2 grass +)
(B2 ^reg1 road +)
(B1 ^reg2 road +)
(B1 ^reg1 car +)
(U1 ^highest sky +)
(S1 ^allowed B5 +)
(S1 ^allowed B4 +)
(S1 ^allowed B3 +)
(S1 ^allowed B2 +)
(S1 ^allowed B1 +)
(S1 ^allowed U1 +)
=>WM: (22: B5 ^reg2 trees)
=>WM: (21: B5 ^reg1 grass)
=>WM: (20: B4 ^reg2 trees)
=>WM: (19: B4 ^reg1 sky)
=>WM: (18: B3 ^reg2 trees)
=>WM: (17: B3 ^reg1 road)
=>WM: (16: B2 ^reg2 grass)
=>WM: (15: B2 ^reg1 road)
=>WM: (14: B1 ^reg2 road)
=>WM: (13: B1 ^reg1 car)
=>WM: (12: U1 ^highest sky)
=>WM: (11: S1 ^allowed U1)
=>WM: (10: S1 ^allowed B1)
=>WM: (9: S1 ^allowed B2)
=>WM: (8: S1 ^allowed B3)
=>WM: (7: S1 ^allowed B4)
=>WM: (6: S1 ^allowed B5)
Firing rule1
-->
(A1 ^reg2 trees +)
(A1 ^reg1 grass +)
(S1 ^adjacent A1 +)
Firing rule2
-->
(A2 ^reg2 grass +)
(A2 ^reg1 trees +)
(S1 ^adjacent A2 +)
Firing rule1
-->
(A3 ^reg2 trees +)
(A3 ^reg1 sky +)
(S1 ^adjacent A3 +)
Firing rule2

-->
(A4 ^reg2 sky +)
(A4 ^reg1 trees +)
(S1 ^adjacent A4 +)
Firing rule1
-->
(A5 ^reg2 trees +)
(A5 ^reg1 road +)
(S1 ^adjacent A5 +)
Firing rule2
-->
(A6 ^reg2 road +)
(A6 ^reg1 trees +)
(S1 ^adjacent A6 +)
Firing rule1
-->
(A7 ^reg2 grass +)
(A7 ^reg1 road +)
(S1 ^adjacent A7 +)
Firing rule2
-->
(A8 ^reg2 road +)
(A8 ^reg1 grass +)
(S1 ^adjacent A8 +)
Firing rule1
-->
(A9 ^reg2 road +)
(A9 ^reg1 car +)
(S1 ^adjacent A9 +)
Firing rule2
-->
(A10 ^reg2 car +)
(A10 ^reg1 road +)
(S1 ^adjacent A10 +)
=>WM: (52: A10 ^reg2 car)
=>WM: (51: A10 ^reg1 road)
=>WM: (50: S1 ^adjacent A1)
=>WM: (49: S1 ^adjacent A2)
=>WM: (48: S1 ^adjacent A3)
=>WM: (47: S1 ^adjacent A4)
=>WM: (46: S1 ^adjacent A5)
=>WM: (45: S1 ^adjacent A6)
=>WM: (44: S1 ^adjacent A7)
=>WM: (43: S1 ^adjacent A8)
=>WM: (42: S1 ^adjacent A9)
=>WM: (41: S1 ^adjacent A10)
=>WM: (40: A9 ^reg2 road)
=>WM: (39: A9 ^reg1 car)
=>WM: (38: A8 ^reg2 road)
=>WM: (37: A8 ^reg1 grass)
=>WM: (36: A7 ^reg2 grass)
=>WM: (35: A7 ^reg1 road)
=>WM: (34: A6 ^reg2 road)
=>WM: (33: A6 ^reg1 trees)
=>WM: (32: A5 ^reg2 trees)
=>WM: (31: A5 ^reg1 road)
=>WM: (30: A4 ^reg2 sky)
=>WM: (29: A4 ^reg1 trees)
=>WM: (28: A3 ^reg2 trees)

=>WM: (27: A3 ^reg1 sky)
=>WM: (26: A2 ^reg2 grass)
=>WM: (25: A2 ^reg1 trees)
=>WM: (24: A1 ^reg2 trees)
=>WM: (23: A1 ^reg1 grass)
Firing propose*ruleg
-->
(L1 ^lab6 road +)
(L1 ^lab5 trees +)
(L1 ^lab4 grass +)
(L1 ^lab3 road +)
(L1 ^lab2 trees +)
(L1 ^lab1 sky +)
(O1 ^result L1 +)
(O1 ^name implement*ruleg +)
(S1 ^operator O1 +)
Firing propose*ruleg
-->
(L2 ^lab6 road +)
(L2 ^lab5 road +)
(L2 ^lab4 grass +)
(L2 ^lab3 road +)
(L2 ^lab2 trees +)
(L2 ^lab1 sky +)
(O2 ^result L2 +)
(O2 ^name implement*ruleg +)
(S1 ^operator O2 +)
Firing propose*ruleg
-->
(L3 ^lab6 grass +)
(L3 ^lab5 trees +)
(L3 ^lab4 road +)
(L3 ^lab3 grass +)
(L3 ^lab2 trees +)
(L3 ^lab1 sky +)
(O3 ^result L3 +)
(O3 ^name implement*ruleg +)
(S1 ^operator O3 +)
Firing propose*ruleg
-->
(L4 ^lab6 grass +)
(L4 ^lab5 car +)
(L4 ^lab4 road +)
(L4 ^lab3 grass +)
(L4 ^lab2 trees +)
(L4 ^lab1 sky +)
(O4 ^result L4 +)
(O4 ^name implement*ruleg +)
(S1 ^operator O4 +)
Firing propose*ruleg
-->
(L5 ^lab6 grass +)
(L5 ^lab5 grass +)
(L5 ^lab4 road +)
(L5 ^lab3 grass +)
(L5 ^lab2 trees +)
(L5 ^lab1 sky +)
(O5 ^result L5 +)
(O5 ^name implement*ruleg +)

(S1 ^operator O5 +)
=>WM: (97: S1 ^operator O5 +)
=>WM: (96: S1 ^operator O4 +)
=>WM: (95: S1 ^operator O3 +)
=>WM: (94: S1 ^operator O2 +)
=>WM: (93: S1 ^operator O1 +)
=>WM: (92: L5 ^lab6 grass)
=>WM: (91: L5 ^lab5 grass)
=>WM: (90: L5 ^lab4 road)
=>WM: (89: L5 ^lab3 grass)
=>WM: (88: L5 ^lab2 trees)
=>WM: (87: L5 ^lab1 sky)
=>WM: (86: O5 ^result L5)
=>WM: (85: O5 ^name implement*ruleg)
=>WM: (84: L4 ^lab6 grass)
=>WM: (83: L4 ^lab5 car)
=>WM: (82: L4 ^lab4 road)
=>WM: (81: L4 ^lab3 grass)
=>WM: (80: L4 ^lab2 trees)
=>WM: (79: L4 ^lab1 sky)
=>WM: (78: O4 ^result L4)
=>WM: (77: O4 ^name implement*ruleg)
=>WM: (76: L3 ^lab6 grass)
=>WM: (75: L3 ^lab5 trees)
=>WM: (74: L3 ^lab4 road)
=>WM: (73: L3 ^lab3 grass)
=>WM: (72: L3 ^lab2 trees)
=>WM: (71: L3 ^lab1 sky)
=>WM: (70: O3 ^result L3)
=>WM: (69: O3 ^name implement*ruleg)
=>WM: (68: L2 ^lab6 road)
=>WM: (67: L2 ^lab5 road)
=>WM: (66: L2 ^lab4 grass)
=>WM: (65: L2 ^lab3 road)
=>WM: (64: L2 ^lab2 trees)
=>WM: (63: L2 ^lab1 sky)
=>WM: (62: O2 ^result L2)
=>WM: (61: O2 ^name implement*ruleg)
=>WM: (60: L1 ^lab6 road)
=>WM: (59: L1 ^lab5 trees)
=>WM: (58: L1 ^lab4 grass)
=>WM: (57: L1 ^lab3 road)
=>WM: (56: L1 ^lab2 trees)
=>WM: (55: L1 ^lab1 sky)
=>WM: (54: O1 ^result L1)
=>WM: (53: O1 ^name implement*ruleg)
--- decision phase ---
=>WM: (108: S2 ^item O1)
=>WM: (107: S2 ^item O2)
=>WM: (106: S2 ^item O3)
=>WM: (105: S2 ^item O4)
=>WM: (104: S2 ^item O5)
=>WM: (103: S2 ^quiescence t)
=>WM: (102: S2 ^choices multiple)
=>WM: (101: S2 ^impasse tie)
=>WM: (100: S2 ^attribute operator)
=>WM: (99: S2 ^superstate S1)
=>WM: (98: S2 ^type state)
    1: ==>S: S2 (operator tie)
```

9.6   An Example of Using Soar for Diagnosis

Here we consider a simple example of using Soar to convert an "expert" diagnosis paradigm into a Soar-based formulation. The diagnostic scenario concerns diagnosing problems when turning on a room light. We are being somewhat imprecise (bulb wattage, etc), but this example is more for the Soar introduction than a final expert system design.

The formulation uses operators and explicitly creates and removes subgoals in the diagnostic process.

9.6.1 "Lightbulb" Diagnosis Formulation

The diagnosis problem is summarized as follows:

If you turn the switch "on" and the light does not go "on" and other lights in the house are on, then check the lightbulb.

If you want to check the lightbulb and the lamp fixture contains a standard (any wattage) light-bulb, then remove the lightbulb and check it.

If you check the bulb and it is OK, then check to see if the lamp is plugged in.

If you check the bulb and it is bad, then replace the bulb.

9.6.2 Operator-Based Soar Formulation and Results

The Soar source shown below implements an operator-based implementation of this paradigm.

```
## lightbulb-diagnosis-oper.soar
## soar implementation of diagnosis
## operator-based version of 'lightbulb' example

sp {propose*initialize-state
    (state <s> ^superstate nil)
-->
(<s> ^operator <o> +)
(<o> ^name initialize)}

sp {apply*initialize-state
    (state <s> ^operator <o>)
    (<o> ^name initialize)
-->
(<s> ^entity <sw>)
(<sw> ^name switch ^status on)  ## light switch on, but
(<s> ^entity <lb>)
(<lb> ^name lightbulb ^status off) ## bulb is not lit
(<lb> ^condition ok) # bulb is ok
##(<lb> ^condition bad) # bulb is not ok
(<s> ^entity <ol>)
(<ol> ^name other-lights ^status on) ## other lights on
(<s> ^entity <lf>)
(<lf> ^name lamp-fixture ^type-bulb standard) ## std. fixture
(<s> ^entity <lp>)
(<lp> ^name lamp-fixture ^condition plugged-in)
(write (crlf) |you must diagnose the lightbulb problem| (crlf))
(<s> ^entity <t>)
(<t> ^name task ^action diagnose ^entity lightbulb-problem ^status todo)}

sp {propose*generate*check*lightbulb*goal
  (state <s> ^entity <t>)
  (<t> ^name task ^action diagnose ^entity lightbulb-problem ^status todo)
-->
(<s> ^operator <o> !)
(<o> ^name check*lightbulb*goal)}
```

```
sp {apply*generate*check*lightbulb*goal
   (state <s> ^operator <o>)
   (<o> ^name check*lightbulb*goal)
   (<s> ^entity <t0>)
   (<t0> ^name task ^action diagnose ^entity lightbulb-problem ^status todo)
-->
(write (crlf) |Check the lightbulb...| (crlf))
(<t0> ^name task - ^action diagnose - ^entity lightbulb-problem - ^status todo -)
(<s> ^entity <t>)
(<t> ^name task ^action check ^entity lightbulb-fixture ^status todo)}


sp {propose*generate*check*lightbulb*fixture*goal
   (state <s> ^entity <t>)
   (<t> ^name task ^action check ^entity lightbulb-fixture ^status todo)
-->
(<s> ^operator <o> !)
(<o> ^name apply*check*lightbulb*fixture*goal)}


sp {apply*generate*check*lightbulb*fixture*goal
   (state <s> ^operator <o>)
   (<o> ^name apply*check*lightbulb*fixture*goal)
   (<s> ^entity <t0>)
   (<t0> ^name task ^action check ^entity lightbulb-fixture ^status todo)
   (<s> ^entity <lf>)
   (<lf> ^name lamp-fixture ^type-bulb standard)
-->
(write (crlf) |You have a standard fixture...| (crlf))
(write (crlf) |Remove and test the lightbulb...| (crlf))
(<t0> ^name task - ^action check - ^entity lightbulb-fixture - ^status todo -)
(<s> ^entity <t>)
(<t> ^name task ^action remove-and-test ^entity lightbulb ^status todo)}


sp {propose*implement*remove*test*lightbulb
   (state <s> ^entity <t>)
   (<t> ^name task ^action remove-and-test ^entity lightbulb ^status todo)
-->
(<s> ^operator <o> !)
(<o> ^name apply*implement*remove*test*lightbulb)}


sp {apply*implement*remove*test*lightbulb
   (state <s> ^entity <t0> ^entity <lb>)
   (<t0> ^name task ^action remove-and-test ^entity lightbulb ^status todo)
   (<lb> ^name lightbulb ^condition ok)
   (<s> ^operator <o>)
   (<o> ^name apply*implement*remove*test*lightbulb)
-->
(write (crlf) |lightbulb is OK...| (crlf))
(write (crlf) |check if lamp is plugged in...| (crlf))
(<t0> ^name task - ^action remove-and-test - ^entity lightbulb - ^status todo -)
(<s> ^entity <t>)
(<t> ^name task ^action see-if-lamp-plugged-in ^status todo)}


sp {propose*generate*check*plugged*in*goal
```

```
   (state <s> ^entity <t>)
   (<t> ^name task ^action see-if-lamp-plugged-in ^status todo)
-->
(<s> ^operator <o> !)
(<o> ^name apply*generate*check*plugged*in*goal)}

sp {apply*generate*check*plugged*in*goal
   (state <s> ^entity <t0> ^entity <lp>)
   (<lp> ^name lamp-fixture ^condition plugged-in)
   (<t0> ^name task ^action see-if-lamp-plugged-in ^status todo)
   (<s> ^operator <o>)
   (<o> ^name apply*generate*check*plugged*in*goal)
-->
(write (crlf) |lamp is plugged in...| (crlf))
(write (crlf) |no obvious solution...| (crlf))
(<t0> ^name task - ^action see-if-lamp-plugged-in - ^status todo -)
(halt)}

sp {generate*replace*lightbulb*goal
   (state <s> ^entity <t> ^entity <lb>)
   (<t> ^name task ^action remove-and-test ^entity lightbulb ^status todo)
   (<lb> ^name lightbulb ^condition bad)
-->
(write (crlf) |lightbulb is bad...| (crlf))
(write (crlf) |Replace the lightbulb...| (crlf))
(halt)}
```

Sample Soar results are shown as follows.

```
watch 3
source "lightbulb-diagnosis-oper.soar"
**********
Total: 11 productions sourced.
Source finished.
step
--- input phase ---
--- propose phase ---
Firing propose*initialize-state
--- decision phase ---
     1: O: O1 (initialize)
step
--- apply phase ---
--- Firing Productions (PE) ---
Firing apply*initialize-state
you must diagnose the lightbulb problem
--- Change Working Memory (PE) ---
--- Firing Productions (IE) ---
Firing propose*generate*check*lightbulb*goal
--- Change Working Memory (IE) ---
--- output phase ---
--- input phase ---
--- propose phase ---
--- decision phase ---
     2: O: O3 (check*lightbulb*goal)
```

```
step
--- apply phase ---
--- Firing Productions (PE) ---
Firing apply*generate*check*lightbulb*goal
Check the lighbulb...
--- Change Working Memory (PE) ---
--- Firing Productions (IE) ---
Firing propose*generate*check*lightbulb*fixture*goal
Retracting propose*generate*check*lightbulb*goal
--- Change Working Memory (IE) ---
--- output phase ---
--- input phase ---
--- propose phase ---
--- decision phase ---
     3: O: O4 (apply*check*lightbulb*fixture*goal)
step
--- apply phase ---
--- Firing Productions (PE) ---
Firing apply*generate*check*lightbulb*fixture*goal
You have a standard fixture...

Remove and test the lighbulb...
--- Change Working Memory (PE) ---
--- Firing Productions (IE) ---
Firing propose*implement*remove*test*lightbulb
Retracting propose*generate*check*lightbulb*fixture*goal
--- Change Working Memory (IE) ---
--- output phase ---
--- input phase ---
--- propose phase ---
--- decision phase ---
     4: O: O5 (apply*implement*remove*test*lightbulb)
step
--- apply phase ---
--- Firing Productions (PE) ---
Firing apply*implement*remove*test*lightbulb
lightbulb is OK...

check if lamp is plugged in...
--- Change Working Memory (PE) ---
--- Firing Productions (IE) ---
Firing propose*generate*check*plugged*in*goal
Retracting propose*implement*remove*test*lightbulb
--- Change Working Memory (IE) ---
--- output phase ---
--- input phase ---
--- propose phase ---
--- decision phase ---
     5: O: O6 (apply*generate*check*plugged*in*goal)
step
--- apply phase ---
--- Firing Productions (PE) ---
Firing apply*generate*check*plugged*in*goal
lamp is plugged in...
```

```
no obvious solution...
--- Change Working Memory (PE) ---
--- Firing Productions (IE) ---
Retracting propose*generate*check*plugged*in*goal
--- Change Working Memory (IE) ---
This Agent halted.
```

An agent halted during the run.

9.7 Soar Input/Output

Communication (input/output or I/O) may take place on several levels in Soar. Individual Soar agents may communicate with the outside world (including a Soar "user"); agents may communicate with each other; and simple text output is provided for user interaction with an agent.

9.7.1 Simple Text Output

A function to display text strings is provided by Soar, and has been used in several of the previous examples. According to the Soar manual, however:

> *Soar applications that do extensive input and output of text should use Soar Markup Language (SML).*

This is considered an advanced endeavor, and is treated in Section 9.11.

9.7.2 Communication Between Soar Agents and the Outside World

As of Version 8.6, a command-line interface is no longer part of the Soar kernel. Instead, all communications to Soar should be through the SML interface (more on this in Section 9.11). This section is provided to set the stage for more advanced I/O programming in Soar.

Interaction with an External Environment

A Soar agent's external environment may be as simple as the user of a Java-based debugger or as complex as instrumentation and actuators in the real world. In the latter case, inputs might be measured quantities (temperature, speed, etc.) or the physical location of other agents. Outputs might be actuator control signals or agent movement directives. In any case, input and output is conveyed to Soar by the state (or change) of WMEs and implemented by predefined input-link and output-link structures. Soar input functions are invoked at the start of every execution cycle (most of our Soar logs up to this point have shown this phase to be irrelevant). Similarly, Soar output functions are invoked at the end of every cycle in response to changes in the output-link structure in working memory.

```
print <s>
(S1 ^io I1 ^superstate nil ^type state)
print <ts>
(S1 ^io I1 ^superstate nil ^type state)
print I1
(I1 ^input-link I2 ^output-link I3)
print I2
(I2)
print I3
(I3)
```

Figure 9.14 Input-Output Links (Attributes) Upon Soar Agent Initialization

Soar Structures for Input/Output (I/O)

The input-link and output-link structures mentioned in the previous section are implemented as attributes `input-link` and `output-link` attached to the `io` attribute of the top-level state. Soar provides this predefined `io` attribute (or link) to facilitate input and output with an agent. All input and output in working memory is a substructure of this link. Values of the `input-link` and `output-link` attributes are identifiers used to augment the set of input/output WMEs.

Examining the Predefined Soar IO Links. The previously-mentioned links are best seen with the simple log of the Soar operation in Figure 9.14.

Modifying and Manipulating IO Links. We show a simple example that implements the direct **transfer** of input link values to output link values within an agent. Note that the simplistic situation shown is only intended to convey the pragmatics of the process; in an actual application an agent would almost certainly process the input link values to produce the output link values. The Soar source for this effort is shown in Figure 9.15. The corresponding log of the session is shown in Figure 9.16.

9.8 Impasses, Subgoaling, and Learning (Chunking)

9.8.1 Why Soar Is Different

Many production systems (e.g., CLIPS) employ conflict resolution schemes for rule/production selection. A conflict set is formed, and a rule/production is chosen (usually from among many); the process stops when this set is empty.

Soar is different in several aspects:

1. Soar distinguishes between productions used in the elaboration phase and those used to implement *operators*; and

2. Soar is a *problem-solving architecture*. Soar does not just "choose among things it could do," but rather requires a *clear, unambiguous* choice of the "best" operator to proceed.

```
## agent 1 in 2-agent IO example
## prelude to 2-agent communication
## agent1IO-ex2-start.soar
## use operator to set output link
##     from input link with O-support

sp {initial-state
   (state <s> ^superstate nil
              -^agent-status initialized)
-->
   (<s> ^operator <o> +)
   (<o> ^name initializeAgent)}

## note link status is state, not io link, attribute
## temp debug: to give input link a value and status
##  in practice will be set by user or other agent

sp {apply*initializeAgent
   (state <s> ^io.input-link <i2>)
   (<s> ^io.output-link <i3>)
   (<s> ^operator <o>)
   (<o> ^name initializeAgent)
-->
   (<s> ^agent-name agent1
        ^number 86 ^agent-status initialized)
   (write (crlf) |Hello from Agent 1|)
   (<i2> ^data <v>)
   (<v> ^val1 123 ^val2 456)
   (<i3> ^data empty)
   (<s> ^io-link-status changed)}

sp {propose*transfer*io*link
   (state <s> ^agent-status initialized)
   (<s> ^io-link-status changed)
-->
   (<s> ^operator <o> +)
   (<o> ^name transfer-link-value)}

## can transfer input-> output link data if changed
##  code example from Soar planner:
##        (<b1> ^cell <x> ^contents <t1> - <t2>) # out and in
##   cannot delete input/output links; must work at level below

sp {implement*transfer*io*link
   (state <s> ^operator <o>)
   (<o> ^name transfer-link-value)
   (<s> ^io-link-status changed)
   (<s> ^io <i1>)
   (<i1> ^input-link <i2>)
   (<i1> ^output-link <i3>)
   (<i2> ^data <d>)
   (<i3> ^data <prev>)
-->
   (<i3> ^data <prev> - <d>) ## here's the switch
   (<s> ^io-link-status changed - read)} ## change to 'read'

##  TTD: print data on output link ->
##  ultimately read by c++ program
```

Figure 9.15 Soar Agent Productions to Transfer (Single) Agent Input Link Values to the Output Link

```
source "agent1IO-ex2-start.soar"
****
Source finished.
step
Firing initial-state
=>WM: (7: S1 ^operator O1 +)
=>WM: (6: O1 ^name |initializeAgent|)
=>WM: (8: S1 ^operator O1)
     1: O: O1 (|initializeAgent|)
Firing |apply*initializeAgent|
Hello from Agent 1
=>WM: (16: S1 ^io-link-status changed)
=>WM: (15: I3 ^data empty)
=>WM: (14: V1 ^val2 456)
=>WM: (13: V1 ^val1 123)
=>WM: (12: I2 ^data V1)
=>WM: (11: S1 ^agent-status initialized)
=>WM: (10: S1 ^number 86)
=>WM: (9: S1 ^agent-name agent1)
Firing propose*transfer*io*link
Retracting initial-state
=>WM: (18: S1 ^operator O2 +)
=>WM: (17: O2 ^name transfer-link-value)
<=WM: (7: S1 ^operator O1 +)
<=WM: (8: S1 ^operator O1)
<=WM: (6: O1 ^name |initializeAgent|)
print <s>
(S1 ^agent-name agent1 ^agent-status initialized ^io I1
     ^io-link-status changed ^number 86 ^operator O2 + ^superstate nil
     ^type state)
print I1
(I1 ^input-link I2 ^output-link I3)
print I2
(I2 ^data V1)
print V1
(V1 ^val1 123 ^val2 456)
print I3
(I3 ^data empty)
step
=>WM: (19: S1 ^operator O2)
     2: O: O2 (transfer-link-value)
Firing implement*transfer*io*link
=>WM: (21: S1 ^io-link-status read)
=>WM: (20: I3 ^data V1)
<=WM: (16: S1 ^io-link-status changed)
<=WM: (15: I3 ^data empty)
Retracting propose*transfer*io*link
<=WM: (18: S1 ^operator O2 +)
<=WM: (19: S1 ^operator O2)
<=WM: (17: O2 ^name transfer-link-value)
print <s>
(S1 ^agent-name agent1 ^agent-status initialized ^io I1 ^io-link-status read
     ^number 86 ^superstate nil ^type state)
print I1
(I1 ^input-link I2 ^output-link I3)
print I2
(I2 ^data V1)
print I3
(I3 ^data V1)
print V1
(V1 ^val1 123 ^val2 456)
```

Figure 9.16 Log of the Soar Link Value Transferal Process Shown in Figure 9.15

It is for these reasons that Soar operator impasses frequently occur. While they are (perhaps) an impediment for novice Soar developers, impasses are integral to both the Soar problem-solving philosophy and the built-in Soar learning mechanism (chunking).

9.8.2 An Impasse

In a situation where the available preferences unambiguously indicate a single operator, Soar operation is relatively straightforward—the operator is applied and the process continues. However, when it is not possible to use preference memory to select a new operator, an (*operator*) *impasse* occurs in Soar. Viewed another way, an impasse results when Soar detects a lack of knowledge necessary to continue the problem solution.

To resolve an impasse, Soar generates a new state, with augmentations indicating the type of impasse and other relevant information. The superstate of this new state is the state wherein the impasse occurred, i.e., the new state is a substate of the state containing the impasse. Impasses may also occur in this substate, in which case another substate is generated. Once impasses are resolved in each substate, control returns to the superstate of each, ultimately returning to the state that originally generated the impasse.

Impasses may be caused by:

◆ A tie in operator preference;

◆ A conflict, wherein two or more operators are preferred over each other, but a third ("best") operator does not exist;

◆ A constraint-failure, wherein conflicting necessity preferences exit; or

◆ A "no-change" situation, wherein the elaboration phase achieves *quiescence* and no new operator is proposed (no preferences are in working memory) or the state does not change.

An impasse arises and is reported by Soar when there is insufficient knowledge to decide upon the next action of the agent. Note, again, this is in contrast to most production systems wherein conflict resolution strategies guarantee some production will be chosen. The Soar philosophy is more "do the right thing to solve *this* problem" than "find something that could be done." Appendix D of the Soar User's Manual (Version 8.6) shows the eight-step sequence used to determine the outcome of the preference resolution process.

9.8.3 Soar's Impasse Resolution Activity

To facilitate handling of an impasse situation, Soar automatically generates a new (sub)state and augments this state with a number of attribute-value pairs describing the impasse (see the Soar manual). This allows the user to define productions that test for impasses. Viewed another way, when Soar reaches an impasse, it *subgoals*, that is, it modifies the problem state in an attempt to resolve the impasse. Specifically, Soar creates a new state that indicates the type of impasse and a link to the original state. The goal for Soar, given this new state, is to resolve the impasse.

9.8.4 Impasse (Tie) Example

Soar Actions in Encountering an Impasse

The excerpt from Soar shown in Figure 9.17 shows the creation of an impasse. The impasse is an operator tie, and resulted in the creation of state S2 (S1 existed at the time). Operators O5 and

```
=>WM: (154: S1 ^operator O6 +)
=>WM: (153: S1 ^operator O5 +)
=>WM: (152: O6 ^t2 T2)
    .
    .
    .
=>WM: (162: S2 ^item O5)
=>WM: (161: S2 ^item O6)
=>WM: (160: S2 ^quiescence t)
=>WM: (159: S2 ^choices multiple)
=>WM: (158: S2 ^impasse tie)
=>WM: (157: S2 ^attribute operator)
=>WM: (156: S2 ^superstate S1)
=>WM: (155: S2 ^type state)

    5:    ==>S: S2 (operator tie)
```

Figure 9.17 Example of Soar State Information Related to Impasse Detection

O6 have equal preference. Notice the information available in the newly-created state regarding the impasse.

Productions to Recognize an Operator Impasse

To facilitate resolving the preceding impasse example, an impasse-recognition production is shown in Figure 9.18. Notice how the available impasse-state information was used to recognize the situation. The output in Figure 9.19 was produced by this user production that recognized the impasse indicated in Figure 9.17:

```
## production to recognize impasse
## where impasse is a tie

sp {checkerboard*recognize*tie*impasse
   (state <s2> ^impasse tie ^choices multiple
               ^attribute operator ^quiescence t
               ^superstate <s>)
   (<s> ^superstate nil ^name checkerboard-problem)
-->
   (write (crlf) |Operator tie --|)
   (write (crlf) |impasse reached|)
   (write (crlf) |impasse resolution necessary| (crlf))}
```

Figure 9.18 Example of Soar Production to Detect Impasse of Figure 9.17

```
Operator tie --
impasse reached
impasse resolution necessary
```

Figure 9.19 Example of Output Produced by Soar Impasse Detection Production

```
## from the soar library (typical structure)

sp {default*select*indifferent-and-worst*tied
   "Indifferent an object if it leads to a tie that can not be solved."
   :default
   (state <s2> ^impasse tie ^choices multiple
                ^attribute operator ^quiescence t
                ^item <op>
                ^superstate <s>)
   (<s> ^superstate nil ^name checkerboard-problem
        ^operator <op> +)
   -->
   (<s> ^operator <op> =, < )}
```

Figure 9.20 Example of Soar Default Impasse Resolution Production (tie)

9.8.5 Handling Impasses: Available Impasse Resolution Productions in the Default Library

The Soar user must develop productions to recognize and resolve operator impasses. The Soar library, however, contains many useful and somewhat "generic" productions to facilitate impasse resolution. One example is shown in Figure 9.20.

9.8.6 Chunks and Learning

A *chunk* is a Soar production that is created that is applicable in the situation that caused the impasse. The actions of the chunk production produce changes to preference memory that resolve the impasse. The Soar architecture directs the creation of a chunk whenever an impasse is resolved. This (learning) mechanism may be viewed as creating new (long-term) knowledge in the form of productions and as an experience-based learning technique.

9.9 Debugging Soar Representations

Since Soar is a production or rule-based language, not an imperative language, Soar IS implementations may not be easily debugged with tools commonly used with other language paradigms. For example, in C it is common to insert `printf` statements at various points in the C source code. While it is possible to insert `write` function statements at various points in the Soar source code, this may be of limited utility.

9.9.1 The Soar Visual Debugger

The Soar IDE contains many useful features for understanding and debugging Soar programs. While it is possible to use Soar from the command line (and numerous examples in this chapter employ this display), a visual interface is provided. Figure 9.21 shows an example of the Java-based visual debugger, using the example of Section 9.3.12.

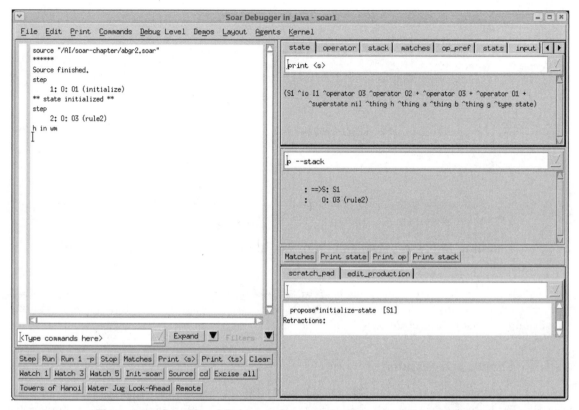

Figure 9.21 Soar Visual Debugger Showing the Example of Section 9.3.12

Numerous windows are presented in the (default) Soar debugger configuration. For example, when a production is not firing as (the user) expected, the "productions" window of the Soar IDE may help explain why. The Soar debugger allows customization of these windows.

9.9.2 Additional Debugging Techniques

The following may be useful Soar debugging approaches in certain circumstances:

1. Single-step Soar.

2. Log the session to a log file.

3. Examine the system state through a careful trace of wm elements. If the situation represented by the contents of wm is complex, "ASCII art" or Tk-based visualizations (enabled by user-written productions) may help.

4. Turn on watch productions and/or watch preferences. This may be done via a pulldown menu or by the command line:

```
watch 1 productions -on preferences -on
```

In this case, O- and I-support are displayed.

5. Be sure to distinguish between I- and O-support for WMEs.

6. Write a smaller, simpler Soar program to check understanding of vs. actual Soar behavior. Carefully tracing (single-stepping with lots of watching of quantities) may indicate potential discrepancies. Sometimes the voluminous amount of display data can be daunting when debugging a large and complex Soar program.

9.10 Soar, Ontologies, and Other Development Aids

9.10.1 Background

The concept and utility of an ontology was developed in Chapter 2, and use of the Protégé ontology editor was shown. Furthermore, in Chapter 8 (Section 8.4) it was shown how a Protégé-developed ontology may be directly imported into CLIPS. This section addresses a similar question, namely:

Is it possible to develop an ontology (perhaps using an ontology editor) and import this information into Soar?

9.10.2 Herbal

The quick answer to the question posed in Section 9.10.1 is a guarded "yes." Recall that Soar is more than a simple CLIPS-like production system. Therefore, integrating ontologically-derived information into Soar is somewhat more involved.

To this end, the Herbal project at http://acs.ist.psu.edu/projects/Herbal/ provides the Herbal IDE. This IDE is based upon the Protégé Ontology Editor, and provides a number of Protégé extensions, especially the Herbal compiler. More importantly, the Herbal IDE distribution includes Protégé project and resource description framework (RDF) files that enable production of Soar source code from Protégé-based descriptions.

There is an available Herbal Viewer; this functions as (yet another) Soar debugger. Herbal and Protégé both require Java 1.4 or higher.

9.11 Soar "Under the Hood": So You Really Want to Develop Embedded, Autonomous Agents?

9.11.1 A Note About Different Soar Platforms/Implementations

Soar is available for linux, Windows, and OS-X. The discussion here is centered on the Soar source included with the linux distribution. The discussion of C++ functions is common to all three distributions.

9.11.2   The Soar Computational Architecture

Soar 8.6.1 (and later versions) uses the Soar Markup Language (SML) for communication with the kernel on (default) port 12121. In addition, it is possible to make a connection to a kernel running on a remote machine with a known IP address and appropriate permissions. The SML is based upon communication of XML packets. Unlike earlier versions, there is no built-in command line interface to the kernel. The included Java-based Soar debugger may be used to start a (or connect to a running) kernel, start (or connect to running) multiple agents, and issue commands. In addition, utility applications such as `TestCommandLineInterface` and `TestClientSML` are included.[3]

9.11.3   The Soar Kernel

The Soar kernel is the "engine" of Soar. By creating one or more Soar agents, we are able to implement the Soar architecture. In practice, the kernel is implemented as a thread of the current process.

Note that a single kernel may (and does, as many of our examples show) support multiple agents. They are maintained in a linked list in a kernel data structure. Agents are local to their "enabling" kernels; a kernel cannot create or run agents outside the local process.

9.11.4   Agents and the Soar Kernel

What Is a (Soar) Agent?

Chapter 8, Section 8.9 considers agent technology in more detail. For now, we propose two definitions; the latter is the most relevant to Soar implementation.

Agent: Definition #1.   An agent is an active, persistent software component that perceives, reasons, acts, and communicates.

Agent: Definition #2.   A Soar agent is an independent (i.e., it has no knowledge of other agents) software structure maintained by a Soar kernel.

Why Implement Agents and Not Just a Monolithic Set of Productions?

Consider the following (somewhat whimsical, yet illustrative) application example:

> *Develop a Soar simulation of two blocks,* `block1` *and* `block2`*. Both blocks are situated on an $n \times n$ checkerboard at initially different locations. Each block may sense its location as well as the location of the other block. In addition, each block may move into an adjacent cell. The objective (motivation) of* `block2` *is to move toward and overtake* `block1` *(get to the same location).* `block1` *has a very different objective (motivation)—that is, to not be overtaken or caught.*

Figure 9.22 illustrates the problem.

---

[3]Windows versions have an extension `exe`.

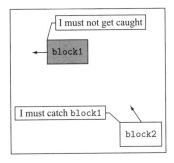

Figure 9.22 An Obvious Agent-Based Scenario

It is possible to implement this scenario in Soar (or any other production system) using a single agent. However, an agent-based implementation is a better-suited IS design for the following reasons:

1. It is desirable to isolate, encapsulate, and implement the reasoning and goal ("motivation") of each block as a separate agent (see Agent: Definition #1);

2. It is desirable to restrict the input of each block to the quantities indicated. A monolithic (single agent) implementation would allow productions to "see" all of the current state.

3. The representation is extendable, e.g., consider adding a second "chasing" block (block3).

The Soar Kernel and Agents

The situation is shown in Figure 9.23. Soar agent creation is implemented by the Soar kernel in the following steps:

1. The requested agent name is checked to be sure it is unique within the kernel;

2. Memory is allocated for the agent structure;

3. Agent parameters and settings are initialized; and

4. A top state and IO links are created for the agent.

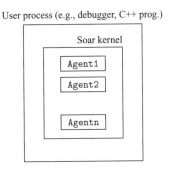

Figure 9.23 The Process, Soar Kernel, and Agents

Example: Multiple Java Debuggers, Agents, and Kernels

Our first example shows the relationships among multiple Java debuggers, kernels, and running agents. This example is straightforward and only requires the use of the Soar Java debugger. The reader is encouraged to replicate and extend this example.

The example initially requires starting three copies of the Java debugger. It is important to note that three debugger processes have been created on the host machine. Also, by default, each debugger instance creates a separate, freestanding kernel thread; thus three instances of the Soar kernel exist. Furthermore, each agent (`soar1`) is local to the respective kernel, i.e., even though the (default) agent name[4] is the same (`soar1`), *they are not the same agent.* They are three independent agents in three independent kernel threads in three independent processes.

If we now use the debugger menu commands

`Kernel|Delete local Soar kernel instance`

for two of the debuggers, we are left with two debuggers without Soar kernels (or agents). Again using the Java debugger menu, we issue the command

`Kernel|Connect to remote Soar`

in debuggers two and three.

Note that now we have one agent (`soar1`) being examined by three debuggers (one running the kernel; two via a remote connection to this kernel). A more interesting situation arises if we now issue the command

`Agents|Create Agent- Same Window`

in debuggers two and three. The result is the existence of three agents, all running in the kernel thread of the first debugger. Each debugger provides a "window inside" the respective agent. Note that although the three agents are all running in the same kernel, they do not interact with each other. To show the independence of the three agents, we could load a separate Soar source file into each agent. These files are shown in Figure 9.24. Of course, we could load any three distinct Soar files for this example (e.g., a blocks-world planner, a checkerboard planner, and the lightbulb diagnosis example). Figure 9.25 shows the results. Notice the agent-specific results in each window.

```
## agent 1 initialization          ## agent 2 initialization          ## agent 3 initialization
## agent1.soar                      ## agent2.soar                      ## agent3.soar

sp {initial-state                   sp {initial-state                  sp {initial-state
    (state <s> ^superstate nil)         (state <s> ^superstate nil)        (state <s> ^superstate nil)
-->                                 -->                                -->
(<s> ^agent-name agent1             (<s> ^agent-name agent2            (<s> ^agent-name agent3
    ^number 007 ^status running)        ^number |Number 2| ^status running)   ^number 86 ^status running)
(write (crlf) |Hello from Agent 1|)}  (write (crlf) |Hello from Agent 2|)}  (write (crlf) |Hello from Agent 3|)}
```

Figure 9.24 Soar Files Loaded into Respective Agents (via the respective debuggers)

---

[4]Displayed in the debugger window title.

Figure 9.25 After Loading Three Separate Soar Source Files into Each Agent and Running One Cycle. Three debuggers are shown (with resized windows, for illustration).

This example illustrates the relationships among debuggers, kernels, and agents in Soar. We now turn our attention to a more versatile agent interface using C++.

9.11.5 C++ Interfaces to Soar Using SML

Why the Debugger?

Section 9.11.4 showed the use of (multiple copies of) the Java debugger in starting a Soar kernel and managing agents. *In what follows, the Soar kernel and agents are implemented as threads in a C++ process. The Java-based debugger is used* **only** *to provide an external view of the operation of the C++ code that implements the agents.*

Key Documentation and Distribution Files for C++ Development

Interfacing to Soar using SML and C++ is not a trivial undertaking. Useful resources include[5]:

1. "The Soar Users Manual," especially Section 3.5;

2. "The SML Quick Start Guide";

3. The Slide Presentation: `Soar25-SML-ANewInterfaceintoSoar` (contains perspective, history, and C++ functions overview);

4. File `sml_ClientKernel.h`: Header file for `ClientSML.cpp` application; contains documented Kernel class (discussed in the following subsection);

5. File `sml_ClientAgent.h`: Another header file for `ClientSML.cpp` application; contains documented agent class (discussed in the following subsection); and

6. C++ source for applications: `TestClientSML` and `ClientSML`.

Key C++ Kernel and Agent Classes and Methods (Functions)

The kernel and agent C++ classes are the foundation for implementing Soar agents in C++. Especially important are the functions that start the (or connect to a remote) kernel, create agents, and provide access to the aforementioned IO links. We illustrate and highlight some (but not all) of the useful methods in the following subsection.

Programming Note. Many of the class-specific methods (functions) provided return pointers to various objects. Especially important is the creation of instances of the agent class using methods provided in the kernel class. In this case, a pointer to the agent (object) created is returned. Function calls to class methods (functions) thus take the sample forms:

```
pAgent1 = pKernel->CreateAgent("agent1");
pAgent1->LoadProductions("agent1IOinit.soar");
```

---

[5]In the SoarSuite/Documentation subdirectory.

where pKernel is a pointer to a running kernel instance and the class method CreateAgent is used to create an agent in this kernel and return a pointer to the agent. In the second line, LoadProductions is a method from the agent class.

The Kernel and (Starting) Agents: Using C++

The following examples are some key classes and related methods for a C++ interface to the Soar kernel using SML. The reader is encouraged to study the documentation provided in the respective header files for each.

```
// file: sml_ClientKernel.h

class Kernel : public ClientErrors

static Kernel* CreateRemoteConnection(bool sharedFileSystem,
                                      char const* pIPaddress,
                                      int port = kDefaultSMLPort,
                                      bool ignoreOutput = false) ;


static Kernel* CreateKernelInCurrentThread(char const* pLibraryName,
                                           bool optimized = false,
                                           int portToListenOn = kDefaultSMLPort) ;

static Kernel* CreateKernelInNewThread(char const* pLibraryName, int     portToListenOn = kDefaultSMLPort) ;

Agent* CreateAgent(char const* pAgentName) ;

char const* ExecuteCommandLine(char const* pCommandLine, char const* pAgentName, bool echoResults = false) ;

//file: sml_ClientAgent.h

bool LoadProductions(char const* pFilename, bool echoResults = true) ;

Identifier* GetInputLink() ;
Identifier* GetOutputLink() ;

Identifier* FindIdentifier(char const* pID, bool searchInput,
                           bool searchOutput, int index = 0) ;

StringElement* CreateStringWME(Identifier* parent, char const* pAttribute,
                               char const* pValue);

IntElement* CreateIntWME(Identifier* parent, char const* pAttribute,
                         int value) ;

Identifier* CreateIdWME(Identifier* parent, char const* pAttribute) ;

 void Update(StringElement* pWME, char const* pValue) ;
 void Update(IntElement* pWME, int value) ;
 void Update(FloatElement* pWME, double value) ;

char const* RunSelf(unsigned long numberSteps,
                    smlRunStepSize stepSize = sml_DECISION) ;
```

Example 1: Three Agents and a Kernel Implemented Using C++

In this example, we use C++ to accomplish results similar to that of Section 9.11.4. We start a kernel, create three agents, and load and run agent-specific Soar source files. The C++ code to accomplish this is shown as follows. The agent-specific files are those used in Section 9.11.4. Note the use of polled input to "halt" the program execution and allow connection of a Java debugger to each agent. Results (with a partial log of the C++ program execution) are shown in Figure 9.25.

C++ Source Code for a Three-Agent Example.   The C++ source code is shown here.

```
// this is  a c++ example of Soar 8.6.4 interface
// file: 3agentsSML.cpp
// objective: create 3 agents in 1 kernel thread and
// interface via 3 debugger copies (remote connections)
// sequences the events with pauses for debugger analysis

#include <iostream.h>
#include "stdio.h"
#include <string.h>
#include "sml_Client.h"

using namespace sml;

// pausing function
int pause(void)
{
int response;
cout << "\n** Enter 1 to continue =>\n";
cin >> response;
while (response != 1) cin >> response;
return (1);
}

int main(void)
{

sml::Agent *pAgent1, *pAgent2, *pAgent3;

// start of c++ interface to Soar 8.6.4
cout << "\n\n *** Welcome to a Soar 8.6.4 c++ interface example ***\n\n";

cout << "\n1. I'm now creating an instance of the Soar kernel;\n";
cout << "\nYou may use the debugger(s) to connect to it.\n";

// Create an instance of the Soar kernel in our process
Kernel* pKernel = Kernel::CreateKernelInNewThread("SoarKernelSML") ;

// Check that nothing went wrong.
if (pKernel->HadError())
{
cout << pKernel->GetLastErrorDescription() << endl ;
return 0;
}
```

```
// press 1 to continue
pause();

cout << "\n2. I'm now creating 3 agents in this Soar kernel;\n";
cout << "\nYou may use debugger(s) to connect to them.\n";

// Create 3 Soar agents named 'agent1', 'agent2', 'agent3'
pAgent1 = pKernel->CreateAgent("agent1") ;
// Check that nothing went wrong in agent creation
if (pKernel->HadError())
{
cout << pKernel->GetLastErrorDescription() << endl ;
return 0;
}

pAgent2 = pKernel->CreateAgent("agent2") ;
if (pKernel->HadError())
{
cout << pKernel->GetLastErrorDescription() << endl ;
return 0;
}

pAgent3 = pKernel->CreateAgent("agent3") ;
if (pKernel->HadError())
{
cout << pKernel->GetLastErrorDescription() << endl ;
return 0;
}

// press 1 to continue
pause();

cout << "\n3. I'm now loading a specific production \n \
for each of the agents in this Soar kernel;\n";

// Load a specific production for each of the agents
pAgent1->LoadProductions("agent1.soar") ;

if (pAgent1->HadError())
{
cout << pAgent1->GetLastErrorDescription() << endl ;
return 0;
}

pAgent2->LoadProductions("agent2.soar") ;

if (pAgent2->HadError())
{
cout << pAgent1->GetLastErrorDescription() << endl ;
return 0;
}
pAgent3->LoadProductions("agent3.soar") ;

if (pAgent3->HadError())
```

```
{
cout << pAgent1->GetLastErrorDescription() << endl ;
return 0;
}

// press 1 to continue
pause();

cout << "\n4. I'm now running each agent for 1 decision (in sequence)\n";

// Run Soar for 1 decision for each agent
pAgent1->RunSelf(1) ;
pAgent2->RunSelf(1) ;
pAgent3->RunSelf(1) ;

// press 1 to continue
pause();

cout << "\n5. I'm now shutting down and cleaning up\n";

// Shutdown and clean up
pKernel->Shutdown() ; // delete all agents (unless using a remote connection)
delete pKernel ; // deletes the kernel thread

return 1;}
```

Results of executing this code were shown in Figure 9.25 (debugger display) and the corresponding log file of Figure 9.26.

Example 2: Putting It All Together—Two-Agent Communication in Soar

Objective. The objective of this example is to show multiple agent communication using C++ in Soar. This example facilitates a general, multiagent computation scheme involving interagent communication. *Note, however, that communication between agents is restricted to sharing input and output link values and enforced (or enabled) by the C++ agent interface.* Specifically, a C++ implementation is developed that allows two agents to trade location values (assumed to be integer coordinates). Each agent begins with an empty ^io.input-link value. The current agent location is stored as the values of the ^io.output link. The C++ implementation shown facilitates the following series of events:

1. Agent1 io.output-link values are read by the C++ program.

2. The C++ program writes these as the io.input-link values for Agent2. Thus, Agent1 has sent a message (concerning location data) to Agent2.

3. In an analogous manner, Agent2's position (on Agent2's ^io.output-link) is passed, via the C++ interface, to Agent1 (and received as Agent1's ^io.input-link values).

The situation is shown in Figure 9.27.

```
$ ./3AgentsSML


 *** Welcome to a Soar 8.6.4 c++ interface example ***


1. I'm now creating an instance of the Soar kernel;

You may use the debugger(s) to connect to it.

Random Seed = 1
Listening on port 12121

** Enter 1 to continue =>
Received a connection
Got new connection
1

2. I'm now creating 3 agents in this Soar kernel;

You may use debugger(s) to connect to them.

** Enter 1 to continue =>
1

3. I'm now loading a specific production
 for each of the agents in this Soar kernel;

** Enter 1 to continue =>
1

4. I'm now running each agent for 1 decision (in sequence)

** Enter 1 to continue =>
```

Figure 9.26 Log of C++ Execution of Soar Kernel with Three Independent Agents

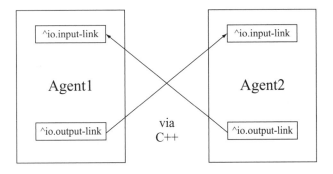

Figure 9.27 Agent Communication Example Objective Using C++ Interface to SML

```
## agent 1 in 2-agent IO example          ## agent 2 in 2-agent IO example
## agent1IO-ex2.soar                       ## agent2IO-ex2.soar
## use operator to set output link         ## use operator to set output links
##    with O-support                       ##    with O-support

sp {initial-state                          sp {initial-state
   (state <s> ^superstate nil                 (state <s> ^superstate nil
            -^agent-status initialized)                -^agent-status initialized)
-->                                        -->
   (<s> ^operator <o> +)                      (<s> ^operator <o> +)
   (<o> ^name initializeAgent)}               (<o> ^name initializeAgent)}

sp {apply*initializeAgent                  sp {apply*initializeAgent
   (state <s> ^io.output-link <i3>)           (state <s> ^io.output-link <i3>)
   (<s> ^operator <o>)                        (<s> ^operator <o>)
   (<o> ^name initializeAgent)                (<o> ^name initializeAgent)
-->                                        -->
   (<s> ^agent-name agent1                    (<s> ^agent-name agent2
       ^number 1 ^agent-status initialized)       ^number 2 ^agent-status initialized)
   (<i3> ^loc1 101 ^loc2 102)                 (<i3> ^loc1 203 ^loc2 204)
   (<s> ^io-link-status changed)}             (<s> ^io-link-status changed)}
```

Figure 9.28   Soar Source Files Used for Two-Agent Communication Example

Initial Status of Soar Agents (Agent1, Agent2).   The output link initializations used are shown in the Soar agent source files in Figure 9.28.

C++ Source for Two-agent Communication.

```
// file: 2agents-IOlinks.cpp
// sample use of c++, SML and state IO links
// agents pass location information to each other

#include <iostream.h>
#include "stdio.h"
#include <string.h>
#include "sml_Client.h"

using namespace sml;

// pausing function
int pause(void)
{
int response;
cout << "\n** Enter 1 to continue =>\n";
cin >> response;
while (response != 1) cin >> response;
return (1);
}
```

```
int main(void)
{
Kernel* pKernel;
WMElement* oLinkChild;
Identifier* pID1;
Identifier* pID2;
Identifier* pInputLink1;
Identifier* pInputLink2;
Identifier* pOutputLink1;
Identifier* pOutputLink2;
sml::Agent* pAgent1;
sml::Agent* pAgent2;
//IntElement* pWMEx;
//IntElement* pWMEy;
int numchild,i;
// we assume locations are integer pairs
// temp: use strings for reading
// loc[0][] is agent1 data; loc[1][] is agent2 data
const char* loc[2][2];

cout << "\n\n *** 2 Agent Soar 8.6.4 c++ Communication Example ***\n\n";

cout << "\nCreating an instance of the Soar kernel;\n";

// Create an instance of the Soar kernel in our process
pKernel = Kernel::CreateKernelInNewThread("SoarKernelSML") ;

if (pKernel->HadError())
{
cout << pKernel->GetLastErrorDescription() << endl ;
return 0;
}
cout << "\nCreating 2 agents (agent1, agent2) in this Soar kernel;\n";
cout << "\nYou may now use debugger(s) to watch them.\n";

// create Soar agents named 'agent1' and 'agent2'
pAgent1 = pKernel->CreateAgent("agent1") ;
// check that nothing went wrong in agent creation
if (pKernel->HadError())
{
cout << pKernel->GetLastErrorDescription() << endl ;
return 0;
}

pAgent2 = pKernel->CreateAgent("agent2") ;
if (pKernel->HadError())
{
cout << pKernel->GetLastErrorDescription() << endl ;
return 0;
}

pause();

cout << "\nLoading specific (initialization) productions for \n \
```

```
each of the  2 agents in this Soar kernel;\n";

// Load a specific production for each of the agents
pAgent1->LoadProductions("agent1IO-ex2.soar") ;

if (pAgent1->HadError())
{
cout << pAgent1->GetLastErrorDescription() << endl ;
return 0;
}

pAgent2->LoadProductions("agent2IO-ex2.soar") ;

if (pAgent2->HadError())
{
cout << pAgent1->GetLastErrorDescription() << endl ;
return 0;
}

pause();

cout << "\nRunning each agent for 1 decision (in sequence)\n";

// Run Soar for 1 decision for each agent (initialization)
pAgent1->RunSelf(1) ;
pAgent2->RunSelf(1) ;

cout << "\nUse a debugger to examine the IO link values for agent1 and agent2\n";

pause();

// First objective: read agent1's output link and
// set this pair as the input link values for agent2

cout <<"\nFirst, we read agent1's output link and set this pair as the input link values for agent2";

pOutputLink1 = pAgent1->GetOutputLink();
if (pOutputLink1) {
        numchild = pOutputLink1->GetNumberChildren();
        cout << "\nAgent1: number of output link children = " << numchild << "\n";
// now read and display the output link WMEs
        for(i=0;i<numchild;i++){
        oLinkChild = pOutputLink1->GetChild(i);
//cout << "\n Attribute: " << oLinkChild->GetAttribute();
loc[0][i] = oLinkChild->GetValueAsString();
cout << "\n Value (as int): " << loc[0][i];
                }
        }
  else
   {cout << "Error getting agent1 output link" << endl ;
    return(0);}

pause();
```

```
// Agent2 input link is set after reading agent1 output link

pInputLink2 = pAgent2->GetInputLink();
if (!pInputLink2) cout << "Error getting agent2 input link" << endl ;

// create (I3 ^agent1-loc <X>)(<X> ^xloc locx ^yloc locy)
// on agent2's input link with specified coordinates

// void Update(IntElement* pWME, int value) ;
pID2 = pAgent2->CreateIdWME(pInputLink2, "agent1-loc") ;
pAgent2->CreateIntWME(pID2, "xloc", atoi(loc[0][0]));
pAgent2->CreateIntWME(pID2, "yloc", atoi(loc[0][1]));

// commit agent1 changes to working memory
pAgent2->Commit() ;

cout << "\nYou may now use the debugger to check \n the agent 1 location data on agent2's input link\n";

pause();

// Second objective: read agent2's output link and
// set this pair as the input link values for agent1

cout <<"\nSecond, we read agent2's output link and set this pair as the input link values for agent1";

pOutputLink2 = pAgent2->GetOutputLink();
if (pOutputLink2) {
        numchild = pOutputLink2->GetNumberChildren();
        cout << "\nAgent2: number of output link children = " << numchild << "\n";
// now read and display the output link WMEs
        for(i=0;i<numchild;i++){
        oLinkChild = pOutputLink2->GetChild(i);
//cout << "\n Attribute: " << oLinkChild->GetAttribute();
loc[1][i] = oLinkChild->GetValueAsString();   // problem here
cout << "\n Value (as int): " << loc[1][i];
                }
            }
  else
    {cout << "Error getting agent2 output link" << endl ;
     return(0);}

pause();

// Agent1 input link is set after reading agent2 output link

pInputLink1 = pAgent1->GetInputLink();
if (!pInputLink1) cout << "Error getting agent1 input link" << endl ;

// create (I3 ^agent2-loc <X>)(<X> ^xloc locx ^yloc locy)
// on agent1's input link with specified coordinates

// void Update(IntElement* pWME, int value) ;
pID1 = pAgent1->CreateIdWME(pInputLink1, "agent2-loc") ;
pAgent1->CreateIntWME(pID1, "xloc", atoi(loc[1][0]));
```

```
pAgent1->CreateIntWME(pID1, "yloc", atoi(loc[1][1]));

// commit agent1 changes to working memory
pAgent1->Commit() ;

cout << "\nYou may now use the debugger to check the agent2 location data \n on agent1's input link\n";

cout <<"\nAfter that, I'll clean up and shutdown\n";

pause();

cout << "\nShutting down and cleaning up\n";

// shutdown and clean up

pKernel->Shutdown() ;
delete pKernel ;

return 1;}
```

Log of the Two-Agent Communication Example.   This is shown in Figure 9.29.

Resulting Agent States.   Using a Java-based debugger for each agent, Figure 9.30 validates the two-agent communication results.

9.12   Soar Resources and References

The Soar home page is at http://sitemaker.umich.edu/soar/home. This page contains links for downloading and installing Soar. The Soar appearance and behavior is the same on all platforms. Versions of Soar are available for Mac OS X, Windows, and linux. The Soar wiki page is at http://winter.eecs.umich.edu/soarwiki/. Both pages contain links to Soar references, tutorials, and examples.

```
$ ./2agents-IOlinks


 *** 2 Agent Soar 8.6.4 c++ Communication Example ***


Creating an instance of the Soar kernel;

Random Seed = 1
Listening on port 12121

Creating 2 agents (agent1, agent2) in this Soar kernel;

You may now use debugger(s) to watch them.

** Enter 1 to continue =>
Received a connection
Got new connection
1

Loading specific (initialization) productions for
 each of the  2 agents in this Soar kernel;

** Enter 1 to continue =>
1

Running each agent for 1 decision (in sequence)

Use a debugger to examine the IO link values for agent1 and agent2

** Enter 1 to continue =>
1

First, we read agent1's output link and set this pair as the input link values for agent2
Agent1: number of output link children = 2

 Value (as int): 101
 Value (as int): 102
** Enter 1 to continue =>
1

You may now use the debugger to check
 the agent 1 location data on agent2's input link

** Enter 1 to continue =>
1

Second, we read agent2's output link and set this pair as the input link values for agent1
Agent2: number of output link children = 2

 Value (as int): 203
 Value (as int): 204
** Enter 1 to continue =>
1

You may now use the debugger to check the agent2 location data
 on agent1's input link

After that, I'll clean up and shutdown

** Enter 1 to continue =>
```

Figure 9.29 Log of the Two-Agent Communication Example

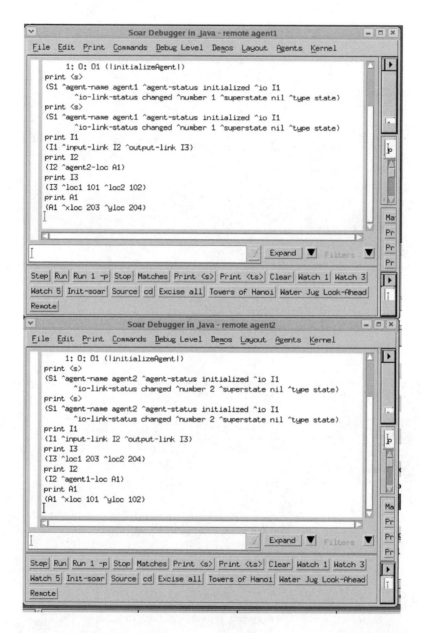

Figure 9.30   Respective Debugger Interfaces Showing `Agent1` and `Agent2` IO Links After Using the C++ Interface to Facilitate Interagent Communication in Soar

9.13 Exercises

1. Develop a table that compares CLIPS and Soar.

2. As indicated in Section 9.3.6 and Figure 9.5, Soar employs a systematic procedure to select the single best (proposed) operator (or generates an impasse). The purpose of this problem is to explore whether it is possible to force Soar to emulate a much simpler (and less focused) production system. Specifically, operator selection consists of simply choosing a proposed operator randomly. How can this be achieved? (Hint: See Section 5 of the Soar Users Manual.)

3. The following presents an interesting problem: After studying the concepts and architecture of Soar, suppose you have a CLIPS implementation and desire the functionality of Soar. Can a CLIPS database be designed such that features of Soar, such as:

   ◆ The concept of a state;
   ◆ Hierarchical representations in wm;
   ◆ Operator proposal;
   ◆ Subgoaling;
   ◆ State elaboration; and
   ◆ wm I/O support

   are emulated?

4. (a) Distinguish between an operator and a production in Soar.
   (b) Cite instances wherein a Soar program that uses state elaboration (and thus produces WMEs with I-support) is preferable to an implementation employing operators (and thus produces WMEs with O-support).

5. Modify the Soar program in Figure 9.8 with one or more productions to specify a goal and indicate when the goal has been reached by halting Soar.

6. Implement the sorting approach from CLIPS in Soar.

7. In Soar, what is the difference between using `halt` vs. `interrupt`?

8. Distinguish between Soar and a "conventional" rule-based system (RBS).

9. In Section 9.2.7 we showed the distinction between I- and O-support. Consider the alternative approach shown here:

```
## example of not as predicate and remove as action
## objective is to alternate wm contents

sp {example*propose*initialize
   (state <s> ^superstate nil
           -^name)
```

```
-->
   (<s> ^operator <o> +)
   (<o> ^name initialize-example)}

sp {example*create*initial-and-desired-states
   (state <s> ^operator <o>)
   (<o> ^name initialize-example)
-->
   (<s> ^name example-problem
        ^previous thingA)  # to start
}

## example of not and remove in productions
## wmes have I-support

sp {example*putA
   (state <s> ^name example-problem)
   (<s> -^previous thingA)
-->
   (<s> ^previous thingB -) # remember it has
   (<s> ^previous thingA)   # I-support
}

sp {example*putB
   (state <s> ^name example-problem)
   (<s> -^previous thingB)
-->
   (<s> ^previous thingA -)
   (<s> ^previous thingB)
}
```

The objective is to alternate wm contents, as in Section 9.2.7. Single-step this Soar implementation and cite the difference in behavior and indicate why.

10. Continue the Soar implementation of the image labeling problem from Section 9.5. Consider (i.e., implement) the following:

   (a) Using only the adjacency constraint; and

   (b) Using the unary constraints "highest" and "moving" with the adjacency constraint.

In both cases, consider producing the labelings using state elaboration as well as producing the labelings using operators for O-support of labelings.

11. Compare the structure of Soar with that of ACT-R.

12. The operator-based labeling formulation of Section 9.5 has a significant shortcoming. If the log of the Soar execution (by phases) were continued, the results shown below would appear:

```
run 1 --phase
--- output phase ---
run 1 --phase
```

```
--- input phase ---
run 1 --phase
--- propose phase ---
run 1 --phase
--- decision phase ---
=>WM: (112: S2 ^item O2)
=>WM: (111: S2 ^item O3)
=>WM: (110: S2 ^item O4)
=>WM: (109: S2 ^item O5)
=>WM: (108: S2 ^item O6)
=>WM: (107: S2 ^quiescence t)
=>WM: (106: S2 ^choices multiple)
=>WM: (105: S2 ^impasse tie)
=>WM: (104: S2 ^attribute operator)
=>WM: (103: S2 ^superstate S1)
=>WM: (102: S2 ^type state)
      2: ==>S: S2 (operator tie)
```

Notice that the next Soar cycle with this formulation results in an operator-based impasse. In other words, the only thing keeping Soar from repeatedly generating the same set of labelings at each cycle is the impasse. Revise the Soar formulation of Figure 9.13 to eliminate this behavior.

13. This problem is a variation on the two-agent communication example presented in Section 9.11.5. Develop a two-agent simulation using C++, Soar, SML, and state IO links that implements the following:

   1. User enters Agent1 location to set Agent1 io.input-link;

   2. Agent1 transfers this information to its output link;

   3. We read the Agent1 output link;

   4. Set Agent2's input link to these values; and

   5. (Finally) Agent2 writes the output link information.

14. Compare and contrast the execution cycle of Soar with that of CLIPS. Specifically:

   (a) Enumerate the process for each. Be quantitative.

   (b) Show parts that are common, or similar.

   (c) Show parts that are unique to either Soar or CLIPS.

15. Compare and contrast Soar and CLIPS in terms of overall design, features, capabilities, system architecture, embedding capabilities, and intended use.

16. Using the Soar representation of Section 9.2.5, sketch the blocks-world state.

17. This problem illustrates "not" condition elements and wm element removal. Consider the Soar source shown in Figure 9.31 . The intent of the example is to alternate wm entities thingA and thingB at each cycle. This is done by two operators, operator*putA and operator*putB, as shown in the figure. Generate a log of the Soar session and verify that the desired alternation is achieved.

```
## example of not as predicate and remove as action
## objective is to alternate wm contents

sp {example*propose*initialize
   (state <s> ^superstate nil
             -^name)
-->
   (<s> ^operator <o> +)
   (<o> ^name initialize-example)}

sp {example*create*initial-and-desired-states
   (state <s> ^operator <o>)
   (<o> ^name initialize-example)
-->
   (<s> ^name example-problem
        ^previous thingA)  # to start
}


## example of not and remove in productions

## proposal of operators
## proposal wmes have I-support

sp {example*propose*operator*putA
   (state <s> ^name example-problem)
   (<s> -^previous thingA)
-->
   (<s> ^operator <o> +)
   (<o> ^name putA)
}

sp {example*propose*operator*putB
   (state <s> ^name example-problem)
   (<s> -^previous thingB)
-->
   (<s> ^operator <o> +)
   (<o> ^name putB)
}


## application of operators
## application yields wmes O-support

sp {example*apply*operator*putA
   (state <s> ^operator <o>)
   (<o> ^name putA)
-->
   (<s> ^previous thingB -) # remember it has
   (<s> ^previous thingA)   # O-support
}

sp {example*apply*operator*putB
   (state <s> ^operator <o>)
   (<o> ^name putB)
-->
   (<s> ^previous thingA -)
   (<s> ^previous thingB)
}
```

Figure 9.31 Soar Source for Example Showing "not" and Removal of the **wm** Element

18. Another strategy for removing a WME is using the Soar `retract-wme` command. Show a simple example using this command.

19. Develop Soar source code for the image labeling problem of Section 9.5 using state elaboration. Use the adjacency and highest constraints and show a log of the resulting five solutions (labelings).

20. Develop a state elaboration-based Soar formulation for the lightbulb diagnosis example of Section 9.6.2. Show the log of Soar operation and compare the result with that of Section 9.6.2.

21. The following Soar source code

```
sp {initial-state
    (state <s> ^superstate nil)
-->
(<s> ^clearup no ^locob right ^clearleft yes)}

sp {move-rule1
    (state <s> ^clearup no ^locob right ^clearleft yes)
-->
(<s> ^move? left)
(write (crlf) |based upon the current state attributes,|
        (crlf) |the block may move left| (crlf))}
```

after firing production **move-rule1**, produces a state:

```
Firing move-rule1
-->
based upon the current state attributes,
the block may move left
(S1 ^move? left +)
=>WM: (9: S1 ^move? left)
--- decision phase ---
=>WM: (15: S2 ^quiescence t)
=>WM: (14: S2 ^choices none)
=>WM: (13: S2 ^impasse no-change)
=>WM: (12: S2 ^attribute state)
=>WM: (11: S2 ^superstate S1)
=>WM: (10: S2 ^type state)
     1: ==>S: S2 (state no-change)
```

and then a succession of states each with the same attributes. Use Soar to verify this.

The purpose of this problem is to write an additional production to recognize this situation and halt Soar. Develop, implement, and test your production using Soar.

22. In Chapter 2, the concepts of a system state and corresponding state space were developed. Soar also involves the concept of a state (or states, if subgoaling occurs). Relate the two concepts of state (Soar vs. system or problem state). Show where they contain similar information and where they are different.

Representing and Manipulating Uncertainty in IS, Part 1: Confidence Factors, Probability, Belief Networks, and Multivalued Logic

10.1 Introduction

10.1.1 Representing and Manipulating Uncertainty

In this chapter and the next, we consider aspects of IS representation and manipulation involving uncertainty. Commonly encountered types of uncertainty include imprecision or vagueness, ambiguity, and generality. Uncertainty in measurement, reasoning, control, modeling, estimation, etc., is inherent in real-world situations. Numerous IS approaches have been developed to allow uncertainty. This includes probability, multivalued logic, confidence factors, and fuzzy logics. In this chapter we address the first three; Chapter 11 considers fuzzy approaches.

10.1.2 Expressing Uncertainty in Statements

Uncertainty in statements or propositions may be represented in a number of ways:

1. By attaching confidence factors to representation elements. The numerical value of the confidence factor is intended to indicate confidence, certainty, or "comfort" with the element. Typically confidence factors are associated with facts and rules.

   For example, we could assign a confidence value to a statement that is a numerical value in the interval [0, 1]. A value of 1, for example, represents absolute certainty in the statement (i.e., confidence that the statement is TRUE), whereas a value of 0 indicates absolute certainty that the statement is FALSE. A truth value of 0.75, for example, might indicate that the statement is "fairly true."

2. By allowing a statement to assume a truth value other than TRUE or (exclusive or) FALSE (multivalued logic). One approach is to define and use a multivalued logic. For example, truth values TRUE, FALSE, and MAYBE might be used in a three-valued logic. Another approach is to expand the space of allowable truth values between definite truth and falsity, thus defining an interval of truth values. Within this approach there are numerous alternatives. Multivalued logic research is not new. Much of the seminal work occurred in the 1920s [Pos21].

3. By assigning a probability measure to the truth value of a statement. For example, define a probability-based confidence measure for statement S in the form:

P (statement S is TRUE) $= 0.8$ (or simply $P(S) = 0.8$)

For example, if

$P(S) = 1.0$

we indicate absolute certainty that S is true. This approach is considered later.

10.1.3 Approaches to Uncertainty

The summary of Figure 10.1, shows that there are a number of different (but in some cases related) approaches to the problem of representation and manipulation of uncertainty in IS.

10.2 Use and Limitations of Probability in IS

We digress briefly to consider the manipulation of probabilities and the necessary underlying assumptions for those manipulations to be valid. The probability of an event, H, is denoted as $P(H)$; recall we have defined an event as the occurrence of a particular statement being TRUE.

10.2.1 Conditional Probability

The conditional probability of an event H, given the information available up to this event (i.e., the knowledge of the occurrence of other events that may be related to H), is denoted

$$P(H|E)$$

where E is the evidence available. Thus, we view $P(H|E)$ as the conditional probability that event H is TRUE, in light of the evidence E. The formulation does not represent the attention that should be given to or the significance of event H, it merely reflects its probability of occurrence. For example, if H is the occurrence of an (unlikely but) deadly disease, we need an alternative formulation to indicate its significance.

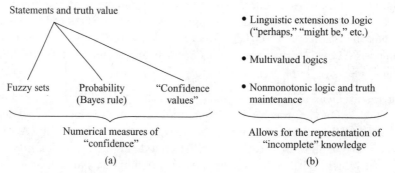

Figure 10.1 Some Approaches to Representation and Manipulation of Uncertainty

10.2.2 Bayes Rule

One of the most useful formulations relates the conditional probability of an event to the joint occurrence of two events as:

$$P(H \cap E) = P(H|E)P(E)$$

and

$$P(H \cap E) = P(E|H)P(H)$$

It is this result from which Bayes' rule is derived:

$$P(H|E) = \frac{P(E|H)P(H)}{P(E)}$$

to relate conditional probabilities.

Sample Application of Bayes Rule in Inference. Suppose we had the events:

  H: patient has lung cancer
  E: patient smokes

and we are interested in developing a quantitative assessment of

$$P(H|E) = P(\text{patient has lung cancer}|\text{patient smokes})$$

given $P(H)$ is the probability of lung cancer in the general population, we may also formulate:

$$P(E|H) = P(\text{patient is a smoker}|\text{patient has lung cancer})$$

Assume $P(E|H)$ may be obtained from experience or history, i.e., we know the percentage of all persons diagnosed to have lung cancer who are smokers. For a given patient, in the absence of any evidence, it is easy to show that the confidence in our diagnosis (statement H is TRUE) is $P(H)$. This is simply the probability that anyone in the general population has lung cancer. However, if we are given evidence, E, that the patient smokes, we may refine our confidence in the diagnosis using Bayes rule as:

$$P(H|E) = \frac{P(E|H)P(H)}{P(E)}$$

10.2.3 Independence

Two events, H and E, are independent in a probabilistic sense if

$$P(H|E) = P(H)$$

Thus, given the logical formulation

$$C = A \cap B$$

the assumption of independence allows us to write the following:

$$P(C) = P(A \cap B) = P(A)P(B)$$

10.2.4   Limitations of the Probabilistic Approach

One shortcoming of the probabilistic approach is that it does not directly lead to representations of "ignorance" (as perceived by humans). For example, if evidence E supports hypothesis, H, through $0 < P(H|E) < 1$, then according to the rules of probability, it would also have to partially support the negative of the hypothesis, H, since probability requires

$$P(H|E) + P(\neg H|E) = 1$$

Humans, in contrast, tend to classify evidence as either supporting or refuting a hypothesis.

Another difficulty occurs in mapping the truth value of a statement into a probability when the statement contains variables. We could view this as spawning the need for an "extended" predicate function.

10.2.5   A Simple Example of Probability Limitation Leading Up to Confidence Factors

Suppose a rule has two antecedents, A and B. The logical interpretation that leads to firing of the rule and generation of consequent C is AB. We now proceed, given $P(A)$ and $P(B)$ to determine $P(C)$. Moreover, we show how the assumption of independence in the initial database facts does not lead to the assumption of independence as we get deeper in the inference net. Therefore employing the independence assumption in the calculation of probability-based confidence measures yields (probabilistically speaking) incorrect results.

Refer to the two-level inference net in Figure 10.2. Assuming initial facts A and B are independent (which might be a reasonable assumption), we derive $P(C)$ using `Rule-p` as:

$$P(C) = P(A)P(B)$$

Again employing the independence assumption for the second level of inference with `Rule-q` (since $D = C \cap A$) yields

$$P(D) = P(C) \cap P(A) = [P(A)]^2 P(B)$$

This result is incorrect, since the firing of `Rule-p` has introduced dependence into the antecedents (C and A) of `Rule-q`.

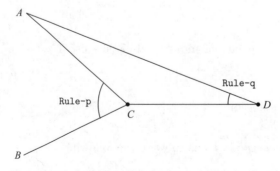

Figure 10.2 Inference Net for Probability Analysis

Considering Dependence (Conditional Probabilities).   If the problem is now reformulated by accounting for the dependence of propagated fact probabilities, we get:

$$P(D) = P(A \cap C) = P(A)P(C|A)$$

Since

$$P(C|A) = \frac{P(C \cap A)}{P(A)} = \frac{P(A \cap B \cap A)}{P(A)} = \frac{P(A \cap B)}{P(A)} = \frac{P(A)P(B)}{P(A)} = P(B)$$

Accounting for the probabilistic dependence of the inputs to `Rule-q` yields:

$$P(D) = P(A)P(C|A) = P(A)P(B)$$

which is correct according to the probabilistic interpretation. It is also obvious from the inference net of Figure 10.2. Moreover, several important observations regarding the intuitive correctness of this result may be made:

1. The approach based upon an assumption of independence, for a given rule, returns a probability-based confidence measure that is lower than one that accounts for dependence. (Compare this result with $P^2(A)P(B)$ in the previous case.)

2. The approach that accounts for dependence includes the case where the rule consequents are independent, i.e., when $P(C|A) = P(C)$.

3. As illustrated by the example, even if the initially given facts are independent, the rule-based production system introduces significant dependence. Thus, at some level in the inference net, the assumption of independence is not reasonable. This introduces significant analytical and practical complexity. The rule-based inference net will produce facts that are dependent, thus the assumption of dependence (even if it is difficult to quantify) is more reasonable than that of independence.

Thus, several characteristics of the probabilistic approach with the independence assumption are noteworthy:

◆ It yields a very "lossy" system, in terms of confidence measure propagation. Since the probability of any event is 1.0, the successive multiplication of these probabilities, as we progress through the inference net, yields monotonically nonincreasing confidence measures. Restoration of confidence in a fact is not possible without modification of the approach.

◆ In the case of rules with a large number of antecedents, the resulting consequent probability decreases quickly, due to the product of a number of terms, all whose value is 1.0.

10.2.6   Joint Probability (Conjunction) Propagation

This example introduces a major limitation with propagation of joint probabilities. Suppose, in implementation of an IS, for statements or events $S1$ and $S2$ we need to determine the measure $P(S1 \cap S2)$. Furthermore, suppose the probabilities associated with the individual statements are given, i.e., define

$$P(S1) = p1 \quad \text{and} \quad P(S2) = p2 \tag{10.1}$$

We seek to determine how the joint probabilities associated with logical combinations of statements $S1$ and $S2$ are related to the probabilities $p1$ and $p2$. More importantly, we wish to know if the probability measures in Equation 10.1 may be used to determine the joint distributions. There are four logical combinations involving the conjunction of the truth states of $S1$ and $S2$.

We define the corresponding joint probabilities:

i. $P(S1 \cap S2) = p_{tt}$

ii. $P(S1 \cap \neg S2) = p_{tf}$

iii. $P(\neg S1 \cap S2) = p_{ft}$

iv. $P(\neg S1 \cap \neg S2) = p_{ff}$

The marginal probabilities of statements $S1$ and $S2$ may be formed from the joint probabilities. Since

$$P(S1) = P(S1 \cap S2) + P(S1 \cap \neg S2)$$
$$= p_{tt} + p_{tf}$$
$$= p1$$

Similarly

$$P(S2) = P(S1 \cap S2) + P(\neg S1 \cap S2)$$
$$= p_{tt} + p_{ft}$$
$$= p2$$

Given $p1$ and $p2$, and desiring p_{tt}, we have two equations and three unknowns. (Note also that p_{ff} was not required.) This result indicates the principal problem with the strictly probabilistic approach, namely that $p1$ and $p2$ alone are insufficient for the determination of the joint probability functions. Furthermore, in an n-statement rule this approach is also impractical, since for n statements there are 2^n joint probability measures that must be considered.

10.2.7 Bayes Rule for Information Fusion

A Notational Note. Heretofore we have denoted conjunction of events using $\cap$, e.g., writing $P(A \cap B)$. An alternative, and commonly encountered notation is simply $P(A, B)$, where (,) denotes AND. We use this notation in subsequent sections.

Considering Bayes Rule for three variables yields a number of possible rewritings, including:

$$P(A, B, C) = P(C|A, B)P(A, B) = P(A|B, C)P(B, C))$$

Now consider the following problem where we have a hypothesis, C, and observed "evidence," A and B. Our objective is to combine the individual evidence, i.e., measures $P(C|A)$ and $P(C|B)$ into $P(C|A, B)$. From the preceding equation:

$$P(C|A, B) = \frac{P(A|B, C)P(B, C)}{P(A, B)}$$

We make two assumptions regarding independence:

1. $P(A, B) = P(A)P(B)$

2. $P(A|B, C) = P(A|C)$.

Under these conditions,

$$P(C|A, B) = \frac{P(A|C)P(B|C)P(C)}{P(A)P(B)}$$

The formulation is even more interesting if we employ Bayes rule again to yield:

$$\frac{P(A|C)}{P(A)} = \frac{P(C|A)}{P(C)}$$

and

$$\frac{P(B|C)}{P(B)} = \frac{P(C|B)}{P(C)}$$

so that

$$P(C|A, B) = [\frac{P(C|A)}{P(C)}][\frac{P(C|B)}{P(C)}]P(C)$$

This formulation makes clear the modification, refinement, or propagation of $P(C)$, given probabilistic "evidence" regarding A and B.

10.3 From Probability to Confidence Factors

10.3.1 Introduction

On the basis of the previous section, one might conclude that the probabilistic approach to reasoning with uncertainty, due to its rigorous foundation in mathematics, and despite the aforementioned complexities, is the paradigm of choice in developing rule-based systems that reason with uncertainty. This is not the case for at least two reasons:

1. It has been observed that "experts," when faced with a problem, do not choose approaches that embody standard probabilistic approaches.

2. The difficulty (particularly with respect to the independence assumption) in incorporating strict probabilistic approaches practically precludes its use.

Thus, a search for systematic techniques for the representation of uncertainties in the inference process yields two main avenues to pursue: i) the identification and emulation of the (nonprobabilistic) approaches observed to be used by experts; and ii) approaches "similar" to, but not founded in, probability.

10.3.2 Confidence Factors

Experts have been observed to use "certainty factors" in their problem solving. For example, in the expert system MYCIN, a confidence scale of $[-1, 1]$ is used to represent the range of confidence associated with a particular fact or assertion (conclusion). A value of -1 indicates total lack of confidence (i.e., complete confidence the assertion is FALSE), whereas a measure of 1 represents complete certainty the assertion is TRUE. If, after exhausting all search possibilities, the cumulative confidence measure associated with a hypothesis is in the interval $[-0.2, 0.2]$, the hypothesis is regarded as unconfirmed. Of course, this is an empirically determined range that is subject to modification or alternate interpretation in a particular application.

Furthermore, the expert system CASNET, also used for medical diagnosis (specifically for the identification of glaucoma), uses a scale of confidence factors in the range $[1, 5]$, where 1 indicates "rarely causes" and 5 indicates "almost always causes." The somewhat novel feature of this approach, however, is that the numerical values of certain observations are converted into confidence factors for the associated fact. For example, if "intraocular pressure" is measured to be 15 mm Hg, the corresponding fact might have the confidence factor 3, but an observation of 30 mm Hg might yield a confidence factor of 4.

10.3.3 A Heuristic Approach

The development of confidence factors requires corresponding development of a mechanism to combine and propagate these factors. In MYCIN, given a rule that incorporates the conjunction (AND-ing) of n antecedents, the confidence measure associated with the consequent obtained by firing this rule is the minimum of the confidence measures of the individual antecedents. Alternately, given a rule that incorporates the disjunction (OR-ing) of n antecedents, the confidence of this rule is the maximum of the confidence measures of the individual antecedents.

10.3.4 Comparison of the Heuristic Approach with Probability

For illustration, a two-antecedent rule (conjunction) is used. Given confidence measures denoted X and Y corresponding to two events A and B, i.e., $X = conf(A)$, $Y = conf(B)$, we compare the results for the calculation of $Z = conf(C)$. Using the heuristic approach of Section 10.3.3, we get Z_H, where

$$Z_H = min(X, Y)$$

whereas the confidence in the probability-based approach assuming independence, denoted Z_P

$$Z_P = XY$$

This is shown in Table 10.1 for various values of the confidence measures.

Intuitive and Analytical Comparison. Table 10.1 suggests a number of comparisons.

1. The heuristic approach is less conservative than the probabilistic approach, i.e., the resulting confidence measures vis-a-vis the probabilistic approach are higher.

X	Y	XY	$min(X,Y)$
0	0	0	0
.1	.9	.09	.10
.25	1.0	.25	.25
.25	.25	.06	.25
.5	1.0	.5	.5
.5	.5	.25	.5
.75	1.0	.75	.75
.75	.75	.56	.75
1.0	1.0	1.0	1.0

Table 10.1 Comparison of Propagated Confidence Factors

2. The heuristic approach resembles the probabilistic approach with dependence considerations. This is straightforward to show since

$$P(C) = P(A \cap B)$$

and

$$P(A \cap B) = P(A|B)P(B) \le P(B)$$

and

$$P(A \cap B) = P(B|A)P(A) \le P(A)$$

Thus,

$$P(A \cap B) \le min\{P(A), P(B)\}$$

so that the heuristic is a reasonable, albeit conservative, bound on the confidence of C. It also happens to have an explanation using probability.

10.3.5 Positive and Negative Reinforcement in the Heuristic Approach

The reasonableness of the heuristic approach vis-a-vis the probabilistic approach is further illustrated by the following two cases. We consider both positive and negative reinforcement of A and B.

Case 1: $P(A|B) \approx 1$; $P(B) < P(A|B)$ **(Positive Reinforcement).** In this case:

$$P(A|B) = \frac{P(A \cap B)}{P(B)} \approx 1$$

therefore,

$$P(C) = P(A \cap B) = P(A|B)P(B) \approx P(B)$$

So we would be correct in choosing $P(B)$ as $conf(C)$.

Case 2: $P(A|B) \approx 0$ **(Negative Reinforcement).** In this case, A and B don't jointly occur, i.e., $P(A \cap B) \approx 0$. Either $P(A|B) \approx 0$ or $P(B|A) \approx 0$. Suppose $P(\neg A|B) \approx 1$. Since $P(\neg A) \geq P(\neg A|B)$, we surmise that $P(\neg A) \approx 1$, therefore $P(A) = 0$, which yields the correct propagated confidence using $conf(C) = min\{P(A), P(B)\}$.

10.3.6   Extension of the Heuristic Approach to OR Formulations

For OR formulations, MYCIN and other inference systems use the confidence factor propagation heuristic

$$conf(C) = max\ conf(A), conf(B)$$

The reader is encouraged to repeat the analysis of the AND-based heuristic for this case, to verify the reasonableness of this approach as well as its relation to probability.

10.3.7   Confidence Factors Are Implemented in CLIPS

The CLIPS extension fuzzyCLIPS is introduced in Chapter 11, Section 11.6. fuzzyCLIPS incorporates both fuzzy reasoning and confidence factors. Confidence factors are treated in Section 11.6.2 of Chapter 11.

10.4   Belief Networks

A Belief Network (BN) [Pea88] is a multi-use tool for reasoning with uncertainty. Specifically, a BN may be used to:

1. Provide a systematic approach to the incorporation of dependencies (e.g., conditional probabilities) for events (see Sections 10.2.1 and 10.2.5); or

2. Provide a formalism for reasoning with uncertainty when partial beliefs are available.

A Belief Network may be visualized as a tree-structured network. The computation of beliefs using a BN involves a belief propagation algorithm. However, *the most challenging part of the endeavor is learning the BN from observed evidence.*

10.4.1   Definitions

A BN is a 4-tuple:

$$BN = \{X, D, G, P\}$$

where

$X = \{X_1, X_2, \ldots, X_n\}$ is a set of random variables;

D is a set of domains corresponding to the RVs in X; and

G is a directed, acyclic graph over X and P where

$$P = \{p_1, p_2, \ldots, p_n\}$$

and

$$p_i = P(X_i = x_i|pa_i)$$

where pa_i denotes the parents of X_i in G.

The BN represents the probability distribution over X in product form, i.e.,

$$P(x_1, x_2, \dots, x_n) = \prod_{i=1}^{i=n} P(x_i|x_{pa_i})$$

Given a set of instantiated variables, $x_1, x_2, \dots, x_n$, or a so-called *evidence set*, the probability of this evidence set may be computed.

10.4.2 BN Example and Use

Suppose our problem involves RVs $A, B, \dots, G$ where:

A is an independent RV;

B depends upon A;

C depends upon A;

D depends upon A and C;

E depends upon D and C;

F depends upon B and C; and

G depends upon E and F.

Figure 10.3 shows the BN for this case. Referring to Figure 10.3, note that

$$P(g, f, e, d, c, b, a) = P(g|f, e)P(f|b, c)P(e|c, d)P(d|a, c)P(c|a)P(b|a)P(a)$$

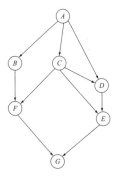

Figure 10.3 Sample Belief Network for Random Variables A thru G

10.5   Multivalued Logic

10.5.1   Review of Two-Valued Logic

In classical or two-valued logic, facts are either absolutely TRUE or absolutely FALSE. The representation of facts and rules as axioms in a logic-based approach allows deduction to proceed as theorem proving. This is mathematically sound, however, it lacks expressiveness and leads to "brittle" reasoning strategies that do not allow uncertainty. Often, rules or facts provided by experts are accompanied by some quantification of certainty (descriptors such as "in most cases," "often," "seldom," etc., are used in statements).

10.5.2   Extension to Multivalued Logics

Allowing a statement to assume a truth value other than TRUE or FALSE introduces many-valued logics (MVL). Notice an alternative viewpoint is that the statements no longer reside in the set of TRUE statements OR[1] the set of FALSE statements, but rather may have a degree of membership in each.

Many valued logics have been around at least since Aristotle, who proposed four "shades" of truth:

◆ necessity

◆ contingency

◆ possibility

◆ impossibility

The generalization to a many-valued propositional logic, in its modern form, is often attributed to Post [Pos21]. Other comprehensive and more modern surveys, such as those of Turner [Tur84] and DiZenzo [DiZ88] appear in the references.

10.5.3   A Simple Heuristic Three-Valued Logic System Example

Consider a three-valued logic, wherein a statement, S, can take on one of three truth values: TRUE (denoted 1), FALSE (denoted 0), and MAYBE (denoted 1/2). Given this logic, immediate concerns include the ability to propagate truth values using logical connectives. Specific connectives of immediate interest include AND, OR, NOT, and implication. A second issue is the combination and relating of these connectives (e.g., recall in classical two-valued logic

$$(p \rightarrow q) \equiv (\neg p \cup q)) \tag{10.2}$$

---

[1]exclusive OR.

An obvious choice, which parallels that of confidence measure propagation, follows. Letting $T(S)$ denote the truth value of statement S, we arrive at the following paradigm:

$$T(\neg S) = 1 - T(S) \tag{10.3}$$
$$T(S_1 \cap S_2) = min\{S_1, S_2\} \tag{10.4}$$
$$T(S_1 \cup S_2) = max\{S_1, S_2\} \tag{10.5}$$

Thus, we have an extension of two-valued logic, with the addition of $\neg maybe = maybe$. We now formalize this approach and show examples of its utility.

10.5.4 Formalizing MVL: Truth Sets and Truth Values

Our formulation for a many-valued logic applicable to uncertain reasoning uses an Extended Post formulation [DiZ88]. We begin with the following variable definitions:

p: the number of truth values in a p-valued logic.[2]

$V(p)$: the truth set or set of possible truth values. Restricting truth values to the range $[0, 1]$ for a p-valued logic $V(p) = \{0, 1/p - 1, ..., (p - 2)/(p - 1), 1\}$. Note in a two-valued logic $V(2) = \{0, 1\}$.

For notational convenience, we rewrite $V(p)$ to index truth values by m, where

$$V(p) = \{u(m)\} \quad m = 0, 1, ...p - 1 \tag{10.6}$$

so the mth truth value $u(m)$ is given by

$$u(m) = m/p - 1 \tag{10.7}$$

For example, consider the following three-valued logic ($p = 3$) formulation:

$$V(3) = 0, 1/2, 1 \tag{10.8}$$

Note that truth value $u(m) = 1/2$, i.e., the value corresponding to truth index $m = 1$, intuitively corresponds to the notion of "maybe" or "possibly." This yields the correspondence between the truth index and the truth value, shown for the $p = 3$ case in Table 10.2.

---

[2] $p = 2$ is conventional two-valued or binary logic with truth values TRUE and FALSE.

| m to $u(m)$ Mapping ||
m	$u(m)$
0	0
1	1/2
2	1

Table 10.2 Example of Truth Index to Truth Value Mapping for $m = 3$

10.5.5 "Weak" Connectives in Multivalued Logic

We denote the truth value of a statement, a, as $T(a)$. The following "weak" interpretations of the $\neg$ (not), $\cap_m$ (and), and $\cup_m$ (or) logical connectives are defined.

Weak Negation ($\neg$).

$$T(\neg a) = 1 - T(a) \tag{10.9}$$

i.e., note that the unary negation operator is not dependent upon m.

Weak Conjunction ($\cap_m$).

$$T(a \cap_m b) \begin{cases} = max\{T(a), T(b)\} & \text{if } \{T(a) < m \ AND \ T(b) < m\} \\ & OR \ \{T(a) \geq m \ AND \ T(b) \geq m\} \\ = min\{T(a), T(b)\} & \text{otherwise} \end{cases} \tag{10.10}$$

Weak Disjunction ($\cup_m$).

$$T(a \cup_m b) \begin{cases} = min\{T(a), T(b)\} & if \ \{T(a) \geq m \ AND \ T(b) \geq m\} \\ & OR \ \{T(a) < m \ AND \ T(b) < m\} \\ = max\{T(a), T(b)\} & \text{otherwise} \end{cases} \tag{10.11}$$

Weak Implication ($\rightarrow_m$).   Weak implication is defined via the equivalence

$$T(a \rightarrow_m b) = T(\neg a U_m b) \tag{10.12}$$

These connectives are summarized for the $p = 3$ case in Tables 10.3, 10.4, 10.5, and 10.6. Notice that increasing m yields truth tables that are, in a sense, more conservative. Alternative truth table-based definitions for the logical connectives in a $p = 3$ valued logic are explored in Chapter 3 of [Tur84]. The logics of Lukesiewicz [Luk67], Kleene [Kle52], and Bochvar [Boc39] are summarized in Tables 10.7, 10.8, and 10.9.

		$m = 0$	$m = 1$	$m = 2$	$p = 2$ logic
a	b	$a \cap_0 b$	$a \cap_1 b$	$a \cap_2 b$	$a \cap b$
0	0	0	0	0	0 (F)
0	1	1	0	1	—
0	2	2	0	0	0 (F)
1	0	1	0	1	—
1	1	1	1	1	—
1	2	2	2	1	—
2	0	2	0	0	0 (F)
2	1	2	2	1	—
2	2	2	2	2	2 (T)

Table 10.3 $a \cap_m b$ for Various Values of m

a	b	$a \cup_0 b$	$a \cup_1 b$	$a \cup_2 b$	$a \cup b^3$
0	0	0	0	0	0 (F)
0	1	0	1	0	—
0	2	0	2	2	2 (T)
1	0	0	1	0	—
1	1	1	1	1	—
1	2	1	1	2	—
2	0	0	2	2	2 (T)
2	1	1	1	2	—
2	2	2	2	2	2 (T)

Table 10.4 $a \cup_m b$ for Various Values of m

		$p = 2$ logic
a	$\neg a$	$\neg a$
0	2	2 (T)
1	1	—
2	0	0 (F)

Table 10.5 $\neg a$ for $p = 3$ Valued Logic

p	q	$\neg p$	$m=0$ $p \cup_m q$	$m=1$ $p \cup_m q$	$m=2$ $p \cup_m q$	$p=2$ logic $p \rightarrow q$
0	0	2	0	2	2	2 (T)
0	1	2	1	1	2	—
0	2	2	2	2	2	2 (T)
1	0	1	0	1	0	—
1	1	1	1	1	1	—
1	2	1	1	1	2	—
2	0	0	0	0	0	0 (F)
2	1	0	0	1	0	—
2	2	0	0	2	2	2 (T)

Table 10.6 Weak Implication $(p \rightarrow_m q)$

a	$\neg a$
t	f
f	t
u	u

Negation $(\neg)$ from Kleene

a	b	$a \cap b$	$a \cup b$	$a \rightarrow b$
f	f	f	f	t
f	u	f	u	t
f	t	f	t	t
u	f	f	u	u
u	u	u	u	u
u	t	u	t	t
t	f	f	t	f
t	u	u	t	u
t	t	t	t	t

Other Logical Connectives from Kleene

Table 10.7 Logical Connectives (Kleene). t: TRUE, f: FALSE, u: UNDECIDED

a	b	a → b
f	f	t
f	i	t
f	t	t
i	f	i
i	i	t
i	t	t
t	f	f
t	i	i
t	t	t

Table 10.8 Lukasiewicz Multivalued Logic (¬, ∩, ∪ same as in Kleene) i: indeterminate (cannot be assigned the value of t or f)

a	$\neg a$
t	f
f	t
m	m

Not (¬)

a	b	$a \cap b$	$a \cup b$	$a \rightarrow b$
f	f	f	f	t
f	m	m	m	m
f	t	f	t	t
m	f	m	m	m
m	m	m	m	m
m	t	m	m	m
t	f	f	t	f
t	m	m	m	m
t	t	t	t	t

Table 10.9 Three-Valued Logic from Bochvar (m: meaningless)

10.5.6 Using Multivalued Logic for Inference

Notice that implied in Equations 10.10–10.12 and Table 10.3 is choice of m, which also serves as a "threshold" or "level of significance." For a p-valued logic, this enables p logically complete subsystems or "logical planes," each indexed by a particular value of m. Given some measure of desired inference significance, one conceptually obvious approach is to fix the significance measure m and use only this logical plane (with the corresponding truth tables for its logical connectives). For example, consider a $p = 100$ valued logic. If we were using this logic for diagnosis of cancer, we might choose a relatively high level of significance, e.g., the $m = 90$ plane. Conversely, if we are using the logic for a very speculative mineral exploration, a lower (e.g., $m = 40$) level might be chosen.

The previous approach, while straightforward, may be improved upon by mixing planes, as shown in [DiZ88].

10.6 Exercises

1. This problem is intended to help you visualize a multivalued logic function. Consider the two-input exclusive-OR (XOR) logic function.

   (a) Plot the two-input(XOR) logic function using values 0 and 1.

   (b) Define XOR in terms of the NOT, AND, and OR connectives.

   (c) Using the simple three-valued logic system of Section 10.5.3 and the preceding result, determine the truth table for a three-valued version of XOR. Use $\frac{1}{2}$ for the third logic value.

   (d) Plot the two-input(XOR) three-valued logic function.

2. Compare the weak formulation of multivalued logic connectives of Tables 10.3, 10.4, 10.5, and 10.6 with the heuristic formulation of Section 10.5.3.

3. As shown, the assumption of independence allows considerable simplification in the propagation of conditional probabilities. Given events x, y, and z, *with x and y conditionally independent,* prove the following axioms result:

$$P(x, y|z) = P(x|z)P(y|z)$$

$$P(x|y, z) = P(x|z)$$

$$P(x, y, z) = P(x|z)P(y, z)$$

4. This problem explores the capabilities and limitations of probability. Here are some questions:

   ◆ Does probability exhaustively model uncertainty?

   ◆ Is uncertainty the same as randomness?

   ◆ Is being unsure the same as "chance"?

   ◆ Does probability exhaustively model vagueness?

   ◆ Why do statisticians hate fuzzy theory?

5. Draw the corresponding Belief Network for the events shown in Figure 10.2.

6. Figure 10.4 shows a BN with random variables a thru j. Determine $P(j, i, h, g, f, e, d, c, b, a)$.

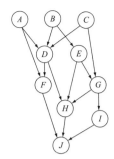

Figure 10.4 Belief Network for Random Variables A thru J

7. Repeat the analysis of Section 10.2.6 for the case of a three-input or three-statement probability propagation.

Representing and Manipulating Uncertainty in IS, Part 2: Fuzzy Systems and FuzzyCLIPS

This chapter begins our look at "soft computing" via fuzzy representation and manipulation. Soft computing is described by attempts to characterize the inevitable imprecision and uncertainty of real-world models and problems. Soft computing includes elements of fuzzy logic, neural computing, pattern recognition, and genetic (or evolutionary) computing. Key elements of soft computing include:

◆ Computational methods that tolerate (not encourage) imprecision and uncertainty;

◆ Approximate rather than categorical reasoning; and

◆ Presentation of computation results in linguistic terms.

11.1 Fuzzy Sets and Fuzzy Logic

Fuzzy systems provide a mathematical framework to capture uncertainty. Fuzzy approaches are an *alternative* technology for both system control and IS representation and manipulation. Practically speaking, fuzzy approaches are about 40 years old.

11.1.1 Examples of Fuzzy Concepts, Connotations, and Use

Arguably, we seem to be surrounded by fuzziness. Examples include statements such as:

"the number of head injuries dropped dramatically;"

"administrator's raises were significantly higher than faculty;" and

"congressional committees agreed to less severe but still significant reductions."

An obvious question is: Why would someone choose a fuzzy approach? There are many different answers, including:

◆ Uncertainty is involved;

◆ The domain of discourse falls naturally into a fuzzy set-based description; or

◆ All the other approaches failed or are "too hard." This may be a subtle, yet very popular rationale for the use of fuzzy techniques.

For context, we cite two premises put forth by Lotfi Zadeh [Zad92]:

"...traditional methods of system analysis are unsuited for dealing with systems in which relations between variables do not lend themselves to representation in terms of differential or difference equations..."

"...everything is fuzzy, to some degree..."

Distinctions Between Probability and Fuzziness.   Bezdek [Bez93] uses a simple example to reinforce this distinction. Suppose you were faced with dehydration and offered two unlabeled[1] bottles, denoted A and B, from which to (possibly) drink. Consider Case 1, a probability specification, namely you are given: P(bottle A is potable) = 0.9. As an alternative consider Case 2, a fuzzy membership specification, namely that Member(bottle B potable liquids) = 0.90. Which would you drink, and why?

11.1.2 Sample Fuzzy Applications

Process Control.   Applications for fuzzy logic-based solutions include process control. In fuzzy approaches to modeling, control, and inference a common strategy is to incorporate the "experience" of humans into the system design. Often this is in lieu of process details. This may lead to "rule of thumb" strategies. This is useful, for example, when a device or plant can be controlled with better results by an experienced human operator than by conventional automatic controllers. A long and detailed example is shown later in this chapter.

Appliance Control.   Control of home appliances is a popular fuzzy application domain: For example, Sanyo/Fisher incorporates a fuzzy controller in their 8mm camcorder to evaluate focus and lighting conditions, and Matsushita employs a fuzzy controller for camcorder image stabilization. Matsushita uses a fuzzy controller for washing machine control with rules employing antecedants such as: "*small* load with *large* amount of grease" and "*large* load of *slightly* soiled clothes." Panasonic produces an electric shaver with fuzzy logic, and Mitsubishi Heavy Industries has an air conditioning control system that employs 25–50 fuzzy rules and has shown a 24% reduction in energy consumption in comparison to previous (nonfuzzy) controllers. Other noteworthy application areas include optimization, image processing, and pattern recognition.

On-Line Portfolio Selection.   Decision making (especially stock picking), often incorporates fuzzy concepts. PORSEL (PORtfolio SELector) [ZM99] is a system for selection of stocks. PORSEL uses a fuzzy rule-based system to perform fundamental analysis. PORSEL has shown excellent performance when compared with the S&P 500. Sample results[2] are shown in Table 11.1. In the results shown in

---

[1] In the sense that the contents were not identified.

[2] Note these results represent retrospective, and not prospective, performance.

Year	Equal proportion	Variable proportion	S&P 500 index
1989	55.5	58.8	31.49
1990	73.06	89.5	-3.17
1991	109.3	226.5	30.55
1992	29.1	-4.0	7.67
1993	567.4	573.5	9.99
1994	38.1	44.4	-1.50
Average	145.41	164.78	12.5

Table 11.1 Sample PORSEL Performance

Table 11.1, all shares were purchased at the beginning of the year, held for the entire year, and sold at the year's end. PORSEL then selected twenty new stocks for the next year. "Equal proportion" means that the same amount was invested in each of the selected stocks whereas "Variable proportion" indicates that PORSEL also optimized the relative amount invested in each selected stock.

Fuzzy Expert Systems.   A *fuzzy expert system* is an expert system that uses a collection of fuzzy membership functions and rules to implement reasoning. When a production system architecture is used, and the rules (productions) in the production system involve fuzzy quantities, the productions are referred to as *fuzzy productions* in a *fuzzy production system*.

11.2 Fundamental Fuzzy System Concepts

Fundamental fuzzy systems concepts include:

1. The notion and quantification of fuzzy sets, especially the all-important notion of membership functions for (fuzzy and nonfuzzy, i.e., crisp) sets;

2. Linguistic variables, labels, and hedges;

3. The process of fuzzification;

4. The propagation of fuzzy information via fuzzy productions (rules) and associated compositional rules of inference (CRI); and

5. The process of defuzzification.

11.2.1 Representing Sets with Membership Functions

Membership functions characterize (both fuzzy and crisp) sets. The manipulation of fuzzy quantities is therefore carried out by manipulation of fuzzy set membership functions. This manipulation includes set complement, intersection, and union as well as fuzzification and defuzzification. *Using fuzzy sets requires that we develop a means to propagate (fuzzy) set membership through conventional logic connectives.*

Crisp Sets

Quite simply, in conventional (or crisp) sets, *an element is either a member of a set or not.* Thus, a membership function for a crisp set S, denoted $\mu_S()$, is a binary valued function that implements:

$$\mu_S(x) = \begin{cases} 1 & if \;\; x \in S \\ 0 & otherwise \end{cases} \tag{11.1}$$

Logic functions or *predicates* [Sch90] implement membership functions, where the (crisp) sets are the sets of TRUE or[3] FALSE statements (or more generally outcomes, e.g., values of logic gates). In the case of binary or two-valued logic, values of m_S are truth values. It is straightforward to indicate the members of a crisp set; either by enumeration or by a closed-form expression.

Fuzzy Sets

Fuzzy sets generalize the notion of crisp sets, as defined in Section 11.2.1. The set membership function is no longer binary-valued. Thus, one definition of a fuzzy set is a set whose boundary is not crisp or sharp. Extending the definition of a membership function for a crisp set to describe fuzzy set membership illustrates the point in a more quantitative manner. The membership function for fuzzy set X, denoted $\mu_X()$, *is no longer a binary valued function.* Instead, the set X is mapped onto the real interval $[0, 1]$. A sample fuzzy set membership function could be:

$$\mu_X(x) = 1 - x \tag{11.2}$$

Of course, the membership function is chosen to suit the specific problem representation. The general role of the membership function is shown in Figure 11.1.

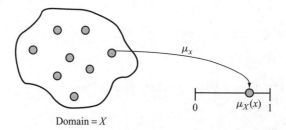

Domain $= X$

Figure 11.1 Definition of a Fuzzy Set Through a Membership Function

---

[3]Exclusive-OR

Therefore, in a crisp set, membership is dichotomous ("yes-or-no"), whereas in a fuzzy set we allow the concept of graded membership ("more-or-less"). Alternately, the question: "does $x \in X$ belong to set A?" has different answers in each domain. In the crisp domain, x belongs to A or (xor) not, whereas in the fuzzy domain x has a (possibly zero) degree of membership in all sets, including A.

Summary. Any fuzzy or crisp set, A, is defined via a membership function:

$$A = \{(\mu_A(x), x)\} \; for \; x \in X \tag{11.3}$$

If the set is crisp, $\mu_A \in \{0, 1\}$. If the set is fuzzy, $0 \leq \mu_A \leq 1$, i.e., there is no clear-cut transition from "belongingness" to "nonbelongingness" in the fuzzy set.

Examples of Crisp and Fuzzy Sets

Consider the crisp formulation:

$$A_{=6} = \text{``numbers equal to 6''} \Rightarrow \mu_A(x) = \begin{cases} 1 & if \; x = 6 \\ 0 & otherwise \end{cases}$$

and compare this with the fuzzy description:

$$A_{close \; to \; 6} = \text{``numbers close to 6''} \Rightarrow \mu_A(x) = \frac{1}{1 + (6 - x)^2}$$

Another example, using linguistic variables, is shown in Figure 11.2.

Determining Membership Functions, μ_i

There are a number of ways to acquire the necessary μ_i for a fuzzy system. These include:

1. Subjective evaluation and elicitation (experts specify membership function curves appropriate to a given problem).

2. Ad-hoc functional forms (most actual fuzzy control operations draw from a very small set of different curves).

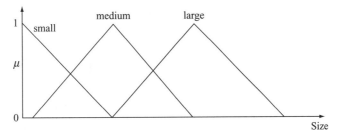

Figure 11.2 Example of Fuzzy Membership Functions Using Linguistic Variables for the Sets Small in Size, Medium in Size, etc.

3. Converted frequencies or probabilities. (However, we must remember that membership functions are NOT probabilities.)

4. Physical measurement.

5. Learning and adaptation.

Mathematical Forms and Characteristics of Membership Functions

Closed-form mathematical representations are often useful for membership functions. Parametric adjustment of these representations is used in membership function (MF) development.

Note in many of the examples shown, the membership function peaks in the middle of the domain and attains its lowest values at the edges or limits of the domain. Thus, a plethora of membership functions are triangular or trapezoidal. Other membership functions, based upon parametrically controlled sigmoidal and trapezoidal functions, are shown in Figure 11.3. A triangular MF, denoted μ_{tri}, is specified by four parameters as follows [JS95]:

$$\mu_{tri}(x; a, b, c, d) = max(min(\frac{x-a}{b-a}, \frac{c-x}{c-b}), 0) \tag{11.4}$$

Similarly, a trapezoidal MF, denoted μ_{trap} is given by:

$$\mu_{trap}(x; a, b, c, d) = max(min(\frac{x-a}{b-a}, 1, \frac{d-x}{d-c}), 0) \tag{11.5}$$

Generalized bell MFs are given by:

$$\mu_{bell}(x; a, b, c) = \frac{1}{1 + |\frac{x-c}{a}|^{2b}} \quad b > 0 \tag{11.6}$$

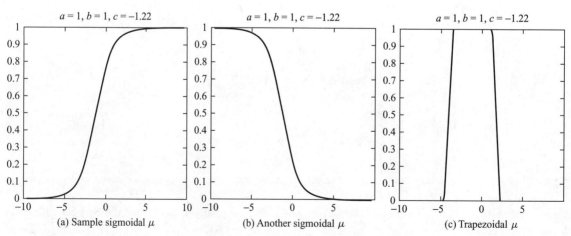

(a) Sample sigmoidal μ (b) Another sigmoidal μ (c) Trapezoidal μ

Figure 11.3 Sample Membership Functions

Additional membership functions are shown in Figure 11.3.

One especially important membership function is the Gaussian MF, denoted μ_g, and defined by two parameters, c and σ:

$$\mu_g(x; c, \sigma) = \exp^{-(\frac{x-c}{\sigma})^2} \tag{11.7}$$

11.2.2 Membership Functions Resulting from Set-Theoretic Operations

Numerous application domains require the computation of a membership function resulting from an algebraic operation on one or more sets, resulting in an output set. Important aspects of fuzzy sets, conveyed through their respective membership functions follow.

Fuzzy Set Equality

$$A = B \text{ iff } \mu_A(x) = \mu_B(x) \; \forall \; x \in X \tag{11.8}$$

Notice there is no fuzziness in equality, i.e., it is a crisp concept.

Fuzzy Set Complement

A^c is complement of A iff:

$$\mu_{A^c}(x) = 1 - \mu_A(x) \tag{11.9}$$

Fuzzy Set Union

The union of fuzzy sets $A, B \subset X$, written $A \cup B$ is defined as:

$$\mu_{A \cup B}(x) = \mu_A(x) \cup \mu_B(x) \; \forall \; x \in X \tag{11.10}$$

where $a \cup b = max(a, b)$.

Fuzzy Set Intersection

The intersection of fuzzy sets $A, B \subset X$, written $A \cap B$ is defined as:

$$\mu_{A \cap B}(x) = \mu_A(x) \cap \mu_B(x) \; \forall \; x \in X \tag{11.11}$$

where $a \cap b = min(a, b)$.

11.2.3 The Extension Principle

The extension principle is an oft-cited way to relate lots of things to two-valued logic. Notice that the use of Equations 11.8–11.11 with discrete membership values of 0 and 1 results in two-valued logic. This is called the *Extension Principle*, which claims that the classical results of Boolean logic are a subset of fuzzy logic. The claim is also made that fuzzy logic is a *generalization* of classical logic, but this does not necessarily give it validity.

11.3 General Fuzzy System Structure

11.3.1 Major Components

As shown by Figure 11.4, a general structure for a system employing fuzzy concepts consists of three entities:

- A fuzzification process that converts nonfuzzy (crisp) inputs into their fuzzy counterparts;

- A fuzzy computational mechanism (CRI) that maps fuzzy quantities into fuzzy quantities; and

- A defuzzification interface that converts the fuzzy-domain results into nonfuzzy (crisp) outputs.

Not all three components are required. Only the heart of the system shown, i.e., the fuzzy computational mechanism, is required. In the case of a system based upon linguistic (fuzzy) inputs, fuzzification is not required. Similarly, if a linguistic (fuzzy set) output is sufficient, defuzzification is not required.

11.3.2 Linguistic Variables

Perhaps the most fundamental element in fuzzy systems is the notion of a linguistic variable, i.e., a variable whose values are *words rather than numbers*. For example, consider the use of the linguistic variable temperature in the fuzzy expression: "the temperature is **hot**," as compared with the crisp interpretation: "the temperature is 56.00108709023°C." Linguistic variables also allow qualifiers on the fuzzy set or linguistic label/descriptor, for example, valid expressions are "the temperature is **very hot**," "the temperature is NOT hot" and "the temperature is NOT very hot."

We refer back to Figure 11.2 to develop some nomenclature. The x-axis in this figure corresponds to values of a *linguistic variable*. Examples of linguistic variables are temperature, height, size (used in Figure 11.2), speed, and voltage. Each linguistic variable has an associated set of *linguistic labels*, for example two linguistic labels for temperature are hot and cold. Three linguistic labels for speed

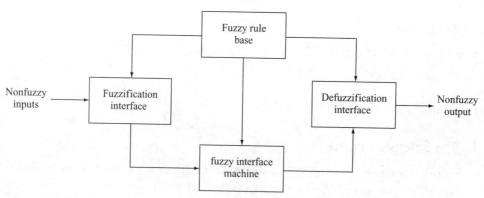

Figure 11.4 Typical Fuzzy System (crisp I/O shown for example)

are slow, moderate, and fast. Often we see a general formulation of a linguistic variable used in rules as:

IF x is A ...

for example,

"IF temperature is hot."

In this formulation, x is a linguistic variable and A is a linguistic label. In the most elementary form, the linguistic label is the name of a fuzzy set, for example the set of hot temperatures. The value used by the fuzzy system in subsequent processing is the membership function corresponding to the fuzzification of the crisp input value. Of course, this depends upon the linguistic label used. Therefore, for each linguistic variable, there are usually many linguistic values, one for each linguistic label. For example, the linguistic variable "temperature" has linguistic values for both linguistic labels "hot" and "cold."

11.3.3 Fuzzy Antecedents and Rules

The structure of an antecedent in a fuzzy rule is:

$$v \text{ is } V \Rightarrow \text{"input temperature is hot"}$$

This leads to the rule form[4]:

$$IF\ (x\ is\ A)\ and\ (y\ is\ B)\ THEN\ z\ is\ C \tag{11.12}$$

where

◆ A and B denote fuzzy sets over the input domains X and Y of linguistic variables x and y.

◆ C is a fuzzy set over the output domain Z of linguistic variable z.

Rule 11.12 relates x and y to z *linguistically. Therefore, fuzzy rules relate fuzzy sets.* The propagation of and computation with fuzzy variables and values is necessary. This is often referred to as fuzzy inference.

11.4 Fuzzy System Design Procedures

11.4.1 Principal Tasks

The main tasks in applying fuzzy techniques to a specific problem are:

1. Selection of a set of input linguistic variables that are both natural to the application and whose crisp values are available;

---

[4]In several sections we show fuzzy rules with two antecedants for ease of illustration. Extension to n antecedants is obvious.

2. Selection of a set of output linguistic variables that are both natural to the application and whose crisp values are needed;

3. Determination of membership functions for all linguistic labels of the linguistic variables;

4. Selection of fuzzification and defuzzification techniques;

5. Development of a knowledge base of fuzzy rules—often these are designed to be human-readable;

6. Selection of or development of a fuzzy inference strategy; and

7. System prototyping, testing, and documentation.

11.4.2 Fuzzy Computational Mechanisms

A fuzzy rule has the general form:

> IF (statements with linguistic variables) THEN (consequent)

Notice the antecedants may be connected via conjunction, disjunction, and the NOT connective may be used. In what follows, we assume conjunction (AND-ing) of the antecedents for illustration. For example,

> IF the engine is very noisy AND the fuel mileage is poor THEN the car should be serviced soon

involves the linguistic variable "soon" in the consequent.

As indicated by Figure 11.4, the overall strategy is subdivided into the following steps.

Fuzzification

In this (first) step, crisp inputs are converted into fuzzy representations. System inputs are assumed to be available as the crisp output of sensors. Thus, a single (crisp) number for each input must be converted into the fuzzy domain for each linguistic label. Given the appropriate membership functions, this involves mapping the input variable to a fuzzy set membership value. This step only requires evaluation of membership functions corresponding to rule antecedents.

Applying Compositional Rules of Inference (CRI)

Fuzzy rules, together with the chosen CRI, are used to produce linguistic consequents. This is the fuzzy domain computation.

Defuzzification of Linguistic (Fuzzy) Outputs

Defuzzification is usually necessary in order to provide crisp outputs. For example, in a control application, the output of the fuzzy controller must be an exact voltage, current, flow setting, etc. We cannot expect physical systems to be able to "speed up slightly" (a fuzzy linguistic concept), but rather the controller must specify "speed = 30 ips." This was shown in Figure 11.4. There are several methods of defuzzification; they are treated in detail in Section 11.5.1.

11.4.3 The Plethora of Fuzzy CRI and Defuzzification Strategies

There are numerous fuzzy CRIs and associated defuzzification approaches. A few are [JS95]: The Mamdani fuzzy inference system with min-max propagation; the Mamdani fuzzy inference system with $prod - max$ propagation; the Sugeno fuzzy inference system; and the Tsukamoto fuzzy inference system. We emphasize the use of the Mamdani strategy in detail in Section 11.4.4.

11.4.4 Applying Compositional Rules of Inference (CRI)

The overall process consists of the following (typical) steps[5]:

1. Given crisp inputs (e.g., x and y), compute grade of proposition, denoted w_i, on antecedent (the Mamdani CRI rules are shown here) for each fuzzy rule

$$w_i = \mu_{A_i}(x) \cap \mu_{B_i}(y) \tag{11.13}$$

   Thus, w_i represents the firing "strength" of the ith rule, where $\cap = min$.

2. Compute the function:

$$\mu^*_{C_i}(z) = w_i \times \mu_{C_i}(z) \tag{11.14}$$

   that indicates the strength of antecedent-consequent (fuzzy sets) coupling.

3. Scale the membership function for ith rule consequent.

   Note that there exist alternatives to scaling, e.g.,

$$\mu^*_{C_i}(z) = min\{w_i, \mu_{C_i}(z)\} \tag{11.15}$$

   A comparision of these approaches is shown in Figure 11.5

4. Compute the aggregate membership function for the output fuzzy set:

$$\mu_C(z) = \bigcup_{i=1}^{n} \mu^*_{C_i}(z) \tag{11.16}$$

   Recall $\cup = max$, and notice Equations 11.13–11.16 yield:

$$\mu_C(z) = \bigcup_{i=1}^{n} \{\mu_{A_i}(x) \cap \mu_{B_i}(y)\} \mu_{C_i}(z) \tag{11.17}$$

   i.e., *a static mapping from inputs to outputs results.*

5. Defuzzify $\mu_C(z)$ to a crisp value. For example:

$$z_o = \frac{\int z \mu_C(z) dz}{\int \mu_C(z) dz} \tag{11.18}$$

   Equation 11.18 illustrates the enter of gravity (COG) approach. Other defuzzification strategies exist as shown in Section 11.5.1.

---

[5] A two-antecedent fuzzy rule is used for illustration.

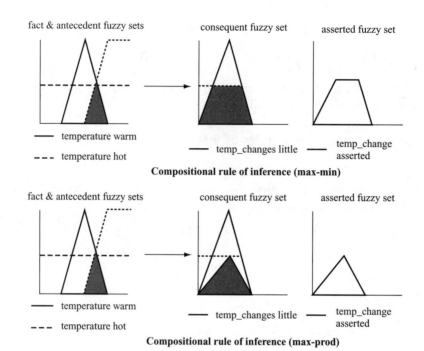

Figure 11.5 Two Approaches to the CRIs. Adapted from the FuzzyCLIPS Manual.

11.5 A Fuzzy System Application (Control) Example

The objective of this example is to control propeller speed as a function of process temperature and motor torque. The fuzzy rules are summarized in Table 11.2. Note the column index is the membership function for linguistic variable "temperature," and the row index is the membership function for linguistic variable "torque." The uppercase fuzzy sets shown in the table correspond to membership functions for linguistic variable "speed."

This formulation yields nine control rules over three values (each) of two (input) linguistic variables. Sample membership functions are shown in Figure 11.6.

(output) Speed		(input) Temperature		
		cool	warm	hot
(input) Torque	low	HIGH	NORMAL	NORMAL
	normal	HIGH	NORMAL	LOW
	high	NORMAL	LOW	LOW

Table 11.2 Table of Nine Rules for Control of Propeller Speed. Fuzzy Sets for (output) Linguistic Variable "Speed" Shown in Uppercase.

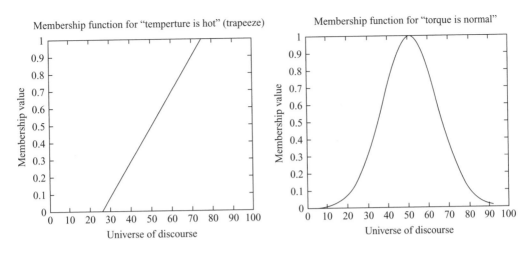

Figure 11.6 Sample Membership Functions Used for Fuzzy Speed Controller Example

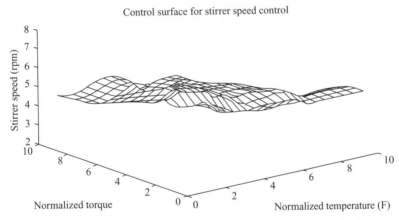

Figure 11.7 Resulting Control Surface (coarse quantization)

The composite effect of these nine rules is shown in the resulting control surface of Figure 11.7. This example is continued in Section 11.6. Many details are shown using a FuzzyCLIPS implementation.

11.5.1 The Plethora of Defuzzification Techniques

Defuzzification is an inherently underconstrained process. Many defuzzification approaches exist. Several examples follow. The exercises provide pointers to many other defuzzification techniques.

COG Defuzzification

Let set U denote the set of possible fuzzy output values resulting from the application of system rules, i.e.,

$$U = \{U_1, U_2, \ldots U_n\} \tag{11.19}$$

The objective is to defuzzify the U_i values to achieve a crisp output, denoted U_{crisp}. *Center of Gravity Defuzzification* computes the output (crisp) value U_{out}^{COG} using:

$$U_{out}^{COG} = \frac{\sum_{i=1}^{n} \mu_i U_i}{\sum_{i=1}^{n} \mu_i} \tag{11.20}$$

COG defuzzification can lead to "prohibited control command" problems, and tends to produce a uniform distribution for the output set as the number of rules increases.

MOM Defuzzification

The mean of maximum (MOM) technique is an alternative to the COG. Let G be the subset of U consisting of those values that are maxima of μ, i.e.,

$$G = \{u^* | \mu(u^*) = \frac{max}{u} \mu(u)\} \tag{11.21}$$

Let $|G|$, i.e., the cardinality of G be m. MOM computes the crisp output using:

$$U_{out}^{MOM} = \frac{\sum_{U_i \in G} U_i}{m} \tag{11.22}$$

[FY91] shows that COG and MOM defuzzification approaches have a common basis in terms of probability distributions.

A Generalized Defuzzification, BAsic Defuzzification Distribution (BADD) Method

This method, introduced by Filev and Yager [FY91], generalizes both the COG and MOM methods. The BADD technique can switch between the COG and MOM methods using a single parameter α. The crisp output d is formulated as

$$d_G = \frac{\sum_{i=1}^{n} w_i^{\alpha} u_i}{\sum_{i=1}^{n} w_i^{\alpha}} \tag{11.23}$$

where the u_i are the elements of the discrete output universe and the w_i are the elements of the fuzzy output set. COG is achieved for $\alpha = 1$, and MOM is reached when $\alpha \to \infty$. The BADD defuzzification method can be used to influence the shape of the control surface from smooth ($\alpha \approx 1$) to more step-shaped.

Sugeno's CRI Method

The Sugeno model proposed by Takagi, Sugeno, and Kang [JS95] is an effort to develop a systematic approach to the generation of fuzzy rules. Typical Sugeno rules have a different form than the rule structure discussed in Section 11.3.3. Instead, they have the form:

$$IF\ [x]\ is\ [A]\ and\ [y]\ is\ [B]\ THEN\ [z]\ =\ f(x, y) \tag{11.24}$$

where A and B are fuzzy sets in the antecedent and $z = f(x, y)$ is a crisp function. The output of each rule is then weighted by the rule's firing strength, ω. The overall output d is formulated by

$$d = \frac{\sum_{i=1}^{m} w_i u_i}{\sum_{i=1}^{m} w_i} \tag{11.25}$$

where w_i are the elements of the fuzzy output set, u_i are the elements of the discrete output universe, and m is the number of fuzzy Sugeno rules. The method was not used in the vitrification research either because it requires the special rule structure.

11.5.2 Fuzzy Approach Shortcomings

Numerous issues are yet to be resolved regarding fuzzy system technology. They include:

- The low portability of rule bases. They tend to be application specific and thus lack standard libraries or modules for general applications;

- Significant sensitivity of control surface to small changes in the fuzzy rulebase or membership functions;

- Required time to identify and tune membership functions; and

- Validating a fuzzy system, especially for safety-critical applications.

11.6 Exploring Uncertainty and Fuzzy Concepts with CLIPS

11.6.1 Introduction to FuzzyCLIPS

FuzzyCLIPS is an enhanced version of CLIPS developed at the National Research Council of Canada. FuzzyCLIPS facilitates the implementation of fuzzy systems for reasoning with uncertainty. A good source of information is the users manual ("User's Guide"), which accompanies FuzzyCLIPS Version 6.10d.[6] FuzzyCLIPS is available without cost as a noncommercial download. The current URL is http://www.iit.nrc.ca/IR_public/fuzzy/fuzzyClips/FuzzyCLIPSIndex2.html or ftp://ai.iit.nrc.ca/pub/fzclips/.

We show the use of FuzzyCLIPS for implementing a fuzzy production system that incorporates uncertainty in facts and rules. Specifically, both confidence factors and fuzzy sets are implemented in FuzzyCLIPS. Note that enhancing a production system like CLIPS to achieve this capability is a nontrivial venture. Several example applications are used.

---

[6]Written by Bob Orchard; dated October, 2004.

Notes on FuzzyCLIPS and CLIPS COOL and Protégé. FuzzyCLIPS implements the COOL functions described in Chapter 8, Section 8.3. This is important, since preexisting crisp (nonfuzzy) class-based representations may need to be "fuzzified," or serve as the basis for a fuzzy representation. In addition, preexisting ontologies (with instances defined) developed in Protégé may also be used with FuzzyCLIPS. It is noteworthy, however, that instances of classes used with FuzzyCLIPS defined in Protégé (Chapter 8) must be explicitly declared "reactive," i.e., able to be matched against object patterns in the CE to a rule. Otherwise, a FuzzyCLIPS error results.

11.6.2 Implementing Confidence Factors in FuzzyCLIPS

In FuzzyCLIPS, confidence factor-based uncertainty and fuzziness can be modeled simultaneously. First, we consider confidence factors. FuzzyCLIPS allows the use of confidence or "certainty" factors as follows:

```
(defrule flight-rule
(declare (CF 0.95)) ;declares certainty factor of the rule
(animal type bird)
 =>
(assert (animal can fly))
)
```

This rule signifies that there is a 95% confidence in the rule stating that if an animal is a bird, then it can fly. In FuzzyCLIPS, if a certainty factor of a rule is not declared, it is assumed to be equal to 1.0. This is shown in the following example.

Default Behavior of FuzzyCLIPS

We begin by extending a previous CLIPS example containing no uncertainty. The CLIPS source is repeated here:

```
;; clips implementation of a sample database
;; file: ars-clips.clips

;; template for memory
(deftemplate primitive
(slot name))

;; a rule
(defrule rule1
  (primitive (name a))
  (primitive (name r))
=>
  (assert (primitive (name b))))

;; initial facts
(deffacts startup
  (primitive (name a))
  (primitive (name r))
  (primitive (name s)))
```

Suppose we use FuzzyCLIPS and load and run this file. The results are shown as follows:

```
FuzzyCLIPS> (load "ars-clips.clips")
Defining deftemplate: primitive
Defining defrule: rule1 +j+j
Defining deffacts: startup
TRUE
FuzzyCLIPS> (facts)
f-0     (initial-fact) CF 1.00
f-1     (primitive (name a)) CF 1.00
f-2     (primitive (name r)) CF 1.00
f-3     (primitive (name s)) CF 1.00
For a total of 4 facts.
FuzzyCLIPS> (run)
FuzzyCLIPS> (facts)
f-0     (initial-fact) CF 1.00
f-1     (primitive (name a)) CF 1.00
f-2     (primitive (name r)) CF 1.00
f-3     (primitive (name s)) CF 1.00
f-4     (primitive (name b)) CF 1.00
For a total of 5 facts.
```

Notice that FuzzyCLIPS has appended confidence factors to the facts and indicated a CF of 1.0 (certainty).

Fact and Rule Confidence Factors: Syntax and Propagation

In the confidence factor-based extension to CLIPS, a fact is composed of two parts: the fact with the standard CLIPS syntax and an accompanying certainty factor. The propagated certainty factor for facts produced by a rule is

$$CF_{rule} \times min(CF_1, ..., CF_n)$$

where CF_{rule} is the certainty factor for the rule and the CF_i are the respective certainty factors for the facts that matched the LHS CEs of the rule.

Examples of Confidence Factor Definition and Propagation

The first example illustrates the use of a confidence factor on only the rule (facts default to 1.0). The second shows confidence factor definition and propagation in both facts and rules.

Example 1.

```
;; modified clips example
;; ars-clips-fuzzy-CF1.clips
;; for FuzzyCLIPS

;; template for memory
(deftemplate primitive
(slot name))

;; a rule
```

```
(defrule rule1
  (declare (CF 0.8))      ;; only uncertainty
   (primitive (name a))   ;; in rule
   (primitive (name r))
 =>
   (assert (primitive (name b))))

;; initial facts
(deffacts startup
  (primitive (name a))
  (primitive (name r))
  (primitive (name s)))

FuzzyCLIPS> (load "ars-clips-fuzzy-CF1.clips")
Defining deftemplate: primitive
Defining defrule: rule1 +j+j
Defining deffacts: startup
TRUE
FuzzyCLIPS> (reset)
FuzzyCLIPS> (facts)
f-0      (initial-fact) CF 1.00
f-1      (primitive (name a)) CF 1.00
f-2      (primitive (name r)) CF 1.00
f-3      (primitive (name s)) CF 1.00
For a total of 4 facts.
FuzzyCLIPS> (run)
FuzzyCLIPS> (facts)
f-0      (initial-fact) CF 1.00
f-1      (primitive (name a)) CF 1.00
f-2      (primitive (name r)) CF 1.00
f-3      (primitive (name s)) CF 1.00
f-4      (primitive (name b)) CF 0.80
For a total of 5 facts.
FuzzyCLIPS>
```

Example 2.

```
;; further modified clips example
;; for FuzzyCLIPS
;; using confidence factors

;; template for memory
(deftemplate primitive
(slot name))

;; rules

(defrule rule1
  (declare (CF 1.0))    ;; no uncertainty in rule
   (primitive (name a))
   (primitive (name r))
 =>
   (assert (primitive (name b))))
```

```
(defrule rule2
 (declare (CF 0.75))    ;; uncertainty in rule
  (primitive (name a))
  (primitive (name s))
=>
  (assert (primitive (name g))))


;; initial facts
(deffacts startup
  (primitive (name a)) CF 0.7
  (primitive (name r)) CF 0.6
  (primitive (name s)) CF 0.45
)


FuzzyCLIPS> (load "ars-clips-fuzzy-CF2.clips")
Defining deftemplate: primitive
Defining defrule: rule1 +j+j
Defining defrule: rule2 =j+j
Defining deffacts: startup
TRUE
FuzzyCLIPS> (reset)
FuzzyCLIPS> (facts)
f-0      (initial-fact) CF 1.00
f-1      (primitive (name a)) CF 0.70
f-2      (primitive (name r)) CF 0.60
f-3      (primitive (name s)) CF 0.45
For a total of 4 facts.
FuzzyCLIPS> (run)
FuzzyCLIPS> (facts)
f-0      (initial-fact) CF 1.00
f-1      (primitive (name a)) CF 0.70
f-2      (primitive (name r)) CF 0.60
f-3      (primitive (name s)) CF 0.45
f-4      (primitive (name g)) CF 0.34
f-5      (primitive (name b)) CF 0.60
For a total of 6 facts.
FuzzyCLIPS>
```

Using Threshold Tests on Certainty Factors

FuzzyCLIPS makes it is possible (see Users Manual, Section 5.3.4) to set a threshold certainty factor value such that no rule may be fired unless the rule has a calculated certainty factor value greater than or equal to the threshold value. This feature prevents chaining with very low certainty factors and thus produces facts with no significant confidence measure. The default is a threshold certainty factor of 0.0.

11.6.3   Implementing Fuzzy Sets and Reasoning in CLIPS

In FuzzyCLIPS, fuzzy set membership is represented by enhancing the CLIPS `deftemplate` and `deffacts` constructs, and extending the rule condition element (CE) syntax. Furthermore, it is possible to directly display and manipulate fuzzy sets, as the examples in the following sections show.

`deftemplate` Extensions for Fuzzy Variables

In FuzzyCLIPS, all fuzzy variables must be defined before use with the `deftemplate` construct, which is an extension of the standard `deftemplate` construct in CLIPS. The extended syntax is:

```
(deftemplate <name> ["<comments>"]
             <from> <to> [<unit>]          ; universe of discourse
                 (
                    t1
                    .
                    .     ; list of primary terms
                    .
                    tn
                 )
           )
```

where `<name>` is the identifier used for the fuzzy variable, `<from>` and `<to>` are floating point numbers, and a primary term `ti (i=1, ..., n)` has the form

```
(<pname> <description of fuzzy set>)
```

where `<pname>` represents the name of the the fuzzy set, and `<description of fuzzy set>` defines a corresponding membership function.

Membership Functions

FuzzyCLIPS allows a membership function to be described using several techniques:

1. A so-called singleton representation, where points on the membership function are specified and interpolation is used in between these points;

2. A standard (including built-in) function representation; or

3. A linguistic expression that uses terms defined previously in a fuzzy `deftemplate` definition.

Built-in functions include the functions S (or s), Z (or z), and PI (or pi), as shown in Figure 11.8. A specification for these membership functions has the following syntax:

```
<standard> ::= (S a c) | (s a c) | (Z a c) | (z a c) | (PI d b) | (pi d b)
```

where a, b, c, and d are the parameters of the respective functions.

Extension of `deffacts`

The `deffacts` construct has been expanded to allow the declaration of fuzzy facts with the syntax:

```
(deffacts <deffacts-name> [<comment>]
                 <RHS-pattern>*
        )
```

where `<RHS-pattern>` has been extended as follows:

```
<RHS-pattern> ::=        <ordered-RHS-pattern> |
                            <template-RHS-pattern> |
                            <fuzzy-template-RHS-pattern>
```

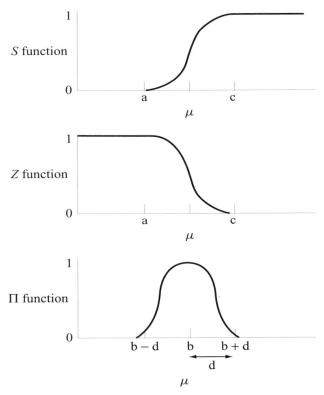

Figure 11.8 Built-in FuzzyCLIPS Membership Functions

```
<ordered-RHS-pattern> ::= (<symbol> <RHS-field>+)
                          [CF <certainty factor> | <certainty factor expression>]

<template-RHS-pattern> ::= (deftemplate-name> <RHS-slot>*)
                          [CF <certainty factor> | <certainty factor expression>]

<fuzzy-template-RHS-pattern> ::=
                          (<fuzzy-template-name> <description of fuzzy set>)
                          [CF <certainty factor> | <certainty factor expression>]
```

Example of Fuzzy Set Definition, Display, and Manipulation

We now show the use of a number of previously described constructs and topics via an example.

Consider the fuzzy representation of the concept of age. We begin with an example consisting of two principles:

1. "age" is a fuzzy variable that has membership in the fuzzy sets "young," "middle," and "old."

2. An entity (in this example, a person) has a nonfuzzy slot with value "name" and a fuzzy slot representing the fuzzy variable age.

The FuzzyCLIPS representation for this is shown as follows:

```
;; examples of linguistic variable "age"

;; first using piecewise linear ennumeration

(deftemplate age
 0 100 ; universe
 ( (young  (0 1) (25 1) (40 0.5) (55 0))
   (middle (0 0) (25 0.5) (40 1.0) (55 0.5) (70 0))
   (old    (0 0) (40 0) (55 0.5) (70 1) (80 1)) )
)

;; using 'standard function' representation
;; note: fuzzy sets may be different from above

(deftemplate sfage
 0 100 ; universe
 ( (young  (z 30 55))
   (middle (pi 15 40))
   (old    (s 40 70)) )
)

;; instances of entities with fuzzy attribute
;; first the fuzzy deftemplate

(deftemplate person
 (slot name)
 (slot age (type FUZZY-VALUE age))
)

;; instances (fuzzy facts)

(deffacts startup
 (person (name bob) (age middle))
 (person (name katie) (age young))
)
```

Before considering other aspects of the representation, we note that numerous manipulations with this fuzzy database in FuzzyCLIPS are possible. Some are shown here.

```
FuzzyCLIPS> (get-u age)
0.00 - 100.00
FuzzyCLIPS> (get-fuzzy-inference-type)
max-min
FuzzyCLIPS> (plot-fuzzy-value t + nil nil (create-fuzzy-value age middle)
)

Fuzzy Value: age
Linguistic Value: middle (+)
```

```
1.00                +
0.95               + +
0.90
0.85            .  +   +
0.80              +     +
0.75             +       +
0.70
0.65           +       +
0.60          +         +
0.55         +           +
0.50        +
0.45       +             +
0.40      +               +
0.35     +                 +
0.30    ++
0.25    +                    +
0.20   +                      +
0.15  +                        +
0.10  ++
0.05 +                          +
0.00+                 +++++++++++++++++
    |----|----|----|----|----|----|----|----|----|----|
   0.00    20.00    40.00    60.00    80.00   100.00
```

Universe of Discourse: From   0.00 to 100.00

FuzzyCLIPS> (plot-fuzzy-value t + nil nil (create-fuzzy-value sfage middle))

Fuzzy Value: sfage
Linguistic Value: middle (+)

```
1.00                  +
0.95                 + +
0.90
0.85             +     +
0.80
0.75
0.70
0.65             +       +
0.60
0.55
0.50
0.45           +         +
0.40
0.35
0.30
0.25           +         +
0.20
0.15
0.10         +             +
0.05        +               +
0.00++++++++++++          ++++++++++++++++++++++++
    |----|----|----|----|----|----|----|----|----|----|
   0.00    20.00    40.00    60.00    80.00   100.00
```

Universe of Discourse: From   0.00 to 100.00

FuzzyCLIPS> (plot-fuzzy-value t + nil nil (create-fuzzy-value sfage young))

Fuzzy Value: sfage
Linguistic Value: young (+)

```
  1.00+++++++++++++++++
  0.95                  +
  0.90                   +
  0.85
  0.80                     +
  0.75
  0.70                      +
  0.65
  0.60
  0.55                       +
  0.50
  0.45
  0.40                         +
  0.35
  0.30
  0.25                          +
  0.20
  0.15                           +
  0.10                            +
  0.05                           +
  0.00                             +++++++++++++++++++++++++
      |----|----|----|----|----|----|----|----|----|----|
     0.00    20.00    40.00    60.00    80.00   100.00
```

Universe of Discourse: From   0.00 to 100.00

FuzzyCLIPS> (plot-fuzzy-value t + nil nil (create-fuzzy-value sfage old))

Fuzzy Value: sfage
Linguistic Value: old (+)

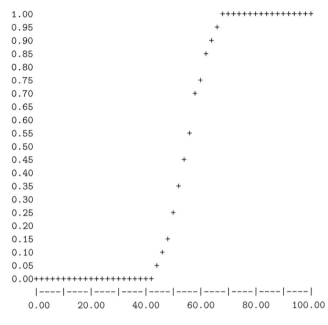

```
1.00                      +++++++++++++++++
0.95                            +
0.90                           +
0.85                          +
0.80
0.75                         +
0.70                        +
0.65
0.60
0.55                      +
0.50
0.45                    +
0.40
0.35                   +
0.30
0.25                 +
0.20
0.15               +
0.10              +
0.05             +
0.00+++++++++++++++++++++
     |----|----|----|----|----|----|----|----|----|----|
     0.00    20.00    40.00    60.00    80.00   100.00
```

Universe of Discourse: From   0.00 to 100.00

FuzzyCLIPS>

Fuzzy Set Operations

Here we consider the simple fuzzy set operations of union, intersection, and complement (not). First, consider the membership functions plotted in the following subsections for some simple fuzzy sets.

Fuzzy Sets for Low, Medium, and High Speed.

FuzzyCLIPS> (plot-fuzzy-value t + nil nil (create-fuzzy-value speed low))

Fuzzy Value: speed
Linguistic Value: low (+)

```
1.00+++++++++++++++++
0.95                 +
0.90                  +
0.85
0.80                  +
0.75
0.70                   +
0.65
0.60
0.55                    +
0.50
0.45
0.40                     +
0.35
0.30
0.25                      +
0.20
0.15                       +
0.10                        +
0.05                         +
0.00                 ++++++++++++++++++++++++++
     |----|----|----|----|----|----|----|----|----|----|
    0.00     20.00    40.00    60.00    80.00   100.00
```

Universe of Discourse: From   0.00 to 100.00

FuzzyCLIPS> (plot-fuzzy-value t + nil nil (create-fuzzy-value speed medium))

Fuzzy Value: speed
Linguistic Value: medium (+)

```
1.00                  +
0.95                +  +
0.90
0.85              +     +
0.80
0.75
0.70
0.65            +       +
0.60
0.55
0.50
0.45          +         +
0.40
0.35
0.30
0.25        +             +
0.20
0.15
0.10      +                 +
0.05    +                     +
0.00++++++++++++++        ++++++++++++++++++++++++
     |----|----|----|----|----|----|----|----|----|----|
    0.00     20.00    40.00    60.00    80.00   100.00
```

Universe of Discourse: From   0.00 to 100.00

FuzzyCLIPS> (plot-fuzzy-value t + nil nil (create-fuzzy-value speed high))

Fuzzy Value: speed
Linguistic Value: high (+)

```
 1.00                           +++++++++++++++++
 0.95                         +
 0.90                        +
 0.85                       +
 0.80
 0.75                    +
 0.70                   +
 0.65
 0.60
 0.55                 +
 0.50
 0.45               +
 0.40
 0.35             +
 0.30
 0.25           +
 0.20
 0.15         +
 0.10        +
 0.05       +
 0.00+++++++++++++++++++++
    |----|----|----|----|----|----|----|----|----|----|
   0.00    20.00    40.00    60.00    80.00    100.00
```

Universe of Discourse: From   0.00 to 100.00

Example of Fuzzy Set Union.

FuzzyCLIPS> (plot-fuzzy-value t "abc" nil nil
        (create-fuzzy-value speed low) ;; 1st set to plot
        (create-fuzzy-value speed high) ;; 2nd set to plot
        (fuzzy-union (create-fuzzy-value speed low)
                     (create-fuzzy-value speed high)) ;; 3rd set
)

Fuzzy Value: speed
Linguistic Value: low (a), high (b), [low] OR [high] (c)

```
1.00ccccccccccccccccc            ccccccccccccccccc
0.95                c              c
0.90                c              c
0.85                               c
0.80                c
0.75                             c
0.70                c           c
0.65
0.60
0.55              c       c
0.50
0.45                        c
0.40              c
0.35                    c
0.30
0.25                 c c
0.20
0.15                   c
0.10                  b a
0.05                  b   a
0.00bbbbbbbbbbbbbbbbbbbbbbbb    aaaaaaaaaaaaaaaaaaaaaaaaa
    |----|----|----|----|----|----|----|----|----|----|
    0.00    20.00    40.00    60.00    80.00    100.00
```

Universe of Discourse: From   0.00 to 100.00

Example of Fuzzy Set Intersection.

```
FuzzyCLIPS> (plot-fuzzy-value t "abc" nil nil
       (create-fuzzy-value speed low)  ;; 1st set to plot
       (create-fuzzy-value speed high) ;; 2nd set to plot
       (fuzzy-intersection (create-fuzzy-value speed low)
                 (create-fuzzy-value speed high)) ;; 3rd set
)
```

Fuzzy Value: speed
Linguistic Value: low (a), high (b), [low] AND [high] (c)

```
1.00aaaaaaaaaaaaaaaaaaa                    bbbbbbbbbbbbbbbbbbb
0.95                 a              b
0.90                 a             b
0.85                               b
0.80                 a
0.75                           b
0.70                a          b
0.65
0.60
0.55                  a          b
0.50
0.45                           b
0.40               a
0.35                        b
0.30
0.25                    a b
0.20
0.15                      c
0.10                    c c
0.05                  c     c
0.00ccccccccccccccccccccc      cccccccccccccccccccccc
    |----|----|----|----|----|----|----|----|----|----|
   0.00      20.00     40.00     60.00     80.00    100.00
```

Universe of Discourse: From   0.00 to 100.00

Example of Fuzzy Set Complement (not).

```
FuzzyCLIPS> (plot-fuzzy-value t "+-" nil nil
    (create-fuzzy-value speed low)
    (fuzzy-modify (create-fuzzy-value speed low) not)
)
```

Fuzzy Value: speed
Linguistic Value: low (+), not low (-)

```
1.00++++++++++++++++         -----------------------
0.95                +        -
0.90                +        -
0.85                         -
0.80              +
0.75                       -
0.70            +
0.65
0.60                     -
0.55              +
0.50
0.45                   -
0.40                +
0.35                   -
0.30
0.25                   +
0.20                 -
0.15                   +
0.10               -     +
0.05               -       +
0.00----------------        +++++++++++++++++++++++++
    |----|----|----|----|----|----|----|----|----|----|
    0.00     20.00    40.00    60.00    80.00    100.00
```

Universe of Discourse: From   0.00 to 100.00

Defuzzification

COG and MOM defuzzification is provided. This is shown in the examples that follow.

```
;; defuzzification of linguistic variable 'age'

;; first using piecewise linear ennumeration

(deftemplate age
 0 100 ; universe
 ( (young  (0 1) (25 1) (40 0.5) (55 0))
   (middle (0 0) (25 0.5) (40 1.0) (55 0.5) (70 0))
   (old    (0 0) (40 0) (55 0.5) (70 1) (80 1)) )
)


;; using 'standard function' representation
;; note: fuzzy sets may be different from above

(deftemplate sfage
 0 100 ; universe
 ( (young  (z 30 55))
   (middle (pi 15 40))
   (old    (s 40 70)) )
)


;; instances of entities with fuzzy attribute
;; first the fuzzy deftemplate
```

```
(deftemplate person
 (slot name)
 (slot age (type FUZZY-VALUE age))
)


;; sample rule for COG-defuzzification

(defrule age-defuzz-cog
 ?any <- (person (name ?Who) (age ?FSet))
=>
(printout t "person:  " ?Who crlf
            "has COG-defuzzified age= " (moment-defuzzify ?FSet)
            crlf crlf)
)


;; sample rule for MOM-defuzzification

(defrule age-defuzz-mom
 ?any <- (person (name ?Who) (age ?FSet))
=>
(printout t "person:  " ?Who crlf
            "has MOM-defuzzified age= " (maximum-defuzzify ?FSet)
            crlf crlf)
)


;; instances (fuzzy facts)

(deffacts startup
 (person (name bob) (age middle))
 (person (name katie) (age young))
)

FuzzyCLIPS> (load "age-defuzz.fclips")
Defining deftemplate: age
Defining deftemplate: sfage
Defining deftemplate: person
Defining defrule: age-defuzz-cog +j
Defining defrule: age-defuzz-mom +j
Defining deffacts: startup
TRUE
FuzzyCLIPS>(reset)
FuzzyCLIPS>(facts)
f-0     (initial-fact) CF 1.00
f-1     (person (name bob) (age middle)) CF 1.00
( (0.0 0.0) (25.0 0.5) (40.0 1.0) (55.0 0.5) (70.0 0.0)  )
f-2     (person (name katie) (age young)) CF 1.00
( (25.0 1.0) (40.0 0.5) (55.0 0.0)  )
For a total of 3 facts.
FuzzyCLIPS> (run)
person:  katie
has COG-defuzzified age= 20.9375

person:  katie
has MOM-defuzzified age= 12.5
```

```
person:  bob
has COG-defuzzified age= 37.82051282051282

person:  bob
has MOM-defuzzified age= 40.0
```

Implementing Fuzzy Productions in FuzzyCLIPS: Compositional Rules of Inference

In this section, we show the ability to represent and propagate uncertainty in productions. The example in Section 11.3.3 is used.

Fuzzy Production Structure. As noted in the FuzzyCLIPS Manual, productions may involve both crisp and fuzzy quantities in both the condition elements and actions. We digress to consider a less general case. A sample fuzzy production is:

$$IF\ (x\ is\ A)\ and\ (y\ is\ B)\ THEN\ z\ is\ C \tag{11.26}$$

where A and B are fuzzy set descriptors for fuzzy variables x and y and C is a fuzzy set descriptor for fuzzy variable z. Alternately, we may view the fuzzy rule or production in (11.26) as relating three fuzzy sets: the two antecedant fuzzy sets ($x\ is\ A$ and $y\ is\ B$) and the consequent fuzzy set ($z\ is\ C$). For ease of explanation, consider rewriting the fuzzy production in terms of three fuzzy sets:

$$IF\ A' \cap B'\ THEN\ C' \tag{11.27}$$

where the meaning of fuzzy sets A', B', and C' is evident.

It is reasonably clear that this fuzzy production involves conjunction of the antecedent fuzzy sets A' and B'. However, an extremely important question arises: How are fuzzy sets A' and B' unified with the contents of working memory (i.e., the facts database), and how does this result influence fuzzy set C'? The answer is easier if we first consider a further simplification, i.e., assume the situation is:

$$IF\ A'\ THEN\ C' \tag{11.28}$$

and we have fuzzy set A_f in **wm**. The new question is thus:

> *How do you unify the two fuzzy sets, namely A' and A_f, and what gets propagated to fuzzy set C'?*

Section 5.3.1.3 of the FuzzyCLIPS manual addresses this issue in general as a "FUZZY_FUZZY Simple Rule" The behaviour of the CRI used is easy to show by example.

Example of Fuzzy Set Matching. The exercises consider a fuzzy production-based card playing strategy. Suppose **wm** contains the fuzzy set (A_f) or "small chip stack." The CE to the simple fuzzy production in situation (11.28) is the fuzzy set A' or "medium chip stack." To show the effect of matching and fuzzy set propagation, we define a consequent set whose membership function is 1.0

```
;; fuzzyunify.fclips
;; to show unification of antecedent with wm

(deftemplate chipStack
 0 100 ; universe
 ( (small  (z 30 60))
   (medium (pi 15 45))
   (large  (s 30 60)) )
)

(deftemplate flatset
 0 100 ; universe
 ( (flat (0 1)) )
)

;; intersect CE fuzzy set with wm fuzzy set

(defrule unify-CE-and-wm
   (chipStack medium)  ;; intersection here
   =>
   (assert (flatset flat)) ;; observe value
)

(deffacts wmFact (chipStack small))
```

Figure 11.9 FuzzyCLIPS Source to Illustrate Fuzzy Set Matching

over the universe ("flatset" in the following example). The FuzzyCLIPS source for this example is shown in Figure 11.9.

First, we show the intersection of fuzzy sets A_f ("small chip stack") and A′ ("medium chip stack") in Figure 11.10.

Notice the $min(\mu_{A_f}, \mu_{A'}) = 0.75$. This quantity is used to scale the output membership function, yielding the overall fuzzy set propagation shown in Figure 11.11. In this case, the FuzzyCLIPS `max-min` CRI is employed.

FuzzyCLIPS provides another strategy (similar to the Mamdani rules) called `max-prod`. The FuzzyCLIPS function `set-fuzzy-inference-type` is used to control the choice of CRI.

FuzzyCLIPS Extensions for Fuzzy Productions

As shown previously, the `defrule` syntax is expanded to allow the use of fuzzy CEs in the rule antecedents. To allow propagation of fuzzy sets, the syntax of the `assert` construct is enhanced as follows:

```
(assert
                 (<crisp fact>
                 | fuzzy-variable-name <description of fuzzy set>
                 | template-name <slot-description>+
                 ) [CF <certainty factor> | <certainty factor expression>]
         )
```

```
FuzzyCLIPS> (plot-fuzzy-value t smi nil nil
  (create-fuzzy-value chipStack small)  ;; 1st plot
  (create-fuzzy-value chipStack medium) ;; and plot
(fuzzy-intersection
  (create-fuzzy-value chipStack small)
  (create-fuzzy-value chipStack medium)) ;; 3rd plot
)

Fuzzy Value: chipStack
Linguistic Value: small (s),  medium (m),  [ small ] AND [ medium ] (i)

 1.00sssssssssssssssss        m
 0.95                s     mm
 0.90                 s   m   m
 0.85                 s
 0.80
 0.75                 i     m
 0.70                 i
 0.65
 0.60
 0.55              i   i   m
 0.50
 0.45                  i
 0.40
 0.35              i     i   m
 0.30
 0.25                  i
 0.20
 0.15              i     i m
 0.10                   i
 0.05             i        im
 0.00iiiiiiiiiiiiiiiii        iiiiiiiiiiiiiiiiiiiiiii
    |----|----|----|----|----|----|----|----|----|----|
    0.00     20.00    40.00    60.00    80.00    100.00

Universe of Discourse:  From   0.00  to  100.00
```

Figure 11.10 FuzzyCLIPS Fuzzy Sets in Working Memory and Production Antecedant (with set intersection shown)

```
where
        + indicates that there are one or more <slot-description> entries and at least
        one of these is a <fuzzy-slot-description> and
where
          <fuzzy-slot-description> is of the form:
          ( fuzzy-slot-name <description of fuzzy set>)
```

Recall further that the certainty factor is optional and, if not specified, a CF of 1.0 is assumed.

Example Using Extended (Fuzzy) Productions

Consider one of the nine productions used in the example of Section 11.5, namely:

"IF temperature is cool and torque is low THEN speed is high."

```
FuzzyCLIPS> (reset)
FuzzyCLIPS> (run)
FuzzyCLIPS> (facts)
f-0     (initial-fact) CF 1.00
f-1     (chipStack small) CF 1.00
( (30.0 1.0) (33.75 0.9688) (37.5 0.875) (41.25 0.7188) (45.0 0.5)
  (48.75 0.2812) (52.5 0.125) (56.25 0.03125) (60.0 0.0)  )

f-2     (flatset ???) CF 1.00
( (0.0 0.7647)  )

For a total of 3 facts.
FuzzyCLIPS> (plot-fuzzy-value t f nil nil 2)

Fuzzy Value: flatset
Linguistic Value: ??? (f)

 1.00
 0.95
 0.90
 0.85
 0.80
 0.75ffffffffffffffffffffffffffffffffffffffffffffffffffffffffffffffff
 0.70
 0.65
 0.60
 0.55
 0.50
 0.45
 0.40
 0.35
 0.30
 0.25
 0.20
 0.15
 0.10
 0.05
 0.00
     |----|----|----|----|----|----|----|----|----|----|
    0.00    20.00   40.00   60.00   80.00   100.00

Universe of Discourse:  From   0.00  to  100.00
```

Figure 11.11 FuzzyCLIPS Sample Propagation of Fuzzy Sets in Production (11.28)

Implementation of this fuzzy production first requires definition of the linguistic variables temperature, torque, and speed and the respective fuzzy sets cool, low, and high. The FuzzyCLIPS implementation is shown in Figure 11.12. Use of this FuzzyCLIPS database is shown in Figure 11.13.

Linguistic Hedges in FuzzyCLIPS

A rich set of qualifiers on the fuzzy set are allowed, including not, somewhat, very, extremely, slightly, and more-or-less. See the FuzzyCLIPS User's Guide, Section 6.3, for more details of the

```
;; implementation example: propeller (fan) speed control
;; definitions of linguistic variables
;; using 'standard function' representation

;; file: propeller-ex.fclips

(deftemplate temperature
 0 100 ; universe
 ( (cool  (z 30 55))
   (warm  (pi 15 40))
   (hot   (s 40 70)) )
)

(deftemplate torque
 0 100 ; universe
 ( (low    (z 30 55))
   (medium (pi 15 40))
   (high   (s 40 70)) )
)

(deftemplate speed
 0 100 ; universe
 ( (low    (z 30 55))
   (medium (pi 15 40))
   (high   (s 40 70)) )
)

;; instances of entities with fuzzy attribute
;; first the fuzzy deftemplate

(deftemplate input
 (slot temp (type FUZZY-VALUE temperature))
 (slot torq (type FUZZY-VALUE torque))
)

(deftemplate output
 (slot propspeed (type FUZZY-VALUE speed))
)

;; Fuzzy production to propagate sets

(defrule rule1of9
 (input (temp cool) (torq low))
=>
 (assert (output (propspeed high)))
)

;; for illustration as a controller--
;; sample rule for COG-defuzzification of output

(defrule speed-defuzz-cog
 (output (propspeed ?SpeedFSet))
=>
 (printout t "output propeller speed" crlf
         "has COG-defuzzified value= " (moment-defuzzify ?SpeedFSet)
         crlf crlf)
)

;; instances (fuzzy facts)

(deffacts startup
 (input (temp cool) (torq low))
)
```

Figure 11.12 FuzzyCLIPS Partial Implementation (single fuzzy production) of Propeller Speed Control

```
FuzzyCLIPS> (load "propeller-ex.fclips")
Defining deftemplate: temperature
Defining deftemplate: torque
Defining deftemplate: speed
Defining deftemplate: input
Defining deftemplate: output
Defining defrule: rule1of9 +j
Defining defrule: speed-defuzz-cog +j
Defining deffacts: startup
TRUE
FuzzyCLIPS> (reset)
FuzzyCLIPS> (facts)
f-0     (initial-fact) CF 1.00
f-1     (input (temp cool) (torq low)) CF 1.00
( (30.0 1.0) (33.12 0.9688) (36.25 0.875) (39.38 0.7188) (42.5 0.5)
  (45.62 0.2812) (48.75 0.125) (51.88 0.03125) (55.0 0.0)  )
( (30.0 1.0) (33.12 0.9688) (36.25 0.875) (39.38 0.7188) (42.5 0.5)
  (45.62 0.2812) (48.75 0.125) (51.88 0.03125) (55.0 0.0)  )
For a total of 2 facts.
FuzzyCLIPS> (run)
output propeller speed
has COG-defuzzified value= 77.05729166666667

FuzzyCLIPS> (facts)
f-0     (initial-fact) CF 1.00
f-1     (input (temp cool) (torq low)) CF 1.00
( (30.0 1.0) (33.12 0.9688) (36.25 0.875) (39.38 0.7188) (42.5 0.5)
  (45.62 0.2812) (48.75 0.125) (51.88 0.03125) (55.0 0.0)  )
( (30.0 1.0) (33.12 0.9688) (36.25 0.875) (39.38 0.7188) (42.5 0.5)
  (45.62 0.2812) (48.75 0.125) (51.88 0.03125) (55.0 0.0)  )
f-2     (output (propspeed high)) CF 1.00
( (40.0 0.0) (43.75 0.03125) (47.5 0.125) (51.25 0.2812) (55.0 0.5)
  (58.75 0.7188) (62.5 0.875) (66.25 0.9688) (70.0 1.0)  )
For a total of 3 facts.
FuzzyCLIPS>
```

Figure 11.13 Sample Use of the FuzzyCLIPS Implementation of Figure 11.12

implementation and effect of these modifiers. Here we show examples using the fuzzy sets defined in Section 11.6.3.

```
FuzzyCLIPS> (plot-fuzzy-value t "+sve" nil nil
    (create-fuzzy-value speed normal)
    (fuzzy-modify (create-fuzzy-value speed normal) somewhat)
    (fuzzy-modify (create-fuzzy-value speed normal) very)
    (fuzzy-modify (create-fuzzy-value speed normal) extremely)
)

Fuzzy Value: speed
Linguistic Value: normal (+),  somewhat normal (s),  very normal (v),  extremely normal (e)
```

```
1.00                   e
0.95                  s s
0.90                 s    s
0.85                 +v  v+
0.80               s ee s
0.75
0.70               v    v
0.65              s+      +s
0.60               e    e
0.55
0.50            s           s
0.45            +           +
0.40            v           v
0.35
0.30          s  e      e  s
0.25            +          +
0.20            v          v
0.15         s                s
0.10          + e        e +
0.05          + v        v +
0.00eeeeeeeeeeeeeeee        eeeeeeeeeeeeeeeeeeeeeeeee
    |----|----|----|----|----|----|----|----|----|----|
    0.00    20.00    40.00    60.00    80.00    100.00
```

Universe of Discourse: From   0.00 to 100.00

　　　Linguistic hedges may also be applied in fuzzy productions, as the following example illustrates.

```
;; examples of two rules using linguistic hedges

(defrule rule1of9
 (input (temp extremely cool) (torq extremely low))
=>
 (assert (speed high))
)

(defrule rule9of9
 (input (temp extremely hot) (torq extremely high))
=>
 (assert (speed low))
)
```

Example: Fuzzy Speed Controller Using FuzzyCLIPS
Additional FuzzyCLIPS Source (Eight Additional Fuzzy Productions).

```
;; propeller (fan) speed control extended
;; all 9 of 9 fuzzy productions
;; other definitions shown previously

(defrule rule1of9
 (input (temp cool) (torq low))
=>
 (assert (output (propspeed high)))
)
```

```
(defrule rule2of9
 (input (temp cool) (torq normal))
=>
 (assert (output (propspeed high)))
)

(defrule rule3of9
 (input (temp cool) (torq high))
=>
 (assert (output (propspeed normal)))
)

(defrule rule4of9
 (input (temp warm) (torq low))
=>
 (assert (output (propspeed normal)))
)

(defrule rule5of9
 (input (temp warm) (torq normal))
=>
 (assert (output (propspeed normal)))
)

(defrule rule6of9
 (input (temp warm) (torq high))
=>
 (assert (output (propspeed low)))
)

(defrule rule7of9
 (input (temp hot) (torq low))
=>
 (assert (output (propspeed normal)))
)

(defrule rule8of9
 (input (temp hot) (torq normal))
=>
 (assert (output (propspeed low)))
)

(defrule rule9of9
 (input (temp hot) (torq high))
=>
 (assert (output (propspeed low)))
)
```

Results Using Fuzzy Controller Productions (Linguistic Input).   This implementation returns defuzzified output speed values in the format shown.

```
FuzzyCLIPS> (assert (input (temp hot) (torq high)))
FuzzyCLIPS> (facts)
```

```
f-0     (initial-fact) CF 1.00
f-1     (input (temp hot) (torq high)) CF 1.00
( (40.0 0.0) (43.75 0.03125) (47.5 0.125) (51.25 0.2812) (55.0 0.5)
  (58.75 0.7188) (62.5 0.875) (66.25 0.9688) (70.0 1.0)  )
( (40.0 0.0) (43.75 0.03125) (47.5 0.125) (51.25 0.2812) (55.0 0.5)
  (58.75 0.7188) (62.5 0.875) (66.25 0.9688) (70.0 1.0)  )
For a total of 2 facts.
FuzzyCLIPS> (run)
given the input (linguistic) conditions,
output propeller speed
has COG-defuzzified value= 29.80024563612018

... after retracting all but f-0 ...

FuzzyCLIPS> (assert (input (temp cool) (torq low)))
<Fact-11>
FuzzyCLIPS> (facts)
f-0     (initial-fact) CF 1.00
f-11    (input (temp cool) (torq low)) CF 1.00
( (30.0 1.0) (33.12 0.9688) (36.25 0.875) (39.38 0.7188) (42.5 0.5)
  (45.62 0.2812) (48.75 0.125) (51.88 0.03125) (55.0 0.0)  )
( (30.0 1.0) (33.12 0.9688) (36.25 0.875) (39.38 0.7188) (42.5 0.5)
  (45.62 0.2812) (48.75 0.125) (51.88 0.03125) (55.0 0.0)  )
For a total of 2 facts.
FuzzyCLIPS> (run)
given the input (linguistic) conditions,
has COG-defuzzified value= 64.75940123235469

... after retracting all but f-0 ...

FuzzyCLIPS> (assert (input (temp extremely hot) (torq extremely high)))
<Fact-21>
FuzzyCLIPS> (run)
given the input (linguistic) conditions,
output propeller speed
has COG-defuzzified value= 23.51899913545348

... after retracting all but f-0 ...

FuzzyCLIPS> (assert (input (temp extremely cool) (torq extremely high)))
<Fact-31>
FuzzyCLIPS> (run)
given the input (linguistic) conditions,
output propeller speed
has COG-defuzzified value= 28.66841476070781

... after retracting all but f-0 ...

FuzzyCLIPS>  (assert (input (temp extremely cool) (torq extremely low)))
<Fact-41>
FuzzyCLIPS> (run)
given the input (linguistic) conditions,
output propeller speed
has COG-defuzzified value= 67.72392471853919
```

11.7 Exercises

1. Given the FuzzyCLIPS membership functions Z, S, and PI in Section 11.6.3, show:

    (a) $Z(u, a, c) = 1 - S(u, a, c)$

    (b) $PI(u, d, b) = S(u, b - d, d), \quad u \leq b$

    (c) $PI(u, d, b) = Z(u, b, b + d), \quad b < u$

2. Using the FuzzyCLIPS implementation in Section 11.6.3, implement the remaining eight rules from the propeller speed control example of Section 11.5.

3. Modify the FuzzyCLIPS controller in Section 11.6.3 to allow specification of crisp input, i.e., implement fuzzification.

4. Shown in Figure 11.14 are four set membership functions. Which are NOT fuzzy sets?

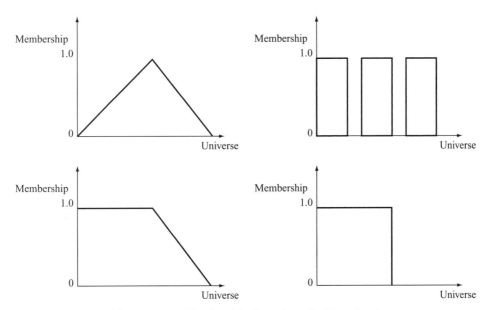

Figure 11.14 Membership Functions for Exercise 4.

5. Validating an IS designed using fuzzy approaches raises a number of issues. After some research, pose some fundamental questions to address validation.

6. Develop membership functions for the fuzzy sets:

    (a) "the engine is very noisy"

    (b) "the fuel mileage is poor"

7. The text noted that a plethora of defuzzification techniques exist. Define and compare each of the following approaches. Where possible, show a graph of the strategy using an arbitrary membership function. (Hint: you may find [Cox94] useful.)

   (a) The Center of Mass defuzzification method

   (b) The Far and Near Edges method

   (c) The Center of Maximums method

   (d) The Average of Support Region method

   (e) The Bisector of Area method

8. Is each of the following statements TRUE or FALSE (explain each answer)?

   ◆ **Randomness** and **uncertainty** are two different concepts.

   ◆ The **probability** that X is a Y is different from the **similarity** of X with Y.

   ◆ The measure of **whether** an event occurs is different from a measure of **the degree to which** it occurs.

   ◆ Both probability and fuzzy sets treat uncertainty numerically.

9. Probability and fuzziness also exhibit many similarities. Find three similarities.

10. Compare fuzzy systems with crisp rule-based reasoning. Begin with the general form of the rules.

11. Draw the two fuzzy sets indicated by the following FuzzyCLIPS extended `deftemplate` specification:

```
(deftemplate age ;definition of fuzzy variable 'age'
  0 120 years
( (young (25 1) (50 0))
(old (50 0) (65 1)))
)
```

12. Suppose you are building a fuzzy controller using FuzzyCLIPS and are using crisp inputs. Describe, quantitatively, how you would implement fuzzification in FuzzyCLIPS.

13. In Section 7.2.2, the CLIPS-based implementation of a part of a card game was introduced in order to show some basic CLIPS use. In this problem, we develop elements of an implementation based upon fuzzy productions.

   (a) A player's actions may be governed by the size of his/her current stack of chips. Define and implement in FuzzyCLIPS, membership functions for small, medium, and large chip stacks.

(b) An important strategy, implemented as a fuzzy production, is the player's betting strategy. Implement the following expert strategy as a FuzzyCLIPS production:

```
"IF
            I have a large stack of chips
            AND
            I have a pretty good starting hand
            AND
            I perceive my opponent is weak
            AND
            My opponent has a small stack of chips
        THEN
            I will bet a large amount"
```

Define any additional necessary fuzzy sets.

Planning in IS

12.1 Introduction

Planning is a problem-solving technique that involves determining a course (or sequence) of actions that take a system from an initial state to a desired, or goal, state.

The ability to plan is a fundamental property of intelligent behavior. For our purposes, the focus is on the *autonomous generation of plans*, to be used in applications such as intelligent agents, autonomous robots, and unmanned vehicles. In this sense, we are developing autonomous *planners*.

In this chapter, we approach planning as a heuristic-guided search procedure. Alternate viewpoints exist, including formulation of planning problems as satisfiability problems in logical representations (see Chapter 4).

For our purposes, a plan consists of a sequence of actions or operators or "agents" (the literature is not consistent). As in rule-based inference, this sequential, time-dependent, or ordered set of operators is seldom unique. Like rule-based inference, planning may be accomplished by either moving the system state from an initial state, S_i, to the goal state, S_g, using forward state propagation (FSP), or by working backward from S_g through the conditional application of operators using backward state propagation (BSP), to S_i. Parallelism in planning leads to multioperator plans, while we consider following the development of single-operator (serial) planning.

Planning problems are ubiquitous. For example, the Hubble Space Telescope uses two planning systems: a short-term system named SPSS and a long-term experiment planning system named Spike. SPSS software is used to schedule instrumentation configurations required by specific scientific experiments. Spike provides a general Constraint Satisfaction Problem (CSP)-based approach to experiment planning and scheduling, including ground-based telescope scheduling. Technical details concerning Spike are found in [JM94].

In this chapter, two simple examples are used to study planning algorithm development and complexities (search). As shown in Figure 12.1, they are a "checkerboard" path planner and a "blocks world" planner. The last two sections of the chapter show implementations in CLIPS and Soar. The reader is encouraged to review the relevant CLIPS and Soar chapters before exploring these implementations.

417

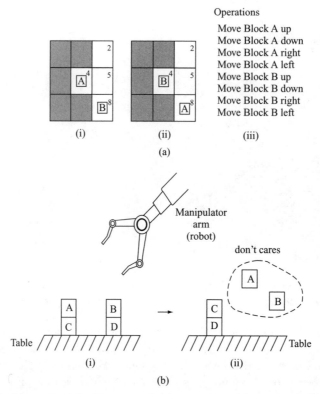

Figure 12.1 Planning Problems Used for Illustration. (a) "Checkerboard" Path Planning; (b) "Blocks-World Problem."

12.1.1 Path Planning

The first example in Figure 12.1(a) illustrates path planning [DM84], which in its most general form, involves choosing how to move several objects in two or three spatial dimensions without collisions. The scenario consists of an area containing obstacles, object(s) to be moved, and the specified goal location(s) of the object(s). A typical application is that of navigation planning for mobile robots. The shortest possible path is usually desired, with the additional constraint that a path should be acyclic.

12.1.2 Blocks World

In Figure 12.1(b) a manipulator arm is used to (perhaps using vision and tactile feedback) move blocks on a table. Given the mobility constraints of the manipulator, specification of a goal state, and specification (or autonomous recognition) of an initial situation (e.g., the present state of the blocks on the table), it is desired to generate a sequence of actions that achieve the goal state.

12.1.3 Planning Related to a Production System

Planning and rule-based inference share a number of similarities. For example, given suitable representations, both problems are often pattern-directed and involve matching to determine applicable rules or operators. In addition, considerable complexities with search usually occur. Plans may be generated with production system architectures like Soar and CLIPS.

Several significant differences also exist, namely:

◆ Problem representations for planning are often different and more complex;

◆ Planning almost always requires a revocable control strategy due to a noncommutative production system; and

◆ The strong possibility of producing conflicting subgoals due to operator interaction exist.

Planning is also closely related to a number of other topics, most significantly inference, production systems, control, temporal reasoning, the frame problem, and search.

In what follows, list form is used for both representations of "clauses" to form state descriptions and operators. Notice in this list-based formulation variables are lowercase and constants (e.g., block names) are uppercase.

12.1.4 Planning Representations

The development of a suitable problem representation is critical for planning. This representation requires:

(a) A means to describe the problem "world" or the problem state; and

(b) A means to describe how the application of an operator (an action) changes the state.

12.1.5 Representation Choice: Explicit Representation of Everything or Allowing Derivable Information

In the exploration of representation issues related to planning, often a trade-off arises—should the planning representation:

◆ Contain all the information about the current state; or

◆ Contain enough information such that other, relevant aspects of the state may be derived.

For example, if a block occupies a space, should the state representation explicitly contain (`location BlockA (10,10)`) and (`occupied (10,10)`), or just the first clause (from which the second is derivable via a separated inference computation)?

It appears there is no consensus on this topic. Soar updates `wm` with derivable information prior to conflict resolution whereas CLIPS does not.

12.1.6 The Frame Problem in Planning

The frame problem in IS involves efficiently quantifying the "persistence" of facts. Fortunately, much information is persistent. Unfortunately, it is inefficient to explicitly enumerate this persistence. Figure 12.2 provides another simple illustration of the frame problem. Movement of Block A "allows" B to "spring" into location 0, i.e., the statement (`location B 3`) is not persistent under the action of operator (`move-right A`). That is, there are two effects of operator (`move-right A`), namely the direct effect that causes (`location A 1`) and the indirect or side effect that causes (`location B 0`) (`empty 3`). Other examples are shown in Figure 12.2(b).

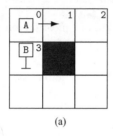

(a)

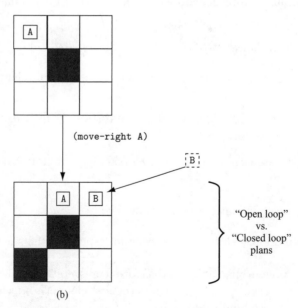

(b)

Figure 12.2 The Frame Problem—Quantifying the "Persistence" of Facts

12.1.7 Developing a Representation

Figure 12.2(a) shows a graphical example of a two-dimensional block movement problem. From this description, the initial state might be described using the clauses:

```
(occupied 0)
(location A  0)
(blocked 8)
(empty 1)
(empty 2)
   .
   .
   .
(empty 7)
```

Note that some of the information in the preceding representation is derivable, i.e., a sample rule is

```
(location A 0) ->
                (occupied 0)
```

12.1.8 Plan Generation As a Control Problem

The problem of plan generation may be visualized using the problem (familiar to many engineers) that involves control of a system or "plant." The system state is changed through the generation of input or control signals, which may be potentiometer settings, valve positions, voltages, etc., in a physical plant. Furthermore, a closed loop or "feedback" formulation is often chosen for a variety of reasons, including robustness and ease of implementation. Characterizing the discrete closed loop control approach is the use of the current system state to form the next inputs, which in turn determine the succeeding system state. Figure 12.3(a) shows the typical structure, where in Part (i) the state error, (i.e., the deviation of the current state from the goal) is used to form the next control input. A more general controller is shown in Part (ii).

For comparison, a planning production system strategy is shown in Part (b) of Figure 12.3. Note the similarity—the plan generation algorithm requires the current or present state as well as the goal state, and chooses the selected operator or action on the basis of these entities. This action, when applied (as an "input") to the system, changes the system state. In addition, the closed loop nature of the two situations in Figure 12.3 is evident.

A closed loop planning or control mechanism is not necessary in either case (a) or (b) of Figure 12.3. Rather, "open loop" strategies are possible, wherein other information is used to form inputs that adjust the system to a desired state. More importantly, in the case of the control system in 12.3(a), open loop control implies a priori knowledge that a specific input will result in a certain, known, output state. Correspondingly, in the case of the planning system, this implies the same type of a priori information, i.e., knowledge of current state, action, and future state relationships.

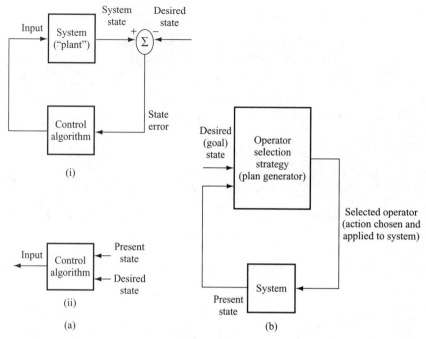

Figure 12.3 Planning and Control

12.1.9 Planning Difficulties: Local Actions and Global Objectives

One of the foremost difficulties in the development of planning strategies (that parallel that of search) stems from the fact that *planning involves a series of local actions with the objective of achieving some global objective.* Often, as in optimization problems, it is not possible to "see" the goal or reliably estimate the distance to the goal. Additionally, plans often appear to contradict intuition, in the sense that they may appear to move the system state in an incorrect or opposite direction from the goal state. An example might be found in the football running back who runs backward to avoid the defense (apparently moving farther from the end zone, or goal state). The local action of running away from the goal may seem incorrect, however, if the running back avoids the defense and scores a touchdown the goal is achieved. This example illustrates the fact that local planning may be globally inefficient. This is illustrated further by the somewhat whimsical example in Figure 12.4.

12.1.10 Cycles

In the plan generation process, it is easy for cycles to be generated. A cycle is defined as a succession of operators that move the system from some state, S_o, through one (or more) states and eventually back to S_o. For example, the successive application of operator (`pickup A`) followed by (`putdown A`) results in an obvious cycle, with no apparent benefit. Typically, cycles are not so easy to identify. In most practical applications, they serve no useful purpose. Identification of cycles requires keeping track of previously explored states.

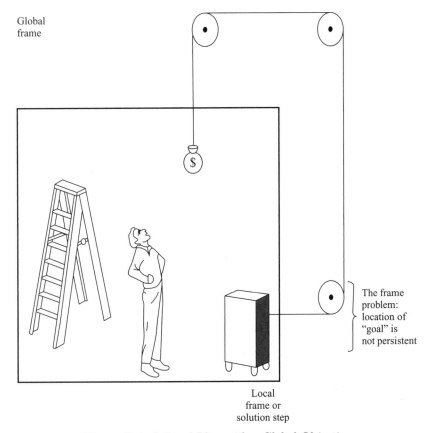

Figure 12.4 A Local Plan with a Global Objective

How Do We "Break" a Cycle?   Since a cycle may invoke the successive application of n operators and n corresponding states, once a cycle has been identified an obvious question is "where" to break the cycle. Given numerous operator selection alternatives along the path that led to the cycle, significant choice as to which decision(s) should be revised to eliminate the cycle exist. Unfortunately, except in simplistic cases, it is not possible to generally state a solution.

12.1.11 Unreachable States

Recall that planning problems typify IS difficulties in that nondeterministic algorithms result. Thus, it is quite easy to specify a problem with operators and S_i and S_g for which no possible plan exists. A related problem is that of unreachable states, as shown in Figure 12.5. The identification of impossible (i.e., unachievable) goals (and subgoals) is critical to the practical success of a planner. Impossible subgoals include those that are (i) unreachable (a path does not exist) or those that are (ii) contradictory (e.g., conflicting). As mentioned, it is desirable to check for impossible subgoals in order to avoid wasting computational resources (in the search process).

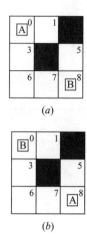

(a)

(b)

Figure 12.5 A Questionable Planning Problem (unreachable states). (a) Initial State; (b) Goal State.

12.1.12 Trade-offs

In studying the autonomous generation of planning algorithms, one noteworthy distinction is the trade-offs between *the complexity of the resulting plan vs. the complexity of the planning algorithm*. A simplistic plan generation algorithm (e.g., GAT) could implement lengthy (number of steps) and thus relatively poor plans. On the other hand, a more sophisticated search/planning algorithm (e.g., A*) might, with considerably more computational expense, generate shorter, more direct, plans.

12.2 Representation and STRIPS

STRIPS, the **S**tanford **R**esearch **I**nstitute **P**roblem **S**olver, was developed by Fikes and Nilsson in 1971 [FN71]. Whereas the formulation in [FN71] concerns both a representation and a planning algorithm, we focus on the representation here.

12.2.1 Operator Characterization in STRIPS

As mentioned, it would be quite cumbersome to develop a planning representation to enumerate, following every action, the state components that remain unchanged or are persistent. STRIPS is a planning representation wherein the clauses that are not subject to the direct effect of an action are assumed persistent. Thus, the STRIPS representation provides a solution for the frame problem by indicating state changes due to an action by specifying only which clauses in the state clauses are assumed persistent.

Specifically, each operator is characterized by the following four fields in a STRIPS representation:

1. An action descriptor, which is a statement, in words, of what the operator accomplishes. This is significant only for human understanding and documentation of the operator;

2. A set of state preconditions, in the form of clauses that must be verified prior to application of the operator;

3. A set of clause-based ("old") facts that are to be deleted from current system description following operator application, since they are no longer true; and

4. A set of clause-based ("new") facts that are to be added to the updated system description.

12.2.2 STRIPS Blocks–World Example

Consider the so-called "blocks-world" problem, introduced in Figure 12.1(b). Given an arrangement of blocks on a table (the initial state) and the availability of a manipulator arm, the problem is that of determining an appropriate sequence of manipulator arm actions such that the goal state of Figure 12.1(b) is achieved. We note immediately that this sequence of actions is unlikely to be unique, and some may be perceived as "better" than others.

Assume the horizontal relationship of blocks on the table is inconsequential, and instead concentrate on the top–bottom relationship among the blocks. Also, assume that the manipulator arm may only grasp one block at a time and that only the topmost block of a stack may be grasped. These constraints must be converted into a manipulable operator representation.

Using Figure 12.1, the system initial and goal states are quantified using a set of self-explanatory clauses entered in list form as:

```
Initial State, Si

        (on A C)
        (on B D)
        (ontable C)
        (ontable D)
        (clear A)        ;nothing on top
        (clear B)
        (empty)          ;state of the manipulator arm
```

The clause "(on x y)" is used to signify the state attribute of block x being on top of block y. The clause "(clear x)" indicates that there is not another block on top of block x, and "(empty)" signifies that the manipulator arm is empty, i.e., no block is being grasped by the arm. Similarly:

```
Goal State, Sg

        (on C D)
        (clear C)
        (ontable D)
```

Notice the goal state specification is somewhat ambiguous in that the orientation of Blocks A and B is unspecified and the arm is not constrained to be empty.

STRIPS Operator Representation for Example. The following STRIPS representation is used for operator specification.

A. Table-based block manipulation operators

    1. (pickup x)   action: picks up block x (from the table)
                          preconditions: (ontable x), (clear x), empty.
                          delete facts: (ontable x), (clear x), (empty).
                          add facts: (hold x)

    2. (putdown x)   action: puts block x down (on the table)
                          preconditions: (hold x)
                          delete facts: (hold x)
                          add facts: (ontable x), (clear x), (empty)

B. Block-based block manipulation operators

    3. (takeoff x y) action: takes block x off block y
                          preconditions: (on x y), (clear x), empty
                          delete facts: (on x y), (clear x), (empty)
                          add facts: (clear y), (hold x)

    4. (puton x y)   action: puts block x on top of block y
                          preconditions: (hold x), (clear y)
                          delete facts: (hold x), (clear y)
                          add facts: (on x y), (clear x), (empty)

12.2.3 Another Simple STRIPS (Robot) Example

The STRIPS example in Figure 12.6 was taken from [PL05].

12.3 Plan Generation Algorithms

The overall planning situation is shown in Figure 12.7. The details of any planning algorithm are related to the specific operator selection (search) methodology and related heuristics employed. We

```
Action:          Move-Arm(q₁,q₂)
preconditions:   if(X²-Y²<cos(I²-J²)-sin(I²-J²))then move-arm
Effects:         q₁ = atan(Y/X)
                 q₂ = acos((I²-J²+B²)/(2*I*B))
```

Figure 12.6 STRIPS Representation for a Robot Action

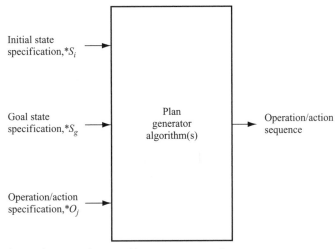

*Dependent upon chosen problem state representation

Figure 12.7 An Overall View of the Planning (plan generation) Problem

consider both forward state propagation (FSP) and backward state propagation (BSP) approaches. We show several examples of the use of these algorithms.

12.3.1 Generate-and-Test

The first example shown exemplifies generate-and-test (GAT), which is a brute-force, albeit systematic, procedure to generate possible solutions. GAT, as the name implies, simply generates a possible solution path and tests its feasibility. GAT is useful only when the number of possible solutions is small, otherwise, the potential combinatorial explosion of the solution space makes the approach at best inefficient, and more likely, impractical. GAT is applicable to both forward and backward state propagation approaches.

12.3.2 An Algorithm for FSP

A skeletal algorithm in shown in Figure 12.8.

An Example. The state transitions possible are illustrated in Figure 12.9.

Planning algorithm 1: forward state propagation (FSP) without heuristics, (i.e., "generate and test")

$0(a)$, Represent initial and goal state, S_i and S_g respectively (in clause form).

$0(b)$, Represent operator (O_i) capacity as mappings of states (in clause form).

$0(c)$, Set the current state to be the initial state, S_i.

$0(d)$, Check if $S_g \subseteq S_i$. If so, no plan is necessary.

1.   Form L_0, where L_0 only contains operators O_i, whose preconditions are satisfied by S_i. If $L_0 = \emptyset$ we must backup. If no alternatives for backup exist, a path (plan) cannot be found.

2.   Choose one operator, $O_i \in L_0$ (see note 1), and tentatively form S_{i+1} resulting from the application of O_i to S_i

$3(a)$. Check for conflicting subgoals in S_{i+1}. If one or more exist, revise operator selection.

$3(b)$. Check for a cycle (see note 2)

   $a)$ IF a cycle exists, backup (note 3) to a previous state and, if possible, revise a previous operator selection.

   $b)$ IF no cycle exists, go to step 4.

4.   Check if S_g is contained in S_{i+1}. If so SUCCESS, otherwise set $S_i \leftarrow S_{i+1}$ and go to step 1.

Notes:
1. This may invoke heuristics, state-difference functions, and so on (shown later).
2. A cycle is defined as a state in which the system has been previously.
3. There exist many possible ways to do this.

Figure 12.8   FSP Algorithm

12.4 Cataloging (Remembering) and Re-Using a Plan

In this section we give a brief overview of the formation, use, and properties of *triangle tables* [FN71]. After generation of a plan, our interest in triangle tables is motivated by the following questions:

1. What has been learned in the planning process?

2. Is anything in this plan reusable?

3. Is anything in this plan extendable?

12.4.1 The Triangle Table

We employ the STRIPS operator and state representation for this section. Refer to Section 12.2.2 for the STRIPS characterization of the table and block-based operators.

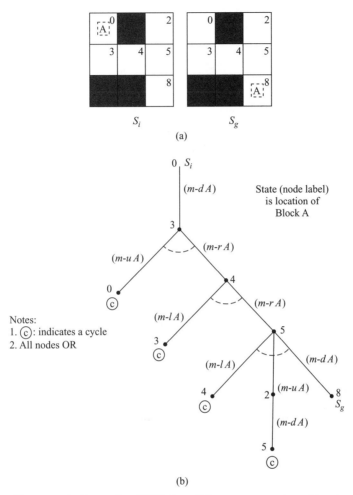

Figure 12.9 Example of FSP (possible state space transitions)

Definition

Suppose a plan consists of a sequence of p operators. A triangle table is a lower-triangular matrix consisting of $p+1$ rows and $p+1$ columns. Rows are indexed by n, where $n \in [0, \ p]$ and columns are indexed by m, where $m \in [0, \ p]$. All columns where $p > 0$ are labeled with the operator used.

Rules for Forming the Triangle Table

The table is formed recursively, beginning with cell $(0, 0)$. Figure 12.10 summarizes the rules for forming the triangle table.

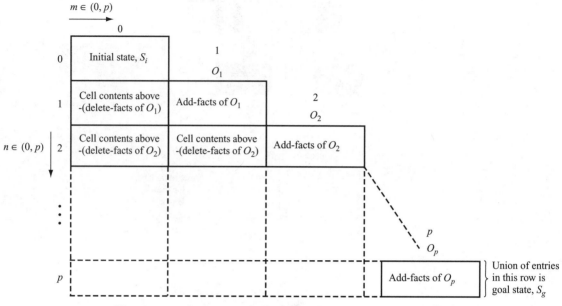

Figure 12.10   Structure and Rules for Forming a Triangle Table

12.4.2   Example: A Triangle Table for a Blocks–Moving Problem

The Plan: Graphical View and the Corresponding Triangle Table

Using the initial state in Figure 12.11 and the STRIPS operator characterization of Section 12.2.2, the triangle table is generated using the rules of Figure 12.10. The reader is encouraged to verify this table.

12.4.3   Properties and Use of the Triangle Table

The sequence of single-step or elementary operators comprising a generated plan may be viewed as yielding a composite, perhaps higher level, "macro" operator. A triangle table is a useful tool to store or catalog this resulting macro operator. However, several additional benefits arise.

Using the table generation rules of Figure 12.10, it is easily shown that the summation of the clauses in any row of the table comprises a state. Thus, the triangle table actually stores a number of "subplans," consisting of one or more operators in the sequence. Thus, a triangle table yields a library of macro or composite operators. The reader should verify this in Figure 12.12.

A second use of the triangle table is to enable a somewhat limited "reactive" agent, capable of operation in unpredictable or uncertain environments. The table allows the observed world state

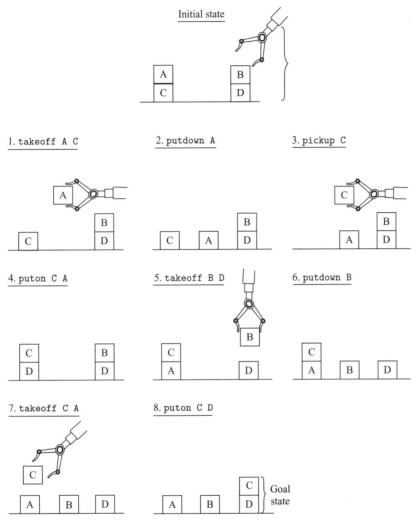

Figure 12.11 Graphical View of Blocks-Moving Plan Used for Triangle Table

resulting from application of an operator to be compared with the (predicted) table state. In this manner, unexpected changes of the real world would preclude the blind application of subsequent steps in the plan. This process is sometimes referred to as *execution monitoring*.

Additional aspects of the triangle table are left to the exercises.

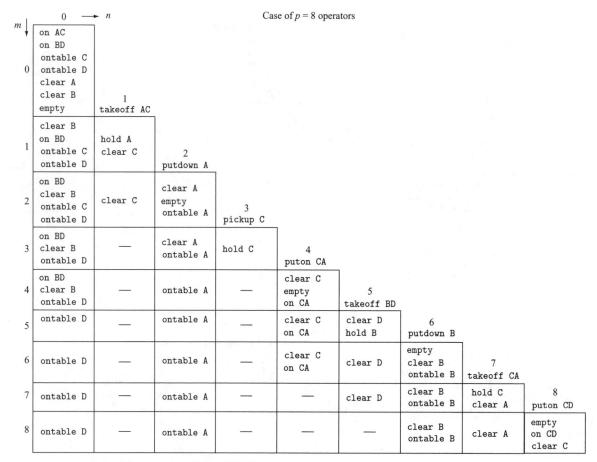

Figure 12.12 Triangle Table for Blocks-Moving Plan of Figure 12.11

12.5 Planning, Abstraction, and Subgoals

12.5.1 Details, Details, and Defeating Search Complexity

Any real-world problem domain has a potentially large (or even unmanageable) quantity of representational detail. Typically, with a high-detail or high-resolution representation, the number of possible states is large. Consequently, the search space is huge, often to the extent that the generation of a complete plan is unachievable with reasonable computational resources.

A good or even "optimal" planner typically seeks to minimize the number of operators necessary to map the initial state to the goal state. That is, the "best" plan contains the fewest steps. The search space for a given planning problem can be generated in a variety of ways. Simple planners might generate the search space by enumerating all possible states. The problem then is only to find a path, or paths, connecting the initial state to the goal state. The computational complexity of this approach leads to alternative search space considerations.

Planning systems are prone to suffer from representations with inappropriate levels of detail. Extremes range from a cumbersome amount of extraneous detail to an insufficient amount of detail. In realistic planning problems, the detailed representation that models the real-world domain is prone to produce a computationally expensive search space. Conversely, if the representation is (over) simplified to the point where the search is significantly reduced, the resulting representation often no longer adequately models the real-world problem domain. A number of planning strategies have been developed to address this situation, including planning in abstract spaces and planning with subgoals.

In this section we show the skeletal implementation of a checkerboard (path planning) planner that uses subgoals generated from abstraction space.

12.5.2 Planning in Abstraction Space

Abstraction of the planning representation is often effective in pruning the search space and thus reducing the computational complexity of the planning process [Sac74]. One approach is to plan in a simpler, "abstract" space and then *amplify* the abstract system states into higher resolution (intermediate) states that may serve as subgoals.

Abstraction

The goal of abstraction of the full-detail (concrete) representation is to reduce detail while preserving significant information necessary for plan generation. An example is shown in Figure 12.13.

Unfortunately, there are no universally applicable strategies for developing an abstract representation. Engineering judgment and often trial and error are necessary.

With an abstract state representation, abstract specification of S_i and S_g is possible. An example is shown in Figure 12.14.

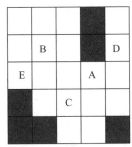
Concrete (ground space) Checkerboard Representations

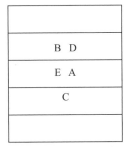
Abstract Versions of the Representation

Figure 12.13 Example of Representation Abstraction (checkerboard path planning problem)

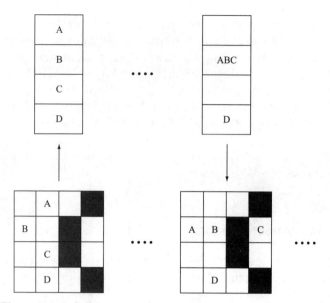

Figure 12.14 Concrete and Abstract Specification of S_i and S_g

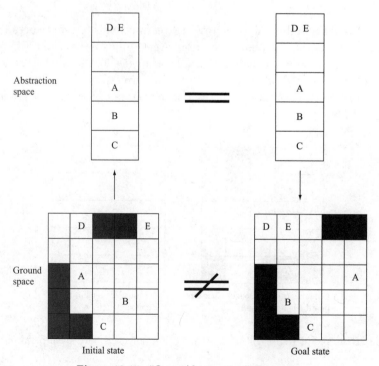

Figure 12.15 "Over-Abstraction" Example

Notice that "over-abstraction" is possible, as shown in Figure 12.15. This is considered further in the problems.

Using the Abstract Representation to Generate a Skeletal Plan

Abstract specification of S_i and S_g may be accompanied by abstraction of operators. This allows the generation of a simple plan in abstraction space comprised of a succession of abstract states from S_i to S_g.

Amplification

Amplification is, in essence, the inverse of abstraction. Using amplification, a state in the abstract representation is "amplified" in detail to form a corresponding concrete representation. Unfortunately, amplification is not a 1-to-1 mapping. In some abstractions, it is possible for an abstract state to correspond to many concrete states.

12.5.3   Planning Using Subgoals Generated from Abstract Space

Once an abstract plan, or succession of abstract states, has been generated, a number of alternatives exist to aid in generating a complete plan in the original problem domain, or "ground space." One method of utilizing abstract planning involves amplifying intermediate abstract states to corresponding ground space representations where these states can serve as subgoals. The use of subgoals prunes the search tree in the ground space and consequently guides the planning process. An example is shown in Figure 12.16.

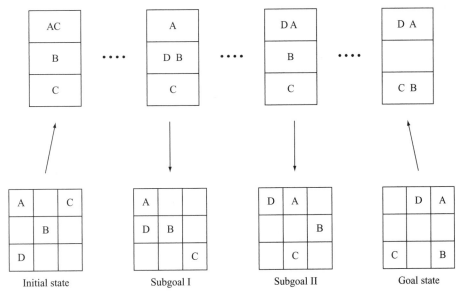

Figure 12.16 Succession of Subgoals Generated in Abstract Planning Space

12.6   Parallel Actions in Planning

12.6.1   More Is Better?

An interesting extension to our previous planning algorithms is considering the generation of plans where operators may be applied simultaneously, i.e., in parallel. Often this is referred to as multiagent or parallel planning. We explore this concept using the checkerboard example and the four operators (move-up-x), (move-down-x), (move-right-x), and (move-left-x) where x is a variable representing the name of a specific block. For example, we could attempt simultaneous application of operators (move-right-x) (move-left-x) where x takes on the values A or B. This is shown in Figure 12.17. The difficulty, which arises initially on an intuitive level, is that certain parallel combinations of operators yield illegal states, as shown in Figure 12.17. Note this is due to representation of the effect of each operator independently.

One of the obvious objectives of multioperator planning is the generation of plans that are "superior" to those that invoke only a single action at each step. Measures of "superior" might include fewer overall steps from the initial state to the goal state. This is explored in the problems.

12.6.2   Extending Operator Representations to Multiagents or Parallel Actions

To avoid the multioperator difficulty shown in Figure 12.17, we return to fundamental considerations in operator representation. Recall that an operator may be formally characterized as a relation on the system state. For example, in the system state space shown for the two-block case of Figure 12.18, consider specification of the operator (move-right-A). In specifying the system state in the relation, the shorthand (A O) is used to signify that Block A is at grid (single operator) location O.

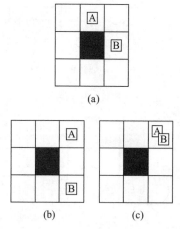

(a)

(b)   (c)

Figure 12.17 Problems in Planning with Parallel Actions

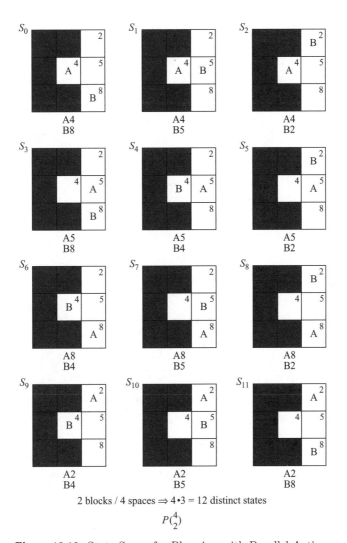

2 blocks / 4 spaces ⇒ 4·3 = 12 distinct states

$P\binom{4}{2}$

Figure 12.18 State Space for Planning with Parallel Actions

Characterization of (move-right-A) and (move-down-B) as Single Operators

(move-right-A) =

{((A4, B8), (A5, B8)), ((A4, B2), (A5, B2))}

Similarly, consider the representation of (move-down-B).

(move-down-B) =

{((A8, B2), (A8, B5)), ((A2, B5), (A2, B8)),

((A4, B5), (A4, B8)), (A4, B2), (A4, B5))}

Note in both operator characterizations, the location of the block not moved is considered persistent. In multioperator cases, this is not necessarily true.

Parallel (Extended) Representations

Consider a generalization leading to the parallel representation of (`move-right-A`):

```
(move-right-A)p =
{
((A4, B8), (A5, B8))          ; same as before B stationary
((A4, B5), (A5, B8))          ; parallel with (m-d-B)
((A4, B5), (A5, B2))          ; parallel with (m-u-B)
((A4, B2), (A5, B2))}         ; same as before
```

Similarly, a parallel representation of (`move-down-B`) is:

```
(move-down-B)p =

{((A4, B5), (A4, B8))         ; same as before
((A4, B5), (A5, B8))          ; parallel with (m-r-A)
((A4, B2), (A4, B5))          ; same as before
((A5, B2), (A8, B5))          ; parallel with (m-d-A)
((A8, B2), (A8, B5))          ; same as before
((A2, B5), (A2, B8))          ; same as before
((A2, B5), (A5, B8)           ; parallel with (m-d-A)
((A5, B2), (A4, B5))}         ; parallel with (m-l A)
```

Referring to Figure 12.18, consider the possibility of simultaneous application of the operators (`move-right-A`) and (`move-down-B`), designated with a "|":

```
(move-right-A) | (move-down-B) = {((A4, B5), (A5, B8))}
```

In this representation we assume both operators were applied. The resulting parallel operator characterization may be achieved by locating states wherein parallel operator application does not yield succeeding states that are illegal. It is significant that

```
(move-right-A) | (move-down-B) =
          intersect{(move-right-A)p,(move-down-B)p}
```

Thus, a more structured approach is to form the extended representations and use the intersection of these relations (denoted as sets) to form the parallel operator representation.

12.7 Planning Implementations in CLIPS

12.7.1 The Sample Problem

Figure 12.19 depicts the situation. We only consider Part (b) of the figure, and assume eight operators whose effect upon the system state space is somewhat obvious:

1. $move - up - x$,

2. $move - down - x$,

3. $move - left - x$, and

4. $move - right - x$

where x is the name of a block, i.e., $x \in \{A, B\}$ in Figure 12.19.

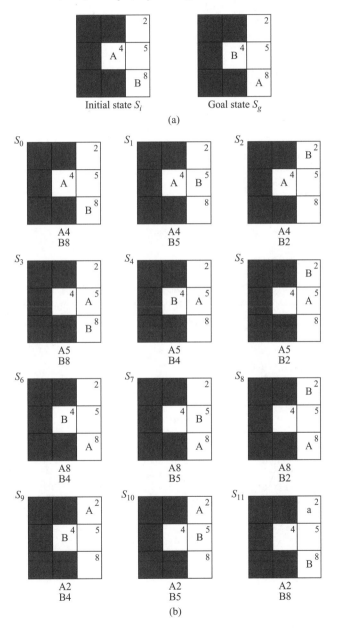

Figure 12.19 The (simplistic) "Checkerboard" Problem. (a) Sample Initial and Goal States. (b) Graphical Depiction of the 12 States.

12.7.2   The Desired Solution

The objective is to design and implement a planning algorithm for this situation in CLIPS. As shown in the following section, we choose suitable CLIPS representations for the system state and operators. We also should be able to specify initial and desired goal states and have CLIPS generate the sequence of actions and corresponding states leading to the goal state. Implementation results are shown with several examples.

12.7.3   Sample CLIPS Solutions

The First Attempt

The initial planner design in CLIPS is shown here.

```
;; file clipsplan1.clips
;; clips planner for checkerboard

;; this approach uses forward chaining

;; the concept of a cell and immediate neighbors

(deftemplate cell
          (slot name
             (allowed-symbols '0' '1' '2' '3'
                              '4' '5' '6' '7' '8'))
          (slot contents
             (allowed-symbols A B empty blocked))
)

(deftemplate neighbors
            (slot name
               (allowed-symbols '0' '1' '2' '3'
                                '4' '5' '6' '7' '8'))
            (slot left
               (allowed-symbols '0' '1' '2' '3'
                                '4' '5' '6' '7' '8' NONE))
            (slot right
               (allowed-symbols '0' '1' '2' '3'
                                '4' '5' '6' '7' '8' NONE))
            (slot up
               (allowed-symbols '0' '1' '2' '3'
                                '4' '5' '6' '7' '8' NONE))
            (slot down
               (allowed-symbols '0' '1' '2' '3'
                                '4' '5' '6' '7' '8' NONE))
)

;; contents of wm will be state

;; create initial state

(defrule create-inital-state
?Start <- (initial-fact)
```

```
  =>
  (assert (cell (name '0') (contents blocked)))
  (assert (cell (name '1') (contents blocked)))
  (assert (cell (name '2') (contents empty)))
  (assert (cell (name '3') (contents blocked)))
  (assert (cell (name '4') (contents A)))
  (assert (cell (name '5') (contents empty)))
  (assert (cell (name '6') (contents blocked)))
  (assert (cell (name '7') (contents blocked)))
  (assert (cell (name '8') (contents B)))
  (retract ?Start)
)

;; check goal state

(defrule check-goal-state
  (cell (name '0') (contents blocked))
  (cell (name '1') (contents blocked))
  (cell (name '2') (contents empty))
  (cell (name '3') (contents blocked))
  (cell (name '4') (contents B))
  (cell (name '5') (contents empty))
  (cell (name '6') (contents blocked))
  (cell (name '7') (contents blocked))
  (cell (name '8') (contents A))
  =>
  (printout t crlf
   "goal state reached" crlf)
  (halt)
)

;; sample production to show neighbors (for illustration only)

(defrule show-neighbors
  (neighbors (name ?Who) (left ?left) (right ?right)
            (up ?up) (down ?down))
  =>
  (printout t crlf
  "cell: " ?Who " has neighbors as follows:" crlf
  "left cell is: " ?left " right cell is: " ?right crlf
  "up cell is: " ?up " down cell is: " ?down crlf crlf)
  )


;; block-moving productions -- very simple
;; the following formulation is verbose, but illustrative
;; could leave block name and directions
;;        as variables (L.A.E.)

(defrule move-block-A-left
  ?Initial <- (cell (name ?Current-A) (contents A))
   (neighbors (name ?Current-A) (left ?Status))
  ?Fill <- (cell (name ?Status) (contents empty))
  =>
```

```
(printout t crlf "moving block A to " ?Status crlf)
(modify ?Initial (contents empty))
(modify ?Fill (contents A))
)

(defrule move-block-A-right
?Initial <- (cell (name ?Current-A) (contents A))
 (neighbors (name ?Current-A) (right ?Status))
?Fill <- (cell (name ?Status) (contents empty))
=>
(printout t crlf "moving block A to " ?Status crlf)
(modify ?Initial (contents empty))
(modify ?Fill (contents A))
)

(defrule move-block-A-up
?Initial <- (cell (name ?Current-A) (contents A))
 (neighbors (name ?Current-A) (up ?Status))
?Fill <- (cell (name ?Status) (contents empty))
=>
(printout t crlf "moving block A to " ?Status crlf)
(modify ?Initial (contents empty))
(modify ?Fill (contents A))
)

(defrule move-block-A-down
?Initial <- (cell (name ?Current-A) (contents A))
 (neighbors (name ?Current-A) (down ?Status))
?Fill <- (cell (name ?Status) (contents empty))
=>
(printout t crlf "moving block A to " ?Status crlf)
(modify ?Initial (contents empty))
(modify ?Fill (contents A))
)

;; block B

(defrule move-block-B-left
?Initial <- (cell (name ?Current-B) (contents B))
 (neighbors (name ?Current-B) (left ?Status))
?Fill <- (cell (name ?Status) (contents empty))
=>
(printout t crlf "moving block B to " ?Status crlf)
(modify ?Initial (contents empty))
(modify ?Fill (contents B))
)

(defrule move-block-B-right
?Initial <- (cell (name ?Current-B) (contents B))
 (neighbors (name ?Current-B) (right ?Status))
?Fill <- (cell (name ?Status) (contents empty))
=>
(printout t crlf "moving block B to " ?Status crlf)
(modify ?Initial (contents empty))
```

```
(modify ?Fill (contents B))
)

(defrule move-block-B-up
?Initial <- (cell (name ?Current-B) (contents B))
 (neighbors (name ?Current-B) (up ?Status))
?Fill <- (cell (name ?Status) (contents empty))
=>
(printout t crlf "moving block B to " ?Status crlf)
(modify ?Initial (contents empty))
(modify ?Fill (contents B))
)

(defrule move-block-B-down
?Initial <- (cell (name ?Current-B) (contents B))
 (neighbors (name ?Current-B) (down ?Status))
?Fill <- (cell (name ?Status) (contents empty))
=>
(printout t crlf "moving block B to " ?Status crlf)
(modify ?Initial (contents empty))
(modify ?Fill (contents B))
)


;; defining the checkerboard representation
;; to date, only the non-blocked cells represented
;; could extend to entire checkerboard

(deffacts layout
  (neighbors (name '2') (left NONE) (right NONE)
                        (up NONE) (down '5'))
  (neighbors (name '4') (left NONE) (right '5')
                        (up NONE) (down NONE))
  (neighbors (name '5') (left '4') (right NONE)
                        (up '2') (down '8'))
  (neighbors (name '8') (left NONE) (right NONE)
                        (up '5') (down NONE))
)
```

Results using this planner are shown here.

```
CLIPS> (load "clipsplan1.clips")
Defining deftemplate: cell
Defining deftemplate: neighbors
Defining defrule: create-inital-state +j
Defining defrule: check-goal-state +j+j+j+j+j+j+j+j
Defining defrule: show-neighbors +j
Defining defrule: move-block-A-left +j+j+j
Defining defrule: move-block-A-right =j=j+j
Defining defrule: move-block-A-up =j=j+j
Defining defrule: move-block-A-down =j=j+j
Defining defrule: move-block-B-left +j+j+j
Defining defrule: move-block-B-right =j=j+j
Defining defrule: move-block-B-up =j=j+j
Defining defrule: move-block-B-down =j=j+j
```

```
Defining deffacts: layout
TRUE
CLIPS> (reset)
CLIPS> (run 1)

cell: '8' has neighbors as follows:
left cell is: NONE right cell is: NONE
up cell is: '5' down cell is: NONE

CLIPS> (run 1)

cell: '5' has neighbors as follows:
left cell is: '4' right cell is: NONE
up cell is: '2' down cell is: '8'

CLIPS> (run 1)

cell: '4' has neighbors as follows:
left cell is: NONE right cell is: '5'
up cell is: NONE down cell is: NONE

CLIPS> (run 1)

cell: '2' has neighbors as follows:
left cell is: NONE right cell is: NONE
up cell is: NONE down cell is: '5'

CLIPS> (run 1)
CLIPS> (run 1)

moving block B to '5'
CLIPS> (run 1)

moving block B to '2'
CLIPS> (run 1)

moving block B to '5'
CLIPS> (run 1)

moving block B to '2'
CLIPS> (run 1)

moving block B to '5'
CLIPS> (run 1)

moving block B to '2'
CLIPS> (run 1)

moving block B to '5'
CLIPS> (run 1)

moving block B to '2'
CLIPS> (run 1)
```

```
moving block B to '5'
CLIPS>
```

The Second Attempt: Addressing Cycles

To avoid cycles, the CLIPS planner is modified as shown.

```
;; file clipsplan2.clips
;; clips planner for checkerboard
;; enhancements added for cycle prohibition

;; the concept of a cell and immediate neighbors

(deftemplate cell
            (slot name
                (allowed-symbols '0' '1' '2' '3'
                                 '4' '5' '6' '7' '8'))
            (slot contents
                (allowed-symbols A B empty blocked))
)

(deftemplate neighbors
              (slot name
                (allowed-symbols '0' '1' '2' '3'
                                 '4' '5' '6' '7' '8'))
              (slot left
                (allowed-symbols '0' '1' '2' '3'
                                 '4' '5' '6' '7' '8' NONE))
              (slot right
                (allowed-symbols '0' '1' '2' '3'
                                 '4' '5' '6' '7' '8' NONE))
              (slot up
                (allowed-symbols '0' '1' '2' '3'
                                 '4' '5' '6' '7' '8' NONE))
              (slot down
                (allowed-symbols '0' '1' '2' '3'
                                 '4' '5' '6' '7' '8' NONE))
)

;; for remembering the state
;; could use multivalued slot

(deftemplate priorState
   (slot whereA
     (allowed-symbols '0' '1' '2' '3'
     '4' '5' '6' '7' '8'))
   (slot whereB
     (allowed-symbols '0' '1' '2' '3'
     '4' '5' '6' '7' '8'))
)

;; contents of wm will be state
;; create initial state
```

```
(defrule create-inital-state
?Start <- (initial-fact)
=>
  (assert (cell (name '0') (contents blocked)))
  (assert (cell (name '1') (contents blocked)))
  (assert (cell (name '2') (contents empty)))
  (assert (cell (name '3') (contents blocked)))
  (assert (cell (name '4') (contents A)))
  (assert (cell (name '5') (contents empty)))
  (assert (cell (name '6') (contents blocked)))
  (assert (cell (name '7') (contents blocked)))
  (assert (cell (name '8') (contents B)))
  (assert (priorState (whereA '4') (whereB '8')))
  (retract ?Start)
)

;; check goal state

(defrule check-goal-state
  (cell (name '0') (contents blocked))
  (cell (name '1') (contents blocked))
  (cell (name '2') (contents empty))
  (cell (name '3') (contents blocked))
  (cell (name '4') (contents B))
  (cell (name '5') (contents empty))
  (cell (name '6') (contents blocked))
  (cell (name '7') (contents blocked))
  (cell (name '8') (contents A))
=>
  (printout t crlf
   "goal state reached" crlf)
  (halt)
)

;; block-moving productions
;; here we don't allow a cycle by checking
;;   and updating history via priorState

(defrule move-block-A-left
?Initial <- (cell (name ?Current-A) (contents A))
 (neighbors (name ?Current-A) (left ?Status))
?Fill <- (cell (name ?Status) (contents empty))
 (cell (name ?Bloc) (contents B))
 (not (priorState (whereA ?Status) (whereB ?Bloc)))
=>
(printout t crlf "moving block A to " ?Status crlf)
(modify ?Initial (contents empty))
(modify ?Fill (contents A))
(assert (priorState (whereA ?Status) (whereB ?Bloc)))
)

(defrule move-block-A-right
?Initial <- (cell (name ?Current-A) (contents A))
 (neighbors (name ?Current-A) (right ?Status))
```

```
?Fill <- (cell (name ?Status) (contents empty))
 (cell (name ?Bloc) (contents B))
 (not (priorState (whereA ?Status) (whereB ?Bloc)))
=>
(printout t crlf "moving block A to " ?Status crlf)
(modify ?Initial (contents empty))
(modify ?Fill (contents A))
(assert (priorState (whereA ?Status) (whereB ?Bloc)))
)

(defrule move-block-A-up
?Initial <- (cell (name ?Current-A) (contents A))
 (neighbors (name ?Current-A) (up ?Status))
?Fill <- (cell (name ?Status) (contents empty))
 (cell (name ?Bloc) (contents B))
 (not (priorState (whereA ?Status) (whereB ?Bloc)))
=>
(printout t crlf "moving block A to " ?Status crlf)
(modify ?Initial (contents empty))
(modify ?Fill (contents A))
(assert (priorState (whereA ?Status) (whereB ?Bloc)))
)

(defrule move-block-A-down
?Initial <- (cell (name ?Current-A) (contents A))
 (neighbors (name ?Current-A) (down ?Status))
?Fill <- (cell (name ?Status) (contents empty))
 (cell (name ?Bloc) (contents B))
 (not (priorState (whereA ?Status) (whereB ?Bloc)))
=>
(printout t crlf "moving block A to " ?Status crlf)
(modify ?Initial (contents empty))
(modify ?Fill (contents A))
(assert (priorState (whereA ?Status) (whereB ?Bloc)))
)

;; block B

(defrule move-block-B-left
?Initial <- (cell (name ?Current-B) (contents B))
 (neighbors (name ?Current-B) (left ?Status))
?Fill <- (cell (name ?Status) (contents empty))
 (cell (name ?Aloc) (contents A))
 (not (priorState (whereA ?Aloc) (whereB ?Status)))
=>
(printout t crlf "moving block B to " ?Status crlf)
(modify ?Initial (contents empty))
(modify ?Fill (contents B))
(assert (priorState (whereA ?Aloc) (whereB ?Status)))
)

(defrule move-block-B-right
?Initial <- (cell (name ?Current-B) (contents B))
 (neighbors (name ?Current-B) (right ?Status))
```

```
?Fill <- (cell (name ?Status) (contents empty))
 (cell (name ?Aloc) (contents A))
 (not (priorState (whereA ?Aloc) (whereB ?Status)))
=>
(printout t crlf "moving block B to " ?Status crlf)
(modify ?Initial (contents empty))
(modify ?Fill (contents B))
(assert (priorState (whereA ?Aloc) (whereB ?Status)))
)


(defrule move-block-B-up
?Initial <- (cell (name ?Current-B) (contents B))
 (neighbors (name ?Current-B) (up ?Status))
?Fill <- (cell (name ?Status) (contents empty))
 (cell (name ?Aloc) (contents A))
 (not (priorState (whereA ?Aloc) (whereB ?Status)))
=>
(printout t crlf "moving block B to " ?Status crlf)
(modify ?Initial (contents empty))
(modify ?Fill (contents B))
(assert (priorState (whereA ?Aloc) (whereB ?Status)))
)


(defrule move-block-B-down
?Initial <- (cell (name ?Current-B) (contents B))
 (neighbors (name ?Current-B) (down ?Status))
?Fill <- (cell (name ?Status) (contents empty))
 (cell (name ?Aloc) (contents A))
 (not (priorState (whereA ?Aloc) (whereB ?Status)))
=>
(printout t crlf "moving block B to " ?Status crlf)
(modify ?Initial (contents empty))
(modify ?Fill (contents B))
(assert (priorState (whereA ?Aloc) (whereB ?Status)))
)



;; defining the checkerboard representation
;; to date, only the non-blocked cells represented
;; could extend to entire checkerboard

(deffacts layout
  (neighbors (name '2') (left NONE) (right NONE)
                        (up NONE) (down '5'))
  (neighbors (name '4') (left NONE) (right '5')
                        (up NONE) (down NONE))
  (neighbors (name '5') (left '4') (right NONE)
                        (up '2') (down '8'))
  (neighbors (name '8') (left NONE) (right NONE)
                        (up '5') (down NONE))
)
```

Results using the revised planner are shown here.

```
CLIPS> (clear)
CLIPS> (load "clipsplan2.clips")
Defining deftemplate: cell
Defining deftemplate: neighbors
Defining deftemplate: priorState
Defining defrule: create-inital-state +j
Defining defrule: check-goal-state +j+j+j+j+j+j+j+j
Defining defrule: move-block-A-left +j+j+j+j
Defining defrule: move-block-A-right =j+j+j+j
Defining defrule: move-block-A-up =j=j+j+j+j
Defining defrule: move-block-A-down =j=j+j+j
Defining defrule: move-block-B-left +j+j+j+j
Defining defrule: move-block-B-right =j=j+j+j+j
Defining defrule: move-block-B-up =j=j+j+j
Defining defrule: move-block-B-down =j=j+j+j
Defining deffacts: layout
TRUE
CLIPS> (reset)
CLIPS> (run)

moving block A to '5'

moving block A to '2'

moving block B to '5'

moving block B to '4'

moving block A to '5'

moving block A to '8'

goal state reached
CLIPS>
```

12.8 Planning Implementations Using Soar

In this section, we combine the concepts of planning and Soar. A prerequisite is a good understanding of both concepts.

Several examples of Soar planning applications (i.e., the blocks-world and eight-puzzle implementations) accompany the distribution and tutorials. In this section, we consider a different, but related, planning application.

In assessing the "quality" of our planning algorithm(s), we consider the cardinality of the state space vs. the (average) number of states explored in the generation of a plan. For the 4×4 checkerboard configuration example there are 90 possible states. If our planner takes an average of 140 (block-moving) applications to achieve the goal state, the quality is suspect. Cycles, where avoidable, are not desired in the solution.

12.8.1   A Simple "Warm-Up" Problem: Using a Single Block and a 3 × 3 Checkerboard

Problem Specification

Refer to Figure 12.9. This is the case of a single block in a 3×3 checkerboard. S_i and S_g are indicated. Cycles, where avoidable, are not desired in the solution.

We develop a Soar implementation to solve this planning problem. To facilitate structure in the solution, the following set of (self-explanatory) Soar productions is used:

```
checkerboard*propose*initialize
checkerboard*create*initial-and-desired-states
checkerboard*propose*operator*move-blockA
checkerboard*apply*operator*move-blockA
checkerboard*recognize*impasse
checkerboard-display*state
checkerboard*check*for*goal*state
```

In addition, we anticipate and handle impasses. Additional constraints include:

◆ The block must be moved into an open cell.

◆ Only moves to an adjacent or "neighbor" cell are permitted.

◆ We also inhibit an operator that moves the block back to the position it just came from, by reducing the preference on the operator. However, since this might actually be necessary, in the case of an impasse this action is allowed.

Soar Model and Solution

The structure of the Soar problem representation is a modified version of the eight-puzzle implementation. The Soar source is shown as follows.

State Representation and Initialization.

```
## 3 × 3 checkerboard problem version 3
## adds previous cell attribute to avoid repeats (cycles)
## this file creates the initial and desired states
## the OPEN and BLOCKED are redundant and derivable (elaborations)

sp {checkerboard*propose*initialize
   (state <s> ^superstate nil
           -^name)
-->
   (<s> ^operator <o> +)
   (<o> ^name initialize-checkerboard-problem)}

sp {checkerboard*create*initial-and-desired-states
   (state <s> ^operator <o>)
   (<o> ^name initialize-checkerboard-problem)
-->
   (<s> ^name checkerboard-problem
        ^current <i> ^goal <d> ^previous |nil|)
```

```
## specified initial state
   (<i> ^bindings <b0> <b1> <b2> <b3> <b4>
                  <b5> <b6> <b7> <b8>)
   (<b0> ^cell <c11> ^contents <t1>)
   (<b1> ^cell <c12> ^contents <t0>)
   (<b2> ^cell <c13> ^contents <t2>)
   (<b3> ^cell <c21> ^contents <t2>)
   (<b4> ^cell <c22> ^contents <t0>)
   (<b5> ^cell <c23> ^contents <t2>)
   (<b6> ^cell <c31> ^contents <t0>)
   (<b7> ^cell <c32> ^contents <t0>)
   (<b8> ^cell <c33> ^contents <t0>)
## cell neighbors
   (<c11> ^name c11 ^cell <c12> ^cell <c21>)
   (<c12> ^name c12 ^cell <c11> ^cell <c13> ^cell <c22>)
   (<c13> ^name c13 ^cell <c12> ^cell <c23>)
   (<c21> ^name c21 ^cell <c11> ^cell <c31> ^cell <c22>)
   (<c22> ^name c22 ^cell <c21> ^cell <c12>
          ^cell <c23> ^cell <c32>)
   (<c23> ^name c23 ^cell <c22> ^cell <c33> ^cell <c13>)
   (<c31> ^name c31 ^cell <c32> ^cell <c21>)
   (<c32> ^name c32 ^cell <c31> ^cell <c22> ^cell <c33>)
   (<c33> ^name c33 ^cell <c32> ^cell <c23>)
## cell contents
   (<t0> ^name | OPEN |)
   (<t1> ^name | blockA|)
   (<t2> ^name |BLOCKED|)
## specified goal state
   (<d>  ^bindings <d0> <d1> <d2> <d3> <d4> <d5>
                   <d6> <d7> <d8>)
   (<d0> ^cell <c11> ^contents <t0>)
   (<d1> ^cell <c12> ^contents <t0>)
   (<d2> ^cell <c13> ^contents <t2>)
   (<d3> ^cell <c21> ^contents <t2>)
   (<d4> ^cell <c22> ^contents <t0>)
   (<d5> ^cell <c23> ^contents <t2>)
   (<d6> ^cell <c31> ^contents <t0>)
   (<d7> ^cell <c32> ^contents <t0>)
   (<d8> ^cell <c33> ^contents <t1>)}
```

State Display.

```
#  'ascii art' to draw the state
#  for illustration and debugging

sp {checkerboard-display*state
   (state <s> ^name checkerboard-problem
              ^current <i>)
   (<i> ^bindings       <b0> <b1> <b2>
                        <b3> <b4> <b5>
                        <b6> <b7> <b8>)
   (<b0> ^cell.name c11 ^contents.name <n1>)
   (<b1> ^cell.name c12 ^contents.name <n2>)
   (<b2> ^cell.name c13 ^contents.name <n3>)
```

```
   (<b3> ^cell.name c21 ^contents.name <n4>)
   (<b4> ^cell.name c22 ^contents.name <n5>)
   (<b5> ^cell.name c23 ^contents.name <n6>)
   (<b6> ^cell.name c31 ^contents.name <n7>)
   (<b7> ^cell.name c32 ^contents.name <n8>)
   (<b8> ^cell.name c33 ^contents.name <n9>)
-->
   (write (crlf) |       ------------------------------|  | | (crlf) | | )
   (write |      \||  | | <n1>  | | |\||  | | <n4>  | | |\||  | | <n7>  | | |\||  | | (crlf) | | )
   (write |      \|---------\|---------\|---------\||  | | (crlf) | | )
   (write |      \||  | | <n2>  | | |\||  | | <n5>  | | |\||  | | <n8>  | | |\||  | | (crlf) | | )
   (write |      \|---------\|---------\|---------\||  | | (crlf) | | )
   (write |      \||  | | <n3>  | | |\||  | | <n6>  | | |\||  | | <n9>  | | |\||  | | (crlf) | | )
   (write |      ------------------------------|  | | (crlf) | | )}
```

Block Moving Operator and Productions.

```
## checkerboard block moving version 3
## we propagate all the matching work
##    via an elaboration of <o>


## operator proposal

sp {checkerboard*propose*operator*move-blockA
   (state <s> ^name checkerboard-problem
              ^current <i>
              ^previous <g>)
   (<i> ^bindings <b1> <b2> { <> <b1> <b2>})
   (<b1> ^cell <x> ^contents <t1>) # contents.name ?
   (<t1> ^name | blockA|) # we've found blockA
   (<x>  ^cell <y> {<y> <> <g>}) # no cycle
   (<b2> ^cell <y> {<y> <> <x>} ^contents <t2>)
   (<t2> ^name |  OPEN |) # we've found an empty neighbor
-->
   (<s> ^operator <o> +)
   (<o> ^name move-blockA ^b1 <b1> ^t1 <t1>  # save the
                          ^x <x> ^y <y>      # matching
                          ^b2 <b2> ^t2 <t2>)}


## operator application

sp {checkerboard*apply*operator*move-blockA
   (state <s> ^operator <o>
              ^name checkerboard-problem ^current <i>
              ^previous <g>)
   (<o> ^name move-blockA ^b1 <b1> ^t1 <t1>
                          ^x <x> ^y <y>
                          ^b2 <b2> ^t2 <t2>)
-->
   (<s> ^name checkerboard-problem ^current <i>
        ^previous <g> - <x>)
   (<i> ^bindings <b1> <b2>) # revise the bindings
   (<b1> ^cell <x> ^contents <t1> - <t2>) # out and in
   (<b2> ^cell <y> ^contents <t2> - <t1>)}
```

Impasses and Resolution.

```
## recognition and handling of impasses

## production to recognize impasse
## where impasse is a tie

sp {checkerboard*recognize*tie*impasse
    (state <s2> ^impasse tie ^choices multiple
                ^attribute operator ^quiescence t
                ^superstate <s>)
    (<s> ^superstate nil ^name checkerboard-problem)
-->
    (write (crlf) |Operator tie --|)
    (write (crlf) |impasse reached|)
    (write (crlf) |impasse resolution necessary| (crlf))}


## from the soar library (default.soar)

sp {default*select*indifferent-and-worst*tied
    "Indifferent an object if it leads to a tie that can not be solved."
    :default
    (state <s2> ^impasse tie ^choices multiple
                ^attribute operator ^quiescence t
                ^item <op>
                ^superstate <s>)
    (<s> ^superstate nil ^name checkerboard-problem
        ^operator <op> +)
    -->
    (<s> ^operator <op> =, < )}


## for the impasse where we paint ourselves in a corner
## and must backtrack to get out
## essentially checkerboard*propose*operator*move-blockA
## with the previous cell check (immediate cycle)
## restriction removed

sp {checkerboard*allow*previous*state
    (state <s2> ^impasse no-change ^choices none
                ^attribute state
                ^superstate <s>)
    (<s> ^superstate nil ^name checkerboard-problem
            ^current <i>) # don't check previous
    (<i> ^bindings <b1> <b2> { <> <b1> <b2>})
    (<b1> ^cell <x> ^contents <t1>) # contents.name ?
    (<t1> ^name | blockA|) # we've found blockA
    (<x>  ^cell <y>)
    (<b2> ^cell <y> {<y> <> <x>} ^contents <t2>)
    (<t2> ^name |  OPEN |) # we've found an empty neighbor
-->
    (<s> ^operator <o> +)
    (<o> ^name move-blockA ^b1 <b1> ^t1 <t1>  # save the
                           ^x <x> ^y <y>        # matching
                           ^b2 <b2> ^t2 <t2>)}
```

Testing for the Goal State.

```
# testing for goal state

sp {checkerboard*check*for*goal*state
   (state <s> ^name checkerboard-problem
              ^current <i> ^goal <d>)
   (<i> ^bindings <x11> <x12> <x13>
                  <x21> <x22> <x23>
                  <x31> <x32> <x33>)
   (<x11> ^cell.name c11 ^contents <o11>)
   (<x12> ^cell.name c12 ^contents <o12>)
   (<x13> ^cell.name c13 ^contents <o13>)
   (<x21> ^cell.name c21 ^contents <o21>)
   (<x22> ^cell.name c22 ^contents <o22>)
   (<x23> ^cell.name c23 ^contents <o23>)
   (<x31> ^cell.name c31 ^contents <o31>)
   (<x32> ^cell.name c32 ^contents <o32>)
   (<x33> ^cell.name c33 ^contents <o33>)
   (<d> ^bindings <d11> <d12> <d13>
                  <d21> <d22> <d23>
                  <d31> <d32> <d33>)
   (<d11> ^cell.name c11 ^contents <o11>)
   (<d12> ^cell.name c12 ^contents <o12>)
   (<d13> ^cell.name c13 ^contents <o13>)
   (<d21> ^cell.name c21 ^contents <o21>)
   (<d22> ^cell.name c22 ^contents <o22>)
   (<d23> ^cell.name c23 ^contents <o23>)
   (<d31> ^cell.name c31 ^contents <o31>)
   (<d32> ^cell.name c32 ^contents <o32>)
   (<d33> ^cell.name c33 ^contents <o33>)
-->
   (<s> ^success <d>)
   (write (crlf) |Congratulations!|)
   (write (crlf) |*** You have reached the goal state ***| (crlf))
   (halt)}
```

Loading All the Soar Source Files.   To efficiently load the entire set of Soar source files, we source a file with the following contents:

```
# file to load all checkerboard sources
source initialize-checkerboard3.soar
source move-block3.soar
source state-display.soar
source impasse.soar
source goal-test.soar
```

Sample Results

The following is an abbreviated log of several runs of the Soar solution to this problem using the formulation of Section 12.8.1.

```
**** log opened ****

    0: ==>S: S1
    1:    O: O1 (initialize-checkerboard-problem)
         ------------------------------
         | blockA | BLOCKED |  OPEN   |
         |--------|---------|---------|
         |  OPEN  |  OPEN   |  OPEN   |
         |--------|---------|---------|
         | BLOCKED | BLOCKED |  OPEN  |
         ------------------------------

    2:    O: O2 (|move-blockA|)
         ------------------------------
         |  OPEN  | BLOCKED |  OPEN   |
         |--------|---------|---------|
         | blockA |  OPEN   |  OPEN   |
         |--------|---------|---------|
         | BLOCKED | BLOCKED |  OPEN  |
         ------------------------------

    3:    O: O3 (|move-blockA|)
         ------------------------------
         |  OPEN  | BLOCKED |  OPEN   |
         |--------|---------|---------|
         |  OPEN  | blockA  |  OPEN   |
         |--------|---------|---------|
         | BLOCKED | BLOCKED |  OPEN  |
         ------------------------------

    4:    O: O4 (|move-blockA|)
         ------------------------------
         |  OPEN  | BLOCKED |  OPEN   |
         |--------|---------|---------|
         |  OPEN  |  OPEN   | blockA  |
         |--------|---------|---------|
         | BLOCKED | BLOCKED |  OPEN  |
         ------------------------------

    5:    ==>S: S2 (operator tie)
Operator tie --
impasse reached
impasse resolution necessary

    6:    O: O6 (|move-blockA|)
         ------------------------------
         |  OPEN  | BLOCKED |  OPEN   |
         |--------|---------|---------|
         |  OPEN  |  OPEN   |  OPEN   |
         |--------|---------|---------|
         | BLOCKED | BLOCKED | blockA |
         ------------------------------

Congratulations!
```

```
*** You have reached the goal state ***

System halted.
All Soar WMEs have been removed.


     0: ==>S: S1
     1:    0: O1 (initialize-checkerboard-problem)
     ------------------------------
     | blockA | BLOCKED |  OPEN  |
     |--------|--------|--------|
     |  OPEN  |  OPEN  |  OPEN  |
     |--------|--------|--------|
     | BLOCKED | BLOCKED |  OPEN  |
     ------------------------------

     2:    0: O2 (|move-blockA|)
     ------------------------------
     |  OPEN  | BLOCKED |  OPEN  |
     |--------|--------|--------|
     | blockA |  OPEN  |  OPEN  |
     |--------|--------|--------|
     | BLOCKED | BLOCKED |  OPEN  |
     ------------------------------

     3:    0: O3 (|move-blockA|)
     ------------------------------
     |  OPEN  | BLOCKED |  OPEN  |
     |--------|--------|--------|
     |  OPEN  | blockA |  OPEN  |
     |--------|--------|--------|
     | BLOCKED | BLOCKED |  OPEN  |
     ------------------------------

     4:    0: O4 (|move-blockA|)
     ------------------------------
     |  OPEN  | BLOCKED |  OPEN  |
     |--------|--------|--------|
     |  OPEN  |  OPEN  | blockA |
     |--------|--------|--------|
     | BLOCKED | BLOCKED |  OPEN  |
     ------------------------------

     5:    ==>S: S2 (operator tie)
Operator tie --
impasse reached
impasse resolution necessary
```

```
 6:    O: O5 (|move-blockA|)
       -------------------------------
       |  OPEN  | BLOCKED |  blockA |
       |---------|---------|---------|
       |  OPEN  |  OPEN   |  OPEN   |
       |---------|---------|---------|
       | BLOCKED | BLOCKED |  OPEN   |
       -------------------------------


 7:    ==>S: S3 (state no-change)
 8:    O: O7 (|move-blockA|)
       -------------------------------
       |  OPEN  | BLOCKED |  OPEN   |
       |---------|---------|---------|
       |  OPEN  |  OPEN   |  blockA |
       |---------|---------|---------|
       | BLOCKED | BLOCKED |  OPEN   |
       -------------------------------


 9:    ==>S: S4 (operator tie)
Operator tie --
impasse reached
impasse resolution necessary


10:    O: O9 (|move-blockA|)
       -------------------------------
       |  OPEN  | BLOCKED |  OPEN   |
       |---------|---------|---------|
       |  OPEN  |  OPEN   |  OPEN   |
       |---------|---------|---------|
       | BLOCKED | BLOCKED |  blockA |
       -------------------------------


Congratulations!
*** You have reached the goal state ***

System halted.
**** log closed ****
```

12.8.2 More Elaborate Planning (and Soar) Using a 4 × 4 Checkerboard and Two Blocks

The Expanded Problem

We extend the planning problem of Section 12.8.1 to a larger state space and multiple blocks. These blocks are denoted blockA and blockB. Thus, the choice of operator is specific to a block (blockA or blockB). Our effort concerns the design of a solution where operator selection (or impasse resolution) is guided by one or more heuristics to achieve the goal.

Sample S_g and S_i.

The goal state is:

```
-----------------------------------------
|  blockB  |   OPEN   | BLOCKED | BLOCKED |
|----------|----------|---------|---------|
|   OPEN   | BLOCKED  |   OPEN  |   OPEN  |
|----------|----------|---------|---------|
|   OPEN   |   OPEN   |   OPEN  |   OPEN  |
|----------|----------|---------|---------|
| BLOCKED  | BLOCKED  | BLOCKED |  blockA |
-----------------------------------------
```

The initial state is:

```
-----------------------------------------
|  blockA  |   OPEN   | BLOCKED | BLOCKED |
|----------|----------|---------|---------|
|   OPEN   | BLOCKED  |   OPEN  |   OPEN  |
|----------|----------|---------|---------|
|   OPEN   |   OPEN   |   OPEN  |   OPEN  |
|----------|----------|---------|---------|
| BLOCKED  | BLOCKED  | BLOCKED |  blockB |
-----------------------------------------
```

Approach #1: Extending the "Warm-up" Formulation

The solution provided below is basically an extension of the "warm-up" formulation from Section 12.8.1, with an extension to two block-specific operators and the corresponding productions.

State Representation and Initialization in 4 × 4, Two-Block Problem.

```
## 4 × 4 checkerboard problem version
## adds previous cell to avoid repeats
## this file creates the initial and desired states
## the OPEN and BLOCKED are redundant and derivable (elaborations)

sp {checkerboard*propose*initialize
   (state <s> ^superstate nil
            -^name)
-->
   (<s> ^operator <o> +)
   (<o> ^name initialize-checkerboard-problem)}

sp {checkerboard*create*initial-and-desired-states
   (state <s> ^operator <o>)
   (<o> ^name initialize-checkerboard-problem)
```

```
-->
   (<s> ^name checkerboard-problem
         ^current <i> ^goal <d>
         ^previousA |nil| ^previousB |nil|)
## specified initial state
   (<i> ^bindings <b11> <b21> <b31> <b41>
                  <b12> <b22> <b32> <b42>
                  <b13> <b23> <b33> <b43>
                  <b14> <b24> <b34> <b44>)
   (<b11> ^cell <c11> ^contents <t1>)
   (<b21> ^cell <c21> ^contents <t0>)
   (<b31> ^cell <c31> ^contents <t2>)
   (<b41> ^cell <c41> ^contents <t2>)
   (<b12> ^cell <c12> ^contents <t0>)
   (<b22> ^cell <c22> ^contents <t2>)
   (<b32> ^cell <c32> ^contents <t0>)
   (<b42> ^cell <c42> ^contents <t0>)
   (<b13> ^cell <c13> ^contents <t0>)
   (<b23> ^cell <c23> ^contents <t0>)
   (<b33> ^cell <c33> ^contents <t0>)
   (<b43> ^cell <c43> ^contents <t0>)
   (<b14> ^cell <c14> ^contents <t2>)
   (<b24> ^cell <c24> ^contents <t2>)
   (<b34> ^cell <c34> ^contents <t2>)
   (<b44> ^cell <c44> ^contents <t3>)
## cell neighbors
   (<c11> ^name c11 ^cell <c12> ^cell <c21>)
   (<c12> ^name c12 ^cell <c11> ^cell <c13> ^cell <c22>)
   (<c13> ^name c13 ^cell <c12> ^cell <c23> ^cell <c14>)
   (<c14> ^name c14 ^cell <c13> ^cell <c24>)
   (<c21> ^name c21 ^cell <c11> ^cell <c31> ^cell <c22>)
   (<c22> ^name c22 ^cell <c12> ^cell <c21>
                    ^cell <c32> ^cell <c23>)
   (<c23> ^name c23 ^cell <c13> ^cell <c22>
                    ^cell <c33> ^cell <c24>)
   (<c24> ^name c24 ^cell <c14> ^cell <c23> ^cell <c34>)
   (<c31> ^name c31 ^cell <c21> ^cell <c41> ^cell <c32>)
   (<c32> ^name c32 ^cell <c22> ^cell <c31>
                    ^cell <c42> ^cell <c33>)
   (<c33> ^name c33 ^cell <c23> ^cell <c32>
                    ^cell <c43> ^cell <c34>)
   (<c34> ^name c34 ^cell <c24> ^cell <c33> ^cell <c44>)
   (<c41> ^name c41 ^cell <c31> ^cell <c42>)
   (<c42> ^name c42 ^cell <c32> ^cell <c41> ^cell <c43>)
   (<c43> ^name c43 ^cell <c33> ^cell <c42> ^cell <c44>)
   (<c44> ^name c44 ^cell <c34> ^cell <c43>)
## cell contents
   (<t0> ^name |  OPEN |)
   (<t1> ^name | blockA|)
   (<t2> ^name |BLOCKED|)
   (<t3> ^name | blockB|)
```

```
## specified goal state
   (<d> ^bindings <d11> <d21> <d31> <d41>
                  <d12> <d22> <d32> <d42>
                  <d13> <d23> <d33> <d43>
                  <d14> <d24> <d34> <d44>)
   (<d11> ^cell <c11> ^contents <t3>)
   (<d21> ^cell <c21> ^contents <t0>)
   (<d31> ^cell <c31> ^contents <t2>)
   (<d41> ^cell <c41> ^contents <t2>)
   (<d12> ^cell <c12> ^contents <t0>)
   (<d22> ^cell <c22> ^contents <t2>)
   (<d32> ^cell <c32> ^contents <t0>)
   (<d42> ^cell <c42> ^contents <t0>)
   (<d13> ^cell <c13> ^contents <t0>)
   (<d23> ^cell <c23> ^contents <t0>)
   (<d33> ^cell <c33> ^contents <t0>)
   (<d43> ^cell <c43> ^contents <t0>)
   (<d14> ^cell <c14> ^contents <t2>)
   (<d24> ^cell <c24> ^contents <t2>)
   (<d34> ^cell <c34> ^contents <t2>)
   (<d44> ^cell <c44> ^contents <t1>)
}
```

Moving Blocks.

```
## checkerboard block moving version for 4 × 4
## we propagate all the matching work
##    via an elaboration of <o>


## proposal

sp {checkerboard*propose*operator*move-blockA
   (state <s> ^name checkerboard-problem
              ^current <i>
              ^previousA <g>)
   (<i> ^bindings <b1> <b2> { <> <b1> <b2>})
   (<b1> ^cell <x> ^contents <t1>) # contents.name ?
   (<t1> ^name | blockA|) # we've found blockA
   (<x>  ^cell <y> {<y> <> <g>}) # no cycle
   (<b2> ^cell <y> {<y> <> <x>} ^contents <t2>)
   (<t2> ^name |  OPEN |) # we've found an empty neighbor
-->
   (<s> ^operator <o> +)
   (<o> ^name move-blockA ^b1 <b1> ^t1 <t1>  # save the
                          ^x <x> ^y <y>       # matching
                          ^b2 <b2> ^t2 <t2>)}

sp {checkerboard*propose*operator*move-blockB
   (state <s> ^name checkerboard-problem
              ^current <i>
              ^previousB <g>)
   (<i> ^bindings <b1> <b2> { <> <b1> <b2>})
   (<b1> ^cell <x> ^contents <t1>) # contents.name ?
```

```
   (<t1> ^name | blockB|) # we've found blockB
   (<x>  ^cell <y> {<y> <> <g>}) # no cycle
   (<b2> ^cell <y> {<y> <> <x>} ^contents <t2>)
   (<t2> ^name |  OPEN |) # we've found an empty neighbor
-->
   (<s> ^operator <o> +)
   (<o> ^name move-blockB ^b1 <b1> ^t1 <t1>  # save the
                          ^x <x> ^y <y>       # matching
                          ^b2 <b2> ^t2 <t2>)}

## application

sp {checkerboard*apply*operator*move-blockA
   (state <s> ^operator <o>
              ^name checkerboard-problem ^current <i>
              ^previousA <g>)
   (<o> ^name move-blockA ^b1 <b1> ^t1 <t1>
                          ^x <x> ^y <y>
                          ^b2 <b2> ^t2 <t2>)
-->
   (<s> ^name checkerboard-problem ^current <i>
        ^previousA <g> - <x>)
   (<i> ^bindings <b1> <b2>) # revise the bindings
   (<b1> ^cell <x> ^contents <t1> - <t2>) # out and in
   (<b2> ^cell <y> ^contents <t2> - <t1>)}

sp {checkerboard*apply*operator*move-blockB
   (state <s> ^operator <o>
              ^name checkerboard-problem ^current <i>
              ^previousB <g>)
   (<o> ^name move-blockB ^b1 <b1> ^t1 <t1>
                          ^x <x> ^y <y>
                          ^b2 <b2> ^t2 <t2>)
-->
   (<s> ^name checkerboard-problem ^current <i>
        ^previousB <g> - <x>)
   (<i> ^bindings <b1> <b2>) # revise the bindings
   (<b1> ^cell <x> ^contents <t1> - <t2>) # out and in
   (<b2> ^cell <y> ^contents <t2> - <t1>)}
```

Expanded State Display.

```
## 'ascii art' to draw the 4 × 4 state(s)
## for illustration and debugging

## current state

sp {checkerboard-display*current*state
   (state <s> ^name checkerboard-problem
              ^current <i>)
   (<i> ^bindings    <b0> <b1> <b2> <b3>
                     <b4> <b5> <b6> <b7>
                     <b8> <b9> <b10> <b11>
                     <b12> <b13> <b14> <b15>)
   (<b0> ^cell.name c11 ^contents.name <n1>)
   (<b1> ^cell.name c12 ^contents.name <n2>)
   (<b2> ^cell.name c13 ^contents.name <n3>)
   (<b3> ^cell.name c14 ^contents.name <n4>)
   (<b4> ^cell.name c21 ^contents.name <n5>)
```

```
      (<b5> ^cell.name c22 ^contents.name <n6>)
      (<b6> ^cell.name c23 ^contents.name <n7>)
      (<b7> ^cell.name c24 ^contents.name <n8>)
      (<b8> ^cell.name c31 ^contents.name <n9>)
      (<b9> ^cell.name c32 ^contents.name <n10>)
      (<b10> ^cell.name c33 ^contents.name <n11>)
      (<b11> ^cell.name c34 ^contents.name <n12>)
      (<b12> ^cell.name c41 ^contents.name <n13>)
      (<b13> ^cell.name c42 ^contents.name <n14>)
      (<b14> ^cell.name c43 ^contents.name <n15>)
      (<b15> ^cell.name c44 ^contents.name <n16>)
-->
      (write (crlf) |The current state is:| (crlf))
      (write (crlf) |      --------------------------------------|  | | (crlf) | | )
      (write |      \||  | | <n1>  | | |\||  | | <n5>  | | |\||  | | <n9>  | | |\||  | | <n13>  | | |\||  | | (crlf) | | )
      (write |      \|---------\|---------\|---------\|---------\||  | | (crlf) | | )
      (write |      \||  | | <n2>  | | |\||  | | <n6>  | | |\||  | | <n10>  | | |\||  | | <n14>  | | |\||  | | (crlf) | | )
      (write |      \|---------\|---------\|---------\|---------\||  | | (crlf) | | )
      (write |      \||  | | <n3>  | | |\||  | | <n7>  | | |\||  | | <n11>  | | |\||  | | <n15>  | | |\||  | | (crlf) | | )
      (write |      \|---------\|---------\|---------\|---------\||  | | (crlf) | | )
      (write |      \||  | | <n4>  | | |\||  | | <n8>  | | |\||  | | <n12>  | | |\||  | | <n16>  | | |\||  | | (crlf) | | )
      (write |      --------------------------------------|  | | (crlf) | | )
      (write (crlf))}


## for goal state

sp {checkerboard-display*goal*state
      (state <s> ^name checkerboard-problem
                 ^previousA |nil|
                 ^previousB |nil|
                 ^goal <i>)
      (<i> ^bindings        <b0> <b1> <b2> <b3>
                            <b4> <b5> <b6> <b7>
                            <b8> <b9> <b10> <b11>
                            <b12> <b13> <b14> <b15>)
      (<b0> ^cell.name c11 ^contents.name <n1>)
      (<b1> ^cell.name c12 ^contents.name <n2>)
      (<b2> ^cell.name c13 ^contents.name <n3>)
      (<b3> ^cell.name c14 ^contents.name <n4>)
      (<b4> ^cell.name c21 ^contents.name <n5>)
      (<b5> ^cell.name c22 ^contents.name <n6>)
      (<b6> ^cell.name c23 ^contents.name <n7>)
      (<b7> ^cell.name c24 ^contents.name <n8>)
      (<b8> ^cell.name c31 ^contents.name <n9>)
      (<b9> ^cell.name c32 ^contents.name <n10>)
      (<b10> ^cell.name c33 ^contents.name <n11>)
      (<b11> ^cell.name c34 ^contents.name <n12>)
      (<b12> ^cell.name c41 ^contents.name <n13>)
      (<b13> ^cell.name c42 ^contents.name <n14>)
      (<b14> ^cell.name c43 ^contents.name <n15>)
      (<b15> ^cell.name c44 ^contents.name <n16>)
-->
      (write (crlf) |The goal state is:| (crlf))
      (write (crlf) |      --------------------------------------|  | | (crlf) | | )
      (write |      \||  | | <n1>  | | |\||  | | <n5>  | | |\||  | | <n9>  | | |\||  | | <n13>  | | |\||  | | (crlf) | | )
      (write |      \|---------\|---------\|---------\|---------\||  | | (crlf) | | )
      (write |      \||  | | <n2>  | | |\||  | | <n6>  | | |\||  | | <n10>  | | |\||  | | <n14>  | | |\||  | | (crlf) | | )
      (write |      \|---------\|---------\|---------\|---------\||  | | (crlf) | | )
      (write |      \||  | | <n3>  | | |\||  | | <n7>  | | |\||  | | <n11>  | | |\||  | | <n15>  | | |\||  | | (crlf) | | )
      (write |      \|---------\|---------\|---------\|---------\||  | | (crlf) | | )
      (write |      \||  | | <n4>  | | |\||  | | <n8>  | | |\||  | | <n12>  | | |\||  | | <n16>  | | |\||  | | (crlf) | | )
      (write |      --------------------------------------|  | | (crlf) | | )
      (write (crlf))}
```

Impasse Resolution.

```
## recognition and handling of impasses

## production to recognize impasse
## where impasse is a tie

sp {checkerboard*recognize*tie*impasse
    (state <s2> ^impasse tie ^choices multiple
                ^attribute operator ^quiescencent
                ^superstate <s>)
    (<s> ^superstate nil ^name checkerboard-problem)
-->
    (write (crlf) |Operator tie --|)
    (write (crlf) |impasse reached|)
    (write (crlf) |impasse resolution necessary| (crlf))}


## from the soar library (default.soar)

sp {default*select*indifferent-and-worst*tied
    "Indifferent an object if it leads to a tie that can not be solved."
    :default
    (state <s2> ^impasse tie ^choices multiple
                ^attribute operator ^quiescencent
                ^item <op>
                ^superstate <s>)
    (<s> ^superstate nil ^name checkerboard-problem
         ^operator <op> +)
    -->
    (<s> ^operator <op> =, < )}

## for the impasse where we paint ourselves in a corner
## and must backtrack to get out
## essentially checkerboard*propose*operator*move-blockA
## with the previous cell check (immediate cycle)
## restriction removed

sp {checkerboard*allow*previous*stateA
    (state <s2> ^impasse no-change ^choices none
                ^attribute state
                ^superstate <s>)
    (<s> ^superstate nil ^name checkerboard-problem
             ^current <i>) # don't check previousX
    (<i> ^bindings <b1> <b2> { <> <b1> <b2>})
    (<b1> ^cell <x> ^contents <t1>) # contents.name ?
    (<t1> ^name | blockA|) # we've found blockA
    (<x>  ^cell <y>)
    (<b2> ^cell <y> {<y> <> <x>} ^contents <t2>)
    (<t2> ^name | OPEN |) # we've found an empty neighbor
-->
    (<s> ^operator <o> +)
    (<o> ^name move-blockA ^b1 <b1> ^t1 <t1> # save the
                           ^x <x> ^y <y>     # matching
                           ^b2 <b2> ^t2 <t2>)}
```

```
sp {checkerboard*allow*previous*stateB
   (state <s2> ^impasse no-change ^choices none
                   ^attribute state
                   ^superstate <s>)
   (<s> ^superstate nil ^name checkerboard-problem
           ^current <i>) # don't check previousX
   (<i> ^bindings <b1> <b2> { <> <b1> <b2>})
   (<b1> ^cell <x> ^contents <t1>) # contents.name ?
   (<t1> ^name | blockB|) # we've found blockA
   (<x>   ^cell <y>)
   (<b2> ^cell <y> {<y> <> <x>} ^contents <t2>)
   (<t2> ^name |  OPEN |) # we've found an empty neighbor
-->
   (<s> ^operator <o> +)
   (<o> ^name move-blockA ^b1 <b1> ^t1 <t1>  # save the
                           ^x <x> ^y <y>        # matching
                           ^b2 <b2> ^t2 <t2>)}
```

Checking for the Goal State.

```
# testing for goal state

sp {checkerboard*check*for*goal*state
   (state <s> ^name checkerboard-problem
                 ^current <i> ^goal <d>)
   (<i> ^bindings <b11> <b21> <b31> <b41>
                  <b12> <b22> <b32> <b42>
                  <b13> <b23> <b33> <b43>
                  <b14> <b24> <b34> <b44>)
   (<b11> ^cell.name c11 ^contents <t1>)
   (<b21> ^cell.name c21 ^contents <t2>)
   (<b31> ^cell.name c31 ^contents <t3>)
   (<b41> ^cell.name c41 ^contents <t4>)
   (<b12> ^cell.name c12 ^contents <t5>)
   (<b22> ^cell.name c22 ^contents <t6>)
   (<b32> ^cell.name c32 ^contents <t7>)
   (<b42> ^cell.name c42 ^contents <t8>)
   (<b13> ^cell.name c13 ^contents <t9>)
   (<b23> ^cell.name c23 ^contents <t10>)
   (<b33> ^cell.name c33 ^contents <t11>)
   (<b43> ^cell.name c43 ^contents <t12>)
   (<b14> ^cell.name c14 ^contents <t13>)
   (<b24> ^cell.name c24 ^contents <t14>)
   (<b34> ^cell.name c34 ^contents <t15>)
   (<b44> ^cell.name c44 ^contents <t16>)
## specified goal state
   (<d> ^bindings <d11> <d21> <d31> <d41>
                  <d12> <d22> <d32> <d42>
                  <d13> <d23> <d33> <d43>
                  <d14> <d24> <d34> <d44>)
   (<d11> ^cell.name c11 ^contents <t1>)
   (<d21> ^cell.name c21 ^contents <t2>)
   (<d31> ^cell.name c31 ^contents <t3>)
```

```
        (<d41> ^cell.name c41 ^contents <t4>)
        (<d12> ^cell.name c12 ^contents <t5>)
        (<d22> ^cell.name c22 ^contents <t6>)
        (<d32> ^cell.name c32 ^contents <t7>)
        (<d42> ^cell.name c42 ^contents <t8>)
        (<d13> ^cell.name c13 ^contents <t9>)
        (<d23> ^cell.name c23 ^contents <t10>)
        (<d33> ^cell.name c33 ^contents <t11>)
        (<d43> ^cell.name c43 ^contents <t12>)
        (<d14> ^cell.name c14 ^contents <t13>)
        (<d24> ^cell.name c24 ^contents <t14>)
        (<d34> ^cell.name c34 ^contents <t15>)
        (<d44> ^cell.name c44 ^contents <t16>)
-->
        (<s> ^success <d>)
        (write (crlf) |Congratulations!|)
        (write (crlf) |*** You have reached the goal state ***| (crlf))
        (halt)}
```

Sample Use.

```
0: ==>S: S1
      1:   0: O1 (initialize-checkerboard-problem)
The goal state is:

        ---------------------------------------
        | blockB |  OPEN   | BLOCKED | BLOCKED |
        |--------|---------|---------|---------|
        |  OPEN  | BLOCKED |  OPEN   |  OPEN   |
        |--------|---------|---------|---------|
        |  OPEN  |  OPEN   |  OPEN   |  OPEN   |
        |--------|---------|---------|---------|
        | BLOCKED | BLOCKED | BLOCKED | blockA |
        ---------------------------------------


The current state is:

        ---------------------------------------
        | blockA |  OPEN   | BLOCKED | BLOCKED |
        |--------|---------|---------|---------|
        |  OPEN  | BLOCKED |  OPEN   |  OPEN   |
        |--------|---------|---------|---------|
        |  OPEN  |  OPEN   |  OPEN   |  OPEN   |
        |--------|---------|---------|---------|
        | BLOCKED | BLOCKED | BLOCKED | blockB |
        ---------------------------------------


      2:    ==>S: S2 (operator tie)
Operator tie --
impasse reached
impasse resolution necessary
```

```
    3:      O: O2 (|move-blockB|)
The current state is:

        -----------------------------------------
        | blockA |   OPEN  | BLOCKED | BLOCKED |
        |---------|---------|---------|---------|
        |  OPEN  | BLOCKED |   OPEN  |   OPEN  |
        |---------|---------|---------|---------|
        |  OPEN  |   OPEN  |   OPEN  | blockB |
        |---------|---------|---------|---------|
        | BLOCKED | BLOCKED | BLOCKED |   OPEN  |
        -----------------------------------------


    4:    ==>S: S3 (operator tie)
Operator tie --
impasse reached
impasse resolution necessary

    5:      O: O6 (|move-blockB|)
The current state is:

        -----------------------------------------
        | blockA |   OPEN  | BLOCKED | BLOCKED |
        |---------|---------|---------|---------|
        |  OPEN  | BLOCKED |   OPEN  |   OPEN  |
        |---------|---------|---------|---------|
        |  OPEN  |   OPEN  | blockB |   OPEN  |
        |---------|---------|---------|---------|
        | BLOCKED | BLOCKED | BLOCKED |   OPEN  |
        -----------------------------------------


    6:    ==>S: S4 (operator tie)
Operator tie --
impasse reached
impasse resolution necessary

    7:      O: O4 (|move-blockA|)
The current state is:

        -----------------------------------------
        |  OPEN  |   OPEN  | BLOCKED | BLOCKED |
        |---------|---------|---------|---------|
        | blockA | BLOCKED |   OPEN  |   OPEN  |
        |---------|---------|---------|---------|
        |  OPEN  |   OPEN  | blockB |   OPEN  |
        |---------|---------|---------|---------|
        | BLOCKED | BLOCKED | BLOCKED |   OPEN  |
        -----------------------------------------
```

```
 8:    O: O9 (|move-blockA|)
The current state is:

    ----------------------------------------
    |  OPEN   |  OPEN   | BLOCKED | BLOCKED |
    |---------|---------|---------|---------|
    |  OPEN   | BLOCKED |  OPEN   |  OPEN   |
    |---------|---------|---------|---------|
    | blockA  |  OPEN   | blockB  |  OPEN   |
    |---------|---------|---------|---------|
    | BLOCKED | BLOCKED | BLOCKED |  OPEN   |
    ----------------------------------------


 9:    O: O10 (|move-blockA|)
The current state is:

    ----------------------------------------
    |  OPEN   |  OPEN   | BLOCKED | BLOCKED |
    |---------|---------|---------|---------|
    |  OPEN   | BLOCKED |  OPEN   |  OPEN   |
    |---------|---------|---------|---------|
    |  OPEN   | blockA  | blockB  |  OPEN   |
    |---------|---------|---------|---------|
    | BLOCKED | BLOCKED | BLOCKED |  OPEN   |
    ----------------------------------------


10:    O: O7 (|move-blockB|)
The current state is:

    ----------------------------------------
    |  OPEN   |  OPEN   | BLOCKED | BLOCKED |
    |---------|---------|---------|---------|
    |  OPEN   | BLOCKED | blockB  |  OPEN   |
    |---------|---------|---------|---------|
    |  OPEN   | blockA  |  OPEN   |  OPEN   |
    |---------|---------|---------|---------|
    | BLOCKED | BLOCKED | BLOCKED |  OPEN   |
    ----------------------------------------


11:    ==>S: S5 (operator tie)
Operator tie --
impasse reached
impasse resolution necessary

12:    O: O12 (|move-blockA|)
The current state is:
```

```
-------------------------------------------
|  OPEN   |  OPEN   | BLOCKED | BLOCKED |
|---------|---------|---------|---------|
|  OPEN   | BLOCKED |  blockB |  OPEN   |
|---------|---------|---------|---------|
|  OPEN   |  OPEN   |  blockA |  OPEN   |
|---------|---------|---------|---------|
| BLOCKED | BLOCKED | BLOCKED |  OPEN   |
-------------------------------------------
```

```
    13:    O: O13 (|move-blockA|)
The current state is:
```

```
-------------------------------------------
|  OPEN   |  OPEN   | BLOCKED | BLOCKED |
|---------|---------|---------|---------|
|  OPEN   | BLOCKED |  blockB |  OPEN   |
|---------|---------|---------|---------|
|  OPEN   |  OPEN   |  OPEN   |  blockA |
|---------|---------|---------|---------|
| BLOCKED | BLOCKED | BLOCKED |  OPEN   |
-------------------------------------------
```

```
    14:    ==>S: S6 (operator tie)
Operator tie --
impasse reached
impasse resolution necessary
```

```
    15:    O: O11 (|move-blockB|)
The current state is:
```

```
-------------------------------------------
|  OPEN   |  OPEN   | BLOCKED | BLOCKED |
|---------|---------|---------|---------|
|  OPEN   | BLOCKED |  OPEN   |  blockB |
|---------|---------|---------|---------|
|  OPEN   |  OPEN   |  OPEN   |  blockA |
|---------|---------|---------|---------|
| BLOCKED | BLOCKED | BLOCKED |  OPEN   |
-------------------------------------------
```

```
    16:    O: O15 (|move-blockA|)
The current state is:
```

```
-------------------------------------------
|  OPEN   |  OPEN   | BLOCKED | BLOCKED |
|---------|---------|---------|---------|
|  OPEN   | BLOCKED |  OPEN   |  blockB |
|---------|---------|---------|---------|
|  OPEN   |  OPEN   |  OPEN   |  OPEN   |
|---------|---------|---------|---------|
| BLOCKED | BLOCKED | BLOCKED |  blockA |
-------------------------------------------
```

```
17:    O: O16 (|move-blockB|)
The current state is:

        ----------------------------------------
        |   OPEN  |   OPEN  | BLOCKED | BLOCKED |
        |---------|---------|---------|---------|
        |   OPEN  | BLOCKED |   OPEN  |   OPEN  |
        |---------|---------|---------|---------|
        |   OPEN  |   OPEN  |   OPEN  |  blockB |
        |---------|---------|---------|---------|
        | BLOCKED | BLOCKED | BLOCKED |  blockA |
        ----------------------------------------


    18:    O: O17 (|move-blockB|)
The current state is:

        ----------------------------------------
        |   OPEN  |   OPEN  | BLOCKED | BLOCKED |
        |---------|---------|---------|---------|
        |   OPEN  | BLOCKED |   OPEN  |   OPEN  |
        |---------|---------|---------|---------|
        |   OPEN  |   OPEN  |  blockB |   OPEN  |
        |---------|---------|---------|---------|
        | BLOCKED | BLOCKED | BLOCKED |  blockA |
        ----------------------------------------


    19:    ==>S: S7 (operator tie)
Operator tie --
impasse reached
impasse resolution necessary

    20:    O: O18 (|move-blockB|)
The current state is:

        ----------------------------------------
        |   OPEN  |   OPEN  | BLOCKED | BLOCKED |
        |---------|---------|---------|---------|
        |   OPEN  | BLOCKED |  blockB |   OPEN  |
        |---------|---------|---------|---------|
        |   OPEN  |   OPEN  |   OPEN  |   OPEN  |
        |---------|---------|---------|---------|
        | BLOCKED | BLOCKED | BLOCKED |  blockA |
        ----------------------------------------
```

21:     O: O20 (|move-blockB|)
The current state is:

```
-----------------------------------------
|  OPEN   |   OPEN  | BLOCKED | BLOCKED |
|---------|---------|---------|---------|
|  OPEN   | BLOCKED |  OPEN   | blockB  |
|---------|---------|---------|---------|
|  OPEN   |   OPEN  |  OPEN   |  OPEN   |
|---------|---------|---------|---------|
| BLOCKED | BLOCKED | BLOCKED | blockA  |
-----------------------------------------
```

22:     O: O21 (|move-blockB|)
The current state is:

```
-----------------------------------------
|  OPEN   |   OPEN  | BLOCKED | BLOCKED |
|---------|---------|---------|---------|
|  OPEN   | BLOCKED |  OPEN   |  OPEN   |
|---------|---------|---------|---------|
|  OPEN   |   OPEN  |  OPEN   | blockB  |
|---------|---------|---------|---------|
| BLOCKED | BLOCKED | BLOCKED | blockA  |
-----------------------------------------
```

23:     O: O22 (|move-blockB|)
The current state is:

```
-----------------------------------------
|  OPEN   |   OPEN  | BLOCKED | BLOCKED |
|---------|---------|---------|---------|
|  OPEN   | BLOCKED |  OPEN   |  OPEN   |
|---------|---------|---------|---------|
|  OPEN   |   OPEN  | blockB  |  OPEN   |
|---------|---------|---------|---------|
| BLOCKED | BLOCKED | BLOCKED | blockA  |
-----------------------------------------
```

24:     ==>S: S8 (operator tie)
Operator tie --
impasse reached
impasse resolution necessary

25:     O: O23 (|move-blockB|)
The current state is:

```
----------------------------------------
|  OPEN   |  OPEN   | BLOCKED | BLOCKED |
|---------|---------|---------|---------|
|  OPEN   | BLOCKED |  blockB |  OPEN   |
|---------|---------|---------|---------|
|  OPEN   |  OPEN   |  OPEN   |  OPEN   |
|---------|---------|---------|---------|
| BLOCKED | BLOCKED | BLOCKED |  blockA |
----------------------------------------
```

26:     O: O25 (|move-blockB|)
The current state is:

```
----------------------------------------
|  OPEN   |  OPEN   | BLOCKED | BLOCKED |
|---------|---------|---------|---------|
|  OPEN   | BLOCKED |  OPEN   |  blockB |
|---------|---------|---------|---------|
|  OPEN   |  OPEN   |  OPEN   |  OPEN   |
|---------|---------|---------|---------|
| BLOCKED | BLOCKED | BLOCKED |  blockA |
----------------------------------------
```

27:     O: O26 (|move-blockB|)
The current state is:

```
----------------------------------------
|  OPEN   |  OPEN   | BLOCKED | BLOCKED |
|---------|---------|---------|---------|
|  OPEN   | BLOCKED |  OPEN   |  OPEN   |
|---------|---------|---------|---------|
|  OPEN   |  OPEN   |  OPEN   |  blockB |
|---------|---------|---------|---------|
| BLOCKED | BLOCKED | BLOCKED |  blockA |
----------------------------------------
```

28:     O: O27 (|move-blockB|)
The current state is:

```
----------------------------------------
|  OPEN   |  OPEN   | BLOCKED | BLOCKED |
|---------|---------|---------|---------|
|  OPEN   | BLOCKED |  OPEN   |  OPEN   |
|---------|---------|---------|---------|
|  OPEN   |  OPEN   |  blockB |  OPEN   |
|---------|---------|---------|---------|
| BLOCKED | BLOCKED | BLOCKED |  blockA |
----------------------------------------
```

```
    29:    ==>S: S9 (operator tie)
Operator tie --
impasse reached
impasse resolution necessary

    30:    O: O29 (|move-blockB|)
The current state is:


        ----------------------------------------
        |  OPEN   |  OPEN   | BLOCKED | BLOCKED |
        |---------|---------|---------|---------|
        |  OPEN   | BLOCKED |  OPEN   |  OPEN   |
        |---------|---------|---------|---------|
        |  OPEN   | blockB  |  OPEN   |  OPEN   |
        |---------|---------|---------|---------|
        | BLOCKED | BLOCKED | BLOCKED | blockA  |
        ----------------------------------------


    31:    O: O30 (|move-blockB|)
The current state is:


        ----------------------------------------
        |  OPEN   |  OPEN   | BLOCKED | BLOCKED |
        |---------|---------|---------|---------|
        |  OPEN   | BLOCKED |  OPEN   |  OPEN   |
        |---------|---------|---------|---------|
        | blockB  |  OPEN   |  OPEN   |  OPEN   |
        |---------|---------|---------|---------|
        | BLOCKED | BLOCKED | BLOCKED | blockA  |
        ----------------------------------------


    32:    O: O31 (|move-blockB|)
The current state is:


        ----------------------------------------
        |  OPEN   |  OPEN   | BLOCKED | BLOCKED |
        |---------|---------|---------|---------|
        | blockB  | BLOCKED |  OPEN   |  OPEN   |
        |---------|---------|---------|---------|
        |  OPEN   |  OPEN   |  OPEN   |  OPEN   |
        |---------|---------|---------|---------|
        | BLOCKED | BLOCKED | BLOCKED | blockA  |
        ----------------------------------------
```

```
  33:    0: 032 (|move-blockB|)
The current state is:


      ----------------------------------------
      | blockB |   OPEN  | BLOCKED | BLOCKED |
      |--------|---------|---------|---------|
      |  OPEN  | BLOCKED |   OPEN  |   OPEN  |
      |--------|---------|---------|---------|
      |  OPEN  |   OPEN  |   OPEN  |   OPEN  |
      |--------|---------|---------|---------|
      | BLOCKED | BLOCKED | BLOCKED | blockA |
      ----------------------------------------



Congratulations!
*** You have reached the goal state ***

System halted.
**** log closed ****
```

Approach #2: Holding Blocks in Goal Positions

This formulation is similar to that of the previous section, except that once a block is in the desired
goal state cell, we reduce the operator preference for moving that block. Only the moving operator-
related Soar source is shown.

```
## checkerboard block moving version for 4 × 4
## this version tries to hold a block in the goal
## state position by reduced operator preference

## proposal

sp {checkerboard*propose*operator*move-blockA
   (state <s> ^name checkerboard-problem
              ^current <i>
              ^previousA <g>)
   (<i> ^bindings <b1> <b2> { <> <b1> <b2>})
   (<b1> ^cell <x> ^contents <t1>) # contents.name ?
   (<t1> ^name | blockA|) # we've found blockA
   (<x>  ^cell <y> {<y> <> <g>}) # no cycle
   (<b2> ^cell <y> {<y> <> <x>} ^contents <t2>)
   (<t2> ^name |  OPEN |) # we've found an empty neighbor
-->
   (<s> ^operator <o> +)
   (<o> ^name move-blockA ^b1 <b1>  ^t1 <t1>  # save the
                          ^x <x> ^y <y>       # matching
                          ^b2 <b2>  ^t2 <t2>)}

sp {checkerboard*propose*operator*move-blockB
   (state <s> ^name checkerboard-problem
              ^current <i>
              ^previousB <g>)
   (<i> ^bindings <b1> <b2> { <> <b1> <b2>})
   (<b1> ^cell <x> ^contents <t1>) # contents.name ?
```

```
   (<t1> ^name | blockB|) # we've found blockB
   (<x>  ^cell <y> {<y> <> <g>}) # no cycle
   (<b2> ^cell <y> {<y> <> <x>} ^contents <t2>)
   (<t2> ^name |  OPEN |) # we've found an empty neighbor
-->
   (<s> ^operator <o> +)
   (<o> ^name move-blockB ^b1 <b1> ^t1 <t1>  # save the
                          ^x <x> ^y <y>       # matching
                          ^b2 <b2> ^t2 <t2>)}


## sample elaboration (writes only)
## to check if a block is in a goal state position

sp {checkerboard*check*for*goal*state*blockA*print
   (state <s> ^name checkerboard-problem
              ^current <i> ^goal <d>)
   (<i> ^bindings <ba>)
   (<ba> ^cell <cla> ^contents.name | blockA|)
   (<cla> ^name <what>)
   (<d> ^bindings <bg>)
   (<bg> ^cell <clg> ^contents.name | blockA|)
   (<clg> ^name <what>) ## same cell in initial and goal states
-->
   (write (crlf) |** blockA is in goal state position **| (crlf))
}


## reduce preference of any operator proposed for a block
## already in a goal state position
## *** note we may still paint ourselves into a corner

sp {checkerboard*check*for*goal*state*blockA
   (state <s> ^name checkerboard-problem
              ^current <i> ^goal <d>)
   (<i> ^bindings <ba>)
   (<ba> ^cell <cla> ^contents.name | blockA|)
   (<cla> ^name <what>)
   (<d> ^bindings <bg>)
   (<bg> ^cell <clg> ^contents.name | blockA|)
   (<clg> ^name <what>) ## blockA in same cell, initial and goal states
   (<s> ^operator <oany> +)
   (<oany> ^name move-blockA ^x <cla>)
-->
   (<s> ^operator <oany> <) # reduce preference
   (write (crlf) | blockA is in goal state position|)
   (write (crlf) | *** leave it alone ***|)}


## same for blockB

sp {checkerboard*check*for*goal*state*blockB*print
   (state <s> ^name checkerboard-problem
              ^current <i> ^goal <d>)
   (<i> ^bindings <ba>)
   (<ba> ^cell <cla> ^contents.name | blockB|)
   (<cla> ^name <what>)
```

```
    (<d> ^bindings <bg>)
    (<bg> ^cell <clb> ^contents.name | blockB|)
    (<clb> ^name <what>) ## same cell in initial and goal states
-->
    (write (crlf) |** blockB is in goal state position **| (crlf))
}

sp {checkerboard*check*for*goal*state*blockB
    (state <s> ^name checkerboard-problem
               ^current <i> ^goal <d>)
    (<i> ^bindings <ba>)
    (<ba> ^cell <clb> ^contents.name | blockB|)
    (<clb> ^name <what>)
    (<d> ^bindings <bg>)
    (<bg> ^cell <clg> ^contents.name | blockB|)
    (<clg> ^name <what>) ## same cell in initial and goal states
    (<s> ^operator <oany>)
    (<oany> ^name move-blockB ^x <clb>)
-->
    (<s> ^operator <oany> <)
    (write (crlf) | blockB is in goal state position|)
    (write (crlf) | *** leave it alone ***|)}


## application

sp {checkerboard*apply*operator*move-blockA
    (state <s> ^operator <o>
               ^name checkerboard-problem ^current <i>
               ^previousA <g>)
    (<o> ^name move-blockA ^b1 <b1> ^t1 <t1>
                           ^x <x> ^y <y>
                           ^b2 <b2> ^t2 <t2>)
-->
    (<s> ^name checkerboard-problem ^current <i>
         ^previousA <g> - <x>)
    (<i> ^bindings <b1> <b2>) # revise the bindings
    (<b1> ^cell <x> ^contents <t1> - <t2>) # out and in
    (<b2> ^cell <y> ^contents <t2> - <t1>)}



sp {checkerboard*apply*operator*move-blockB
    (state <s> ^operator <o>
               ^name checkerboard-problem ^current <i>
               ^previousB <g>)
    (<o> ^name move-blockB ^b1 <b1> ^t1 <t1>
                           ^x <x> ^y <y>
                           ^b2 <b2> ^t2 <t2>)
-->
    (<s> ^name checkerboard-problem ^current <i>
         ^previousB <g> - <x>)
    (<i> ^bindings <b1> <b2>) # revise the bindings
    (<b1> ^cell <x> ^contents <t1> - <t2>) # out and in
    (<b2> ^cell <y> ^contents <t2> - <t1>)}
```

Approach #3: Use of Distances to Guide Operator Selection (and Holding in Goal State Positions)

The planning heuristics we have employed so far include:

1. Inhibiting an operator that moves the block immediately back to the previous position.

2. Checking if a block is in the desired goal state cell.

The next extension is to compute and use the proposed next state cell distance to goal state to control operator preference. To achieve this, two-dimensional cell locations are added to the state representation and operator proposal productions compute this distance. Following this, operator preferences are adjusted based upon distance. Higher distances yield lower preferences. Only the relevant modifications are shown.

Soar State Representation Modifications to Allow Distances.

```
## 4 × 4 checkerboard problem version
## adds previous cell to avoid repeats
## this file creates the initial and desired states
## this version enables inter-cell distance computations
##  used for impasse resolution
## rjs 9-29-04
## the OPEN and BLOCKED are redundant and derivable (elaborations)

sp {checkerboard*propose*initialize
   (state <s> ^superstate nil
             -^name)
-->
   (<s> ^operator <o> +)
   (<o> ^name initialize-checkerboard-problem)}


sp {checkerboard*create*initial-and-desired-states
   (state <s> ^operator <o>)
   (<o> ^name initialize-checkerboard-problem)
-->
   (<s> ^name checkerboard-problem
        ^current <i> ^goal <d>
        ^previousA |nil| ^previousB |nil|)
## specified initial state
   (<i> ^bindings <b11> <b21> <b31> <b41>
                  <b12> <b22> <b32> <b42>
                  <b13> <b23> <b33> <b43>
                  <b14> <b24> <b34> <b44>)
   (<b11> ^cell <c11> ^contents <t1>)
   (<b21> ^cell <c21> ^contents <t0>)
   (<b31> ^cell <c31> ^contents <t2>)
   (<b41> ^cell <c41> ^contents <t2>)
   (<b12> ^cell <c12> ^contents <t0>)
   (<b22> ^cell <c22> ^contents <t2>)
   (<b32> ^cell <c32> ^contents <t0>)
   (<b42> ^cell <c42> ^contents <t0>)
   (<b13> ^cell <c13> ^contents <t0>)
   (<b23> ^cell <c23> ^contents <t0>)
```

```
    (<b33> ^cell <c33> ^contents <t0>)
    (<b43> ^cell <c43> ^contents <t0>)
    (<b14> ^cell <c14> ^contents <t2>)
    (<b24> ^cell <c24> ^contents <t2>)
    (<b34> ^cell <c34> ^contents <t2>)
    (<b44> ^cell <c44> ^contents <t3>)
## cell neighbors
    (<c11> ^name c11 ^cell <c12> ^cell <c21>)
    (<c12> ^name c12 ^cell <c11> ^cell <c13> ^cell <c22>)
    (<c13> ^name c13 ^cell <c12> ^cell <c23> ^cell <c14>)
    (<c14> ^name c14 ^cell <c13> ^cell <c24>)
    (<c21> ^name c21 ^cell <c11> ^cell <c31> ^cell <c22>)
    (<c22> ^name c22 ^cell <c12> ^cell <c21>
                    ^cell <c32> ^cell <c23>)
    (<c23> ^name c23 ^cell <c13> ^cell <c22>
                    ^cell <c33> ^cell <c24>)
    (<c24> ^name c24 ^cell <c14> ^cell <c23> ^cell <c34>)
    (<c31> ^name c31 ^cell <c21> ^cell <c41> ^cell <c32>)
    (<c32> ^name c32 ^cell <c22> ^cell <c31>
                    ^cell <c42> ^cell <c33>)
    (<c33> ^name c33 ^cell <c23> ^cell <c32>
                    ^cell <c43> ^cell <c34>)
    (<c34> ^name c34 ^cell <c24> ^cell <c33> ^cell <c44>)
    (<c41> ^name c41 ^cell <c31> ^cell <c42>)
    (<c42> ^name c42 ^cell <c32> ^cell <c41> ^cell <c43>)
    (<c43> ^name c43 ^cell <c33> ^cell <c42> ^cell <c44>)
    (<c44> ^name c44 ^cell <c34> ^cell <c43>)
## cell distances: <cjk> at ^xloc <j> ^yloc <k>
    (<c11> ^xloc 1 ^yloc 1)
    (<c12> ^xloc 1 ^yloc 2)
    (<c13> ^xloc 1 ^yloc 3)
    (<c14> ^xloc 1 ^yloc 4)
    (<c21> ^xloc 2 ^yloc 1)
    (<c22> ^xloc 2 ^yloc 2)
    (<c23> ^xloc 2 ^yloc 3)
    (<c24> ^xloc 2 ^yloc 4)
    (<c31> ^xloc 3 ^yloc 1)
    (<c32> ^xloc 3 ^yloc 2)
    (<c33> ^xloc 3 ^yloc 3)
    (<c34> ^xloc 3 ^yloc 4)
    (<c41> ^xloc 4 ^yloc 1)
    (<c42> ^xloc 4 ^yloc 2)
    (<c43> ^xloc 4 ^yloc 3)
    (<c44> ^xloc 4 ^yloc 4)
## cell contents
    (<t0> ^name |  OPEN |)
    (<t1> ^name | blockA|)
    (<t2> ^name |BLOCKED|)
    (<t3> ^name | blockB|)
## specified goal state
    (<d> ^bindings <d11> <d21> <d31> <d41>
                   <d12> <d22> <d32> <d42>
                   <d13> <d23> <d33> <d43>
                   <d14> <d24> <d34> <d44>)
```

```
   (<d11> ^cell <c11> ^contents <t3>)
   (<d21> ^cell <c21> ^contents <t0>)
   (<d31> ^cell <c31> ^contents <t2>)
   (<d41> ^cell <c41> ^contents <t2>)
   (<d12> ^cell <c12> ^contents <t0>)
   (<d22> ^cell <c22> ^contents <t2>)
   (<d32> ^cell <c32> ^contents <t0>)
   (<d42> ^cell <c42> ^contents <t0>)
   (<d13> ^cell <c13> ^contents <t0>)
   (<d23> ^cell <c23> ^contents <t0>)
   (<d33> ^cell <c33> ^contents <t0>)
   (<d43> ^cell <c43> ^contents <t0>)
   (<d14> ^cell <c14> ^contents <t2>)
   (<d24> ^cell <c24> ^contents <t2>)
   (<d34> ^cell <c34> ^contents <t2>)
   (<d44> ^cell <c44> ^contents <t1>)
}
```

Soar Operator Production Modifications with Distances.

```
## checkerboard block moving version for 4 × 4
## this version uses a distance-based heuristic
##     to resolve impasses
## also hold blocks in goal state positions
## we propagate all the matching work
##     via an elaboration of <o>


## proposal: <y> is the cell where the block would go
## we augment the operator with (distance to goal)^2
##     from here

sp {checkerboard*propose*operator*move-blockA
   (state <s> ^name checkerboard-problem
              ^current <i> ^goal <d>
              ^previousA <g>)
   (<i> ^bindings <b1> <b2> { <> <b1> <b2>})
   (<b1> ^cell <x> ^contents <t1>) # contents.name
   (<t1> ^name | blockA|) # we've found blockA
   (<x>  ^cell <y> {<y> <> <g>}) # no cycle
   (<b2> ^cell <y> {<y> <> <x>} ^contents <t2>)
   (<t2> ^name |  OPEN |) # we've found an empty neighbor
## compute distance
   (<y> ^xloc <xy> ^yloc <yy>)
   (<d> ^bindings <ba>)
   (<ba> ^cell <which> ^contents.name | blockA|)
   (<which> ^xloc <xw> ^yloc <yw>)
-->
   (<s> ^operator <o> +)
   (<o> ^name move-blockA ^b1 <b1> ^t1 <t1>  # save the
                          ^x <x> ^y <y>       # matching
                          ^b2 <b2> ^t2 <t2>)
```

```
## remember arithmetic is prefix notation
   (<o> ^sqdist (+ (*
                      (- <xy> <xw>)
                      (- <xy> <xw>))
                   (*
                      (- <yy> <yw>)
                      (- <yy> <yw>))))
## following is for illustration and debugging
   (write (crlf) |*** for operator move-block-A --->|)
   (write (crlf) |i.e., | <o> )
   (write (crlf) |for proposed next cell | <y>)
   (write (crlf) |located at | <xy> | | <yy>)
   (write (crlf) |with goal to be at | <xw> | | <yw>)
   (write (crlf) |distance squared is |
                 (+ (*
                      (- <xy> <xw>)
                      (- <xy> <xw>))
                   (*
                      (- <yy> <yw>)
                      (- <yy> <yw>))))
   (write (crlf))
}

sp {checkerboard*propose*operator*move-blockB
   (state <s> ^name checkerboard-problem
              ^current <i> ^goal <d>
              ^previousB <g>)
   (<i> ^bindings <b1> <b2> { <> <b1> <b2>})
   (<b1> ^cell <x> ^contents <t1>) # contents.name
   (<t1> ^name | blockB|) # we've found blockB
   (<x>  ^cell <y> {<y> <> <g>}) # no cycle
   (<b2> ^cell <y> {<y> <> <x>} ^contents <t2>)
   (<t2> ^name |  OPEN |) # we've found an empty neighbor
## compute distance
   (<y> ^xloc <xy> ^yloc <yy>)
   (<d> ^bindings <ba>)
   (<ba> ^cell <which> ^contents.name | blockB|)
   (<which> ^xloc <xw> ^yloc <yw>)
-->
   (<s> ^operator <o> +)
   (<o> ^name move-blockB ^b1 <b1> ^t1 <t1>  # save the
                          ^x <x> ^y <y>       # matching
                          ^b2 <b2> ^t2 <t2>)
## remember arithmetic is prefix notation
   (<o> ^sqdist (+ (*
                      (- <xy> <xw>)
                      (- <xy> <xw>))
                   (*
                      (- <yy> <yw>)
                      (- <yy> <yw>))))
## following is for illustration and debugging
   (write (crlf) |*** for operator move-block-B --->|)
   (write (crlf) |i.e., | <o> )
   (write (crlf) |for proposed next cell | <y>)
```

```
        (write (crlf) |located at | <xy> | | <yy>)
        (write (crlf) |with goal to be at | <xw> | | <yw>)
        (write (crlf) |distance squared is |
                    (+ (*
                        (- <xy> <xw>)
                        (- <xy> <xw>))
                       (*
                        (- <yy> <yw>)
                        (- <yy> <yw>))))
        (write (crlf))
}


## application of operators

sp {checkerboard*apply*operator*move-blockA
    (state <s> ^operator <o>
               ^name checkerboard-problem ^current <i>
               ^previousA <g>)
    (<o> ^name move-blockA ^b1 <b1> ^t1 <t1>
                           ^x <x> ^y <y>
                           ^b2 <b2> ^t2 <t2>)
    -->
    (<s> ^name checkerboard-problem ^current <i>
         ^previousA <g> - <x>)
    (<i> ^bindings <b1> <b2>) # revise the bindings
    (<b1> ^cell <x> ^contents <t1> - <t2>) # out and in
    (<b2> ^cell <y> ^contents <t2> - <t1>)}

sp {checkerboard*apply*operator*move-blockB
    (state <s> ^operator <o>
               ^name checkerboard-problem ^current <i>
               ^previousB <g>)
    (<o> ^name move-blockB ^b1 <b1> ^t1 <t1>
                           ^x <x> ^y <y>
                           ^b2 <b2> ^t2 <t2>)
    -->
    (<s> ^name checkerboard-problem ^current <i>
         ^previousB <g> - <x>)
    (<i> ^bindings <b1> <b2>) # revise the bindings
    (<b1> ^cell <x> ^contents <t1> - <t2>) # out and in
    (<b2> ^cell <y> ^contents <t2> - <t1>)}


## USING DISTANCE --
## distance-based operator preference modification
## the best operator has the shortest distance
## only rank within A or B
## else just tend to move one block for too long

sp {checkerboard*rank*operators
    (state <s> ^operator <o1> + ^name <opname>)
    (<s> ^operator <o2> + ^name <opname>) #same block
    (<o1> ^sqdist <do1>)
    (<o2> ^sqdist <do2> {<do2> < <do1>})
# closer
```

```
-->
## to enable trying various preference modifications
##    (<s> ^operator <o2> >)
##    (<s> ^operator <o1> -)  # best wins
##    (<s> ^operator <o2> > <o1>) # ranked
   (<s> ^operator <o1> = 50)
   (<s> ^operator <o2> = 100) # ranked indifferent


}


## the above production DOES NOT CHECK IF THE BLOCK
## TO BE MOVED IS IN THE GOAL POSITION, THEREFORE
## CHECK IF THE BLOCK IS IN THE GOAL STATE POSITION
## reduce preference of any operator applied to a block
## already in a goal state position
## *** note we may still paint ourselves into a corner

sp {checkerboard*check*for*goal*state*blockA
   (state <s> ^name checkerboard-problem
              ^current <i> ^goal <d>)
   (<i> ^bindings <ba>)
   (<ba> ^cell <cla> ^contents.name | blockA|)
   (<cla> ^name <what>)
   (<d> ^bindings <bg>)
   (<bg> ^cell <clg> ^contents.name | blockA|)
   (<clg> ^name <what>) ## A in same cell, initial and goal states
   (<s> ^operator <oany> +)
   (<oany> ^name move-blockA ^x <cla>)
-->
   (<s> ^operator <oany> <) # reduce preference
   (write (crlf) | blockA is in goal state position|)
   (write (crlf) | *** leave it alone ***|)}

sp {checkerboard*check*for*goal*state*blockB
   (state <s> ^name checkerboard-problem
              ^current <i> ^goal <d>)
   (<i> ^bindings <ba>)
   (<ba> ^cell <clb> ^contents.name | blockB|)
   (<clb> ^name <what>)
   (<d> ^bindings <bg>)
   (<bg> ^cell <clg> ^contents.name | blockB|)
   (<clg> ^name <what>) ## B insame cell, initial and goal states
   (<s> ^operator <oany> +)
   (<oany> ^name move-blockB ^x <clb>)
-->
   (<s> ^operator <oany> <)
   (write (crlf) | blockB is in goal state position|)
   (write (crlf) | *** leave it alone ***|)}
```

Approach #4: Alternating Blocks and Resolving Block–Moving Operators

One of the problems with the distance-based formulation proposed previously is that it tends to continue to move a single block toward its goal position. This would be acceptable if the path to this position, and the goal cell position itself, were OPEN. If not, it is advisable to move other blocks. For this reason, we show a formulation that alternates block movement. The use of distance and "goal state holding" is carried over to this formulation.

Soar State Representation Modifications for Alternating Block Movement.

```
## 4 × 4 checkerboard problem version
## adds previous cell to avoid repeats
## this file creates the initial and desired states
## this version enables inter-cell distance computations
## used for impasse resolution
## rjs 10-15-04
## alternates block movements

sp {checkerboard*propose*initialize
   (state <s> ^superstate nil
            -^name)
-->
   (<s> ^operator <o> +)
   (<o> ^name initialize-checkerboard-problem)}

sp {checkerboard*create*initial-and-desired-states
   (state <s> ^operator <o>)
   (<o> ^name initialize-checkerboard-problem)
-->
   (<s> ^name checkerboard-problem
        ^current <i> ^goal <d>
        ^previousA |nil| ^previousB |nil|
        ^prev-moved blockA)  # to start
## specified initial state
   (<i> ^bindings <b11> <b21> <b31> <b41>
                  <b12> <b22> <b32> <b42>
                  <b13> <b23> <b33> <b43>
                  <b14> <b24> <b34> <b44>)
   (<b11> ^cell <c11> ^contents <t1>)
   (<b21> ^cell <c21> ^contents <t0>)
   (<b31> ^cell <c31> ^contents <t2>)
   (<b41> ^cell <c41> ^contents <t2>)
   (<b12> ^cell <c12> ^contents <t0>)
   (<b22> ^cell <c22> ^contents <t2>)
   (<b32> ^cell <c32> ^contents <t0>)
   (<b42> ^cell <c42> ^contents <t0>)
   (<b13> ^cell <c13> ^contents <t0>)
   (<b23> ^cell <c23> ^contents <t0>)
   (<b33> ^cell <c33> ^contents <t0>)
   (<b43> ^cell <c43> ^contents <t0>)
   (<b14> ^cell <c14> ^contents <t2>)
   (<b24> ^cell <c24> ^contents <t2>)
   (<b34> ^cell <c34> ^contents <t2>)
   (<b44> ^cell <c44> ^contents <t3>)
## cell neighbors
   (<c11> ^name c11 ^cell <c12> ^cell <c21>)
   (<c12> ^name c12 ^cell <c11> ^cell <c13> ^cell <c22>)
```

```
    (<c13> ^name c13 ^cell <c12> ^cell <c23> ^cell <c14>)
    (<c14> ^name c14 ^cell <c13> ^cell <c24>)
    (<c21> ^name c21 ^cell <c11> ^cell <c31> ^cell <c22>)
    (<c22> ^name c22 ^cell <c12> ^cell <c21>
                    ^cell <c32> ^cell <c23>)
    (<c23> ^name c23 ^cell <c13> ^cell <c22>
                    ^cell <c33> ^cell <c24>)
    (<c24> ^name c24 ^cell <c14> ^cell <c23> ^cell <c34>)
    (<c31> ^name c31 ^cell <c21> ^cell <c41> ^cell <c32>)
    (<c32> ^name c32 ^cell <c22> ^cell <c31>
                    ^cell <c42> ^cell <c33>)
    (<c33> ^name c33 ^cell <c23> ^cell <c32>
                    ^cell <c43> ^cell <c34>)
    (<c34> ^name c34 ^cell <c24> ^cell <c33> ^cell <c44>)
    (<c41> ^name c41 ^cell <c31> ^cell <c42>)
    (<c42> ^name c42 ^cell <c32> ^cell <c41> ^cell <c43>)
    (<c43> ^name c43 ^cell <c33> ^cell <c42> ^cell <c44>)
    (<c44> ^name c44 ^cell <c34> ^cell <c43>)
## cell distances: <cjk> at ^xloc <j> ^yloc <k>
    (<c11> ^xloc 1 ^yloc 1)
    (<c12> ^xloc 1 ^yloc 2)
    (<c13> ^xloc 1 ^yloc 3)
    (<c14> ^xloc 1 ^yloc 4)
    (<c21> ^xloc 2 ^yloc 1)
    (<c22> ^xloc 2 ^yloc 2)
    (<c23> ^xloc 2 ^yloc 3)
    (<c24> ^xloc 2 ^yloc 4)
    (<c31> ^xloc 3 ^yloc 1)
    (<c32> ^xloc 3 ^yloc 2)
    (<c33> ^xloc 3 ^yloc 3)
    (<c34> ^xloc 3 ^yloc 4)
    (<c41> ^xloc 4 ^yloc 1)
    (<c42> ^xloc 4 ^yloc 2)
    (<c43> ^xloc 4 ^yloc 3)
    (<c44> ^xloc 4 ^yloc 4)
## cell contents
    (<t0> ^name |  OPEN |)
    (<t1> ^name | blockA|)
    (<t2> ^name |BLOCKED|)
    (<t3> ^name | blockB|)
## specified goal state
    (<d> ^bindings <d11> <d21> <d31> <d41>
                   <d12> <d22> <d32> <d42>
                   <d13> <d23> <d33> <d43>
                   <d14> <d24> <d34> <d44>)
    (<d11> ^cell <c11> ^contents <t3>)
    (<d21> ^cell <c21> ^contents <t0>)
    (<d31> ^cell <c31> ^contents <t2>)
    (<d41> ^cell <c41> ^contents <t2>)
    (<d12> ^cell <c12> ^contents <t0>)
    (<d22> ^cell <c22> ^contents <t2>)
    (<d32> ^cell <c32> ^contents <t0>)
    (<d42> ^cell <c42> ^contents <t0>)
    (<d13> ^cell <c13> ^contents <t0>)
```

```
   (<d23> ^cell <c23> ^contents <t0>)
   (<d33> ^cell <c33> ^contents <t0>)
   (<d43> ^cell <c43> ^contents <t0>)
   (<d14> ^cell <c14> ^contents <t2>)
   (<d24> ^cell <c24> ^contents <t2>)
   (<d34> ^cell <c34> ^contents <t2>)
   (<d44> ^cell <c44> ^contents <t1>)
}
```

Soar Operator Production Modifications for Alternating Block Movement.

```
## checkerboard block moving version for 4 × 4
## this version uses a distance-based heuristic
##     to resolve impasses
## also hold blocks in goal state positions
## forces alternating block movements
## we propagate all the matching work
##     via an elaboration of <o>


## proposal: <y> is the cell where the block would go
## we augment the operator with (distance to goal)^2
##     from here

sp {checkerboard*propose*operator*move-blockA
   (state <s> ^name checkerboard-problem
               ^current <i> ^goal <d>
               ^previousA <g>)
   (<s> -^prev-moved blockA)
   (<i> ^bindings <b1> <b2> { <> <b1> <b2>})
   (<b1> ^cell <x> ^contents <t1>) # contents.name
   (<t1> ^name | blockA|) # we've found blockA
   (<x>  ^cell <y> {<y> <> <g>}) # no cycle
   (<b2> ^cell <y> {<y> <> <x>} ^contents <t2>)
   (<t2> ^name |  OPEN |) # we've found an empty neighbor
## compute distance
   (<y> ^xloc <xy> ^yloc <yy>)
   (<d> ^bindings <ba>)
   (<ba> ^cell <which> ^contents.name | blockA|)
   (<which> ^xloc <xw> ^yloc <yw>)
-->
   (<s> ^operator <o> +)
   (<o> ^name move-blockA ^b1 <b1> ^t1 <t1>  # save the
                          ^x <x> ^y <y>       # matching
                          ^b2 <b2> ^t2 <t2>)
## remember arithmetic is prefix notation
   (<o> ^sqdist (+ (*
                   (- <xy> <xw>)
                   (- <xy> <xw>))
                   (*
                   (- <yy> <yw>)
                   (- <yy> <yw>))))
## following is for illustration and debugging
   (write (crlf) |*** for operator move-block-A --->|)
```

```
    (write (crlf) |i.e., | <o> )
    (write (crlf) |for proposed next cell | <y>)
    (write (crlf) |located at | <xy> | | <yy>)
    (write (crlf) |with goal to be at | <xw> | | <yw>)
    (write (crlf) |distance squared is |
                (+ (*
                    (- <xy> <xw>)
                    (- <xy> <xw>))
                  (*
                    (- <yy> <yw>)
                    (- <yy> <yw>))))
    (write (crlf))
}

sp {checkerboard*propose*operator*move-blockB
    (state <s> ^name checkerboard-problem
               ^current <i> ^goal <d>
               ^previousB <g>)
    (<s> -^prev-moved blockB)
    (<i> ^bindings <b1> <b2> { <> <b1> <b2>})
    (<b1> ^cell <x> ^contents <t1>) # contents.name
    (<t1> ^name | blockB|) # we've found blockB
    (<x>   ^cell <y> {<y> <> <g>}) # no cycle
    (<b2> ^cell <y> {<y> <> <x>} ^contents <t2>)
    (<t2> ^name |  OPEN |) # we've found an empty neighbor
## compute distance
    (<y> ^xloc <xy> ^yloc <yy>)
    (<d> ^bindings <ba>)
    (<ba> ^cell <which> ^contents.name | blockB|)
    (<which> ^xloc <xw> ^yloc <yw>)
-->
    (<s> ^operator <o> +)
    (<o> ^name move-blockB ^b1 <b1> ^t1 <t1>  # save the
                           ^x <x> ^y <y>        # matching
                           ^b2 <b2> ^t2 <t2>)
## remember arithmetic is prefix notation
    (<o> ^sqdist (+ (*
                    (- <xy> <xw>)
                    (- <xy> <xw>))
                  (*
                    (- <yy> <yw>)
                    (- <yy> <yw>))))
## following is for illustration and debugging
    (write (crlf) |*** for operator move-block-B --->|)
    (write (crlf) |i.e., | <o> )
    (write (crlf) |for proposed next cell | <y>)
    (write (crlf) |located at | <xy> | | <yy>)
    (write (crlf) |with goal to be at | <xw> | | <yw>)
    (write (crlf) |distance squared is |
                (+ (*
                    (- <xy> <xw>)
                    (- <xy> <xw>))
                  (*
                    (- <yy> <yw>)
```

```
                          (- <yy> <yw>))))
    (write (crlf))
}


## application of operators

sp {checkerboard*apply*operator*move-blockA
   (state <s> ^operator <o>
               ^name checkerboard-problem ^current <i>
               ^previousA <g>)
   (<o> ^name move-blockA ^b1 <b1> ^t1 <t1>
                          ^x <x> ^y <y>
                          ^b2 <b2> ^t2 <t2>)
-->
   (<s> ^name checkerboard-problem ^current <i>
        ^previousA <g> - <x>)
   (<s> ^prev-moved blockB -) # remember it has
   (<s> ^prev-moved blockA)   # O-support
   (<i> ^bindings <b1> <b2>) # revise the bindings
   (<b1> ^cell <x> ^contents <t1> - <t2>) # out and in
   (<b2> ^cell <y> ^contents <t2> - <t1>)}

sp {checkerboard*apply*operator*move-blockB
   (state <s> ^operator <o>
               ^name checkerboard-problem ^current <i>
               ^previousB <g>)
   (<o> ^name move-blockB ^b1 <b1> ^t1 <t1>
                          ^x <x> ^y <y>
                          ^b2 <b2> ^t2 <t2>)
-->
   (<s> ^name checkerboard-problem ^current <i>
        ^previousB <g> - <x>)
   (<s> ^prev-moved blockA -)
   (<s> ^prev-moved blockB)
   (<i> ^bindings <b1> <b2>) # revise the bindings
   (<b1> ^cell <x> ^contents <t1> - <t2>) # out and in
   (<b2> ^cell <y> ^contents <t2> - <t1>)}


## USING DISTANCE --
## distance-based operator preference modification
## the best operator has the shortest distance
## only rank within A or B
## else just tend to move one block for too long

sp {checkerboard*rank*operators
   (state <s> ^operator <o1> + ^name <opname>)
   (<s> ^operator <o2> + ^name <opname>) #same block
   (<o1> ^sqdist <do1>)
   (<o2> ^sqdist <do2> {<do2> < <do1>}})
# closer
-->
## to enable trying various preference modifications
##   (<s> ^operator <o2> >)
##   (<s> ^operator <o1> -)  # best wins
```

```
##   (<s> ^operator <o2> > <o1>) # ranked
    (<s> ^operator <o1> = 50)
    (<s> ^operator <o2> = 100) # ranked indifferent


}


## the above production DOES NOT CHECK IF THE BLOCK
## TO BE MOVED IS IN THE GOAL POSITION, THEREFORE
## CHECK IF THE BLOCK IS IN THE GOAL STATE POSITION
## reduce preference of any operator applied to a block
## already in a goal state position
## *** note we may still paint ourselves into a corner

sp {checkerboard*check*for*goal*state*blockA
    (state <s> ^name checkerboard-problem
               ^current <i> ^goal <d>)
    (<i> ^bindings <ba>)
    (<ba> ^cell <cla> ^contents.name | blockA|)
    (<cla> ^name <what>)
    (<d> ^bindings <bg>)
    (<bg> ^cell <clg> ^contents.name | blockA|)
    (<clg> ^name <what>) ## same cell in initial and goal states
## blockA is in goal cell; don't move it
    (<s> ^operator <oany>)
    (<oany> ^name move-blockA ^x <cla>)
-->
    (<s> ^operator <oany> -) # reduce preference
    (write (crlf) | blockA is in goal state position|)
    (write (crlf) | *** leave it alone ***|)}

sp {checkerboard*check*for*goal*state*blockB
    (state <s> ^name checkerboard-problem
               ^current <i> ^goal <d>)
    (<i> ^bindings <ba>)
    (<ba> ^cell <clb> ^contents.name | blockB|)
    (<clb> ^name <what>)
    (<d> ^bindings <bg>)
    (<bg> ^cell <clg> ^contents.name | blockB|)
    (<clg> ^name <what>) ## same cell in initial and goal states
## blockB is in goal cell; don't move it
    (<s> ^operator <oany>)
    (<oany> ^name move-blockB ^x <clb>)
-->
    (<s> ^operator <oany> -)
    (write (crlf) | blockB is in goal state position|)
    (write (crlf) | *** leave it alone ***|)}
```

Extending the Solution: Additional Heuristics

1. Favor moving any block that is in a goal state cell and not the block desired in this cell. This (at least temporarily) "clears" the cell for the desired block.

2. Use of different distance measures. For example, perhaps just the maximum of the x and y

distances, i.e., a one-dimensional distance measure.

3. Rather than alternating block movements, randomly choose a block to be considered for movement.

4. Rank an operator preference on the basis of the number of blocked neighbors in the proposed destination cell. This attempts to avoid painting the blocks into a corner.

12.9 Exercises

1. Consider the blocks-world states shown in Figure 12.20.

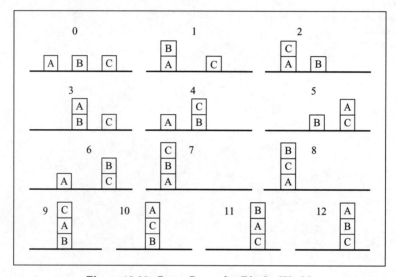

Figure 12.20 State Space for Blocks World

States are labeled 0–12. For this problem, we will modify the operators used in the earlier STRIPS representation. Note that x, y, and z are variables that take on specific block names.

The operator representation is as follows:

Operator #1: t-to-b(x,y)

Action: moves Block x from the table to on top of Block y

Preconditions:

(ontable x) (clear x) (clear y)

Add Facts:

(on x y)

Delete Facts:

(ontable x) (clear y)

Operator #2: b-to-t(x,y)

Action: moves Block x (currently on Block y) from a stack to the table

Preconditions:

(on x y) (clear x)

Add Facts:

(ontable x) (clear y)

Delete Facts:

(on x y)

Operator #3: s-s(x,y,z)

Action: moves Block x from one stack (on y) to another (on z)

Preconditions:

(on x y) (clear x) (clear z)

Add Facts:

(on x z) (clear y)

Delete Facts:

(on x y) (clear z)

(a) Describe the *serial* operator *t-to-b(B,A)* as a relation.

(b) Describe the operators *t-to-b(B,A)* and *b-to-t(C,A)* as relations *in the parallel representation.* Assume two independent "arms" are available for block movement. Also assume any timing problems with two operators may be resolved in our favor, i.e., as we did in the "tic-tac-toe" problem. In other words, if two operators are being considered for use "simultaneously," and it is possible for one to be used first and thus yield preconditions required by the other operator, consider this parallel combination possible. To avoid overextending the concept of "parallel," consider only initial states where (ontable B) holds for parallel execution in *t-to-b(B,A)$_p$*. Likewise, consider only initial states where (on C A) holds for development of *b-to-t(C,A)$_p$*.

(c) Using the results from Part (b), describe the parallel operator *t-to-b(B,A)|b-to-t(C,A)* as a relation.

2. This problem involves Prolog for knowledge representation and manipulation.

   (a) Revise the checkerboard as shown in Figure 12.21. Add a third block (C). How many states are there in this problem state space?

   (b) Implement a planning solution in Prolog. This requires a state representation and a planning algorithm. Extend the operators to Block C, namely *move-up-x, move-down-x, move-left-x,* and *move-right-x.*

   Do not try to enumerate or draw the state space.

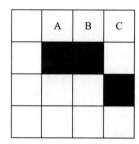 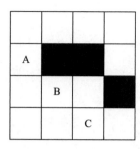

Figure 12.21 Initial (left) and Goal (right) States

(c) Show, using your Prolog implementation, the generation of a solution for the beginning and end state specification in Figure 12.21.

3. The Prolog code that follows is an early attempt at a Prolog planner.

```
/* file: planner5.pro */
/**************************************
describe state of 3 × 3 checkerboard

0 1 2
3 4 5
6 7 8

as 9-element list indicating, by place, what is there

[0 1 2 3 4 5 6 7 8]

e.g.,

A 1 B
3 C 5
6 7 8

looks like state:

[a,0,b,0,c,0,0,0,0]

recall

nth0(?Index, ?List, ?Elem)
    Succeeds when the Index-th element of List unifies with Elem.

*********************************************/

free(Cell, PresentState) :- nth0(Cell,PresentState,0).

location(A, PresentState, Where) :- nth0(Where,PresentState,A).
```

```
can-use(m-r,A,PresentState) :-
                            location(A,PresentState,Where),
                            not(equal(A,0)),
                            right-of(Where,OnRight),
                            free(OnRight,PresentState).

/* inelegant, but works */

right-of(0,1).
right-of(1,2).
right-of(2,blocked).
right-of(3,4).
right-of(4,5).
right-of(5,blocked).
right-of(6,7).
right-of(7,8).
right-of(8,blocked).

equal(X,X).

/* below to avoid typing initial state */

initialState([a,0,b,0,c,0,0,0,0]).
```

Show ALL solutions, if any, for each of the following goals:

```
?- initialState(Init),location(a,Init,Where).

?- initialState(Init),location(b,Init,Where).

?- initialState(Init), free(Which,Init).

?- initialState(Init),can-use(m-r,Which,Init).
```

4. How does "over-abstraction" result in Figure 12.15? How could it be detected? Suggest an alternative abstraction such that this problem does not occur.

5. Using the abstraction of Figure 12.13, show that it is possible for an abstract state to correspond to many concrete states.

6. Section 12.4.1 introduced the notion of a triangle table for plans. How could a triangle table be used:

   (a) To identify cycles in a plan; and

   (b) To break, or remove, cycles from a plan.

7. Section 12.4.3 indicated that a triangle table actually catalogued a number of macro (i.e., composite single-step) operators. For a plan consisting of p operators ($p > 2$), how many possible macro operators result? Verify your result using the example table of Figure 12.12.

8. A graph of the state space of a planing system is shown in Figure 12.22. Each arc between nodes represents two STRIPS operator applications. For the shortest path between "start" and "goal," label the path with the STRIPS operators (including specific block names) used.

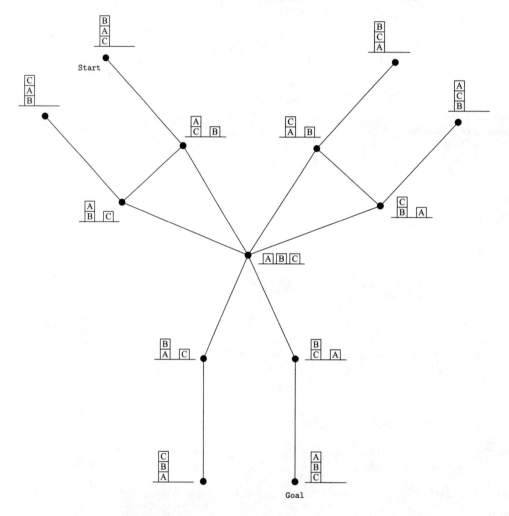

Figure 12.22 Blocks-Table Planning Search Space

Biologically-Inspired Computing and IS: Neural Networks (Part 1)

13.1 Conceptual Background and Motivation

In this chapter, we begin to look at biologically-inspired approaches to IS. In this context, the topic of artificial neural networks (ANNs) is both relevant and popular. We begin by making some overall observations and comparisons. Then we introduce biological and neural units. After that, we move on to multiunit architectures, applications, and training approaches based upon a multilayer feedforward (MLFF) structure. Other families of ANNs are treated in subsequent chapters.

13.2 Relationship of IS to ANNs

ANNs provide a set of tools for solving some IS problems that are difficult or impractical to solve with other methods.[1] To compare these two topics, we must be clear about what we mean with respect to each. For example, we must be clear about *which* IS approach and which ANN we refer to.

At some level, IS and ANN-based development strategies share a number of similarities. Here are a few:

◆ Both classical or conventional IS and ANN technologies are approaches to building systems with, what is perceived to be, intelligent behavior.

◆ Both are problem-solving tools, i.e., both provide classes of useful solutions in certain problem domains.

◆ Both are strongly oriented toward learning (or training).

◆ Both have their origin in biological systems.

◆ Both concern building models of mind/brain (natural and artificial).

---

[1]Reference: V. Honavar and L. Uhr (eds). *Artificial Intelligence and Neural Networks–Steps Toward Principled Integration*. Academic Press, San Diego, CA, 1994.

13.3   Biology and ANN Building Blocks

We first explore the actual building blocks of biological neural systems. There are over 40 properties of biological neurons that influence their information processing capability, therefore only a summary explanation of this process is provided.

13.3.1   Physical (Biological) Neurons

Nerve Cells: Types, Functional Classification, and Morphology

The nervous system consists of two classes of cells: *neurons*, or nerve cells, and *glia*, or glial cells. Neurons are the basic building blocks of biological information processing systems [KSJ00]. A biological neuron, typical of those found in vertebrates, is shown in Figure 13.1.[2] This cell has three major morphologically defined portions. Each component makes a specific contribution to the processing of signals. They are:

◆ A *cell body*, or *soma*, which consists of the cell nucleus and perikaryon. The cell body is typically $50\mu m$ or larger in diameter.

◆ The *axon*, a tubular construct with a diameter ranging from 0.2 to $20\mu m$ with length up to $1m$. The axon begins at the *axon hillock* that generates the cell action potential. The axon is the main conduction mechanism of the neuron.

◆ *Dendrites*, which branch out in tree-like fashion. Most neurons have multiple, and often many, dendrites. Dendrites of one neuron are connected to axons of other neurons via *synaptic connections*, or synapses. This is how biological networks are formed. The multipolar neurons shown in Figure 13.1 have two types of dendrites, namely, *apical* and *basal*. Basal dendrites can facilitate both excitory and inhibitory functions in axon signal generation.

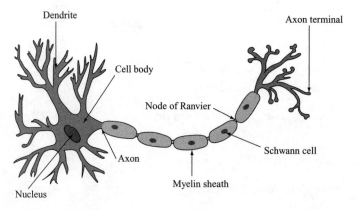

Figure 13.1 Expanded View of Single Neuron Morphology

---

[2]Originally Neuron.jpg (public domain). Source: "Anatomy and Physiology" by the U.S. National Cancer Institute's Surveillance, Epidemiology, and End Results (SEER) Program. Modified by the author.

Physical (biological)	Artificial
(neuron) Cell	"Unit"
Synapse	Interconnection weight
Excitatory input	(large) Positive interconnection weight
Inhibitory input	(large) Negative interconnection weight
Activation by ("spiking") frequency	DC level
Range of activation limited by cell physics	Activation limited by "squashing" function

Table 13.1 Comparing Physical and Artificial Neurons

13.3.2 Abstracting Biological Mechanisms into Artificial Unit Characteristics

Our previous review of elements of neural science suggests numerous biological mechanisms for signal or information processing that could form the basis for artificial neuron units. Table 13.1 summarizes typical relationships between a biological neuron and an artificial unit.

The Neural Unit Weight Convention.   Each artificial neuron input has an associated weight, indicating the strength of its connection with either an external input or another neuron output. Although the literature is somewhat inconsistent on this topic, we adopt the following convention: w_{ij} *represents the strength of the connection TO neuron unit i FROM (either) neuron unit j or input j*. Thus, a large positive value of w_{ij} indicates a strongly excitory input from unit or input j to unit i, whereas a large negative weight value could be used to represent a highly inhibitory input.

13.3.3 Two–Part Unit Models: Activation and Squashing

Many, but not all, of the artificial neural unit models involve two important processes:

1. Forming a *unit net activation*, denoted by the scalar net_j for unit j, by (somehow) combining (perhaps different classes) of inputs. Most commonly, a weighted linear input combination (WLIC) is used:

$$net_j = \underline{w}^T \underline{i} \quad where \quad \underline{w}_j = \overset{d \times 1}{\begin{pmatrix} w_{j1} \\ w_{j2} \\ \vdots \\ w_{jd} \end{pmatrix}} \quad and \quad \underline{i} = \overset{d \times 1}{\begin{pmatrix} i_1 \\ i_2 \\ \vdots \\ i_d \end{pmatrix}} \tag{13.1}$$

From the viewpoint of geometry, the unit output is formed by projection of the unit input onto the unit weight vector $\underline{w}_j$. The weight vector is a specific set of parameters of the unit that models unit interconnection strengths from other sources of stimuli in the network.

2. Mapping this activation value into the artificial unit output. This mapping may be as simple as using the identity function, or as complex as using a nonlinear mapping function with memory (dynamics). Commonly, the logistic function (Section 13.3.4) is used.

13.3.4 The Sigmoid (Logistic) Squashing Function

The particular functional form that is often used for the *sigmoid* or *"logistic"* activation function is:

$$o_j = f(net_j) = \frac{1}{1 + e^{-net_j}} \tag{13.2}$$

which yields $o_j \in [0, 1]$. This is shown in Figure 13.2.

The sigmoid is important and popular for several reasons:

1. It "squashes";

2. It is semilinear.[3] This influences its use with certain training approaches;

3. It is expressible in a closed-form expression;

4. Modifications/extensions lead to or relate to other squashing functions;

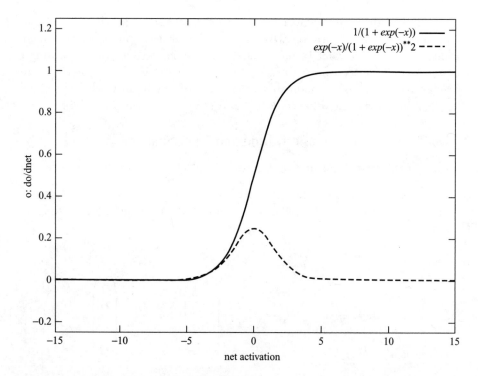

Figure 13.2 Sigmoid Activation Function and Derivative for the Artificial Neuron. Note saturation regions.

---

[3]Nondecreasing and differentiable everywhere.

5. The derivative of the sigmoid w.r.t. net_i is very easy to form (shown in the following section); and

6. It has a biological basis. The average firing frequency of biological neurons, as a function of excitation, follows a sigmoidal characteristic.

13.3.5 The Sigmoid Derivative

The derivative of the logistic function is:

$$\frac{\partial o_j}{\partial net_j} = \frac{\partial f(net_j)}{\partial net_j} = \frac{e^{-net_j}}{(1 + e^{-net_j})^2} \tag{13.3}$$

Note from Figure 13.2 that the derivative in Equation 13.3 is symmetric about zero and more peaked in the center than the (0,1) Gaussian density. Since this quantity will be computed many times during the training phase, one computationally advantageous feature is that Equation 13.3 simplifies to:

$$\frac{\partial o_j}{\partial net_j} = o_j \cdot (1 - o_j) \tag{13.4}$$

13.4 The Multilayer Feedforward Structure, Architectures, and Notation

The design of an FF net for a specific application involves many issues, most of which require problem-dependent solutions. Some are shown in Figure 13.3.

The overall computational approach we use for exploring the FF net and training algorithm is shown in Figure 13.4. The situation may be viewed as two parts: feedforward (implementation) of the learned mapping, and training of the multilayer network. The training algorithm will use the feedforward implementation as part of training; in this sense they are coupled.

Topology. The *feedforward network* considered here is composed of two or more mutually exclusive sets of neurons or layers. The first, or input layer, serves as a holding site for the inputs applied to the network. The last, or output, layer is the point at which the overall mapping of the network input is available. Between these two extremes lie zero or more layers of *hidden units*; it is in these internal layers that additional remapping or computing takes place.

Interconnections. Links, or weights, connect each unit in one layer to only those in the next-higher layer. There is an implied directionality in these connections, in that the output of a unit, scaled by the value of a connecting weight, is fed forward to provide a portion of the activation for the units in the next-higher layer. Figure 13.5 illustrates the typical feedforward network. The network as shown consists of a layer of d input units, (L_i), a layer of c output units, (L_o), and a variable number (5 in this example) of internal or "hidden" layers (L_{h_i}) of units. Observe the *feedforward* structure, where

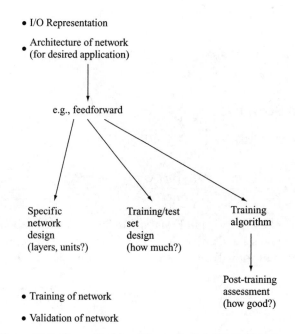

- I/O Representation
- Architecture of network
  (for desired application)

e.g., feedforward

Specific
network
design
(layers, units?)

Training/test
set
design
(how much?)

Training
algorithm

Post-training
assessment
(how good?)

- Training of network
- Validation of network

Figure 13.3 Some Problem-Dependent ANN Design Issues

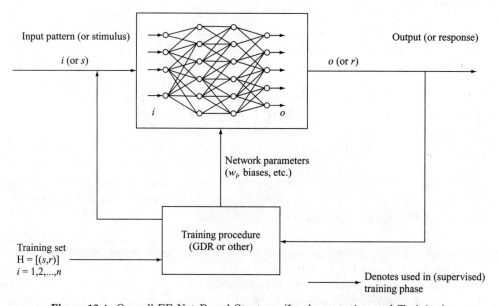

Input pattern (or stimulus)

i (or s)

Output (or response)

o (or r)

Network parameters
(w_i, biases, etc.)

Training set
H = [(s,r)]
$i = 1,2,...,n$

Training procedure
(GDR or other)

Denotes used in (supervised)
training phase

Figure 13.4 Overall FF-Net Based Strategy (Implementation and Training)

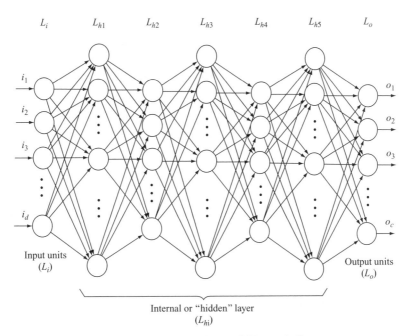

Figure 13.5 Layered Feedforward Network Structure

the inputs are directly connected to only units in L_o, and the outputs of layer L_k units are only connected to units in layer L_{k+1}. [4]

The Role of Input Units. As detailed in Section 13.5.2, the role of the input layer is somewhat fictitious, in that input layer units are only used to "hold" input values and distribute these values to units in the next layer. Thus, the input layer units do not implement a separate mapping or conversion of the input data, and their weights, strictly speaking, do not exist.

Constrained Information Flow in the FF Structure. From Figure 13.5, note that the information flow in the network is restricted to flow only layer-by-layer from the input to the output. Each layer, based upon its input, computes an output vector, and propagates this information to the succeeding layer. Thus, from an architectural viewpoint, the FF network allows parallelism (parallel processing) within each layer, but the flow of interlayer information is necessarily serial.

"Slash" or "Cross" Notation. We adopt a "slash" or cross-like notation to designate the numbers of input, hidden, and output units in each layer (as well as the number of hidden layers). For example, a general three-layer network is an $I/H/O$ or $I \times H \times O$ network, where

I is the number of input (hold) units;

---

[4]Or are outputs, if $L_k = L_o$.

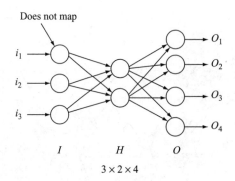

Figure 13.6 Example of a 3/2/4 (3 × 2 × 4) Network

H is the number of hidden units in the *single* hidden layer; and

O is the number of output units.

This is shown in Figure 13.6. Describing a four-layer network is analogous; we use the notation $I/H1/H2/O$ or $I \times H1 \times H2 \times O$.

In addition, unless indicated otherwise, we assume each layer is totally interconnected with the succeeding and previous layers. In other words, there is a connection from the output of every unit in L_k to the input of every unit in L_{k+1}.

Note that the slash or cross notation does not indicate unit characteristics in each layer, nor the use (or lack thereof) of a bias input. It may be extended to show this, assuming all units in a given layer have the same activation function and or bias characteristic. For example, a three-layer network with sigmoidal hidden units (with a bias) and a linear output layer without bias could be designated $I/H_{sigmoid;bias}/O_{linear;no\ bias}$.

To simplify the following discussion, we further extend the notation as follows: $o_i^{L_x}$ is the output of unit i in layer L_x, where x denotes the particular layer. Specifically,

x = 0 is the input layer

x = 1 is the first hidden layer, i.e., the layer that receives input directly from the input layer

x = 2 is the second hidden layer, i.e., the layer that receives input from hidden layer L_1

x = p is the output layer

Note that the outputs of layer L_k are inputs to layer L_{k+1}, for $k \leq p - 1$. We could denote an entire layer (L_x) with the notation $\underline{o}^{L_x}$

13.5 Training the MLFF Network: The Generalized Delta Rule

13.5.1 Training Considerations

Once an appropriate network structure is chosen, much of the effort in designing an ANN for a specific application involves the design of a reasonable training strategy. This necessitates engineering judgment in considering the following training concerns:

- Whether to train by pattern or epoch[5];

- Whether to use *momentum* and the appropriate value;

- Sequential vs. random ordering of the training set data;

- Determining whether the training algorithm has diverged, converged, is oscillating, or "stuck" at a local error minimum;

- Determining and training "suitable" unit biases (if applicable); and

- Determining appropriate initial conditions on biases, weights, etc.

13.5.2 Overview of the Generalized Delta Rule (GDR)

The GDR is a weight adjustment strategy for a feedforward, multiple-layer, structured neural network that uses *gradient descent*. Network weights are adjusted to minimize an error based upon a measure of the difference between desired and actual feedforward network output. Desired input/output behavior is given in the training set, H.

The process consists of the following steps:

1. Initialize all unit weights in the network.

2. Apply input (stimulus) vector to the network.

3. "Feedforward" or propagate the input vector to determine all unit outputs.

4. Compare unit responses in output layer with desired or target response.

5. Compute and propagate an error sensitivity measure backward (starting at the output layer) through the network, using this as the basis for weight correction.

6. Minimize the overall error at each stage through unit weight adjustments.

The following are defined:

i input pattern (vector),

o corresponding output pattern or response (vector),

---

[5]The term epoch commonly refers to a single pass through the training set.

$\underline{w}$ network weights (vector), and

$\underline{t}$ desired (or target) system output (vector).

Initially, a two-layer network (that is, a structure with no "hidden" units) is considered. Thus, $\underline{i}$ denotes the state of the input layer, and $\underline{o}$ denotes the state of the output layer. Recall that weight w_{ji} denotes the strength of interconnection FROM unit i (or network input i) TO unit j.[6] Using this structure, we develop the delta rule (DR). We later extend this formulation to the multilayer case, to develop the generalized GDR.

Gradient Descent Approaches for Training.   The basis of the algorithms derived as follows is **gradient descent**. Specifically, to adjust network weights we define and compute (or estimate) a mapping error, E, and the gradient $\frac{\partial E}{\partial w_{ji}}$. The weight adjustment $\triangle w_{ji}$, is then set proportional to $\frac{-\partial E}{\partial w_{ji}}$.

The Training Set.   The training set for this type of network consists of ordered pairs of vectors and is denoted

$$H = \{(\underline{i}^k, \underline{t}^k)\} \qquad k = 1, 2, \dots, n \tag{13.5}$$

where, for the pth input/output pair $i_i^p \in \underline{i}^p$ is the ith input value (also denoted i_{pi} in the literature). Similarly, o_j^p (also denoted o_{pj} in the literature) and t_j^p (or t_{pj}) are the jth elements of $\underline{o}^p$ and $\underline{t}^p$ respectively where $\underline{o}^p$ is the actual network output resulting from input $\underline{i}^p$ and the current set of network weights, $\underline{w}$. Given a preselected network structure, the goal is to develop a learning or training algorithm that uses $\underline{i}^p$, $\underline{o}^p$, and $\underline{t}^p$ to adjust the network weights.

An Initial Error Measure.   Define an output error *vector* for the pth pattern pair as

$$\underline{e}^p = \underline{t}^p - \underline{o}^p \tag{13.6}$$

A scalar measure of the output error based upon the pth training sample is denoted E^p and defined as:

$$E^p = \frac{1}{2}(\underline{e}^p)^T \underline{e}^p = \frac{1}{2} \parallel \underline{e}^p \parallel^2 \tag{13.7}$$

From Equations 13.6 and 13.7,

$$E^p = \frac{1}{2} \parallel \underline{t}^p - \underline{o}^p \parallel^2 \tag{13.8}$$

---

[6]Although the notation may bother some readers, we consider w_{ji} (as opposed to w_{ij}) in order to develop a notation that is consistent with most (not all) of the literature.

or

$$E^p = \frac{1}{2}\sum_j (t_j^p - o_j^p)^2 \tag{13.9}$$

We could also develop an alternative formulation by considering the total *epoch error*:

$$E = \sum_p E^p \tag{13.10}$$

The quantities $2E$ and $2E^p$ are therefore sums of squared errors incurred in the pattern mappings obtained.

Unit Activation Function.   Assume an activation function for the jth unit of the form:

$$o_j^p = f_j(w_{ji}, \underline{i}^p) \tag{13.11}$$

where f_j is a *nondecreasing* and *differentiable* function with respect to each of its arguments. Typically, f_j is constant over j (at least within a layer), that is, all units have the same activation function. Commonly, f is chosen to be a sigmoid function, i.e.,

$$f(net_j) = \frac{1}{1 + e^{-net_j}} \tag{13.12}$$

For WLIC units, the artificial neuron activation for unit j is formed from the weighted linear sum of the inputs to unit j:

$$net_j = \sum_i w_{ji}i_i \tag{13.13}$$

where i_i is the ith input to unit j. In the case where a unit bias is incorporated in the model:

$$net_j = \sum_i w_{ji}i_i + bias_j \tag{13.14}$$

Note that Equation 13.14 shows a model of a neural unit where the bias is added directly to net_j. The training of the bias input is considered in Section 13.5.5.

Error Sensitivity and the Chain Rule.   The quantity $\frac{\partial E^p}{\partial w_{ji}}$ is paramount in the gradient descent-based GDR training algorithm. Several forms of the chain rule may be used to develop the GDR

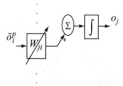

Figure 13.7 Sensitivity of o_j to Weight w_{ji}

training algorithm. For example, one formulation obtainable from the chain rule is:

$$\frac{\partial E^p}{\partial w_{ji}} = \frac{\partial E^p}{\partial o_j^p} \frac{\partial o_j^p}{\partial w_{ji}}$$

(13.15)

that represents the incremental change in E^p due to the incremental change in network weight w_{ji}. Alternately, this is the sensitivity of E^p to w_{ji}. The first term in Equation 13.15, $\frac{\partial E_p}{\partial o_j^p}$, is the effect on E^p due to the output of the jth unit, whereas the second term, $\frac{\partial o_j^p}{\partial w_{ji}}$, measures the change on o_j^p as a function of ∂w_{ji}. This sensitivity is shown in Figure 13.7.

Nomenclature: "All Inputs in the MLFF ANN Are Unit Outputs." The MLFF ANN will have many unit outputs forming the inputs to units in the next layer. In order to generalize our results to hidden units, a general representation for the ith *input* to neuron j, denoted $\tilde{o}_i^p$ is developed. $\tilde{o}_i^p = o_i^p$ if this input is the output of another neuron in the hidden or output layers. $\tilde{o}_i^p = i_i$ if this input is a direct input to the network. Thus, network external inputs are the "outputs" of the (fictitious) input layer.

13.5.3   A Formulation Introducing Delta

A more useful and general alternative to Equation 13.15, still using the chain rule, is to form the components of the gradient vector as:

$$\frac{\partial E^p}{\partial w_{ji}} = \frac{\partial E^p}{\partial net_j^p} \frac{\partial net_j^p}{\partial w_{ji}}$$

(13.16)

where

$$net_j^p = \sum_i w_{ji} \tilde{o}_i^p$$

(13.17)

From Equation 13.17, the rightmost term of Equation 13.16 is easy to compute and is:

$$\frac{\partial net_j^p}{\partial w_{ji}} = \tilde{o}_i^p \qquad (13.18)$$

Introducing Delta. The sensitivity of the pattern error on the net activation of the jth unit is defined to be the first term on the right-hand side of Equation 13.16. Thus:

$$\delta_j^p = -\frac{\partial E^p}{\partial net_j^p} \qquad (13.19)$$

so Equation 13.16 may be written

$$\frac{\partial E^p}{\partial w_{ji}} = -(\delta_j^p)\tilde{o}_i^p \qquad (13.20)$$

Learning Rate. Recall the iterative weight correction procedure using the pth training sample is:

$$\triangle^p w_{ji} = -\epsilon\left(\frac{\partial E^p}{\partial w_{ji}}\right) \qquad (13.21)$$

where ϵ is a positive constant, referred to as the *learning rate.*

The learning rate determines what amount of the calculated error sensitivity to weight change will be used for the weight correction. The "best" value of the learning rate depends on the characteristics of the error surface, i.e., a plot of E vs. w_{ij}. If the surface changes rapidly, the gradient calculated only on local information will give poor indication of the true "right path." In this case, a smaller rate is desirable. On the other hand, if the surface is relatively smooth, then a larger learning rate will speed convergence. This rationale, however, is based upon knowledge of the shape of the error surface, which is rarely available. Some indication may be given by the calculation of E at each iteration and observation of the impact of previous weight corrections. A general rule might be to use the largest learning rate that works and does not cause oscillation. A rate that is too large may cause the system to oscillate, and thereby slow or prevent the network's convergence.

Gradient Descent Using Delta. To move in a direction opposite the gradient, the weight correction becomes:

$$\triangle^p w_{ji} = \epsilon\delta_j^p\tilde{o}_i^p \qquad (13.22)$$

Note that Equation 13.22 holds for any (mapping) unit, anywhere in the MLFF network. It is necessary to compute δ_j^p for every unit. For the jth unit we may again use the chain rule on Equation 13.19 to yield:

$$\frac{\partial E^p}{\partial net_j^p} = \frac{\partial E^p}{\partial o_j^p} \frac{\partial o_j^p}{\partial net_j^p} \tag{13.23}$$

Choice of certain activation functions makes computation of the rightmost term in Equation 13.23 easier. For example, if a sigmoidal characteristic is used, the rightmost term in Equation 13.23 becomes:

$$\frac{\partial o_j^p}{\partial net_j^p} = o_j^p(1 - o_j^p) \tag{13.24}$$

We are then left with computation of $\frac{\partial E^p}{\partial o_j^p}$. *The computation of this quantity depends on the location of the specific unit.* We consider two cases as follows.

13.5.4 Output Unit Weight Corrections

For an output unit, the error definition in Equation 13.9 yields:

$$\frac{\partial E^p}{\partial o_j^p} = -(t_j^p - o_j^p) \tag{13.25}$$

Therefore, *in the case of output unit*, using Equations 13.19 and 13.23:

$$\delta_j^p = (t_j^p - o_j^p)f_j'(net_j^p) \tag{13.26}$$

and the sample-based weight correction for output units from Equation 13.21 becomes:

$$\triangle^p w_{ji} = \epsilon(t_j^p - o_j^p)f_j'(net_j^p)\tilde{o}_i^p \tag{13.27}$$

Notice that Equation 13.27 involves the quantity $f_j'(net_j^p)$. Thus the correction will be minimized whenever units are in "inactive regions," i.e., where this derivative is small. This is a serious concern in networks where weights are randomly initialized and units with squashing functions in the saturation region(s) occur. For example, in the case of sigmoidal units, using Equation 13.24, $f_j'(net_j^p) = o_j(1 - o_j)$. If a unit, or collection of units, has a net activation value that causes saturation, despite high values of the gain ϵ and error, the δ value(s) will be small, thus yielding slow corrections. This situation has been referred to as "premature saturation" of units in the network.

13.5.5 A Modified Procedure for Hidden Units: The GDR

Layers other than (the fictitious) input and output are denoted *hidden layers* and contain so-called *hidden units*. These were shown in Figure 13.5. The formulation for training hidden units is a little more complex than that of output units. This is due to the "indirect" effect of hidden unit weights on E^p. Alternately, *there are no target outputs for hidden units*.

For weights in units that are not output units, a method for computing $\triangle w_{ji}$ is sought. Consequently, an estimate of $\frac{\partial E^p}{\partial w_{ji}}$ for these weights is desired. Recall E^p is based upon comparing the outputs of *output units* with desired or target values. For a three-layer (input, hidden, output) network with hidden unit, u_k, first consider how the weights for u_k affect E^p:

1. The output of u_k feeds (activates) neurons in the output layer; and

2. The output of u_k is a function of its inputs,[7] weights, and activation function.

These effects are illustrated in Figures 13.8 and 13.9.
On this basis, we reformulate our approach for hidden unit u_k by considering its influence on the other n output units and again employ the chain rule as follows:

$$\frac{\partial E^p}{\partial o_k^p} = \sum_n \frac{\partial E^p}{\partial net_n^p} \frac{\partial net_n^p}{\partial o_k^p} = \sum_n (-\delta_n^p w_{nk}) \tag{13.28}$$

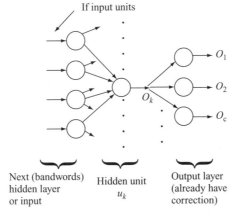

Figure 13.8 The Role of Hidden Unit u_k

---

[7]These are the prespecified inputs, $\underline{i}^p$, in a three-layer network. In n-layer ($n > 3$) networks, these may be the outputs of other (hidden) units.

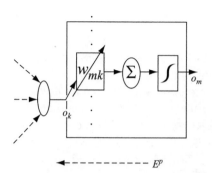

Figure 13.9 Back Propagation of Unit Influence on E^p

The result in Equation 13.28 incorporates Equation 13.19 and differentiation of Equation 13.13. Therefore, Equations 13.19 and 13.23 yield:

$$\delta_k^p = -\frac{\partial E^p}{\partial o_k^p} f_k'(net_k^p) \tag{13.29}$$

This, combined with Equation 13.28, yields the *recursive formulation* for a back propagation-based update of the hidden layer weights:

$$\delta_k^p = f_k'(net_k^p) \sum_n \delta_n^p w_{nk} \tag{13.30}$$

where δ_n^p is obtained from the output layer.

Analysis of GDR Equations

Equations 13.29 and 13.30 illustrate the necessarily serial nature of the GDR or back propagation (BP) algorithm. First, note the possibility of premature saturation (PS) in hidden layer units. However, there is an even more significant possible shortcoming due to the recursive formulation. Since Equation 13.30 computes $\delta_k^p = f_k'(net_k^p) \sum_n \delta_n^p$, additional concerns are:

1. The effect of small δ in a previous layer (perhaps due to PS) could be further exaggerated in the cascaded combination of two saturated units. If unit k is saturated, the weighting $f_k'(net_k^p)$ further reduces the correction.

2. This process may continue backward, from the output layer, until weight corrections at internal layers are inconsequential. This partially explains why networks with large numbers of hidden layers train poorly using the GDR strategy.

Back Propagation—Summary of the Multistep Procedure

Beginning with an initial (possibly random) weight assignment for a three-layer feedforward network, proceed as follows:

Step 1: Present $\underline{i}^p$, form outputs, o_i, of all units in the network.

Step 2: Use Equation 13.27 to update w_{ji} for the output layer.

Step 3: Use Equations 13.22 and 13.30 to update w_{ji} for hidden layer(s).

Step 4: Stop if updates are insignificant or error is below a preselected threshold, otherwise proceed to Step 1.

This leads to an adjustment scheme based upon *back propagation*. This is shown in Figure 13.10. The GDR equations are summarized in Table 13.2.

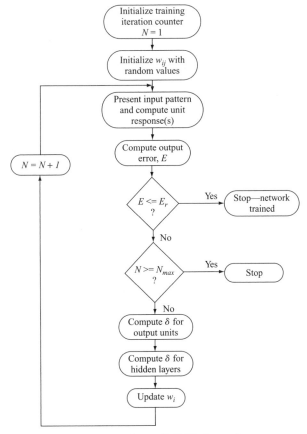

Figure 13.10 Overall GDR Procedure

(pattern) error measure	$E^p = \frac{1}{2}\sum_j (t_j^p - o_j^p)^2$	Equation 13.9
(pattern) weight correction	$\triangle^p w_{ji} = \epsilon \delta_j^p \tilde{o}_i^p$	Equation 13.22
(output units) (internal units)*	$\delta_j^p = (t_j^p - o_j^p)f_j'(net_j^p)$ $\delta_j^p = f_j'(net_j^p)\sum_n \delta_n^p w_{nj}$ * where δ_n^p are from next layer (L^{k+1})	Equation 13.26 Equation 13.30
output derivative (assumes sigmoidal characteristic)	$f_j'(net_j^p) = o_j^p(1 - o_j^p)$	Equation 13.24

Table 13.2 Summary of the GDR Equations for Training Using Back Propagation

Weight Initialization (Starting Points)

The ideal situation for avoiding unit saturation is for units to be in their active regions for maximum weight correction; this explains why a "good" initialization procedure would be to initialize units (with random weights) such that the expected value of unit activation is zero.

Pattern Presentation and Weight Updating Strategies

Given the power of the weight correction strategies developed in Section 13.5, numerous options are possible. We explore some of the rationale for these strategies in the following subsections. Most importantly, we consider training by sample vs. training by epoch.

Training by Sample. We could correct the network weights for the pth training set pair and thus implement *training by sample* or *pattern-based training*. The pattern mode of training is simpler to implement, and, coupled with random pattern selection strategies, allows a weight correction that is somewhat random in nature. This may help when entrapment in a local error minimum is possible.

Training by Epoch. Weight corrections based upon individual input patterns have been derived. These guide the gradient descent procedure. If it is desired to use the epoch error, E, to guide the gradient descent procedure, the gradient $\frac{\partial E}{\partial w_{ji}}$ is required. Fortunately, this does not require a separate derivation. Referring to Equations 13.7 and 13.10 it is straightforward to show:

$$\frac{\partial E}{\partial w_{ji}} = \sum_p \frac{\partial E^p}{\partial w_{ji}} \tag{13.31}$$

Thus, an alternative is training by epoch, where we form

$$\triangle w_{ji} = \sum_p \triangle^p w_{ji} \tag{13.32}$$

This represents an overall or accumulated correction to the weight set after each sweep of all pattern pairs in the training set, or training "epoch." This approach is also referred to as "batch" training. Epoch-based training represents a smoothing of the weight corrections.

Error Trajectories During Training

The GDR is a procedure based upon first-order gradient descent and therefore *will find a local minimum in E*. Unfortunately, as shown in Figure 13.11, local minima found by the solution procedure may correspond to suboptimal solutions with respect to the global minima. In addition, the particular minimum found, and corresponding network weights, are a function of many parameters, including $\underline{w}(0)$. This is shown in Figure 13.12.

GNU Octave is a high-level language, primarily intended for numerical computations.

Another valuable tool for monitoring training is to plot E as a function of iteration. This may take many forms, including quick, direct convergence, oscillatory behavior (both stable and unstable), and "plateauing," as shown in Figure 13.13.

Training the Unit Bias Inputs

Equation 13.14 showed a unit model that included an (assumed) adjustable bias term, $bias_j$. We could extend the previous derivations to compute $\frac{\partial E^p}{\partial bias_j}$ and form a bias adjustment strategy for unit j. However, a simpler alternative, using the unit bias structure of Equation 13.14, is to note that an equivalent formulation is that of an additional input to unit j. This extra input is denoted i_b, with corresponding weight w_{jb}. If we *assume i_b is the output of a unit that is always ON*, i.e., $\tilde{o}_{bias_j} = 1.0$, $bias_j$ may be adjusted through changes in w_{jb}. Therefore, the previous weight adjustment (training) procedure is directly applicable, and no new algorithm is required.

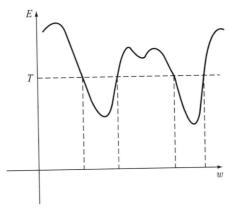

Figure 13.11 Possible Minima of $E(w)$ Found in Training

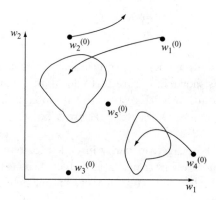

Figure 13.12 Possible Weight Trajectories During Training

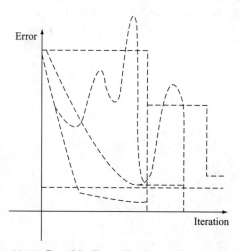

Figure 13.13 Possible Error Evolution During Training

Adding Momentum to the Training Procedure

Examination of the change in E as a function of $\triangle w_{ji}$ at each iteration suggests that care must be taken in choosing the learning parameter ϵ. Often, in gradient descent approaches, this scaling parameter is adjusted as a function of the iteration, e.g., $\epsilon(n) = \frac{\epsilon_o}{n}$. This type of adjustment allows for large initial corrections, yet avoids weight oscillations around the minimum when near the solution. To add *momentum* to the weight update at the $(n+1)$st iteration, the correction $\triangle w_{ji}(n+1)$ is modified:

$$\triangle w_{ji}(n+1) = \epsilon\{-\frac{\partial E}{\partial w_{ji}}\}(n+1) + \alpha \triangle w_{ji}(n) \tag{13.33}$$

where α is the momentum weight.

Two significant aspects of momentum are:

1. In training formulations involving *momentum*, when $\frac{\partial E}{\partial w_{ij}}$ has the same algebraic sign on consecutive iterations, Δw_{ij} grows in magnitude and so w_{ij} is modified by a large amount. Thus, momentum tends to accelerate descent in steady downhill directions, i.e., giving "momentum" to the correction.

2. In training formulations involving *momentum*, when $\frac{\partial E}{\partial w_{ij}}$ has alternating algebraic signs on consecutive iterations, Δw_{ij} becomes smaller and so the weight adjustment is small. Thus, momentum has a stabilizing effect on learning.

13.6 MLFF ANN: Internal/Hidden Layers and Network Mapping Ability

The internal layers *remap* the inputs and results of other (previous) internal layers. Often, it is illustrative to examine the structure of the internal layer remapping that evolves from training. Another viewpoint is that internal layers provide an intermediate mapping to a possibly higher-dimensional vector space.

13.6.1 How Many Hidden Layers Are Needed?

This is possibly one of the most interesting, commonly asked, and difficult questions related to multilayer, feedforward networks. A corollary is: "How many units should be in a (the) hidden layer?"

The choice of the number of hidden units in a feedforward structure design often involves considerable engineering judgment. Often, trade-offs between training time and mapping accuracy lead to iterative adjustment of the network using simulation. For a given problem, the design of an appropriately- sized hidden layer is often nonobvious. This question is also related to the applicability of a specific MLFF network architecture for a particular task.

13.6.2 A Theoretical Result for Continuous Activation Functions

Using the general definition of a sigmoidal function, Cybenko [Cyb89] approached the problem of identifying classes of functions that can be approximated by networks that implement the following mapping:

$$o_i = g(\underline{i}) = \sum_{j=1}^{N} \alpha_j \sigma(\underline{w}_i^T \underline{i} + b_i) \qquad (13.34)$$

Equation 13.34 represents a three-layer (two-mapping layer) network, comprised of a layer of units that each implement $\sigma(\underline{w}_i^T \underline{i} + b_i)$, followed by a layer of linear units. [Cyb89] shows that sums of the form of Equation 13.34 are dense in the space of continuous functions over the unit cube (a subspace of R^d) if σ is any continuous function. Most importantly, the emphasis is on approximation, rather than exact representation.

Thus, an FF ANN with one hidden layer and a family of well-known activation functions are capable of approximating continuous functions with arbitrary precision if:

1. No constraints are placed on the size of the hidden layer[8] (i.e., N); and

2. No constraints are placed on the magnitude of the weights.

13.7 Comprehensive MLFF ANN Training and Application Examples

We show a number of illustrative examples, in order of increasing complexity (and difficulty) in the following section. The GNU Octave language is used. GNU Octave is a high-level language, primarily intended for numerical computations.[9] GNU Octave is freely redistributable software licensed under the terms of the GNU General Public License (GPL). While Octave is not required for ANN simulation, it is quite convenient. Octave is very similar to the commercial MATLAB tool.

13.7.1 Fruit Classification

The fruit classification problem is treated in Chapter 16 from both the ID3 algorithm point of view as well as generalization. Refer to Table 16.14 for the training data. Here we address the problem in the context of an FF ANN.

Converting Inputs for the ANN

The symbolic-valued inputs to this problem are first converted into inputs suitable for ANN. This is shown in Figure 13.14 and Table 13.3.

Single Layer Solution

The Octave code to implement and train a single layer ANN accompanies the web page for this text.

Training results (TSS error vs. epoch) for the no-hidden-layer case are plotted in Figure 13.15.

---

[8]For example, it may grow exponentially in terms of the number of inputs.

[9]See http://www.gnu.org/software/octave/

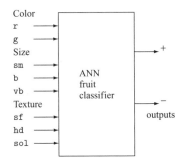

Figure 13.14 Input Structure for Fruit Classification Network

Color		Size			Texture			Class
r	g	sm	b	vb	sf	hd	sol	
1	0	0	0	1	1	0	0	+
0	1	0	1	1	0	1	0	+
0	1	1	0	0	0	1	0	+
1	0	0	1	0	0	1	0	-
1	0	1	0	0	0	1	0	-
1	0	0	0	1	0	0	1	-

Table 13.3 ANN Binary Training Inputs for Fruit Problem

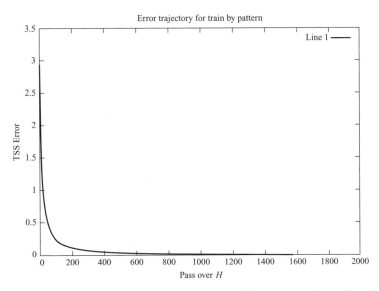

Figure 13.15 Training Results for a Single Layer ANN Used for Fruit Classification

Fruit Classification Mapping Results

Abbreviated Octave results are shown here. While a two-layer solution appears unnecessary, it is left to the problems for comparison.

```
d = 8
n = 6
t =

  1  1  1  0  0  0
  0  0  0  1  1  1

c = 2
lr = 0.25000
niter = 2000
w1 =

 Columns 1 through 6:

   -3.1428296    3.5939010    0.0091509   -0.6861817    2.0213275    3.9263531
    3.1428296   -3.5939010   -0.0091509    0.6861817   -2.0213275   -3.9263531

 Columns 7 and 8:

   -0.6770309   -2.7982509
    0.6770309    2.7982509

b1 =

   0.45107
  -0.45107

o1 =

   0.9628853   0.9910142   0.9669809   0.0170406   0.0335810   0.0302166
   0.0371147   0.0089858   0.0330191   0.9829594   0.9664190   0.9697834

init_tss_error = 3.1018
final_tss_error = 0.0097717
```

Effect of Weight Initialization

Note that initial weights (including bias) are $w_{ij} = 0 \; \forall \; ij$ in the network. The symmetry of the weights in the solution, as a result of the GDR, is evident.

13.7.2 Blocks Movement

In this section, we show a two-layer solution for the blocks moving problem. A one-layer solution (and comparison) is left to the problems. The training data is taken from Table 16.13 in Section 16.4.9. It is repeated here in Table 13.4.

locOB	clearUp	clearLeft	clearRight	clearDown	move?
up	yes	yes	yes	yes	up
up	no	yes	yes	yes	left
up	no	no	yes	yes	right
up	no	no	no	yes	down
down	yes	yes	yes	yes	down
down	no	yes	yes	no	right
down	yes	no	no	no	up
down	no	no	yes	no	right
left	yes	yes	yes	yes	left
left	no	no	yes	yes	down
left	yes	yes	yes	no	left
left	yes	no	no	yes	up
right	yes	yes	yes	yes	right
right	yes	yes	no	yes	up
right	no	no	no	yes	down
right	no	yes	no	no	left

Table 13.4 Multiple Outcome Blocks Movement Training Examples. (This data is used for both ANN and ID3 training examples.)

Converting Blocks World Inputs for the ANN

As in the previous example, inputs to this problem are first converted into binary-valued inputs suitable for the ANN. This is shown in Figure 13.16 and in the Octave implementation that follow.

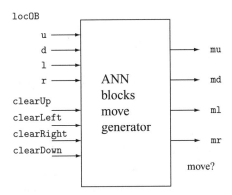

Figure 13.16 Input Strategy Used for ANN-Based Blocks Moving Example (others are possible)

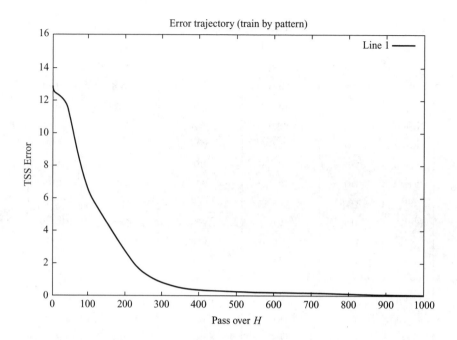

Figure 13.17 Training Error Trajectory for Two-Layer ANN Used for Blocks Movement

Two-Layer Blocks Solution

Using the input-output structure of Section 13.7.2, Octave was used to implement and train a two-layer ANN with 16 hidden units. The Octave implementation for this problem is available from the text's website. Training results (TSS error) are plotted in Figure 13.17.

Training Set Mapping Results

These results are shown in Figure 13.18. Using the weights determined by training, the absolute value of the difference between the target and actual output for each of the four ANN outputs is computed. This is shown for all 16 patterns in H. The absolute value of the error for any of the four outputs and any training set pattern is at most 0.06; therefore suitable rounding of output values (to 0 or 1) produces a perfect mapping over H.

In addition, it is necessary to consider the generalization of the block-moving network using inputs not in the training set. This is left to the exercises. A one-layer solution, for comparison, is also left to the exercises.

13.7.3   Learning an A/D Converter Function

In this example, we attempt to implement a 4-bit A/D converter by training an MLFF neural network with a suitable architecture. The specifications are summarized here:

1. (Analog) input in the range $[0, 1)$;

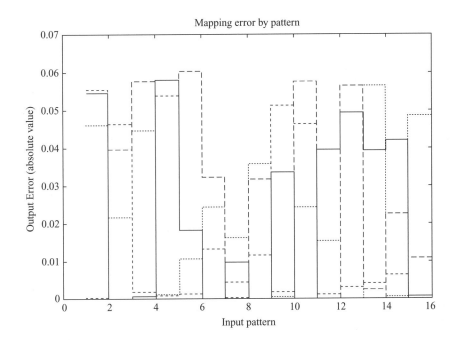

Figure 13.18 Training Results (over H) for a Two-Layer ANN Used for Blocks Movement

2. Sigmoidal units and WLIC formation of *net*;

3. For an input (in the input range) of value $\frac{n}{16}$, output is 4-bit unsigned binary representation of n; and

4. Training using the GDR.

The A/D converter function is much more of a challenge, particularly since correct generalization (interpolation) is required.

Results

Results using Octave are shown in Figure 13.19. Note "Line 1" represents the ideal mapping characteristic (with an infinite number of bits). "Line 2" represents the ideal case with 4-bit quantization, and "Line 3" is the mapping actually obtained from the trained ANN.

13.8 Resources

The Usenet newsgroup comp.ai.neural-nets is quite useful for beginners. In addition, archives and a complete, but somewhat outdated, FAQ may be found at ftp://ftp.sas.com/pub/neural/FAQ.html.

An interesting reference for biologically-inspired computing is http://www.egr.msu.edu/~hujianju/Biologically_inspired.htm.

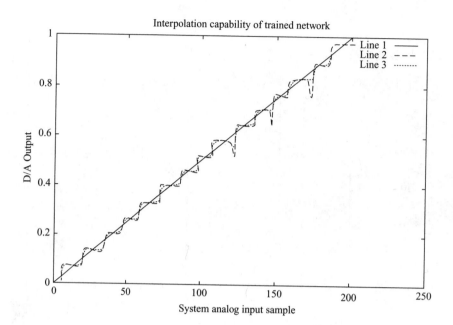

Figure 13.19 Training Results for Two-Layer ANN Used for A/D Converter

13.9 References

The history of feedforward ANNs is partially rooted in attempts to extend the use and training of linear mapping functions (considered in Chapter 4). The seminal paper is [RM86]. A comparison of neural mapping approaches is found in [HL87]. A geometrical analysis of ANN mapping capabilities is shown in [WL87]. An important consideration in neural implementations with limited precision analog or digital circuits is the network sensitivity to weight errors. An excellent examination of this effect is [SW90]. Numerous extensions to the GDR algorithm analysis exist. One particularly important concept is the adjustment of the learning rate, leading to adaptive learning algorithms. Interesting references are [Jac88] and [SA90].

13.10 Exercises

1. Design a feedforward network (using GDR training) that implements a 4-bit digital-to-analog (D/A) converter. Use a single output $o_1 \in [0, 1]$ and consider the input bit pattern $i_1\ i_2\ i_3\ i_4$ to be a binary number with i_1 the MSB.

2. Design and train feedforward networks that, given binary inputs A and B, implement:

    (a) The logical three-input AND function;

    (b) The logical three-input OR function; and

    (c) The logical function $\bar{A}\bar{B} + AB$. (This function is useful in matching binary patterns.)

3. Suppose we are designing an NN to determine if an input pattern (of varying length) corresponds to the binary representation of an (unsigned) even or odd number. For our purposes, consider the input pattern to be fixed length, with "0"s in the higher order bit positions, e.g.,

$000101_2 = 3_{10}$ is in class *odd*; and

$010000_2 = 16_{10}$ is in class *even*.

Choose an NN structure and develop a training set. Determine the NN weights. After training, does your NN place as much significance on the least significant bit as a human would?

4. Referring to Figure 13.20, the initial weight values are as shown.

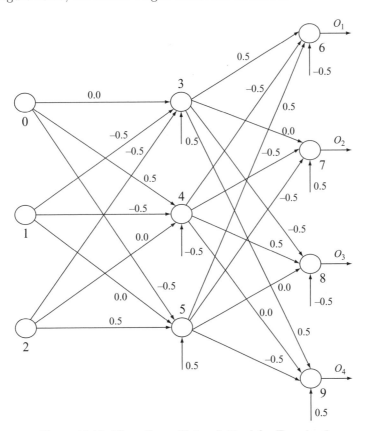

Figure 13.20 Three-Layer Network Used for Exercise 4

The network uses sigmoidal units with unity gain. The learning rate, $\epsilon = 1.0$. For the following input:

$$\underline{i}^p = \begin{pmatrix} 1 \\ 1 \\ 0 \end{pmatrix} \tag{13.35}$$

and corresponding target:

$$\underline{t}^p = \begin{pmatrix} 0 \\ 1 \\ 0 \\ 1 \end{pmatrix} \tag{13.36}$$

determine δ_4 for the first iteration.

5. A more general activation function is of the form:

$$o_j = f(net_j) = \frac{1}{1 + e^{-\{\frac{(net_j - \theta_j)}{\theta_o}\}}} \tag{13.37}$$

(a) Show how the parameter θ_j serves as a threshold and "positions" f.

(b) Show how θ_o determines the abruptness of the transition of f.

(c) Suggest applications for each of the parameters in (a) and (b).

(d) Discuss how the parameters θ_j and θ_o could be obtained from training.

6. TRUE or FALSE: If an $E = 0$ solution to a mapping problem with a fixed architecture exists, the GDR with a single random initialization will find it.

7. Given the GDR weight correction equations of Section 13.5.5, discuss whether $\{-1, 1\}$ or $\{0, 1\}$ inputs are more desirable.

8. Suppose the pattern error to be minimized by the GDR is $E^p = \frac{1}{2}||\underline{e}^p||_R^2$, where R is diagonal. Re-derive the equations for weight correction $\triangle^p w_{ji} = \epsilon \delta_j^p \tilde{o}_i^p$ for both output and hidden units.

9. This problem concerns the application of the GDR equations "by hand." Refer to the $1 \times 1 \times 2$ FF ANN shown in Figure 13.21. The hidden unit has a bias (w_{2b}); output units do not. Thus, there are four parameters (w_{21}, w_{2b} (the bias), w_{32}, and w_{42}) to be determined. Units are referred to

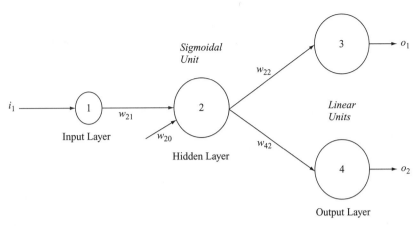

Figure 13.21 Network for "Hand-Worked" GDR Problem

by numbers that are shown inside the unit. The training set, H, consists of a single target-input pair[10] as follows:

$$H = \{(\begin{pmatrix} -3 \\ 3 \end{pmatrix}, 3)\} \tag{13.38}$$

Additional parameters and constraints are:

- Initial weights are $w_{ij} = 0$ for all ij, including bias;
- Output units are linear: $f(net) = net$;
- The hidden unit uses logistic function for squashing;
- Only the hidden unit has a bias;
- The learning rate, $\epsilon = 0.5$; and
- All weights are updated after each entire back propagation phase is complete (i.e., hidden layer δ_2 uses the "old" output weights).

Show the first two iterations of the GDR, and show all intermediate quantities, (E, δ_k, Δw_{ij}, net_k, $f(net_k)$, $f'(net_k)$, and so on), as well as the weights after each complete iteration. Also, compute E at the start, and after iterations #1 and #2. Does E decrease?

10. Section 13.7.3 considered "learning" the A/D converter function using an MLFF ANN. For reference, research the conventional design of A/D converters. Does the ANN-based approach have any similarity?

---

[10]This is not realistic, but a larger cardinality H would only make the problem more complicated and not aid in testing whether you understand the GDR computations.

11. In Chapter 16, Section 16.5.1, the use of ID3 for learning fruit classification rules is shown. In addition, Section 13.7.1 showed the realization of a fruit classifier by training an MLFF ANN.

    Compare and contrast these approaches. Especially significant are any similarities you find. Issues to address include:

    ◆ The learning or training process used;

    ◆ The form of the training data;

    ◆ The amount of human intervention necessary in the process;

    ◆ Alternative uses for/extensions of the resulting classifier;

    ◆ The resulting generalization of the solution implemented; and

    ◆ Any other relevant issues.

12. In Section 13.7.1, the resulting weights for the fruit classifier network are shown.

    (a) Draw the network and label the weights.

    (b) Carefully examine the resulting GDR-produced weights. Does the network weight structure indicate anything about the relative significance of the inputs in determining the classification?

13. Use a two-layer FF ANN to implement the fruit classification problem. Compare your results with those of the one-layer solution in Section 13.7.1.

14. Develop and compare a one-layer FF ANN solution to the blocks movement problem of Section 13.7.2.

15. An IS engineer was interested in developing the fastest and most minimal ANN implementation possible for an intelligent, ANN-based "black-box" blocks mover. The training data used is the same data as for the previous problem (see Table 13.4).

    The engineer decided to use a single unit with a bias. The activation function was a sigmoid. The engineer decided to use the input and output representation shown as follows (MATLAB or Octave format).

```
% inputs:
%% locOB: u,d,l,r binary (one-of) inputs
%% clearUP,clearLeft,clearRight,clearDown:
%%          each a single binary input
%%          0=no; 1=yes

% {u d l r} cU cL cR cD
p=[1 0 0 0  1 1 1 1;
   1 0 0 0  0 1 1 1;
   1 0 0 0  0 0 1 1;
   1 0 0 0  0 0 0 1;
   0 1 0 0  1 1 1 1;
   0 1 0 0  0 1 1 0;
```

```
        0 1 0 0   1 0 0 0;
        0 1 0 0   0 0 1 0;
        0 0 1 0   1 1 1 1;
        0 0 1 0   0 0 1 1;
        0 0 1 0   1 1 1 0;
        0 0 1 0   1 0 0 1;
        0 0 0 1   1 1 1 1;
        0 0 0 1   1 1 0 1;
        0 0 0 1   0 0 0 1;
        0 0 0 1   0 1 0 0]'

%% output
% use midpoints of regions

%       up:    [0-0.25];  use   0.125
%       left:  [0.25-0.50]; use 0.375
%       down:  [0.5-0.75];  use 0.625
%       right: [0.75-1];    use 0.875

t=[0.125;   %up
   0.375;   %left
   0.875;   %right
   0.625;   %down
   0.625;   %down
   0.875;   %right
   0.125;   %up
   0.875;   %right
   0.375;   %left
   0.625;   %down
   0.375;   %left
   0.125;   %up
   0.875;   %right
   0.125;   %up
   0.625;   %down
   0.375]'  %left
```

After training, the resulting single unit weights and bias are given here.

```
w1 =  -0.73602   0.42045  -0.59893   0.97817  -1.13033  -1.13875   2.23212   0.19779

b1 = -0.27242
```

It is your job to quantitatively assess this solution. An answer such as "It is good" or "It is bad" is not acceptable. Only consider the 16 inputs given (in other words, ignore generalization).

16. Chapter 16, Table 16.14 shows a set of exemplars ($E1$–$E6$) for learning fruit classification. In addition, the Chapter 16 problems contain a problem that is considered a valid (but not necessarily optimal) generalization for class $+$.

Use this data with the ANN from Section 13.7.1 to test the generalization of the resulting network.

17. The ID3 algorithm of Chapter 16 allows multiple outcomes for the same attribute values. In this case the most frequent output is incorporated into the tree. How would the training and operation of an FF ANN be influenced by this type of data?

18. Section 16.4.10 of Chapter 16 considers the development of an ID3 tree for a five-input parity detection function. The input consists of five binary-valued attributes, $x1$ through $x5$. The binary-valued outcome, denoted out? is 1 if the attribute values consist of an even number of "1"s. Develop an ML FF ANN for this function.

19. Table 16.15 in the Exercises section of Chapter 16 shows training data provided by aspiring politicians for U.S. health care insurance solutions. (Our interest is apolitical.) Determine the suitability of this problem for an MLFF ANN solution. Implement the solution and show your results.

Neural Networks (Part 2): Recurrent Networks and IS Applications

14.1 Introduction

Recurrent networks have closed loops in the network topology. The outputs of all units comprise the network (or system) state. A recurrent ANN maps *states* into *states*.

We explore a form of a recurrent neural network suitable for autoassociative, (content) addressable memory (AM or CAM), and optimization and constraint satisfaction applications. First, a nonlinear, totally interconnected, recurrent, and symmetric network is developed. This network is often referred to as a "Hopfield" net. Patterns stored in this configuration correspond to the stable states of a nonlinear system. This device is able to recall as well as *complete* partially specified inputs. The network is trained via a *storage prescription* that forces stable states to correspond to (local) minima of a network "energy" function. The memory capacity, or allowable number of stored states, is shown to be related to the location of the particular states, network size, and the training algorithm.

The "Hopfield" net, honors John Hopfield of Caltech, who seems to have popularized the strategy. The pioneering work actually occurred over 10 years prior to Hopfield's publications by Amari [Ama72b]. Amari proposed the recurrent structure and a correlation-based learning prescription while providing considerable insight into network performance in 1972. The Hopfield approach serves as a *framework* or exemplar for other related neural network design paradigms. The Hopfield structure is somewhat paradoxical in that it is easily described with a few equations, yet gives rise to complex mathematical analysis. In addition, the energy-minimization characteristic of the Hopfield net leads to interesting applications in constraint satisfaction and optimization.

14.2 Basic Parameters and Recurrent Network Design

We initially follow the approach of Hopfield [Hop82], [Hop84], [HT85], [HT86], in developing a recurrent neural computational paradigm.

14.2.1 Network Parameters

The following variables are defined:

o_i: the output state of the ith neuron. Therefore, the vector $\underline{o}$ represents the outputs of all units and therefore the state of the entire network.

α_i: the activation threshold of the ith neuron.

w_{ij}: the interconnection weight, i.e., the strength of the connection **FROM** the output of neuron j **TO** neuron i. Thus, $\Sigma_j w_{ij} o_j$ is the total input or activation (net_i) to neuron i. To begin, assume $w_{ij} \in R$, although other possibilities (e.g., binary interconnections) are possible. With the constraints developed as follows, for a d-unit network there are $\frac{d(d-1)}{2}$ possibly nonzero and unique weights.

In the Hopfield network, every neuron is allowed to be connected to all other neurons, although the value of w_{ij} varies (it may also be 0 to indicate no unit interconnection). To avoid false reinforcement of a neuron state, the constraint $w_{ii} = 0$ is employed. *Thus, no self-feedback is allowed in the Hopfield formulation.*

Hopfield Unit Characteristic

Threshold or hardlimiter unit characteristics are commonly used, although in some cases this firing characteristic requires careful interpretation, since the network behavior may be different when $\alpha_i = 0^-$ vs. $\alpha_i = 0^+$. Hopfield's original work suggested a slight modification of the hardlimiter characteristic, where the interpretation of the unit output at the threshold value is somewhat different; the unit output is unchanged from its previous value. We refer to this as the "leave it alone" characteristic, given by:

$$o_i = \begin{cases} 1 & if \sum_{j;\ j \neq i} w_{ij} o_j > \alpha_i \\ o_i \quad (previously) & if \sum_{j;\ j \neq i} w_{ij} o_j = \alpha_i \\ 0 & otherwise \end{cases} \tag{14.1}$$

Commonly, $\alpha_i = 0$. Notice from Equation 14.1, the neuron activation characteristic is nonlinear. Commonly, the threshold $\alpha_i = 0$. Notice from Equation 14.1, where $\alpha_i = 0\ \forall i$, there is no impetus for the system to move from the state $\underline{o}(t_k) = \underline{0}$.

The Unit Cube and Related Concepts

In the case of a discrete system with $o_i \in \{a, b\}$, we note that the system state "lives" or exists only on the vertices of a d-dimensional hypercube. The most common case is where $o_i \in \{0, 1\}$, in which case this is the unit hypercube. State transitions are movements from vertex to vertex. It is worth noting that in a d-unit Hopfield net, whether discrete units have $\{0, 1\}$ or $\{-1, 1\}$ outputs, there are 2^d states in state space.

14.2.2 Network Dynamics

State Initialization and Trajectory

The Hopfield net is started in state $\underline{o}(0)$ by initializing all unit outputs to some values. Viewing the state of a d-neuron Hopfield network at time (or iteration) t_k as a $d \times 1$ vector, $\underline{o}(t_k)$, the state of the system at time t_{k+1} (or iteration $k+1$ in the discrete case) may be described by the nonlinear state transformation:

$$\underline{o}(t_{k+1}) = \underline{f}(W\underline{o}(t_k)) \tag{14.2}$$

or

$$W\underline{o}(t_k) \stackrel{*}{\Rightarrow} \underline{o}(t_{k+1}) \tag{14.3}$$

where the $\stackrel{*}{\Rightarrow}$ operator indicates the element-by-element state transition characteristic that is used to form $\underline{o}(t_{k+1})$. In order to see the two-part process (net activation formation and subsequent squashing), the preceding formulation uses matrix multiplication for the formation of the LHS of Equation 14.3. This represents a vector of activations at time t_k, $\underline{net}(t_k)$, whose ith element is $net_i(t_k)$. The $\stackrel{*}{\Rightarrow}$ in Equation 14.3 does not imply equality or assignment, however, unless the units have a linear input/output characteristic. It is merely a convenient notational shorthand, and allows an interpretation of stable network states in a manner analogous to a linear algebra formulation.

Unit Bias. Equation 14.3 may be generalized for each unit to accommodate an additional vector of unit bias inputs, i.e.,

$$\left[(W\underline{o}(t_k) + \underline{i}(t_k)\right] \stackrel{*}{\Rightarrow} \underline{o}(t_{k+1}) \tag{14.4}$$

For example, using a hardlimiter as the activation function, Equation 14.4 may be written for unit i as

$$o_i(t_{k+1}) = \mu_s\left(\sum_j w_{ij}o_j(t_k) + i_i\right) \tag{14.5}$$

where i_i is the external or bias input to unit i and μ_s is the unit step function,

$$\mu_s(x) = \begin{cases} 1 & x > 0 \\ 0 & x \le 0 \end{cases} \tag{14.6}$$

Network Updating Strategies

The timing of the updating of units in a recurrent network offers several possibilities. Obvious extremes are:

◆ All units are updated simultaneously.

◆ Units are randomly updated without any concern for synchronization with the updating of other units.

It is interesting to explore the effects of varying the relative timing of the unit updates. Another way to visualize this effect is that we are controlling, to some extent, the allowable trajectories of the state vector in state space. For example, if we update only one unit at a time, we are forcing the system to either stay at the current vertex or move to one that is a Hamming Distance (HD) of 1 away. Clearly, the network convergence properties, and converged state, may be influenced by these constraints.

The network state propagation given by Equation 14.3 suggests that the unit transitions are synchronous, that is, each unit, in lockstep fashion with all other units, computes its net activation and subsequent output. While this is achievable in (serial) simulations, it is not necessary.

14.2.3 Determining and Quantifying Network States and Behavior

The notion of a system equilibrium state is one of the central themes in systems analysis. For a continuous system, states where $\underline{\dot{o}}(t) = \underline{0}$ are equilibrium states. For a discrete system, states where $\underline{o}(k+1) = \underline{o}(k)$ are equilibrium states. As shown in the following subsections, equilibrium states may be stable, unstable, or neutrally stable. Given any initial state, $\underline{o}(0)$, the recurrent network equations define a state trajectory, $\underline{o}(k) = \phi(k, \underline{o}_0)$, for all time steps $k \in \{0, 1, \cdots, \infty\}$. More is said about this in dealing with CSPs.

Equilibrium Versus Stable States. Stable states are equilibrium states with special local properties, namely the influence of the state trajectory for small perturbations from the equilibrium point. If the system returns to $\underline{o}_e$ then the point is also stable. Stable points are denoted $\underline{o}^s$. In what follows, we show why the ability to store and recall equilibrium/stable states is useful.

State Energy Formulation. To explore the dynamics of a system, we use an energy-based formulation. The *energy analogy* model likens the state-dependent energy to the state of a ball on a hill. The one-dimensional case for various starting states ($\underline{o}_0$) is shown in Figure 14.1.

Notice from Figure 14.1 that points B, D, E, F, and G correspond to system equilibrium states. Left alone, the system has no physical motivation to change state. Points B, E, and G are stable points, i.e., for small perturbations the system returns to these points. Note that they correspond to local minima in the energy function. Points D and F are neutrally stable equilibrium points. Points A and C are not equilibrium points. If the system is started in either of these points, it will not remain there but rather tend to other states with a lower energy value that are local energy minima.

For associative memory applications, after the storing process, a number of fundamental states are learned that are desired to be asymptotically stable equilibrium points. However, in addition to the learned states, spurious states [BGM94] can exist that negatively affect the performance of the system. A *spurious state* is a stable state (asymptotically or oscillatory) that is not part of the learned pattern set. These spurious states are not desirable, yet they exist in most of the neural implementations of associative memory.

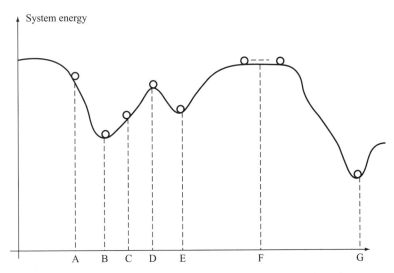

Figure 14.1 System Energy as a Function of Various Possible States (A–G) for a Ball on a Hill

14.3 Weight Storage Prescription and Network Capacity
14.3.1 Weight Prescriptions

The storage prescriptions shown as follows lead to symmetric network interconnection matrices with zero diagonal entries. This is a popular form, although others, as shown in the References, exist.

Units Outputs $\in \{0, 1\}$.   First we treat the case of $\{0, 1\}$ unit outputs, no bias input,[1] and $\alpha_i = 0$. This leads to the rule for determination of w_{ij}, from Equations 14.9 and 14.1, together with a set of desired stored states $\underline{o}^s, s = 1, 2, ...n$, from the the training set (stored states) $H = \{\underline{o}^1, \underline{o}^2, \ldots, \underline{o}^n\}$. The prescription given by Hopfield is:

$$w_{ij} = \sum_{s=1}^{n}(2o_i^s - 1)(2o_j^s - 1) \qquad i \neq j \tag{14.7}$$

with the additional "no self-activation" constraint

$$w_{ii} = 0 \tag{14.8}$$

It is paramount to note that stable (stored) states correspond to minima of the following energy function:

$$E = -\frac{1}{2}\sum_{i \neq j}\sum w_{ij}o_i o_j \tag{14.9}$$

---

[1] The effect and use of the bias is addressed later.

Assessment.   When employing the Hopfield network in certain constraint satisfaction problems, the energy of a state can be interpreted [He81] as the extent to which a combination of hypotheses or instantiations fit the underlying neural-formulated model. Thus, low energy values indicate a good level of constraint satisfaction. This is considered later.

Weight Prescription and Energy for $\{-1, 1\}$ Units.   For $\{-1, 1\}$ units, the storage prescription of Equation 14.7 becomes even simpler:

$$w_{ij} = \sum_{s=1}^{n} o_i^s o_j^s \qquad i \neq j \tag{14.10}$$

with the previous constraint

$$w_{ii} = 0 \tag{14.11}$$

The energy function of Equation 14.9 remains applicable.

14.3.2 Additional Characterizations of the Storage Prescription

Relation to Outer-Product (Hebbian) Learning.   The storage prescription of Equation 14.10 is a Hebbian or outer-product formulation. Note that w_{ij} is formed by considering the joint states of units o_i and o_j, and that equal unit output values yield a positive reinforcement, whereas unequal (complementary) unit output values lead to negative values of the weight.

Symmetry of the Hopfield Learning Prescription.   The storage prescription of Equations 14.7 or 14.10 yield a network with considerable interconnection symmetry. For example, with $\{0, 1\}$ units:

$$w_{ji} = \sum_{s}(2o_j^s - 1)(2o_i^s - 1) = w_{ij} \tag{14.12}$$

It is left to the reader to verify the symmetry with $\{-1, 1\}$ units.

System Energy Concepts, Part I.   For the discrete-in-time and "high-gain" case and units without bias, an energy function identical to Equation 14.9 is formulated using the quadratic form:

$$E(\underline{o}) = -\frac{1}{2}\underline{o}^T W \underline{o} \tag{14.13}$$

where network interconnection matrix $W = [w_{ij}]$ is symmetric with $w_{ii} = 0$. This function defines, over the state space of $\underline{o}$, an energy landscape. The objective is for minima of E to correspond to stored states of the CAM. From Equation 14.10, since W corresponds to the superposition of a number of pattern-specific weight matrices, i.e.,

$$W = W_1 + W_2 + \ldots W_n \tag{14.14}$$

Equation 14.13 may be rewritten as:

$$E = -\frac{1}{2}\underline{o}^T[W_1 + W_2 \ldots W_n] = E_1 + E_2 + \ldots E_n \tag{14.15}$$

The interaction of these individual energy "landscapes" leads to spurious local minima, which may be a problem.

Comparison with Discrete Time Linear Dynamic Systems.   The determination of neural network state evolution in the formulation of Equation 14.3 parallels that of the unforced or homogeneous discrete *linear* time invariant system: $\underline{x}(t_{k+1}) = A\underline{x}(t_k)$. For example, given A, there may be states such that as $k \to \infty$, $\underline{x}(t_{k+1}) = \underline{x}(t_k)$. These are analogous to the stable states of the nonlinear system of Equation 14.3. It is well known that these states are given by the eigenvectors of the A matrix, which correspond to eigenvalues of unity.

14.3.3 Network Capacity Estimation

Unfortunately, the simplicity of the Hopfield approach is not without its limitations. These include limited and sometimes unpredictable stored state capacity as well as limited and sometimes unpredictable state trajectories. A reasonable question is therefore: "As a rough rule of thumb, how many patterns should be able to be stored in a net?" More quantitatively, the convergence of the network also involves the Hamming distance between the initial state and the desired stable state. Different stable states that are close in Hamming distance are undesirable, since convergence to an incorrect stable state may result. Hopfield [Hop82] suggested that a d-neuron network allows approximately $0.15d$ stable states, if the states are well separated in state space.

Other researchers have proposed more conservative bounds [AMJ85]. McEliece [MV87] presents a detailed analysis of the memory capacity, which covers both synchronous and asynchronous unit updating with symmetric interconnections. In this study, the network capacity, C, to store randomly generated patterns (with uniform distribution), is found to be bounded by:

$$\frac{n}{4ln(n)} < C < \frac{n}{2ln(n)} \tag{14.16}$$

where n is the total number of units. For example, the boundary values for a 100-neuron network (using Equation 14.16) are about 5.4 to 10.8 stored states.

14.4 Recurrent Network Design Procedures and Example CAM Applications
14.4.1 General Design Procedure

Training Set Design and Determining W.   The design procedure is summarized as:

1. Determine the training set (and therefore W);

2. Initially test for desired CAM properties using the training set to verify recall of the stored patterns;

3. Check E in this process; and

4. Modify the network, E, and the training set if operation is not satisfactory and repeat the preceding steps.

Verifying CAM Properties. Following initial design, the emphasis shifts to assessment of system performance. Specifically:

1. We need to consider (relatively small) perturbations of stored characters as the initial state and explore the resulting state dynamics/trajectories;

2. We need to assess the performance of the net as an associative memory;

3. We need to examine E as a function of the state[2] for each state trajectory; and

4. We need to identify other important network characteristics, such as "spurious" states.

14.4.2 Another CAM Example: Design of a Simple Hopfield Network—Storing and Accessing Stable States

Problem Specification. Assume the neuron threshold, $\alpha_i = 0$, and a binary, i.e., $\{0, 1\}$ output. The network is required to store the following stable state:

$$\underline{o}^s = \begin{pmatrix} 1 \\ 0 \\ 1 \\ 0 \end{pmatrix}$$

First we determine the unit interconnections and verify that $\underline{o}_s$ is a stable state. For a four-neuron network, there are $16 - 4 = 12$ possibly nonzero network weights or coefficients. Due to the symmetry of the network, six are unique. From the storage prescription of 14.12, given the number of stable states $n = 1$, weights are

$$w_{ij} = (2o_i^s - 1)(2o_j^s - 1)$$

where

$$\underline{o}^s = \begin{pmatrix} o_1^s \\ o_2^s \\ o_3^s \\ o_4^s \end{pmatrix} = \begin{pmatrix} 1 \\ 0 \\ 1 \\ 0 \end{pmatrix}$$

Therefore, $w_{12} = (2o_1^s - 1)(2o_2^s - 1) = (2-1)(-1) = -1$ and similarly $w_{13} = (2-1)(2-1) = +1 = w_{31}$, $w_{14} = (2-1)(-1) = -1 = w_{41}$, $w_{23} = (-1)(2-1) = -1 = w_{32}$, $w_{24} = (-1)(-1) = +1 = w_{42}$, and

---

[2]Here we mean iteration number; the state dimensionality precludes a plot of E vs. the state.

$w_{34} = (2-1)(-1) = -1 = w_{43}$. Recall also the constraint $w_{11} = w_{22} = w_{33} = w_{44} = 0$. The network state is propagated using Equation 14.3:

$$\begin{pmatrix} 0 & -1 & 1 & -1 \\ -1 & 0 & -1 & 1 \\ 1 & -1 & 0 & -1 \\ -1 & 1 & -1 & 0 \end{pmatrix} \underline{o}(t_k) \stackrel{*}{\Rightarrow} \underline{o}(t_{k+1})$$

where $\stackrel{*}{\Rightarrow}$ denotes the nonlinear activation to output mapping.

Checking for Stable States.   Notice for $\underline{o}(t_k) = \underline{o}^s$;

$$W\underline{o}^s = \begin{pmatrix} 1 \\ -2 \\ 1 \\ -2 \end{pmatrix}$$

therefore $\underline{o}(t_{k+1}) = \underline{o}^s$. Thus, $\underline{o}^s$ is indeed a stable state, and any trajectory that includes $\underline{o}^s$ converges to $\underline{o}^s$.

Assessment of Network Trajectory for Other Initial States.   Since there are only 16 possible distinct states, it is relatively easy to explore and enumerate state trajectories as a function of $\underline{o}(t_0)$. When the network is started in initial states other than $\underline{o}^s$, we explore the resulting state trajectories. Denote these initial states as $\underline{o}^1$, $\underline{o}^2$, and $\underline{o}^3$, where

$$\underline{o}^1(t_o) = \begin{pmatrix} 1 \\ 0 \\ 0 \\ 1 \end{pmatrix} \qquad \underline{o}^2(t_o) = \begin{pmatrix} 1 \\ 0 \\ 0 \\ 0 \end{pmatrix} \qquad \underline{o}^3(t_o) = \begin{pmatrix} 0 \\ 0 \\ 0 \\ 1 \end{pmatrix}$$

Given $\underline{o}^1(t_o)$, $\underline{o}(t_1)$ is found from

$$W\underline{o}^1(t_o) = \begin{pmatrix} -1 \\ 0 \\ 0 \\ -1 \end{pmatrix} \stackrel{*}{\Rightarrow} \begin{pmatrix} 0 \\ 0 \\ 0 \\ 0 \end{pmatrix} = \underline{o}^1(t_1)$$

Furthermore, at t_2

$$W\underline{o}^1(t_1) = \begin{pmatrix} 0 \\ 0 \\ 0 \\ 0 \end{pmatrix} \stackrel{*}{\Rightarrow} \underline{o}^1(t_2) = \underline{o}^1(t_1)$$

and the network is in a stable state, *but not one that was explicitly stored.* Thus, $\underline{o}(t_k) = \underline{0}$ is another stable state. For $o^2(t_k)$,

$$W\underline{o}^2(t_o) = \begin{pmatrix} 0 \\ -1 \\ 1 \\ -1 \end{pmatrix} \overset{*}{\Rightarrow} \begin{pmatrix} 1 \\ 0 \\ 1 \\ 0 \end{pmatrix} = \underline{o}^2(t_1) = \underline{o}^s$$

The network therefore converges from initial state $\underline{o}^2(t_o)$ to $\underline{o}^s$ after one iteration. For $\underline{o}^3(t_k)$, a very interesting case occurs:

$$W\underline{o}^3(t_o) = \begin{pmatrix} -1 \\ 1 \\ -1 \\ 0 \end{pmatrix} \overset{*}{\Rightarrow} \begin{pmatrix} 0 \\ 1 \\ 0 \\ 0 \end{pmatrix} = \underline{o}^3(t_1)$$

$$W\underline{o}^3(t_1) = \begin{pmatrix} -1 \\ 0 \\ -1 \\ 1 \end{pmatrix} \overset{*}{\Rightarrow} \begin{pmatrix} 0 \\ 0 \\ 0 \\ 1 \end{pmatrix} = \underline{o}^3(t_2) = \underline{o}^3(t_0)$$

The system is therefore in a *cycle*.

14.4.3 CAM Example: Association of Simple Two–Dimensional Patterns

Input Patterns.   Consider the storage of the 5×5 patterns shown in Figure 14.2. Two-dimensional inputs are converted to vectors using row concatenation.

Checking Stored States.   Figure 14.3 shows the behavior of the network as a CAM, using the stored states from H as input.

Performance Using Perturbed Input Patterns.   Results are shown in Figure 14.4.

14.5 Recurrent Networks: Energy Function Characterization

In this section, we take a more in-depth look at recurrent network state energy, especially as it relates to convergence properties. The primary sources of reference are [RV87], [Hir89], [Kob91], [PB94], and [AF90].

The Russian mathematician Liapunov devised a stability test that is based upon energy-like (or Liapunov) functions [Bro74] denoted $E(\underline{o})$. Determining suitable Liapunov functions in general is difficult. Fortunately, many problems allow the use of constrained quadratic forms. *Local minima* of the energy function correspond to *locally stable* system or network states.

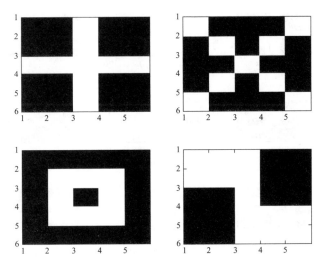

Figure 14.2 5 × 5 CAM: Patterns Used in H for CAM Example

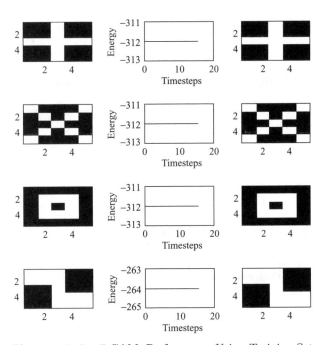

Figure 14.3 5 × 5 CAM: Performance Using Training Set

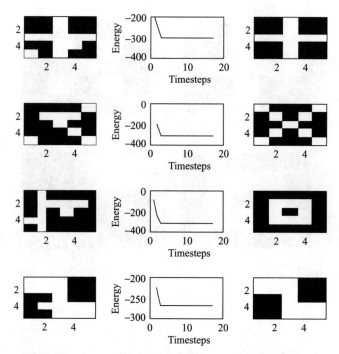

Figure 14.4 5 × 5 CAM: Response for Distorted Input Patterns

14.5.1 Energy Analysis or "Why Hopfield Networks Work"

We alluded to the concept of an *energy function* in Section 14.2.3. For the discrete and "high-gain" case of $\alpha_i = 0$ in Equation 14.1, an energy function is defined using the quadratic form:

$$E(\underline{o}) = -\frac{1}{2}\underline{o}^T W \underline{o} \tag{14.17}$$

where network interconnection matrix $W = [w_{ij}]$ is symmetric with $w_{ii} = 0$. Alternately, Equation 14.17 may be rewritten as

$$E(\underline{o}) = -\frac{1}{2}\sum_{i \neq j}\sum w_{ij}o_i o_j \tag{14.18}$$

Computing $\frac{\partial E(\underline{o})}{\partial \underline{o}}$ yields (see Chapter 2)

$$\frac{\partial E(\underline{o})}{\partial \underline{o}} = -W\underline{o} \tag{14.19}$$

or

$$\frac{\triangle E(\underline{o})}{\triangle o_i} = -\sum_{i \neq j} w_{ij}o_j \tag{14.20}$$

Relating the result of Equation 14.20 with Equation 14.1 is quite interesting. If the right-hand side of Equation 14.20 is negative, then it must be that

$$\sum_{i \neq j} w_{ij} o_j > 0 \tag{14.21}$$

From the neural unit activation characteristic of Equation 14.1, Equation 14.21 requires either $\triangle o_i > 0$ (if o_i were initially 0) or $\triangle o_i = 0$ (if o_i were already 1). Thus, $\triangle o_i$ in Equation 14.20 cannot be negative, and consequently any change in energy function, E, *cannot be positive* in this network. From Equation 14.17, since each o_i is bounded, i.e., $o_i \in [0, 1]$, E is bounded. Therefore, network dynamics, viewed in terms of unit transitions, must be such that the E either decreases or remains the same. Clearly, "separation" of stable states that correspond to local minima is desirable. This is related to the issue of memory capacity. This brief convergence analysis yields some insight into the dynamics of the Hopfield network structure.

14.5.2 Example: $d = 4$ Network Energy Function

Recall the network that was developed in Section 14.4.2 to store the vector:

$$\varrho^s = \begin{pmatrix} 1 \\ 0 \\ 1 \\ 0 \end{pmatrix}$$

that yielded the weight matrix:

$$W = \begin{pmatrix} 0 & -1 & 1 & -1 \\ -1 & 0 & -1 & 1 \\ 1 & -1 & 0 & -1 \\ -1 & 1 & -1 & 0 \end{pmatrix}$$

The reader should verify that

$E[\varrho^s] = -1,$
$E[\varrho^1(t_o)] = +1,$
$E[\varrho^1(t_1)] = 0,$
$E[\varrho^2(t_o)] = 0,$
$E[\varrho^2(t_1)] = E[\varrho^s] = -1,$

and, most interestingly, for the cycle

$E[\varrho^3(t_o)] = E[\varrho^3(t_1)] = E[\varrho^3(t_2)] = -1.$

Furthermore, using Equation 14.17 yields:

$$E(\varrho) = -\frac{1}{2}\varrho^T W \varrho = \ldots = o_1 o_2 + o_1 o_4 + o_2 o_3 + o_3 o_4 - (o_1 o_3 + o_2 o_4) \tag{14.22}$$

The reader should verify that negative contributions on Equation 14.22 correspond to joint values of the elements of $\underline{o}$ that, when nonzero, lead to a reduction in E. This explains why vectors

$$\begin{pmatrix} 1 & 0 & 1 & 0 \end{pmatrix}^T$$

and

$$\begin{pmatrix} 0 & 1 & 0 & 1 \end{pmatrix}^T$$

correspond to stable states. A similar remark may be made for positive elements in Equation 14.22. It is also quite illustrative to relate the system state changes (trajectory) to the Hamming Distance between the given initial state and the stored states. This is left as an exercise for the reader.

14.5.3 Summary of the Generalized Hopfield Network Equations

Discrete Case.

$$\underline{net}(k+1) = W\underline{o}(k) + \underline{i}_b \tag{14.23}$$

$$\underline{o}(k+1) = \underline{f}\{\underline{net}(k+1)\} \tag{14.24}$$

When an (optional) bias is used, the corresponding energy equation is [AF90]:

$$E(\underline{o}) = -\frac{1}{2}\underline{o}^T W \underline{o} - \underline{i}_b^T \underline{o} \tag{14.25}$$

We note that the formulation of Equation 14.25 appears in the literature in an attempt to characterize the continuous unit case; it is, strictly speaking, incorrect.

14.6 Recurrent ANN Constraint Satisfaction and Optimization Applications

There exist many other significant applications of recurrent networks based upon CAM functionality. For example, face recognition and other biometric applications are popular. However, an equally important application domain is in the solution of constraint satisfaction and related problems.

14.6.1 Optimization and CSP Problems

Optimization problems require the adjustment of some quantities to minimize or maximize some *objective function*. For example, in a system with n adjustable quantities $o_1, o_2, \ldots o_n$,[3] the problem is formulated as:

$$min\{J(o_1, o_2 \ldots o_n)\} \tag{14.26}$$

---

[3]The similarity in naming of these variables and the outputs of Hopfield network units is obviously not accidental.

Thus, we may use recurrent nets as *Optimization Networks*. Many optimization problems also require that constraints among the variables be observed; this gives rise to *constrained optimization problems*, formulated as:

$$min\{J(o_1, o_2 \ldots o_n)\} \quad subject\ to \quad \underline{f}(o_1, o_2 \ldots o_n) = 0 \tag{14.27}$$

In addition to the subsequent Set Partitioning and Traveling Salesman Problems (TSP), applications for recurrent network optimization/CSP formulations include image labeling, fitting points to lines, the N-queens problem, map coloring (left as an exercise), and stereo vision (the correspondence problem). Another potential utility of recurrent (Hopfield-like) networks is in problems involving relational constraint satisfaction such as matching of attributed graphs.

14.6.2 Mapping Constraints and Objectives into Recurrent Networks

The nature of the Hopfield network is one of energy minimization; given W and an initial state, $\underline{o}(t_0)$, the network seeks to minimize $E(\underline{o})$. Thus, if it is desired to minimize[4] a certain function of some variables, it is possible to use the Hopfield net if we are able to map the objective function into an energy function and the variables into unit outputs, $\underline{o}$.

14.6.3 Other Interpretations of E

Unfortunately, many useful optimization problems involve *minimization of an objective function subject to additional constraints*. Additional constraints include linear and/or nonlinear equalities and/or inequalities. This requires a further extension of the definition of E for minimization purposes. We define an error measure for the constrained minimization problem as:

$$E = E^{opt(min)} + \lambda E^{constraints} \tag{14.28}$$

where λ determines the relative sensitivity to E of the minimization component and the constraint. When $\lambda = 1$, the optimization and constraint problems are weighted equally; when $\lambda \ll 1$ we are signifying that the solution should emphasize the optimization, not the satisfaction of the constraints. A similar remark holds for $\lambda \gg 1$. More generally,

$$E = E^{opt(min)} + A_1 E^{constraint_1} + A_2 E^{constraint_2} + \ldots + A_n E^{constraint_n} \tag{14.29}$$

Note in both Equations 14.28 and 14.29 that it is typical to formulate E such that the minimum value is 0.

Several problems regarding the formulation of Equation 14.29 exist, including:

◆ Determining good or reasonable values of the A_i, or the relative weighting of the A_i

◆ Sensitivity of the solutions to the A_i values

◆ The fact that neural solutions may not converge to "interpretable" solutions, as evidenced by many simulations.

---

[4]Notice we can also maximize by appropriate rewriting of our objective.

Formulating problem constraints and optimization (minimization) measures via E lead to the following observations:

- Minimum values of Equation 14.29 correspond to (local) minima of the corresponding net. The lower the value of E, the better the solution.

- The best solution to the constraints of Equation 14.29 is the global minimum.

14.6.4 The Overall Design Process

Basically, the process consists of the following steps:

1. Development of a network structure so that unit output has some relevance to the problem solution;

2. Design of energy function components whose minima correspond to satisfaction of problem constraints;

3. Determination of network weights; and

4. Simulation of the network and assessment as to the validity of the solution produced.

14.6.5 Unit Characteristics and Weights

In our prior efforts, we used the Hopfield storage prescription (or an alternative) to get W from a specification of desired stored states, $\underline{o}^s$. Here, since these states are unknown[5] we adopt an alternative viewpoint driven by E.

Once E is formulated, the problem of determining E may be solved in several ways:

1. By expanding E in terms of $\underline{o}$, and equating coefficients with the Hopfield energy function. This is only practical in small problems.

2. By noticing

$$w_{ij} = -\frac{\partial^2 E}{\partial o_i \partial o_j} = \frac{\partial net_i}{\partial o_j} \tag{14.30}$$

and

$$net_i = -\frac{\partial E}{\partial o_i} \tag{14.31}$$

This yields a straightforward, albeit tedious, technique to find unit weights and biases.

---

[5]If we knew the solution, why solve the problem?

14.7 Example: Partitioning of Sets

In what follows, we present a design methodology for application of recurrent networks to solving constraint satisfaction and/or optimization problems. We introduce the subject in order of increasing complexity of examples.

We consider two subcases for this problem:

Case #1: A CSP problem (no "performance" measure or quantity to be minimized); just satisfaction of constraints; and

Case #2: A constrained optimization problem, using the constraints of Case #1, but with a cost of each partition.

Case #1 is considered first, since it is the simplest.

14.7.1 Problem Statement, Case #1

Consider the partitioning of a set, $A = \{a, b, c, d, e\}$ of five elements into *two mutually exclusive subsets, each consisting of exactly two nonidentical elements.* For example, $\{(a, b), (c, d)\}$ is a valid solution; $\{(a, b), (a, e)\}$ and $\{(a, a), (c, b)\}$ are not.

14.7.2 Problem Representation

State Vector

We use a $5 \times 2 = 10$ unit network and the following notation **to link unit output states to the problem solution**. This gives each unit output "meaning" in the overall solution. The state vector is a 10×1 vector:

$$\underline{o} = \left(o_{X,i} \right) \quad \text{where} \quad X \in \{a, b, c, d, e\} \text{ and } i = 1, 2 \tag{14.32}$$

More importantly, the output of unit $\{X, i\}$, i.e., $o_{X,i}$ corresponds to element X in partition i. If $o_{X,i} = 1$ in the solution, this signifies that element X is in partition i. Specifically, by concatenation of the table columns we arrive at:

$$\underline{o} = \begin{pmatrix} o_{a,1} \\ o_{b,1} \\ o_{c,1} \\ o_{d,1} \\ o_{e,1} \\ o_{a,2} \\ o_{b,2} \\ o_{c,2} \\ o_{d,2} \\ o_{e,2} \end{pmatrix} \tag{14.33}$$

This makes interconnection or weight matrix W a 10×10 matrix.

Tabular Form of Network Output

	1	2
a	1	0
b	1	0
c	0	1
d	0	1
e	0	0

Table 14.1 Problem Representation—Unit Outputs in Tabular Form. Solution shown is $\{(a,b),(c,d)\}$.

Referring to Table 14.1, notice that the column headings denote *which subset*, i.e., in the result shown the first subset consists of elements $\{a,b\}$, since $o_{a,1} = 1$ and $o_{b,1} = 1$. Similarly, the second subset shown in Table 14.1 is $\{c,d\}$, since $o_{c,2} = 1$ and $o_{d,2} = 1$.

As a prelude to developing constraint with this problem representation, consider some other possible situations shown in Tables 14.2–14.5.

	1	2
a	0	0
b	1	0
c	0	1
d	1	0
e	0	1

Table 14.2 Set Partitioning Solution $\{(b,d),(c,e)\}$

	1	2
a	1	0
b	1	0
c	1	0
d	0	1
e	0	1

Table 14.3 Set Partitioning Solution $\{(a,b,c),(d,e)\}$ (Illegal Solution)

14.7.3 Constraints

Based on our tabular representation of the solution, consider the required properties of row and columns in the tabular (or matrix) representation for a valid solution. To enforce the constraint that

	1	2
a	1	0
b	0	0
c	0	0
d	0	1
e	0	1

Table 14.4 Set Partitioning Solution $\{(a),(d,e)\}$ (Illegal Solution)

	1	2
a	1	0
b	1	0
c	1	0
d	1	0
e	0	0

Table 14.5 Set Partitioning Solution $\{(a,b,c,d),()\}$ (Illegal Solution)

no element can be in both partitions, we could use the constraint:

$$o_{X,1} + o_{X,2} \leq 1 \quad X \in \{a,b,c,d,e\} \tag{14.34}$$

An alternate constraint[6] might be:

$$o_{X,1}o_{X,2} = 0 \quad X \in \{a,b,c,d,e\} \tag{14.35}$$

Notice, in terms of the tabular form of the preceding problem representation developed, that either constraint places a restriction on a row of the solution. Similarly, to enforce the constraint that each subset must contain exactly two elements, we could use:

$$\sum_{X \in \{a,b,c,d,e\}} o_{X,j} = 2 \ for \ j = 1,2 \tag{14.36}$$

Note that this represents a column-based constraint on the solution in tabular form.

14.7.4 Network Energy Functions

Corresponding to the constraint in Equation 14.35, we develop the following energy function:

$$E_1 = \frac{A}{2} \sum_{X \in \{a,b,c,d,e\}} o_{X,1}o_{X,2} \tag{14.37}$$

---

[6]Here, for implementation purposes, we could index X from 1 to 5.

Note $E_1 = 0$ if the constraint is satisfied, otherwise $E_1 > 0$. Similarly,

$$E_2 = \frac{B}{2} \sum_{j=1}^{2} ((\sum_{X \in \{a,b,c,d,e\}} o_{X,j}) - 2)^2 \tag{14.38}$$

E_2 has a minimum at 0, corresponding to exactly two ON units in each column. Therefore, the total energy function to be minimized is $E_1 + E_2$ (for Case #1). The weighting parameters A and B must also be determined. The interconnection matrix, W, and unit biases are determined by equating of coefficients or differentiation of E, as shown later.

14.7.5 Solving for Weights and Biases

E_1

Recall the constraint of Equation 14.35 that corresponds to E_1 in Equation 14.37. In this case, unit biases are not an issue, and only Equation 14.30 is necessary. Expanding:

$$E_1 = \frac{A}{2} \sum_{X \in \{a,b,c,d,e\}} o_{X,1} o_{X,2} = \frac{A}{2} \{o_{a,1} o_{a,2} + o_{b,1} o_{b,2} + o_{c,1} o_{c,2} + o_{d,1} o_{d,2} + o_{e,1} o_{e,2}\} \tag{14.39}$$

Since we are determining the interconnection weights between any two units and since our unit indices with the chosen problem representation correspond to units $o_{X,i}$ and $o_{Y,j}$, we rewrite Equation 14.30 as:

$$w_{o_{X,i}, o_{Y,j}} = -\frac{\partial^2 E}{\partial o_{X,i} \partial o_{Y,j}} = \frac{\partial net_{X,i}}{\partial o_{Y,j}} \tag{14.40}$$

Notice[7] differentiation of 14.39 using Equation 14.40 yields:

$$w_{o_{X,i}, o_{Y,j}} = -\frac{\partial^2 E}{\partial o_{X,i} \partial o_{Y,j}} = \begin{cases} -\frac{A}{2} & \text{if } X = Y \text{ and } j \neq i \\ 0 & \text{otherwise} \end{cases} \tag{14.41}$$

Equation 14.41 may be simplified by introduction of the Kroneker delta defined by:

$$\delta(x) = \begin{cases} 1 & \text{if } x = 0 \\ 0 & \text{otherwise} \end{cases} \tag{14.42}$$

so

$$\delta(p - q) = \begin{cases} 1 & \text{if } p = q \\ 0 & \text{otherwise} \end{cases} \tag{14.43}$$

therefore, Equation 14.41 may be written:

$$w_{o_{X,i}, o_{Y,j}} = -\frac{\partial^2 E}{\partial o_{X,i} \partial o_{Y,j}} = -\frac{A}{2} \delta(X - Y)[1 - \delta(i - j)] \tag{14.44}$$

---

[7]The reader should verify this.

E_2

This part of the energy formulation is a little more challenging. Expanding Equation 14.38 yields:

$$E_2 = \frac{B}{2}[(o_{a,1} + o_{b,1} + o_{c,1} + o_{d,1} + o_{e,1} - 2)^2 + (o_{a,2} + o_{b,2} + o_{c,2} + o_{d,2} + o_{e,2} - 2)^2] \qquad (14.45)$$

In a manner analogous to that used in Section 14.7.5, we find

$$w_{o_{X,i}, o_{Y,j}} = -\frac{\partial^2 E}{\partial o_{X,i} \partial o_{Y,j}} = -B\delta(i - j) \qquad (14.46)$$

Revisiting the Bias

In typical AM applications of recurrent networks, there is no defined role for the unit bias.[8] However, in the present application the role of the bias is significant. The bias is a constant addition to the unit net activation. When an (optional) bias is used, recall the corresponding energy equation is:

$$E(\underline{o}) = -\frac{1}{2}\underline{o}^T W \underline{o} - i_b^T \underline{o} \qquad (14.47)$$

Referring to the general energy formulation of Equation 14.47, observe that terms in $E(\underline{o})$ that are linear in $\underline{o}$ involve the bias. Furthermore, since,

$$net_i = -\frac{\partial E}{\partial o_i} \qquad (14.48)$$

any constant terms that result from differentiation of Equation 14.47 must be the corresponding unit biases. To find the unit bias in this problem, we simply expand Equation 14.38 and make use of the reasoning discussed here:

$$E_2 = \frac{B}{2} \sum_{i=1}^{2} \left\{ \left[\left(\sum_X o_{X,i} \right) \left(\sum_Y o_{Y,i} \right) \right] - 4 \sum_X o_{X,i} + 4 \right\} \qquad (14.49)$$

Therefore, from Equation 14.49,

$$bias_{o_{X,i}} = \text{constant term from } -\frac{\partial E_2}{\partial o_{X,i}} = \left(-\frac{B}{2}\right)(-4) = 2B \qquad (14.50)$$

14.7.6 Looking at W

With the results from Section 14.7.5, we now have the network weights. The reader should look at them and determine, intuitively, the reasonableness of these results.

14.7.7 Case #2: Optimization Measure and Associated E

Costs for Two-Element Assignments

In this extension of the problem, there is a cost associated with each two-element assignment. For example, putting a and b in a subset has an associated cost of 4. Table 14.6 shows the associated

---

[8]Note the Hopfield storage prescription did not provide a means to compute a bias.

Cost	a	b	c	d	e
a	-	4	2	4	4
b	4	-	2	5	3
c	2	2	-	2	6
d	4	5	2	-	1
e	4	3	6	1	-

Table 14.6 Costs of Associations for Constrained Optimization Example

costs. The objective here is to both satisfy the previous CSP as well as minimize the resulting overall cost of the partition. This is a constrained optimization problem.

Examples

Using the costs of Table 14.6, the (assignment) cost of the result in Table 14.1 is the cost of pairing a with b plus the cost of pairing c with d or $4 + 2 = 6$. Similarly, the (assignment) cost of the result in Table 14.2 is the cost of pairing b with d plus the cost of pairing c with e or $5 + 6 = 11$.

Incorporation of the optimization measure in E is straightforward, and results in the following additional term:

$$E_3 = \frac{C}{2} \sum_{i,j} \sum_{X \in \{a,b,c,d,e\}} \sum_{\substack{Y \in \{a,b,c,d,e\} \\ Y \neq X}} o_{X,i} o_{Y,i} c_{X,Y} \tag{14.51}$$

Therefore, the total energy function to be minimized is $E_1 + E_2$ for Case #1 and $E_1 + E_2 + E_3$ for Case #2.

14.8 Example: State Representation and the Traveling Salesman Problem

In ANN-based solutions to CSP and optimization problems, one of the initial challenges is mapping the problem representation into the network representation such that problem solutions correspond to preferred network states. For example, consider the Traveling Salesman Problem (TSP), originally proposed by Hopfield and Tank [HT85]. In this problem, a two-dimensional array of units is used, arranged as shown in Table 14.7.

The row index is the name of a city; the column index is the step the city is visited in the solution sequence. Every entry in this two-dimensional array is represented by the output of a unit in a Hopfield network; here we have a 5×5 or $d = 25$ unit network. In the example shown in Table 14.7, the resulting path or sequence is C-A-E-B-D.

Each unit in the $d \times d$ array is indexed with row and column indices. For example, unit $o_{C,3}$ corresponds to city C at time 3. If this unit is active (ON) in a particular solution, it signifies that city C was visited at Step 3 in this solution. In this manner, the constraints cited in Section 14.8.1 may be enforced.

City	Step Visited in Solution				
	1	2	3	4	5
A	0	1	0	0	0
B	0	0	0	1	0
C	1	0	0	0	0
D	0	0	0	0	1
E	0	0	1	0	0

Table 14.7 Matrix Representation for TSP

14.8.1 Embedding Constraints in E

The preceding $d = 25$ unit network has a corresponding energy function, E, determined by W. The objective in this section is to show how E, and consequently W, may be determined by the problem constraints and objective function. Consider a few constraint cases:

1. Suppose each city should be visited exactly once on the tour. This requires that the sum of the active units in any row be exactly 1.

2. Since each stop in the tour presumably occurs at a different time, we cannot visit more than one city simultaneously. This requires the sum of active units in each column to be at most 1. Furthermore (the problems explore this), if we stipulate that a city must be visited at each step (a logical constraint for a five city tour and five steps), the sum of active units in each column must then be exactly 1.

14.8.2 Mapping Constraints and Objectives into E

The reader is encouraged to expand several of the sums that follow to verify that the desired constraints are achieved.

In order to require that a solution contains **at most** one nonzero entry per row, we use a term of the form:

$$E_1 = \frac{\hat{A}}{2} \sum_X \sum_i \sum_{j;\ j \neq i} o_{X,i} o_{X,j} \tag{14.52}$$

Similarly, to enforce the constraint that **at most** one neuron corresponding to each column is active, we add the term:

$$E_2 = \frac{\hat{B}}{2} \sum_i \sum_X \sum_{Y;\ X \neq Y} o_{X,i} o_{Y,i} \tag{14.53}$$

to the overall E. The constraint that exactly n neurons (5 here) be active is enforced by addition of the term:

$$E_3 = \frac{\hat{C}}{2} \left(\sum_X \sum_i o_{X,i} - n \right)^2 \tag{14.54}$$

Finally, the cost of the path, as constrained by Table 14.6, is added via incorporation of:

$$E_4 = \frac{\hat{D}}{2} \sum_X \sum_{X \neq Y} \sum_i d_{XY}(o_{X,i})(o_{Y,i+1} + o_{Y,i-1}) \tag{14.55}$$

into the overall network energy function. Note the weighting terms $\hat{A}$, $\hat{B}$, $\hat{C}$, and $\hat{D}$ in the preceding equations allow (relative) unequal weighting of each of the individual terms in the overall energy function.

14.8.3   Unit Characteristics and Weights

Basic Weight Determination.   Once E is formulated, the problem of determining E may be solved in several ways:

1. By expanding the problem E, and equating coefficients with the Hopfield energy function.

2. By observing, from Equation 14.9, or, more generally, Equation 14.47 in Section 14.5.3, that:

$$w_{ij} = -\frac{\partial^2 E}{\partial o_i \partial o_j} = \frac{\partial net_i}{\partial o_j} \tag{14.56}$$

and recalling

$$net_i = -\frac{\partial E}{\partial o_i} \tag{14.57}$$

In the case of the previous TSP formulation, Equation 14.56 yields:

$$w_{Xi,Yj} = -\hat{A}\delta_{XY}(1 - \delta_{ij}) - \hat{B}\delta_{ij}(1 - \delta_{XY}) - \hat{C} - \hat{D}d_{XY}(\delta_{j,i+1} + \delta_{j,i-1}) \tag{14.58}$$

where δ_{ab} is used to denote the Kroneker delta function, that is,

$$\delta_{ab} = \delta(a - b) = \begin{cases} 1 & if\ a = b \\ 0 & otherwise \end{cases} \tag{14.59}$$

14.8.4   The Role of the Hopfield Unit Bias

Notice in Equation 14.58 that every term is either zero or negative. Thus, the resulting W matrix would yield a system wherein all initial states would be driven to the origin. However, we have ignored the role of the unit bias. Referring to the general energy formulation of Equation 14.47, observe that terms in $E(\underline{o})$ that are linear in $\underline{o}$ are due to the bias. In addition, term E_3 (Equation 14.54) leads to an overall network energy function that contains terms linear in the values of $\underline{o}$. Therefore, equating coefficients in Equations 14.47 and 14.54 leads to the prescription for unit biases as:

$$b_{X,i} = \hat{C}n \tag{14.60}$$

where $b_{X,i}$ is the bias for unit X, i. This provides a positive offset for the unit net activation value.

14.8.5   Discrete or Continuous Unit Models

The units used in the optimization formulation may have continuous ("analog") or discrete (usually bilevel or "digital") outputs. As we have shown in Section 14.2.1, units with bilevel discrete output only have two states; continuous units have an infinite number. Since the discrete network must live on the vertices of a cube in 2^d, the state trajectory is a series of jumps from one vertex to another, possibly making the search for an E minimum somewhat random. Continuous unit state vectors, on the other hand, since they are guided by a differential equation, usually lead to a "smoother" form of search [KPW90]. However, the discrete network lends itself to a faster and more direct implementation; the continuous net requires the solution of a set of coupled nonlinear differential equations. Finally, there are claims and empirical evidence suggesting the E landscape of the analog network is better suited to optimization problems [KPW90].

14.8.6   Sample Results

In addition to the problem of determining $\underline{o}(t_0)$ and the required choice of a number of coefficients for weighting or "tuning" various energy terms [HT85], another limitation of the recurrent network-based optimization/CSP strategy is that *not all local minima discovered by the network correspond to optimal, or even valid solutions*. For example, in [HT85], in solving the TSP, it was noted that after network tuning 16 of 20 starting states produced valid tours, and 50% of the trials produced one of the two shortest paths.

14.8.7   Other Sample CSP Applications

Other CSPs involving image labeling, power system protection interpretation, and natural language processing were considered in Chapters 4 and 5. Solutions using Prolog and other approaches are shown. These problems are also suitable for an ANN implementation. This effort is continued as an exercise.

14.9   The Psychology of "Recall" and ANN Bidirectional Associative Memory (BAM) Structures

This section introduces the Bidirectional Associative Memory (BAM) structure. It is attributed to Kosko [Kos87]–[Kos88]. First, we consider some relevant aspects of psychology that help to support the BAM computational framework.

14.9.1   The Order of Thought

Many of the concepts popularized by "connectionist" computing and associative behavior of artificial neural networks, were proposed by noted psychologist William James in 1890 [Jam90]. James studied and formulated a number of hypotheses regarding the *order of ideas* in thought. Specifically, he was curious how the sequence of mental imagery in a temporal sample of thought could be explained. Clearly this sequence contained transitions between ideas and concepts. Some were very smooth or continuous; others were quite abrupt. In many cases, however, the thought path contains logical *links*.

Many of James' assertions suggest a knowledge representation that is "connectionist" in nature. We explore a few highlights here.

14.9.2 Discrimination, Association, and Principles of Connection (James)

James postulated the two fundamental operations involving thought (ideas) were *discrimination* and *association*. James postulated these links are describable by *principles of connection*, which explain the succession or coexistence of ideas in mental imagery. For example, a common subpath in thought might be expressed as:

Thinking about A leads to thinking about B, where A and B are concepts.

Concepts A and B are somehow connected. James explained this as a result of training or experience, which is learned, and postulated that:

♦ There is no other elementary causal law of association than the *law of neural habit*:

"When two elementary brain-processes have been active *together* or in *immediate succession* (emphasis added), one of them, on [recurring], tends to propagate its excitement into the other."

♦ An extension of the elementary principle for *many processes* (each process excited by conjunction of many others) is the following corollary:

"The amount of activity at any given point in the brain-cortex is the sum of the tendencies of all other points to discharge into it, such tendencies being proportionate:

1. To the number of times the excitement of each other point may have accompanied that of the point in question;

2. To the intensity of such excitements; and

3. To the absence of any rival point functionally disconnected with the first point, into which the discharges might be diverted."

Items 1–3 are closely related to the notion of Hebbian or correlation-based learning.

14.9.3 Relevant Principles of Association

Conceptual (Temporal) Links. James postulated that the structure of memory processes involved inter- (activation) and intra- (resonance) concept *connections*. Sample interconcept connections and intraconcept "nerve tracts" are shown in Figure 14.5. For example, notice:

♦ Concept B nerve tract "l" is excited by elementary nerve tracts "a," "b," and "c" in concept A.

♦ Nerve tract "o" in concept B is excited by concept A nerve tracts "b," "d," and "e."

In addition, nerve tracts "a," "b," "c," "d," "e," and "l," "m," "n," "o," "p" also "vibrate in unison" or resonate *within the concept*. This observation will also become significant in our exploration of BAM.

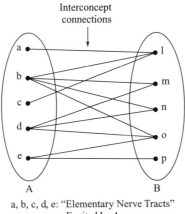

a, b, c, d, e: "Elementary Nerve Tracts"
Excited by A
l, m, n, o, p: "Nerve Tracts" for Concept B

Figure 14.5 Links Between Concepts A and B

Total Recall. Total recall is a process whereby the mind is in a "perpetual treadmill" of reminiscences, with perfect detail. All corresponding nerve tracts for an active concept are excited. The sequence of concepts that is mentally replayed is determined by the interconnections and initial resonances. Total recall is not a plausible model for thinking, except in cases of mental disorder [Jam1890].

Partial Recall. Partial recall is a powerful basis for learning/forgetting and recall and association models in ANN structures, and leads to implementations involving self-adaptation. The most important characterizations of the concept of *partial recall*, are:

◆ In no revival of a past experience are all the items of our thought equally operative in determining what the next thought shall be. Always some ingredient is prepotent over the rest.

◆ Prepotent items are those that appeal most to our *interest*.

These observations suggest stored representations are time-varying; extremes are one part of a process (Concept A or B) that could be fading, decaying, or becoming indistinct (losing "vividness"). Another part of the same process (that possesses a strong internal *interest*) resists this tendency, thereby becoming relatively stronger. In other words, an internal representation *evolves* and certain portions become *dominant*.

Focalized Recall. Partial recall leads to *focalized recall*, or *association by similarity*, as shown in Figure 14.6. In focalized recall, one entity (nerve tract) invokes an entire other concept, i.e., not all entities are needed to "address" or "invoke" a concept.

Summary and Utility. Over time (experience) concepts are modified by evolution and *interest*. Some entities become *dominant*, where dominance of a concept is based upon *reinforcement* (Hebbian learning).

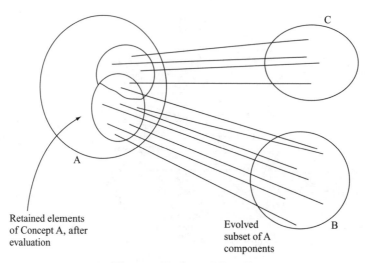

Retained elements
of Concept A, after
evaluation

Evolved
subset of A
components

Figure 14.6 Partial Recall

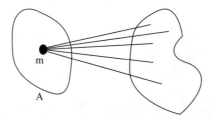

Figure 14.7 Focalized Recall. An Individual Component of Concept A is Used.

Most importantly:

1. Figure 14.5 suggests a network architecture or structure; and

2. Figures 14.6 and 14.7 suggest an approach for implementing recall.

14.9.4   BAM Evolution from Hopfield (Totally Recurrent) Structure

A Word about BAM Notation.   In the literature, (for some reason) the BAM often appears described with row vectors, rather than the more commonly used column vectors used throughout this text. While this does not change the fundamentals of the BAM technology, it nonetheless may be a source of confusion. Thus readers are cautioned to transpose all vectors and matrices originating with the row vector formulation.

Consider a simple four-unit topology. If we allow total interconnection (with the constraint $w_{ii} = 0 \quad \forall i$, as before), the Hopfield net of Figure 14.8 results. Alternately, a more constrained interconnection strategy combined with an interpretation of "layers," as shown in Figure 14.9, yields

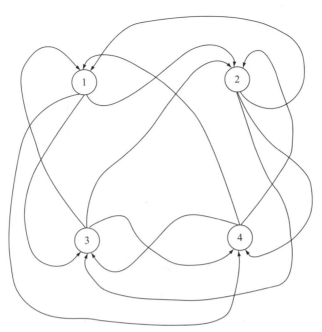

Figure 14.8 Use of Four Units as Hopfield Net

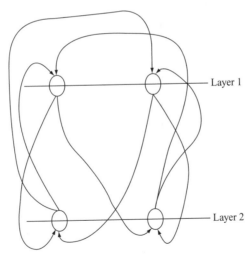

Figure 14.9 Interpretation of Four Units as BAM

an example of bidirectional associative memory (BAM). Thus, the BAM concept may be developed as a Hopfield derivative. Nonetheless, it possesses a number of interesting properties and applications, and we consider it separately.

14.9.5 Architecture

The basic BAM architecture is a two-layer network shown in Figure 14.10. Note that weighted connections exist *between the layers, but not within them.*

14.9.6 Training and Connections

The BAM stores *vector associations* in a two-layer structure. In this sense there are two sets of "outputs" of the network, one for each layer. The BAM units typically have $\{-1, 1\}$ outputs (bipolar), and therefore we must convert $\{0, 1\}$ (binary) inputs to the bipolar notation.

Training Set

A training set consists of N pattern associations[9]

$$H = \{(\underline{a}_i, \underline{b}_i)\} \quad i = 1, 2, \ldots N \tag{14.61}$$

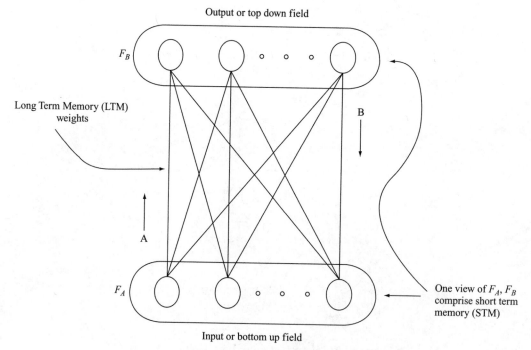

Output or top down field

F_B

Long Term Memory (LTM) weights

B

A

F_A

One view of F_A, F_B comprise short term memory (STM)

Input or bottom up field

Figure 14.10 BAM Structure

---

[9]Note here that these are not input and target patterns as in the FF structure, but rather the desired converged states of each of the two layers.

where $\underline{a}_i$ is $n \times 1$ and $\underline{b}_i$ is $p \times 1$. These are desired pattern associations. The patterns in H (see Equation 14.61) are assumed binary ($\{0, 1\}$) and converted to bipolar representation ($\{-1, 1\}$) before use.

Interlayer Mapping Matrix

A matrix, denoted M, is used to facilitate recall. M is a linear mapping between the output of F_A and the net activation to F_B:

$$M : R^n \rightarrow R^p \tag{14.62}$$

which is less general than the nonlinear mapping:

$$T : R^n \rightarrow R^p \tag{14.63}$$

BAM Recall

BAM recall is based upon vector-matrix multiplication of M and the outputs of one layer to find the net activation for the other layer. Subsequently, application of a nonlinear squashing function yields the layer output, which is propagated back to the first layer. Formation of the net activation for the first layer, followed by application of a nonlinear squashing function yields this layer output, and so on. Thus, the BAM layers iterate outputs between layers until convergence is reached.

The procedure for applying an input vector $\underline{a}$ to the network begins by converting $\underline{a}$ to bipolar form. Denote the bipolar form of $\underline{a}$ as $\underline{o}_0$. $\underline{o}_0$ is now applied[10] to the BAM network, resulting in:

$$M\underline{o}_0 = \underline{i}^B \tag{14.64}$$

where $\underline{i}^B$ is now the vector of net activations to Layer B (F_B). With this interpretation, element $m_{ji} \in M$ is the connection from element o_i in vector $\underline{o}_0$ to element i_j^B in $\underline{i}^B$. Alternately, m_{ji} may be viewed as the synaptic interconnection strength between unit j in F_B and unit i in F_A, where unit j in F_B is the receiving unit.

Unit i in layer F_B then forms its output using a squashing function:

$$o_i^B = S(i_i^B) \tag{14.65}$$

where S could be any activation function. Here we use the Hopfield "leave it alone" characteristic of Equation 14.1, namely

$$o_i = S(net_i) = \begin{cases} 1 & net_i > 0 \\ unchanged & net_i = 0 \\ -1 & net_i < 0 \end{cases} \tag{14.66}$$

---

[10]Applied here means the outputs of Layer A (F_A) units are set to the respective values of the bipolar representation of $\underline{a}$, namely $\underline{o}_0$.

So far we have described a unidirectional mapping from F_A to F_B. The bipolar output of layer F_B is then propagated back to Layer F_A using an analogous procedure:

$$M^T \underline{o}^B = \underline{i}^A \tag{14.67}$$

where $\underline{i}^A$ is the vector of net activations to the units in Layer A (F_A). Layer A units then use Equation 14.66 to form their outputs and the process continues. Thus, we have described a bidirectional mapping procedure.

BAM and Partial Recall

The BAM acts as a nonlinear heteroassociative memory with feedback. The structure of BAM dynamics may be shown as:

$$\underline{a} \to \underline{o}_0 \to M \to \underline{i}^B \to \underline{o}^B \to M^T \to \underline{i}^A \to \underline{o}^A \to M \to \underline{i}^B \to \underline{o}^B \dots \tag{14.68}$$

Thus, information reverberates or resonates in the network.

BAM Convergence

Anytime the outputs of F_A and F_B are both satisfied, in the sense that all unit inputs and outputs are commensurate with the unit activation function, the network is in an equilibrium state and no further changes take place.

Determination of M

The storage prescription for M is both simple and familiar. For the ith pair of H, form:

$$M_i = \underline{y}_i \underline{x}_i^T \tag{14.69}$$

where $\underline{x}_i$ and $\underline{y}_i$ are the bipolar counterparts of $\underline{a}_i$ and $\underline{b}_i$ in Equation 14.61, respectively. The overall "forward" mapping matrix is then:

$$M = \sum_{i=1}^{N} M_i \tag{14.70}$$

From Equations 14.69 and 14.70, the Hebbian-based nature of the training is evident. Note that there is only one matrix to determine during the training phase; its transpose is used for the companion or "backward" mapping, as shown in Equation 14.67.

14.9.7   BAM Examples

Example #1: Small (Hand–Worked) BAM

The vector associations shown in Table 14.8 are to be used to design a BAM. Recall the BAM uses bipolar ($\{-1, 1\}$) units, so we must convert these binary inputs to the $\{-1, 1\}$ representation before use.

BAM Specifications		
i	$\underline{a}_i^T$	$\underline{b}_i^T$
1	$(0\ 0\ 0\ 1)$	$(0\ 1)$
2	$(1\ 0\ 1\ 0)$	$(1\ 0)$
3	$(0\ 1\ 0\ 1)$	$(0\ 0)$
4	$(1\ 0\ 0\ 1)$	$(1\ 1)$

Table 14.8 Data for BAM Example

Determination of the Storage Matrix, M. Using Equations 14.69 and 14.70, we find

$$M = \begin{pmatrix} 4 & -2 & 2 & -2 \\ 0 & -2 & -2 & 2 \end{pmatrix} \tag{14.71}$$

Determination of Subsequent BAM Behavior. Using $\underline{a}_1$ as input:

$$\underline{x}_1 = \begin{pmatrix} -1 \\ -1 \\ -1 \\ 1 \end{pmatrix} \tag{14.72}$$

so

$$M\underline{x}_1 = M \begin{pmatrix} -1 \\ -1 \\ -1 \\ 1 \end{pmatrix} = \begin{pmatrix} -6 \\ 6 \end{pmatrix} \tag{14.73}$$

so $\underline{y}_1^T = (-1\quad 1)$, with corresponding binary representation $\underline{b}_1^T = (0\quad 1)$. Thus

$$M^T \underline{y}_1 = \begin{pmatrix} -4 \\ 0 \\ -4 \\ 4 \end{pmatrix} \tag{14.74}$$

which, with the characteristic of Equation 14.66 yields the updated F_A outputs as:

$$\underline{x}_1 = \begin{pmatrix} -1 \\ -1 \\ -1 \\ 1 \end{pmatrix} \tag{14.75}$$

corresponding to the binary equivalent

$$\underline{a}_1 = \begin{pmatrix} 0 \\ 0 \\ 0 \\ 1 \end{pmatrix} \tag{14.76}$$

Thus, this pattern association is stored. The reader is left to verify the status of the remaining patterns, $\underline{a}_2$, $\underline{a}_3$, and $\underline{a}_4$, using the storage matrix and procedures as determined.

Energy Analysis.   Kosko claims that, for any $(\underline{x}_i, \underline{y}_i)$ state of the network, i.e., $(\underline{\alpha},\underline{\beta})$, each cycle of decoding (iteration) reduces the energy function:

$$-\alpha^T M \beta$$

The reader is left to verify this using the input pattern $\underline{a}_i = (1101)$.

Second BAM Example: Formulation and Results

Problem Description.   We show a simple BAM implementation using 5×1 vectors in F_A and 2×1 vectors in F_B. H consists of three stored associations, arranged as corresponding columns in matrices $a1$ and $a2$ as follows:

$$a1 = \begin{pmatrix} 1 & 1 & 1 \\ -1 & 1 & -1 \\ -1 & -1 & 1 \\ 1 & -1 & -1 \\ -1 & 1 & -1 \end{pmatrix} \tag{14.77}$$

$$a2 = \begin{pmatrix} -1 & 1 & -1 \\ -1 & -1 & 1 \end{pmatrix} \tag{14.78}$$

Sample Results.   Figure 14.11 shows H and the response of the BAM to H. Figure 14.12 shows the response of the BAM to an additional input.

Example: Character Association Using BAM

Figure 14.13, from [Kos87], shows a BAM application involving the recall of associated characters. Approximately six neurons are updated per iteration, and the character associations (S, F), (M, V), and (G, N) are stored. Layer F_A contains 140 units; layer F_B contains 106. A noise corrupted version of (S, E) is used to start the BAM network.

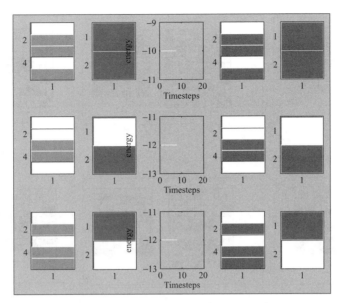

Figure 14.11 BAM Training Set and Response. Each set of 5×1 and 2×1 vectors used to initialize F_A and F_B are shown on the left; converged network layer outputs are shown on the right. Three examples are shown. Dark values indicate negative quantities.

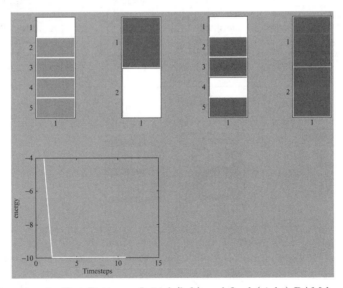

Figure 14.12 BAM Response to Test Pattern—Initial (left) and final (right) BAM layer outputs and E as a function of iteration

Figure 14.13 BAM Recall for Associated Character Patterns (from [Kosko1987]). A Succession of 11 States Is Shown with Input on Left and Output on Right. Courtesy of B. Kosko. Adaptive bidirectional associative memories. *Applied Optics*, 26(23):4947–4960, December 1987.

14.9.8 BAM as Partitioned Bipolar Hopfield and Other Connection Matrices

The BAM may be viewed as a Hopfield net where the state vector has been partitioned into two parts (the F_A and F_B unit fields), together with two-step update. This is one of a number of possible

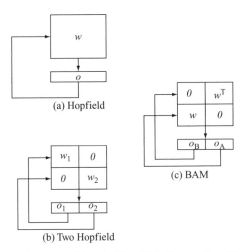

(a) Hopfield

(c) BAM

(b) Two Hopfield

Figure 14.14 Networks Derivable via Hopfield Connection Matrix Partitioning

variations on the Hopfield connection matrix, W, and updating strategy. Several examples are shown in Figure 14.14.

14.10 References

In 1972, Amari proposed the use of a fully interconnected network of threshold elements to store a set of patterns as stable states encoded in the interconnection weights [Ama72a]. In his analysis, the dynamical system concepts and definitions are used to describe and quantify the system recall capability. In 1982, a similar network was proposed by Hopfield in [Hop82] and [Hop84]. Hopfield showed that correlation-like learning (Hebbian learning) could be used to design an associative network (CAM) using a single layer of fully interconnected neurons. The interconnection matrix used is symmetric with zero diagonal elements. Using this model, Hopfield was able to show that the system would seek a local minima of a certain energy function. Studies of this architecture from applications, capacity, and dynamics points of view were reported in various works [Hop84], [HT85], [GB88], [SS91], [MV87], and [Lip87]. An extensive analysis of the Hopfield network capacity is shown in [AMJ85].

Numerous alternative learning algorithms for recurrent networks have been proposed [KS87], [ZW95], [Wik94], and [Olu94]. Genetic approaches, as in feedforward structures, have also been considered [ASP94]. Learning continues to be an active area of research.

The characteristics and applications of recurrent neural networks continue to be an active area of research. Applications include solutions of optimization problems such as the Traveling Salesman Problem [HT85] and constraint satisfaction problems such as image labeling [JS88]. Fitting of curves is treated in [KPW90]. [MS94] shows the use of Hopfield-like nets for solving the correspondence problem in stereo vision. Another application is that of time series prediction [CMA94]. The general topic of associative neural memories is treated in a series of papers in [Has93]. In addition, the relationship between finite-state automata and recurrent networks continues to be investigated [AS95].

14.11   Exercises

1. Develop a solution to the image labeling problem[11] using a recurrent network. For a starting representation, see Figure 14.15.

2. This problem extends our look at recurrent ANN architectures used for constraint satisfaction/optimization problems. The objective is to solve the "map coloring problem" for several maps and with several different choices of colors.

Each part of this problem is based upon a systematic procedure. This procedure is based upon formulating E_i and thus E, differentiation of E to find weights and biases, implementation of the recurrent network, tuning of energy function parameters (coefficients of E_i such as A, B, etc.), and validation.

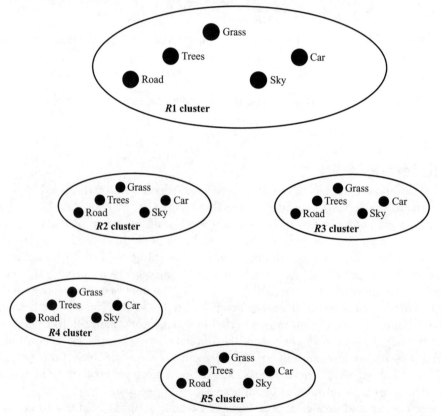

Figure 14.15 Possible Unit Representation for Image Labeling Problem

---

[11]Using both the 42 solution constraints (only "adjacent-to") as well as the unique solution constraints (adding "highest" and "sky").

Test Maps. Refer to Figures 14.16 and 14.17. These are used to test your results.

(a) Phase 1

The objective of this part is to use Figure 14.16 with three colors (RGB) and develop a recurrent structure for the coloring solution. Specifically do all of the following:

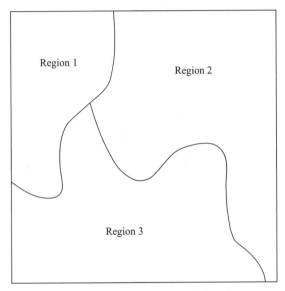

Figure 14.16 Map to be Colored

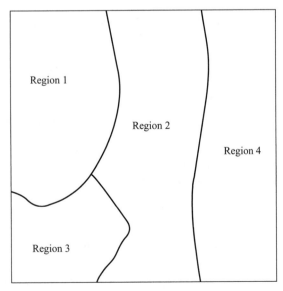

Figure 14.17 Second Map for Verification

    i. Using three colors, how many solutions are there? (Just the number.)

    ii. State the coloring problem constraints.

    iii. Determine a unit "meaning" in order to map o into valid solutions.

    iv. How many units are required? The set partitioning and TSP solutions should give you some insight here.

    v. Determine the component E_i to satisfy the coloring constraints, and thus E. Leave the influence of each component adjustable in E, i.e., $E = A * E_1 + B * E_2 + ...$

    vi. Show E for various "hand-worked" valid and invalid solutions.

    vii. Determine $w_{i,j}$ and thus W. This is to be done via differentiation of E.

    viii. Determine unit bias.

    ix. Using the weights and biases, sketch the overall network and comment on the reasonableness of the weights in terms of the coloring constraints. Is this the interconnection strategy you would expect?

    x. Implement the network, start at randomly generated $o(t_0)$ and show the state evolution.

    xi. Show the effect of changing the relative values of A, B, etc.

    xii. Does the state converge upon a solution (try many cases)?

    xiii. Plot $E(o(t))$ for each case, and assess this in view of the solution.

(b) Phase 2

Repeat the three-color effort of Phase 1, but using the map of Figure 14.17.

(c) Phase 3

Repeat the effort of Phase 1 (Figure 14.16, but use four colors (RGBW).

(d) Phase 4

Repeat the effort of Phase 2 (Figure 14.17, but use four colors).

(e) Phase 5

This effort repeats the efforts of Phases 3 and 4, but using *up to four colors*. In other words, *minimize the total number of colors used*. This must be done by addition of another E_i to implement the measure of optimization.

(f) Draw the resulting network(s) corresponding to the example in Section 14.4.2.

3. Repeat the example of Section 14.4.2, but only update alternate (e.g., even or odd) units at each iteration. Compare the convergence of the network with this procedure with that of a global update, and assess relative computational costs.

4. This problem makes an excellent project. We desire a neural network that connects patterns that are not connected. A connected binary pattern is defined as one in which each location, p_i, which is "ON" (contains a "1") has at least one neighbor in a 3×3 region, centered at p_i, which is also ON.

Using an $n \times n$ array to represent the pattern, develop a Hopfield network that ideally takes fragments of a connected curve that have been disconnected and "connects" these fragments to form a connected curve. Determine a suitable n in order that a reasonable number of sample connected patterns may be stored, yet the number of weights is not excessive. Recall the earlier problem used $n = 5$. Train the network and show sample responses to fragmented patterns.

5. The addition of a bias to all units in a Hopfield network corresponds to adding a plane to the energy surface, or landscape. Show how the direction of this plane relates to the values of the unit bias.

6. In biological networks, the "updating" of neuron activity is highly asynchronous. In Equation 14.3, a highly synchronous version of the updating is shown. This problem is intended to explore the alternatives available for such nets in simulation. Discuss ramifications (and implement them in simulations, if possible) of the following:

(a) At each iteration, Equation 14.3 is used. Notice if the units are updated serially, some activations using "old" o_i values are used.

(b) In contrast with (a), at each iteration the current activation and consequent output of the unit is computed using the latest available o_i values.

(c) The unit updating is random. At each iteration, only a certain percentage of the units are updated.

7. Show that for a change of unit state from o_j to $-o_j$, the network energy change is given by $\Delta E_j = -2o_j net_j$.

8. The Hopfield formulation of Equation 14.9 prohibited self feedback—a unit could neither reinforce nor reduce its output using w_{ii}. This was shown in Equation 14.8. This problem concerns what would change if we allowed nonzero values for w_{ii}. Specifically, consider influence on the following:

◆ Unit output

◆ Energy function

◆ State trajectory

◆ Storage prescription

9. Show how the Hopfield net may be used to *maximize* an objective function by recasting the objective as one to be minimized.

10. In the CSP/optimization problem of Section 14.8, suppose we did not explicitly require a city to be visited at each step. Reformulate the constraints to allow this. Be sure to fully explain your solution.

11. Determine whether the following statement is TRUE OR FALSE:

For Hopfield units with $\{0, 1\}$ outputs and no bias, the energy of the system is the sum of all the weights of connecting units that happen to be ON ($= 1$), scaled and inverted in sign.

12. (a) A $d = 2$ discrete network with $\{0, 1\}$ units is used to store the state: $\underline{\varrho}^s = \begin{pmatrix} 0 \\ 1 \end{pmatrix}$. Determine the corresponding weight matrix.

(b) Find all equilibrium states of this system.

(c) Determine the value of the energy function for each state in this system.

(d) (Assume Hopfield unit characteristics, and a synchronous unit update.) If the system is started in state $\underline{\varrho} = \begin{pmatrix} 1 \\ 1 \end{pmatrix}$, determine subsequent system behavior. Relate this to your answer in Part (c).

Neural Networks (Part 3): Self-Organizing Systems

In this chapter, neural-based examples of "unsupervised" learning are shown. Specifically, networks used to determine natural clusters or feature similarity from given input data are explored. The "cluster discovery" capability of such networks leads to the descriptor *self-organizing*. Biological implications, extensions, and modifications of these approaches are significant, however we only consider the most elementary related concepts here.

15.1 Biological Justification

Biological neural systems often exhibit, on the basis of significant learning or training, an organization of function by local arrangement or structuring of neurons. Thus, a significance to the *geometrical arrangement of neurons* arises. Perhaps the best example is the localization of function of the human brain.

15.2 Self-Organization via Clustering

Self-organizing approaches attempt to develop a network structure on the basis of given sample data. One popular and somewhat obvious approach is *clustering*, or *mode separation*.

15.2.1 Determining "Natural Clusters"

The objective is to design a mechanism that "clusters" data, perhaps by computing similarity. As shown later, there are neural networks with this feature.

In many applications, the data falls into natural, easily observed groups. However, the more difficult and commonly encountered case is where the number of clusters, and the separation between clusters, is not visually obvious. Unfortunately, a solution procedure to handle the latter case is not obvious. In this context, clustering may be conceptualized as "how do we build fences around the data?"

15.2.2 Clustering Similarity Measures

Assume the network input training data is given in vector form. This set is denoted $H_u = \{\underline{v}_p\}$ $p = 1, 2, \ldots, n$. If the input consists of two-dimensional characters represented by matrices, these matrices may be row- or column-concatenated to form vectors. In general, we desire a clustering measure, $d(\underline{v}_i, \underline{v}_j)$, for two vectors, $\underline{v}_i$ and $\underline{v}_j$, such that

$$d(\underline{v}_i, \underline{v}_j) = \begin{cases} \textit{"large"} & \text{when } \underline{v}_i \text{ and } \underline{v}_j \text{ belong in different clusters;} \\ \textit{"small"} & \text{when } \underline{v}_i \text{ and } \underline{v}_j \text{ belong in the same cluster.} \end{cases} \tag{15.1}$$

Using this as a distance measure, we would require $d(\underline{v}_i, \underline{v}_i) = 0$. Using measure $d(\underline{v}_i, i_j)$, we can develop a skeletal threshold-based clustering procedure:

$$\text{assign } \underline{v}_i \text{ and } \underline{v}_j \text{ to } \begin{cases} \text{the same cluster} & \text{if } d(\underline{v}_i, i_j) \leq d_T \\ \text{different clusters} & \text{if } d(\underline{v}_i, \underline{v}_j) > d_T \end{cases} \tag{15.2}$$

Of course, determination of d_T is critical. If d_T is large (i.e., we are fairly loose in our assessment of similarity), we end up with a few "widespread" clusters. Conversely, if d_T is small (we are fairly critical), we may end up with many sparse clusters. Thus, the clustering problem involves choosing $d(\underline{v}_i, \underline{v}_j)$ and d_T and classifying all elements of H_u such that:

- $d(\underline{v}_i, \underline{v}_j)$ is "small" for all pairs $(\underline{v}_i, \underline{v}_j)$ in the same cluster.

- $d(\underline{v}_i, \underline{v}_j)$ is "large" when $\underline{v}_i$ and $\underline{v}_j$ are in different clusters.

This involves a consideration of *inter- and intracluster similarity,* which in turn relies on general distance or similarity measures. The case of distance measures for non-numerical (symbolic) features is left to the exercises.

15.2.3 Clustering Complexity

Efficient and robust clustering algorithms are desirable. A *partition*, denoted P, of a set H, is a set of disjoint subsets of H, i.e., $P = \{H_1, H_2, \ldots, H_m\}$ with $H_i \cap H_j = \phi$ unless $i = j$ and $\cup_{j=1}^{m} H_j = H$. We desire a *partition* of H_u

$$H_u = \{H_1, H_2, \ldots, H_m\} \tag{15.3}$$

where m is chosen such that a clustering function, J_e, is extremized (minimized or maximized). J_e reflects both intra- and intercluster similarity measures.

There are

$$\frac{1}{c!} \sum_{k=1}^{c} \binom{c}{k} (-1)^{c-k} k^n \approx \frac{c^n}{c!} \tag{15.4}$$

possible partitions of n vectors into c nonempty subsets. For example, given the apparently innocuous case of $n = 100$ vectors and $c = 10$ sets, there are approximately $\frac{10^{100}}{10!} \approx 3 \times 10^{93}$ possible partitions. Clearly, exhaustive search procedures are impractical.

15.2.4 Clustering Algorithm Parameters

We illustrate a number of examples of clustering, or generally unsupervised learning, algorithms in the following sections. A key issue in many of these algorithms is design choices involving architectures and parameter determination. Many of these choices are not easy, nor are good guidelines available. This issue is, of course, also common to many other neural network and IS approaches.

For example, c-means requires determining a distance measure, initial means, and c. Self-organizing feature maps (SOFM) require a choice of a spatial architecture, neighborhood "shrinking" schedule, initial weights, and learning rate. Neural gas also requires the determination of several similar parameters. These choices often dictate whether a good solution is obtained from the algorithm. Finally, one of the major difficulties in relating the neural-based results in this chapter to the more conventional syntactic and statistical solutions is the lack of a good set of "benchmark" problems.

15.3 The *c*–Means Algorithm

15.3.1 Algorithm Description

Given a set of input vectors, $H_u = \{\underline{v}_p\}$ $p = 1, 2, \ldots, n$ the algorithm processes H as follows:

1. Choose the number of clusters, c.[1]

2. Determine exemplars for each cluster in H_u, denoted $\underline{\mu}_i(0)$. Often the $\underline{\mu}_i$ are randomly chosen cluster means, which explains the algorithm name.

3. Classify each input vector. Typically this is done using a similarity or distance measure as described in Section 15.2.2, i.e., input $\underline{v}_i$ is assigned to the class represented by exemplar $\underline{\mu}_j$ if

$$d(\underline{v}_i, \underline{\mu}_j) = \overset{min}{q} \{d(\underline{v}_i, \underline{\mu}_q)\} \tag{15.5}$$

4. Recompute the estimates for the exemplar using the results of Step 3.

5. If the exemplars are consistent, STOP, otherwise go to Step 1, 2, or 3.

---

[1] In cases where the number of classes or clusters is not known a priori, this may be done iteratively. Nonetheless, it presents a significant challenge. The ISODATA algorithm provides some help.

Notice the essence of this approach is to achieve a self-consistent partitioning of the data. Choice of initial parameters (c and $\underline{\mu}_i(0)$) is still a challenging issue. This spawns an area of study concerning *cluster validity*.

In determining the validity of the overall clustering, each sample is compared with a "representative" of the ith cluster, namely $\underline{\mu}_i$. Those that are close to $\underline{\mu}_i$ are seen to form a natural grouping, falling within some distance of (and centered around) $\underline{\mu}_i$. There exist many other clustering measures that are also intended to produce "natural clusters."

15.3.2   A Simple 1D c–Means Example and Visual Interpretation

We begin with a simple, easy to visualize, two-cluster example, and investigate the behavior of c-means with varying values of c.

Input Vectors

To illustrate the process, a set of 200 randomly generated 2-D training or input vectors was used. In this set, there are randomly generated Gaussian vectors from two classes with mean vectors and covariance matrices as follows:

Class 1: $\underline{\mu}_1 = \begin{pmatrix} 50 \\ 50 \end{pmatrix}$ and $\Sigma_1 = \begin{pmatrix} 100 & 0 \\ 0 & 100 \end{pmatrix}$.

Class 2: $\underline{\mu}_2 = \begin{pmatrix} -50 \\ -50 \end{pmatrix}$ and $\Sigma_1 = \begin{pmatrix} 100 & 0 \\ 0 & 100 \end{pmatrix}$.

Results and Means Trajectory

Figure 15.1 indicates the quick and direct convergence of the $c = 2$-means to the cluster centers in this example. As shown in the figure, initial means were:

$$\underline{\mu}_1(0) = \begin{pmatrix} 31.3488 \\ 2.6328 \end{pmatrix} \text{ and } \underline{\mu}_2(0) = \begin{pmatrix} 19.2116 \\ -38.6717 \end{pmatrix}$$

and the final (converged) means are:

$$\underline{\mu}_1(2) = \begin{pmatrix} 50.855 \\ 50.866 \end{pmatrix} \text{ and } \underline{\mu}_2(2) = \begin{pmatrix} -50.679 \\ -51.600 \end{pmatrix}$$

Interestingly, each final mean represents a cluster comprised of (the nearest) 100, i.e., half of the input vector set. Only two iterations were required for convergence. The favorable results provided by this example are somewhat optimistic due to a number of factors, including well-separated clusters, favorable choices of initial means, and accurate knowledge of c.

Results for c = 2, 3, 4, 10

In this case, c-means exhibits some nonideal behavior. The convergence of the algorithm to local minima is evident in Figure 15.2.

Input Data and Trajectory of *c*-means (*c* = 2) Vectors

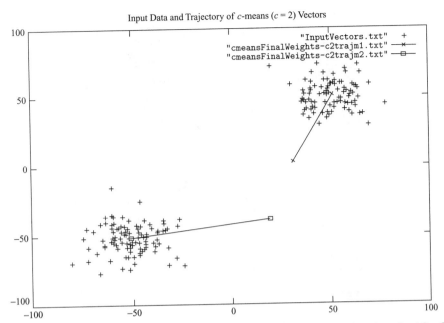

Figure 15.1 $c = 2$-Means Showing Initial to Final Means Trajectory. Two Iterations Required for Convergence.

Input Data and Resulting *c*-means (*c* = 2,3,4,10) Vectors

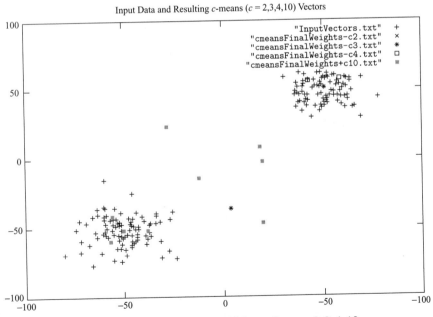

Figure 15.2 Initial and Final Means for $c = 2, 3, 4, 10$

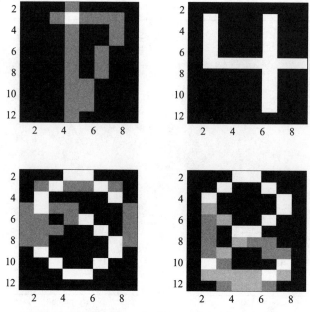

Figure 15.3 Results of c-Means ($c = 4$) on Digits

This example is continued in Section 15.4.7 using a SOFM for comparison.

15.3.3 Example: Clustering Digits ($0, 1, 2, \dots, 9$)

In this example, we use the $n = 10$ digit training set from Chapter 14. Each digit is considered an 88×1 vector[2] and $c = 4$-means are sought. Figure 15.3 shows sample results. The exercises continue this example using alphabetic characters.

15.4 Self-Organizing Feature Maps (SOFM)

15.4.1 Introduction

Kohonen ([Koh84], [Koh82b], [Koh82a], [Koh87], [KKL90]) has shown a neural learning structure involving networks that perform dimensionality reduction through conversion of feature space to yield *topologically ordered* similarity graphs or maps or clustering diagrams (with potential statistical interpretations). In addition, the training algorithm implements a form of local competitive learning.

15.4.2 Unit Topologies

Figures 15.4 and 15.5 show possible 1-D and 2-D configurations of units to form feature or pattern dimensionality reducing maps. For example, a 2-D topology yields a planar map, indexed by a 2-D

---

[2]Although we choose to visualize the results by resizing the vector into an 11×8 array.

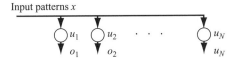

Figure 15.4 One-Dimensional Unit Topology

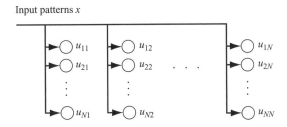

Figure 15.5 Two-Dimensional Unit Topology

coordinate system. Of course, 3-D and higher dimensional maps are possible. Notice each unit, regardless of the topology, receives the input pattern $\underline{v} = (i_1, i_2 \ldots i_d)^T$ in parallel. The unit output is inconsequential. Considering the topological arrangement of the chosen units, the d-D feature space is mapped into 1-D, 2-D, 3-D, etc. The coordinate axes used to index the unit topology, however, have no explicit meaning or relation to feature space. They may, however, reflect a similarity relationship between units in the reduced dimensional space, where topological distance is proportional to dissimilarity.

Choosing the dimension of the feature map involves engineering judgment. Some IS applications naturally suggest a certain dimension, for example a 2-D map may be developed for speech recognition applications, where 2-D unit clusters represent phonemes. The dimensions of the chosen topological map may also influence the training time of the network. It is noteworthy, however, that powerful results have been obtained by just using 1-and 2-dimensional topologies.

15.4.3 Defining Topological Neighborhoods ("Bubbles")

Once a topological dimension is chosen, the concept of an equivalent dimension neighborhood (or cell or bubble), around each neuron may be introduced. Examples for a 2-D map are shown in Figure 15.6.

This neighborhood, denoted N_c, is centered at neuron u_c, and the cell or neighborhood size (characterized by its radius in 2-D, for example) may vary with time or iteration in the training phase. For example, initially N_c may start as the entire 2-D network, and the radius of N_c shrinks as iteration (described subsequently) proceeds. As a practical matter, the discrete nature of the 2-D net allows the neighborhood of a neuron to be defined in terms of its nearest neighbors, e.g., with

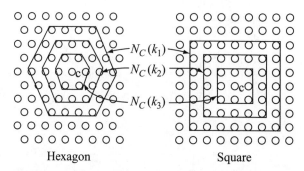

Figure 15.6   Sample 2-D Neighborhood Definitions and Evolution Over Iteration

a square array the four nearest neighbors of u_c are its N, S, E, and W neighbors; the eight nearest neighbors would include the "corners."[3] In 1-D, a simple distance measure may be used.

15.4.4   Network Learning Algorithm

The set of vectors to be explored is denoted $H_u = \{\underline{v}_p\}$ $p = 1, 2, \ldots, n$. Each unit, hereafter denoted u_i, in the network has the same number of weights as the dimension of the input vector, and receives the input vector $\underline{v}$ in parallel. The goal of the self-organizing network, given a large, unlabeled training set, is to have individual neural clusters self-organize to reflect input pattern similarity. Defining a weight vector for neural unit u_i as $\underline{m}_i = (w_{i1}, w_{i2}, \ldots w_{id})^T$, the overall structure may be viewed as *an array of matched filters, which competitively adjust unit input weights on the basis of the current weights and goodness of match.* A useful viewpoint is that each unit tries to become a matched filter, in competition with other units. This learning concept is now more fully quantified.

Assume the network is initialized with the weights of all units chosen randomly. Thereafter, during training step k, input pattern $\underline{v}(k)$ is presented to the SOFM. A distance measure $d(\underline{v}(k), \underline{m}_i(k))$ is employed. This measure may be an inner product measure (correlation), Euclidean distance, or another suitable measure. For simplicity, we proceed using the Euclidean distance. For input $\underline{v}(k)$, the *matching phase* defines a "winner" unit u_c, containing weight vector $\underline{m}_c(k)$, using

$$\parallel \underline{v}(k) - \underline{m}_c(k) \parallel = \overset{min}{i} \left\{ \parallel \underline{v}(k) - \underline{m}_i(k) \parallel \right\} \tag{15.6}$$

Thus, at training step k, for input vector $\underline{v}(k)$, c is the index of the best matching spatial unit. The weight training affects all units in the currently defined cell, bubble, or cluster surrounding u_c, $N_c(k)$ through the global network *updating phase* as shown in Equation 15.7. The $\underline{m}_i(k)$ for input vector $\underline{v}(k)$ are updated using:

$$\underline{m}_i(k+1) = \begin{cases} \underline{m}_i(k) + \alpha(k)\left[\underline{v}(k) - \underline{m}_i(k)\right] & i \in N_c(k) \\ \\ \underline{m}_i(k) & i \notin N_c(k) \end{cases} \tag{15.7}$$

---

[3]The reader may observe that a hexagonal array makes the nearest neighbors of u_c equidistant.

Each unit vector $\underline{m}_i$ may be updated many times in one pass through H_u if it is in the neighborhood of multiple winners. We update $\underline{m}_i(k)$ immediately and use that value with the next input. In other words, we change the winning vectors in the neighborhood and then use these new values for the next input vector.

Iterations Versus Epochs and Parameter Adjustment Schedules.   Equation 15.7 indicates several iteration-dependent parameters ($N_c(k)$ and learning rate $\alpha(k)$). We have indicated the neighborhood function is $N_c(k)$ "shrinking;" typically this may be done after each epoch (where k is an integer multiple of n).

The updating strategy in Equation 15.7 corresponds to a discretized version of the differential adaptation law:

$$\frac{d\underline{m}_i(t)}{dt} = \alpha(\underline{v}(t) - \underline{m}_i(t)) \qquad i \in N_c \tag{15.8}$$

$$\frac{d\underline{m}_i(t)}{dt} = 0 \qquad i \notin N_c \tag{15.9}$$

Equation 15.8 indicates that $d(\underline{v}, \underline{m}_i)$ is decreased for units inside N_c, by moving $\underline{m}_i$ in the direction $(\underline{v} - \underline{m}_i)$. Therefore, after the adjustment, the weight vectors in N_c are closer to input pattern $\underline{v}$. Weight vectors for units outside N_c are left unchanged. The competitive nature of the algorithm is evident, since after the training iteration units outside N_c are *relatively* further from $\underline{v}$. That is, there is an opportunity cost of not being adjusted.

15.4.5 Network Coordinate Systems—Topological and Weight Spaces

One of the crucial aspects in grasping SOFM concepts is the distinction between the *spatial location* of a unit and *unit weights*. There is no required relation between the dimensionalities of these spaces, however the literature is replete with cases involving $d = 2$-dimensional input (and correspondingly weight) spaces and 2-D spatial arrays. This is used to facilitate confirmation that:

◆ Unit weights eventually self-organize to "span" the input space; and

◆ Spatial organization or localization takes place.

Thus, a SOFM employs two coordinate systems. Each unit is indexed by two sets of coordinates: fixed physical coordinates (denoted $(u, v)_p$) and weight space values (denoted $(w_u, w_v)_w$). *Only values of $(w_u, w_v)_w$ change in the SOFM formation process.* Often, as the example in Section 15.4.7 shows, neighboring units in physical space are shown by connecting weight coordinates with lines.

15.4.6 Algorithm Properties and Discussion

Parameter Choices

The resulting accuracy of the mapping depends upon the choices of $N_c(k)$, $\alpha(k)$, and the number of iterations. Kohonen cites the use of 10,000–100,000 iterations as typical. Furthermore, $\alpha(k)$ should start with a value close to 1.0, and gradually decrease with k.

Neighborhood Evolution or "Shrinking"

The neighborhood size, $N_c(k)$, deserves careful consideration in SOFM algorithm design. Too small a choice of $N_c(0)$ may lead to maps without topological ordering. Therefore, it is reasonable to let $N_c(0)$ be fairly large (Kohonen suggests one-half the diameter of the map) shrinking $N_c(k)$ (perhaps linearly) with epoch to the fine-adjustment phase, where $N_c(k)$ only consists of the nearest neighbors of unit u_c. A limiting case is where $N_c(k)$ becomes one unit, namely the winner.

15.4.7   A Simple 1-D SOFM Example

We begin with a simple, easy to visualize, example using a 10-unit 1-D topological array. Unit weights are in 2-D, and this allows graphical visualization of the self-organizing effects (assuming they occur). The input data of Section 15.3.2 is (re-)used. This allows comparison of the different approaches and corresponding results.

Initial Unit Weights

Figure 15.7 shows the spatial organization of the initial one-dimensional SOFM (before training).

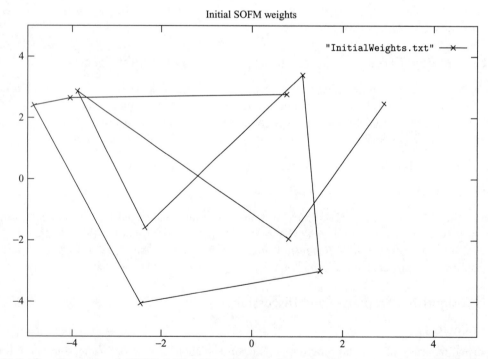

Figure 15.7 One-Dimensional SOFM Initial Unit Weights. Line segments are used to indicate the nearest physical space neighbor. Note the "unorganized" nature of the initial weights.

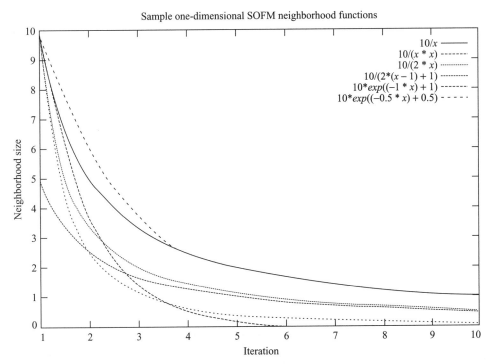

Figure 15.8 Possible One-Dimensional Spatial Neighborhood Shrinking Strategies. Here iteration = epoch.

Neighborhood "Shrinking" Strategies

In this example, the original neighborhood size is chosen to be the entire extent of the 1-D spatial array. The neighborhood shrinks with iteration (epoch). Several possible alternatives are shown in Figure 15.8.

In designing a SOFM, it is advisable to coordinate the neighborhood shrinking schedule with the total number of iterations.

Final Unit Weights

Recall from Section 15.3.2, there are two (visually apparent) clusters in the input training vector set. The initial and final unit weights are shown (connected by line segments indicating nearest physical neighbors) in Figure 15.9.

In this example, the neighborhood and neighborhood shrinking schedule for the 10-unit spatial array was defined by parameter $diameter(epoch) = 10/epoch^2$. All units within a distance of $diameter$ of the winning unit are considered to be in the neighborhood, i.e., a unit at spatial location i is in the neighborhood of the winner at spatial location i_c if $((i - i_c)^2 < diameter^2$.

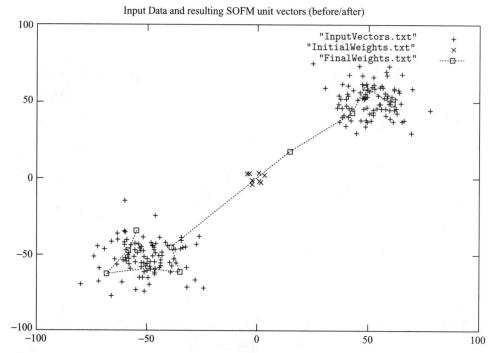

Figure 15.9 One-Dimensional SOFM Input Vectors with Initial and Final Unit Weights

15.4.8 Validation and Interpretation of the Resulting SOFM

While the formal validation of SOFMs[4] is a complex and open subject [L06], it is useful to be able to conceptualize "good" and "bad" SOFM results. There are a number of ways to interpret a successfully self-organized SOFM. Recall the training algorithm causes the weights of *all units* in a "winning" neighborhood to be adjusted toward the current input vector, $\underline{v}(k)$. As a result, repeated presentations of input vectors that are close (in input space) leads to the development, or organization, of spatial neighborhoods where spatially close units contain similar, or close (in distance), weight vectors. Therefore, the SOFM forms a spatially organized map where similar inputs are mapped close together and dissimilar input vectors are mapped farther apart. If there exist clusters of vectors in high-dimensional input space, these clusters are reflected in the SOFM as spatial clusters of units with similar weight values. Following training, the SOFM may contain a number of such spatial clusters.

Another interpretation is to consider the inverse of the input space-to-SOFM mapping, where SOFM unit weights may be visualized as "pointers" back into input space. The spatial distribution of these weights in the SOFM forms a discrete approximation to the distribution of the training vectors in input space. (Spatially) large neighborhoods of units in the SOFM containing similar weights "point" to regions in input space with high-input vector concentration. Conversely, small or 1-unit spatial neighborhoods in the SOFM point to regions of input space that are sparsely populated.

---

[4]And, for that matter, neural gas and other related computational architectures.

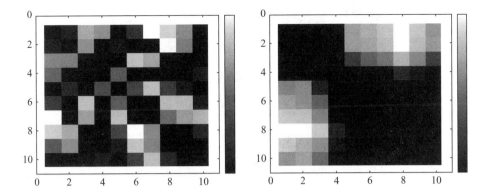

Figure 15.10 Visual Display of Initial (left) and Final (right) Weight Differences (squared) for 1-D SOFM Array of Example (see Figure 15.9)

Use of This Property and SOFM Solution Constraints. Either interpretation from Section 15.4.8 leads to the following assertion:

If there exist clusters in the training set (input space), they are reflected as spatial clusters in the 1-D SOFM.

Note that in low-dimensional (2-D) cases, plotting of vectors allows a human visual interpretation of clusters. It is more important to develop an automated process applicable to higher-dimensional vectors. To this end, we compute and display the squared distance from every vector in the SOFM to every other vector in the SOFM, both initially and following application of the SOFM training algorithm. The significance of this distance data to validate the self-organizing property is easy to see using the example of Figure 15.9. Figure 15.10 shows the results.

15.4.9 Another Example: 2–D SOFM Application to 11 × 8 Digits

To show the development of a 2-D SOFM, we employ 11 × 8 arrays used to represent the digits $(0, 1, 2 \ldots, 9)$. Digits are converted into 88 × 1 vectors by row concatenation of the 11 × 8 matrix representation. The 2-D spatial array consists of 5 × 5 units. Although all inputs and unit weights are 88 × 1 vectors, unit weights are displayed in the 11 × 8 format to enhance visualization of the results.

Initial SOFM Weights. These are generated by a random number generator and are shown in Figure 15.11. Note that there is little apparent visual similarity with the initial weights of the SOFM and any digits.

Resulting SOFM (Weights Viewed as Digits). These are shown in Figure 15.12. The self-organizing nature of the 2-D array is evident in the similarity of weights of adjacent units.

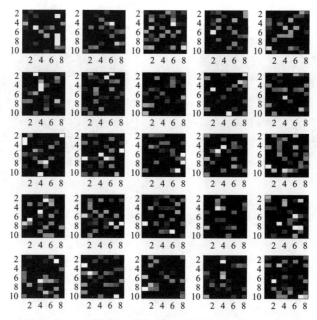

Figure 15.11 Initial Weight Values in SOFM for Digit Application

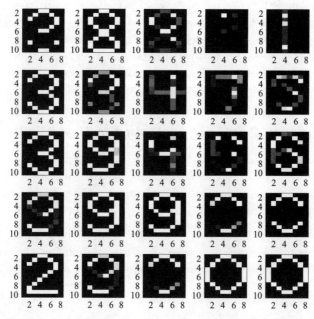

Figure 15.12 Resulting SOFM Array for Digits. Note clustering is evident in the similarity of spatially adjacent unit weights.

15.5 The Neural Gas (NG) Self–Organizing Network

In the NG approach, no spatial neighborhood is used. **NG is ordering-based rather than topology-driven.**[5] We first present the algorithm as originally proposed, i.e., with the notion of explicit sorting. This helps convey the underlying algorithm concepts. Later we show only implicit sorting is necessary.

15.5.1 NG Algorithm

As in SOFM, define the training set as $H_u = \{\underline{v}_p\}$ $p = 1, 2, \ldots, n$. For an NG network consisting of N weights,

$$||\underline{v} - \underline{w}_i|| i = 1, 2, \ldots, N$$

or, using a non-Euclidean R-norm

$$||\underline{v} - \underline{w}_i||_R   i = 1, 2, \ldots, N$$

is computed for each weight vector, $\underline{w}_i$.

As in SOFM there is not an adjustment to a single "winner," but (assuming presentation of $\underline{v}$) adjustments to unit weights are based upon **order** in terms of distance from $\underline{v}$. Thus, the sorted NG weight set (denoted **w**) is:

$$\mathbf{w} = \{\underline{w}_{i_0}, \underline{w}_{i_1}, \underline{w}_{i_2}, \ldots, \underline{w}_{i_k}, \ldots, \underline{w}_{i_{N-1}}\}$$

where $\underline{w}_{i_0}$ is the closest to $\underline{v}$, $\underline{w}_{i_1}$ is next closest to $\underline{v}$, and so on until $\underline{w}_{i_{N-1}}$ is the furthest away from $\underline{v}$. Note that a general property of any unit weight vector, denoted $\underline{w}_{i_k}$ $k = 0, 1, \ldots, N - 1$, in the ordered weight set, is that there are k unit weight vectors, $\underline{w}_j$, for which

$$||\underline{v} - \underline{w}_j|| < ||\underline{v} - \underline{w}_{i_k}||$$

Although somewhat obvious, we observe that each unit weight vector's **position** in the ordered array is a function of:

◆ $\underline{v}$

◆ All the (**current**) unit weights in the network, denoted as the set $\mathbf{w} = \{\underline{w}_1, \underline{w}_2, \ldots, \underline{w}_N\}$

The position of unit weight vector $\underline{w}_i$ is denoted[6] $k_i(\underline{v}, \mathbf{w})$.

The distance ordering, based upon $\underline{v}$, maps each unit weight vector, $\underline{w}_i$ in **w** into some relative position in the sorted array. Thus in the sorted array, the weight vector appears at position $\underline{w}_{i_k}$. For example, if $\underline{w}_i$ is the closest, it is at position i_0. If $\underline{w}_i$ is the furthest, it is at position i_{N-1}.

---

[5]Relating the two comes later.
[6]Or could be thought of as the result of a mapping function $k = f(\underline{v}, \underline{w}_i, \mathbf{w})$.

15.5.2   How Is the NG Sorted Array Used?

The adaptation for each unit weight vector, $\underline{w}_i \in \mathbf{w}$, relies on its position in the sorted weight array and is given by:

$$\Delta \underline{w}_i = \epsilon h_\lambda(k_i(\underline{v}, \mathbf{w}))(\underline{v} - \underline{w}_i) \quad i = 1, 2, \ldots, N \tag{15.10}$$

where ϵ is the learning or adaptation rate, and the "rewarding" function $h_\lambda(k_i(\underline{v}, \mathbf{w}))$ weights or scales the amount of adaptation based upon distance from $\underline{v}$, as indicated by relative position in the sorted array. For example, if

$$h_\lambda(k_i(\underline{v}, \mathbf{w})) = \delta(k_i)$$

where $\delta(k_i)$ is the Kronecker delta function,[7] only the closest unit weight vector is updated. This parameter choice yields the LVQ algorithm.

More often, $h_\lambda(x)$ is chosen to be a decaying function of increasing x, so that nonzero corrections are made to $\underline{w}_{i_0}, \underline{w}_{i_1}, \underline{w}_{i_2}$, and so on, but with less correction to $\underline{w}_{i_1}$ than to $\underline{w}_{i_0}$, less correction to $\underline{w}_{i_2}$ than to $\underline{w}_{i_1}$, and so on. Typically, h_λ is a monotonically decreasing function parameterized by an iteration-dependent λ (i.e., $\lambda(k)$). For example, Equation 15.11 indicates one "schedule" for h_λ.

$$h_\lambda(k_i(\underline{v}, \mathbf{w})) = e^{-\dfrac{k_i(\underline{v}, \mathbf{w})}{\lambda}} \tag{15.11}$$

Parameter λ controls how quickly the weight corrections "decay" as a function of distance from the winner or closest unit weight vector. As the algorithm starts, λ is chosen to be large, therefore weights that may be a considerable distance from $\underline{v}$ are corrected. As the iterations proceed, λ decreases. Similarly, the learning rate, ϵ, may be iteration-dependent. This is shown in the example of Section 15.5.4.

15.5.3   Engineering and Pragmatic Concerns

Some remarks on computational costs and the alternatives of sorting vs. finding the minimum distance "winner" are in order. First, for N weight vectors, N distance calculations are needed to find the winner. In considering sorting for N weight vectors, there are $N!$ possible permutations of the weight vector set. The computational complexity [Joh86] of the sort is $O(N log_2 N)$. There is therefore some interest in making the algorithm less costly.

Explicit Sorting Is Not Necessary.   Up to this point, we have conveyed the NG algorithm using the notion of an (explicitly) sorted array. Strictly speaking, this is not necessary. Note the weight adjustments or corrections are based upon the *relative position in the sorted array, i.e., the ordered distance from $\underline{v}$*. Consider the following alternative [AS98]:

$$m_i = \frac{d_i - d_{min}}{d_{max} - d_{min}} \tag{15.12}$$

---

[7] $\delta(0) = 1$; otherwise $\delta(k) = 0$.

where d_{min} and d_{max} are the minimum and maximum distances between $\mathbf{w}$ and $\underline{v}$ respectively, and d_i is the distance corresponding to vector $\underline{w}_i$. Thus,

$$m_i \in [0, 1]$$

where $m_i = 0$ if $\underline{w}_i$ is the closest to $\underline{v}$ (d_{min}) and $m_i = 1$ if $\underline{w}_i$ is the farthest from $\underline{v}$ (i.e., a distance of d_{max}).

Based upon Equation 15.12, weight corrections or adjustments may be formulated as:

$$\Delta\underline{w}_i = \epsilon h_{\lambda'}(m_i(\underline{v}, \mathbf{w}))(\underline{v} - \underline{w}_i) \quad i = 1, 2, \ldots, N \tag{15.13}$$

where

$$h_{\lambda'}(m_i) = \exp(-m_i/\lambda'(t))$$

and

$$\lambda'(t) = \lambda(t)/(N - 1)$$

Thus, the weight correction is still based upon relative distance to $\underline{v}$, but explicit sorting of the weight set is not necessary.

Another Approximation: Partial Sorting. If we don't update an entire sorted list, another approximation results. Implementation of this [AS98] is by modification (truncation) of $h_\lambda(k_i(\underline{v}, \mathbf{w}))$, defined in Equation 15.11 and used in Equation 15.10:

$$h_\lambda(k_i(\underline{v}, \mathbf{w})) = \begin{cases} e^{-\frac{k_i(\underline{v}, \mathbf{w})}{\lambda}} & \text{if } k_i \leq m \\ 0 & \text{otherwise} \end{cases} \tag{15.14}$$

Notice that the effect of this truncation is a function of how quickly h_λ is approaching 0.

15.5.4 NG Example

Using implicit sorting, the control of $h_\lambda(k_i(\underline{v}, \mathbf{w}))$ is straightforward. Figure 15.13 shows various possible "schedules."

Applying NG. Here we show an illustrative NG example (again, on low-dimensional data to facilitate algorithm behavior visualization). This example uses the input data of Section 15.4.7.

Figure 15.14 shows sample algorithm results using the same input vector data used for c-means and SOFM. The results after 5, 10, and 100 iterations are shown. In this example, the parameters used (each is with respect to the total number of iterations) were: initial $\lambda = 10$, final $\lambda = 1$, initial $\epsilon = 0.05$, and final $\epsilon = 0.001$.

15.5.5 Validation of NG Example

To show the NG-induced ordering of the initial weight set, we repeat the analysis of Section 15.4.8. The visual renditions of the distance-squared matrices for the initial NG weight sets and for 5, 10, and 100 iterations are shown in Figure 15.15. The interpretation of the evolution of these matrices is left to the exercises.

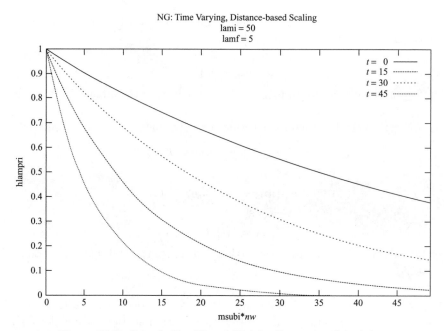

Figure 15.13 Sample Families of Weight Correction Schedules

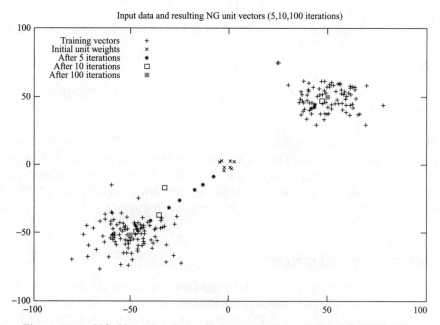

Figure 15.14 NG Algorithm Input Vectors—Initial and Final Unit Weights

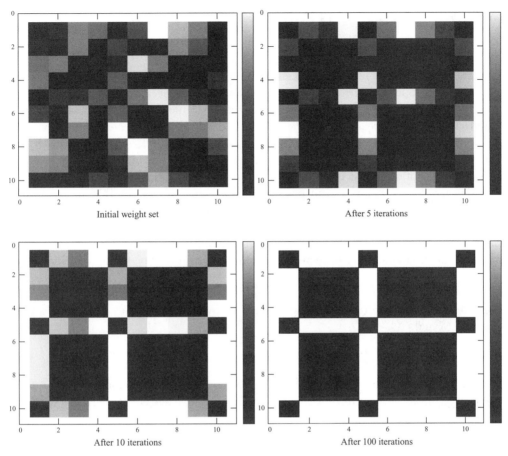

Figure 15.15 Visual Display of NG Network Weight Differences (squared) for 5, 10, and 100 iterations (see Figure 15.14)

15.5.6 Neural Gas Statistical Characterization

[TMMS93] has shown that, given $H_u = \{\underline{v}_p\}$ $p = 1, 2, \ldots, n$, the weights resulting from NG training minimize:

$$E = \int p(\underline{v}) ||\underline{v} - \underline{w}_i||^2 \underline{dv} \tag{15.15}$$

by a suitable choice of "reference" vectors, $\underline{w}_i$.

15.6 Growing Neural Gas (GNG)

15.6.1 Algorithm Description

Growing Neural Gas [Fri95] (GNG) is an example of an unsupervised neural network that is able to generate the network topology during the learning phase. It is not necessary to prespecify the number of units or the GNG topology. However, a number of fixed parameters must be chosen. Typically, the network is stopped when a specified network size is obtained, although other criteria are possible.

Like our previous networks, the GNG network consists of a set, A, of units with each unit containing a d-dimensional vector. Units may be connected by insertion of an undirected edge between them. Denote the set of all connected unit pairs as $C \subset A \times A$. (Alternately, a data structure such as a connection matrix $c(i, j)$ for all unit pairs u_i, u_j may be used to store this information. Entries in this matrix may also be used to hold the current edge age.) The transitivity of the "connected" relation and the current set of edges defines clusters of connected units. The main strategy of the GNG is to successively add new units to the (initially minimal) network based upon previous training error measures. Furthermore, edges have an associated "age" and may be removed during the training process.

The GNG training procedure is somewhat more complex than SOFM and NG. A skeletal version is summarized as follows. The reader will notice that many of the steps or computations are similar to those of SOFM and NG.

Skeletal GNG Training Algorithm.

1. Initialize the network with two units, u_a and u_b, containing respective randomly-generated vectors $\underline{w}_{u_a}$ and $\underline{w}_{u_b}$. Initialize the interunit connection array, c, edge age counter array, and unit specific error accumulator array, $E(u_i)$.

2. For an input, $\underline{v}(k)$, from the training set, H_u, find the first and second nearest units, denoted s_1 and s_2. This requires a distance computation similar to SOFM and NG, but with a "second" winner.

3. Increment the age of all edges emanating from winner s_1.

4. Update the entry in the error accumulator array, E, for unit s_1 using:

$$\Delta E(s_1) = ||\underline{w}_{s_1} - \underline{v}(k)||^2$$

5. Adjust the weight vectors in unit s_1 and its **direct topological neighbors**[8] toward $\underline{v}(k)$ via:

$$\Delta w_{s_1} = \epsilon_b(\underline{v}(k) - \underline{w}_{s_1})$$

and

$$\Delta w_{u_k} = \epsilon_n(\underline{v}(k) - \underline{w}_{u_k})$$

6. If $(s_1, s_2) \in C$, set the age of this edge to 0. If not, insert an edge between units s_1 and s_2 with age 0.

---

[8]Direct topological neighbors of s_1 are defined as $N_{s_1} = \{u_k | (s_1, u_k) \in C\}$.

7. Prune edges whose age is greater than a_{max}. If, after this step, there are units in the network that have no emanating edges (they are totally unconnected), remove these units.

8. If k is an integer multiple of a parameter, λ, insert a new unit. This requires determining where topologically to place the unit, as well as the unit parameters. The insertion action is carried out in several steps:

(a) Determine the unit, u_q, with the maximum accumulated error in the network at this time, i.e., where $E(u_q)$ is maximum.

(b) Determine the direct topological neighbor of u_q, denoted u_f, with the largest accumulated error.

(c) Insert a new unit, u_r, whose weight vector is given by:

$$\underline{w}_{u_r} = \frac{1}{2}(\underline{w}_{u_q} + \underline{w}_{u_f})$$

(d) Remove the edge between u_q and u_f. Add zero-age edges connecting u_r and u_q and u_r and u_f.

(e) Modify $E(u_q)$ and $E(u_f)$ using parameter α:

$$\Delta E(u_k) = \alpha E(u_k) \quad k = q, f$$

(f) Set $E(u_r) = E(u_q)$. Note the new (recently updated) value of $E(u_q)$ is used.[9]

9. Decrease all errors in E using parameter d:

$$\Delta E(u_k) = (1 - d)E(u_k)$$

10. Check to see if the training algorithm should stop. This may be done based upon maximum network size (number of units) or some other criteria (see the exercises). If not, go to Step 2.

15.6.2 GNG Example

We show sample GNG algorithm results in Figure 15.16. This example uses the same input data as in Sections 15.3.2, 15.4.7, and 15.5.4 for comparison. For this example, the parameters $\lambda = 1500$, $e_b = 0.05$, $e_n = 0.0006$, $\alpha = 0.5$, $d = 0.9995$, $a_{max} = 50$, and stopping of training was enforced using $maxunits = 15$.

15.7 "Batch" SOFM and NG Approaches

Recall from Sections 15.4 and 15.5.1 that input vectors $\underline{v}(k)$ are presented serially to the network units during training. These are often termed the "online" versions of the algorithms. "Batch" approaches [MCV] for SOFM and NG implementation have a number of computational advantages, especially in facilitating parallel implementation of the training. We assume all inputs in $H_u = \{\underline{v}_p\}$ $p = 1, 2, \ldots, n$ are available prior to training.

---

[9]An alternative to this step that sometimes appears in the literature is to set $E(u_r) = \frac{1}{2}(E(u_q) + E(u_f))$.

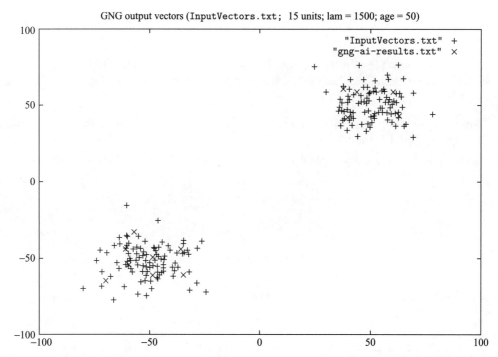

Figure 15.16 GNG results for the data of Sections 15.3.2 (*c*-means), 15.4.7 (SOFM), and 15.5.4 (NG)

15.7.1 Batch SOFM

The description from Kohonen, available at http://www.cis.hut.fi/projects/somtoolbox/theory/ somalgorithm.shtml is paraphrased here. Notice it results in a "unit-centric" approach to SOFM. Also, note a spatial neighborhood is still used.

1. Initialize the SOFM unit vectors, i.e., $u_i(\underline{w}_i)$.

2. For each unit, u_i, collect a list of *all the inputs* whose most similar SOFM unit vector belongs to the neighborhood set, N_i, of u_i.

3. Update each unit vector with the mean over the respective list of vectors for N_i.

4. Repeat Step 2.

15.7.2 Batch NG

Recall from Section 15.5.1 (the explicitly sorted formulation) and Equation 15.10 that the NG weight correction uses $h_\lambda(k_i(\underline{v}, \mathbf{w}))$ to adjust $\underline{w}_i$, given $\underline{v}$. We use the two-step formulation proposed in [MCV]:

1. Define (and compute):

$$k_{ij} = k_i(\underline{v}_j, \mathbf{w})$$

2. Using k_{ij}, set

$$\underline{w}_i = \frac{\sum_{j=1}^{n} h_\lambda(k_{ij})\underline{v}_j}{\sum_{j=1}^{n} h_\lambda(k_{ij})}$$

15.8 References

The popularity and utility of unsupervised learning [DJ80], including clustering has spawned a sizable and varied library of clustering algorithms [BAM82]. Two of the most popular are the c-means and ISODATA clustering approaches in statistical pattern recognition [Sch92], [DJ76]. Other background references for clustering include [For65], [Har75], [Fuk72], and [Pat72].

Additional details regarding Kohonen's self-organizing nets are found in [Koh84], [Koh82b], [Koh82a], [Koh87], [Koh88], [Koh90], and [KKL90]. LVQ, extensions, and the Kohonen nets are covered in [GS91]. Convergence properties of topology preserving networks are derived in [LYB93]. Finally, another solution to the Traveling Salesman Problem (TSP) is shown using Kohonen self-organizing feature maps in [AVT88].

Neural gas and efficient algorithms are found in [TMMS93] and [AS98]. The Growing Neural Gas algorithm is introduced in [Fri95]. Unification of these approaches, and consideration of "batch" approaches, is treated comprehensively in [MCV].

15.9 Exercises

1. The Kohonen self-organizing or adaptation law of Equation 15.8, for each element of $\underline{m}_i$ and $\underline{v}$, may be rearranged as

$$\frac{dw_{ij}(t)}{dt} = \alpha(i_j - w_{ij}) \tag{15.16}$$

which is a specific case of the more general adaptation equation [Koh84]

$$\frac{dw_{ij}(t)}{dt} = \alpha(t)\{u_i(t)i_i(t) - \gamma u_i(t)w_{ij}(t)\} \tag{15.17}$$

where $u_i(t)$ is taken to be unity.

(a) Show that Equation 15.17 represents a form of Hebbian or correlation learning with a "forgetting" term.

(b) What conditions are necessary to simplify Equation 15.17 into Equation 15.16?

2. This problem makes an excellent project. Use a random number generator to generate 100 $d = 2$ dimensional samples from each of $c = 2$ classes to form a set of Kohonen SOFM inputs set, denoted H_u. Choose the random number of parameters such that there is some class overlap.

(a) Apply the c-means algorithm to this data, with the cases $c = 2, 3, 4$. For each case:

    i. Choose $\underline{\mu}_i(0)$, $i = 1, 2, \ldots c$. Use some judgment to get "reasonable" starting values.

    ii. Use the 1-NNR for sample classification.

    iii. Choose, and justify, a stopping criteria.

    iv. Plot $\underline{\mu}_i(k)$ $k > 0$ (k is the iteration number).

(b) Repeat part (a) using a Kohonen SOFM. Consider:

    i. a 2-D unit topology; and

    ii. a 1-D unit topology.

Assess your results.

Given the results from a Kohonen SOFM, how might we determine the number of classes or clusters in the data?

3. In the generation of an SOFM, can the order in which input samples are presented influence the results of the algorithm? Provide justification for your answer.

4. Design both 1-D and 2-D SOFMs for alphabetical characters. Use the 26 uppercase letters: $A, B, \ldots, Z$. The problem consists of these tasks:

(a) Using the SOFM to get feature maps (1-D and 2-D);

(b) Assessing the resulting SOFM; and

(c) Comparing this with the use of the c-means algorithm.

5. Consider the case of a "tie" in the implementation of the SOFM algorithm. Recall in the matching phase, or process of determining a "winner" unit u_c, with weight vector $\underline{m}_c$, (as defined by Equation 15.6), we used the measure $\overset{min}{i} \{\| \underline{v}(k) - \underline{m}_i(k) \|\}$. Suppose for a given $\underline{v}(k)$ there are two or more values of $\underline{m}_i(k)$ for which this similarity measure is a minimum. Suggest one or more methods to determine a "winner" unit in this case.

6. The development and application of distance measures for numerical input data in self-organizing and data mining algorithms is straightforward. A very significant and open research problem is *clustering non-numerical* data. There are many ways this situation could occur, for example:

    ♦ Inputs may be arrangements (e.g., sequences) of symbolic entities such as characters, strings, or files of text.

    ♦ Attributes of entities may be non-numerical, e.g., color, texture, or TRUE/FALSE.

A myriad of approaches to this problem have been proposed. Research this subject and prepare a summary of these approaches.

7. Section 15.5.3 indicated a potentially practical alternative to NG implementation, namely that complete sorting may be avoided, and determining only a few "top" positions in the (ordered) list is sufficient. Discuss (and verify via simulation) the relative importance of sorting accuracy vs. sorting completeness. Consider two approaches:

(a) Partial, exact sorting: the "top" or closest winning unit weights are sorted exactly, remaining weights are left alone (unsorted).

(b) Complete, noisy sorting: the "top" or closest winning unit weights are sorted exactly, remaining weights are subjected to inexact sorting (via the addition of noise).

8. For the GNG training algorithm in Section 15.6, identify computational steps that are similar to:

(a) SOFM

(b) NG

9. As noted in Section 15.6, typically, GNG network is stopped when a specified network size (number of units) is reached. Suggest and justify alternative stopping criteria.

10. In Section 15.5.5, visual renditions of the distance-squared matrices for the initial NG weight sets and for 5, 10, and 100 iterations are shown. Observe that the input data is comprised of two clusters. Discuss the evolution of these interweight distances, especially the final (100 iteration) matrix. Speculate what the matrix might look like if there were three clusters in the input data.

11. In Section 15.6.1, the steps of the GNG algorithm were shown. For each step, indicate the "objective" of the computation. For example:

(a) What is the purpose of edge ages and discarding "old" edges?

(b) What is the underlying philosophy in adding a unit?

(c) Why are winning and runner-up units s_1 and s_2 connected?

12. It was noted that in designing an SOFM, it is advisable to coordinate the neighborhood shrinking schedule with the total number of iterations. Discuss the effect of two (poorly chosen) design extremes:

(a) The neighborhood shrinks to a single unit and the majority of the training iterations have not yet occurred.

(b) The maximum number of training iterations is reached, and the current neighborhood is still quite large compared with the spatial extent of the SOFM.

13. How do the parallel or "batch" implementations of the NG and SOFM algorithms compare with c-means?

14. This problem concerns the design, implementation, and use of c-means (as a possible reference); 1-D SOFM; NG; and batch NG and SOFM neural networks. 2500 $d = 8$ dimensional training vectors are available on the book's web page in the file `ch15simulation.txt`. Each line in the file contains the transpose of a single 8×1 vector, i.e., the file has 2500 lines.

(a) Apply c-means to this data. Does it tell you anything?

(b) Design and implement a 1-D SOFM.

(c) Train the SOFM, using the data given. This requires a number of SOFM algorithm parameter choices. Determine data clusters, if any, from the SOFM.

(d) Design and implement NG. Train the NG network, using the data given. This requires a number of NG algorithm parameter choices. Implicit sorting is recommended.

(e) Determine data clusters, if any from the NG network.

(f) Repeat using batch formulations for SOFM and NG.

15. The Kohonen SOFM algorithm was run for $d = 4$ input vectors and a 2-D topological space consisting of 12 units arranged in a 3×4 spatial array. Resulting unit weight vectors from the 3×4 2-D SOFM are shown here. Each vertical 4-tuple in the 3×4 array is the resulting unit weight vector at that spatial location.

```
0.5133    0.8415    0.4679    0.5717
0.5911    0.2693    0.2872    0.8024
0.8460    0.4154    0.1783    0.0331
0.4121    0.5373    0.1537    0.5344


0.4985    0.8907    0.2128    0.2746
0.9554    0.6248    0.7147    0.0030
0.7483    0.8420    0.1304    0.4143
0.5546    0.1598    0.0910    0.0269


0.7098    0.3175    0.6813    0.1475
0.9379    0.8870    0.3858    0.5872
0.2399    0.6521    0.3877    0.8456
0.1809    0.1503    0.4997    0.5901
```

Assess, as best you can, the self-organizing results of this network. Be quantitative.

Learning in IS

16.1 Introduction to Machine Learning (ML)

16.1.1 Preface

We begin with a question. Suppose an IS system solves a problem, e.g., generates a plan, labels an image, or provides a diagnostic result based upon expert-generated rules. Once the solution is available (the IS computation has terminated), we ask the following question:

Was anything learned (by the IS)?

Most likely, we need to answer "no," and realize that the IS, presented with the identical problem next week, will simply repeat the computation.

In general, there are many aspects of "learning." It is difficult to precisely quantify (or perhaps even to define) the concept of human learning. Nonetheless, some form of autonomous learning may be fundamental to IS system development. Perhaps the immediate question is: "What or how do you want the IS to learn?"

As IS application areas mature, the automation of human learning will become necessary to develop adaptable and robust systems that can aggregate experience and relevant information in an opportunistic manner.

Does Learning Ability Indicate Intelligence or Vice Versa? Arguably, the concepts of an IS and learning are indistinguishable; for a deployed system to be considered "intelligent," it should have the capacity for learning. In this chapter, we explore aspects of machine learning (ML), or the automation of several learning paradigms. ML is a growing and very diverse field.

16.1.2 Where Do We Integrate Learning in an IS?

Learning algorithms could be integrated into IS systems as a "shell" around the IS system, or developed as an integral part of the system. The amount of choice an IS system designer has in this respect is due to the potential coupling of the chosen knowledge structure and the learning algorithm(s). In some cases it may be inappropriate or impossible to separate these functions.

16.1.3   Learning about Learning

Many of the various machine learning approaches have a number of common or overlapping conceptual and practical aspects. Learning capability is often related to a number of interrelated actions:

1. Self-improvement or adaptation (to new or different circumstances);

2. Concept formulation and revision (e.g., generalization or specialization of the underlying conceptual model); and

3. Solution reuse and refinement.

Learning as Refinement.   In this chapter, we consider learning as refinement of the representation, perhaps on the basis of experience in solving previous problems. Experience may result from interaction between the existing system and the outside world, including exposure to new or updated data.

Refinement or adaptation of an existing IS model is common to many learning strategies, and may even be thought of as the core of or a replacement for the IS design process itself. For example, once the architecture is designed, an FF ANN (see Chapters 13, 14, and 15) becomes a trainable structure that "learns" to solve problems.

Learning as Opportunistic Reuse.   The reader should note a number of systems described as follows employ the reuse (or reuse with modification) of previous system results. This is also considered in Chapter 12, where a triangle table was suggested for reuse and modification of a previously-developed plan.

Rote Learning.   This is equivalent to the memorization of facts and actions. Understanding of the data (in the sense of any action other than recollection) is not required. In this context the "opposite" of learning is "forgetting." We equate rote learning with explicit programming.

Advice Taking.   Given control information, e.g., heuristics, the IS is modified. This is also simplistic, in the sense that it represents the creation of additional rules, e.g., advice may be phrased as "IF ... THEN ... ." The possibility of advice that conflicts with information in the current database must also be considered. Furthermore, if we allow the "advice generation" mechanism to examine past inference results, and perhaps to incorporate performance evaluation or provide "criticism," we arrive at performance-driven learning.

Learning Concepts from Examples.   This is a common and powerful learning paradigm, and may be implemented in a variety of ways. Several aspects are:

◆ Learning from examples directly exemplifies generalization of knowledge as learning. In particular, the process of induction is used to generalize a portion of the existing knowledge structure using the "example" information.

◆ Learning from examples may be used to generate totally new rules.

◆ Learning from examples allows the potential of learning by analogy, in the sense that new actions or conclusions are based upon the similarity of structure with previous actions or conclusions. The autonomous recognition of analogy, however, is a challenging problem.

Learning by Exploration.   Nature provides the best example of this paradigm for adaptation (or learning) through the random perturbations or adaptation of a system and consequent survival of those systems whose perturbation is beneficial.

Learning by Analogy.   This involves the use of available, perhaps previously developed, and similar information. For example, in the generation of a plan, once a problem has been solved, the solution (in this case a plan) could be applicable to other similar situations. In addition, the solution to a specific problem may often provide useful guidelines on how to approach related problems. Past experience, perhaps in the structure of the solution, may be modified or adapted to solve a new problem.

Observation/Explanation-Based Learning.   This is a popular topic and is usually treated at the conceptual/philosophical level. It is based upon the study of human observation-based learning principles [Osm08] and appears somewhat difficult to implement.

Learning Through Building Models and Structural Links.   In learning as model building, we view experience as instances or realizations of a process that is either generated by or constrained by a model. Larger conceptual models may be built from smaller building blocks (e.g., concepts) and experience. A rule or mechanism to organize concepts into larger structures is the *schema*.

16.1.4 Learning History and Psychology

The study of learning, like the study of intelligence itself, is not new. The German psychologist Johann Friedrich Herbart in 1816 formulated an intuitively plausible conjecture that is referred to as the "apperceptive mass explanation" of learning. Paraphrased [Wat63]:

> "Combined ideas form wholes and a combination of related ideas form an apperceptive mass, into which relevant ideas are welcomed but irrelevant ones are excluded."

Conversely, psychologists eschewing the behaviorist notion promoted the "conditioning" interpretation of learning. Conditioning may be an unconscious process wherein behavior changes after a number of examples of correct behavior, i.e., accumulated evidence. Behaviorism attempts to characterize and achieve correct stimulus-response (S-R) action. A neural network that adapts its interconnection structure on the basis of a training set typifies this approach.

Piaget [Pia68] proposed a categorization of learning based on the type of change in the stored knowledge representation. Assimilation of new information into an existing and unchanged structure (e.g., a schemata) is differentiated from accommodation, wherein the existing structure is modified on the basis of new information. This taxonomy has been extended to three categories [RN78]:

1. Accretion: basically the same as assimilation.

2. Schema tuning: minor changes to the structure (e.g., addition of new properties or defaults, generalization) are allowed.

3. Restructuring: major reorganization of schemata, allows induction of new concepts (similar to accommodation).

Thus, accommodation encompasses both tuning and restructuring.

16.1.5　Learning Definition(s) and Examples of Automated Learning Paradigms

A reasonable interpretation of machine learning is the following:

Learning Definition #1.　The development of systems capable of learning involves the development or identification and implementation of algorithms ("learning algorithms") that enable other algorithms (IS algorithms) to improve their performance.

On the basis of this definition, a general notion of learning is not simply the acquisition of additional raw data (e.g., additional explicit programming). There is a distinct difference between reasoning and recollection.

Learning Definition #2.　(Inductive) learning systems form plausible internal descriptions that explain observed evidence and are useful for the prediction of new evidence.

IS Research Approaches.　A number of research approaches to IS learning are identifiable:

1. Neural Modeling: In this approach, learning (or training) takes place via adaptation of network connection strengths.

2. Case-Based Reasoning: Previous solutions may be reused or refined to solve similar problems, and (modified) solutions are archived.

3. Decision Theoretic Techniques: Evidence, i.e., $A1$, $A2$, ..., An is used to update $P(E|A1, A2, ..., An)$ from $P(E)$.

4. Symbolic Concept Acquisition (SCA): Proceeds by constructing or modifying stored representations of concepts. Representations may be in the form of logic, production rules, or semantic networks.

5. Constructive Induction [Mi86]: This major area includes learning from examples or observations (as in concept acquisition) and learning by analogy.

A long-term objective of automated learning research is the development of precise computational models for the learning mechanism. As with other aspects of IS, research into learning methodologies must consider the potential contribution of the human behavior model. Through the study and attempted modeling of the cognitive development of babies and young children in key areas such as the development or acquisition of language understanding [Sel86], development of the capacity to understand humor, and the ability to count, key aspects related to the automation of learning capability may result.

16.2 Case–Based Reasoning and Learning

Case-Based Reasoning (CBR) could be viewed as an extension of learning by analogy; we treat it separately. In CBR, the process of solving new problems is based upon the solution(s) to previously encountered, similar problems. CBR is a commonly-observed behavior in human problem solving. Figure 16.1 illustrates the overall approach.

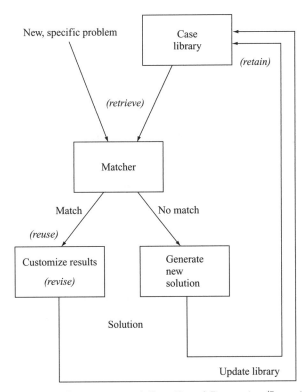

Figure 16.1 Components of Case-Based Reasoning/Learning

16.2.1   Components of a CBR System

CBR assumes a library of stored (previous) scenarios or *cases*. Already this presents practical challenges, since the cases must be stored in a representation such that:

1. The cases are reusable; and

2. A similarity measure is available to identify new cases or situations as similar to one or more previously seem.

Notice this raises the "manipulation" issue. CBR applications include:

◆ Computer diagnosis (e.g., the "help desk"): Many problems are common, as are their solutions.

◆ Medical diagnosis: Case-based diagnosis systems attempt to retrieve past cases whose symptoms are similar in nature to that of the current case and suggest diagnoses based on the best matching retrieved cases. One could argue this also partially defines the behavior of human physicians.

◆ Design: Human designers in architectural and industrial domains often retrieve past design cases and use parts of these as the basis of new designs.

◆ Legal reasoning (see Section 16.2.5)

◆ Information retrieval

16.2.2   The Four "R"s of CBR

Case-based reasoning has been adapted for ML as a four-step process [AP94, Lea96, SRK94]:

1. **Retrieve** case(s) from a case library that are relevant to solving the current problem. This requires a problem similarity measure. At the minimum, a case representation includes a formal description of the problem and a corresponding solution. Optionally, an annotation of the solution derivation is included.

2. **Reuse** the solution from the previous case to solve the current problem.

3. **Revise** the prior solution(s) for the new challenge. This may involve adaptation, refinement, or extension of the previous solution. It also requires testing the revised solution and, if necessary, further revision. Revising the case solution selected for reuse is necessary if the previous solution proves inadequate for the current problem. This step provides another opportunity for learning.

4. **Retain** or catalog the revised solution as either a generalized version of the prior solution or a new case.

These steps are shown in Figure 16.1.

16.2.3 Case Representation Structure and Determining Case Similarity

Arguably, the core of a CBR system is the *problem matcher*, used to retreive similar cases. If cases are indexed by a set of features (perhaps both numeric and symbolic in nature), a similarity measure is necessary. This is a significant CBR system design challenge with many aspects commonly found in syntactic and self-organizing pattern recognition systems [Sch92]. Often, the retrieving process begins with a partial, incomplete problem description or specification.

Use of the Similarity Measure

Given a similarity measure, subsequent challenges include dealing with matching situations as follows:

Exact match: No problem—just reuse old results. This is based upon "memorization" of a previous solution.

Multiple Case Matches: Should we use one of these, all of these, or try to distill all the cases and use the "fused" results?

Inexact Matches: (the likely case)

1. Extract additional relevant problem features or aspects (this is an art) and continue the match;

2. Find the closest match and either reuse or modify; or

3. Treat the problem as entirely new and formulate, then archive, the new solution.

Case Representation Structure and Contents

As noted in the previous section, a significant concern is the efficiency and practicality of access to previous cases. This suggests the need for a quick, efficient indexing of the case database and perhaps a structured (e.g., hierarchical) representation of cases.

CBR system expertise is embodied in a library of previously solved cases. This is in stark contrast to other knowledge representation strategies, such as encoding the expertise in a rule-based format. A case typically contains the (previous) problem description together with the solution (and/or outcome). The knowledge and reasoning process used by an expert to solve the problem is therefore not explicitly archived, rather it is implicit in the case solution.

16.2.4 Issues with CBR

There are potential drawbacks to using CBR. The most obvious is lack of a sufficiently rich case library [Ris06]. In addition, CBR systems may inherit possible bias associated with a prior solution [Wat97]. CBR systems may fail to recognize the true lack of problem similarity, i.e., the current problem may actually be unique.

16.2.5   Case-Based Reasoning and the U.S. Legal System

CBR has a strong similarity to certain operational aspects of the U.S. legal system. A deciding court considers and follows previously decided, relevant cases in determining the outcome of a new case. Decisions involving the same, or a very similar, issue are made by courts on a precedent basis following the doctrine of *stare decisis* ("let the decision stand"). Precedent-setting court decisions or "case law" are published[1] and facilitate legal research to support a position.

16.3   Learning through Description Generalization/Specialization

Much of the behavior of learning in an IS system involves the transition from the specific to generalizations (or vice versa). The generalization/specialization dichotomy of knowledge is one vehicle in which to explore learning.

Generalization-based learning paradigms may involve:

1. The elimination of constraints in certain expressions (this makes them more general); or

2. The substitution of variables for constants. This is due to the observation that constants are specific whereas variables are general. On this basis, we formulate the definition [DM81]:

16.3.1   General-to-Specific (G–S) and Specific-to-General (S–G) Approaches

Learning through generalization or specialization may be cast in a number of ways. In some instances, the ability to derive more specific information may be desirable, whereas the generalization of existing information is also useful. In specific-to-general (S–G) approaches, the goal is to find a minimal description that includes (generalizes) all possible instances of some concept in the database, without including any negative instances. Often this type of learning (in nonconstructive inductive inference) involves search through concept space. The examples or evidence used may consist of labeled samples that may be positive instances (i.e., exemplars of a given concept) or negative instances. The concept space in realistic problems is likely to be large.

Example.

(hypothesis) h: all birds can fly

evidence:

    (e-1): sparrows are birds

    (e-2): sparrows can fly

Evidence (e-1) and (e-2) may be used to conclude h. However, if the database contained negative instances of this, for example

---

[1]For example, online services such as Westlaw and Lexis market research assistance for locating case law on specific topics.

(e-3) newborn sparrows cannot fly

(e-3) newborn sparrows are birds

the generalization would fail. This type of reasoning, particularly with respect to the exceptions, is related to nonmonotonic reasoning. Generalization of this type may also be categorized as instance-to-class or part-to-whole.

Generalization Operators. The achievement of generalization through application of inductive reasoning involves a transformation of less general descriptions into more general ones. This is accomplished via generalization operators.

16.3.2 Representations and Descriptions

Assume a chosen problem representation that includes:

1. A set of elemental descriptors (primitives). For example, a problem representation could be based on a set of clauses. Sets of these clauses form concept descriptions, denoted c_i. A set of concept descriptions is denoted C.

2. A set of generalization/specialization operators.

   The key to this type of learning is modification of the concept descriptions through generalization (or specialization). This may involve elimination, addition, and/or modification of descriptors in the c_i in C.

16.3.3 The Training Sets

To initiate learning, we assume we are given sets of exemplars or instances. The positive exemplar set, denoted P, consists of positive examples, whereas the negative exemplar set, denoted N, consists of negative examples (or counterexamples). Note that C, P, and N consist of descriptors in a chosen representation.

16.3.4 Consistency and "Covering"

A description, c_i, "covers" an exemplar iff:

1. It is consistent (i.e., unifies with) with a positive exemplar; and

2. It is inconsistent with a negative exemplar (shown as follows).

   The determination of "consistency" requires a matching process. This is shown in Figure 16.2. A set of descriptions, C, covers an exemplar iff each member of C covers the exemplar. On this basis, a minimal goal for concept learning from examples is to derive C such that all exemplars in the training set are covered. This is shown in Figure 16.3.

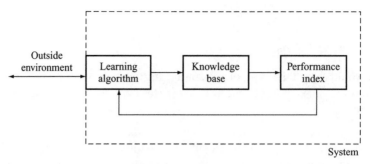

Figure 16.2 Overall Learning Objective

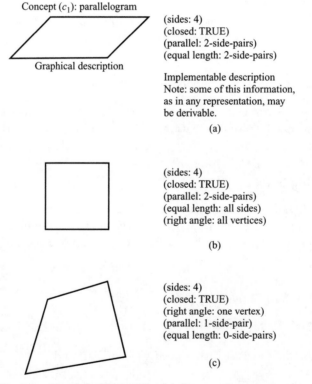

Concept (c_1): parallelogram

Graphical description

(sides: 4)
(closed: TRUE)
(parallel: 2-side-pairs)
(equal length: 2-side-pairs)

Implementable description
Note: some of this information,
as in any representation, may
be derivable.

(a)

(sides: 4)
(closed: TRUE)
(parallel: 2-side-pairs)
(equal length: all sides)
(right angle: all vertices)

(b)

(sides: 4)
(closed: TRUE)
(right angle: one vertex)
(parallel: 1-side-pair)
(equal length: 0-side-pairs)

(c)

Figure 16.3 Positive and Negative Exemplars Example. (a) Concept Description (parallelogram) (b) Positive Exemplar (square) (c) Negative Exemplar (quadrilateral)

16.3.5 Algorithmic Goals for Generalization/Specialization–Based Learning

Specifically, using the given exemplars (the training set), goals of the two approaches are as follows:

Specific-to-General (S–G):   produce a set of general concept descriptions

General-to-Specific (G–S):   produce a set of most specific concept descriptions

In both cases the resulting descriptions must cover all the positive and negative exemplars in the training set. It is also desirable that the resulting descriptions possess the property that they are likely to cover future (extended) data. This is shown in Figure 16.4.

16.3.6 Description Modification

In what follows, we adopt a "conservative" approach to the modification of descriptions in the sense that a description is only extended (generalized) or specialized as much as is needed at each step in the process. By modifying descriptions as little as possible, (attempt to) avoid the generation of modified descriptions that are easily disproved. The issue of nonconstructive vs. constructive description modification is addressed in a subsequent section.

16.3.7 Specific to General (S–G) ("Opening" the Description) Approach

Given C, a set of (possibly empty) current concept descriptions, and a set of positive exemplars (instances), P, where

$$P = p_0, p_1, ..., p_n \tag{16.1}$$

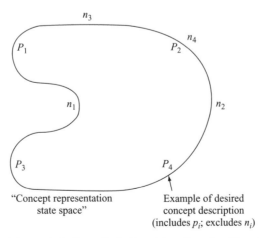

Figure 16.4 Graphical View of Desired S–G or G–S Algorithm Results. Note in G–S the coverage "shrinks" whereas in S–G the coverage "grows."

and a set of negative exemplars, N, where

$$N = n_0, n_1, ..., n_m \qquad (16.2)$$

there exist many strategies for the sequential use of elements of P and N to refine C.

S–G Algorithm.

1. If $C = \emptyset$, initialize C to cover one (or more) of the p_i that have not previously been elements of C.

2. Generalize C to cover one or more remaining elements of P.

3. Thin C by:

   (a) removing generalizations, c_i, which cover any element n_i of N; and

   (b) removing any c_i that are overly general, i.e., they are more general than (or subsume) another element in C.

   If C becomes empty, go to Step 1.

4. If every c_i covers both P and N, STOP, otherwise go to Step 2.

16.3.8 General–to–Specific (G–S) ("Narrowing" the Description) Approach

Using the preceding definitions, an alternative learning strategy is shown. The G–S approach begins with an overly general description, and successively refines C using P and N.

G–S Algorithm.

1. If $C = \emptyset$, initialize C to the most general positive exemplar, p_i, or another (a priori known) set of general descriptions.

2. Using N, specialize each c_i so that it is not consistent with any n_i.

3. Thin C by:

   (a) eliminating any c_i that does not cover a p_i (therefore, it is overly specific);

   (b) eliminating any c_i that is more specific than another c_i.

   If C becomes empty, go to Step 1.

4. If every c_i in C covers both P and N, STOP, otherwise go to Step 2.

The S–G approach leads to the set of most general concept descriptors, whereas the G–S approach leads to the most specific set. The choice of one approach over the other, like many IS choices, is probably application-dependent. Table 16.1 summarizes the role of the exemplars in each approach. Of course, hybrid generalization approaches, explored in the problems, are possible. Note also that both algorithms invoke choices of different concept description/modification paths. Thus, an underlying search problem is also present in the formulation.

	Positive exemplar (p_i)	Negative exemplar (n_i)
Specific-to-general (S–G)	Generalize C^a	Filter C
General-to-specific (G–S)	Filter C^b	Make C more specific

[a](eliminate overly general alternatives).
[b](eliminate overly specific alternatives).

Table 16.1   Utility of Exemplars in Generalization Formulations

16.3.9   Example: Learning 2–D Geometric Descriptors

The following extended example is intended to illustrate the overall approach. Figure 16.5 shows the chosen representation and the training sets (P and N). The desired concept to be learned is

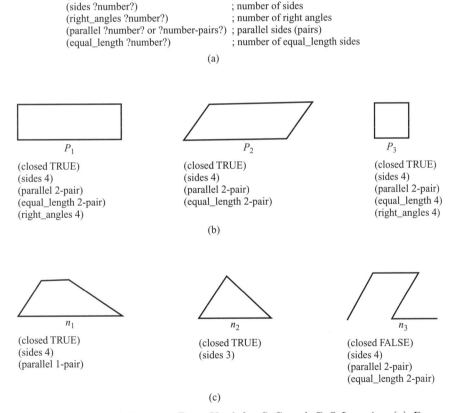

```
(closed ?status?)                        ; is the figure closed?
(sides ?number?)                         ; number of sides
(right_angles ?number?)                  ; number of right angles
(parallel ?number? or ?number-pairs?)    ; parallel sides (pairs)
(equal_length ?number?)                  ; number of equal_length sides
```

(a)

P_1

(closed TRUE)
(sides 4)
(parallel 2-pair)
(equal_length 2-pair)
(right_angles 4)

P_2

(closed TRUE)
(sides 4)
(parallel 2-pair)
(equal_length 2-pair)

P_3

(closed TRUE)
(sides 4)
(parallel 2-pair)
(equal_length 4)
(right_angles 4)

(b)

n_1

(closed TRUE)
(sides 4)
(parallel 1-pair)

n_2

(closed TRUE)
(sides 3)

n_3

(closed FALSE)
(sides 4)
(parallel 2-pair)
(equal_length 2-pair)

(c)

Figure 16.5   Representation and Training Data Used for S–G and G–S Learning (a) Representation (b) Positive Exemplars (c) Negative Exemplars

1. Assume $C = \Phi$ Initialize C to be equal to p_1.

```
C = {c₁} = {((closed TRUE)
                (sides 4)
                (right_angles 4)
                (parallel 2-pair)
                (equal_length 2-pair))}
```

2. Generalize C to cover one or more of the remaining elements of P.

   Generalize c_1 to cover p_2 by deleting the (descriptor) clause

```
(right_angles x) where x = 4
```

   since from p_2, one of the possible values of x is 0.

```
C = {c₂} = {((closed TRUE)
                (sides 4)
                (parallel 2-pair)
                (equal_length 2-pair))}
```

3. Thin C by removing any c_1 that does not cover any N_1 (i.e., any c_1 that is consistent with N).

```
c₂ does not cover any element of N so go to 4.
```

4. If every c_1 covers both P and N, STOP. Otherwise go to Step 2.

```
c₂ does not cover p₃. so generalize c₂:
```

```
C = {c₃} = {((closed TRUE)
                (sides 4)
                (parallel 2-pair)
                (equal_length x)
                        where x ∈ (2,4))}
```

5. Since every c_1 covers both P and N, STOP.

```
c₃ is the minimal description that covers all p₁
```

Figure 16.6   Example of the S–G Algorithm Applied to the Problem of Figure 16.5

"parallelogram." Figure 16.6 shows sample results for the S–G algorithm. Figure 16.7 shows the application of the G–S approach.

16.3.10   Inductive Reasoning and Truth/Falsity Preservation

One difficulty with inductive inferences [Mich83], for example, generalization, is that *inductive generalization is only falsity-preserving*, not truth-preserving. For example, if we declare the statement

$$(\forall X)\ computer(X), has\_chips(X) \rightarrow electronic\_device(X)$$

1. Initialize

```
C₁ = {((closed x)
        (sides a)
        (right_angles b)
        (parallel c)
        (equal_length d)}
            where a. b. c. d ∈ 1 and x ∈ {TRUE.FALSE})
```

This is the most general description available.

2. Using N, specialize each element of C (c_1) so it covers (i.e., is inconsistent with) each n_1. (Not all possible specializations shown.)

Generalize c_1 to cover p_2 by deleting the (descriptor) clause

```
C1 = {((closed TRUE)                        C2 = {((closed TRUE)
        (sides x)          x ≠ 4                    (sides x)          x ≠ 3
        (right_angles y)   y ∈ 1                    (right_angles y)   y ∈ 1
        (parallel z)       z ≠ 1 pair               (parallel z)       z ∈ 1
        (equal_length z)   z ≠ 0.3)}                (equal_length w)   w ∈ 1}

C3 = {((closed FALSE)                        C4 = {((closed TRUE)
        (sides x)          x ≠ 4                    (sides x)          x ≠ 4
        (right_angles y)   y ∈ 1                    (right_angles y)   y ∈ 1
        (parallel z)       z ≠ 1 pair               (parallel z)       z ≠ 2 pair
        (equal_length w)   w ∈ 1}                   (equal_length w)   w ≠ 2 pair}

C5 = {((closed FALSE)                        C6 = {((closed TRUE)
        (sides x)          x ≠ 4                    (sides 4)
        (right_angles y)   y ∈ 1                    (right_angles x)   x ∈ 1
        (parallel z)       z ∈ 1                    (parallel 2-pair)
        (equal_length w)   z ∈ 1}                   (equal_length 2-pair)}
```

3. Thin C in Step 2 by elimination of any c, which does not cover a p_1 (this eliminates $c_1, c_2, c_3,$ $c_4,$ and c_5).

4. Since the description of c_6 covers each p_1 and n_1, STOP

Figure 16.7 Example of the G–S Algorithm Applied to the Problem of Figure 16.5

is TRUE, we are able to correctly deduce that if X is a computer and X has chips, then X is an electronic device. An inductive generalization of this is:

$$(\forall X)\ computer(X) \rightarrow electronic\_device(X)$$

that may or may not be TRUE. However, if the first statement is FALSE, the second must also be FALSE (hence the falsity-preserving characteristic of generalization).

16.3.11 Generalization Operators

In the preceding examples, the set of generalization or specialization operators was left unspecified. In this section, using the nomenclature of [DM81], the process of generalization is viewed as the application of generalization operators to intermediate descriptions. The application of a generalization operator, denoted G, to an expression $S1$ produces a more general expression $S2$. Of course, the operator is applied to $S1$ based upon some subset of the cumulative knowledge and experience available, collectively denoted E. In other words, denoting this generalization operator:

$$S2 = G(S1, E) \tag{16.3}$$

This means that an implication derived from 16.3 (note carefully the direction of this implication) must be TRUE:

$$S2 \rightarrow S1 \tag{16.4}$$

where now the knowledge contained in $S1$ is a specialized case of that in $S2$, as desired. Based upon this observation, we use the notation $\Leftarrow$ to indicate the generalization. Thus $A \Leftarrow B$ denotes "A may be generalized to B." For example, the operation in 16.3 is denoted:

$$S1 \Leftarrow S2 \tag{16.5}$$

and read as "$S1$ may be generalized to $S2$." Note:

- A nonconstructive generalization operator uses only the descriptors in $S1$ to produce $S2$.

- A constructive generalization operator creates one or more new descriptors in $S2$, thus changing the representational space of the problem.

The problem of computational complexity, i.e., search for the "best" set of generalization operators in a given problem is significant. At any given time, there may be an enormous number of statements that may be generalized, a large number of ways (e.g., different variables) in which individual generalization operators may be applied, and a large number of applicable generalization operators.

Examples of Generalization Operators

A number of nonconstructive generalization operators exist. We use the Prolog notation of predicate calculus to show their effect.[2] They may be combined to form even broader generalizations. Several of these operators are:

1. The dropping condition operator. We may relax the conditions on one or more of the components in the description, e.g.,

$$must\_have(dell\_computer), must\_have(dell\_monitor) \Leftarrow$$
$$must\_have(dell\_computer) \tag{16.6}$$

---

[2]Recall "," denotes AND, ";" denotes OR, and variables are uppercase.

2. The constants to variables operator.

$$must\_have(dell\_computer), must\_have(dell\_monitor) \Leftarrow$$
$$must\_have(A\_computer), must\_have(A\_monitor) \quad (16.7)$$

(16.7) includes the case of the variable that always match, i.e., the anonymous variable in Prolog (denoted "_"). For example, when the generalization to require a computer, but any computer is acceptable, we may have the generalization:

$$must\_have\_computer(dell), must\_have(dell\_monitor) \Leftarrow$$
$$must\_have\_computer(\_), must\_have(dell\_monitor) \quad (16.8)$$

3. The disjunction operator. Allowing additional possibilities through disjunction is a form of generalization. For example, in Generalization (16.6) "*must_have_computer(dell)*" may be generalized through disjunction in several ways. For example,

$$must\_have\_computer(dell) \Leftarrow$$
$$must\_have\_computer(dell);$$
$$must\_have\_computer(toshiba);$$
$$must\_have\_computer(gateway);$$
$$must\_have\_computer(apple). \quad (16.9)$$

4. The closing interval operator. This is an extension of the previous example. A constraint on the range of a variable is relaxed. For example,

$$num \in (lower, upper] \Leftarrow num \in [lower, \infty] \quad (16.10)$$

5. The hierarchy-generation generalization operator. This operator is based upon generation of generalizations satisfying hierarchical relationships.

6. The specialization exception operator. If, during the process of generalization, a description becomes overgeneralized, or a generalization is inhibited due to a small number of exceptions, (due perhaps to the observation of a number of negatively-reinforcing or counterexamples), rather than inhibit the generalization we achieve generalization with exceptions. Recall this was addressed in our examination of frames, property inheritance, and the "is_a" hierarchical representation. In addition, the example of sparrows and the flying capability exemplifies this.

Creating IF–THEN–UNLESS Rules for Generalization with Exceptions

As noted, overgeneralization is possible. One way to control overgeneralization is by exceptions. This approach leads to augmented versions of IF-THEN rules with the form:

$$IF\ a1\ ...\ an\ THEN c1,\ c2\ ...\ cp\ UNLESS\ b1,\ b2,\ ...,\ bm \quad (16.11)$$

where the IS are antecedents, the c_i are (possibly multiple) consequents, and the b_i are m blocking conditions, which inhibit firing of the rule if their disjunction (OR-ing) evaluates to true. An example of an IF-THEN-UNLESS form is from the following generalization:

$$electronic\_device(X) : -computer(X), has\_chips(X) \tag{16.12}$$

that was generalized to

$$electronic\_device(X) : -computer(X) \tag{16.13}$$

The generalization of (16.13) is FALSE, for example, if we consider optical computers (which we assume do not involve electronics). One way to reformulate Generalization (16.13) is therefore

$$electronic\_device(X) : -computer(X)\hat{\ }optical\_dev(X) \tag{16.14}$$

where the "$\hat{\ }$" denotes "unless."

Constructive Inductive Generalization

This type of learning is considerably more difficult to analyze, and, not surprisingly, to achieve. A constructive generalization operator creates one or more new descriptors and thus changes the representational space of the problem. Examples of constructive generalization rules are given in [Mic80].

16.4 Learning Decision Trees

This section presents an introduction to a form of learning known as tree induction. The focus is on the ID3 ("Iterative Dichotomizer 3") algorithm [Qui86], [Utg89]. Despite the name, *ID3 is a recursive, entropy-based procedure for implementing a sequence of decisions.* The objective is to use "experience" in the form of training data and to generate or "learn" a decision strategy (in the form of a tree) from this data. The resulting ID3 decision tree may provide significant utility in:

1. Reducing a large, unmanageable data set (and perhaps one wherein visualization of the data is impossible) into a relatively small set of decisions;

2. Providing some insight into the nature of the data (as illustrated by some of the examples in this chapter); and

3. Providing generalization of the decision strategy to a large set of data.

The ID3 algorithm has been implemented in several languages. In this chapter, a CommonLisp representation is used.[3]

---

[3]This Lisp implementation is available as a part of accompanying software.

16.4.1 Synopsis of the ID3 Approach

Basically, *the ID3 algorithm constructs a decision tree by recursively partitioning a set of training data, until every outcome in a partition maps into the same value.*[4] This is the stopping criteria for the recursion.

As we show, partitioning of the input data is based upon individual attribute values. The ordering of the attribute tests (or sequential decisions) is determined by considering the entropy (in an information-theoretic sense) associated with the partitions. Entropy is defined in Section 16.4.4.

Note the ID3 algorithm we consider involves discrete (but not necessarily binary) attribute values and outcomes. Extensions to continuous values are possible.

16.4.2 Sample Exemplars (ID3 Input Data)

Consider the desired attribute/outcome pairings in Table 16.2.

The astute reader will recognize this as the logical OR function. However, suppose the data set were considerably larger and this mapping was not apparent from (human visual) inspection. The ID3 algorithm allows us to:

1. Develop a classifier or sequential mapping procedure to produce the desired outcome, given attribute values for a specific case (and without using the training data for lookup);

2. Determine or explore the structure of the underlying mapping function perhaps implied by the data; and

3. Develop production system rules from the data.

More will be said later regarding incomplete and conflicting data sets.

16.4.3 The Decision Tree: Definition and Tree Components

A decision tree, like any tree, consists of a root node, leaf nodes, and interior nodes, and provides a graphical representation of a sequential decision process. The decisions or outcomes of the tree could correspond to many things, including medical diagnosis, classification of an entity, or selection of a particular action (we will show block movement choice in the following example).

exemplar	$x1$	$x2$	outcome?
$d1$	0	0	0
$d2$	0	1	1
$d3$	1	0	1
$d4$	1	1	1

Table 16.2 Set of Instances Indicating Attribute Values and Outcome. Here $0 = F$; $1 = T$.

---

[4]Note: if this situation does not occur, the algorithm must be extended. This situation is indicative of either a problem with the training data or nondeterminism of the problem.

The decision tree representation involves a number of entities:

1. The root node (in-degree = 0) starts the decision process.

2. Any leaf node represents an outcome or decision.

3. The root and interior nodes implement a (partial) decision. Each partial decision is based upon the observed values of *one* (of perhaps many) problem attribute(s).

4. A path from the root to a leaf corresponds to an observed set of attributes (or, equivalently, the result of a sequence of attribute tests) from a specific instance. This is also the result of applying a set of conjunctive, sequential tests.

16.4.4 The General Concept of (Information) Entropy

Definition, Properties, and an Example

Entropy is a well known measure of uncertainty or "impurity" in a probabilistically-defined problem. Suppose we are given a set, H, of n probabilities, $\{p_1, p_2, \cdots, p_n\}$ summing to 1. Each probability could correspond to a distinct outcome or event. The entropy of this set is defined as:

$$E = \sum_{i=1}^{n} -p_i log_2(p_i) \tag{16.15}$$

Observe:

1. If all outcomes are equally likely ($p_i = \frac{1}{n}$), E is maximum.

2. If the probability of one outcome dwarfs all other outcomes (e.g., $p_1 = 0.99$ and $\sum_{i=2}^{n} p_i = 0.01$) the corresponding entropy (uncertainty) is small.

3. Here we use the log_2 function, but log in general will work. Entropy-derived measures are used in the ID3 algorithm to compare attributes. Recall $log_2(x) = \frac{log_{10}(x)}{log_{10}(2)}$; this may help to facilitate hand computations.

   If the log used is base 2, then the unit of entropy is in bits.

Entropy of a Two-Outcome Example. Many (not all) decision trees involve a binary outcome, such as "go to class" or "don't go to class." In such a $c = 2$ class situation, each outcome or decision must be either class 1 (with probability p_1) or class 2 (with probability p_2). The entropy measure in this case becomes:

$$E = \sum -p_1 log_2(p_1) - p_2 log_2(p_2) \tag{16.16}$$

A plot of entropy for this case is shown in Figure 16.8.

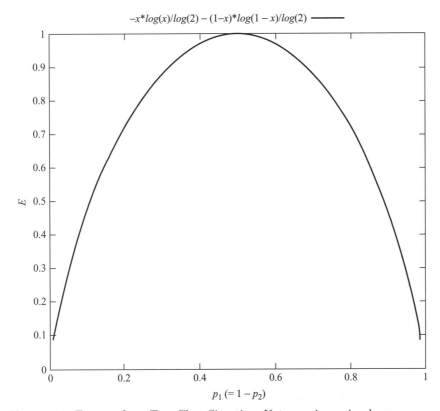

Figure 16.8 Entropy for a Two Class Situation. Note maximum is where $p_1 = p_2$.

Example. Suppose we have a collection of 20 instances; 14 corresponding to the outcome "go fishing" and 6 corresponding to "don't go fishing." E for this set of instances is 0.881.

The Use of Entropy in the Induction of Decision Trees

In the induction of decision trees, entropy is used to determine the relative significance of an attribute test. **For each attribute**, the current data set C is partitioned according to allowable values of the attribute and possible outcomes in C. Entropy is calculated for each such attribute-based partition. A summary measure (E_{xi}^{avg}) is then computed over all attribute partitions. This provides a heuristic to compare attribute significance in the sequence of decisions. The idea is to order attribute tests in terms of increasing entropy of partitions of the instances and values of the attributes. Another viewpoint is that we make the sequential decisions in order of attribute significance—the "big" decisions corresponding to small entropy or large "information gain" are made first.

16.4.5 The ID3 Algorithm

As shown in Section 16.4.5, *the* ID3 *algorithm for inducing decision trees is recursive.* The objective is to learn a *target concept.* The logical OR function with two attributes was shown previously.

ID3 Input Data: Instances, Attributes, Values, and Outcomes

Background.   The ID3 algorithm is given a set of examples or instances, denoted C. Each example in C is based upon a set of attributes. Each attribute has a possible set of values. Each instance corresponds to a certain class or outcome.[5] We only consider discrete-valued attributes and outcomes (classes) here. For example, a CommonLisp formulation for the three-input OR problem is shown in Section 16.4.6. The attributes are **x1**, **x2**, and **x3**; the outcome is a value of out. Possible values for attributes and the outcome are from the set $\{0, 1\}$.

In What Order Should I Build the Decision Tree (i.e., Test Attributes)?

This section illustrates the use of Entropy in attribute selection. The technical rationale is based upon maximizing the concept of information gain in a dataset. Recall the quantitative description of our problem involves the following entities:

C: A set of instances, exemplars, or examples.

A: Set of attributes, each denoted a_i.

V_i: Set of possible values for a_i, each denoted v_{ij} where $j \in [1, |V_i|]$. Recall $|S|$ denotes the cardinality of set S.

P_i: A *partition* of the set of instances, C, according to the values of attribute a_i.

The overall process is recursive. The objective is to compute an entropy or expected information measure, denoted $E_{a_i}(C)$, for each attribute, a_i, at a decision node. This quantity is also related to a measure of information gain, G, defined as $G(C, a_i) = E(C) - E_{a_i}(C)$. Information gain is typically a good measure for deciding the relevance of an attribute.[6] Using these measures, we determine the "best" attribute to employ at each decision tree node, as the tree is developed. $E_{a_i}(C)$ provides a test for choosing attribute relevance. *The attribute with the lowest $E_{a_i}(C)$ score (largest information gain) is preferred.*

Computing Average Attribute Entropy

For c possible outcomes, *each discrete value* of an attribute yields a corresponding partitioning of the set of outcomes C into c subsets, one for each possible outcome or class. Some of these subsets may be empty. The probability of each outcome may be estimated and an E *for each attribute and value* determined. The binary outcome case, i.e., $c = 2$ causes the partition of C to yield two subsets. These subsets are sometimes referred to as positive and negative exemplar sets.

We define (and use in subsequent examples) the average entropy[7] of a specific attribute. This takes into account the entropies of each partition for each possible attribute value. It is defined as follows:

$$E_{a_i}^{avg} = \sum_{v_{ij} \in V_i} num(v_{ij}) * E(P_{v_{ij}}) \tag{16.17}$$

---

[5]Some references refer to this as the *target attribute*.
[6]There are exceptions.
[7]Actually it is scaled by n, the cardinality of C.

where $num(v_{ij})$ is the number of instances in C where $a_i = v_{ij}$ and $E(P_{v_{ij}})$ is the entropy of the partition of C induced by the value v_{ij}. Equation 16.17 thus computes the sum, over all possible values of attribute a_i, of the number of instances in C with a specific value times the entropy of the partition of outcomes corresponding to this value. Note Equation 16.17 refers to a single attribute. It is computed for each attribute in considering each partition of the data.

A Partitioning Example and Sample Average Entropy Computations

The preceding process described is actually simpler than the description would indicate. Sample calculations are shown to help illustrate the process. We use the $E_{a_i}^{avg}$ definition from Section 16.4.5. We begin with a situation corresponding to binary-valued attributes and outcome. Consider the set C shown in Table 16.3. Notice that this represents an exhaustive training set for the three-input logical OR function.

For reference, each instance of the n-instance set C is indexed by a symbol, d_i, $i \in [1, 8]$. We first consider computation E_{x1}^{avg}, i.e., the average entropy of attribute x1. Since x1 has two possible values, observe that x1 = 0 corresponds to the four instances d1, d2, d3, and d4 (denote this P_1) whereas x1 = 1 corresponds to the four instances d5, d6, d7, and d8 (denoted P_2). Within P_1, three of the four possible *outcomes* correspond to or? = 1, thus $p_1 = \frac{3}{4}$ and $p_2 = \frac{1}{4}$. Within P_2, all of the four possible *outcomes* correspond to or? = 1, thus $p_1 = 1$ and $p_2 = 0$. E_{x1}^{avg} is thus computed as:

$$E_{x1}^{avg} = 4 \times E(P_1) + 4 \times E(P_2)$$

or

$$E_{x1}^{avg} = 4(-\frac{3}{4}log_2(\frac{3}{4}) - \frac{1}{4}log_2(\frac{1}{4}) + 4(-1log_2(1)) = 3.246$$

The reader should verify that $E_{x1}^{avg} = E_{x2}^{avg} = E_{x3}^{avg}$.

	x1	x2	x3	or?
d1	0	0	0	0
d2	0	0	1	1
d3	0	1	0	1
d4	0	1	1	1
d5	1	0	0	1
d6	1	0	1	1
d7	1	1	0	1
d8	1	1	1	1

Table 16.3 C for Three-Input OR (exhaustive set of instances)

Entropy Ties.   It is possible, as shown in the preceding example, for a tie in average entropy involving several attributes. Numerous tie-breaking approaches have been proposed. Exploration of tie-breaking approaches is left to the exercises.

Continuation of the Example: Forming a Decision Node and Subsequent Attribute Comparisons.   Suppose the tie-breaking decision is to form the first decision node using attribute x1. For each value of x1 (0 and 1 in this case), it is necessary to form the remainder of the decision tree, i.e., attribute tests involving x2 and x3. This is a recursive process, and we show the next step.

For the x1 = 0 path, Table 16.3 indicates that instances d1, d2, d3, and d4 must be considered. Likewise, for the x1 = 1 path, Table 16.3 indicates that instances d5, d6, d7, and d8 must be considered. We now estimate the average entropy for attributes x2 and x3.

For x2, the value x2 = 0 corresponds to the two instances d1 and d2. In these instances, the or? = 0 outcome occurs once, as does the or? = 1 outcome. x2 = 1 corresponds to instances d3 and d4; the only outcome is or? = 1 (twice). Similarly, for attribute x3, the value x3 = 0 corresponds to the two instances d1 and d3. In these instances, the outcomes or? = 0 and or? = 1 each occur once. For x3 = 1, corresponding to the two instances d2 and d4, the only outcome is or? = 1 (twice).

Although it is possible to compute the average entropy for x2 and x3, it is not necessary, since the preceding analysis indicates it will be equal. Thus, another tie results.

Pseudocode for the Basic ID3 Algorithm

Simple Version.   Given a set of exemplars:

1. If all the exemplars are from exactly one class or outcome, then the decision tree is a leaf node containing that class name or outcome.

2. Otherwise:

   (a) Define a^{best} to be the attribute corresponding to the *lowest*[8] value of $E_a(C)$.

   (b) For each value v_i^{best} of a^{best}, grow a branch from a^{best} to a decision tree constructed recursively from all those instances with values v_i^{best} of attribute a^{best}.

One extension we will incorporate immediately is for the case where there are no more attributes to consider, but multiple outcomes or classes. In this case, the ID3 algorithm defines a leaf node with the outcome or class determined by the *most frequently occurring* outcome.

16.4.6   ID3 Algorithm Examples

An Example of ID3 Learning (Three–Input OR)

This problem was considered in Section 16.4.5. CommonLisp input and results for a three-input OR function with exhaustive training set is shown as follows.

```
(setq tshor
;;format: x1 x2 x3 out
```

---

[8]Notice this yields the largest information gain.

```
    '((0 0 0 0)
      (0 0 1 1)
      (0 1 0 1)
      (0 1 1 1)
      (1 0 0 1)
      (1 0 1 1)
      (1 1 0 1)
      (1 1 1 1)))
> (printTree (id3 tshor '(x1 x2 x3)))
   x1
   1 -> 1
   0
      x2
      1 -> 1
      0
         x3
         1 -> 1
         0 -> 0
t
```

A Four-Outcome, Three-Attribute Example Using Hand Computation and the CommonLisp ID3 Implementation

Here we use the ID3 algorithm to derive the decision tree for the four-class three-attribute problem with data indicated below in Table 16.4. Possible outcomes are c0, c1, c2, and c3. Attributes are binary-valued (yes or no).

exemplar	x1	x2	x3	class?
d1	no	no	no	c0
d2	no	no	yes	c1
d3	no	yes	no	c1
d4	no	yes	yes	c1
d5	yes	no	no	c1
d6	yes	no	yes	c2
d7	yes	yes	no	c2
d8	yes	yes	yes	c3

Table 16.4 Four-Class, Three-Attribute Training Examples

CommonLisp input is shown here:

```
(setq tsmod
;; fmt:  x1 x2 x3 class?
     '((no no no c0)
       (no no yes c1)
       (no yes no c1)
       (no yes yes c1)
```

```
(yes no no c1)
(yes no yes c2)
(yes yes no c2)
(yes yes yes c3)))
```

Hand Computation of E_{x1}^{avg}.   As in Section 16.4.5, we calculate the average entropy for each attribute. Consider attribute x1. For x1 = "no", there are four instances or exemplars (d1–d4) we denote subset P_1 and for attribute x1 = "yes" there are also four instances or exemplars (d5–d8), collectively denoted subset P_2. As a prelude to the entropy calculation, we now consider the outcomes within each subset. Within P_1 outcome c0 occurs once, outcome c1 occurs three times, and c2 and c3 do not occur. Thus

$$E(P_1) = -\frac{1}{4}log_2(\frac{1}{4}) - \frac{3}{4}log_2(\frac{3}{4})$$

Similarly, within P_2 outcome c0 does not occur, outcome c1 occurs once, outcome c2 occurs twice, and outcome c3 occurs once. Thus

$$E(P_2) = -\frac{1}{4}log_2(\frac{1}{4}) - \frac{1}{2}log_2(\frac{1}{2}) - \frac{1}{4}log_2(\frac{1}{4})$$

Therefore, for attribute x1 the average entropy is:

$$E_{x1}^{avg} = 4 \times E(P_1) + 4 \times E(P_2) = 9.245$$

The reader should verify that

$$E_{x2}^{avg} = E_{x3}^{avg} = 12.0$$

Therefore x1 is the lowest (average) entropy attribute and used as the first attribute test at the root node of the ID3 tree.

Continuation of the Hand Example.   Once the x1 attribute test has been applied, the resulting training data partitions P_1 and P_2 are considered for the remaining test. The recursive nature of the ID3 algorithm, on a diminishing set of exemplars, is evident. Refer to Tables 16.5 and 16.6 for P_1 and P_2.

exemplar	x2	x3	class?
d1	no	no	c0
d2	no	yes	c1
d3	yes	no	c1
d4	yes	yes	c1

Table 16.5 Four-Class, Two-Attribute Training Examples Remaining After x1 = no Attribute Test (subset P_1)

exemplar	x2	x3	class?
d5	no	no	c1
d6	no	yes	c2
d7	yes	no	c2
d8	yes	yes	c3

Table 16.6 Four-Class, Two-Attribute Training Examples Remaining After x1 = yes Attribute Test (subset P_2)

Working with P_1 (Table 16.5). It is left for the reader to compute the entropy of attributes x2 and x3 for the data of P_1.

Working with P_2 (Table 16.6). Similarly, the reader should compute the entropy of attributes x2 and x3 for the data of P_2.

For Comparison (and Validation): Algorithm Results Using the CommonLisp Implementation. The decision tree is shown here.

```
> (printTree (id3 tsmod '(x1 x2 x3)))
   x1
   yes
      x2
      yes
         x3
         yes -> c3
         no -> c2
      no
         x3
         yes -> c2
         no -> c1
   no
      x2
      yes -> c1
      no
         x3
         yes -> c1
         no -> c0
t
```

16.4.7   An ID3 Application: Learning Musical Structures

In this Section, we show a "musical" application of the ID3 algorithm.[9] We investigate ID3 learning to classify chord quality as a function of the input component musical notes. An implementation of the ID3 algorithm in CommonLisp is used. The reader is encouraged to compare the results of the various cases.

---

[9]Nonmusicians should merely interpret the input data as symbolic data.

Triads

We begin with a simple example. The input is restricted to three notes, and the ID3 output is restricted to major and minor triads. For musical purists, we consider only root, first, and second inversions. The exercises consider a "nonmusical" extension. Even to a nonmusical observer, it is evident that the significant distinction is the presence of either the third (3) or the lowered third (b3).

Training Data.

```
;; chords-id3-training.l
(setq chords
;; format: note1 note2 note3 type?
'((1 3 5 Maj)
  (3 5 1 Maj)
  (5 1 3 Maj)
  (1 b3 5 Min)
  (b3 5 1 Min)
  (5 1 b3 Min)))
```

ID3 Results.   The reader should draw the resulting tree. Note the tree is validated, and two inputs (one a part of the training data, the other not) are also checked using the tree.

```
>(printTree (id3 chords '(note1 note2 note3)))
   note1
   5
      note3
      b3 -> min
      3 -> maj
   b3 -> min
   1
      note2
      b3 -> min
      3 -> maj
   3 -> maj
t
> (tree-validate  chords '(note1 note2 note3))

"tree successfully validated"
t
> (setq resultant-tree  (id3 chords '(note1 note2 note3)))
(note1 (5 (note3 (b3 min) (3 maj))) (b3 min) (1 (note2 (b3 min) (3 maj)))
 (3 maj))
> (tree-outcomes '((b3 5 1)) resultant-tree  '(note1 note2 note3))
(min)
> (tree-outcomes '((5 3 1)) resultant-tree  '(note1 note2 note3))
(nil)
```

Heavy Metal/Grunge Extension of Training Data

The data of the initial example is modified to allow two note "power" chords or diads, as shown here.

Revised Training Data.

```
(setq chords-extended2
;; format: note1 note2 note3 type?
'((1 3 5 Maj)
  (3 5 1 Maj)
  (5 1 3 Maj)
  (1 1 5 HM) ;; requires Marshall stack
  (1 5 5 HM)
  (1 5 1 HM)
  (1 b3 5 Min)
  (b3 5 1 Min)
  (5 1 b3 Min)
))
```

ID3 Results with Revised Training Data.

```
>  (printTree (id3 chords-extended2 '(note1 note2 note3)))
   note1
   5
      note3
      b3 -> min
      3 -> maj
   b3 -> min
   1
      note2
      b3 -> min
      5 -> hm
      1 -> hm
      3 -> maj
   3 -> maj
t
>
```

The reader should compare the resulting ID3 tree in this case with the original example.

Considering Four-Note Chords

The objective is to consider a wider class of chords, therefore we allow an additional input note. As a preface however, and to show the effect of a constant attribute upon entropy (and the resulting ID3 tree), consider the following four-note chord data.

Four-Note Data with Constant Attribute.

```
(setq chords-extended3
;; format: note1 note2 note3 note4 type?
'((1 3 5 *none* Maj) ;; original data
  (3 5 1 *none* Maj)
  (5 1 3 *none* Maj)
  (1 b3 5 *none* Min)
  (b3 5 1 *none* Min)
  (5 1 b3 *none* Min)
))
```

ID3 Tree Result with Constant-Attribute Data.

```
> (printTree (id3 chords-extended3 '(note1 note2 note3 note4)))
  note1
  5
     note3
     b3 -> min
     3 -> maj
  b3 -> min
  1
     note2
     b3 -> min
     3 -> maj
  3 -> maj
t
>
```

The reader should compare this tree with earlier results.

Adding 7th Chords: ID3 Input Data.

```
(setq chords-extended4
;; format: note1 note2 note3 note4 type?
'((1 3 5 *none* Maj) ;; original data
  (3 5 1 *none* Maj)
  (5 1 3 *none* Maj)
  (1 b3 5 *none* Min)
  (b3 5 1 *none* Min)
  (5 1 b3 *none* Min)
  (1 3 5 7 Maj7) ;; some root pos 7ths
  (1 3 5 b7 Dom7)
  (1 b3 5 b7 Min7)
))
```

Corresponding ID3 Tree Results.

```
> (printTree (id3 chords-extended4 '(note1 note2 note3 note4)))
  note4
  b7
     note2
     b3 -> min7
     3 -> dom7
  7 -> maj7
  *none*
     note1
     5
        note3
        b3 -> min
        3 -> maj
     b3 -> min
     1
        note2
        b3 -> min
        3 -> maj
     3 -> maj
t
```

16.4.8   Another ID3 Handworked Example: Results and Ramifications

Consider the data shown in Table 16.7. Note this is a modification of the data from the problem in Section 16.4.6. Possible outcomes are c0, c1, c2, and c3. Attributes are binary-valued (here, "yes" or "no").

The ID3 algorithm is used to derive the decision tree for this four-class, three-attribute problem. However, two additional topics are considered:

◆ The resulting ID3-derived decision tree and the underlying functional mapping; and

◆ The effect of conflicting data (see Section 16.4.10).

"Handworked" Decision Tree

Root Node Attribute Entropy Computation.   Consider the partitioning of C based upon attribute x1, as shown in Tables 16.8 and 16.9. Partition $P1$ contains exemplars d1, d2, d3, and d4, whereas partition $P2$ contains exemplars d5, d6, d7, and d8. Rather than repeat this reasoning, a summary is presented in Table 16.10.

exemplar	x1	x2	x3	class?
d1	no	no	no	c0
d2	no	no	yes	c0
d3	no	yes	no	c0
d4	no	yes	yes	c0
d5	yes	no	no	c1
d6	yes	no	yes	c1
d7	yes	yes	no	c2
d8	yes	yes	yes	c3

Table 16.7   Another Four-Class, Three-Attribute Training Example

exemplar	x1	x2	x3	class?
d1	no	no	no	c0
d2	no	no	yes	c0
d3	no	yes	no	c0
d4	no	yes	yes	c0

Table 16.8   Partition for Attribute x1 = no ($P1$)

exemplar	x1	x2	x3	class?
d5	yes	no	no	c1
d6	yes	no	yes	c1
d7	yes	yes	no	c2
d8	yes	yes	yes	c3

Table 16.9 Partition for Attribute x1 = yes ($P2$)

			Number of Outcome Occurrences			
Partition	attribute = value		c0	c1	c2	c3
$P1$	x1 = no		4	0	0	0
$P2$	x1 = yes		0	2	1	1
$P3$	x2 = no		2	2	0	0
$P4$	x2 = yes		2	0	1	1
$P5$	x3 = no		2	1	1	0
$P6$	x3 = yes		2	1	0	1

Table 16.10 Summary of Data for Initial Partitions

Using Table 16.10, the determination of E_{xi}^{avg} is straightforward. Notice $P1$ contains only outcome c0, thus we expect a leaf node. The computations are as follows:

$$E_{x1}^{avg} = 4E(P1) + 4E(P2)$$

$$= 4(-4log_2(1)) + 4(-\frac{1}{2}log_2(\frac{1}{2}) - \frac{1}{4}log_2(\frac{1}{4}) - \frac{1}{4}log_2(\frac{1}{4}))$$

$$= 6$$

$$E_{x2}^{avg} = 4E(P3) + 4E(P4)$$

$$4(-\frac{1}{2}log_2(\frac{1}{2}) - \frac{1}{2}log_2(\frac{1}{2})$$

$$+4(-\frac{1}{2}log_2(\frac{1}{2}) - \frac{1}{4}log_2(\frac{1}{4}) - \frac{1}{4}log_2(\frac{1}{4})$$

$$= 10$$

$$E_{x3}^{avg} = 4E(P5) + 4E(P6)$$

$$4(-\frac{1}{2}log_2(\frac{1}{2}) - \frac{1}{4}log_2(\frac{1}{4}) - \frac{1}{4}log_2(\frac{1}{4}))$$

$$+4(-\frac{1}{2}log_2(\frac{1}{2}) - \frac{1}{4}log_2(\frac{1}{4}) - \frac{1}{4}log_2(\frac{1}{4}))$$

$$= 12$$

Thus, x1 is the lowest entropy attribute at the root node. In addition, x1 = no is a leaf node in the decision tree.

Determination of Second Decision Node.   Since it has been determined the root node of the decision tree is the x1 attribute test and the x1 = no branch yielded a leaf node, the remaining sequential tests involve the recursive partitioning of $P2$. $P2$ is shown in Table 16.9. E_{xi}^{avg} for attributes x2 and x3 must be determined. Forming a table for these attributes similar to Table 16.10 yields Table 16.11. From this we compute:

$$E_{x2}^{avg} = 2E(P3) + 2E(P4)$$
$$= 0 + 2(-\frac{1}{2}log_2(\frac{1}{2}) - \frac{1}{2}log_2(\frac{1}{2}))$$
$$= 2$$

and (the reader should verify this)

$$E_{x3}^{avg} = 4$$

Thus, x2 yields the lowest entropy and becomes the next decision node. Note also that x2 = no yields a leaf node. Since x3 is the remaining attribute, it comprises the last decision node and the tree is complete. The resulting hand-computed ID3 tree is shown in Figure 16.9.

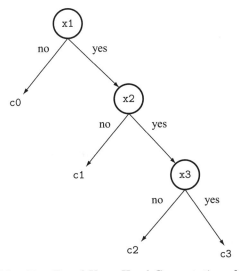

Figure 16.9 Resulting Tree Based Upon Hand Computation of Attribute Entropy

Partition	attribute = value	Number of Outcome Occurrences			
		c0	c1	c2	c3
P3	x2 = no	0	2	0	0
P4	x2 = yes	0	0	1	1
P5	x3 = no	0	1	1	0
P6	x3 = yes	0	1	0	1

Table 16.11   Summary of Modified Data Partitions Remaining After x1 Node Selection (Corresponding to x1 = yes)

CommonLisp ID3 Tree Solution

Using the input data shown, the ID3 tree is obtained.

```
(setq ts
;; fmt:  x1 x2 x3 class?
     '((no no no c0)
        (no no yes c0)
        (no yes no c0)
        (no yes yes c0)
        (yes no no c1)
        (yes no yes c1)
        (yes yes no c2)
        (yes yes yes c3)))

> (printTree (id3 ts '(x1 x2 x3)))
   x1
   yes
      x2
      yes
         x3
         yes -> c3
         no -> c2
      no -> c1
   no -> c0
t
```

Comparison of the ID3 Strategy with the Underlying Mapping

Several observations are noteworthy:

1. It is interesting to note that the logical functions[10] that were used to form the training data in Table 16.7 are as follows:

   $c0 = \overline{x1}$: This requires one attribute test;

---

[10]Here assume $no = 0$ and $yes = 1$ and an outcome occurs if the logical function evaluates to 1.

$c1 = x1\overline{x2}$: This requires two attribute tests;

$c2 = x1x2\overline{x3}$: This requires three attribute tests; and

$c3 = x1x2x3$: This requires three attribute tests.

2. It is also noteworthy that these logic functions may be derived from the resulting ID3 tree, by considering the logical tests employed in each (possible set of) path(s) to a specific outcome, c_i.

16.4.9   Using ID3 for Learning Block Movement Strategies

Here we use the ID3 learning algorithm for a more realistic task, namely the learning of a decision tree for "checkerboard" block move selection. The situation is illustrated in Figure 16.10. Our aim is to derive a decision tree for block movement, where the objective of the block is to get closer (or "catch") the other block. The location of the other block (OB) and various possible obstructions are shown.

Case1: Simple Yes–No Outcome

To get started, consider the simplistic scenario outlined by the examples in Table 16.12.

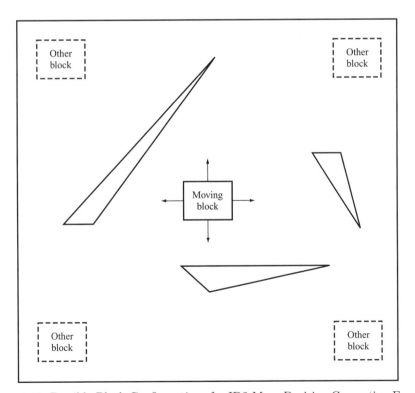

Figure 16.10 Possible Block Configurations for ID3 Move Decision Generation Example

locOB	obstrUp	clearUp	moveUp?
up	yes	no	no
up	yes	yes	yes
up	no	no	no
up	no	yes	yes
down	no	no	no
down	yes	yes	no

Table 16.12 Simple Blocks Movement Training Examples

CommonLisp input corresponding to this case, followed by ID3-based results, is shown here.

```
(setq blocks1
;;;      locOB obstrUp clearUp moveUp?
      '((up yes no no)
        (up yes yes yes)
        (up no no no)
        (up no yes yes)
        (down no no no)
        (down yes yes no)))

> (printTree (id3 blocks1 '(locOB obstrUp clearUp)))
   clearup
   yes
      locob
      down -> no
      up -> yes
   no -> no
t
```

Case 2: Multiple (> 2) Move Outcomes/Decisions

Referring to Figure 16.10, we develop a more complex set of problem outcomes using simple attribute tests. The outcome is no longer a binary decision, but rather indicates the decision to use one of four possible operators. Note that this problem is also considered from the ANN viewpoint in Chapter 13, Section 13.7.2. Table 16.13 enumerates the block movement instances for this scenario.

Training Instances and Resulting Tree.   CommonLisp input of the training data is shown here, followed by the resulting ID3 tree.

```
(setq blocks2
;;; locOB clearUp clearLeft clearRight clearDown move?
' ((up yes yes yes yes up)
   (up no yes yes yes left)
   (up no no yes yes right)
   (up no no no yes down)
   (down yes yes yes yes down)
   (down no yes yes no right)
```

locOB	clearUp	clearLeft	clearRight	clearDown	move?
up	yes	yes	yes	yes	up
up	no	yes	yes	yes	left
up	no	no	yes	yes	right
up	no	no	no	yes	down
down	yes	yes	yes	yes	down
down	no	yes	yes	no	right
down	yes	no	no	no	up
down	no	no	yes	no	right
left	yes	yes	yes	yes	left
left	no	no	yes	yes	down
left	yes	yes	yes	no	left
left	yes	no	no	yes	up
right	yes	yes	yes	yes	right
right	yes	yes	no	yes	up
right	no	no	no	yes	down
right	no	yes	no	no	left

Table 16.13 Multiple Outcome Blocks Movement Training Examples. (This data is used for both ANN and ID3 training examples.)

```
(down yes no no no up)
(down no no yes no right)
(left yes yes yes yes left)
(left no no yes yes down)
(left yes yes yes no left)
(left yes no no yes up)
(right yes yes yes yes right)
(right yes yes no yes up)
(right no no no yes down)
(right no yes no no left) ))

> (treePathspp (id3 blocks2 '(locOB clearUp clearLeft clearRight clearDown)))
  clearup
  no
     locob
     right
        clearleft
        yes -> left
        no -> down
     left -> down
     down -> right
     up
        clearleft
```

```
      no
         clearright
         no -> down
         yes -> right
      yes -> left
yes
   locob
   right
      clearright
      no -> up
      yes -> right
   left
      clearleft
      no -> up
      yes -> left
   down
      clearleft
      no -> up
      yes -> down
   up -> up
```

16.4.10 ID3 Learning, Training Data, and Generalization

Concepts and Questions

The ID3 algorithm produces a decision tree, given C. The reader should question what the ID3 algorithm *learns*, and how properties of C influence the utility of the tree obtained. For example, the following somewhat interrelated questions are relevant (some are left as exercises):

1. What if C contains conflicting data (e.g., the same set of attributes corresponds to two or more outcomes)?

2. What if it is known that the problem has c outcomes, but set C does not contain instances corresponding to all c outcomes?

3. In the previous case, how will the decision tree classify?

4. How comprehensive must C be?

5. How correctly does the decision tree provide an outcome for "new" instances, i.e., those not in C?

6. (How) could the tree be updated, rather than recomputed, when new instances become available?

7. Does the tree suggest any general tests on the attributes, on the basis of classifying all the instances in C?

ID3 Extension: Conflicting Data

When the same set of attributes produce differing outcomes, the ID3 algorithm assigns the most frequently observed outcome to the decision node. An example follows. The reader is encouraged to compute the relevant partitions and entropies.

```
(setq tsmult
;; fmt:  x1 x2 x3 class?
      '((no no no c0)
        (no no no c1)
        (no no no c1)
        (yes yes yes c1)
        (yes yes yes c1)
        (yes yes yes c2)
        (yes yes no c2)
        (yes yes yes c3)))

> (printTree (id3 tsmult '(x1 x2 x3)))

"** Warning: out of attributes but multiple outcomes **"

"** Warning: out of attributes but multiple outcomes **"
   x1
   yes
      x3
      yes
         x2
         yes -> c1
      no -> c2
   no
      x2
      no
         x3
         no -> c1
t
```

To further illustrate or answer some of the questions posed in Section 16.4.10, we present two additional examples.

Five-Input AND; Exhaustive and Reduced C

Consider the development of a decision tree that implements a five-input logical AND function. Note that the maximum number of unique instances (i.e., the exhaustive C) consists of $2^5 = 32$ cases. We show the results of developing a decision tree using ID3 for two cases:

1. Using the exhaustive C; and

2. Using half of the instances in the exhaustive C.

Case 1: Exhaustive C.   The data for the exhaustive C are shown here using CommonLisp representation.

```
(setq tsand
;;;     x1 x2 x3 x4 x5 and?
      '((0 0 0 0 0 0)
        (0 0 0 0 1 0)
        (0 0 0 1 0 0)
        (0 0 0 1 1 0)
        (0 0 1 0 0 0)
        (0 0 1 0 1 0)
        (0 0 1 1 0 0)
        (0 0 1 1 1 0)
        (0 1 0 0 0 0)
        (0 1 0 0 1 0)
        (0 1 0 1 0 0)
        (0 1 0 1 1 0)
        (0 1 1 0 0 0)
        (0 1 1 0 1 0)
        (0 1 1 1 0 0)
        (0 1 1 1 1 0)
        (1 0 0 0 0 0)
        (1 0 0 0 1 0)
        (1 0 0 1 0 0)
        (1 0 0 1 1 0)
        (1 0 1 0 0 0)
        (1 0 1 0 1 0)
        (1 0 1 1 0 0)
        (1 0 1 1 1 0)
        (1 1 0 0 0 0)
        (1 1 0 0 1 0)
        (1 1 0 1 0 0)
        (1 1 0 1 1 0)
        (1 1 1 0 0 0)
        (1 1 1 0 1 0)
        (1 1 1 1 0 0)
        (1 1 1 1 1 1)))
```

Resulting Decision Tree for Exhaustive C.

```
> (printTree (id3 tsand '(x1 x2 x3 x4 x5)))
   x1
   1
     x2
     1
       x3
       1
         x4
         1
           x5
           1 -> 1
           0 -> 0
         0 -> 0
       0 -> 0
     0 -> 0
   0 -> 0
t
```

Case 2: Reduced C**.**   For illustration, every other sample in the previous training set is eliminated. Input data is shown here:

```
(setq tsand-reduced
;;;     x1 x2 x3 x4 x5 out?
      '((0 0 0 0 1 0)
        (0 0 0 1 1 0)
        (0 0 1 0 1 0)
        (0 0 1 1 1 0)
        (0 1 0 0 1 0)
        (0 1 0 1 1 0)
        (0 1 1 0 1 0)
        (0 1 1 1 1 0)
        (1 0 0 0 1 0)
        (1 0 0 1 1 0)
        (1 0 1 0 1 0)
        (1 0 1 1 1 0)
        (1 1 0 0 1 0)
        (1 1 0 1 1 0)
        (1 1 1 0 1 0)
        (1 1 1 1 1 1)))
```

Decision Tree for the Reduced C Case.

```
> (printTree (id3 tsand-reduced '(x1 x2 x3 x4 x5)))
   x1
   1
       x2
       1
           x3
           1
               x4
               1 -> 1
               0 -> 0
           0 -> 0
       0 -> 0
   0 -> 0
t
```

In this example, observe that the resulting decision tree differs from the tree obtained using the exhaustive training set.

Five-Input Parity Detector; Exhaustive and Reduced C

As a second example, consider a five-input parity detection function. The input consists of five binary-valued attributes, x1 through x5. The binary-valued outcome, denoted out? is 1 if the attribute values consist of an even number of "1"s.

Exhaustive C**.**   The exhaustive training set and resulting decision tree are shown here.

```
;; out? = 1 if even # of "1"s
(setq tsparity
;;;     x1 x2 x3 x4 x5 out?
```

```
  '((0 0 0 0 0 1)
    (0 0 0 0 1 0)
    (0 0 0 1 0 0)
    (0 0 0 1 1 1)
    (0 0 1 0 0 0)
    (0 0 1 0 1 1)
    (0 0 1 1 0 1)
    (0 0 1 1 1 0)
    (0 1 0 0 0 0)
    (0 1 0 0 1 1)
    (0 1 0 1 0 1)
    (0 1 0 1 1 0)
    (0 1 1 0 0 1)
    (0 1 1 0 1 0)
    (0 1 1 1 0 0)
    (0 1 1 1 1 1)
    (1 0 0 0 0 0)
    (1 0 0 0 1 1)
    (1 0 0 1 0 1)
    (1 0 0 1 1 0)
    (1 0 1 0 0 1)
    (1 0 1 0 1 0)
    (1 0 1 1 0 0)
    (1 0 1 1 1 1)
    (1 1 0 0 0 1)
    (1 1 0 0 1 0)
    (1 1 0 1 0 0)
    (1 1 0 1 1 1)
    (1 1 1 0 0 0)
    (1 1 1 0 1 1)
    (1 1 1 1 0 1)
    (1 1 1 1 1 0)))){sec:id3-parity}

> (printTree (id3 tsparity '(x1 x2 x3 x4 x5)))
  x1
  1
    x2
    1
      x3
      1
        x4
        1
          x5
          1 -> 0
          0 -> 1
        0
          x5
          1 -> 1
          0 -> 0
      0
        x4
        1
          x5
          1 -> 1
```

```
                    0 -> 0
              0
                    x5
                    1 -> 0
                    0 -> 1
        0
            x3
            1
                x4
                1
                    x5
                    1 -> 1
                    0 -> 0
                0
                    x5
                    1 -> 0
                    0 -> 1
            0
                x4
                1
                    x5
                    1 -> 0
                    0 -> 1
                0
                    x5
                    1 -> 1
                    0 -> 0
  0
      x2
      1
          x3
          1
              x4
              1
                  x5
                  1 -> 1
                  0 -> 0
              0
                  x5
                  1 -> 0
                  0 -> 1
          0
              x4
              1
                  x5
                  1 -> 0
                  0 -> 1
              0
                  x5
                  1 -> 1
                  0 -> 0
      0
          x3
          1
```

```
            x4
            1
                x5
                1 -> 0
                0 -> 1
            0
                x5
                1 -> 1
                0 -> 0
        0
            x4
            1
                x5
                1 -> 1
                0 -> 0
            0
                x5
                1 -> 0
                0 -> 1
t
```

Note that this decision tree implementation requires 32 rules. In addition, the resulting tree correctly classifies all 32 possible inputs, as expected.

Using Half of the Exhaustive C Instances. Instead, we use half the available training or instance data. This reduced set C is formed by skipping every other sample used in the previous example. The input data is shown here.

```
;; reduced (even numbers eliminated) data
;; out? = 1 if even # of "1"s
(setq tsparity-reduced
;;;     x1 x2 x3 x4 x5 out?
      '((0 0 0 0 1 0)
        (0 0 0 1 1 1)
        (0 0 1 0 1 1)
        (0 0 1 1 1 0)
        (0 1 0 0 1 1)
        (0 1 0 1 1 0)
        (0 1 1 0 1 0)
        (0 1 1 1 1 1)
        (1 0 0 0 1 1)
        (1 0 0 1 1 0)
        (1 0 1 0 1 0)
        (1 0 1 1 1 1)
        (1 1 0 0 1 0)
        (1 1 0 1 1 1)
        (1 1 1 0 1 1)
        (1 1 1 1 1 0)))
```

The resulting decision tree is shown here:

```
> (printTree (id3 tsparity-reduced '(x1 x2 x3 x4 x5)))
```

```
x1
1
    x2
    1
        x3
        1
            x4
            1 -> 0
            0 -> 1
        0
            x4
            1 -> 1
            0 -> 0
    0
        x3
        1
            x4
            1 -> 1
            0 -> 0
        0
            x4
            1 -> 0
            0 -> 1
0
    x2
    1
        x3
        1
            x4
            1 -> 1
            0 -> 0
        0
            x4
            1 -> 0
            0 -> 1
    0
        x3
        1
            x4
            1 -> 0
            0 -> 1
        0
            x4
            1 -> 1
            0 -> 0
t
```

Some observations regarding these two cases are:

1. Note that the decision tree produced by the reduced C consists of only 16 rules; moreover there is no use of attribute x5.

2. Classifying samples from the exhaustive C using this tree is ill-advised. The outputs produced by this decision tree using samples from the exhaustive C that are not in the reduced C (e.g., those eliminated) are all in error. On this basis, we note that the reduced C is insufficient to produce the desired function.

Outcome (Classification) Errors and Reformulations of the Decision Tree

The problems encountered in Section 16.4.10 spawn a quest for techniques to update the decision tree when newly obtained instances yield outcome or classification errors. While we could simply add the "offending" instances to C and recompute the tree directly, this is often computationally expensive.

Modified Decision Trees and Learning

After forming a decision tree, numerous situations are possible with respect to future inputs encountered. Two of significance are:

1. An instance is incorrectly classified (i.e., yields an incorrect outcome); or

2. An instance cannot be classified (i.e., the decision tree does not have a path to a leaf node for the combination of attribute values given).

Case 1 has been addressed. Even in the case of no errors or lack of classification problems we still might want to modify the tree. One approach is by pruning. The rationale [Qui86] for this extension (often denoted ID4 or ID4.5) is that pruning introduces generalization (at the risk of increased error). In other words, it might be preferable to trade increased classification error rates for a decision tree with greater applicability.

The ID4 algorithm was developed by Schlimmer and Fisher [SF86]. The ID4 algorithm builds decision trees incrementally.

16.4.11   Converting a Decision Tree into a Rule Set

This is relatively straightforward. One approach is shown in Section 16.5. The general strategy is left as an exercise.

16.5   Integrating and Implementing ID3, Generalization, and Rule Determination

16.5.1   Exemplars

Table 16.14 shows, in tabular form, a set of exemplars ($E1$–$E6$) for learning fruit classification. $E1$–$E3$ are positive exemplars for class "+," and $E4$–$E6$ are negative exemplars for class "+."

16.5.2   ID3 Results

Here we show a CommonLisp-based solution for the ID3 tree.

```
> fruitTS
((red very-big soft +) (green big hard +) (green small hard +) (red big hard -)
```

Exemplar	COLOR	SIZE	TEXTURE	CLASS
E_1	red	very-big	soft	+
E_2	green	big	hard	+
E_3	green	small	hard	+
E_4	red	big	hard	-
E_5	red	small	hard	-
E_6	red	very-big	solid	-

Table 16.14 Positive and Negative Exemplars for Fruit Example (also used in exercises).

```
(red small hard -) (red very-big solid -))

> attributes
(color size texture)

> (setq result (id3 fruitTS attributes))
(color (red (texture (solid -) (hard -) (soft +))) (green +))

> (printTree result)
  color
  red
     texture
     solid -> -
     hard -> -
     soft -> +
  green -> +
t
```

The resulting tree shows that the **size** attribute is superfluous. Also notice in the case of positive exemplars this tree reduces to

```
  color
  red
     texture
       soft -> +
  green -> +
```

16.5.3 Validation of the Tree

Again, a CommonLisp-based solution is shown. The strategy is straightforward:

1. Using the resulting tree and the exemplars in the training set, determine the outcome for each exemplar.

2. Compare this outcome with the one specified in the training set. If all tree evaluation-based outcomes are identical to those indicated in the training set, the tree is consistent with this data.

An example is shown here:

```
> (tree-validate fruitTS attributes)

"tree successfully validated"
t
```

16.5.4 Determination of Resulting Classification Rules

Again, a CommonLisp-based implementation is used:

```
> (treePathspp result)
  color
  red
     texture
     solid -> -
     hard -> -
     soft -> +
  green -> +



"the paths are:"

((color green +) (color red texture soft +) (color red texture hard -)
 (color red texture solid -))
```

showing that the size attribute is superfluous. Each path specifies a rule, which could be easily implemented in Soar or CLIPS.

16.6 Exercises

1. What is wrong with the following logic, used in a generalization example:

   ```
   IF I drink bourbon AND water, THEN I get a hangover

   IF I drink scotch AND water, THEN I get a hangover

   IF I drink whiskey AND water, THEN I get a hangover
   ```

   The (incorrect) generalization of this set of observations is:

   ```
   IF I drink water, THEN I get a hangover
   ```

2. This problem explores learning in CLIPS. (Note Soar implements a form of learning called *chunking*). Show how new productions may be generated using the clips build construct.

3. Table 16.14 showed a set of exemplars (*E1–E6*) for learning fruit classification. Using the approaches of Sections 16.3.7 or 16.3.8, determine which of the following are valid (but not necessarily optimal) generalizations for class "+"? (Note: * denotes a don't-care value of an attribute.)

(i)

(COLOR *)(SIZE very-big)(TEXTURE *)

(ii)

(COLOR green)(SIZE *)(TEXTURE hard)

(iii)

(COLOR *) (SIZE big) (TEXTURE hard OR soft)

(iv)

(COLOR *) (SIZE very-big) (TEXTURE hard))

(v)

(COLOR red) (SIZE very-big OR big) (TEXTURE hard)

4. Using the training set of exemplars in Section 16.5.1 (see Table 16.14), and the resulting ID3 tree in Section 16.5.2, validate the resulting tree by hand.

5. The ID3 tree validation procedure of Section 16.5.3 did not address the issue of multiple outcomes for the same attribute values. How would you resolve the validation procedure for this case?

6. The following questions are intended to foster research into aspects of the ID3 tree.

   (a) What is "statistical neutrality" and how does it impact the derivation of a tree? How does "statistical neutrality" affect generalization?

   (b) How would you handle a missing or unknown attribute value?

   (c) How would you handle attributes with cost?

   (d) How would you handle attributes with continuous values?

7. Using the programming language of your choice, implement the ID3 algorithm. Implementation should be recursive and based upon your design of a function id3, with prototype as follows:

```
id3(ts, attributes)
```

where ts is the training set and attributes is a list of the problem attributes. Note attributes is only necessary so that we may form the tree using the attribute names. See the following example. The function should return the resulting ID3 tree.

8. (a) Show a decision tree for a three-input logical AND function.

   (b) Show a decision tree for a three-input logical XOR function.

9. Section 16.4.4 claimed:

   If the probability of one outcome dwarfs all other outcomes (e.g., $p_1 = 0.99$ and $\sum_{i=2}^{n} p_i = 0.01$) the corresponding entropy (uncertainty) is small.

   Choose p_i and compute E for the case $n = 5$ to partially verify this claim.

10. In using $E_{a_i}^{avg}$ to compare attributes, is it necessary to use log_2?

11. Suppose the ID3 algorithm (not the implementation) is used with instance data containing one or more conflicting outcomes, as shown in the following sample data:

```
(setf *data*
;;;     x1 x2 x3 c?
        '((d1 0 0 0 0)
          (d2 0 0 0 1) ;; put the conflict here
```

or an even simpler case:

```
(setf *data*
;;;     x1  c?
        '((d1 0 0)
          (d2 1 1)
          (d3 1 0)  ;; put the conflict here
```

What is the result as far as the generation of a decision tree?

12. When the entropy of two attributes is identical, how would you resolve the attribute test ordering in building the decison tree?

13. For the example given in Section 16.4.5, verify $E_{x1}^{avg} = E_{x2}^{avg} = E_{x3}^{avg}$.

14. The general "learning" capability of the ID3 algorithm is a subject of continued interest. For example, consider the following "black box" function with samples of input and output shown. LISP representation is used.

Input	Output
[]	[]
[a]	a
[a b]	b
[a b c]	c
[a b c d]	d

(a) What is the "black box" function?

(b) Can this problem be cast in a form suitable for the ID3 algorithm? (Consider both the general case and the restriction to a finite length list.)

15. The ID3 algorithm, as presented, assumes discrete values for both attributes and outcomes. How could the ID3 learning algorithm be modified to allow for continuous values for either or both of these entities?

16. In Section 16.4.10 the use of an inexhaustive C led to subsequent errors in classification. A somewhat obvious approach is to recompute the decision tree after including the instances leading to erroneous outcomes. This problem considers a more elegant approach.

How could the tree obtained using the reduced C be *modified* (not recomputed) using the new instance?

17. In Equation 16.15, the quantity $p_i log_2(p_i)$ occurs. Consider the case where $p_i = 0$, or $lim_{p_i \to 0} p_i log_2(p_i)$. What should the value of this quantity be? (*Hint*: avoid intuitive $0 \times \infty$ arguments.)

18. Two desired characteristics of a measure of entropy are:

(a) The entropy measure should be symmetric, i.e., entropy should be unchanged if the outcomes are reordered; and

(b) The addition of an outcome with probability 0 does not change the entropy.

Show that the measure used in Equation 16.15 satisfies both of these desired characteristics.

19. Consider the set of outcomes with p_i: $P = \{\frac{1}{8}, \frac{1}{4}, \frac{1}{16}, \frac{1}{16}, \frac{1}{2}\}$. Compute the entropy of this set.

20. Repeat the previous exercise with p_i: $P = \{\frac{1}{32}, \frac{1}{64}, \frac{1}{16}, \frac{1}{32}, \frac{55}{64}\}$. Compute the entropy of this set.

21. Entropy is also a commonly encountered concept in statistical thermodynamics. Is there any relationship between the notion of entropy in thermodynamics and our Equation 16.15 definition?

22. The purpose of this problem is to compare the ID3 algorithm for learning a functional mapping with that of an MLFF ANN.

(a) How would you determine the MLFF ANN architecture?

(b) Would you expect a similar functional mapping to be learned in both cases?

(c) Verify your response using the training data of Figure 16.10.

23. Section 16.4.4 indicated that when $p_i = \frac{1}{n}$, E is maximum. Prove this.

24. TRUE or FALSE: For a case where all outcomes have equal probabilities, the entropy increases with an increase in the number of outcomes.

25. In the example of Section 16.4.6, consider the initial forming (root) of the ID3 tree. Specifically consider the attribute entropy computations at this node. Given that x1 has the lowest entropy, is there any significance to the fact that there is a tie for the x2 and x3 attribute entropies?

26. A CommonLisp developer was developing an ID3 implementation for a blocks moving problem. Testing yielded the following tree:

```
(clearup
 (yes
  (locob (right (clearright (yes right) (no up)))
   (left (clearleft (yes left) (no up))) (down (clearleft (yes down) (no up)))
   (up up)))
 (no
  (clearleft (no (clearup (up down) (down right) (left down) (right down)))
   (yes left)))))
```

What is wrong with this ID3 algorithm output? (*Hint*: draw the tree.)

27. Using the blocks moving problem of Section 16.4.9, translate the resulting ID3 tree into a set of CLIPS productions.

28. Table 16.15 shows exemplars provided by politicians intended to solve problems with U.S. health care insurance. Our interest is apolitical; we merely want to determine the ID3 decision tree.

party	has-job	has-insurance	votes	action?
democrat	yes	yes	yes	leave-alone
democrat	yes	no	yes	leave-alone
democrat	yes	no	no	force-into
democrat	no	no	yes	leave-alone
democrat	no	no	no	force-into
republican	yes	yes	yes	leave-alone
republican	yes	no	yes	leave-alone
republican	yes	no	no	force-into
republican	no	no	yes	leave-alone
republican	no	no	no	force-into

Table 16.15   Instances Indicating Political Strategies for Health Care

(a) Derive the resulting ID3 tree;

(b) Draw the tree; and

(c) Assess your result.

29. The first example of Section 16.4.7 only included simple three note triad chord inversions (ordering of notes). Suppose a student proposed the following (somewhat "nonmusical") extensions of the training data:

```
(setq chords-extended
;; format: note1 note2 note3 type?
'((1 3 5 Maj)
  (3 5 1 Maj)
  (5 1 3 Maj)
  (5 3 1 Maj) ;; non-musical extensions
  (3 1 5 Maj) ;; just the other perturbations
  (1 5 3 Maj) ;; of 1-3-5
  (1 b3 5 Min)
  (b3 5 1 Min)
  (5 1 b3 Min)
  (5 b3 1 Min) ;;min permutations also
  (b3 1 5 Min)
  (1 5 b3 Min)
))
```

30. The computational complexity of the ID3 algorithm, as a function of the number of training instances or exemplars (denoted n), is of interest. Explore the ID3 literature and verify that this complexity is

$$\mathcal{O}(nlog(n))$$

31. Table 16.13 indicated there were 16 combinations of inputs used to determine one of 4 possible blocks moves. Compare this with the ID3 tree *paths* resulting from Section 16.4.9.

32. An IS engineer was interested in applying an S–G based learning algorithm to the problem of blocks moving. Table 16.13 is the training data used for the blocks movement case.

On the basis of this data (only), which of the entries in Table 16.16 are valid (but not necessarily optimal) generalizations for outcome move? = up? *Consider each potential generalization separately.* The answer for each possible generalization (1–10) is either yes or no.

Notes:

* denotes a don't-care value of an attribute.

{a, b, c,...} denotes a set of possible values of an attribute.

		locOB	clearUp	clearLeft	clearRight	clearDown	ANSWER
1		*	yes	yes	yes	yes	
2		up	yes	yes	*	yes	
3		up	*	yes	yes	yes	
4		{up,down}	yes	*	*	*	
5		up	yes	*	yes	yes	
6		down	yes	*	no	no	
7		{down,left}	yes	no	no	*	
8		{down,left}	*	no	no	*	
9		left	yes	*	*	yes	
10		right	*	*	no	yes	

Table 16.16 10 Possible Generalizations of the Concept move? = up

33. Provide a reasoned response to each of the following assertions:

(a) CBR does not need an explicit knowledge domain model, thus knowledge elicitation becomes a task of cataloging case histories.

(b) Implementation of CBR reduces to identifying significant features that describe a case.

34. Suppose we generate (see Chapter 12) a large number of planners for blocks-world applications. How could a CBR-based structure be used to facilitate reuse? What type of case features would you employ, and how would the matcher compare these features?

35. Suppose we have solved a CSP, e.g., image labeling. Is there a way for this solution to contribute to future image labelings, i.e., does it allow reuse? Justify your answer.

Genetic Algorithms, Swarm Intelligence, and Other Evolutionary Computing Concepts in IS

17.1 Biology Suggests a Computation

Biomimetics is a term used to describe the engineering of a process or system that mimics nature. Genetic, swarm, and evolutionary algorithms and artificial neural networks are examples of biomimetics.

The observed adaptation of biological systems to their environment is often impressive. This adaptation process, if successfully modeled and implemented, could serve as the basis for the development of artificial systems where performance increases over time and adapts to changing environments.

Evolutionary algorithms provide a potentially attractive and opportunistic approach to the search for solutions in a variety of problem domains [Koz92], including some that are nonobvious [CR04].

17.2 Genetic Algorithms

Evolution is a remarkable process for optimization and the long-term solution of problems. One of these problems may be to optimize the "fitness" of a species to accommodate the environmental pressure of its surroundings. In addition, much of the diversity in the natural world is due to the adaptation and mutation of living organisms.

Adaptation of biological systems (presumably with improved performance or fitness) may occur either through environmental pressures or evolution. Over the course of many generations, genetic modifications due to natural selection and random variation (mutation) determine the behavior of individuals and populations due to the demands of their environment.

Genetic algorithms (GAs) represent one element of an emerging computing area known as *evolutionary computing*. Genetic algorithms attempt to solve problems by mimicking the mechanisms of biological evolution in computing structures.[1] Since they are inherently based upon adaptation, they are good choices for applications that require adaptive problem-solving strategies and exploration, or search, over wide domains.

---

[1]This is an oversimplification.

17.2.1   Applications

Genetic algorithms have been used in many areas, including control, image processing, signal process-ing, pattern recognition, economics, and VLSI. In this section, we develop and use a variant of the "genetic programming paradigm," which breeds populations of computer programs to solve problems. We consider applications ranging from training neural networks to determining optimal compiler flags with gcc.

   Note that genetic breeding produces an extremely slow evolution in biological system time frames (e.g., millions of years), whereas artificial implementations generate, evaluate, and propagate an entire generation in the time necessary for one computational iteration (perhaps milliseconds).

17.2.2   Chromosomes, Genes, the Genome, and Genotypes and Phenotypes

Biological Terminology and Background

First, we introduce some terminology and background:

Chromosome.   In biological systems, a chromosome is a strand of DNA that carries a package of genes. The human genome is divided into 23 pairs of chromosomes. During (human) reproduction, each parent contributes one chromosome to each pair in the offspring. In other words, a human child gets half of their chromosomes from their mother and half from their father. In many artificial genetic algorithms, however, a single chromosome is used and the transferal of genetic information is simplified.

Gene.   A gene is a genetic "unit" that occupies a specific location on a chromosome and determines a particular characteristic in an organism.

Genome: Generally, the genome is all the (functional) genes in an organism. For our purposes, the genome is the total genetic content contained in a single chromosome.[2]

Genotype.   The genotype of an organism is *stored genetic information*. At the time of cell division (or reproduction), this information is propagated to members of the next generation. For our purposes, the genotype provides a system for representation of all or part of the genome of an organism and the propagation of genetic information.

   In biological systems, genetic representations are coded in DNA molecules. Remarkably, every cell contains a complete genetic description of not only its own phenotype but of the whole organism encompassing it.

Phenotype.   Phenotype is defined as the observable structure, function, or behavior of an organism. A simple example is the appearance of a trait. Generally, specific genes (from the genotype)

---

[2]From the biological perspective, this applies to bacteria or the DNA or RNA of viruses. In more complex life forms, the genome is the total genetic content in *a set of* chromosomes and (remarkably) contains a complete set of instructions, or blueprint, for making an organism.

determine specific inherited characteristics of an organism. Thus genotype has a major influence on the phenotypic attributes of the organism[3] and how the organism interacts with the environment.

(Artificial) genetic approaches to computation are derived from observations of the mechanisms of, and relationships between, genotypes and phenotypes in biological systems or living organisms. However, almost all artificial approaches are extreme simplifications of the actual processes found in nature. In addition, it is probably fair to say that, at this point in history, understanding of phenotypes is far more complete than understanding of genotypes.

Representation of the Genotype Versus Evaluation of the Phenotype

Problem representation in evolutionary computing is a key concern. The resulting performance of the genetic solution is strongly coupled with the chosen representation. In the following sections, we will see that major efforts in applying genetic approaches to IS problems are:

1. The encoding and propagation of the genetic information (the genotype); and

2. The mapping of the genetic information into the behavior or measurable performance of an element of the population, i.e., *the mapping from genotype to phenotype and evaluation of the (relative) fitness of the phenotype.*

This aspect of GA design and application is usually a challenging problem. The phenotype is often a far more complex structure (usually capable of some form of computation) than the genotype (which is basically a straightforward data structure). In the following sections, we show a number of examples.

17.2.3   GA as a Search and Optimization Technique

One viewpoint of GAs is that of search or optimization algorithms. In this mode, GAs offer alternatives to more conventional search/optimization algorithms. Computational cost is, however, a significant concern. However, the computations using GAs are inherently parallel, since their search for the best solution is over (large) populations of generations. Genetic structures provide the building blocks for the possible solutions. Figure 17.1 puts the role of GAs in search/optimization problems in perspective.

Definition: Artificial Genetic Algorithm

(Artificial) Genetic Algorithms are algorithms that transform populations of mathematical *objects*. The objects may be strings, lists, or graphical structures such as neural nets.

Primary Genetic Concepts: Reproduction and Crossover.   Depending upon the problem representation, objects are transformed into new populations using operators that follow or emulate biological systems. These operations are: *reproduction*, which is (almost always) proportional to an object's performance relative to that of population ("survival of the fittest"), and *crossover*, an

---

[3]Here we touch upon the age-old argument about the influence of genotype vs. environment on an organism's phenotype.

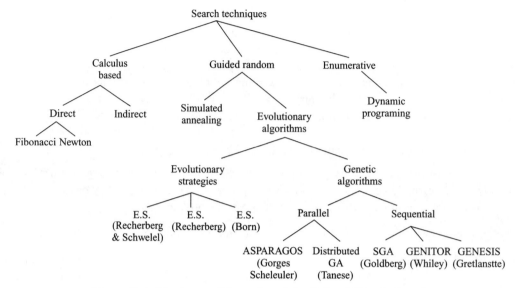

Figure 17.1 The Larger Viewpoint of the Role of GAs In Search

exchange of parts of two objects (akin to sexual recombination). While they are related, we distinguish reproduction as the decision to create new objects in the population from crossover, which is one mechanism to do so.

Mutation.   A third concept (operator) is *mutation*, which modifies the representation of a single object. Mutation is not a dominant operator in biological systems, and the probability of mutation is usually very small. An important concept in artificial implementations is *adaptive mutation*, where mutation occurs according to the level of diversity in the population. For example, when the population is very diverse (or "covers" solution space well), there is a small amount of mutation. Usually this occurs early in the breeding. Alternately, when the population diversity decreases (usually later in the breeding), it is desirable to increase the rate of mutation to keep the search sufficiently broad.

Other Genetic Operators.   Two other possible genetic operators are *transposition* and *gene duplication*. These secondary genetic operators appear to have little use in GA application. However, their existence suggests that in the nonbiological implementation of GA one could conceivably formulate and implement other genetic operators.

Transposition is the movement of genetic elements (genes) from place to place within the genome. The effects of transposition are drastic in nature (especially across species boundaries), and are usually (but not always) detrimental.

The exact workings of the mechanism of gene duplication in biological systems are unknown. However, it appears that occasionally a gene is copied twice during replication. This allows two copies of the gene to evolve independently, facilitating increased diversity in the population.

Repair Operators. In some cases, genetic manipulation produces chromosomes that do not correspond to an allowable solution. We see this in the crossover of the blueprint representation of trees, wherein nonsensical trees are produced. The simplest approach is to cull these offspring from the population. Alternately, a so-called "repair" operator could be used to convert illegal offspring into allowable potential solutions. As we see in the TSP solution, a number of genetic representation approaches lead to offspring that either must be culled or repaired.

The Significance of Search. Genetic algorithms are another search/optimizing procedure. Search proceeds by forming new solutions in the "population." Genetic algorithms, like the ROM methods, and unlike gradient descent, *do not tend to become trapped in local minima.*

Adaptation Approaches. In **cumulative selection**, each successful adaptation is the basis for the next generation. This means we can transform a random process into a nonrandom one. Conversely, in **single-step selection** no cumulative solution structure is used, i.e., each adaptation is independent of past adaptations.

17.2.4 Critical Aspects of a Genetic (Programming) Solution

Critical choices in the design and application of a genetic programming algorithm are:

1. Choice of *representation*, i.e., objects to manipulate. Note genetic algorithms *directly manipulate* the representation. This data structure is often chosen to be relatively simple, e.g., a string. From this object, the phenomes, or individual elements of the population are derived.

   As noted, a string representation is often used in genetic approaches. The string may consist of binary or decimal digits, characters or letters, or almost any set of meaningful symbols. An extension of the genetic representation to other entities, such as matrices, is also considered. Any chosen representation is only useful if it allows or facilitates genetic manipulations.

2. Choice of genetic operators. For this, nature provides some guidance.

3. Choice of a *performance measure, objective function, or measure of "fitness."* This measure is applied to each phenome and guides the genetic adaptation strategy. An associated, but different concern, is the choice of how entire populations evolve from one generation to the next.

   Other important aspects are:

4. Forming the initial population. This is denoted $P(0)$ and is typically chosen by randomly generating objects.[4]

5. Implementing a stopping criteria. A genetic algorithm usually has no obvious stopping criteria. Examples of stopping criteria include:

   ◆ When the average performance of the succeeding generation decreases

---

[4]Where no a priori information is needed.

- When the performance of some (or many) of the current population is quite good with respect to an absolute performance measure

- When the gene pool becomes so narrow or inbred such that successive populations have little or no genetic diversity; this is shown in the examples of Section 17.3.

- When a certain number of iterations, or generations, have been considered

Notice all but the last of these criteria require the recording of statistics as the simulation proceeds.

6. "Time" or iterations are measured in discrete intervals between *generations*, denoted $P(t)$ or $P(n)$.

7. The computing capability required is *significant to enormous*. In fact, this is the limiting factor in the solution search and makes GAs great candidates for *parallel computing*.

8. The detailed design of genetic operators to be used is significant.

9. Parent-offspring replacement properties must be chosen carefully.

17.2.5 Genetic Algorithm Simulation Parameters

The overall computational strategy is outlined in Figure 17.2. While genetic algorithms operate on populations of objects with the objective of producing a better performing population, to achieve artificial implementations it is necessary to define and choose a number of parameters. The following critical parameters are:

$P(t)$: The current population (may be a function of t, the generation); and

$P(0)$: The initial population, often randomly generated as previously described.

Population size (N): That should be large in order to cover the problem space, and avoid "evolution" to a local, as opposed to a global, solution.

Crossover rate (C_r): The frequency, or rate, at which the crossover operator is applied at each generation. In each generation, $N \times C_r$ objects undergo crossover.

Mutation rate (μ_r): If used, controls the rate of mutation. This typically changes with t, the current generation and an estimate of population "diversity." The examples that follow show the significance of mutation in avoiding "inbreeding" in solutions.

Generation gap (G): This measure controls the percentage of the population, P, which is replaced at each succeeding generation. $P(n + 1)$ is formed by replacing $N \times G$ members of $P(n)$. $G = 1$ corresponds to replacement of the entire population at each generation.

Selection strategy (S): An example is reproduction in proportion to "fitness" or performance.

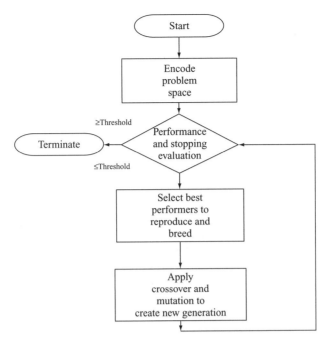

Figure 17.2 Flowchart for Genetic Algorithm

Extensions. Many genetic algorithms are presented as simple evaluate-select-crossover iterations. However, there exist numerous extensions and options for a genetic approach, including:

- Alternative selection strategies. Although we concentrate on fitness-proportional selection probability, this strategy [Whitley01overview.pdf] has some shortcomings. Alternatives include:

  1. Nonrandom selection according to (relative) fitness rank; and

  2. Tournament processes.

- Multipopulation breeding. It is possible to breed some number of generations (> 1) prior to evaluation and selection.

String Representation Example: Crossover. Many GA approaches represent a chromosome as a fixed-length 1-D string that represents one element of a population and thus is a candidate problem solution. The reproduction process is accomplished using the string representation. Suppose X and Y are two string structures chosen from the population pool, either at random or by the application of some "fitness" criteria, to breed. The concept is shown in Figure 17.3. The crossover point(s) could be selected randomly. Notice that crossover *only explores those subspaces of the solution space that*

X and Y represent two string structures chosen from the population pool, either at random or by the application of some "fitness" criteria, to breed.

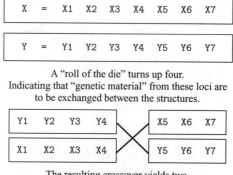

A "roll of the die" turns up four.
Indicating that "genetic material" from these loci are to be exchanged between the structures.

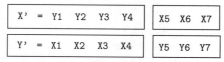

The resulting crossover yields two new string X' and Y' following the partial exchange

| X' | = | Y1 | Y2 | Y3 | Y4 | | X5 | X6 | X7 |

| Y' | = | X1 | X2 | X3 | X4 | | Y5 | Y6 | Y7 |

Figure 17.3 Example of Crossover (String Example)

are already represented in $P(t)$. For example, if for every e_k in $P(t)$ contains a 0 in the same position, i.e.,

$$e_k = x \ldots x 0 x \ldots x \quad \forall k \tag{17.1}$$

crossover cannot generate a 1 in this position. However, that suggests one important use for mutation.

17.3 A Simple Genetic Algorithm Example

We begin our look at genetic programming with a simple example, adapted from Goldberg [Gol89]. Many parameter choices have been made to simplify the presentation.

17.3.1 Problem Formulation

The approach is to find an integer argument to minimize a specified function, i.e, an objective function. The GA-related representation of the integer is based upon the (unsigned) binary representation. In this representation, each bit is a chromosome in the GA representation. Consider a 6-bit (6-chromosome) representation and a population at each generation of 10. Of course, these parameters may be modified.

Given 6 bits for representation of x, we know that $0 < x < 63$. The initial population is formed by randomly generating 10 integers in this interval and then converting each to a binary representation.

For example, consider the initial population:

```
index  initial population of chromosomes
0        1 1 1 1 0 0
1        1 1 0 0 0 1
2        1 0 1 1 1 1
3        0 0 1 0 1 1
4        0 0 1 1 0 1
5        1 0 0 0 1 1
6        0 1 0 1 0 0
7        0 1 0 1 1 1
8        1 1 1 0 1 1
9        1 1 0 0 0 1
```

17.3.2 Objective Function

The initial function to be maximized is

$$f(x) = \frac{1000}{10 + (t - x)^2}$$

i.e., we want to breed populations of solutions with the objective of getting x as close to target, t, as possible. In the initial examples, we choose $t = 32$. This function is plotted in Figure 17.4.

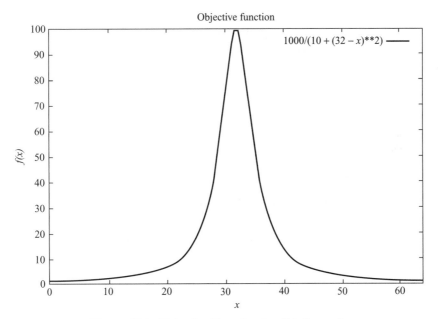

Figure 17.4 Objective Function for GA Example

17.3.3 Selection, Crossover, and Mutation

Fitness and Selection

In this example, selection involves randomly choosing five pairs of parents in the current generation so each pair, using crossover, produces two offspring. Thus, the entire population is replaced at each generation.

It is important to note that *the selection process is not deterministic*, rather the process is random. However, the probability of selection of a member of the population is proportional to performance, or fitness, of the member in the current generation. We define the sum of fitness values to be:

$$fit_{sum} = \sum f(x)$$

and thus the relative fitness of population member x is

$$fit_{rel}(x) = \frac{f(x)}{fit_{sum}}$$

Notice to control the algorithm and measure performance gains by the new population we also define

$$fit_{avg} = \frac{fit_{sum}}{n}$$

where n is the population size.

"Roulette-Wheel" Selection.   There are many ways to implement selection with $P(selected) \sim fit_{avg}$. One of the most popular is the so-called Roulette-wheel method, suggested by Goldberg. In this approach, each candidate string, with associated $fit_{rel}(x)$, is represented on a roulette wheel in proportion to $fit_{rel}(x)$. Strings with a high fitness value therefore occupy a large share or portion of the wheel. Selection is made by "spinning the wheel" N times to determine N parents for the next generation. The actual implementation of the Roulette-wheel strategy is exemplified by the C code snippet shown here:

```
sum = 0;
r = (double)(rand() % (int)sum_fitness);
/* Note rand() % sum_fitness in [0, sum_fitness) */
for (i=0; (i < POPULATION_SIZE)&&(sum <= r); i++)
        sum += fitness[i];
return (--i);        /* return selected string index */
```

Note that this selection strategy does not guarantee that a string with a high fitness value is automatically selected or that one with a low fitness value is never selected. In fact, unless a string has a fitness value of 0, there is a nonzero probability of selection. This selection process is implemented in the examples in Sections 17.3.4.

Crossover

String crossover has been described previously. The crossover point of the two strings is chosen randomly.

Controlling the Generation Gap, *G*

Recall from Section 17.2.5 that G controls the percentage of the population, P, which is replaced at each succeeding generation. $P(n + 1)$ is formed by replacing $N \times G$ members of $P(n)$. In the simulation examples that follow, the population remains constant over generations. To achieve this and to also allow $G > 0$, a parameter PCROSS is used. PCROSS is the probability that crossover is actually used for a pair of (selected) chromosomes. If PCROSS = 1, crossover will take place; if PCROSS = 0 the pair of (selected) chromosomes simply propagate without crossover into the next generation. For 0 < PCROSS < 1, G is randomly determined on the basis of PCROSS.

Mutation

Mutation is implemented to keep the population diverse.

Convergence or Stopping

Define "improvement" from generation n to generation $n + 1$ to be

$$improvement = \frac{fit_{avg}^{(\text{in generation } n+1)}}{fit_{avg}^{(\text{in generation } n)}}$$

We stop the GA when either a predetermined number of generations have been considered (here 50) or the improvement between generations is less than 2%. The latter (improvement-based) constraint is not necessarily good; it might be wiser to allow a generation to have poorer average performance in the hope that better genes will be propagated to the next generation.

17.3.4 Sample Results

Base Case.   The initial example is straightforward. The probability of crossover is 100%, i.e., $G = 1$. As in all the simulations, the crossover point is randomly selected. No mutation is allowed; thus, the probability of a gene mutation is set to 0. The (constant) population consists of 20 elements. The fitness function and target are defined by $f(x) = \frac{1000}{10+(32-x)^2}$.

```
$ ./ga11

*** Genetic Algorithm Simulation ***

Enter the (unsigned integer) target
in the range [0,63]:   32

Parameters of this simulation are:
POP_SIZE  CHROM_LENGTH   PCROSS   PMUT   TARGET   MAX_GEN  STOP_CRIT  SPREAD
   20          6         1.000   0.000     32       10      1.000      1.0

Initial population of chromosomes--

index  genotype   phenotype      f(x)
   0      100111      39        16.9492
   1      010110      22         9.0909
```

2	101011	43	7.6336
3	001001	9	1.8553
4	001101	13	2.6954
5	110000	48	3.7594
6	100010	34	71.4286
7	011011	27	28.5714
8	001001	9	1.8553
9	001110	14	2.9940
10	001111	15	3.3445
11	111011	59	1.3532
12	001101	13	2.6954
13	011101	29	52.6316
14	111001	57	1.5748
15	100101	37	28.5714
16	001110	14	2.9940
17	001111	15	3.3445
18	011000	24	13.5135
19	001100	12	2.4390

For generation 0, average fitness is 12.964749

From generation 0; individuals selected,
based upon relative performance, are:
15-15 13-7 6-6 6-16 6-13 6-18 7-0 6-6 12-6 13-4

This yields generation 1 ==>

index	offspring	new phenotype	new f(x)
0	100101	37	28.5714
1	100101	37	28.5714
2	011101	29	52.6316
3	011011	27	28.5714
4	100010	34	71.4286
5	100010	34	71.4286
6	100110	38	21.7391
7	001010	10	2.0243
8	100010	34	71.4286
9	011101	29	52.6316
10	100010	34	71.4286
11	011000	24	13.5135
12	011111	31	90.9091
13	100011	35	52.6316
14	100010	34	71.4286
15	100010	34	71.4286
16	001101	13	2.6954
17	100010	34	71.4286

```
18    011101       29        52.6316
19    001101       13         2.6954
```

fitness change = (new avg fitness/old avg fitness) = 3.585945
For generation 1, average fitness is 46.490873

From generation 1; individuals selected,
based upon relative performance, are:
13-11 14-13 18-9 5-17 2-15 0-15 17-10 13-10 8-10 18-5

This yields generation 2 ==>

index	offspring	new phenotype	new f(x)
0	100011	35	52.6316
1	011000	24	13.5135
2	100010	34	71.4286
3	100011	35	52.6316
4	011101	29	52.6316
5	011101	29	52.6316
6	100010	34	71.4286
7	100010	34	71.4286
8	011010	26	21.7391
9	100101	37	28.5714
10	100010	34	71.4286
11	100101	37	28.5714
12	100010	34	71.4286
13	100010	34	71.4286
14	100011	35	52.6316
15	100010	34	71.4286
16	100010	34	71.4286
17	100010	34	71.4286
18	011010	26	21.7391
19	100101	37	28.5714

fitness change = (new avg fitness/old avg fitness) = 1.127878
For generation 2, average fitness is 52.436055

From generation 2; individuals selected,
based upon relative performance, are:
14-15 15-3 2-3 2-19 2-7 17-15 11-4 12-13 7-15 4-8

This yields generation 3 ==>

index   offspring new phenotype new f(x)

0	100010	34	71.4286
1	100011	35	52.6316
2	100011	35	52.6316
3	100010	34	71.4286
4	100011	35	52.6316
5	100010	34	71.4286
6	100101	37	28.5714
7	100010	34	71.4286
8	100010	34	71.4286
9	100010	34	71.4286
10	100010	34	71.4286
11	100010	34	71.4286
12	101101	45	5.5866
13	010101	21	7.6336
14	100010	34	71.4286
15	100010	34	71.4286
16	100010	34	71.4286
17	100010	34	71.4286
18	011010	26	21.7391
19	011101	29	52.6316

fitness change = (new avg fitness/old avg fitness) = 1.078647
For generation 3, average fitness is 56.559996

From generation 3; individuals selected,
based upon relative performance, are:
14-16   3-0   3-3   5-2   19-8   3-12   10-8   15-0   8-7   8-0

This yields generation 4 ==>

index	offspring	new phenotype	new f(x)
0	100010	34	71.4286
1	100010	34	71.4286
2	100010	34	71.4286
3	100010	34	71.4286
4	100010	34	71.4286
5	100010	34	71.4286
6	100011	35	52.6316
7	100010	34	71.4286
8	011101	29	52.6316
9	100010	34	71.4286

```
10      100010          34      71.4286
11      101101          45       5.5866

12      100010          34      71.4286
13      100010          34      71.4286

14      100010          34      71.4286
15      100010          34      71.4286

16      100010          34      71.4286
17      100010          34      71.4286

18      100010          34      71.4286
19      100010          34      71.4286
```

```
fitness change = (new avg fitness/old avg fitness) = 1.171442
For generation 4, average fitness is 66.256773


From generation 4; individuals selected,
based upon relative performance, are:
18-0   13-14   17-14   14-4   3-15   0-18   13-17   16-14   7-3   6-3


This yields generation 5 ==>

index   offspring  new phenotype  new f(x)
    0   100010          34      71.4286
    1   100010          34      71.4286

    2   100010          34      71.4286
    3   100010          34      71.4286

    4   100010          34      71.4286
    5   100010          34      71.4286

    6   100010          34      71.4286
    7   100010          34      71.4286

    8   100010          34      71.4286
    9   100010          34      71.4286

   10   100010          34      71.4286
   11   100010          34      71.4286

   12   100010          34      71.4286
   13   100010          34      71.4286

   14   100010          34      71.4286
   15   100010          34      71.4286

   16   100010          34      71.4286
   17   100010          34      71.4286

   18   100010          34      71.4286
   19   100011          35      52.6316
```

```
fitness change = (new avg fitness/old avg fitness) = 1.063872
For generation 5, average fitness is 70.488722

From generation 5; individuals selected,
based upon relative performance, are:
6-19  16-6  17-15  4-15  12-18  3-10  17-14  1-2  19-4  5-15

This yields generation 6 ==>
```

index	offspring	new phenotype	new f(x)
0	100010	34	71.4286
1	100011	35	52.6316
2	100010	34	71.4286
3	100010	34	71.4286
4	100010	34	71.4286
5	100010	34	71.4286
6	100010	34	71.4286
7	100010	34	71.4286
8	100010	34	71.4286
9	100010	34	71.4286
10	100010	34	71.4286
11	100010	34	71.4286
12	100010	34	71.4286
13	100010	34	71.4286
14	100010	34	71.4286
15	100010	34	71.4286
16	100011	35	52.6316
17	100010	34	71.4286
18	100010	34	71.4286
19	100010	34	71.4286

```
fitness change = (new avg fitness/old avg fitness) = 0.986667
```

Analysis of Selection.   An evaluation of the initial population shows the top six members (ranked high to low, based upon fitness) are 6 (the top performer), 13, 7 and 15 (tie), 0, and 18. Thus, we would expect to see these members chosen in the selection process. As the simulation shows, member 6 was chosen eight times and member 13 was chosen three times in selection of 10 parent pairs from generation 0 to form offspring for generation 1. Furthermore, the next two best performers (members 7 and 15) were each selected twice. Conversely, the four worst performers in the initial population (generation 0) were 11, 14, and 8 and 3 (tie). We would not expect these individuals to be selected as parents. The simulation confirms this.

Analysis of Crossover. As the simulation shows, the first four parent pairs selected from generation 0 were: 15-15, 13-7, 6-6, and 6-16. We do not analyze the first and third of these pairs, since the parents are genetically identical. Considering parents 6-16, in generation 0, i.e.,

```
 6      100010
16      001110
```

we note the offspring (in generation 1) are:

```
 6      100110
 7      001010
```

From this, it is easy to see that the randomly-selected crossover point must have been as shown:

```
 6      100|010
16      001|110
```

Enhancements to the Base Case. In the second example, the probability of crossover is 75%. This allows, on average, 25% of parent pairs, selected on the basis of relative fitness, to enter the next generation rather than produce offspring. The probability of a gene mutation is 5%, and the (constant) population remains 20 elements. As shown by the simulation log that follows, the initial population contains several members (8, 12, 14, and 17; indexed from 0) that are reasonably close to 32 and have large relative fitness values. This is especially true of member 14. Therefore, it is not surprising that, in 20 random selections, 14 was selected eight times.

The GA-determined average fitness change between the initial population (generation 0) and generation 1 is seen to be a substantial 3.01. Notice also, that by generation 5, 75% of the population (15 of 20 members) have $f(x) > 90$.

```
$ ./ga11

*** Genetic Algorithm Simulation ***

Enter the (unsigned integer) target
in the range [0,63]:  32

Parameters of this simulation are:
POP_SIZE  CHROM_LENGTH   PCROSS   PMUT   TARGET   MAX_GEN  STOP_CRIT  SPREAD
   20           6        0.750    0.050    32        10     1.000      1.0

Initial population of chromosomes--

index   genotype   phenotype      f(x)
  0      011000        24        13.5135
  1      101001        41        10.9890
  2      001011        11         2.2173
  3      110010        50         2.9940
  4      010100        20         6.4935
  5      101101        45         5.5866
  6      010100        20         6.4935
  7      111000        56         1.7065
  8      100101        37        28.5714
```

9	001001	9	1.8553
10	001100	12	2.4390
11	001000	8	1.7065
12	011101	29	52.6316
13	101101	45	5.5866
14	100001	33	90.9091
15	101011	43	7.6336
16	111111	63	1.0299
17	011010	26	21.7391
18	010101	21	7.6336
19	111111	63	1.0299

For generation 0, average fitness is 13.637972

From generation 0; individuals selected,
based upon relative performance, are:
8-14   12-15   14-4   12-15   17-12   14-14   17-14   5-14   8-12   14-14

This yields generation 1 ==>

index	offspring	new phenotype	new f(x)
0	100001	33	90.9091
1	100111	39	16.9492
2	010101	21	7.6336
3	101011	43	7.6336
4	100001	33	90.9091
5	010100	20	6.4935
6	011001	25	16.9492
7	101011	43	7.6336
8	011101	29	52.6316
9	011010	26	21.7391
10	111001	57	1.5748
11	100101	37	28.5714
12	011010	26	21.7391
13	100001	33	90.9091
14	101101	45	5.5866
15	100001	33	90.9091
16	100101	37	28.5714
17	011101	29	52.6316
18	100001	33	90.9091
19	100001	33	90.9091

fitness change = (new avg fitness/old avg fitness) = 3.012885
For generation 1, average fitness is 41.089640

From generation 1; individuals selected,
based upon relative performance, are:
17-15   17-1   19-8   16-15   4-19   13-0   19-4   16-11   15-15   4-13

This yields generation 2 ==>

index	offspring	new phenotype	new f(x)
0	011101	29	52.6316
1	100001	33	90.9091
2	110111	55	1.8553
3	101101	45	5.5866
4	100001	33	90.9091
5	011101	29	52.6316
6	100101	37	28.5714
7	101001	41	10.9890
8	100001	33	90.9091
9	100000	32	100.0000
10	100001	33	90.9091
11	100011	35	52.6316
12	100001	33	90.9091
13	100001	33	90.9091
14	100111	39	16.9492
15	100101	37	28.5714
16	100001	33	90.9091
17	100001	33	90.9091
18	100001	33	90.9091
19	100001	33	90.9091

fitness change = (new avg fitness/old avg fitness) = 1.532635
For generation 2, average fitness is 62.975427

From generation 2; individuals selected,
based upon relative performance, are:
13-12   4-0   6-19   4-16   18-0   4-19   19-18   8-12   14-17   11-9

This yields generation 3 ==>

index	offspring	new phenotype	new f(x)
0	100001	33	90.9091
1	100001	33	90.9091
2	100001	33	90.9091
3	011101	29	52.6316
4	000101	5	1.3532

5	100001	33	90.9091
6	100001	33	90.9091
7	100001	33	90.9091
8	100001	33	90.9091
9	011101	29	52.6316
10	100001	33	90.9091
11	100011	35	52.6316
12	100101	37	28.5714
13	100001	33	90.9091
14	100001	33	90.9091
15	100001	33	90.9091
16	100111	39	16.9492
17	100001	33	90.9091
18	000010	2	1.0989
19	100100	36	38.4615

fitness change = (new avg fitness/old avg fitness) = 1.060126
For generation 3, average fitness is 66.761901

From generation 3; individuals selected,
based upon relative performance, are:
2-17 7-0 11-17 7-15 0-12 14-14 19-6 1-17 14-7 12-14

This yields generation 4 ==>

index	offspring	new phenotype	new f(x)
0	000001	1	1.0299
1	100001	33	90.9091
2	100001	33	90.9091
3	100001	33	90.9091
4	100011	35	52.6316
5	100001	33	90.9091
6	000001	1	1.0299
7	100001	33	90.9091
8	100001	33	90.9091
9	100101	37	28.5714
10	100001	33	90.9091
11	100001	33	90.9091
12	100100	36	38.4615
13	100001	33	90.9091

14	100001	33	90.9091
15	100001	33	90.9091
16	100001	33	90.9091
17	100001	33	90.9091
18	100101	37	28.5714
19	101001	41	10.9890

```
fitness change = (new avg fitness/old avg fitness) = 1.005890
For generation 4, average fitness is 67.155145
```

```
From generation 4; individuals selected,
based upon relative performance, are:
13-8  7-11  18-13  7-7  7-1  1-3  2-12  15-1  8-5  5-13
```

```
This yields generation 5 ==>
```

index	offspring	new phenotype	new f(x)
0	100001	33	90.9091
1	100001	33	90.9091
2	100001	33	90.9091
3	100001	33	90.9091
4	100101	37	28.5714
5	100001	33	90.9091
6	100100	36	38.4615
7	100001	33	90.9091
8	100001	33	90.9091
9	100001	33	90.9091
10	100001	33	90.9091
11	100001	33	90.9091
12	100000	32	100.0000
13	100100	36	38.4615
14	100101	37	28.5714
15	100001	33	90.9091
16	110001	49	3.3445
17	100001	33	90.9091

```
lso consider
```

18	100001	33	90.9091
19	100000	32	100.0000

```
fitness change = (new avg fitness/old avg fitness) = 1.131133
For generation 5, average fitness is 75.961430
```

```
From generation 5; individuals selected,
based upon relative performance, are:
```

```
3-10   11-5   8-18   3-5   18-0   0-17   15-15   11-17   1-11   13-9
```

This yields generation 6 ==>

index	offspring	new phenotype	new f(x)
0	000001	1	1.0299
1	100001	33	90.9091
2	000001	1	1.0299
3	000001	1	1.0299
4	100001	33	90.9091
5	100001	33	90.9091
6	100001	33	90.9091
7	100001	33	90.9091
8	100011	35	52.6316
9	100001	33	90.9091
10	100001	33	90.9091
11	100001	33	90.9091
12	100001	33	90.9091
13	101000	40	13.5135
14	100001	33	90.9091
15	100001	33	90.9091
16	100001	33	90.9091
17	100001	33	90.9091
18	100100	36	38.4615
19	100000	32	100.0000

```
fitness change = (new avg fitness/old avg fitness) = 0.914618
```

17.3.5   Other Simulation Parameters and Examples

We show some other examples for illustration. In the following example we consider the effect of small populations, with and without the use of mutation to increase diversity.

Small Population, No Mutation.   In the example shown here, $P(mutation) = 0$ and a population of $N = 4$ and $G = 0$ is used. Note the effect of inbreeding.

```
$ ./ga11

*** Genetic Algorithm Simulation ***

Enter the (unsigned integer) target
in the range [0,63]:  32

Parameters of this simulation are:
```

```
POP_SIZE  CHROM_LENGTH  PCROSS  PMUT  TARGET  MAX_GEN  STOP_CRIT  SPREAD
   4           6         1.000  0.000    32      10      1.000      1.0
```

Initial population of chromosomes--

```
index  genotype  phenotype    f(x)
  0     010111      23      10.9890
  1     110011      51       2.6954
  2     011010      26      21.7391
  3     000000       0       0.9671
```

For generation 0, average fitness is 9.097669

From generation 0; individuals selected,
based upon relative performance, are:
0-2 0-2

This yields generation 1 ==>

```
index  offspring  new phenotype  new f(x)
  0     011010         26        21.7391
  1     010111         23        10.9890

  2     010110         22         9.0909
  3     011011         27        28.5714
```

fitness change = (new avg fitness/old avg fitness) = 1.934300
For generation 1, average fitness is 17.597620

From generation 1; individuals selected,
based upon relative performance, are:
2-0 2-3

This yields generation 2 ==>

```
index  offspring  new phenotype  new f(x)
  0     010110         22         9.0909
  1     011010         26        21.7391

  2     010110         22         9.0909
  3     011011         27        28.5714
```

fitness change = (new avg fitness/old avg fitness) = 0.973035

Larger Population, P(Mutation) = 40%. Notice how the effect of a large mutation rate keeps the search diverse, as compared with the previous example. Also note that a larger population is used.

```
./ga11
```

```
*** Genetic Algorithm Simulation ***
```

```
Enter the (unsigned integer) target
```

in the range [0,63]:   32

Parameters of this simulation are:

POP_SIZE	CHROM_LENGTH	PCROSS	PMUT	TARGET	MAX_GEN	STOP_CRIT	SPREAD
10	6	1.000	0.400	32	10	1.000	1.0

Initial population of chromosomes--

index	genotype	phenotype	f(x)
0	010110	22	9.0909
1	111110	62	1.0989
2	011110	30	71.4286
3	010000	16	3.7594
4	011110	30	71.4286
5	011010	26	21.7391
6	100111	39	16.9492
7	101001	41	10.9890
8	111101	61	1.1751
9	011010	26	21.7391

For generation 0, average fitness is 22.939786

From generation 0; individuals selected,
based upon relative performance, are:
4-6   4-5   5-2   2-2   2-4

This yields generation 1 ==>

index	offspring	new phenotype	new f(x)
0	011110	30	71.4286
1	110110	54	2.0243
2	001100	12	2.4390
3	011101	29	52.6316
4	101011	43	7.6336
5	011011	27	28.5714
6	110101	53	2.2173
7	010100	20	6.4935
8	010001	17	4.2553
9	011110	30	71.4286

fitness change = (new avg fitness/old avg fitness) = 1.085987
For generation 1, average fitness is 24.912317

From generation 1; individuals selected,
based upon relative performance, are:
0-0   3-5   3-3   9-9   0-0

This yields generation 2 ==>

index   offspring   new phenotype   new f(x)

```
0    101100     44      6.4935
1    111101     61      1.1751

2    011011     27     28.5714
3    011010     26     21.7391

4    111111     63      1.0299
5    001001      9      1.8553

6    101010     42      9.0909
7    101100     44      6.4935

8    110100     52      2.4390
9    001110     14      2.9940
```

fitness change = (new avg fitness/old avg fitness) = 0.328680

Effect of Getting "Lucky" and Inbreeding.   This example shows that with randomly generated initial populations, it is possible for one member to dominate subsequent generations. Note the dominance of member 6 in the result shown here.

```
$ ./ga11

*** Genetic Algorithm Simulation ***

Enter the (unsigned integer) target
in the range [0,1023]:  300

Parameters of this simulation are:
POP_SIZE  CHROM_LENGTH  PCROSS  PMUT   TARGET  MAX_GEN  STOP_CRIT  SPREAD
   10          10       1.000   0.000   300      10      1.000      1.0

Initial population of chromosomes--

index  genotype   phenotype      f(x)
   0    0101000000     320       2.4390
   1    1101000010     834       0.0035
   2    1111010100     980       0.0022
   3    1010010011     659       0.0078
   4    0011010010     210       0.1233
   5    0001101010     106       0.0266
   6    0100101001     297      52.6316
   7    0000001001       9       0.0118
   8    0111010010     466       0.0363
   9    1110111000     952       0.0024

For generation 0, average fitness is 5.528434

From generation 0; individuals selected,
based upon relative performance, are:
4-6  6-6  6-6  6-6  6-6

This yields generation 1 ==>
```

index	offspring	new phenotype	new f(x)
0	0011010010	210	0.1233
1	0100101001	297	52.6316
2	0100101001	297	52.6316
3	0100101001	297	52.6316
4	0100101001	297	52.6316
5	0100101001	297	52.6316
6	0100101001	297	52.6316
7	0100101001	297	52.6316
8	0100101001	297	52.6316
9	0100101001	297	52.6316

```
fitness change = (new avg fitness/old avg fitness) = 8.570376
For generation 1, average fitness is 47.380752

From generation 1; individuals selected,
based upon relative performance, are:
6-3  6-9  5-6  1-6  8-5


This yields generation 2 ==>
```

index	offspring	new phenotype	new f(x)
0	0100101001	297	52.6316
1	0100101001	297	52.6316
2	0100101001	297	52.6316
3	0100101001	297	52.6316
4	0100101001	297	52.6316
5	0100101001	297	52.6316
6	0100101001	297	52.6316
7	0100101001	297	52.6316
8	0100101001	297	52.6316
9	0100101001	297	52.6316

```
fitness change = (new avg fitness/old avg fitness) = 1.110822
For generation 2, average fitness is 52.631579

From generation 2; individuals selected,
based upon relative performance, are:
6-8  9-9  0-5  4-9  6-6


This yields generation 3 ==>
```

index	offspring	new phenotype	new f(x)
0	0100101001	297	52.6316
1	0100101001	297	52.6316

2	0100101001	297	52.6316
3	0100101001	297	52.6316
4	0100101001	297	52.6316
5	0100101001	297	52.6316
6	0100101001	297	52.6316
7	0100101001	297	52.6316
8	0100101001	297	52.6316
9	0100101001	297	52.6316

```
fitness change = (new avg fitness/old avg fitness) = 1.000000
```

17.3.6 Extension: Modifying the Fitness Function

As noted, the fitness function may have a strong influence on the behavior of the genetic algorithm. For example, consider a parametric generalization of $f(x)$ as defined in Section 17.3.2. This is shown in Figure 17.5.

Here the function "spread" or sensitivity is controlled via the modified fitness function:

```
double evaluate(int value)
{
    return(1000.0/(10.0+(pow((double)(target-value),2.0))/SPREAD));
}
```

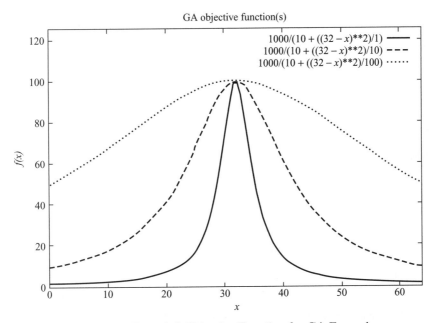

Figure 17.5 Extended Objective Function for GA Example

An additional example using SPREAD = 50 is shown in the following simulation. We also show the effect of a larger chromosome; this increases the cardinality of the search space.

```
$ ./ga11

*** Genetic Algorithm Simulation ***

Enter the (unsigned integer) target
in the range [0,1023]:  32

Parameters of this simulation are:
POP_SIZE  CHROM_LENGTH  PCROSS  PMUT   TARGET  MAX_GEN  STOP_CRIT  SPREAD
   10          10       1.000   0.000    32      10      1.000     50.0

Initial population of chromosomes--

index  genotype    phenotype     f(x)
  0    0001010100      84       15.6055
  1    1011101111     751        0.0966
  2    1010101111     687        0.1164
  3    0001011100      92       12.1951
  4    0010101111     175        2.3867
  5    1000100000     544        0.1904
  6    1100110101     821        0.0803
  7    1111111110    1022        0.0510
  8    1010001101     653        0.1295
  9    0011110111     247        1.0701

For generation 0, average fitness is 3.192159

From generation 0; individuals selected,
based upon relative performance, are:
0-4  3-3  0-3  0-0  9-0

This yields generation 1 ==>

index   offspring  new phenotype   new f(x)
  0     0000101111       47        68.9655
  1     0011010100      212         1.5198

  2     0001011100       92        12.1951
  3     0001011100       92        12.1951

  4     0001011100       92        12.1951
  5     0001010100       84        15.6055

  6     0001010100       84        15.6055
  7     0001010100       84        15.6055

  8     0011110111      247         1.0701
  9     0001010100       84        15.6055

fitness change = (new avg fitness/old avg fitness) = 5.343177
For generation 1, average fitness is 17.056270
```

From generation 1; individuals selected,
based upon relative performance, are:
0-0 0-5 0-0 0-4 2-7

This yields generation 2 ==>

index	offspring	new phenotype	new f(x)
0	0000101111	47	68.9655
1	0000101111	47	68.9655
2	0000101100	44	77.6398
3	0001010111	87	14.1844
4	0000101111	47	68.9655
5	0000101111	47	68.9655
6	0000101100	44	77.6398
7	0001011111	95	11.1882
8	0001011100	92	12.1951
9	0001010100	84	15.6055

fitness change = (new avg fitness/old avg fitness) = 2.839512
For generation 2, average fitness is 48.431477

From generation 2; individuals selected,
based upon relative performance, are:
0-0 1-4 6-1 5-7 5-6

This yields generation 3 ==>

index	offspring	new phenotype	new f(x)
0	0000101111	47	68.9655
1	0000101111	47	68.9655
2	0000101111	47	68.9655
3	0000101111	47	68.9655
4	0000101111	47	68.9655
5	0000101100	44	77.6398
6	0000111111	63	34.2231
7	0001001111	79	18.4570
8	0000101111	47	68.9655
9	0000101100	44	77.6398

fitness change = (new avg fitness/old avg fitness) = 1.283778
For generation 3, average fitness is 62.175274

From generation 3; individuals selected,
based upon relative performance, are:
0-4 9-1 8-1 9-8 4-0

This yields generation 4 ==>

index	offspring	new phenotype	new f(x)
0	0000101111	47	68.9655
1	0000101111	47	68.9655
2	0000101111	47	68.9655
3	0000101100	44	77.6398
4	0000101111	47	68.9655
5	0000101111	47	68.9655
6	0000101111	47	68.9655
7	0000101100	44	77.6398
8	0000101111	47	68.9655
9	0000101111	47	68.9655

fitness change = (new avg fitness/old avg fitness) = 1.137114
For generation 4, average fitness is 70.700364

From generation 4; individuals selected,
based upon relative performance, are:
3-3 5-8 5-6 1-7 3-9

This yields generation 5 ==>

index	offspring	new phenotype	new f(x)
0	0000101100	44	77.6398
1	0000101100	44	77.6398
2	0000101111	47	68.9655
3	0000101111	47	68.9655
4	0000101111	47	68.9655
5	0000101111	47	68.9655
6	0000101100	44	77.6398
7	0000101111	47	68.9655
8	0000101111	47	68.9655
9	0000101100	44	77.6398

fitness change = (new avg fitness/old avg fitness) = 1.024538
For generation 5, average fitness is 72.435211

From generation 5; individuals selected,
based upon relative performance, are:
7-1 5-8 4-6 9-6 0-4

This yields generation 6 ==>

| index | offspring | new phenotype | new f(x) |

0	0000101110	46	71.8391
1	0000101101	45	74.7384
2	0000101111	47	68.9655
3	0000101111	47	68.9655
4	0000101100	44	77.6398
5	0000101111	47	68.9655
6	0000101100	44	77.6398
7	0000101100	44	77.6398
8	0000101111	47	68.9655
9	0000101100	44	77.6398

```
fitness change = (new avg fitness/old avg fitness) = 1.011937
For generation 6, average fitness is 73.299857

From generation 6; individuals selected,
based upon relative performance, are:
0-8  6-5  1-0  6-3  8-0

This yields generation 7 ==>
```

index	offspring	new phenotype	new f(x)
0	0000101111	47	68.9655
1	0000101110	46	71.8391
2	0000101111	47	68.9655
3	0000101100	44	77.6398
4	0000101110	46	71.8391
5	0000101101	45	74.7384
6	0000101100	44	77.6398
7	0000101111	47	68.9655
8	0000101110	46	71.8391
9	0000101111	47	68.9655

```
fitness change = (new avg fitness/old avg fitness) = 0.984173
```

17.4 Applying Genetic Approaches to the Traveling Salesman Problem (TSP)

In this section, we consider the TSP and related genetic solution approaches. We considered alternative solutions using Artificial Neural Networks in Chapter 14. In Section 17.8.6 the Swarm computing paradigm is applied to the TSP.

17.4.1 The TSP

The TSP problem is quite simple to describe, yet difficult to solve for large N. A traveling salesman must determine the minimum travel cost for a tour of N cities where $N \geq 3$. Each city must be visited exactly once and the salesman must end up in the starting city, i.e., the tour is a cycle through the N cities. The cost to travel between any two cities, i and j, is d_{ij}. In the symmetric version of the problem, $d_{ij} = d_{ji}$. Thus, the objective is to find the cyclic permutation, π, of the integers $1, \ldots, N$ that minimizes

$$C(\pi) = \sum_{i=1}^{N-1} d_{\pi(i),\pi(i+1)} + d_{\pi(N),\pi(1)}$$

The remainder of this discussion is limited to the symmetric version of the TSP.

17.4.2 Significance and Computational Complexity of the TSP

Significance

The TSP is a well-known combinatorial optimization that belongs to the class of NP-hard problems. In addition, the TSP is directly related to a number of important routing and scheduling problems. For these reasons, the TSP has become a commonly used test problem for solution approaches and related heuristics.

Computational Cost

For N cities, the computational cost of the TSP is determined by first noting that there are $N!$ permutations of the set of cities. Since the problem involves a cyclic tour and the starting city is arbitrary, N of these permutations correspond to identical, and consequently redundant, tours. Finally, any tour reversed in sequence is also a valid tour. On this basis, one-half of the remaining tours in the set of $(N-1)!$ permutations are also redundant. Therefore, the computational complexity of a brute-force solution involves the evaluation of $\frac{(N-1)!}{2}$ tours.

An Example of Computational Cost. Consider an $N = 30$ city problem. Here

$$\frac{29!}{2} = 4.42 \times 10^{30}$$

Suppose, in a brute-force search approach, we assume it is necessary to perform N additions to evaluate a potential solution. Search of the state space thus requires $\frac{30!}{2} = 1.3 \times 10^{32}$ additions. Assume a machine capable of two GFLOPS is available. The time required for this search is

$$\frac{1.3 \times 10^{32}}{2 \times 10^9} = 6.6 \times 10^{22} \text{ sec}$$

This amounts to 2×10^{15} years.

17.4.3 TSP Representational Issues and Approaches

There are many possible ways to encode potential solutions to the TSP via a chromosome. The simplest, as discussed in the following subsections, is simply a string of cities in the tour. In many cases, however, the effect of conventional or unmodified genetic manipulation operators is the production of an illegal tour. Thus, modification of the genetic operator and/or "repair" operators are also necessary.

Binary Representation

Borrowing from the examples in Section 17.3, suppose each city in the tour is given a unique binary representation. For example, City 1 could be represented as 000, City 2 as 001, City 5 as 100, and so on. A more obvious representation might be an unsigned binary representation of the integer representation of the number of each city. The problems with the binary representation are many-fold:

1. It really is not necessary, i.e., the integer-based strings are more suitable.

2. There exist possible binary representations that do not correspond to cities. They may be produced by blindly applying crossover.

Path Representation

This representational approach is probably the most obvious. Each city is represented by an integer and an integer string is used to hold the sequence of cities visited on a tour. In other words, if City i is the jth element of the string, City i is visited at the jth step of the tour. For example, for $N = 5$, the string 32415 corresponds to the tour: $3 \rightarrow 2 \rightarrow 4 \rightarrow 1 \rightarrow 5$.

Problems with Path Representation. The most apparent problem with path representation is that crossover may produce illegal tours. Consider two valid chromosomes in path representation:

$$12345$$

$$21435$$

The first chromosome corresponds to the tour $1 \rightarrow 2 \rightarrow 3 \rightarrow 4 \rightarrow 5 \rightarrow 1$, whereas the second corresponds to the tour $2 \rightarrow 1 \rightarrow 4 \rightarrow 3 \rightarrow 5 \rightarrow 2$. Crossover of these strings after the second element yields offspring:

$$21345$$

and

$$12435$$

So far so good (we were lucky); these are valid tours. However, subsequent crossover of these strings after the first element yields offspring

$$11345$$

and

$$22435$$

Both are illegal tours.

Modification of Genetic Operators for Path Representation. The "classical" genetic cross-over operator must be modified for use with the path representation. Numerous modifications are possible. For example, *partially mapped crossover* [Gol89] could be used. This approach is best shown by example. Consider the tours (strings): 13254 and 21435. First, two randomly chosen crossover points are selected. Suppose, in this example, these points are after the first and third elements of the strings, i.e.,

$$1|32|54$$

$$2|14|35$$

The sections between the vertical bars are the *mapping sections*. Note that they define the mappings $3 \leftrightarrow 1$ and $2 \leftrightarrow 4$. The skeleton representations of the offspring tours are thus:

$$\text{offspring } 1 \ \Rightarrow x|14|xx$$

$$\text{offspring } 2 \ \Rightarrow x|32|xx$$

where the x's are to be determined. The remainder of the offspring are formed by copying the respective element of the parents into the chromosome, *with the constraint: If a city is already present in the offspring, it is replaced according to the mapping defined by the mapping section.* For example, the first element of offspring 1 would be a 1 (derived from parent 1), however it is already present so it is replaced by a 3. Similarly, the first element of offspring 2 would be a 2 (derived from parent 2); instead it is replaced by 4. So far we have:

$$\text{offspring } 1 \ \Rightarrow 3|14|xx$$

$$\text{offspring } 2 \ \Rightarrow 4|32|xx$$

Subsequent replacements yield:

$$\text{offspring } 1 \ \Rightarrow 3|14|5x$$

$$\text{offspring } 2 \ \Rightarrow 4|32|1x$$

to

$$\text{offspring } 1 \ \Rightarrow 3|14|52$$

$$\text{offspring } 2 \ \Rightarrow 4|32|15$$

Adjacency Representation

This representation also encodes the tour as a string of integers, however it is not a direct path representation. City j is in position i in the string if the tour leads from City i to City j. This is best seen with an example. Consider the adjacency-based tour representation:

$$35421$$

To determine the actual tour, it is convenient to arrange the string indices under the representation, i.e.,

$$35421$$

$$12345$$

The tour is $1 \to 3 \to 4 \to 2 \to 5 \to 1$.

There are several problems with the adjacency representation:

1. The representation allows illegal tours; and

2. The classical crossover operator may create illegal tours.

These are addressed in the exercises.

Matrix Representations

Several (binary) matrix representations have peen proposed. We show two that are typical. Note that implementation of the genetic operators (crossover and mutation) associated with these representations is complex; readers should consult [LKM+99] for complete details.

Tour Representation #1.   In this representation, element $a_{ij} = 1$ iff City i is visited before City j in the tour. For example, in the $N = 4$ city case, the matrix:

$$\begin{pmatrix} 0\ 0\ 0\ 1 \\ 1\ 0\ 1\ 1 \\ 1\ 0\ 0\ 1 \\ 0\ 0\ 0\ 0 \end{pmatrix}$$

requires cities: 1 before 4 (first row); 2 before 1, 3, and 4 (second row); and 3 before 1 and 4 (third row). Thus the tour is $2 \to 3 \to 1 \to 4 \to 2$. The matrix used in this representation has a number of important and useful properties [LKM+99]. To accompany this representation, new genetic operators are defined.

Tour Representation #2.   This matrix representation for the TSP has the following constraint: Element $a_{ij} = 1$ in the matrix iff City j is visited *immediately* after City i in the tour. For example, in the $N = 4$ city case, the matrix:

$$\begin{pmatrix} 0\ 0\ 0\ 1 \\ 0\ 0\ 1\ 0 \\ 1\ 0\ 0\ 0 \\ 0\ 1\ 0\ 0 \end{pmatrix}$$

requires $1 \to 4$ (first row), $2 \to 3$ (second row), $3 \to 1$ (third row), and $4 \to 2$ (fourth row). Thus the tour is $1 \to 4 \to 2 \to 3 \to 1$. In this approach, each row and column in the matrix contains exactly one 1. Note that an arbitrary matrix that satisfies this constraint does not necessarily correspond to a valid tour. In this representation, new crossover and mutation operators are required [LKM+99].

17.5 Application of Genetic Algorithms to ANN Design and Training

A logical question concerns how to apply the genetic approach to "breeding" ANNs. For one, we need an ANN *representation* that facilitates the genetic operators, but must retain the correct input and output dimensions for the subnets that are altered during genetic operations. This process could be viewed as *constrained switching or mutating of subgraphs*. The ANN representation must facilitate the use of genetic operators, which is especially difficult in topology crossover. Viewing the ANN topologies of two parents graphically, we note that the crossover of two arbitrary subgraphs does not, in many cases, make sense. Thus, the representation must allow constraints on the crossover of two parents such that offspring that have meaning are generated.

17.5.1 Topology Optimization and/or Weight Optimization

It is cumbersome to use genetic algorithms for the determination of $\underline{w}$, since the dimensionality of the vector is usually large and individual elements are usually continuous over the interval $[-\infty, \infty]$. The topology, however, is discrete[5] and a better candidate for a genetic solution.

17.5.2 The Blueprint Representation

The blueprint (BP) representation [WSJ92] of a network topology is accomplished in two steps:

1. Starting with the input layer, units are numbered.

2. For each unit, the numbers of preceding units are inserted in the list.

This is best seen by the two-input, one-output example in Figure 17.6.

17.5.3 Blueprint-Based Crossover

Crossover is accomplished by choosing a common point in the blueprint representation and joining two sublists of the parents. This is shown in Figure 17.7.

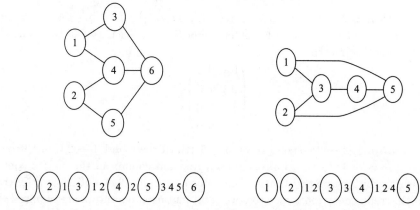

Figure 17.6 Blueprint Representation Example of Two ANN Architectures and Corresponding BP Representations

---

[5] Also, this means derivative-based optimization procedures are inappropriate.

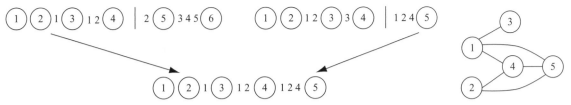

Figure 17.7 Example of Crossover Using the Blueprint Representations of Figure 17.6. Only one offspring is shown. Crossover occurs after Unit 4. Note isolated or "orphan" Unit 3 may be removed.

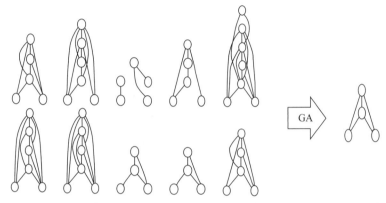

Figure 17.8 GA Solution of the XOR Problem Using the Blueprint Representation (from [WSJ92]). Courtesy of M. Joost, W. Schiffman, and R. Werner.

17.5.4 Sample Blueprint-Based Representation Results

Sample results for the XOR problem, from [WSJ92], are shown in Figure 17.8. Starting nets, generated randomly, are shown on the left. The solution converged to the minimal XOR topology is shown on the right.

17.6 Fusing Learning and a Genetic Application: Meta–Algorithm Development

In this section, we show the utility of genetic algorithms as well as an approach to reuse learned processing capability.

17.6.1 Problem Motivation

Suppose:

◆ Someone came to you with a problem that required development of an algorithm for the solution.

◆ Furthermore, you could specify inputs and (most importantly) could articulate the desired output for this problem.

◆ Parts of, or entire, (tunable) variations of the solution algorithm were already known.

◆ The problem kept changing or evolving. Assume that you did not know, at any given time, which version of the problem you would have to solve.

◆ You did not want to continuously reinvent the wheel.

You might be a candidate for meta-algorithms.

17.6.2   Background

Automatic algorithm generation or refinement is not a new idea [Sax74, Vog89, Sch89]. However, previous work is either restricted to specific operators or impractical. The search space for potentially useful "candidate" algorithm sequences for any problem grows not linearly, but exponentially [Vog90]. Thus, the use of genetic algorithms is commonly suggested [Koz92, Koz94, Mic92].

In this section, we illustrate the development of "algorithms to develop algorithms." The problem domain, for illustration, is restricted to image processing. This meta-algorithm concept is based upon earlier work in dynamic algorithms [SS95].

Dynamic Algorithms.   Dynamic algorithms embed training and archived algorithmic experience in an algorithm graph (AG). Thereafter, the sequence of operations applied to the input data may be dynamically adjusted. Each node in the tree-based representation of a dynamic algorithm without degree greater than 2 is a decision node. At these nodes, the algorithm examines the input data and determines the processing path that will most likely achieve the desired result. One of the principal limitations of this approach is the need for significant human input in the learning phase.

The constrained perturbation of existing algorithm graphs, coupled with a suitable search strategy, offers rich potential for the discovery of new algorithms. This meta-algorithm strategy autonomously generates new dynamic algorithm graphs via genetic recombination of existing algorithm graphs. The AG representation is well suited to this genetic-like perturbation, using the blueprint representation [WSJ92, Sch97]. An overview of the approach is shown in Figure 17.9.

17.6.3   Dynamic Algorithm Graph Representation and Manipulation

A sample dynamic algorithm graph is shown in Figure 17.10. The nodes in the algorithm graph represent data states, and the edges represent operations on the data. Each branch in the tree represents a possible path of execution (in fact, each unique overall path is equivalent to a single, static algorithm), and each leaf node represents output from the graph (algorithm). Decisions are made at each node without degree greater than 1. When input data is to be processed by the dynamic algorithm graph, its overall path through the graph is determined by the set of node classifiers.

Meta-algorithms automatically generate new algorithm graphs. New graphs are typically created by combining aspects of two or more existing graphs. These new dynamic algorithms can then be evaluated by training, and graphs that do not surpass the effectiveness of previous graphs are discarded.

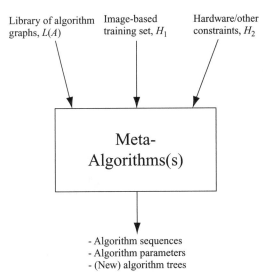

Figure 17.9 Meta-Algorithm Concept

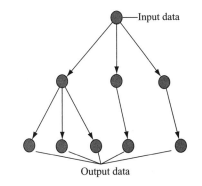

Figure 17.10 Sample Algorithm Graph

17.6.4 The Algorithm Graph Data Structure Representation

The algorithm graph is implemented as a linked list of node data structures. Each node contains links to its first child and the next sibling in the tree. In addition, each node contains a string with the operator assigned to the edge that connects to that node (the edges of the graph are not stored explicitly, so the operator information that pertains to the edges is stored within the nodes). Each node also contains a structure that stores all the training information (feature extraction data) for the node. A sample is shown in Figure 17.11.

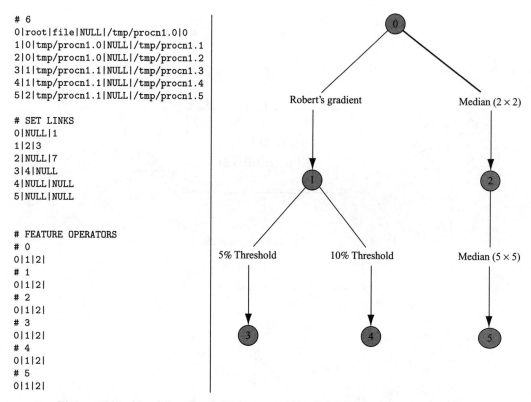

```
# 6
0|root|file|NULL|/tmp/procn1.0|0
1|0|tmp/procn1.0|NULL|/tmp/procn1.1
2|0|tmp/procn1.0|NULL|/tmp/procn1.2
3|1|tmp/procn1.1|NULL|/tmp/procn1.3
4|1|tmp/procn1.1|NULL|/tmp/procn1.4
5|2|tmp/procn1.1|NULL|/tmp/procn1.5

# SET LINKS
0|NULL|1
1|2|3
2|NULL|7
3|4|NULL
4|NULL|NULL
5|NULL|NULL

# FEATURE OPERATORS
# 0
0|1|2|
# 1
0|1|2|
# 2
0|1|2|
# 3
0|1|2|
# 4
0|1|2|
# 5
0|1|2|
```

Figure 17.11 Algorithm Graph Representation—File and Graphical Viewpoints

17.6.5 Genetic Recombination of Graphs

New algorithm graphs are created autonomously via genetic recombination of existing graphs, using the blueprint representation. An example of a small algorithm graph and its corresponding blueprint representation is given in Figure 17.12.

17.6.6 Crossover

The MA forms new dynamic algorithm graphs using the following steps:

1. Two existing algorithm graphs are selected and described in blueprint representation.

2. A node that is common to both graphs is selected at random from a list of all the nodes common to both graphs. This node will be used as the crossover point.

3. The blueprint representations of the original graphs are crossed at the crossover point, creating two new blueprint representations.

4. Two new algorithm graphs are constructed from the new blueprint representations.

Blueprint Representation:

(0) 0 (1) 0 (2) 0 (3) 1 (4) 1 (5) 1 (6) 2 (7)

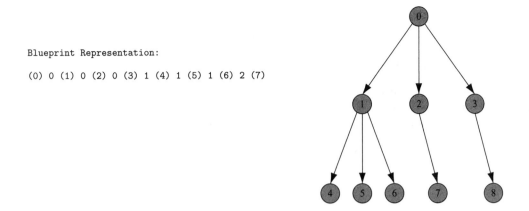

Figure 17.12 Example of an Algorithm Graph in Blueprint Representation

An example of blueprint-based crossover follows. The existing algorithm graph shown in Figure 17.13 is selected for recombination via crossover. The corresponding blueprint representation is:

(0) 0 (1) 0 (2) 0 (3) 2 (4) 2 (5)

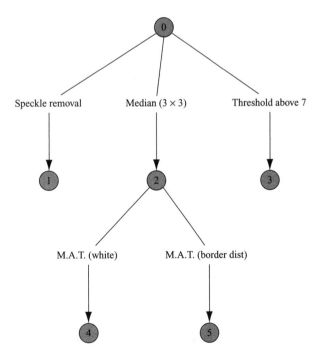

Figure 17.13 First Algorithm Graph Chosen for Crossover

Node 3 is chosen for the crossover point. The second graph selected for crossover is shown in Figure 17.14 and has the corresponding blueprint representation:

(0) 0 (1) 0 (2) 1 (3) 1 (4) 2 (5) 2 (6) 4 (7)

Using the selected crossover point, the graph blueprint representations are crossed by cutting each existing graph blueprint representation immediately after the common node, and then swapping the portions of the string to the right of the common node. This yields two new blueprint representations:

(0) 0 (1) 0 (2) 1 (3) 2 (4) 2 (5)

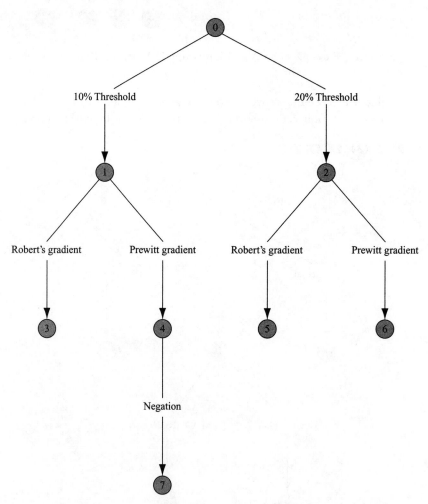

Figure 17.14 Second Algorithm Graph Chosen for Crossover

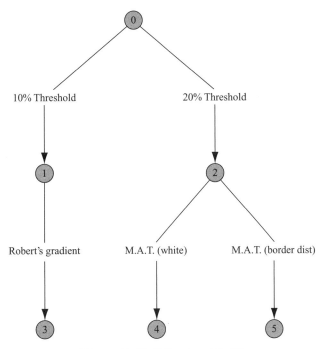

Figure 17.15 Offspring AG #1

and

(0) 0 (1) 0 (2) 0 (3)1 (4) 2 (5) 2 (6) 4 (7)

The resulting blueprint representations then provide two new algorithm graphs, as shown in Figures 17.15 and 17.16.

    With the generation of the two algorithm graphs, the crossover process is complete. The old graphs are not altered by the crossover process, and they may be crossed again using a different common node as the crossover node to generate another set of distinct offspring.

17.7 A Genetic Approach to Optimizing gcc Compiler Options

Many applications or algorithms require a large number of "tuned" parameters to work properly. This includes learning rate and momentum in gradient descent algorithms and filter parameters in signal processing applications [Bev05]. Genetic algorithms are commonly used for the determination of these parameters.

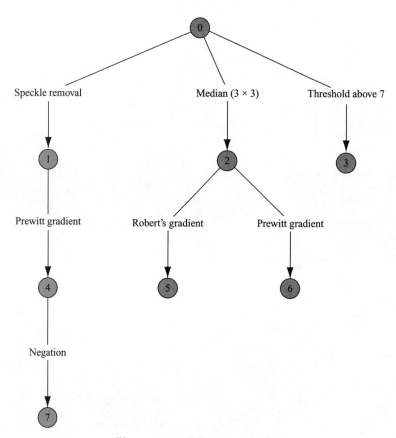

Figure 17.16 Offspring AG #2

Objective

Another interesting example of the use of genetic algorithms for optimization is the approach of **Acovea**: Analysis of Compiler Options via Evolutionary Algorithms. This application implements a genetic algorithm in order to find the "best" `gcc` (compiler) options for compiling a specific C or C++ application. Here "best" is defined as the set of options producing the fastest executable. A brute-force search of all combinations of `gcc` options would need to consider on the order of 10^{18} cases. Thus a GA approach might be a more reasonable alternative. Note this represents a layer of optimization on top of an "optimizing" compiler.

More information, including the source tarball, may be found at http://www.coyotegulch.com/products/acovea/index.html.

Genetic Representation of Compiler Options

An examination of the main page for gcc indicates more than 60 switches or flags that impact the resulting code optimization (in just the case of a specific, i.e., Pentium target architecture). An example is shown here:

```
Optimization Options
    -falign-functions=n  -falign-jumps=n -falign-labels=n
    -falign-loops=n -fbranch-probabilities  -fcaller-saves
    -fcprop-registers -fcse-follow-jumps  -fcse-skip-blocks
    -fdata-sections -fdelayed-branch  -fdelete-null-pointer-checks
    -fexpensive-optimizations  -ffast-math  -ffloat-store -fforce-addr
    -fforce-mem  -ffunction-sections -fgcse  -fgcse-lm  -fgcse-sm
    -floop-optimize  -fcrossjumping -fif-conversion  -fif-conversion2
    -finline-functions  -finline-limit=n  -fkeep-inline-functions
    -fkeep-static-consts  -fmerge-constants  -fmerge-all-constants
    -fmove-all-movables  -fnew-ra  -fno-branch-count-reg
    -fno-default-inline  -fno-defer-pop -fno-function-cse
    -fno-guess-branch-probability -fno-inline  -fno-math-errno
    -fno-peephole  -fno-peephole2 -funsafe-math-optimizations  -ffi-
    nite-math-only -fno-trapping-math  -fno-zero-initialized-in-bss
    -fomit-frame-pointer  -foptimize-register-move -foptimize-sib-
    ling-calls  -fprefetch-loop-arrays -freduce-all-givs  -fregmove
    -frename-registers -freorder-blocks  -freorder-functions -fre-
    run-cse-after-loop  -frerun-loop-opt -fschedule-insns  -fsched-
    ule-insns2 -fno-sched-interblock  -fno-sched-spec
    -fsched-spec-load -fsched-spec-load-dangerous  -fsignaling-nans
    -fsingle-precision-constant  -fssa  -fssa-ccp  -fssa-dce
    -fstrength-reduce  -fstrict-aliasing -ftracer  -fthread-jumps
    -funroll-all-loops  -funroll-loops --param name=value -O  -O0  -O1
    -O2  -O3  -Os
```

Hand-testing of combinations of these is impractical. Note that any filtering of invalid or unreasonable combinations is also not considered.

Representation and Crossover/Mutation.   An element of the population, or an artificial chromosome, of gcc compiler options must be able to represent a specific set of compiler options. Since some options are multivalued (i.e., not binary), a simple binary string is unsuitable. Instead, objects (ultimately lists) are used as shown in the following code snippet:

```
// breed a new options set from two parents
chromosome compiler::breed(const chromosome & a_parent1,
                           const chromosome & a_parent2) const

    // result
    chromosome child;

    // randomly pick an option from one of the parents
    for (int n = 0; n < a_parent1.size(); ++n)
    {
        if (g_random.get_rand() & 1)
            child.push_back(a_parent1[n]->clone());
```

```
        else
            child.push_back(a_parent2[n]->clone());
    }

    // done
    return child;
}

// mutate an option set
void compiler::mutate(chromosome & a_options,
                        double a_mutation_chance) const
{
    for (int n = 0; n < a_options.size(); ++n)
    {
        if (g_random.get_rand_real2() < a_mutation_chance)
            a_options[n]->mutate();
    }
}
```

A population of 40 (default) to 200 organisms is possible.

Fitness. To test fitness of the resulting code produced by a particular chromosome, the specific program is compiled and the runtime of the resulting executable recorded.

Results. A number of test programs were used (FFT, linear algebra, binary trees, etc.). Results of recent tests are available at http://www.coyotegulch.com/products/acovea/acovea_4.html.

17.8 Swarm Intelligence

17.8.1 Natural Behavior

In nature, the behavior of swarms of biological agents, each agent operating independently, often follows easily observed patterns and results in a collective benefit to the swarm. Examples include:

◆ The behavior of ant colonies in finding the shortest path to a food source;

◆ Swarms of wasps working without centralized control to build sophisticated nests; and

◆ Slime mold cells acting collectively as a single multicell organism to survive periods of famine.

In these applications, the collective behavior of the swarm or group is not embedded within, or controlled by, individual members of the group. Furthermore, the collective behavior does not result from a centralized control strategy. Instead, the collective behavior emerges from the behavior of the individual elements of the group and often simple, local interaction. We have also seen this occurrence in ANNs. While it is beyond the scope of this discussion, it should be noted that this framework may also explain the collective social behavior of higher-level biological systems, e.g., birds (penguins) and higher.

17.8.2 Definition

Swarm Intelligence (SI) is a form of observed behavior wherein the collective behavior of (often relatively unsophisticated) members of a population exhibits patterns and is often beneficial to the population as a whole.

17.8.3 Population–Based Processing Approaches

Swarm intelligence and genetic approaches share a characteristic in that they are both instances of *population-based optimization approaches*. In these approaches, interaction, communication, and perhaps competition among members of the population is used to achieve desired global behavior. In genetic approaches, a measure of fitness (or selection) and genetic operators (crossover and mutation) is intended to foster the generation of individual members (offspring) capable of a better problem solution. By contrast, in swarm-based approaches, the behavior of individuals is not evaluated; rather all members are kept in the population. Thus, swarm-based approaches do not embrace the Darwinism principle (survival of the fittest). The notion of a "generation" does not carryover into the swarm-based approaches.

17.8.4 Ant Algorithms (How Real Ant Colonies Find a Minimum Path)

It has been observed that ant colonies are able to easily and reliably find their way to a source of food and back despite the fact that individual ants are effectively blind. Thus, it is not the intelligent functioning of an individual ant, using visual cues and high-level reasoning, that leads the colony to food. Biologists have discovered that the approach seems to be based on a form of local chemical communication in the colony. This communication is based upon a chemical substance called a pheromone.

Definition: Pheromone

> **pheromone** (fer-ə-mōn): A chemical substance produced by an animal. Serves as a stimulus to others of the same species for behavioral response.

Referring to Figure 17.17, we illustrate the natural metaphor used by ant colonies. We later develop artificial variations of this metaphor for other applications. The basic premise of the ant colony metaphor is simple and two-fold:

- Individual ants, while walking, deposit pheromone on the ground beneath them; and
- On a probabilistic basis, ants follow pheromone deposited by other ants.

The Initial Paths and Decision Rule.   Suppose in a path (to food) planning problem, a number of ants are faced with a possible choice in paths. Assuming there is not yet a trail of pheromone, individual ants decide randomly on the path to take. In the absence of other information, assume a uniform distribution of path choice, i.e., for n paths $\frac{1}{n}$ of the initial population of ants chooses each path. Also assume individual ants move at constant speed and deposit pheromone uniformly over time.

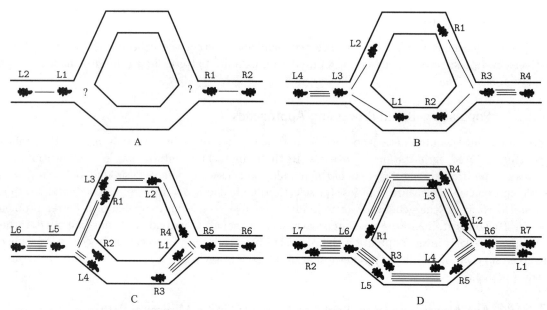

How real ants find a shortest path. A) Ants arrive at a decision point. B) Some ants choose the upper path and some the lower path. The choice is random. C) Since ants move at approximately constant speed, the ants that choose the lower, shorter, path reach the opposite decision point faster than those that choose the upper, longer, path. D) Pheromone accumulates at a higher rate on the shorter path. The number of dashed lines is approximately proportional to the amount of pheromone deposited by ants.

Figure 17.17 How Ants Find the Shortest Path. From [DG96b]. Courtesy of M. Dorigo and L. Gambardella, Ant colony system: A cooperative learning approach to the traveling salesman problem. *IEEE Transactions on Evolutionary Computing*, 1(1), 1997.

Evolution of the Decision Strategy.   Since ants are interested in traveling to the food source and back, those ants (randomly) choosing what turns out to be a shorter path to the source will return more quickly and collectively deposit more pheromone than on a longer path. This, and subsequent individual ant behavior, are the keys to the success of the algorithm. Whereas the initial group of ants chooses a path randomly, after the transient period when new ants come to the path junction (decision point), it is no longer necessary to base the decision on an entirely random basis. At this time, the decision of individual ants will also be based upon accumulated pheromone of each path (we assume the ants are able to sense this). Subsequent ants still choose a path on a probabilistic basis, but the probability of choosing each path reflects accumulated pheromone in each path, i.e., the collective "intelligence" left by previous ant traversals.

Positive Feedback Over Time.   At this point we observe the feedback-like nature of the algorithm. If the probability of choosing a certain path is proportional to the amount of pheromone from previous trips, paths with high levels of pheromone deposits (i.e., shorter paths) will be chosen more frequently, thus further increasing the pheromone deposits along this path and consequently the probability of choosing the shorter path in the future.

17.8.5 Developing and Applying an Artificial Ant Colony Algorithm

Whereas few, if any, IS algorithms are intended to find the shortest path to food, the approach is adaptable to real IS problems. The keys are:

◆ Converting the objective of the problem to one similar to the ant colony problem;

◆ Implementing a randomized decision rule that is influenced by prior results; and

◆ Implementing and using artificial pheromone.

17.8.6 Return to the Traveling Salesman Problem

Recall the Traveling Salesman Problem (TSP):

Let $V = \{a, b, c, \dots, z\}$ be a set of cities to be visited; $A = \{(r, s) : r, s \in V\}$ be the set of paths between cities; and $\delta(r, s)(= \delta(s, r))\}$ be the cost of the path between Cities r and s. The objective is to find the minimum cost associated with visiting each city once and returning to the starting city. Numerous variations on this problem are possible.

17.8.7 Solving the TSP Using the Ant Colony Metaphor

Consider the strategy proposed in [DC96b, DG97]. Suppose the colony consists of m ants. Ant k is currently (or starts) in City r. Furthermore, the set of cities connected to City r, i.e., all $(r, s) \in A$ is known to Ant k. $J_k(r)$ denotes the set of cities remaining in the tour that must be visited by Ant k. $J_k(r)$ is referred to as the "tabu list" in the literature.

The City Selection Probability

After the transient or startup period, Ant k, currently in City r, chooses City s with probability given by $P_k(r, s)$:

$$P_k(r, s) = \begin{cases} \dfrac{[\tau(r,s)] \cdot [\eta(r,s)]^\beta}{\sum_{u \in J_k(r)} [\tau(r,u)] \cdot [\eta(r,u)]^\beta} & \text{if } s \in J_k(r) \\ 0 & \text{otherwise} \end{cases} \tag{17.2}$$

where:

$\tau(r, s)$ is the observed pheromone in the path from City r to City s. Note this equation cannot be used directly in the transient or startup phase since $\tau(r, s) = 0\ \forall s$;

$\eta(r, s) = 1/\delta(r, s)$ is the inverse of the cost from r to s. Note this heuristic is intended to favor lower cost edges; and

$\beta > 0$ is a parameter that allows control of the relative importance of τ (pheromone) and η (local path cost) in the solution.

Notice that Ant k's choice of the next city (path) is still random. Equation 17.2 only specifies the probability of the choice of the next city, although it is influenced by both the amount of observed pheromone as well as the local distance heuristic. This random decision rule must be implemented for each ant at each city as part of the solution.

Individual Tours and Pheromone Updating

All ants in the population (colony) complete tours characterized by Equation 17.2. Following this step, the pheromone is updated for all edges as follows:

$$\tau(r, s) \leftarrow (1 - \alpha) \cdot \tau(r, s) + \sum_{k=1}^{m} \Delta \tau_k(r, s) \tag{17.3}$$

where

$$\Delta \tau_k(r, s) = \begin{cases} 1/L_k & \text{if } (r, s) \in \text{ tour done by ant } k \\ 0 & \text{otherwise} \end{cases} \tag{17.4}$$

where L_k is the length of the tour done by Ant k. Following this update, each ant clears its tabu list in preparation for the next iteration. Notice:

◆ Equation (17.3) incorporates a decay parameter, $0 < \alpha < 1$. If, over time (or iteration), a path "falls out of favor," gradually the pheromone in this path decays. This is also called "pheromone evaporation."

◆ Since L_k is the overall length of the tour done by Ant k, more simulated pheromone is deposited (along the path they visited) by ants completing shorter tours.

Following this pheromone updating, the next iteration over all m ants in the colony commences. This is governed by Equation (17.2). Once a new set of m tours is found, Equations (17.3) and (17.4) are used to globally update the path pheromone values. The process iterates until a stopping criteria is applied.

Results

It is claimed the swarm-based algorithm delivers "good" (in some cases optimal) solutions for small TSPs (i.e., ≤ 30 cities). Unfortunately, the computational cost of applying the algorithm on serial architectures makes it somewhat impractical for larger cases. Sample results for a 30-city problem are shown in Figure 17.18.

17.8.8 Computational Shortcomings of the Artificial Algorithm and the ACS

Due to the aforementioned computational complexity of the algorithm, an alternative algorithm called the Ant Colony System (ACS) was proposed. The ACS differs from the original algorithm in that:

1. A modified and more state-transition function is used. The rule is still probabilistic in nature;

2. The global updating of pheromone is only applied to paths that belong to the best (so far) tour; and

3. While ants are traveling, a local pheromone updating rule is (also) applied.

Best tour length

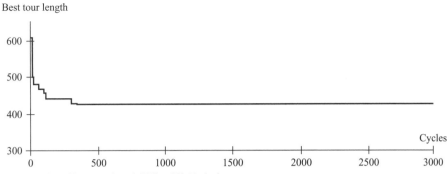

(a) Evolution of best tour length [Oliver30]. Typical run.

Tour length
standard deviation

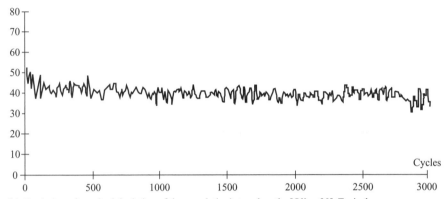

(b) Evolution of standard deviation of the population's tour lengths [Oliver30]. Typical run.

Average node branching

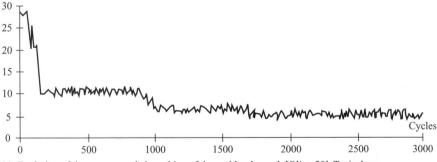

(c) Evolution of the average node branching of the problem's graph [Oliver30]. Typical run.

Figure 17.18 Sample Performance of the Swarm-Based TSP Solver (from [DG97]). Courtesy of M. Dorigo and L. Gambardella, Ant colony system: A cooperative learning approach to the traveling salesman problem. *IEEE Transactions on Evolutionary Computing*, 1(1), 1997.

17.9 References

An excellent introduction to applying genetic algorithms to ANNs is [Whi88]. Classic references for genetic algorithms are [Gol89] and [Dav91]. A compilation of work relating neural nets and genetic algorithms is [SWE92]. [FFP90] compares genetic approaches with the concept of simulated annealing in neural networks.

[DC96b], [DS04], [PV02], and [Cle06] provide good introductions to swarm-computing-based applications. [Ala00] provides a reasonably up-to-date bibliography of genetic algorithms applied to the TSP.

17.10 Exercises

1. Two FF ANN topologies are shown in Figure 17.19.

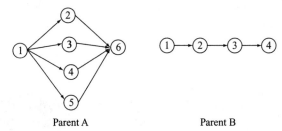

Parent A   Parent B

Figure 17.19 Two Parents in ANN GA Solution Population

(a) Show the blueprint representation for each.

(b) The crossover point is chosen to be just after Unit #3 in each parent's representation. Show the two offspring resulting from crossover of these parents *both in the blueprint representation and graphically.*

2. TRUE or FALSE: In using a genetic algorithm, it is possible for the crossover of two elements of a population to generate a second instance of a member already in the population.

3. The relevant equations from the ant colony-based solution to the TSP are the state-transition equation (see Equation 17.2) and the path/pheromone updating equations (see Equations 17.3 and 17.4). Consider a swarm solution to the TSP problem that requires NC total (overall) cycles, has m ants in the colony, and concerns n cities. (*Hint*: see [DC96b].)

(a) What is the computational complexity of the algorithm?

(b) How does your answer to the previous question compare with the TSP brute-force search solution complexity?

(c) It has been found by experiment that the optimal number of ants is a linear function of the number of cities. In this case, what is the computational complexity of the ant-based algorithm?

(d) What is the effect of $\beta = 0$? What is the effect of $[\tau(r, s)] = k \ \forall s$?

(e) Cite two approaches for initialization of the algorithm. Refer specifically to Equation (17.2).

(f) Cite two techniques for stopping the algorithm.

(g) Suppose Equation (17.4) is updated as follows:

$$\Delta\tau_k(r, s) = \begin{cases} Q/L_k & \text{if } (r, s) \in \text{ tour done by Ant } k \\ 0 & \text{otherwise} \end{cases} \tag{17.5}$$

where Q is a positive constant. How does this modification influence the overall algorithm?

4. This problem concerns the use of a genetic algorithm for solution of the map coloring CSP (see Chapter 4). The objective is to color the regions in a given map using a predefined number of colors such that adjacent regions (i.e., sharing a border) have different colors.

Part 1: Use Chapter 4, Figure 4.8, with three colors (RGB) and develop a genetic algorithm for implementation of the coloring solution.

Part 2: Repeat the three-color effort of Part 1, but using the map of Chapter 4, Figure 4.26.

Part 3: Repeat the effort of Part 1 (see Figure 4.8), but using four colors (RGBW).

Part 4: Repeat the effort of Part 2 (see Figure 4.26), but using four colors (RGBW).

Show (explicit) development of a genotype, phenotype, and $f(x)$, as well as the evolution of the solution for a number of initial populations. Note that (depending upon your chosen genotype), genetic manipulation may produce chromosomes that do not correspond to an allowable representation (e.g., a color that does not exist). You might want to consider a so-called "repair" operator to convert illegal offspring into allowable potential solutions.

5. In the GA example of Section 17.3.4, repeat the analysis shown for parents 13–7 in generation 0 and show the possible crossover points selected.

6. The incorporation of mutation as a genetic operator raises an interesting question: When should mutation occur? Should mutation be implemented before or after the crossover operator? Explain and justify your answer.

7. Compare the (expected or average) search complexity using the genetic approach with that of brute-force search, i.e., exhaustive enumeration and evaluation of the possible states of the problem state space. Note that for a chromosome of length N, there are 2^N possible states.

8. The reader should consider more aspects of the extended example of Section 17.3.6. Specifically, develop GA simulation software that includes the following adjustable simulation parameters:

POP_SIZE

CHROM_LENGTH

PCROSS (probability that crossover actually used for a pair of chromosomes impacts generation gap)

PMUT (for diversity)

MAX_GEN (generation limit)

STOP_CRIT (minimum relative change in **average** fitness to continue)

SPREAD ("spread" of $f(x)$)

By running many sample cases (to achieve statistical significance), determine and comment on:

(a) The relationship between POP_SIZE and CHROM_LENGTH;

(b) The effect of SPREAD;

(c) The effect of MUTATION; and

(d) The effect of PCROSS.

9. In the example of Section 17.3.3, "Roulette-wheel" selection is shown.

(a) The implementation of Roulette-wheel selection shown suffers when sum_fitness is small. In fact, it generates an exception when (int)sum_fitness=0. Why?

(b) A better solution is to normalize sum_fitness to 1.0 and use the following alternative:

```
/* select using the 'roulette wheel' method */

int roulette(void)
{
    int i;
    double r, sum;
    sum = 0;
    r = (double)rand()/(double)RAND_MAX;    /* \in [0,1) */
    for (i=0; (i < SIZE)&&(sum <= r); i++)
        sum += portion[i];
    return (--i);          /* return selected number */
}
```

Verify the validity of this approach using the following values of the wheel "wedges":

```
portion[0]=0.20;
portion[1]=0.10;
portion[2]=0.10;
portion[3]=0.05;
portion[4]=0.05;
portion[5]=0.20;
portion[6]=0.05;
portion[7]=0.05;
portion[8]=0.10;
portion[9]=0.10;
```

by computing a histogram of the indices selected and using 10,000 selections.

10. In the TSP example of Section 17.4.3, using path representation, alternative crossover operators are shown. Use *partially mapped crossover* in each case that follows with the given path representation. For each case, determine the children and verify that they are valid tours.

(a) Consider the previous tours (strings): 13245 and 24135. Assume the two randomly chosen crossover points are after the first and third elements of the strings.

(b) Consider the previous tours (strings): 21543 and 12435. The two randomly chosen crossover points are after the first and third elements of the strings.

(c) Consider the previous tours (strings): 21345 and 12435. The two randomly chosen crossover points are before the first and after the second elements of the strings.

11. Convert the path representation of tour 32415 into the *adjacency representation* of the tour.

12. Convert the adjacency representation of tour 32415 into the path representation of the tour.

13. Here are two TSP tour representation matrices using Tour Representation Strategy #2 from Section 17.4.3:

$$M_1 = \begin{pmatrix} 0 & 1 & 0 & 0 \\ 0 & 0 & 1 & 0 \\ 0 & 0 & 0 & 1 \\ 1 & 0 & 0 & 0 \end{pmatrix} \qquad M_2 = \begin{pmatrix} 0 & 0 & 0 & 1 \\ 1 & 0 & 0 & 0 \\ 0 & 1 & 0 & 0 \\ 0 & 0 & 1 & 0 \end{pmatrix}$$

(a) Verify each is a vaild tour and show the tour.

(b) Suppose a "matrix crossover" operator is developed by analogy with that used for strings. Here we crossover matrix columns. Choosing a crossover point between the second and third columns of each of these matrices, show the resulting matrix children.

(c) Do both of these children correspond to valid tours?

14. (a) If subsequent (other than initial) populations in a genetic solution are determined ONLY by mutation, does the GA simply implement a random search?

(b) Extend the case shown such that the only genetic operator used is mutation.

15. Using the strategy in Tour Representation Strategy #2 from Section 17.4.3, it was noted that not all matrices with a single 1 in each row correspond to valid tours. Does the following matrix correspond to a valid tour?

$$\begin{pmatrix} 0 & 1 & 0 & 0 \\ 1 & 0 & 0 & 0 \\ 0 & 0 & 0 & 1 \\ 0 & 0 & 1 & 0 \end{pmatrix}$$

Fundamentals of Discrete Mathematics

This appendix reviews a number of topics from discrete mathematics that are relevant to IS study.

A.1 Sets

A.1.1 Basic Concepts

Sets provide a rich and powerful framework in which to study many aspects of IS. The following summary is adequate for our purposes:

- A *set* is a collection of objects or *elements*, which are members of the set.

- The *empty set* is a set with nothing in it. It may be denoted $\{\}$ or $\emptyset$.

- Membership of an element, a, of a set, A, is denoted $a \in A$.

- Two sets are *equal* if they contain exactly the same elements. For two sets, A and B, this is denoted $A = B$.

- Two sets, A and B, are *disjoint* if they have no elements in common.

- A is a *subset* of B if every element in A is also in B. This is denoted[1] $A \subset B$. If $A = B$, then $A \subset B$ and $B \subset A$. A set with n elements has 2^n subsets.

- The *cardinal number* or cardinality of a finite set is a nonnegative integer representing the number of elements in the set. This is denoted $|A|$.

- If $A \subset B$ and $A \neq B$, A is a *proper subset* of B.

- The set of all subsets of A, denoted $P(A)$, is the *power set* of A.

- The complement, $\bar{A}$, of a set A is the set of all elements (of a special set, S, the *space or universe*) that are not elements of $\bar{A}$.

---

[1]Some books use the notation $\subseteq$ to denote general subsets and reserve the notation $\subset$ for proper subsets.

A.1.2 Operations on Sets

Intersection.   Intersection is denoted using $\cap$ and defined as follows:

$$A \cap B = \{x | (x \in A) \cap (x \in B)\} \tag{A.1}$$

Union.   Union is denoted using $\cup$ and defined as follows:

$$A \cup B = \{x | (x \in A) \cup (x \in B)\} \tag{A.2}$$

Intersection and union are commutative and associative, and, by recursive use of the definitions, may be defined for more than two sets.

Two sets, A and B, are *mutually exclusive* or *disjoint* if $A \cap B = \emptyset$.

Cartesian Product.   The Cartesian (or direct) product of sets A and B is denoted using $\times$ and is defined as follows:

$$A \times B = \{(a, b) | a \in A \text{ and } b \in B\} \tag{A.3}$$

Our representational framework for constraint satisfaction problems in Chapter 4 makes use of this concept.

Partitions.   A *partition*, P, of a set A, is a collection of mutually exclusive subsets, A_i, which satisfy:

$$A_i \cap A_j = \emptyset \qquad \text{unless } i = j \tag{A.4}$$

and

$$\bigcup_i A_i = A \tag{A.5}$$

Partitions of sets are an extremely useful concept in clustering and grammatical inference.

A.2 Relations

Relations are based upon the notion of set mappings.

If A and B are sets, a *relation* from A to B is a subset of $A \times B$.

Here $A \times B$ denotes the Cartesian product of the sets A and B. Given a set

$$A = \{a, b, c, d, \dots\} \tag{A.6}$$

and

$$B = \{x, y, z, \dots\} \tag{A.7}$$

a relation from A to B, namely R, satisfies $R \subset A \times B$.

This definition is mathematically precise, somewhat esoteric, and defines a *binary relation* since it only involves two sets, and provides a way of "connecting" or relating members of the sets. Specifically, how the sets are connected, and the properties of this connection, or relation, are of interest.

For example, consider the ordered pair of numbers, (x, y). The set of all possible values of x is the *domain* and the set of all possible y values is the *range*. This relation may be enumerated as a set of ordered pairs, for example, relation $R1$ may be defined as:

$$R1 = \{(1, 2), (2, 3), (3, 4), (4, 5)\} \tag{A.8}$$

A.2.1 Properties

The inherent directionality or ordering of relations gives rise to a number of relation properties. We consider three properties of prime importance for a relation R, which form a mapping from sets A to B.

1. *Reflexive*: R is reflexive if, $\forall a \in A, (a, a) \in R$.

2. *Symmetric*: R is symmetric if, $\forall (a, b) \in R, (b, a) \in R$.

3. *Transitive*: R is transitive if, $\forall (a, b) \in R$ and $(b, c) \in R, (a, c) \in R$.

Definition: Equivalence Relation

◆ *A relation that satisfies all three properties (i.e., it is reflexive, symmetric, and transitive) is termed an equivalence relation.*

A.2.2 Relations As Functions

Most scientists and engineers are familiar with a subset of relations called *functions*. Functions are not restricted to numerical quantities. A *function* from A to B is a relation (denoted by the symbol f) such that for every $a \in A, \exists$ one and only one $b \in B s.t. (a, b) \in f$. Usually we show this relation as:

$$f : A \Rightarrow B \tag{A.9}$$

where A is the domain of function f and B is the range. For a particular member of f, i.e., $(a, b) \in f$, we say that b is the *value* of f at a, in other words,

$$b = f(a). \tag{A.10}$$

Another way to view a *function* is a special relation in which each $a_i \in A$ belongs to only one ordered pair in the relation. Thus, given one element of R, i.e., (a_i, b_i) no other element of the form (a_i, c_i) belongs to R unless $b_i = c_i$. This is written as $b_i = f(a_i)$ to denote the function mapping.

Notice the previous definition allows f to contain pairs (a_i, b_i) and (d_i, b_i). If this occurs, the function is not $1 - 1$, and

$$f(a_i) = f(d_i) \xrightarrow{not} a_i = d_i \tag{A.11}$$

A.3 Graphs

A *graph*, G, is an ordered pair

$$G = \{N, R\} \tag{A.12}$$

where N is a set of nodes (or vertices) and R is a subset of $N \times N$, or ordered pairs of nodes. Elements of R represent arcs (or edges) that connect nodes in G. N is denoted the *node set*, and R is denoted the *edge set*.

A.3.1 Subgraphs

A *subgraph* of G is itself a graph, $G_s = \{N_s, R_s\}$ where $N_s \subset N$ and R_s consists of arcs in R that connect only nodes in N_s. A less formal definition is that a G_s is a graph that has some of the nodes and some of the arcs of G.

A.3.2 Directed Graphs (Digraphs)

Often, there is significance attached to the direction of an arc, in the sense that an arc emanates *from* a node and is incident upon another node. Therefore, $(a, b) \in R$ means there is an arc *from* node a *to* node b. This directional significance is characterized a *digraph*. It is *not the case* that $(a, b) \in R$ implies $(b, a) \in R$ in a digraph. When the direction of edges in a graph is not important, i.e., specification of either (a, b) or $(b, a) \in R$ is acceptable, an *undirected graph* results.

A.3.3 Directed Graphs and Intraset Relations

A relationship may be represented graphically by using an arrow to show each element of R. In this way, the "connection" between members of the sets is displayed graphically. When $R \subseteq AXA$, a *directed graph* or *digraph* is a convenient tool to represent the relationship between elements of a set.

Suppose

$$A = \{a, b, c, d\} \tag{A.13}$$

Then

$$A \times A = \{((a, a), (a, b), (a, c), (a, d), (b, a), (b, b), \dots\} \tag{A.14}$$

If we assume, for example, that a relation R is defined as:

$$R = \{(a, b), (b, c), (b, d), (b, a), ((c, c), (d, a)\} \tag{A.15}$$

then we may graphically represent R where *the elements of A are nodes in the graph and the elemental relationships are indicated by arrows from the element in the domain to the corresponding element in the range.* Often we refer to these arrows as *edges*. The use of arrows in the digraph reinforces the notion of a direction to the relation.

Digraphs and "Degree". In the digraph representation of a relation, R, recall a node exists for every $a \in A$ where $(a, b) \in R$. Furthermore, a (directed) arc from node a to node b appears in the digraph. The number of b such that $(a, b) \in R$, or the number of arcs *emanating from node a* in the digraph representation is called the *out-degree of node a*. Similarly, the number of arcs in the digraph *terminating at node b* is the *in-degree* of node a.

A.3.4 Trees

A tree is a data structure that is a finite acyclic (containing no closed loops or paths or cycles) digraph. One node, called the root, has in-degree = 0, and every other node has out-degree ≥ 1, except leaf nodes that have out-degree = 0. There exists exactly one path between any two (distinct) nodes. The set of leaf nodes is often referred to as the *frontier* of the tree. An *n-ary* tree is one where each vertex (or node) has out-degree n or less. A common instance of this is the 2-ary or binary tree, where every node has either 0 or 2 descendants.

Fundamentals of Prolog

This appendix presents a summary and overview of the declarative programming paradigm and the Prolog language. SWI Prolog is used. Prolog pragmatics and references are included in Section B.7.

B.1 Introduction

Two points are fundamental and are intended to help with the Prolog introduction:

1. Prolog is a useful language when the solution to a problem involves satisfaction of a number of constraints relating problem variables. This includes the development of parsers for recognition (and generation) of constrained structural representations.

2. In Prolog, the developer does not concentrate on the specification of program execution sequence, but rather attempts to specify the problem (or situation) through development of a database consisting of clauses. Typically, clauses represent problem constraints. It is left for the built-in Prolog unification mechanism to determine the solution(s), if any exist.

B.2 Predicates, Clauses, Facts, Rules, and Goals

Predicate. A predicate consists of a name and an optional set of arguments. The number of arguments is the *arity* of the predicate.

Clause. The basic statement in Prolog is the clause. A Prolog program is a set of Prolog clauses. Clauses are either rules or facts. Clauses are built using predicates and logical connectives. Often clauses contain (shared) variables that are assumed universally quantified.

- A Prolog clause is comprised of a head and an (optional) body or tail.

- If the body is empty, the clause is a fact, which is interpreted to be true.

- The period (.) ends the clause.

Facts.   As noted, a fact is a clause with an empty tail. In practice, facts have the typical form:

```
predicate_name(term1, term2,...,termn).
```

where the period (`.`) terminates the clause. The following is an example of a database of Prolog facts:

```
is_fact (arg1, arg2).
a_fact_too (Y).
equal (X, X).
another_fact.
wheel_is_round.
round (wheel).
wheel (round).
```

Rules.   A rule is a clause with a head and a nonempty tail. Rules have the typical form (logical representation):

```
predicate_name1(term1, term2,...) :-
              predicate_name2(term1, term2,...),
                        ...
              predicate_nameR(termR, termR,...).
```

The entity `term1` above may be a constant, a variable (capitalized in Prolog syntax), a list, or a functor. A simple example of an easy-to-read Prolog rule containing shared variable `X` is:

```
has_part(X, door) :- is_house (X).
```

Conjunction and Disjunction.   The use of the comma (`,`) in Prolog to separate clauses indicates that the conjunction of these clauses (subgoals) must be satisfied, e.g.,

```
a,b
```

forces both subgoals **a** and **b** to succeed. Prolog systems also provide the disjunction (OR) connective (denoted by ";"). This logical connective allows the disjunction of two predicates in the form

```
a;b
```

This allows alternatives to be specified directly.

B.2.1   Variables

All variables in Prolog begin with a capital (uppercase) letter.

B.2.2   Goals

A Prolog program is incomplete without specification of a goal. A goal, entered at the interpreter prompt (?- in what follows), is a Prolog clause that may be comprised of subgoals, logical connectives, and contain variables. The Prolog system attempts to unify this goal with the database.

B.2.3 Examples

A Simplistic "House" Representation

Suppose the objective were to represent the following:

If an entity is a house, then it has a door. My house is a house.

The following Prolog database accomplishes this.

```
/* simple Prolog representation */
/* file: house.pro  */

has_part(X,door) :- is_house(X).
is_house(my_house).
```

Sample use of this database with a goal is shown here:

```
?- ['house.pro'].
% house.pro compiled 0.00 sec, 0 bytes

Yes
?- has_part(What,door).

What = my_house

Yes
?- has_part(What,fence).

No
?- has_part(What,Item).

What = my_house
Item = door

Yes
```

A More Complex Example

The following Prolog example shows a database comprised of two rules and six facts. We use it to show the Prolog unification process in Section B.2.5.

```
/* smpl-unify1.pro */

goal1(X,Y) :- first(X), second(Y).

goal2(X) :- first(X), second(X).

first(1).
first(2).
first(3).
second(2).
second(4).
second(6).
```

B.2.4 The Anonymous Variable

The anonymous variable is used to represent universal quantification; (when any instantiation of the variable will suffice). It is not necessary to give this variable a name, instead the underbar or "_" is used.

B.2.5 Prolog Uses Term Unification

Prolog will attempt to unify a given goal with the current database. Rules for unification are:

1. Clauses are tested in the order in which they appear in a program (the database).

2. When a subgoal matches the left side (head) of a rule, the right side (tail) becomes a new set of subgoals to unify. The tail of a rule may contain the conjunction or disjunction of a number of predicates. Each of these predicates may, in turn, be the head of one or more rules in the database. It is at this stage that the complexity Prolog solution search becomes an issue.

3. The unifier proceeds from left to right in attempting to satisfy (unify) the predicates in the tail of a rule. Each of these predicates represents a subgoal. When a subgoal is spawned, the unification/search process described in Rule 1 repeats. This represents a depth-first search strategy.

4. A goal is satisfied when a matching fact (a grounded predicate) is found in the database for all the leaves of the goal tree.

5. When two or more clauses in the database with the same predicate name are identified as possible matches, the first clause in the database is chosen (first) for attempted unification. The second (and third, etc.) are marked as points for possible backtracking, and are investigated subsequently if a previous choice fails to unify.

This is shown in the following trace of some goals using the Prolog database of Section B.2.3.

```
?- ['smpl-unify1.pro'].
% smpl-unify1.pro compiled 0.00 sec, 112 bytes

Yes
?- trace(goal1).
%          goal1/2: [call, redo, exit, fail]
```

```
Yes
[debug]  ?- trace(goal2).
%          goal2/1: [call, redo, exit, fail]

Yes
[debug]  ?- trace(first).
%          first/1: [call, redo, exit, fail]

Yes
[debug]  ?- trace(second).
%          second/1: [call, redo, exit, fail]

Yes
[debug]  ?- goal1(A,B).
 T Call: (7) goal1(_G283, _G284)
 T Call: (8) first(_G283)
 T Exit: (8) first(1)
 T Call: (8) second(_G284)
 T Exit: (8) second(2)
 T Exit: (7) goal1(1, 2)

A = 1
B = 2 ;
 T Redo: (8) second(_G284)
 T Exit: (8) second(4)
 T Exit: (7) goal1(1, 4)

A = 1
B = 4 ;
 T Redo: (8) second(_G284)
 T Exit: (8) second(6)
 T Exit: (7) goal1(1, 6)

A = 1
B = 6 ;
 T Redo: (8) first(_G283)
 T Exit: (8) first(2)
 T Call: (8) second(_G284)
 T Exit: (8) second(2)
 T Exit: (7) goal1(2, 2)

A = 2
B = 2 ;
 T Redo: (8) second(_G284)
 T Exit: (8) second(4)
 T Exit: (7) goal1(2, 4)

A = 2
B = 4 ;
 T Redo: (8) second(_G284)
 T Exit: (8) second(6)
 T Exit: (7) goal1(2, 6)

A = 2
```

```
 B = 6 ;
 T Redo: (8) first(_G283)
 T Exit: (8) first(3)
 T Call: (8) second(_G284)
 T Exit: (8) second(2)
 T Exit: (7) goal1(3, 2)

A = 3
B = 2 ;
 T Redo: (8) second(_G284)
 T Exit: (8) second(4)
 T Exit: (7) goal1(3, 4)

A = 3
B = 4 ;
 T Redo: (8) second(_G284)
 T Exit: (8) second(6)
 T Exit: (7) goal1(3, 6)

A = 3
B = 6 ;

No
```

B.2.6 Prolog "help" Notation

In predicate descriptions obtained via SWI `help(<pred-name>)` or in the SWI manual, predicates are shown along with the corresponding arity. For example, in describing (built-in) predicate `member`, the notation `member/2` is used to indicate the arity of the `member` predicate (number of arguments) is 2. Furthermore, `help(member)` indicates the type of arguments to `member`, e.g.,

```
member(?Elem, ?List)
```

followed by a description. In this commonly-used notation,

- ◆ `+Argument` means input (i.e., the argument is bound before invoking the predicate);

- ◆ `-Argument` means output (i.e., the argument is bound to a value, if possible, in the process of finding a solution); and

- ◆ `?Argument` means either (works both ways).

B.2.7 Recursion in Prolog

Recursion is often used in Prolog, and manifests itself as a goal that (perhaps indirectly, i.e., through other clauses) invokes itself. Two simple examples are shown here.

```
/* symmetry */
adjacent-to(R1,R2) :- adjacent-to(R2,R1).

/* transitivity */
related(R1,R3) :- related(R1,R2), related(R2,R3).
```

Prolog, while relentless in its search for a solution, is not able to detect problems with recursion. Especially significant is *infinite recursion*.

B.2.8 Variable Bindings and `is`

Typically, variables get bindings in Prolog via the unification process, however there are exceptions, especially when arithmetic is involved. Prolog provides the infix operator `is` for these cases. The prototypical use of `is` in Prolog is to *force assignment of an expression to a variable*.

B.2.9 Prolog and Arithmetic

Although Prolog is not designed as a "number crunching" language, arithmetic capability is provided. However, the availability of arithmetic operators varies among implementations. Arithmetic involves both predicates that implement floating point and integer arithmetic, as appropriate. As noted, one very noteworthy aspect of arithmetic in Prolog is that *infix notation is used (allowed)* for a number of arithmetic operators. This greatly improves the readability of the Prolog code that concerns arithmetic. Furthermore, for obvious reasons, arithmetic is not done by unification. In most implementations, general arithmetic predicates are compiled.

B.2.10 Predicates to Verify the Type of a Term

Prolog provides a number of predicates for this purpose, including:

`var(+Term)`

that succeeds if `Term` currently is a free (unbound) variable. Similarly,

`nonvar(+Term)`

succeeds if `Term` is currently not a free variable.

B.3 Lists in Prolog

B.3.1 List Representation

Lists are a ubiquitous data structure that are quite useful in many IS representations.

♦ Lists in Prolog consist of elements separated by commas and enclosed in brackets [], i.e.,

```
[a, b, c, d]
```

is a four-element list of the elements `a` thru `d`.

♦ Lists may be used as arguments to predicates. A list is a single argument to a predicate, *regardless of the length of the list.*

♦ Lists may be comprised of variables, constants, and other lists.

Elementary list manipulation is provided somewhat implicitly.[1] The head (X) and tail (Y) of a list are denoted in Prolog statements as:

```
[X | Y]
```

The head is the first element; the tail is the list with the head removed. The empty list is a list without any elements and denoted [ ].

B.3.2 A List Example

```
exactly_one(L,[R1,R2,R3,R4,R5,R6]):-
                  at_least_one(L,[R1,R2,R3,R4,R5,R6]),
                  at_most_one(L,[R1,R2,R3,R4,R5,R6]).
```

B.3.3 Prolog List Membership via Predicate "member"

Definition

This definition provides an example of list use, recursion, and the anonymous variable.

```
member(A, [A|_]).      /* succeeds if A is first element */
member(A, [_|C]) :-
      member(A, C). /* otherwise recurse through list */
```

Member Description (Help)

For help, use ?- help(Topic). or ?- apropos(Word).

```
?- help(member).
member(?Elem, ?List)
    Succeeds  when Elem can be unified with one of the members of List.
    The predicate can be used with any instantiation pattern.
```

B.4 Prolog Databases

B.4.1 Prolog Dynamic Databases

In Prolog, a database predicate may be either dynamic or static. All built-in Prolog predicates are considered static. The previous examples presume static clauses in the Prolog database; these predicates cannot be modified (e.g., redefined) at runtime. Attempting to do so will generate an error. A user-defined predicate is considered static by default unless a **dynamic** directive precedes its definition or it is added to the database[2] using **assert**. Dynamic predicates may be altered.

B.4.2 assert and retract

To dynamically alter the Prolog database, we use dynamic predicates and the built-in predicates **assert** and **retract**.

---

[1]vis-a-vis other languages such as Lisp.
[2]In which case it may not previously exist as a static predicate.

B.5 Backtracking and the cut (!)

The cut (!) is used as a predicate (with a somewhat strange notation) that always succeeds, but with a significant side effect: *all backtracking points (if they exist) up to the cut are erased.* Thus the cut, in a sense, forces commitment to a solution found prior to the occurrence of the cut.

B.5.1 The Concept of Negation as Failure

Prolog provides the **not** predicate, which must be used with care.

The **not** predicate, as would logically be expected, succeeds if unification of its argument fails. Thus, whatever is omitted from the database is treated as logically false. This is known as *negation-as-failure.*

Prolog Notation Compared with Logic. This is shown in Table B.1. *Note $p \rightarrow q$ corresponds to* q :- p.

connective	logical symbol	Prolog syntax
conjunction (and)	$\cap$	,
disjunction (or)	$\cup$	;
implication	$\rightarrow$	:-
negation (not)	$\neg$	not()

Table B.1 Relating Logical Connectives to Prolog Syntax

B.5.2 Logic in Prolog

The logical clause:

$$\{p_1 \cap p_2 \cap p_3\} \rightarrow q$$

may be formulated in Prolog as:

q :- p1,p2,p3.

B.5.3 Prolog and Modus Ponens (MP)

From logic, the pair of statements

    p -> q
    p

is equivalent to the Prolog database

    q:-p.
    p.

B.6 Parsing (Grammatical/Structural Recognition) and Prolog

B.6.1 Using Grammar Rule Notation (the LGN)

Most Prolog implementations contain a built-in feature allowing the direct construction of parsers by entering productions directly using *grammar rule notation*, also known as the LGN (Logic Grammar Notation). It is built around translation of the functor `-->`, which is declared to be an infix operator. The Prolog *preprocessor* converts the LGN to more traditional Prolog clauses.

Assume that the strings to be parsed are represented in Prolog as lists, i.e.,

$$x = aabac$$

is represented as:

```
[a, a, b, a, c]
```

First, consider a simple example. Suppose we had a very minimal set of productions:

$$S \rightarrow AB$$
$$A \rightarrow terma$$
$$B \rightarrow termb$$

where $S, A, B \in V_N$ and $terma, termb \in V_T$. This could be entered *directly* in Prolog LGN as:

```
s --> a, b.
a --> [terma].
b --> [termb].
```

Notice in Prolog the *predicates* are s, a, and b. Consider the following translation and application in Prolog:

```
?- listing(s).

s(A, B) :-
        a(A, C),
        b(C, B).

Yes
```

Notice that Prolog has done all the work in converting the notation to actual predicates. What is even more important is that Prolog has built a parser for us. The LGN-generated clause resulting from the translation of production `s --> a, b.` is:

```
s(A, B) :-
        a(A, C),
        b(C, B).
```

This Prolog clause may be interpreted as implementing the goal:

A is an s with B leftover if A is an a, with C leftover and C is a b with B leftover.

Also notice the following:

1. Shared variables (C in the previous example) in the tail of the goal are used to hold the "leftover" string (list);

2. All predicates in the consumption-based parser are of the form:

```
pred-name(<in-list>, <not-used>)
```

where `<in-list>` is the input string and `<not-used>` is the remainder of the input string after a parse for a substring of `<pred-name>`.

3. Typically B is the empty list; this constrains the parser to use all of the input string (list).

B.6.2 A Significant LGN Utility: Automatic Parsers

By now we know that Prolog, through the LGN, will very easily and directly translate a grammar production of the form:

$$Sentence \rightarrow Nounphrase\ Verbphrase$$

expressed in Prolog as:

```
sentence --> nounphrase, verbphrase.
```

Prolog will automatically convert this into:

```
sentence(A, B) :-
      nounphrase(A, C),
      verbphrase(C, B).
```

where two arguments are automatically added (by Prolog, in the translation) to each predicate. In our *"consumption-based"* parser this means:

List (or string) A is a sentence (with list (or string) B "left over") if list (or string) A contains a noun phrase, with list (or string) C "left over," and list (or string) C contains a verb phrase, with list (or string) B "left over."

B.6.3 Adding Variables in the LGN

Suppose we need to add another variable to the preceding automatically translated LGN rule, e.g., what we really want after LGN translation is:

```
sentence(N, A, B) :-
      nounphrase(N, A, C),
      verbphrase(N, C, B).
```

Here is how we do it in Prolog's LGN:

```
sentence(N) --> nounphrase(N), verbphrase(N).
```

which translates[3] into:

```
sentence(A, B, C) :-
      nounphrase(A, B, D),
      verbphrase(A, D, C).
```

---

[3]The reader should verify this.

B.7   Prolog References and Pragmatics

B.7.1   Books

The classic reference to the Prolog language is [CM03]. This was the first textbook on programming in Prolog and is still a definitive introduction to both the language and the representational methodology. The ISO Prolog standard and programming practice is described in [DC96]. There are numerous books devoted solely to the application of Prolog to IS problems. One of the best known is [Bra00].

B.7.2   Web References

A useful starting web reference is the SWI Prolog home page: www.swi-prolog.org. Here you will find SWI Prolog distributions in various forms, including a self-extracting executable for Windows and an rpm for linux, as well as a User's Guide (pdf). You will also find various additional tools (IDEs, editors, etc.) and Prolog links.

Alternatives to SWI-Prolog include the GNU Prolog compiler (`gprolog`), available at http://www.gnu.org/software/prolog/.

Fundamentals of Linear Algebra

This appendix reviews a number of topics from linear algebra and geometry that will prove useful in IS study. Of particular importance is the developing, training, visualizing, and analyzing of artificial neural networks (ANNs).

C.1 Elementary Matrices

The simplest characterization of an $n \times m$ dimensional matrix, A, is a rectangular arrangement of nm entities (real or complex) in an array of n rows, each with m elements, or m columns, each with n elements. This is denoted

$$A = [a_{ij}] \qquad i = 1, 2, \ldots, n \qquad j = 1, 2, \ldots, m \qquad \text{(C.1)}$$

where a_{ij} is the ijth element, residing at the intersection of the ith row and the jth column. The following are special cases:

1. If $m = n$ the matrix is square.

2. If $m = 1$, the matrix is a column vector, whereas if $n = 1$ the matrix is a row vector.[1] Vectors are denoted with an underbar, i.e. $\underline{x}$ is a vector. Often we are also careful to indicate the length of the vector, which is also the dimension of the vector space within which the vector resides.

3. If $m = n = 1$, the matrix is a scalar.

4. The transpose of matrix A, denoted A^T, is obtained by interchanging rows and columns, i.e.,

$$A^T = [a_{ji}] \qquad j = 1, 2, \ldots, m \qquad i = 1, 2, \ldots, n \qquad \text{(C.2)}$$

5. If $A = A^T$ (or $a_{ij} = a_{ji}$) the matrix is *symmetric*. A must be square to be symmetric.

---

[1] Throughout we will consider vectors, by default, to be column vectors, thus, a row vector $\underline{x}$ is denoted $\underline{x}^T$.

6. It is often convenient to *partition* a matrix, for both visualization and computation. For example, the $n \times m$ matrix, A, may be partitioned as

$$
A = \begin{pmatrix}
\overset{p \times q}{A_1} & \overset{p \times (m-q)}{A_2} \\[2mm]
\underset{A_3}{(n-p) \times q} & \underset{A_4}{(n-p) \times (m-q)}
\end{pmatrix}
\tag{C.3}
$$

where A_1 is $p \times q$, A_2 is $p \times (m-q)$, A_3 is $(n-p) \times q$, and A_4 is $(n-p) \times (m-q)$, and $p \geq 1$ and $q \geq 1$.

7. The most important partitioning of a matrix is into an array of *column vectors*. This is denoted

$$
A = [\underline{a}_1, \underline{a}_2, \dots, \underline{a}_m]
\tag{C.4}
$$

where $\underline{a}_i$ $i = 1, 2, \dots, m$ is an $n \times 1$ dimensional column vector. Columns of a matrix are easily accessed in MATLAB using "colon" notation. For example, `a(:,3)` denotes the third column of a matrix `a`.

Elementary matrix operations include addition, subtraction, multiplication, and scaling. For example, for computer implementation the matrix product $\overset{m \times p}{C} = \overset{m \times n}{A}\,\overset{n \times p}{B}$ is formed via

$$
C = [c_{ij}] \qquad i = 1, 2, \dots, m \qquad j = 1, 2, \dots, p
\tag{C.5}
$$

where

$$
c_{ij} = \sum_{k=1}^{n} a_{ik} b_{kj}
\tag{C.6}
$$

Matrix dimensions must be *conformable* for the specific operation. For example, an $n \times m$ matrix postmultiplied by an $m \times p$ matrix is conformable under multiplication and yields an $n \times p$ product. This serves as a simplistic check on the validity of derivations using matrices and vectors.

C.2 Vectors

For positive integer, d, let R^d be the set of all ordered n-tuples of the form:

$$
\{x_1, x_2, \dots, x_d\}
\tag{C.7}
$$

These could be viewed as the coordinates of a point, x, in d-dimensional space. Of course, the coordinate system must be specified for this interpretation to be meaningful. The x_i coordinates may be arranged in a vector, yielding

$$
\underline{x} = \begin{pmatrix} x_1 \\ x_2 \\ \vdots \\ x_d \end{pmatrix}
\tag{C.8}
$$

C.3 Linearity

A mapping, $\underline{f}(\underline{x})$, is linear[2] if superposition holds, i.e.,

$$\underline{x} = \alpha \underline{x}_1 + \beta \underline{x}_2 \Rightarrow \underline{f}(\underline{x}) = \alpha \underline{f}(\underline{x}_1) + \beta \underline{f}(\underline{x}_2) \tag{C.9}$$

Vector-Matrix Equations. There are several interpretations of the vector-matrix equation[3]:

$$\overset{n \times d}{A} \overset{d \times 1}{\underline{x}} = \overset{n \times 1}{\underline{y}} \tag{C.10}$$

Each may be viewed somewhat abstractly. Notice we have not stated any relationship between n and d. Three cases are possible:

$$n = d \tag{C.11}$$

$$n < d \tag{C.12}$$

$$n > d \tag{C.13}$$

One visualization of Equation (C.10) is the use of A to map vectors from R^d into R^n, as shown in Figure C.1.

However, Equation (C.10) has a particularly important connotation when combined with Equation (C.4) and Equation (C.8), yielding:

$$\underline{y} = \sum_{k=1}^{d} \underline{a}_i x_i \tag{C.14}$$

$\underline{y}$ is formed as a linear combination of the columns of A. The set of all linear combinations (i.e., using any $\underline{x}$) of the columns if A is the *range of A*, denoted $R(A)$. Clearly, in matrix equations of the form

$$A\underline{x} = \underline{y} \tag{C.15}$$

if $\underline{y} \notin R(A)$, finding an $\underline{x}$ that *exactly* satisfies Equation (C.15) is futile.

Figure C.1 Matrices as Vector-Space Mappings

---

[2]Sometimes referred to as *linear in the input-output sense* to distinguish it from other connotations of linearity.
[3]which is written in MATLAB simply as **y=A*x**

Another viewpoint of Equation (C.10) when $n = d$ is that of change of coordinate system (or basis vectors). $\underline{x}$ is the representation of a point in R^d with respect to the original coordinate system, $\underline{y}$ is the representation with respect to a new coordinate system, and A relates the original and new systems.

Matrix Rank.   Equation (C.4) facilitates a discussion of the property of matrix rank. Viewing A in "column form" Equation (C.4), the rank of A is a number, denoted rank(A), which is defined as the number of linearly independent columns of $\overset{n \times d}{A}$ and $n \geq d$, this number is at most d. A square matrix with full rank (i.e., rank(A) $= n = d$) is invertible, and its columns provide a basis set for $R^n = R^d$. Any vector in $R^n = R^d$ may be represented as a linear combination of a basis set.

C.4   Inner and Outer Products and Applications

Inner Product.   If $\underline{x}$ and $\underline{y}$ are real $d \times 1$ vectors, their vector inner product is denoted using braces ($<>$) and defined to be the scalar given by $< \underline{x}, \underline{y} >= (\underline{x})^T \underline{y} = \underline{y}^T \underline{x}$. The inner product, since it is a scalar, is symmetric. Geometrically, $< \underline{x}, \underline{y} >$ is visualized as the projection of $\underline{y}$ onto $\underline{x}$ (or vice versa). The inner product provides a measure of closeness[4] of two vectors.

Outer Products.   The outer product of $\underline{x}$ and $\underline{y}$, denoted $> \underline{x}, \underline{y} <$, is the rank 1 matrix $\underline{x} \, \underline{y}^T$. In contrast with the inner product, $\underline{x}$ and $\underline{y}$ may have unequal dimensions. Thus,

$$> \overset{n \times 1}{\underline{x}}, \overset{m \times 1}{\underline{y}} <= \underline{x}\underline{y}^T = \overset{n \times m}{P} \tag{C.16}$$

and P is generally nonsquare. Expanding Equation (C.16), where $\underline{x} = (x_1, x_2, \ldots, x_n)^T$ and $\underline{y} = (y_1, y_2, \ldots, y_m)^T$ yields

$$\underline{x}\underline{y}^T = P = \begin{pmatrix} x_1 y_1 & x_1 y_2 & \cdots & x_1 y_m \\ x_2 y_1 & x_2 y_2 & & x_2 y_m \\ \vdots & \vdots & & \vdots \\ x_n y_1 & x_n y_2 & & x_n y_m \end{pmatrix} \tag{C.17}$$

When square, the outer product matrix, P, is not necessarily symmetric.

---

[4]This must be further qualified, e.g., relative vector lengths must be considered before we use it as a measure of match.

C.5 Measures of Similarity in Vector Space

Distance is one measure of vector similarity. The Euclidean distance between vectors $\underline{x}$ and $\underline{y}$ is given by

$$d(\underline{x}, \underline{y}) = \| \underline{x} - \underline{y} \| = \sqrt{(\underline{x} - \underline{y})^T (\underline{x} - \underline{y})} \qquad (C.18)$$

$$= +\sqrt{\sum_{i=1}^{d} (x_i - y_i)^2} \qquad (C.19)$$

A related and more general metric is

$$d_p(\underline{x}, \underline{y}) = \left(\sum_{i=1}^{d} |x_i - y_i|^p \right)^{\frac{1}{p}} \qquad (C.20)$$

Equation (C.20) reduces to Equation (C.19) for $p = 2$.

Often, weighted distance measures are used. An example is

$$d_w^2(\underline{x}, \underline{y}) = (\underline{x} - \underline{y})^T R(\underline{x} - \underline{y}) = \| \underline{x} - \underline{y} \|_R^2 \qquad (C.21)$$

Equation (C.21) implements upon a *weighted inner product* or weighted R-norm. The matrix R is often required to be positive definite and symmetric. In this case, R may be factored. Equation (C.21) represents the transformation of a vector space, i.e., the linear transformations

$$\tilde{\underline{x}} = T\underline{x} \qquad (C.22)$$

$$\tilde{\underline{y}} = T\underline{y} \qquad (C.23)$$

yield

$$d^2(\tilde{\underline{x}}, \tilde{\underline{y}}) = (T\underline{x} - T\underline{y})^T (T\underline{x} - T\underline{y}) \qquad (C.24)$$

$$= (\underline{x} - \underline{y})^T T^T T(\underline{x} - \underline{y}) \qquad (C.25)$$

$$= d_w^2(\underline{x}, \underline{y}) \qquad (C.26)$$

When $\underline{x}$ and $\underline{y}$ are binary, measures such as Hamming distance are useful.

C.6 Differentiation of Matrices and Vectors

Differentiation of a Scalar Function with Respect to a Vector.   Let $f(\underline{x})$ be a scalar-valued function of n variables x_i, written as an $n \times 1$ vector $\underline{x}$. The derivative of $f(\underline{x})$ with respect to $\underline{x}$ is an $n \times 1$ vector defined as

$$\frac{df(\underline{x})}{d\underline{x}} = \begin{pmatrix} \frac{\partial f(\underline{x})}{\partial x_1} \\ \frac{\partial f(\underline{x})}{\partial x_2} \\ \vdots \\ \frac{\partial f(\underline{x})}{\partial x_n} \end{pmatrix} \tag{C.27}$$

Equation (C.27) defines the gradient (vector) of f, denoted as $\nabla_x \underline{f}$ or $grad_x \underline{f}$, which is *the direction of maximum increase of function f.*

Differentiation of a Vector Function with Respect to a Vector.   The differentiation of a vector function, i.e., $\underline{f}(\underline{x})$ where $\underline{f}$ is $m \times 1$ and $\underline{x}$ is $n \times 1$ results in an $m \times n$ matrix of the form:

$$\frac{d\underline{f}(\underline{x})}{d\underline{x}} = \begin{pmatrix} \frac{\partial f_1}{\partial x_1} \cdots \frac{\partial f_1}{\partial x_n} \\ \ddots \\ \frac{\partial f_m}{\partial x_1} \cdots \frac{\partial f_m}{\partial x_n} \end{pmatrix} \tag{C.28}$$

where the ijth element of this matrix is $\frac{\partial f_i}{\partial x_j}$ and f_i is the ith element of $\underline{f}$ and x_j is the jth element of $\underline{x}$. This matrix is the Jacobian of $\underline{f}(\underline{x})$, denoted $J_{\underline{x}}$. The differentiation of a matrix with respect to a vector requires a three-dimensional representation and thus employs tensor notation.

Vector-Matrix Differentiation Formulae.   Examples of properties using the preceding definitions may be easily derived and are summarized here. For a matrix A and vectors $\underline{x}$ and $\underline{y}$

$$\frac{d}{d\underline{x}}(A\underline{x}) = A \tag{C.29}$$

$$\frac{d}{d\underline{x}}(\underline{y}^T A\underline{x}) = A^T \underline{y} \tag{C.30}$$

$$\frac{d}{d\underline{x}}(\underline{x}^T A\underline{x}) = (A + A^T)\underline{x} \tag{C.31}$$

C.7 The Chain Rule

To rigorously derive one of the feedforward network training algorithms, we need to consider the *chain rule* and composite (error) functions. Observe:

- A differentiable function of a differentiable function is itself differentiable.

- If $\varsigma = \phi(x, y \ldots)$, $\eta = \phi(x, y \ldots)$, ... are differentiable functions of $x, y, \ldots$, and $f(\varsigma, \eta, \ldots)$ is a differentiable function of $\varsigma, \eta, \ldots$, then $f(\phi(x, y \ldots), \psi(x, y, \ldots), \ldots)$ is a differentiable function of $x, y, \ldots$, [5] with partial derivatives given by

$$\frac{\partial f}{\partial x} = \frac{\partial f}{\partial \phi}\frac{\partial \phi}{\partial x} + \frac{\partial f}{\partial \psi}\frac{\partial \psi}{\partial x} + \ldots \tag{C.32}$$

$$\frac{\partial f}{\partial y} = \frac{\partial f}{\partial \phi}\frac{\partial \phi}{\partial y} + \frac{\partial f}{\partial \psi}\frac{\partial \psi}{\partial y} + \ldots \tag{C.33}$$

$$\vdots \tag{C.34}$$

This result is independent of the number of independent variables $x, y, \ldots$

C.8 Gradient Descent–Based Optimization Procedures

Gradient approaches are optimization procedures used extensively for training of certain classes of ANNs. It is important to become comfortable with the underlying concept.

Steepest (Ascent) Descent Procedures. Since $\nabla_{\underline{x}} f$ in Equation (C.27) defines the direction of maximum increase in the function, we may maximize (or minimize) a scalar function $f(\underline{x})$ by recursively calculating $\nabla_{\underline{x}} f$ and adjusting $\underline{x}$ until we reach a minimum (or maximum). This algorithm for minimization of a function, termed steepest descent, is:
- (a) Choose initial guess, $\underline{x}^0$
- (b) Compute $\nabla_{\underline{x}} f$, i.e.,

$$\frac{df(\underline{x}^0)}{d\underline{x}} \tag{C.35}$$

- (c) Adjust $\underline{x}^0$ to get $\underline{x}^1$ based upon moving in a direction *opposite* to the gradient, i.e.,

$$\underline{x}^1 = \underline{x}^0 - K\left[\frac{df(\underline{x}^0)}{d\underline{x}}\right] \tag{C.36}$$

- (d) Stop when $\underline{x}^{n+1} - \underline{x}^n$ is sufficiently small.

---

[5]Specification of the region, R, over which this holds is also necessary.

Linear Applications and Example.   Consider the equation:

$$A\underline{x} = \underline{y} \tag{C.37}$$

where A is an $n \times n$ matrix and $\underline{x}$ and $\underline{y}$ are $n \times 1$ vectors. In this formulation, consider A and $\underline{y}$ as given, with $\underline{x}$ unknown. Equation (C.36) may be thought of as

1. A matrix equation;

2. A set of n linear constraints of the form

$$\underline{a}_i^T \underline{x} = y_i \tag{C.38}$$

   where $\underline{a}_i^T$ is the ith row of A; or

3. A set of I/O specifications for a neural net, where row i of A and element y_i of $\underline{y}$ are the desired input and output patterns, respectively, and $\underline{x}$ is a set of weights to be determined (see Chapters 4, 5, and 6).

"Batch" Solution (Matrix Inversion).   One solution to Equation (C.37) is to (attempt) to compute the "batch" solution

$$\underline{x} = A^{-1}\underline{y} \tag{C.39}$$

However, we instead explore the ramifications of more general and extendible formulations. Assume that there is *at least* one solution to Equation (C.37). Defining

$$\underline{e} = A\underline{x} - \underline{y} \tag{C.40}$$

note that $\underline{e} = \underline{0}$ when a solution to Equation (C.37) is found.

Error Measures.   Instead of dealing with $\underline{e}$ directly, consider

$$E = \| \underline{e} \|^2 = e_1^2 + e_2^2 + \ldots + e_d^2 \tag{C.41}$$

where $e_i \ i = 1, 2, \ldots, d$ is an element of vector $\underline{e}$. With this choice of *error function* when $E = 0$ a solution is found. $E = 0$ is therefore the minimum error. From Equation (C.40)

$$E = \| \underline{e} \|^2 = <\underline{e}, \underline{e}> = \underline{e}^T \underline{e} = (A\underline{x} - \underline{y})^T (A\underline{x} - \underline{y}) = (\underline{x}^T A^T - \underline{y}^T)(A\underline{x} - \underline{y}) \tag{C.42}$$

$$= \underline{x}^T A^T A\underline{x} - \underline{x}^T A^T \underline{y} - \underline{y}^T A\underline{x} + \underline{y}^T \underline{y} \tag{C.43}$$

Gradient Descent. Computing the gradient of $E(\underline{x})$ with respect to $\underline{x}$ in Equation (C.43) yields

$$\nabla_{\underline{x}} E(\underline{x}) = 2(A^T A)\underline{x} - 2A^T \underline{y} = 2A^T(A\underline{x} - \underline{y}) = 2A^T \underline{e} \tag{C.44}$$

Since the gradient of E defines the direction of *maximum increase in* E, Equation (C.44) is used to form an iterative minimization procedure. Consider a procedure to find $\hat{\underline{x}}$, i.e., the solution vector that minimizes Equation (C.43), of the form:

$$\hat{\underline{x}}^{n+1} = \hat{\underline{x}}^n - \mu(n)\nabla_{\underline{x}} E(\hat{\underline{x}}^n) \tag{C.45}$$

We show this via a simple two-dimensional example. Consider a specific example[6] of Equation (C.37) for $d = 2$, i.e.,

$$\begin{pmatrix} 1 & -1 \\ 2 & 1 \end{pmatrix} \begin{pmatrix} x_1 \\ x_2 \end{pmatrix} = \begin{pmatrix} -1 \\ 4 \end{pmatrix} \tag{C.47}$$

Formulating the error measure of Equation (C.43) yields

$$E(\underline{x}) = \begin{pmatrix} x_1 & x_2 \end{pmatrix} \begin{pmatrix} 5 & 1 \\ 1 & 2 \end{pmatrix} \begin{pmatrix} x_1 \\ x_2 \end{pmatrix} + (-14 \quad -10) \begin{pmatrix} x_1 \\ x_2 \end{pmatrix} + 17 \tag{C.48}$$

or

$$E(\underline{x}) = 5x_1^2 + 2x_1 x_2 + 2x_2^2 - 14x_1 - 10x_2 + 17 \tag{C.49}$$

Therefore, $E(\underline{x})$ is quadratic in x_1 and x_2. Loci of constant E are ellipses, given by

$$5x_1^2 + 2x_1 x_2 + 2x_2^2 - 14x_1 - 10x_2 = k \tag{C.50}$$

Gradient descent procedures are considered for ANN training applications.

---

[6]The "batch" (inverse) solution yields

$$\begin{pmatrix} x_1 \\ x_2 \end{pmatrix} = \begin{pmatrix} 1 \\ 2 \end{pmatrix} \tag{C.46}$$

Fundamentals of Lisp

This appendix presents a summary and overview of the Lisp language.

D.1 The Roots of Lisp

In a seminal paper published in 1960, John McCarthy showed how a small number of (possibly recursive) functions and a data structure (a list) for both code and data could form the basis for a programming language. McCarthy's aim was to develop a programming system to facilitate manipulating symbolic expressions representing declarative and imperative expressions for an application dubbed "Advice Taker." Note the relevance to modern-day IS development. Lisp has had a significant impact on the subsequent development of other functional languages, such as ML and Haskell.

D.2 First Principles

1. The basic Lisp data structures are lists, atoms, and strings.

2. The basic concept is **function application**, i.e., applying **functions** to these data structures. This involves defining (or at least identifying) functions, with particular care to specify **arguments** and function **returned values**.

3. Lisp provides lots of built-in functions. The Lisp programmer achieves additional functionality by using these to define new functions.

4. Frequently **recursion** is used, since it is natural in functional programming and often leads to compact implementations.

D.2.1 Programs and Data Are Lists

Note every one of the examples that follow involves a *list*. Some lists are function definitions, some are function applications, etc. Combinations of these Lisp expressions form programs. The basic data structure is the list. A Lisp program is Lisp data (or so-called "s-expressions"), which may be manipulated by Lisp. This makes (intentionally) self-modifying code easily possible.

D.2.2   The Lisp Top-Level Loop (EVAL)

The read-eval-print loop, (EVAL) evaluates what you type at the interpreter prompt (sometimes called a "form") and acts accordingly:

1. If it is an atom with a value, the value is returned.

```
lisp> pi
3.1415926535897932385L0
```

2. If it is a list, the `car` (first element) of the list is assumed to evaluate to a function that is then applied to the evaluation of the rest of the list elements.[1]

```
lisp> (exp 1)
2.7182817
```

3. If EVAL can't figure out what you want to do,[2] you are sent to the debugger:

```
lisp> (ln (exp 1))

*** - eval: the function ln is undefined
1. Break lisp> abort

lisp> (log (exp 1))
0.99999994
```

4. The quote (`'`) inhibits evaluation by EVAL:

```
lisp> pi
3.1415926535897932385L0
lisp> 'pi
pi
lisp> (quote pi)
pi
```

D.3   Common Lisp Building Blocks

D.3.1   s-expressions (or Forms) and Evaluation

In general, a *form or an s-expression* is either an atom or a list. As noted, if the s-expression is an atom, Lisp's EVAL evaluates it. *Note integers and strings evaluate to themselves.* If the s-expression is a list, the first element (the `car` of the list) is assumed to be the name of a function. The evaluated remaining list elements (the `cdr` of the list) are then passed to the function as arguments.

---

[1]Some functions (special forms) such as `setq` inhibit evaluation of one or more of their arguments.
[2]For example, atoms with no value are entered, or function names that do not correspond to a known function are entered.

D.3.2 Some Special Forms

There are a number of special forms in Common Lisp that look like function calls but, strictly speaking, aren't. These include control constructs such as `if` and `do`, definitions using `defun` and `defstruct` and binding constructs such as `let`. We ignore their special significance and just look at them as if they were functions (usually with side effects).

D.3.3 Basic Function Groups

1. Assignment: (`setf`, `setq`, `defvar`)

2. List manipulation (`car`, `cdr`, `nth`, `cons`, `append`, `assoc`)

3. Sequence (string and array) manipulation (`concatenate`, `subseq`, `substitute`, `position`)

4. Predicates (evaluate and return "non-nil" or nil)

5. Control/branching (`cond`, `if`)

6. Sequential evaluation and iteration (`let`, `do`, `mapcar`)

7. I/O (`read`, `print`, `load`)

8. Math and logical functions (`and`, `or`, `*`, `+`)

9. Function defining functions (`defun`)

10. Tracing/debugging/system calls (`trace`)

Defining Functions: `defun`

`defun` is the built-in Lisp function used for this purpose. For example, we define a function using `defun`:

```
lisp> (defun first-one (x)
    (car x)
        )
first-one
```

Notice the value returned by **defun**. Now let's use the function:

```
lisp>(setq a '(my dog has fleas))

lisp> (first-one a)
my
```

List Manipulation: `car` and `cdr`

The two essential list manipulation functions are **car** and **cdr**. Their use and returned values are easily shown by example.

```
lisp> (setq a '(my dog has fleas))
(my dog has fleas)
lisp> (car a)
my
lisp> (cdr a)
(dog has fleas)
```

D.3.4 Special Symbols

There are two special symbols, t and nil, which are self-evaluating symbols because they evaluate to themselves. Lisp uses t and nil in conjunction with predicates to represent TRUE and FALSE. An example of this use using the if macro is shown in Figure D.1.

```
lisp> (if t 5 6)
5
lisp> (if nil 5 6)
6
lisp> (if 4 5 6)
5
```

Figure D.1 Use of Predicates and a Simple if Example

The All-Important cond

Programmers familiar with the Pascal "case" statement or C's "switch" should find the cond construct in Lisp familiar.

cond Structure

Consider a cond with the typical (pseudocode) form:

```
(cond
    (<pred1> <expr1>)
    (<pred2> <expr2>)
    (<pred3> <expr3>)
        .
        .
        .
    (<predn> <exprn>)
    )
```

Each argument in the cond is a list of the form (<predi> <expri>). The semantics are relatively simple—this cond form *tests its arguments sequentially* and finds the first argument whose <predi> evaluates to non-nil and then evaluates the corresponding <expri>, returning this evaluation as the value of the cond.

More generally, a cond consists of the symbol cond followed by a number of arguments, each of which is a list. The car of each argument to the cond is considered a predicate. The cond form *tests its arguments sequentially* and finds the first argument whose predicate (i.e., car) evaluates to non-nil and then evaluates each of the remaining elements of this argument list, returning the result of the last evaluation. Thus a more general `cond` structure is:

```
(cond
   (<predi> <expr1i> <expr2i> <expr3i> . . . <exprqi>)
   (<predj> <expr1j> <expr2j> <expr3j> . . . <exprpj>)
   .
   .
   .
   )
```

i.e., if `<predi>` evaluates to non-nil, `<expr1i>` `<expr2i>` `<expr3i>` . . .`<exprqi>` are sequentially evaluated and the value returned by the `cond` is the value of `<exprqi>`. Notice:

1. This form allows a `cond` to implement sequential evaluation, as indicated in the preceding example; and

2. In this case, the only role of the evaluations `<expr1i>` `<expr2i>` `<expr3i>` . . . are for side effects. Typically this is for assignments, printing, input, etc.

From `cond` to `if`

Lisp provides the `if` construct that facilitates a clearer representation of this type of a `cond` with the form:

```
(if a b c)
```

In the `if` construct, the first argument determines whether the second or third argument will be evaluated. Other examples were shown in Section D.3.4. Two related forms are **when** and **unless**.

D.4 References

D.4.1 Implementations

CLISP

CLISP is a multiplatform implementation of Common Lisp. Online sources of information and distributions are http://clisp.cons.org/ or http://clisp.sourceforge.net/.

Alternatives to CLISP

There are a number of alternatives to CLISP. Some are commercial products (e.g., see http://www.franz.com/!); others, like CLISP, are covered under the GNU license. This includes `gcl`, the official Common Lisp for the GNU project.

D.4.2   Online Common Lisp Resources and References

As a quick search will show, there are many online Lisp resources. In addition to those cited previously, the following links are quite useful:

www.cs.cmu.edu/afs/cs.cmu.edu/project/ai-repository/ai/html/cltl/cltl2.html. Common Lisp the Language, 2nd Edition (HTML format).

clisp.cons.org/resources.html. Online Repository of Lisp Related Information, Including On-Line References.

http://www-2.cs.cmu.edu/~dst/LispBook/index.html. Common Lisp: A Gentle Introduction to Symbolic Computation.

Bibliography

[AF90]   M. Niranjan, S. V. B. Aiyer, and F. Fallside. A theoretical investigation into the performance of the Hopfield model. *IEEE Trans. Neural Networks*, *1*(2):204–215, 1990.

[AH77]   K. Appel and W. Haken. The solution of the four-color map problem. *Sci. Amer.*, 237:108–121, 1977.

[Ala00] J. T. Alander. An indexed bibliography of genetic algorithms and the traveling salesman problem, 2000 (http://citeseerx.ist.psu.edu).

[All95] J. Allen. *Natural Language Understanding*. Benjamin Cummings, 1995.

[Ama72a] S. I. Amari. Learning patterns and pattern sequences by self-organizing nets. *IEEE Trans. on Computers*, *C-21*(11):1197–1206, November 1972.

[AMJ85] Y. S. Abu-Mostafa and J. M. St. Jacques. Information capacity of the Hopfield model. *IEEE Trans. on Information Theory*, *IT-31*(4):461–464, July 1985.

[AMK88] M. A. Arbib, R. N. Moll, and A. J. Kfoury. *An Introduction to Formal Language Theory*. Springer Verlag, 1988.

[AP94]   A. Aamodt and E. Plaza. Case-based reasoning: Foundational issues, methodological variations, and system approaches. *AI Communications*, *7*(1):39–52, 1994.

[Apt03] K. Apt. *Principles of Constraint Programming*. Cambridge University Press, 2003.

[AS95]   R. Alquezar and A. Sanfeliu. An algebraic framework to represent finite state automata in single-layer recurrent neural networks. *Neural Computation*, *7*(5):931–949, 1995.

[AS98]   A. S. Atukorale and P. N. Suganthan. An efficient neural gas network for classification. *Proc. Intl. Conf. on Control, Automation, Robotics, and Vision (ICARCV-98)*, 1152–1156, December 1998.

[ASP94]   P. J. Angeline, G. M. Saunders, and J. B. Pollack. An evolutionary algorithm that constructs recurrent neural networks. *IEEE Trans. Neural Networks, 5*(1):54–65, 1994.

[ATG92]   A. Acharya, M. Tambe, and A. Gupta. Implementation of production systems on message-passing computers. *IEEE Trans. Parallel and Distributed Systems, 3*(4):477–487, July 1992.

[AVT88]   B. Angeniol, G. D. L. C. Vaubois, and J. Y. L. Texire. Self-organizing feature maps and the traveling salesman problem. *Neural Networks, 1*:289–293, 1988.

[BAM82]   R. K. Blashfield, M. S. Aldenderfer, and L. C. Morey. Cluster analysis software. *Handbook of Statistics,* P. R. Krishniah an L. N. Kanla, eds. 2:245–266, 1982.Volume 2, 245–266. North Holland, 1982.

[BB08]   J. Schaeffer, V. Bulitko and M. Buro. Bots get smart. *IEEE Spectrum*, Vol. 45, Issue 12, 48–56, December 2008.

[BDJT95]   F. Brazier, B. DuninKeplicz, N. R. Jennings, and J. Treur. Formal specifications of multiagent systems: a realworld case. *First International Conference on Multiagent Systems (ICMAS95)*, 25–32, June 1995.

[Bev05]   A. Bevilacqua. Optimizing parameters of a motion detection system by means of a distributed genetic algorithm. *Image and Vision Computing, 23*:815–829, 2005.

[Bez93]   J. C. Bezdek. Fuzzy models—what are they, and why? *IEEE Trans. Fuzzy Systems, 1*(1):1–6, February 1993.

[BFKM86]   L. Brownston, R. Farrel, E. Kant, and N. Martin. *Programming Expert Systems in OPS5: An Introduction to Rule-Based Programming.* Addison-Wesley, 1986.

[BG84]   B. G. Bara and G. Guida. *Computation Models of Natural Language Processing*, Volume 9 of *Fundamental Studies in Computer Science.* North-Holland, 1984.

[BGM94]   M. Bianchini, M. Gori, and M. Maggini. On the problem of local minima in recurrent neural networks. *IEEE Transactions on Neural Networks, 5*(2):167–177, 1994.

[BHM97]   B. Burmeister, A. Haddadi, and G. Matylis. Application of multiagent systems in traffic and transportation. *IEEE Proceedings on Software Engineering, 144*(1):51–60, 1997.

[Bid03]   H. Bidgoli, ed. *Expert and Rule-based Systems.* John Wiley and Sons, 2003.

[Bob67]   D. G. Bobrow. Natural language input for a computer problem solving system. *Semantic Information Processing*, M. L. Minsky, ed. MIT Press, 133–215, 1967.

[Boc39]   D. Bochvar. On three-valued logical calculus and its application to the analysis of contradiction. *Matematiceskij Sbornik, 4*:353–369, 1939.

[BR97]   K. Knight, B. Swartout, R. Patil, and T. Russ. Toward distributed use of large-scale ontologies. *AAAI-97 Spring Symposium Series*, American Association for Artificial Intelligence (AAAI), Menlo Park, CA. March 24–26, 138–148, 1997.

[Bra00]   Ivan Bratko. *Prolog Programming for Artificial Intelligence*, 3rd edition, Addison-Wesley, 2000.

[Bro74]   W. Brogan. *Modern Control Theory.* Quantum, 1974.

[CFPS06]   A. Copestake, D. Flickinger, C. Pollard, and I. Sag. Minimal recursion semantics: an introduction. *Research on Language and Computation, 3*:281–332, 2006.

[Che05]   S. Cherry. Digital dullard. *IEEE Spectrum*, Vol. 42, Issue 12, 46–47, January 2005.

[Cho56]   N. Chomsky. Three models for the description of language. *IRE Trans. Information Theory, 2*:113–124, 1956. Also in Readings in mathematical psychology, R. D. Luce, R. Bush, and E. Galanter, eds., John Wiley and Sons, 105–124, 1965.

[Cle06]   M. Clerc. *Particle Swarm Optimization.* ISTE, 2006.

[CM03]   W. F. Clocksin and C. S. Mellish. *Programming in Prolog: Using the ISO Standard,* 5th edition, Springer Verlag, 2003.

[CMA94]   J. T. Connor, R. D. Martin, and L. E. Atlas. Recurrent neural networks and robust time series prediction. *IEEE Trans. Neural Networks, 5*(2):240–254, 1994.

[Col05]   B. Colwell. Machine intelligence meets neuroscience. *IEEE Computer*, 12–15, January 2005.

[Cov94]   M. A. Covington. *Natural Language Processing for Prolog Programmers.* Prentice-Hall, 1994.

[Cox94]   E. Cox. *The Fuzzy Systems Handbook.* Academic Press, 1994.

[CP92]   N. Cercone and T. Pattabhiraman. Special issue on natural language generation: Introduction. *Computational Intelligence, 8*(1):72–76, February 1992.

[CR04]   E. J. Rothwell, C. M. Coleman, and J. E. Ross. Investigation of simulated annealing, ant-colony optimization, and genetic algorithms for self-structuring antennas. *IEEE Transactions on Antennas and Propagation, 52*(4):1017–1014, 2004.

[CVS04]   E. Compatangelo, W. Vasconcelos, and B. Scharlau. Managing ontology versions with a distributed blackboard architecture. *2004 International Conference on Artificial Intelligence (IC-AI2004)*, June 2004 (http://www.csd.abdn.ac.uk/~bscharla/presentations/AI2004-versioning.pdf).

[Cyb89]   G. Cybenko. Approximation by superpositions of a sigmoidal function. *Mathematics of Control, Signals, and Systems, 2*:303–314, 1989.

[Dav91]   L. Davis. *Handbook of Genetic Algorithms.* Van Nostrand Reinhold, 1991.

[DC96a]   A.-Dbali, P. Deransart, and L. Cervoni. *Prolog: The Standard: Reference Manual.* Springer Verlag, 1996.

[DC96b]   V. Maniezzo, M. Dorigo, and A. Colorni. The ant system: optimization by a colony of cooperating agents. *IEEE Trans. Systems, Man and Cybernetics-Part B, 26*(1):1–13, 1996.

[Dec98]   R. Dechter. Constraint satisfaction. *MIT Encyclopedia of the Cognitive Sciences (MITECS)*. MIT Press, 1998.

[DG97]   M. Dorigo and L. Gambardella. Ant colony system: A cooperative learning approach to the traveling salesman problem. *IEEE Trans. Evolutionary Computing, 1*(1), 1997.

[DiZ88]   S. DiZenzo. A many-valued logic for approximate reasoning. *IBM Journal of Research and Development, 32*(4):552–565, July 1988.

[DJ76]   R. C. Dubes and A. K. Jain. Clustering techniques: The user's dilemma. *Pattern Recognition, 8*:247–260, 1976.

[DJ80]   R. C. Dubes and A. K. Jain. Clustering methodologies in exploratory data analysis. *Advances in Computers*, M. Youits, ed., Academic Press, 1980.

[DM81]   T. G. Dietterich and R. S. Michalski. Inductive learning of structural descriptions. *Artificial Intelligence, 16*:257–294, 1981.

[DM84]   E. Davis and D. McDermott. Planning routes through uncertain territory. *Artificial Intelligence, 22*:107–156, 1984.

[Doy79]   J. Doyle. A truth maintenance system. *Artificial Intelligence, 12*(3):93–116, 1979.

[DS04]   M. Dorigo and T. Stutzle. *Ant Colony Optimization.* MIT Press, 2004.

[EGK+04]   S. Eubank, H. Guclu, V. S. A. Kumar, M. V. Maranthe, A. Srinivasan, Z. Toroczaki, and N. Wang. Modelling disease outbreaks in realistic urban social networks. *Nature, 429*:180–184, 2004.

[Eri05]   K. A. Ericsson. Recent advances in expertise research: a commentary on the contributions to the special issue. *Applied Cognitive Psychology, 19*:233–241, 2005.

[ES91]   K. A. Ericsson and J. Smith, eds. *Toward a General Theory of Expertise: Prospects and Limits.* Cambridge University Press, 1991.

[FER81]   G. Fekete, J. O. Eklundh, and A. Rosenfeld. Relaxation: Evaluation and applications. *IEEE Trans. Pattern Analysis and Machine Intelligence, PAMI-3*(4):459–469, 1981.

[FFMM94]   T. Finin, R. Fritzson, D. McKay, and R. McEntire. "KQML as an Agent Communication Language." in *Proceedings of the 3rd International Conference on Information and Knowledge Management* (CIKM'94), N. Adam, B. Bhargava, and Y. Yesha, Eds. Gaithersburg, MD, USA: ACM Press, 1994. pp. 456–463.

[FFP90]   D. B. Fogel, L. J. Fogel, and V. W. Porto. Evolving neural networks. *Biological Cybernetics, 63*:487–493, 1990.

[Fil88]   R. E. Filman. Reasoning with worlds and truth maintenance in a knowledge-based programming environment. *Communications of the ACM, 31*(4):382–401, April 1988.

[FN71]   R. E. Fikes and N. J. Nilsson. STRIPS: A new approach to the application of theorem proving to problem solving. *Artificial Intelligence, 2*:189–208, 1971.

[For65]   E. W. Forgy. Cluster analysis of multivariate data: efficiency vs. interpretability of classifications. *Biometrics, 21*:768, 1965.

[For82]   C. L. Forgy. Rete: a fast algorithm for the many pattern/many object pattern match problem. *Artificial Intelligence, 19*:17–37, 1982.

[Fox90]   M. S. Fox. Constraint-guided scheduling: a short history of research at CMU. *Computers in Industry, 14*(1–3):79–88, May 1990.

[Fri95]   B. Fritzke. A growing neural gas network learns topologies. *Advances in Neural Information Processing Systems, 7*:625–632, 1995.

[Fri05]   K. J. Friston. Models of brain function in neuroimaging. *Annual Review of Psychology, 56*:57–87, 2005.

[Fu82]   K. S. Fu. *Syntactic Pattern Recognition and Applications.* Prentice-Hall, 1982.

[Fuk72]   K. Fukunaga. *Introduction to Statistical Pattern Recognition.* Academic Press, 1972.

[FY91]   D. P. Filev and R. R. Yager. A generalized defuzzification method via BAD distributions. *International Journal of Intelligent Systems, 6*:687–697, 1991.

[GB88]   A. Guez and J. Barhen. On the stability, storage capacity, and design of nonlinear continuous neural networks. *IEEE Trans. Systems, Man, Cybernet. 18*(1):80–87, January/ February 1988.

[GJL+99]   R. J. Gallimore, N. R. Jennings, H. S. Lamba, C. L. Mason, and B. J. Orenstein. Cooperating agents for 3D scientific data interpretation. *IEEE Trans. Systems Man Cybernet, Part C 29*:110–126, 1999.

[GLC+95]   B. Grosof, D. Levine, H. Chan, C. Parris, and J. Auerbach. Reusable architecture for embedding rule-based intelligence in information agents. In *Proc. of the Workshop on Intelligent Information Agents, ACM Conf. on Information and Knowledge Management (CIKM-95),* December 1995.

[GLC+01]   F. Gobet, P. C. R. Lane, S. Croker, P. C. H. Cheng, G. Jones, I. Oliver, and J. M. Pine. Chunking mechanisms in human learning. *Trends in Cognitive Sciences, 5*:236–243, 2001.

[Gol89]   D. Goldberg. *Genetic Algorithms in Search, Optimization, and Machine Learning.* Addison-Wesley, 1989.

[GR98]   J. Giarratano and G. Riley. *Expert Systems: Principles and Programming*, 3rd edition. Brooks/Cole Publishers, 1998. (Includes a CD-ROM containing CLIPS 6.05 executables, source code, and documentation.)

[GS91]   S. Geva and J. Sitte. Adaptive nearest neighbor pattern classification. *IEEE Trans. Neural Networks, 2*(2):318–322, March 1991.

[Har75]   J. A. Hartigan. *Clustering Algorithms.* John Wiley and Sons, 1975.

[Has93]   M. H. Hassoun. *Associative Neural Memories—Theory and Implementation.* Oxford University Press, 1993.

[Hay79]   P. Hayes. The naive physics manifesto. *Expert Systems in the Microelectronic Age*, D. Michie, ed. Edinburgh University Press, 1979.

[He81]   G. E. Hinton and J. A. Anderson, eds. *Parallel Models of Associative Memory.* Lawrence Erlbaum and Associates, 1981.

[Hir89]   M. W. Hirsch. Convergent activation dynamics in continuous time networks. *Neural Networks, 2*:331–349, 1989.

[HK85]   P. Harmon and D. King. *Expert Systems—Artificial Intelligence in Business.* John Wiley and Sons, 1985.

[HL87]   W. Y. Huang and R. P. Lippmann. Comparison between neural net and conventional classifiers. *Proceedings of the IEEE International Conference on Neural Networks, IV*:485–493, June 1987.

[HLZ96]   M. Henz, S. Lauer, and D. Zimmermann. COMPOzE—intention-based music composition through constraint programming. *Proceedings of the 8th IEEE International Conference on Tools with Artificial Intelligence, 16–19*, IEEE Computer Society Press, 118–121, November 1996.

[Hop82]   J. J. Hopfield. Neural networks and physical systems with emergent collective computational abilities. *Proc. Natl. Acad. Sci., 79* (Biophysics):2554–2558, April 1982.

[Hop84]   J. J. Hopfield. Neurons with graded response have collective computational properties like those of two-state neurons. *Proc. Natl. Acad. Sci., 81* (Biophysics):3088–3092, May 1984.

[HS84]   E. H. Hovy and R. C. Schank. Language generation by computer. *Computation Models of Natural Language Processing* [BG84], 165–195.

[Hsu07]   F. H. Hsu. Cracking go. *IEEE Spectrum, 44*(10):50–55, October 2007.

[HT85]   J. J. Hopfield and D. W. Tank. Neural computation of decisions in optimization problems. *Biological Cybernetics, 52*:141–152, 1985.

[HT86]   J. J. Hopfield and D. W. Tank. Computing with neural circuits: A model. *Science, 233*:625–633, August 1986.

[HZ83]   R. A. Hummel and S. W. Zucker. On the foundations of relaxation labeling processes. *IEEE Transactions on Pattern Analysis and Machine Intelligence, PAMI-5*(3):267–287, May 1983.

[Ish88]   T. Ishida. Optimizing Rules in Production System Programs. In Proceedings of the AAAI-88 Seventh National Conference on Artificial Intelligence, Volume 2, pages 699–704, Los Altos, CA, 1988. Morgan Kaufmann Publishers, Inc.

[Ish91]   T. Ishida. Parallel rule firing in production systems. *IEEE Trans. Knowledge and Data Engineering, 3*(1):11–17, March 1991.

[Jac88]   R. Jacobs. Increased rates of convergence through learning rate adaption. *Neural Networks, 1*, 1988.

[Jam90]   W. James. *Psychology (Briefer Course). Chapter XVI,* Association. Psychology (Briefer Course) (1892) University of Notre Dame Press 1985: ISBN 0-268-01557-0, Dover Publications 2001: ISBN 0-486-41604-6.

[Jen05]   N. R. Jennings. Teaching introductory artificial intelligence using a simple agent framework. *IEEE Trans. Education, 48*(3):382–390, August 2005.

[JM94]   M. Johnston and G. Miller. SPIKE: Intelligent scheduling of hubble space telescope observations. Morgan Kaufmann Publishers, 391–422, 1994.

[JM00]   D. Jurafsky and J. H. Martin. *Speech and Language Processing: An Introduction to Natural Language Processing, Computational Linguistics, and Speech Recognition.* Prentice-Hall, 2000.

[Joh86]   R. Johnsonbaugh. *Discrete Mathematics.* MacMillan, 1986.

[JS88]   T. A. Jamison and R. J. Schalkoff. Image labeling via a neural network approach and a comparison with existing alternatives. *Image and Vision Computing, 6*(4):203–214, November 1988.

[JS95]   J. S. R. Jang and C. T. Sun. Neuro-fuzzy modeling and control. *Proceedings of the IEEE,* March 1995.

[Kas93]   R. Kasper. Typed feature constraint systems: Structures and descriptions. *Feature Formalisms and Linguistic Ambiguity,* H. Trost, ed. Ellis Horwood Limited, 1–19, 1993.

[Kat02]   E. Katz. A multiple rule engine-based agent control architecture. In *Proceedings of the 6th IEEE International Conference on Intelligent Engineering Systems,* May 2002.

[Kay85]   M. Kay. Parsing in functional unification grammar. *Natural Lanugage Parsing: Psychological, Computational, and Theoretical Perspectives,* D. R. Dowty, L. Karttunen, and A. M. Zwioky, eds. Cambridge University Press, 251–278, 1985.

[KB84]   B. Kolman and R. Busby. *Discrete Mathematical Structures for Computer Science.* Prentice-Hall, 1984.

[KC04]   J. A. Kang and A. M. K. Cheng. Shortening matching time in OPS5 production systems. *IEEE Trans. Software Engineering, 30*(7):448–457, 2004.

[KKL90]   J. A. Kangas, T. K. Khonen, and J. T. Laaksonen. Variants of self-organizing maps. *IEEE Trans. Neural Networks, 1*(1):93–99, March 1990.

[KL90]   N. A. Kartam and R. E. Levitt. A constraint-based approach to construction planning of multi-story buildings. *Expert Planning Systems*, Institute of Electrical Engineers, 245–250, 1990.

[KL96]   T. J. Kowalski and L. S. Levy. *Rule-Based Programming.* Kluwer International Series in Engineering and Computer Science, 1996.

[Kle52]   S. Kleene. *Introduction to metamathematics.* 1952.

[Kni89]   K. Knight. Unification: a multidisciplinary survey. *ACM Computing Surveys, 21*(1):93–122, March 1989.

[Knu73]   D. E. Knuth. *The Art of Computer Programming, Volume 3, Sorting and Searching.* Addison-Wesley, 1973.

[Kob91]   Y. Kobuchi. State evaluation functions and lyapunov functions for neural networks. *Neural Networks, 4*:505–510, 1991.

[Kog93]   K. Kogure. Typed feature structure generalization by incremental graph copying. *Feature Formalisms and Linguistic Ambiguity*, H. Trost, ed. Ellis Horwood Limited, 141–158, 1993.

[Koh82a]   T. Kohonen. Analysis of a simple self-organizing process. *Biol. Cybernetics, 44*:135–140, 1982.

[Koh82b]   T. Kohonen. Self-organized formation of topologically correct feature maps. *Biol. Cybernetics, 43*:59–69, 1982.

[Koh84]   T. Kohonen. *Self-Organization and Associative Memory.* Springer Verlag, 1984.

[Koh87]   T. Kohonen. Adaptive, associative, and self-organizing functions in neural computing. *Applied Optics, 26*(3):4910–4918, December 1987.

[Koh88]   T. Kohonen. Self-organizing feature maps. *Course notes from 1988 Conference on Neural Networks*, 1988. Available from the IEEE.

[Koh90]   T. Kohonen. The self-organizing map. *Proceedings of the IEEE, 78*(9):1464–1480, 1990.

[Kos87]   B. Kosko. Adaptive bidirectional associative memories. *Applied Optics, 26*(23):4947–4960, December 1987.

[Kos88]   B. Kosko. Bidirectional associative memories. *IEEE Trans. Systems, Man, and Cybernetics, SMC-18*:42–60, 1988.

[Koz92]   J. R. Koza. *Genetic Programming: On the Programming of Computers by Means of Natural Selection*. MIT Press, 1992.

[Koz94]   J. R. Koza. *Genetic Programming II: Automatic Discovery of Reusable Programs*. MIT Press, 1994.

[KPW90]   B. Kamgar-Parsi and H. Wechsler. Simultaneous fitting of several planes to point sets using neural networks. *Computer Vision, Graphics and Image Processing, 52*:341–359, 1990.

[KS87]   I. Kanter and H. Sompolinsky. Associative recall of memory without errors. *Physical Review A, 35*(1):380–392, 1987.

[KSJ00]   E. R. Kandel, J. H. Schwartz, and T. M. Jessell. *Principles of Neural Science*. 4th edition, McGraw-Hill, 2000.

[L06]   L. Lebart. Assessing self-organizing maps via contiguity analysis. *Neural Networks, 19*:847–854, 2006.

[Lau84]   H. B. Laufer. *Discrete Mathematics and Applied Modern Algebra*. PWS Publishers, 1984.

[LBFL80]   R. K. Lindsay, B. G. Buchanan, E. A. Feigenbaum, and J. Lederberg. *Application of Artificial Intelligence for Chemistry: The DENDRAL Project*. McGraw-Hill, 1980.

[LC02]   P-Y. Lee and A. M. K. Cheng. HAL: A faster match algorithm. *IEEE Trans. Knowledge and Data Engineering, 14*(5):1047–1058, 2002.

[Lea96]   D. Leake. *Case-Based Reasoning: Experiences, Lessons, and Future Directions*. AAAI Press, 1996.

[Len82]   D. Lenat. The nature of heuristics. *Artificial Intelligence, 19*:189–249, 1982.

[Lev02]   D. J. Levitin, ed. *Foundations of Cognitive Psychology: Core Readings*. MIT Press, 2002. Two of the most important and interesting articles are "Can Machines Think?" and "Where an I?"

[Lev06]   D. J. Levitin. *This is Your Brain on Music: The Science of a Human Obsession*. Dutton, 2006.

[Lip87]   R. P. Lippmann. An Introduction to Computing with Neural Nets. *IEEE ASSP Magazine*, 4–22, April 1987.

[LKM$^+$99]   P. Larranaga, C. Kuijpers, R. Murga, I. Inza, and S. Dizdarevic. Genetic algorithms for the traveling salesman problem: A review of representations and operators. *Artificial Intelligence Review, 13*:129–170, 1999.

[LM]   R. D. Levine and W. D. Meurers. *Head-Driven Phrase Structure Grammar Linguistic Approach, Formal Foundations, and Computational Realization*, 2nd edition. Elsevier. (http://www1.elsevier.com/homepage/sal/ell2/).

[LNR87]   J. Laird, A. Newell, and P. Rosenbloom. Soar: An architecture for general intelligence. *Artificial Intelligence, 33*:1–64, 1987.

[LS92]   K. A. Liburdy and R. J. Schalkoff. Model-based object classification using unification grammars and abstract representation. *Proc. SPIE Model-Based Vision Conference*, Vol 1827, November 1992.

[LSK98]   A. Lopez-Suarez and M. Kamel. Reorganizing knowledge to improve performance. *IEEE Transactions on Knowledge and Data Engineering, 10*(1):190–191, 1998.

[Luk67]   J. Lukasiewicz. Many-valued systems of propositional logic. Reprinted in Lukasiewicz, J. (1970). Selected Works (L. Borkowski, ed.). North-Holland Publ. Comp., Amsterdam.

[LYB93]   Z-P. Lo, Y. Yu, and B. Bavarian. Analysis of the convergence properties of topology preserving neural networks. *IEEE Trans. Neural Networks, 4*(2):207–230, March 1993.

[Mac92]   A. K. Mackworth. The logic of constraint satisfaction. *Artificial Intelligence, 58*(1–2): 3–20, 1992.

[MCC00]   R. Malouf, J. Carroll, and A. Copestake. Efficient feature structure operations without compilation. *Natural Language Engineering, 1*(1):1–18, 2000.

[MCV]   A. Hassenfuss, M. Cottrell, B. Hammer, and T. Villmann. Batch and median neural gas. Neural Networks, Vol 19, 2006, 762–771.

[MD80]   D. McDermott and J. Doyle. Non-monotonic logic I. *Artificial Intelligence, 12*(1):41–72, 1980.

[Mi86]   R. S. Michalski, J. G. Carbonell, and T. M. Mitchell. *Machine learning, (an artificial intelligence approach)*, Vol II. Morgan Kaufman, 1986.

[Mic80]   R. S. Michalski. Pattern recognition as rule-guided inference. *IEEE Trans. PAMI, 2*(4):349–361, 1980.

[Mic92]   Z. Michalewicz. *Genetic Algorithms + Data Structures = Evolution Programs*. Springer Verlag, 1992.

[ML91]   D. P. Miranker and B. J. Lofaso. The organization and performance of a TREAT-based production system compiler. *IEEE Trans. Knowledge and Data Engineering, 03*(1):3–10, 1991.

[MS94]   M. Mousavi and R. J. Schalkoff. ANN implementation of stereo vision: Feature extraction and disparity determination. *IEEE Trans. Systems, Man and Cybernetics, 24*(8), August 1994.

[MV87]   R. J. McEliece, E. C. Posner Santosh, and S. Venkatesh. The capacity of the Hopfield associative memory. *IEEE Trans. Inform. Theory, IT-33*(4):461–482, July 1987.

[Neu58]   J. Von Neumann. *The Computer and the Brain*. Yale University Press, 1958.

[New90]   A. Newell. *Unified Theories of Cognition.* Harvard University Press, 1990.

[New92a]   A. Newell. Precis of unified theories of cognition. *Behavioural and Brain Sciences, 15*:425–492, 1992.

[New92b]   A. Newell. Unified theories of cognition and the role of Soar. *Soar: A Cognitive Architecture in Perspective*, J. A. Michon and A. Akyurek, eds. Kluwer Academic Publishers, 1992.

[NGR88]   P. P. Nayak, A. Gupta, and P. S. Rosenbloom. Comparison of the rete and treat production matchers for Soar. *National Conference on Artificial Intelligence*, 693–698, 1988.

[Ni89]   H. P. Ni. Blackboard systems. *The Handbook of Artificial Intelligence*, P. R. Cohen, A. Barr, and E. A. Feingenbaum, eds. Vol IV, Chapter XVI, 1–82, Addison-Wesley, 1989.

[Nil80]   N. J. Nilsson. *Principles of Artificial Intelligence.* Tioga Publishing, 1980.

[NM]   N. F. Noy and D. L. McGuiness. *Ontology development 101: A guide to creating your first ontology.* Available in pdf form from the Protégé documentation website (http://protege.stanford.edu/publications/ontology_development/ontology101.html).

[Nwa96]   H. S. Nwana. Software agents: An overview. *The Knowledge Engineering Review, 11*(3):205–244, October/November 1996.

[Olu94]   O. Olurotimi. Recurrent neural network training with feedforward complexity. *IEEE Transactions on Neural Networks, 5*(2):185–197, 1994.

[Ope]   *Open Music* website. (http://recherche.ircam.fr/equipes/repmus/OpenMusic/).

[Osm08]   M. Osman. Seeing is as good as doing. *The Journal of Problem Solving, 2*, 2008. (http://docs.lib.purdue.edu/jps/vol2/iss1/3).

[OZ99]   A. Omicini and F. Zambonelli. Coordination for internet application development. *Autonomous Agents and MultiAgent Systems, 2*(3):251–269, 1999.

[PA98]   G. A. Papadopoulos and F. Arbab. Coordination models and languages. *Advances in Computers: The Engineering of Large Systems, 46*, August 1998.

[Par91]   D. Partridge. *A New Guide to Artificial Intelligence.* Ablex Publishing Corporation, 1991.

[Pat72]   E. A. Patrick. *Fundamentals of Pattern Recognition.* Prentice-Hall, 1972.

[PB94]   N. Peterfreund and Y. Baram. Second-order bounds on the domain of attraction and the rate of convergence of nonlinear dynamical systems and neural networks. *IEEE Trans. Neural Networks, 5*(4):551–560, 1994.

[Pea84]   J. Pearl. *Heuristics.* Addison-Wesley, 1984.

[Pea88]   J. Pearl. *Probabilistic Reasoning in Intelligent Systems.* Morgan Kaufmann, 1988.

[Pia68]   J. Piaget. *On the Development of Memory and Identity.* Clark University Press, 1968.

[Pin94]   S. Pinker. *The language instinct: How the mind creates language.* William Morrow, 1994.

[PL05]   D. J. Pearson and J. E. Laird. Incremental learning of procedural planning knowledge in challenging environments. *Computational Intelligence, 21*(4):414–439, November 2005. Special Issue on "Learning to Improve Reasoning."

[Pol73]   G. Polya. *How To Solve It: A New Aspect of Mathematical Method.* Princeton University Press, 1973.

[Pos21]   E. L. Post. Introduction to a general theory of elementary propositions. *American Journal of Mathematics, 43*:163–185, 1921.

[Pri93]   A. E. Prieditis. Machine discovery of effective admissible heuristics. *Machine Learning, 12*(1–3):117–141, August 1993.

[PV02]   K. E. Parsopoulos and M. N. Vrahatis. Recent approaches to global optimization problems through particle swarm optimization. *Natural Computing, 1*(2-3):235–306, 2002.

[PZG05]   M. Pantic, R. Zwitserloot, and R. Grootjans. On agent-based software engineering. *Artificial Intelligence, 117*:277–296, 2005.

[Qui86]   J. R. Quinlan. Induction of decision trees. *Machine Learning, 1*(1):81–106, 1986.

[Ris06]   E. L. Rissland. AI and similarity. *IEEE Intelligent Systems, 21*(3):39–49, May/June 2006.

[RLN92]   P. S. Rosenbloom, J. E. Laird, and A. Newell. *The Soar Papers: Research on Integrated Intelligence.* MIT Press, 1992.

[RM86]   D. E. Rummelhart and J. L. McClelland. *Parallel Distributed Processing—Explorations in the Microstructure of Cognition, Volume 1: Foundations.* MIT Press, 1986.

[RN78]   D. E. Rummelhart and D. A. Norman. Accretion, tuning, and restructuring: three modes of learning. *Semantic Factors in Cognition*, J. W. Cotton and R. L. Klatzky, eds. Lawrence Erlbaum, 1978.

[Rob92]   J. A. Robinson. Logic and logic programming. *Communications of the ACM, 35*(3):340–365, March 1992.

[Ros99]   E. Rosch. Reclaiming concepts. *Journal of Consciousness Studies*, (11–12):61–77, 1999. Reprinted in *Reclaiming Cognition: The Primacy of Action, Intention, and Emotion.*, R. Nunez and W. J. Freeman, eds. Imprint Academic, 1999.

[Ros06]   F. Rossi. *Handbook of Constraint Programming.* Elsevier, 2006.

[RV87]   E. R. Rodemich, R. J. McEliece, E.C. Posner, and S. S. Venkatesh. The capacity of the Hopfield associative memory. *IEEE Trans. Information Theory, IT-33*:461–482, 1987.

[SA90]   F. M. Silva and L. B. Almeida. Speeding up backpropagation. In *Advanced Neural Computers*. Elsevier Science Publishers B.V. (North-Holland), 1990.

[Sac74]   E. D. Sacerdoti. Planning in a hierarchy of abstraction spaces. *Artificial Intelligence*, 5:115–135, 1974.

[Sar93]   V. A. Saraswat. *Concurrent constraint programming*. MIT Press, 1993.

[Sax74]   W. O. Saxton. A new computer language for electron image procesing. *Computer Graphics and Image Processing*, 3:266–276, 1974.

[SC94]   H. Kautz, B. Selmen, and B. Cohen. Noise strategies for improved local search. *Proc. AAAI-94*. AAAI Press/MIT Press, 337–343, 1994.

[Sch89a]   R. J. Schalkoff. *Digital Image Processing and Computer Vision*. John Wiley and Sons, 1989.

[Sch89b]   M. Schmitt. Mathematical morphology and artificial intelligence: An automatic programming system. *Signal Processing*, 16(4):389–401, April 1989.

[Sch90]   R. J. Schalkoff. *Artificial Intelligence: An Engineering Approach*. McGraw-Hill, 1990.

[Sch92]   R. J. Schalkoff. *Pattern Recognition: Statistical, Structural and Neural Approaches*. John Wiley and Sons, 1992.

[Sch97]   R. J. Schalkoff. *Artificial Neural Networks*. McGraw-Hill, NY, 1997.

[Sch07]   R. Schalkoff. *Programming Languages and Methodologies*. Jones and Bartlett Publishers, 2007.

[Sel86]   M. Selfridge. A computer model of child language acquisition. *Artificial Intelligence*, 29:171–216, 1986.

[SF86]   J. C. Schlimmer and D. Fisher. A case study of incremental concept induction. In *Proc. Fifth National Conference on Artificial Intelligence*. Morgan Kaufmann, 496–501, 1986.

[She07]   P. C-Y. Sheu. Editorial preface. *International Journal of Semantic Computing*, 1(1):1–9, 2007.

[Shi86]   S. M. Shieber. *An Introduction to Unification-Based Approaches to Grammar*. Center for the Study of Language and Information, Ventura Hall, Stanford University, 1986.

[Sho93]   Y. Shoham. Agent oriented programming. *Artificial Intelligence*, 60(1):51–92, 1993.

[SRK94]   R. Schank, C. Riesbeck, and A. Kass. *Inside Case-Based Explanation*. Lawrence Erlbaum, 1994.

[SS91]   S. I. Sudharsananand and M. K. Sundareshan. Exponential stability and a systematic synthesis of a neural network for quadratic minimization. *Neural Networks*, 4:599–613, 1991.

[SS95]   K. M. Shaaban and R. J. Schalkoff. Image processing and computer vision algorithm selection and refinement using an operator-assisted meta-algorithm. *Proceedings of the SPIE (Visual Information Processing IV)*, *2488*:77–87, April 1995.

[SS00]   I. P. Gent, J. Singer, and A. Small. Backbone fragility and the local search cost peak. *Journal of Artificial Intelligence Research*, *12*:235–270, 2000.

[SW90]   R. Winter, M. Stevenson, and B. Widrow. Sensitivity of feedforward neural networks to weight errors. *IEEE Trans. Neural Networks*, *1*(1):71–80, March 1990.

[SWE92]   J. D. Schaffer, D. Whitley, and L. J. Eshelman. Combinations of genetic algorithms and neural networks: a survey of the state of the art. *Combinations of Genetic Algorithms and Neural Networks*. IEEE Computer Society Press, 1–37, 1992.

[Tar83]   R. E. Tarjan. *Data Structures and Network Algorithms*. SIAM Publications, 1983.

[TB92]   C. J. Thornton and B. Du Boulay. *Artificial Intelligence Through Search*. Kluwer Academic Publishers, 1992.

[TE05]   Z. Toroczaki and S. Eubank. Agent-based modeling as a decision-making tool. *The Bridge*, 22–27, Winter 2005.

[TLA06]   N. A. Taatgen, C. Lebiere, and J. R. Anderson. Modeling paradigms in ACT-R. *Cognition and Multi-Agent Interaction: From Cognitive Modeling to Social Simulation*, R. Sun, ed. Cambridge University Press, 29–52, 2006.

[TMMS93] S. G. Berkovich, T. M. Martinetz, and K. J. Schulten. Neural-gas network for vector quantization and its application to time-series prediction. *IEEE Trans. Neural Networks*, *4*:558–569, July 1993.

[TNR90]   M. Tambe, A. Newell, and P. S. Rosenbloom. The problem of expensive chunks and its solution by restricting expressiveness. *Machine Learning*, *5*:299–348, 1990.

[Tro93]   H. Trost. *Feature Formalisms and Linguistic Ambiguity*. Ellis Horwood, 1993.

[TS90]   P. Trahanias and E. Skordalakis. Syntactic pattern recognition of the ecg. *IEEE Transactions on Pattern Analysis and Machine Intelligence*, *12*(7):648–657, 1990.

[Tur50]   A. M. Turing. Computing machinery and intelligence. *Mind*, *LIX*(236):443–460, 1950. (The full text of Turing's paper and related commentary is available at http://www.abelard.org/turpap/turpap.htm.)

[Tur84]   R. Turner. *Logics for Artificial Intelligence*. John Wiley and Sons, 1984.

[Utg89]   P. E. Utgoff. Incremental induction of decision trees. *Machine Learning*, *4*:161–186, 1989.

[Vla02]   I. Vlahavas. Expernet: An intelligent multiagent system for WAN management. *IEEE Intelligent Systems*, *17*(1):62–72, 2002.

[Vog89]   R. Vogt. *Automatic Generation of Morphological Set Recognition Algorithms*. Springer Verlag, 1989.

[Vog90]   R. C. Vogt. The importance of bandpass operators for automatic algorithm generation systems. *SPIE Volume 1350 (Image Algebra and Morphological Image Processing)*, 103–115, 1990.

[Wat63]   R. I. Watson. *The Great Psychologists from Aristotle to Freud*. Lippincott, 1963.

[Wat97]   I. Watson. *Applying Case-Based Reasoning: Techniques for Enterprise Systems*. Morgan Kaufman, 1997.

[Wei65]   J. Weizenbaum. ELIZA—a computer program for the study of natural language communication between man and machine. *Communications of the Association for Computing Machinery, 9*(1):36–45, January 1965.

[Whi88]   D. Whitley. Applying genetic algorithms to neural net problems. *Neural Networks, 1*:230, 1988.

[Wik94]   H. Wiklicky. On the non-existence of a unversal learning algorithm for recurrent neural networks. *Advances in Neural Information Processing Systems, 6*. Morgan Kaufmann, 431–436, 1994.

[Win72]   T. Winograd. *Understanding Natural Language*. Academic Press, 1972.

[Win83]   T. Winograd. *Language as a Cognitive Process: Syntax*, Volume I. Addison-Wesley, 1983.

[Win08]   J. Wing. Five deep questions in computing. *Communications of the ACM, 51*(1):58–60, January 2008.

[WJ95]   M. Wooldridge and N. Jennings. Intelligent agents: theory and practice. *The Knowledge Engineering Review, 10*(2):115–152, 1995.

[WL87]   A. Wieland and R. Leighton. Geometric analysis of neural network capabilities. *IEEE 1st International Conference on Neural Networks*, III–385, June 1987.

[WSJ92]   R. Werner, W. Schiffmann, and M. Joost. *Synthesis and performance analysis of multilayer neural network architectures*. Technical Report 16/1992, University of Koblenz, Institute für Physics, 1992. (http://citeseerx.ist.psu.edu/viewdoc/summary?doi=10.1.1.54.3794).

[XL00]   K. Xu and W. Li. Exact phase transitions in random constraint satisfaction problems. *Journal of Artificial Intelligence Research, 12*:93–103, 2000.

[Zad92]   L. A. Zadeh. Knowledge representation in fuzzy logic. *An Introduction to Fuzzy Logic Applications in Intelligent Systems*, R. R. Yager and L. A. Zadeh, eds. Kluwer Academic Publishers, 1992.

[ZJOW00] F. Zambonelli, N. R. Jennings, A. Omicini, and M. Wooldridge. Agent-oriented software engineering for internet applications. *Coordination of Internet Agents: Models, Technologies, and Applications*, A. Omicini, F. Zambonelli, M. Klusch, and R. Tolksdorf, eds. Springer Verlag, 2000.

[ZM99]   M. Zargham and S. Mohammad. A web-based information system for stock selection and evaluation. *International Conference on Advance Issues of E-Commerce and Web-Based Information Systems, WECWIS*, 81–83, 1999.

[Zor08]   G. Zorpette. Waiting for the rapture. *IEEE Spectrum*, 34–35, June 2008.

[ZW95]   L. Zhang, B. Zhang, and F. Wu. Programming based learning algorithms of neural networks with self-feedback connections. *IEEE Trans. Neural Networks*, 6(3):771–775, 1995.

Index